O9-ABG-090

THE CIVILIZATION OF THE AMERICAN INDIAN SERIES

TREATISE ON THE HEATHEN SUPERSTITIONS AND CUSTOMS THAT TODAY LIVE AMONG THE INDIANS NATIVE TO THIS NEW SPAIN, 1629

1

Tratado
de las supersticiones de los
Naturales de esta N. E.
Por
el Br. Hernando Ruiz de
Alarcon.

(Escrito en 1627 publicado en los Anales
Tomo VI de la 1a Epoca —)

1

Title page, folio 1r, of the manuscript of the Treatise *in the Museo Nacional de Antropología, Mexico City. This and subsequent illustrations from the manuscript are reproduced with the permission of the Museo Nacional.*

TREATISE ON THE HEATHEN SUPERSTITIONS

That Today Live Among the Indians Native to This New Spain, 1629

By

Hernando Ruiz de Alarcón

Translated and edited by
J. Richard Andrews and Ross Hassig

University of Oklahoma Press : Norman

BY J. RICHARD ANDREWS

Introduction to Classical Nahuatl (Austin, 1975)
Prometheus in Search of Prestige: Juan del Encina (Berkeley and Los Angeles, 1959)
(Translator and editor, with Ross Hassig) Hernando Ruiz de Alarcón *Treatise on the Heathen Superstitions and Customs That Today Live Among the Indians Native to This New Spain, 1629* (Norman, 1984)

BY ROSS HASSIG

(Translator and editor, with J. Richard Andrews) Hernando Ruiz de Alarcón, *Treatise on the Heathen Superstitions and Customs That Today Live Among the Indians Native to This New Spain, 1629* (Norman, 1984)

Library of Congress Cataloging in Publication Data

Ruiz de Alarcón, Hernando.
Treatise on the heathen superstitions and customs that today live among the Indians native to this New Spain, 1629.

(The civilization of the American Indian series; v. 164)
Translation of: Tratado de las supersticiones y costumbres gentilicas que oy viuen entre los indios naturales desta Nueva España.
English and Nahuatlan.
Bibliography: p. 383.
Includes index.
1. Aztecs—Religion and mythology. 2. Aztecs—Medicine. 3. Indians of Mexico—Religion and mythology. 4. Indians of Mexico—Medicine. 5. Aztec language—Texts. I. Andrews, J. Richard (James Richard), 1924- . II. Hassig, Ross, 1945- . III. Title. IV. Series.
F1219.76.R45R8413 1984 299'.792 83-47842
ISBN 0-8061-1832-6

Publication of this work has been made possible in part by a grant from the Andrew W. Mellon Foundation.

The paper in this book meets the guidelines for permanence and durability of the Committee on Production Guidelines for Book Longevity of the Council on Library Resources, Inc.

To Alfredo López Austin

CONTENTS

ILLUSTRATIONS

(From the manuscript in the Museo Nacional de Antropología, Mexico City)

Map

ACKNOWLEDGMENTS

Our indebtedness for scholarly and technical assistance in the preparation of this work extends to many persons. Among those who have given us scholarly help are Gene TeSelle, of the Divinity School, Steven Gauthier, of the Department of French, and Ronald Spores, of the Department of Sociology and Anthropology, all in Vanderbilt University, Nashville, Tennessee; and Jim Fox, of the Department of Anthropology, Stanford University, Stanford, California.

We would like to thank many librarians in Vanderbilt University: Paula Covington, the Latin American Librarian; Paul Wanter, of the Divinity Library; Mary Teloh, the Medical History Librarian; and Lois Griest, Marilyn Jackson, and Lucinda Schrenger, of Interlibrary Loan. Without their able assistance we could not have carried out our research efficiently. We also owe considerable thanks to Phil Sherrod, Maria Perkins, and Dave Palmer, of the Vanderbilt University Computer Center, for spending enormous amounts of time and energy in guiding our efforts in the use of the TEX program in the preparation of the manuscript.

We also wish to express our special gratitude to Lyle Campbell, of the Department of Anthropology, State University of New York at Albany, Albany, New York, for his assistance and encouragement throughout the preparation of this work.

We are also indebted to the Museo Nacional de Antropología, Mexico City, for permitting us to copy and use the manuscript version of Ruiz de Alarcón's *Treatise.*

Also high among those to whom we are indebted, but who are not conventionally acknowledged, are the many Mesoamerican and Nahuatl scholars who preceded us in the study of Ruiz de Alarcón and on whose work we have drawn, particularly Alfredo López Austin.

We would also like to thank the University Research Council of Vanderbilt University for assistance in the research and preparation of this book.

Without the help of the foregoing, the writing of this work would have been immensely more difficult.

Nashville, Tennessee
New York City

J. RICHARD ANDREWS
ROSS HASSIG

EDITORIAL PROCEDURES

Hernando Ruiz de Alarcón's *Treatise* is one of the most important sources of early colonial Mexico dealing with native religion, beliefs, and medicine (Garibay 1971: 316; Gibson 1964:101; Nicholson 1971:396–97; Warren 1973:83–84). Although it was written as a denunciation of continued heathen practices by the Indians and as a call to priests to be vigilant against them, its importance lies in the native incantations, curing practices, and myths in the Nahuatl language that it contains. The *Treatise* has been a major source for writers dealing with these subjects from the seventeenth century forward.

The original manuscript has been lost. Although the situation is not clear, apparently at least two copies of the manuscript were in existence at one time. One was used as a source by Jacinto de la Serna, a contemporary of Ruiz de Alarcón, in writing his *Manual de ministros de indios* in the seventeenth century. This version may have been Ruiz de Alarcón's own copy, but that seems unlikely. Serna (1892: 264) says that, after Ruiz de Alarcón's death in the preceding year, 1646, he visited Atenango del Río, where he found a "large amount of his teachings," but that he has not included any of them in his *Manual* "because I did not solicit them since I did not at that time intend to write this treatise," but that later "there have come into my hands some loose sheets of what I saw concerning the superstitions and idolatries." These loose sheets were the complete text or nearly so, though Serna put them in an order fitting his own purpose. But on at least one occasion Serna (1892:387) apparently used not Ruiz de Alarcón's text but the source of the latter: "Father Friar Augustine Guerra, of the Order of Saint Augustine, who at the time was living in the town of Ocuilan, related this case, and I found out about it from an account of it that I saw written to [not "by"] the Licentiate Don Fernando Ruiz de Alarcón" [the incident is in Treatise I, chapter 7]. Serna goes on to say that he learned of an incident involving Ruiz de Alarcón "from a reliable person of the village [Iguala]," though we find the account of that incident (concerning Mariana and her sister, see Treatise I, chapter 7) in much the same wording as that given by Ruiz de Alarcón. On still another occasion Serna (1892:419), speaking of a general cure for all illnesses and fevers, says, "I found [it] in an account which the Licentiate D. Fernando Ruiz de Alarcón gave to the Licentiate D. Pedro Ponce de León," and yet the wording is close enough to have been copied from Ruiz de Alarcón's *Treatise*. The problem of whether there existed a complete copy of Ruiz de Alarcón's *Treatise* that was used by Serna is further complicated by his failure to give Ruiz de Alarcón credit for much of the material that he took from the *Treatise*; it is as if he was not aware of that material's authorship, since he says (1892:301): "Many other things that happened to this vigilant and zealous minister have come to my notice, but I do not put them here in order not to go on longer in this chapter; and since they are of different subject matter, when I deal with those subjects, I will bring them in in order to support and verify them with his authority." Serna does not, however, acknowledge Ruiz de Alarcón as his source at the appropriate points later on in his work. The result is that some modern scholars (e.g., Brinton 1894) have drawn material from Ruiz de Alarcón unknowingly, since the impression one gains from Serna is that both the commentary and the translated Nahuatl texts are his own, whereas, in fact, the commentary dealing with the incantatory material loosely follows Ruiz de Alarcón's text. Too, although he omits the Nahuatl texts, Serna reproduces Ruiz de Alarcón's Spanish translations exactly or very closely, with certain minor exceptions, which we have pointed out in the Notes.

The other copy of Ruiz de Alarcón's *Treatise* is the manuscript used in this edition. It is presently in the Museo Nacional de Antropología, in Mexico City. The document is a cooperative effort by a number of copyists (at least three), and it shows varying degrees of care and language skill.

In 1892, Francisco del Paso y Troncoso published an edition of this manuscript in the *Anales del Museo Nacional de México.* This edition was later reprinted in 1954 by Editorial Navarro (with a number of misprints and the omission of a few lines). The Paso y Troncoso edition is an excellent work. It is not, however, a strict presentation of what is found in the manuscript. Except for certain apparent misprints, the departures are an attempt to make the Nahuatl more accessible to the reader. The editor has broken up long stretches of the Nahuatl texts into paragraph-like segments, divisions for the most part determined by the structural shifts within the incantations, and has introduced or changed punctuation and, consequently, capitalization. He has spelled out instances of vowels with tildes (e.g., *ĩ* becomes *in*); he has spelled out all abbreviated instances of *qui* and *que;* and he has respelled segmented elements as words (though with an occasional error). With regard to diacritics, he has reproduced the grave, acute, and circumflex accent marks (though with occasional inaccuracies). However, there are two diacritics he apparently misunderstood: since he did not realize that one or two of the copyists used macrons to indicate vowel length, he read them as either acute or grave accents; and since he did not recognize the use of an inverted circumflex (the haček accent) to represent a short vowel, on several occasions he interpreted it as one of the more conventional accents.

Modern scholars working with Ruiz de Alarcón's material have relied on Paso y Troncoso's edition (e.g., Caso 1977; Furst 1976; Gibson 1964; Nicholson 1971; Quezada 1975) for both Ruiz de Alarcón's translation of the Nahuatl texts and his commentaries on them. Others (e.g., Fellowes 1977; Garibay 1958, 1971; Hinz 1970; López Austin 1966, 1967, 1969, 1970, 1975) have dealt exclusively with the Nahuatl, but only in piecemeal fashion, giving their own translations of selected sections of the collection. Of these scholars, López Austin has translated the most extensive stretches of the material and has done so with the most success.

In view of the importance of the work and the reliance placed on it, coupled with the frequent inadequacy of Ruiz de Alarcón's translation and his biased understanding of the Nahuatl material, a new edition is necessary. The nature of the work and the flawed condition of the Nahuatl have determined the manner in which we have presented the text. There are five aspects to this presentation. We have (1) translated into English Ruiz de Alarcón's Spanish exposition, (2) reproduced the Nahuatl as found in the manuscript in the Museo Nacional de Antropología, (3) translated into English Ruiz de Alarcón's Spanish translation of the incantations, (4) rewritten the Nahuatl in a standard form, and (5) made a new translation from this rewritten version.

Translation of the Exposition

In translating Ruiz de Alarcón's commentary, we have attempted to make it as readable as possible without violating unduly the unpolished nature of his style. We have, on occasion, broken a longer sentence into two or more and have introduced paragraph divisions at appropriate places. We have also inserted material in brackets to fill out incomplete sentences, to remedy corrupt grammatical constructions, or to support a possible reading of logical non sequiturs. We have also introduced dashes to separate parenthetical material; consequently, any parentheses in our translation are those found in the manuscript. We have inserted the marginal notes from the manuscript into the body of the text itself but have used braces to distinguish this material from the material (which it at times resembles) that, in the manuscript, is set off by parentheses. We have kept the spelling of Latin quotations as they are found in the manuscript. Whenever we have encountered what we consider an obvious error in the Spanish with no problematic consequences (e.g., *causas* for *cautas*) we have simply given a translation of the corrected item and have made no comment. When, however, a textual error holds the potential for a problem in translation (e.g., *ensierran,* "they lock up," for *entierran,* "they bury") we have explained our reading in a note. Except for capitalization, the Nahuatl in Ruiz de Alarcón's commentary has been retained in the original orthography, with the standard spelling supplied in a note. We have retained the superscript letters that Ruiz de Alarcón occasionally used to key his translation to the Nahuatl.

Reproduction of the Nahuatl Text

In reproducing the Nahuatl text, we have differed from Paso y Troncoso in that we have attempted to be as faithful to the manuscript version as transference from writing to printing permits; the main problem has been the linking or separation of letters and syllables, since word boundaries are not strictly observed (as is common in early texts). A certain degree of arbitrariness has had to enter into a large number of such circumstances; the relative space between letters has been the guiding criterion, though in the instance of division of words at the end of lines we have been guided by treatment of the same word elsewhere in the context or, in the absence of such a word, by our own knowledge of word formation. We believe that, for the most part, the lack of linkage between letters and syllables of words is not a reflection of ignorance concerning word boundaries but is due in part to "mechanical" problems, such as the shape of certain letters that does not permit easy linkage either on the left or on the right, lack of ink on the pen at a given moment, and so forth. Such problems usually do not involve matters that are crucial to a proper decipherment of the text and are therefore of a different nature from those that involve punctuation practices. Because of our decision to reproduce the Nahuatl text of the manuscript as exactly as possible, our transcription also differs from Paso y Troncoso's version with regard to punctuation, capitalization, respelling of tildes, and diacritics. We have, however, largely followed Paso y Troncoso in dividing the incantations into the segments he used (the more serious departures are in the following Treatises and chapters: II:3, II:4, II:6, II:11, IV:1, IV:2, and VI:30). Sometimes the divisions are present in the manuscript, and other times they were introduced by Paso y Troncoso. Our redivisions reflect our understanding of the structure of the incantations (see Appendix F).

Translation of Ruiz de Alarcón's Translation of the Incantations

In translating into English Ruiz de Alarcón's Spanish translation of the Nahuatl, we have tried to adhere even more closely to his language than otherwise, since, as he explains in his Prologue, his curious wording was deliberate: "And if in the translation some clauses and expressions are discordant to readers, let them realize that in the translation I have tried to conform as much as I could to the literal meaning and phrasing of the Indians, especially of those who were practitioners of these superstitions." This statement of his intentions does not fully describe his practice, since his translation is at times more prolix than the Nahuatl (supplying connectives, offering alternative translations, giving explanatory translations, and proposing rationalizing explanations—in other words, in spite of his intention to remain faithful to the Nahuatl, he has Europeanized it by making explicit what is only implicit and by emphasizing logical connections, coordinations, and subordinations). We have deemed it inappropriate to tamper with his style here, our only problem being the proper decision about how to render ambiguous expressions. We should point out, however, that we have introduced punctuation where we have deemed it necessary to make the text readable, though we have left the corresponding Nahuatl text with the punctuation found in the manuscript. All quotations of the Spanish text in the Notes have been left as they are in the manuscript. In our translation we have left Spanish names with the spelling they have in the manuscript: e.g., *Andres Ximenez,* not *Andrés Jiménez; Simon Gomez,* not *Simón Gómez,* and so forth.

Rewriting of Nahuatl Passages

In rewriting the Nahuatl in a standard version, we were guided by two considerations: (1) the Nahuatl exhibits the peculiarities of seventeenth-century orthography and scriptorial practices; for example, the same word may be spelled in more than one way, and spacing is so erratic that not only words but letters, syllables, and short phrases are written as integral elements, set off by spaces; (2) the Nahuatl has a number of grammatical problems resulting either from dialectal differences or from transmission or copyist errors. Since we believe that the manuscript text should be presented as written and since we recognize (as Paso y Troncoso apparently did) that this text would create burdensome difficulties for a reader unless abundant help were given, we felt that the most efficient way to solve this dual problem was to present a regularized version of the Nahuatl in addition to the manuscript version. This meant that we would, first, standardize the spelling in accordance with the orthographic canon presented in Andrews 1975 (which is largely a codification of the logical orthographic practices of colonial writers, i.e., spelling practices that avoid obscuring the morphological and etymological structure of the words) and, second, emend all unexpected or aberrant grammatical formations according to the descriptions of Olmos, Molina, and Carochi and Sahagún's practice. The result should make the Nahuatl of the manuscript more accessible to a larger number of readers and, at the same time, avoid extensive use of *sic* for every oddity or deviancy in spelling and grammar (we have, however, offered notes explaining the more interesting items), since the reader can easily make the comparisons. It should be understood that the errors found in the manuscript version of the

Nahuatl are not our misprints; see, for example, *tlelli* (Treatise II, chapter 4, segment 2), *cuex* (II:7:3), *quicazque* (II:8:13), *macuiltonelleque* (II:8:17), *cocauhque* (II: 11:1), *xxoqui* (VI:3:6), *hueinacoztli* (VI:29:1). Routine corrections of such scribal errors appear in the rewritten version without comment. There are other, more substantive emendations, however, involving more than slips of the pen. In handwritten documents, diacritics are not always as distinctive as one would wish, so that the difference between an accent and a macron is not always clear. In any such case, we have read the diacritic as it should be.

Among the specific changes we have introduced in the rewritten version, the simplest kind involves orthographic changes. These are of several types.

1. The manuscript consistently represents a given phoneme one way, but we have chosen a different spelling; for example, we respell *quauhtli* as *cuāuhtli* (i.e., syllable-initial /kʷ/ is spelled *cu-* instead of *qu-;* we respell *ça* and *ço* as *za* and *zo* (i.e., /s/ before /a/ and /o/ is spelled with *z*). Note that all Nahuatl words, phrases, or sentences occurring in the body of Ruiz de Alarcón's exposition appear in exactly the form they have in the manuscript, including capitalization, punctuation, accentuation, and word divisions. Corrections to such items are given in the Notes, where the Nahuatl words are respelled in the standard manner. Among the respellings of Ruiz de Alarcón's conventions we can include our treatment of the diacritic marks used in the manuscript. We have rewritten them in the normalized version as follows: macron (e.g., ā) = long vowel; acute accent (e.g., á) = short vowel; haček (e.g., ǎ) = short vowel; grave accent (e.g., à) = glottal stop (i.e., h); circumflex (e.g., â) = final glottal stop (i.e., h). The manuscript has also used three abbreviations involving *q* which we have represented in the regularized version as follows: *q́* = *qui;* *q̃* = *que* or *queh;* *q*⁺ (our arbitrary representation of a more elaborate symbol) = *qui* or *que* or *queh*. One of the important facts about the manuscript is that at least some of the copyists used the system found in Carochi's *Arte de la lengua mexicana* (presumably the Museo manuscript is later than Carochi, but there is a remote possibility that these diacritics were included in Ruiz de Alarcón's original manuscript). It should be pointed out, however, that the use of this system is sporadic and at times the assignment of macrons and accents is in error.

2. The manuscript shows variant graphological usages, one standard and the other nonstandard with no pronunciational differences involved. We have changed the nonstandard to the standard form; thus, for *nahui/naui* we spell *nāhui* (i.e., *-u-* is rejected as a spelling for /w/); for *quauhtli/quautli* we spell *cuāuhtli* (i.e., *-u-* is rejected as a spelling for /W/); for *teuctli/tecutli* we spell *tēuctli* (i.e., *-cu-* is rejected as a spelling for syllable-final /kʷ/); for *tiquıxayotız/tic ixayotiz* we spell *tiquīxāyōtīz* (i.e., *c* plus space is rejected as a spelling for /k/ plus /i/ or /e/).

3. The manuscript shows variant graphological usages, one standard and the other possibly reflecting a dialectal pronunciation. We have changed the nonstandard to the standard form; thus, for *nicquıxtıtıuh/niquixtitiuh* (which may have represented the pronunciation /nihki:x.../) we spell *nicquīxtītīuh;* for *niquitta/niquita* we spell *niquitta;* for *amotzahual/ammotzahual/anmotzahual* we spell *amotzāhual* (where the *amo-* is the second person plural possessive prefix, "your," not the subject prefix *am-* plus the reflexive object prefix *-mo-*); similarly, for *amech-/ammech-* we

spell *amēch-*, "you" (second plural object prefix); for *ninotlaloz/ninotlalloz* we spell *ninotlalōz.* The manuscript frequently keeps the *i* of the subject prefixes *ni-* and *ti-* before a vowel, but we respell, for example, *tietic* as *tetic.* Similarly, the manuscript keeps a possessive prefix ending in /o/ when followed by a stem with an initial vowel, but we respell, for example, *moopochcopa* as *mopōchcopa.* It should be obvious, given our purpose, that our respellings do not contest the possibility that the spellings found in the manuscript may represent regional pronunciation practices.

4. Each word, including clitics, is spelled as a separate item: for example, *inic* is rewritten as *in īc, aquin* as *āc in, intlacana* as *in tlā canah,* both *tlein* and *tlen* as *tleh in* [note that when *tleh* is followed by a word beginning with /i/ (as in *tleh in* and *tleh īca*) the glottal stop /h/ is not pronounced].

Another kind of spelling change is more complicated since it concerns the fact that the manuscript shows both standard and nonstandard phonological usages. In each instance we have replaced the dialectal variant with the standard one; thus for *xoxouhqui/xoxoqui* we have spelled *xoxōuhqui* (i.e., /Wk/ is chosen instead of /k/); for *chalchiuhcueye/chalchicueye* we have spelled *chālchiuhcuēyeh* (i.e., /Wk^w/ is chosen instead of /k^w/); for *chiucnahui/chicnahui* we have spelled *chiucnāhui* (i.e., /k^w/ is chosen instead of /k/); for *xihuitl/xiuhtli* we have spelled *xihuitl* (i.e., /wi/ plus a consonant is chosen instead of /W/ plus a consonant).

There is an even more complicated kind of spelling change, that of textual emendation. The text has many copyist errors. Some are minor, involving the already discussed misplaced or incorrect diacritic marks or misspelled words. Others are more serious, involving apparent omissions of words or phrases or curious misplacements of phrases. In extreme cases we have marked the problems with [*sic*]. Another problem with the text is the lack of consistent punctuation. Commas, periods, colons, and question marks are used in a largely imprecise, unsystematic way. At times the Nahuatl text and Ruiz de Alarcón's translation have conflicting indications, thus creating the difficulty of knowing the intended syntactical relationships between adjacent words or even when sentences begin and end.

There are, of course, certain problems that cannot be resolved, either because material is apparently missing or because the errors are too problematic. An example of the latter is the problem of the use of a plural command form (e.g., *xihuālhuiān,* "come [pl]") when the accompanying vocative is singular; for example, *Tlā xihuālhuiān, in nohuēltīuh,* "Come [pl], my sister [sg]." The obvious explanation for this is that it is a matter of a "named partner" construction (see Andrews 1975:201). The example sentence would thus be translated "Come, you and my sister." This is all the more likely because one finds other unquestionable instances of the construction in the second person plural; for example, *Mā ammopīnāuhtihtin, Cōzauhqui Cihuātl,* "Beware of causing yourselves to become ashamed, you and Yellow Woman," where the plurality of "you and" is indicated only in the verb word. It is frequently difficult, however, to translate the command sentence in the plural since the following verb is ordinarily in the singular, the subject of that verb being the named partner of the plural-number command sentence. Another possibility is that Nahuatl speakers had already picked up a Spanish stylistic device, current at that time, of using a second person plural as an honorific second person singular (e.g., *Sed para mí Costantino; / aquel noble emperador / me sed, señora,* "Be

[pl] Constantine for me; be [pl] that noble emperor to me, Lady." Whatever the explanation, in all these instances we have indicated in square brackets the plurality of the verb and have not given a plural vocative. In making these emendations, we have not tried to go beyond the text; that is, we have not tried to rewrite it into an earlier version. We have only clarified what appears in the manuscript. With regard to the vowel length introduced in our rewritten version, we have relied on the works of Carochi (1904) and Ruiz de Alarcón for the seventeenth century and on the modern works of Andrews (1975), Brewer and Brewer (1962), Ramírez de Alejandro and Dakin (1979), and Karttunen (1983). It should be pointed out, however, that we have, for reasons too complex to go into here, on occasion differed from their indications when in our judgment it seemed necessary.

Translation of Rewritten Nahuatl

In presenting a translation of the standardized version of the Nahuatl, we have sought to make available a more accurate picture of post-Conquest cultural practices than is evident in Ruiz de Alarcón's translation. It should be noted, however, that we concur with Ruiz de Alarcón's stated intention of remaining as close as possible to the Nahuatl text. We have not attempted to create a neat, logical, flowing prose because to do so would falsify the nature of the incantations, since their style is frequently irregular, with sudden shifts in thought or abrupt changes in address or changes from second person to third person or vice versa. We have purposefully and deliberately translated the Nahuatl as literally as possible without violating English grammar, and for idiomatic phrases, dialectal usages, and metaphoric expressions we have given their free equivalents (wherever we have been privy to them) in square brackets. It must be remembered that the material found in the incantations was intended to be esoteric. The informants frequently claimed that they did not understand a given expression or incantation, and, even if this was a subterfuge on their part, Ruiz de Alarcón on a number of occasions speaks of the obscurity of the texts.* We have tried to render the Nahuatl in our translation so faithfully that a reader can constantly map the Nahuatl onto the English gloss. There are, of course, many occasions where the grammatical and lexical differences of the two languages make this difficult, if not impossible. With even a slight knowledge of Nahuatl, however, the reader should be able to make the necessary backward or forward leaps to discern the difficulty presented by such incompatibilities.

In our translation, we have, furthermore, had to deal with the problem of names. The text has two kinds of names: names of gods or mythological beings (which may include calendrical names) and metaphorical (or disguising) names (which again may be calendrical names). After careful deliberation, we decided to retain the noncalendrical god names in Nahuatl, putting their translations in Appendix B, and to translate all other names, since to leave them untranslated would mean

*Ruiz de Alarcón apparently had an excellent knowledge of the language; see Serna's (1892:294) characterization of him as "a great preacher in the Mexican language" and the statement that "he had preached and taught all those Indians, principally verses in the Mexican language in devotion to the Most Holy Virgin, Our Lady."

that in some instances the translation would consist, to a large degree, of Nahuatl words and thus would be opaque to the reader. In addition to these two ways of handling names (i.e., nontranslation and translation), we have also given the nonmetaphorical equivalent in brackets whenever that could be determined (we have also included these metaphorical names in Appendix B). Regarding the spelling of nontranslated names, see Appendix B.

To render the material as concisely as possible, we have adopted the following conventions:

1. As stated earlier, the segmenting of the Nahuatl material generally follows that of Paso y Troncoso's edition.

2. The numbers designating segments of incantations are sequential within each chapter and disregard the fact that on occasion a chapter may contain more than one incantation.

3. Square brackets are used for parenthetical material that we have inserted. Parentheses are those found in the manuscript. We have used dashes to set off parenthetical material unmarked in the manuscript.

4. Marginal notes found in the manuscript have been placed in the text at what we have deemed to be appropriate places and have been set off in braces (e.g., {fire}). Our comments to these marginal notes have been placed in the Notes.

5. We have used *Webster's Third New International Dictionary* as a guide for leaving Hispanisms (e.g., *principal, fiscal*) and certain Nahuatlisms (e.g., *copal, peyote*) in the text. There are other Nahuatlisms that, not being listed in *Webster's*, we have kept but have put in italics (e.g., *piciete*). We have listed all Nahuatlisms in the appropriate glossary with a discussion of their meanings. There are certain Spanish words that had a technical meaning in the seventeenth century (e.g., *vicario, visita, doctrina*) which we have also kept, putting them in italics. An explanation of the meaning of these Hispanisms is found in the introductory material and in the Glossary of Nahuatlisms and Hispanisms.

6. The following abbreviations and symbols have been used in the analysis of Nahuatl words and their translations:

*	a hypothetical form
(H)	honorific
sg	singular
pl	plural
//	phonemic representation of sounds
-	division points separating word constituents
( )	beginning and ending boundaries of major wordstems
Ø	silently present constituent

In our infrequent indications of phonemic material in the Notes, the following symbols have been used: /ƛ/ = tl, /W/ = voiceless w sound (as in "wheel"), /h/ = glottal stop, /k^w/ = qu (as in "quality"), /š/ = sh (as in "ship").

7. Nahuatl words are analyzed according to the following formulas:
Noun: person + state + STEM + number
Intransitive verb: person + STEM + tense + number
One-object verb: person + object + STEM + tense + number
Two-object verb: person + object + object + STEM + tense + number

8. References to notes are according to the formula "Treatise: chapter: note," e.g., "note I:2:3." References to Nahuatl segments are according to the formula "Treatise: chapter: segment," e.g., "I:2:3."

9. In our Notes we have used Alonso de Molina's *Vocabulario en lengua castellana y mexicana y mexicana y castellana* and Rémi Siméon's *Dictionnaire de la langue nahuatl ou mexicaine* as the main sources for lexical information and have regularized the spelling of material taken from them since we feel that our readers should not be burdened with more than one spelling convention. Since we rely so heavily on these works and since they are in dictionary form, we have omitted the normal citation procedure. Furthermore, since the native informants of Ruiz de Alarcón's texts were from the area of Guerrero and Morelos, we have considered Forrest Brewer and Jean G. Brewer's *Vocabulario mexicano de Tetelcingo* and Cleofas Ramírez de Alejandro and Karen Dakin's *Vocabulario náhuatl de Xalitla, Guerrero* to have special pertinence in reading the materials recorded by Ruiz de Alarcón, and have used them wherever pertinent. We have also standardized the spelling of material taken from Sahagún.

10. All biblical references are to the Rheims-Douay translation of the Bible from the Latin Vulgate. Also the spelling of biblical names is in accordance with this translation.

11. For the meaning of linguistic terms used in the Notes and in the Appendices, see the Glossary of Linguistic Terms.

POSTSCRIPT

Two books by Eike Hinz (1970, 1978) should be mentioned here. They are studies of the belief systems in "Aztec" texts, the first dealing with Ruiz de Alarcón and the second dealing with books 4 and 6 of Sahagún. Both of these works are important contributions to the study of native thought systems. We have referred to these works only in a very limited way. Much of Hinz's commentary on textual problems deals with the same subject matter that we have dealt with in our Notes, and there is some overlap in the solutions. That we have not referred to them more frequently in our Notes reflects the fact that his interests do not correspond to ours. The thrust of Hinz's works is the analysis of belief systems, an area with which we have not dealt, but we find that we agree in many details of reading. There would undoubtedly have been more points of agreement had Hinz used the original manuscript rather than Paso y Troncoso's edition.

GUIDE TO PRONUNCIATION OF STANDARD SPELLING OF NAHUATL

There are only four vowels. They may be long or short. Long vowels are marked by a macron (e.g., ā) and are pronounced the same as short vowels except for being held longer. Two identical consonants written together are pronounced long. (The symbol *, used below, stands for any consonant or silence. The symbol / stands for "or.")

Letter	*Pronunciation*
a/ā	as in *wad*
e/ē	like *a* in *gate*
i/ī	as in *elite*
o/ō	as in *okra*
c + a/o/*	as in *can*
qu + e/i	like *k* in *kit*
c + e/i	as in *cease*
z + a/o/*	like *s* in *sod*
ch	as in *church*
chu	like *ckw* in *backward*
cu/uc	like *qu* in *quick*
h	as in *hill* (or like the glottal stop between the *e*'s of *re-edit*)
hu	like *w* in *wake*
uh	like *wh* in *wheel*
l	as in *leave* (but before * it is voiceless)
tl	similar to *tl* in *settler*, but a single sound
tz	like *ts* in *hats*
x	like *sh* in *ship*

Pronunciation of the remaining letters *(p, t, m, n, y)* is similar to that of the English letters.

N.B.: The letters consisting of two symbols are considered single letters; therefore, the combination *chu* (= *k* + *w*) consists of two letters.

Stress always falls on the next-to-the-last syllable, with the sole exception of words ending in the vocative *-é*, which always receives the stress (an accent mark is used to show this).

Each syllable has a vowel as its nucleus. There are no diphthongs in Nahuatl; therefore, two adjacent vowels fall in separate syllables; e.g., *āi* = *ā-i*. A single consonant joins a following vowel to constitute a syllable; e.g., *nocal* = *no-cal*. Two consonants are always divided: *āxcān* = *āx-cān; calli* = *cal-li; yehhuātl* = *yeh-huātl*. The digraph letters (*ch, tl, tz, hu, uh, cu,* and *uc*) are considered single letters: *achi* = *a-chi; ātlān* = *ā-tlān; chiucnāhui* = *chiuc-nā-hui*. Notice that *u* does not represent a vowel and is used only to create the digraph letters *hu, uh, cu,* and *uc* (*hu* and *cu* begin a syllable; *uh* and *uc* end a syllable); consequently, *chu* consists of two consonant letters, *c* followed by *hu: cachuah* = *cac-huah*.

TREATISE ON THE HEATHEN SUPERSTITIONS AND CUSTOMS THAT TODAY LIVE AMONG THE INDIANS NATIVE TO THIS NEW SPAIN, 1629

Towns in Mexico mentioned in Ruiz de Alarcon's Treatise

EDITORS' INTRODUCTION: THE HISTORICAL CONTEXT

Little is known of Hernando Ruiz de Alarcón, the author of *Treatise on the Heathen Superstitions and Customs That Today Live Among the Indians Native to This New Spain.* Born in Taxco, Guerrero, Mexico (Warren 1973:83), in the latter part of the sixteenth century, he was one of five sons of Pedro Ruiz de Alarcón, a mine official (Poesse 1972:17–18), and Leonor de Mendoza. One of his brothers was Juan Ruiz de Alarcón (Castro Leal 1943:19; Poesse 1972:17–18), who was to become a famous playwright in Spain. All the brothers attended the University of Mexico. Hernando graduated in 1592, received the degree of *bachiller* (bachelor) in 1597, and became the *cura beneficiado* of Atenango (Toussaint 1931:77). What renown he has is due to his authorship of the *Treatise*, to the incantations in Nahuatl that it contains, and to the good fortune that a copy of the manuscript survived. The reason Ruiz de Alarcón wrote his *Treatise* is related to the confusing and conflicting jurisdictional disputes among the various religious factions in the New World.

THE RELIGIOUS CONTEXT OF THE SPANISH CONQUEST

Religion played a major role in the conquest and colonization of Mexico (New Spain), but conversion of the natives was not a matter of simply imposing the tenets of Roman Catholicism while suppressing native beliefs. Despite the basic theological unity of Roman Catholicism, the manner in which missionization proceeded in the New World reveals considerable internal conflict. There were divisions among the Catholic clergy over who could Christianize the Indians, what powers they could exercise, when they would relinquish those powers, and who could investigate and punish paganism, apostasy, and heresy. The particular circumstances of the discovery and conquest led to the exercise of powers by religious groups that was far beyond their normal scope. Once this exercise of authority was established, competing groups within the church sought to maintain and expand their respective areas of influence. The work of such priests as Ruiz de Alarcón was conditioned by these competing interests and jurisdictional circumscriptions.

The church organizational structure in Mexico was imported from Spain, but the extent and distribution of powers within the church was considerably different in the New World. In Spain, the church's concern with religious orthodoxy had led to the bishops' exercising authority over these matters within their respective dioceses. Jurisdiction over heresy, however, had been removed from the bishops and vested in the office of the Holy Inquisition when it was established in the thirteenth century (Greenleaf 1965:138). While areas of jurisdiction and lines of authority were fairly well recognized in Spain, the transferral of religious functionaries to the New World led to aberrations in authority and power structures and a blurring of areas of responsibility. In the New World the church was brought under the more inclusive framework of the Spanish government.

The colonial government in Mexico was divided into five branches: *gobierno* (civil administration), *justicia* (judiciary), *militar* (military), *hacienda* (treasury), and *eclesiástico* (church affairs) (Gerhard 1972:11). Our concern is primarily with civil, judicial, and church matters, but the distinctiveness of the conceptual divisions was not matched in the way they functioned. The civil government was headed by the viceroy (under the Council of the Indies), under whom were *gobernadores* (governors), and then either *alcaldes mayores* or *corregidores* (see below), all of whom had jurisdiction in civil and criminal cases (Schwaller 1978:32).

The civil government controlled, to a large extent, the religious functionaries in the New World. The king of Spain nominated (in effect, appointed) the higher church dignitaries, while the viceroy and governors nominated the parish priests (Gerhard 1972:17; Haring 1963:167). The American church was essentially a national church, directed and appointed by civil authorities (Haring 1963:169). While this gave the civil government extensive control over church matters, it also permitted the intrusion of ecclesiastical interests into civil affairs. The two realms—civil and religious—often merged; civil law frequently carried religious justifications and sanctions, and ecclesiastics were often appointed to political offices (Gibson 1966:80).

The main division of Roman Catholic clergy was between the secular and regular branches, each organized in distinctly different fashions, subject to different constraints, and pursuing their own goals. The secular branch was composed of those priests who took vows of ordination, normally administered a parish, were under the authority of the archbishop and bishops, but were not bound by vows or rules; they lived in the world, *saeculum* (Gerhard 1972:17; Gibson 1966:77; Schwaller 1978:2). Regulars (such as Franciscans, Augustinians, and Dominicans), however, followed strict rules governing their lives and conduct, often lived in cloistered communities, and took vows of poverty; they lived by the rule, *regula* (Gibson 1966:77; Schwaller 1978:2). When missionization of the New World began at the end of the fifteenth century, the popes granted extensive powers to the rulers of Spain, as patrons of the mission lands. In order to work in areas where the church had never been before, the friars were given great latitude and powers normally reserved for the bishops (Ennis 1977:64–65). Although the initial evangelization of New Spain was conducted by seculars (Schwaller 1978:5), they were too few, and the task fell largely to the regulars, who were permitted to administer the sacraments and perform other duties normally reserved to the secular clergy (Haring 1963:172).* This extraordinary situation rapidly became the norm in the New World, and the regulars, quickly entrenched in their positions, fought the attempts of the bishops to reassert secular control (Gerhard 1972:22; Shiels 1977:112), remaining virtually autonomous well into the seventeenth century.

The seculars were under the bishop of Santo Domingo until 1526, when the first bishopric of New Spain was established in Tlaxcala. The Diocese of Mexico was created the following year, a third was established in 1535 in Antequera (Oaxaca), and a fourth was established in Michoacan in 1538 (Schwaller 1978:6–11).

*Pope Leo X authorized the first of the regulars to go to New Spain. The Franciscans arrived in 1523, the Dominicans in 1526, the Augustinians in 1533, and the Jesuits in 1572. Other orders also arrived but were of minor importance (Braden 1930:132–41; Gerhard 1972:18–19).

Despite the apparent expansion of secular authority, the number of secular priests was limited, but, by papal bull, regulars were given the right to exercise almost all episcopal powers, except ordination, in areas two days distant from a bishop (Greenleaf 1965:138). This struggle for authority by both secular and regular clergy shaped much of the development of the church in the New World.

The structure of the two religious groups differed. The regulars were organized by provinces, the locations of which were determined largely by the order of their entry into Mexico and the areas remaining for missionization. Below the province was the *doctrina*, a parish administered by a regular, called a *doctrinero* (Shiels 1977:112), with its seat in the major town of the region (Cuevas 1946, 2:171–74; Schwaller 1978:115–16). Minor towns within the *doctrina* were called *visitas*. Seculars, however, were subordinate to the bishops and were organized in *partidos* (parishes) which, given the area involved and the sparse population, were often quite large (they were called *parroquias* if they were located within major cities). A priest who administed a parish was normally called a *cura*, or a *cura capellán* until 1565 (Schwaller 1978:115).

The seculars were responsible for the administration of ecclesiastical justice. The highest ecclesiastical judge within the archdiocese, the *vicario general*, was appointed by the archbishop, and subordinate judges were appointed in the outlying territories, many of whom were also *curas*. Only in that case would they also use the title *vicario* (Schwaller 1978:116, 141), but the proliferation of the appointments led to *cura* being virtually a synonym for *vicario*.

Unlike the regulars, who were supported by their orders, the seculars were expected to earn their own support—usually by collecting their wages from Spanish landholders, or directly from the Indians as part of their tribute (Schwaller 1978: 117). This was usually inadequate, however, and by canon law prospective priests were required to demonstrate a permanent source of income, usually called a *beneficio* (benefice) or *congrua*. This financial requirement was one of the main factors limiting the number of seculars during early colonialization. Priests possessing these benefices carried the additional title *beneficiado*. If a *partido* had both a *beneficiado* and a *cura*, the former occupied the senior position (Schwaller 1978: 128), although a *vicario* outranked either. Of the three titles applicable to secular priests—*cura*, *vicario*, and *beneficiado*—the first two titles reflected jurisdiction, while the third referred to income as well. Usually there was only one priest in a *partido*, except for city parishes and mining districts (Schwaller 1978:124). Within the *partidos* priests often used Indian officials as assistants. The elaborate political and religious structures of the pre-Columbian world had been rapidly dismantled, but local-level functionaries persisted, altered both directly and indirectly by the Spaniards. Typically, each *cabecera* had an Indian *gobernador*, often distinguished from the indigenous ruler, or *tlahtoani*, and a *cabildo* (town council). *Cabildos* had two principal officers—*alcaldes* and *regidores*—concerned with political administration; the *alcaldes* also acted as judges in local courts dealing with Indian cases, as did the *gobernadores* (Gibson 1964:167, 180). *Mandones*, *fiscales*, and *alguaciles* held offices in the barrios (town subdivisions) and *estancias* (subordinate Indian communities) (Gibson 1964:182–83). Catholic priests effectively used these officials to carry out the work of conversion. *Fiscales* and *alguaciles* summoned recalcitrant villagers to services, administered minor punishments, and sought out and eliminated unorthodox or pagan religious practices (Gibson 1964:183; Schwaller 1978:126–27).

Much of the conflict between the seculars and the regulars revolved around church finances. The regulars opposed laying additional tribute levies on the hard-pressed and declining Indian population, while the seculars favored it. The issue, though often couched in ethical and humanistic terminology, actually reflected matters of more directly political concern. Generally, the power of the regulars depended on continuing to exclude the seculars, while the power of the seculars depended on expansion, and the goals of each side were tied to the tribute issue (however, the late-arriving Jesuits sided with the seculars against the regulars, whom they regarded as competitors [Schwaller 1978:49]). No increase meant that the regulars could retain their positions with little competition from the seculars, whereas increase meant that the seculars could expand at the expense of the regulars. The crown supported the regulars, since they were more effective, less corrupt, and less costly (Schwaller 1978:17–20).

Until 1571 the Inquisition did not formally exist in New Spain, though bishops had responsibility for enforcing orthodoxy in their capacities as ecclesiastical judges ordinary (Greenleaf 1969:7). Initially, converted Indians were subject to these tribunals, leading to trials and the first burnings in Mexico (Braden 1930:149), but it was soon realized that if embracing Catholicism opened one to such punishment the efforts at conversion would be seriously hindered. Consequently, Charles V decreed, in 1538, that Indians would not be subject to the inquisitional process but would be relegated to the ordinary (i.e., secular) jurisdiction of the bishops (Lea 1922:210). Limits were placed on the corporal punishment that could be inflicted on Indians by the priests; stocks, beatings, and imprisonment were outlawed (Braden 1930:170).

Major changes took place within the Mexican church in the late 1540s. The New Laws of 1542 altered the legal status of the Indians, and the plagues greatly diminished the native population, prompting a further debate over Indian tithes (Schwaller 1978:38). The Diocese of Mexico became an archdiocese in 1547, with jurisdiction over Puebla, Oaxaca, Michoacan, Nueva Galicia, Yucatan, Chiapas, Guatemala, Honduras, and Nicaragua (Schwaller 1978:28). In Europe, the Council of Trent (1545-63) declared that no regular could assume parochial duties without the license of the local bishop and that the bishops had direct control over all parish priests. The scarcity of secular priests in New Spain, however, and the outcry of the regulars prompted King Philip II to seek and receive from the pope a dispensation for Mexico (Greenleaf 1969:117; Schwaller 1978:48; Shiels 1977:113).

In the 1550s and 1560s the first program of *congregación* was carried out. The depopulation was so great that the Indians were persuaded or forced to move from their old townsites to new ones where they could be more easily Christianized (Gerhard 1972:27). This practice was again resorted to after the epidemic of 1576–81.

The ecclesiastical inquisition had proved to be inadequate, owing to the lack of central control and the inadequacy of the personnel (Greenleaf 1969:158). In 1570, Philip II established the Holy Inquisition in Mexico. The main purposes of the Inquisition were to reform the clergy and to eradicate heresy, a directive aimed primarily at lapsed Christianized Jews (Gibson 1966:78–79; Schwaller 1978: 52–53). The Inquisition was equally composed of laity and priests, but its investigations of both regular and secular clergy, as well as its preemption of secular inquisitorial powers, often placed it in opposition to the religious factions (Gibson 1966:79; Lea 1922:199; Schwaller 1978:53). Priests predominated in the Inquisition only at the regional level, serving as local inquisitors in major towns and having charge of collecting testimony and conducting preliminary hearings (Schwaller 1978:53, 149). They had no authority to try cases, but were to forward the accused to the central tribunal (Scholes 1977:28). Although jurisdiction over the natives was denied the Inquisition (it was reserved to the bishops), it continued to investigate instances of native idolatry and superstition (Greenleaf 1965:141; 1969:101, 173–74). The continuation of pagan practices encouraged the gathering of information concerning these practices, and friars of several orders were ordered to provide reports (Greenleaf 1965:144).

The main preoccupation, insofar as the Indians were concerned, was the syncretic nature of their religion. The Indians tended to incorporate the new teachings in a way compatible with their own lives, often in a decidedly non-Christian way, and to view this new religion as complementary rather than exclusive (Gibson 1966:75). Witchcraft was also a major issue (Greenleaf 1969:173), as was the use of hallucinogenic plants for divination, a practice specifically ordered prosecuted by the Holy Inquisition (Guerra 1967:175). In a setting such as this, with poorly trained clergy, widespread indigenous practices, and multiple, crosscutting religious and inquisitional jurisdiction, abuse was not only possible but likely.

In 1614 reports reached the Holy Inquisition in Mexico City of a priest in the Atenango area who was conducting autos-da-fé and punishing Indians—all illegal and an infringement of Inquisition powers. The priest was Hernando Ruiz de Alarcón. The local Inquisition official investigated and forwarded a complete dossier to the tribunal detailing the activities of Ruiz de Alarcón. He had, in fact, been conducting the events alleged—holding offenders up as examples, flogging them, and bringing them from neighboring villages for discipline—but further investigation established to the satisfaction of the Inquisition that he had erred from ignorance, not malice. As a result of his zeal he was appointed ecclesiastical judge in about 1617 (Warren 1973:83), and began informing the Inquisition of instances of idolatry and superstition in his region: he was one of those charged with reporting on pagan practices, a duty that resulted in his *Treatise on the Heathen Superstitions and Customs That Today Live Among the Indians Native to This New Spain.*

THE PERSPECTIVE OF RUIZ DE ALARCÓN

To understand the work of Ruiz de Alarcón, some consideration must be directed to his purposes in writing the *Treatise*—not so much the historical background of his writing as his motivations in collecting and recording these events. As is apparent throughout his *Treatise*, Ruiz de Alarcón felt that he was helping root out paganism and those syncretic elements of the native religion that threatened the purity of Christianity.

There was a danger—long recognized by Spanish clergy (Motolinia 1973:21–23)—that any record of the native ways could permit their continued practice, a danger that Ruiz de Alarcón also recognized. There was, however, a countervailing concern that the clergy were informed of these matters so that they could detect idolatry and paganism when it occurred (Durán 1967, 1:217–19; Ruiz de Alarcón, Prologue). In a less disinterested fashion than that of some of his predecessors (e.g., Durán 1967, 1:41), Ruiz de Alarcón's exasperation led him to adopt an adversary role in both collecting and presenting his evidence. He was convinced that he was recording evil—the only justification for so doing being the eventual eradication of paganism and salvation of the souls being lost. Thus Ruiz de Alarcón's work is neither a comprehensive ethnography, such as Sahagún's work (1951–75), nor a complete treatment of even selected aspects of native life, such as Durán's work (1967). Consequently, his *Treatise* cannot be approached as an exhaustive treatment of native religion and medicine or as a comprehensive study of even those aspects upon which it concentrates most heavily. Much of Ruiz de Alarcón's commentary is the result of misconception. He frequently gives rationalizations for native practices that he does not understand. Because he adopts the view that native practices are diabolical (and hence necessarily and explicitly in opposition to Christianity), rather than being indigenous practices with their own cultural histories and social functions, Ruiz de Alarcón's understanding of them is superficial. Thus the *Treatise* shows evidence of distortion, both as a deliberate act by Ruiz de Alarcón and as a result of misunderstanding the data.

In extracting those matters most injurious to the paganism he sought to eradicate, Ruiz de Alarcón presents only selected materials. As he often mentions in the *Treatise*, there are many additional incantations and practices that are merely alluded to, rather than recorded, once the basic point of what he considers a "typical" practice is made. While not diminishing the value of what is recorded, this selection of examples from among a much larger corpus detracts from the work as a representative cross section of beliefs and practices. Choosing illustrative practices is not, in itself, fatal to the representativeness of the *Treatise*. The selection was not random, however, but carefully sifted to present what Ruiz de Alarcón felt to be the most egregious abuses. While much that is recorded shows distortion, how much he ignored is unknown, as is how much he failed to see (many aspects of native religion that Ruiz de Alarcón fails to discuss are, however, mentioned in the much briefer, contemporary relation of Pedro Ponce; see Appendix A).

Even with the practices he did record, there are further difficulties. While he undoubtedly knew Nahuatl well, he seems to have relied on his native informants or the natives in his household for translation of the material collected, as indicated both by his own statements and by the otherwise strange inconsistency with which certain phrases are translated, as though some informants were more knowledgeable or more forthcoming than others. Ruiz de Alarcón's rationalizations of some of the mistranslated incantations further cloud the picture.

An additional problem in Ruiz de Alarcón's understanding of events, and in our own grasp of exactly what he did and did not know, is his treatment of the native gods. The names of gods in Nahuatl were motivated; that is, the gods had names with transparent significance, unlike our own situation in which most of our proper names have lost motivation (for example, Jesus is a variant of Joshua, meaning "the Lord is salvation"). As a consequence, it is not always clear when Ruiz de Alarcón recognizes a god name as a proper noun, whether a single word or phrase, rather than simply a common noun. He does recognize some gods, such as Quetzalcoatl, and usually leaves those names in Nahuatl, but because he translates other names literally, his recognition of those gods is less certain. Sometimes it is apparent that he recognizes a word as a god name, even when mistranslated, as with Centeotl. At other times, it is obvious that he does not recognize the god (e.g., Tlaloc). Other cases are uncertain, however, and made more so by the Nahuatl fondness for apposition that leads to multiple god names (certainly a common phenomenon in pre-Columbian Mexico) and allusions to gods. To judge by his translations, however, it is apparent that in many instances Ruiz de Alarcón simply fails to recognize gods in the Nahuatl incantations, with the result that his understanding of the text is faulty.*

PRE-COLUMBIAN MEXICAN RELIGION

To understand Ruiz de Alarcón's *Treatise*, a brief overview of pre-Columbian Mexican religion is as necessary as it is difficult. Much of the difficulty arises because the religion was not a perfectly integrated system but the result of thousands of years of development—the gods present at the time of the Conquest being the result of long accretion, the movement of various peoples, and the political fortunes of empires. Although there are difficulties in identifying the gods of the immediate pre-Conquest period with much earlier depictions (Nicholson 1976), the general conservativeness of Mesoamerican religion appears to allow the early identification of Aztec gods or their prototypes.

Tracing the development of gods as illustrated on art objects from as early as 1200 B.C. to the Conquest has been attempted (Covarrubias 1957:62): early Olmec depictions of serpents may have been Quetzalcoatl (Burland 1967:21; Coe 1968:114) and iconographic analysis also suggests the presence of Centeotl, Xipe ToTec, MictlanTeuctli, and a composite of Cipactli, Xiuhcoatl, Xiuhteuctli, and Huehuehteotl (Joralemon 1971:90).

Gods who may be identified as Quetzalcoatl, Huehuehteotl, and Xipe ToTec are depicted throughout the city of Teotihuacan (ca. A.D. 0–700) (Burland 1967:27; Kubler 1967), as is Tlaloc (Kubler 1967; Miller 1973; Pasztory 1974), who appears to be the dominant god—certainly the most commonly represented.

The Toltecs of Tula (ca. A.D. 900–1200) honored Quetzalcoatl and Coatl-Icue (Burland 1967:33), but Tezcatl-Ihpoca became the main god (Chadwick 1971). And with the later rise of the Aztecs, their god Huitzilopochtli became important as well (Nicholson 1971:425–26).

Time was not alone responsible for the incorporation of new gods: contact between different regions and traditions also played a part. Many gods from distant regions and from conquered areas were absorbed into Aztec religion, as their adornment attests. Thus Quetzalcoatl wears a Huastec hat, Tlahzolteotl also wears a Huastec ornament, Centeotl has been identified as Totonac, and Xochiquetzal has been identified as Tlalhuica and Tlaxcalteca (Spence 1923:17, 156, 176, 187, 194). How these gods arose and diffused is not always clear, but the spread of

*God names have been corrected and conventionalized throughout the *Treatise* commentary, the Appendices, and the corrected Nahuatl text, and glottal stops have been included (marked by the use of *h*), but not vowel length. For a fuller discussion of god names, see Appendix B.

Huitzilopochtli was tied to Aztec imperial expansion. As the Aztecs extended their political dominance, Huitzilopochtli was placed among the local gods of conquered peoples, as an addition, not a replacement (see Paso y Troncoso 1905a–c).

A major feature of Mesoamerican religion that facilitated the spread of gods was not simply common cultural elements (Caso 1968) but the qualities of the gods themselves. Although they usually had well-defined characteristics—so that Quetzalcoatl and Tezcatl-Ihpoca could easily be described—the gods possessed few attributes that were exclusively and unambiguously theirs. Instead, qualities, provenances, and powers tended to be diffuse, shared by many gods. For example, several gods had authority over rain, even though Tlaloc is most prominently associated with it. But it was not merely the shading of divine qualities across the supernatural spectrum that fostered the spread of gods and made the analysis of their religion so difficult. There was in Mesoamerican religion a principle of duality, with many gods being divided into masculine and feminine counterparts (e.g., Ome Teotl, who was divided into Ome Teuctli and Ome Cihuatl) (Caso 1958:9; Spence 1923). Moreover, there was an apparent attempt, conscious or unconscious, to rationalize the system of gods, to place them in some understandable relationship to each other and integrate new gods, often reinterpreting them as variants of extant gods. Thus, while he was a separate god, Huitzilopochtli was also conceptualized as the blue Tezcatl-Ihpoca (Caso 1958:10).

In addition to the problem of identifying a particular god as one aspect of another god, a further complicating factor was the multiplicity of names under which the various gods were known. Chicome-Coatl was also known as Chalchiuhcihuatl; Tezcatl-Ihpoca was also known as Titlacahuan; Ome Teuctli and Ome Cihuatl were also known as Citlallatonac and Citlalli Icue; and Chalchihuitl Icue was known variously as Matlalcueyeh, Xochiquetzal, and Macuilxochiquetzal (Clavijero 1979, 1:252; Durán 1967, 1:135; Sahagún 1952:11–12; Torquemada 1976:66, 70, 78). Although the broad outlines of deity origins may be discerned, the incomplete archaeological record and the mutability of godly identity makes such an approach difficult and, in terms of understanding the significance of the gods at any one time, less than satisfactory.

An alternative method of structuring the various gods of the Nahuatl tradition (drawing largely on the Aztecs) is by theogony. Many of the gods were placed in kin relations with one another, much as the Aztecs themselves were, and various accounts record these divine relationships. By one account, Huixtohcihuatl was the sister of the Tlaloqueh, ToCih was the mother of Centeotl or Itztlacoliuhqui, and Coatl Icue was the mother of the Centzonhuitznahuah, Coyolxauhqui, and Huitzilopochtli (Sahagún 1951:13, 86, 112; Sahagún 1952:1–3). No integrated family system is evident, however; different accounts are at variance with one another. For instance, Quetzalcoatl is recorded as the son of Iztac Mixcoatl and either Chimalman or Xochiquetzal in one account, but as the son of Tonacateuctli and Tonacacihuatl in another. The other god relationships are no less confusing, though the relatively recent Huitzilopochtli seems to have suffered the least in this respect (Nicholson 1971:409; Spence 1923).

While adopting an evolutionary approach to the gods sheds some light on their importance and relationships, neither it nor the theogonic approach accounts for them as a coherent, internally consistent group. A third approach is to place the gods in thematic groupings, as various writers have attempted to do. Following Nicholson (1971), we can class the gods in several theme groups sharing common elements and patterns reflecting both the conceptual clustering of the gods and the dominant themes of Mesoamerican religion: (1) Celestial Creativity-Divine Paternalism, (2) Rain-Moisture-Agricultural Fertility, and (3) War-Sacrifice-Sanguinary Nourishment of the Sun and Earth.

The fundamental theme of the Celestial Creativity-Divine Paternalism group was primordial creation. Nicholson further divides this group into several subgroups named for the most prominent god in each; the Ome Teotl complex (concerned with generative power and sexual dualism), the Tezcatl-Ihpoca complex (concerned with the omnipotent, omnipresent, omniscient god), and the Xiuhteuctli complex (concerned with life-giving fire).

The fundamental theme of the Rain-Moisture-Agricultural Fertility group was, of course, agriculture and production. The subgroups include the Tlaloc complex (concerned with the control of rain), the Centeotl:Xochipilli complex (concerned with the cultivation of maize), the Ome-Tochtli complex (concerned with fertility and associated with maguey), the Teteoh Innan complex (concerned with the earth-mother concept), and the Xipe ToTec complex (concerned with sacrifice).

The fundamental theme of the War-Sacrifice-Sanguinary Nourishment of the Sun and Earth was nourishment of the gods as a necessary condition for the continuation of the universe. The several subgroupings include: the Tonatiuh complex (concerned with Ome-Tochtli, the primordial creative deity, and his merger with the sun), the Huitzilopochtli complex (concerned with war and sacrifice), the Mixcoatl: TlahuizcalpanTeuctli complex (concerned with war and ancestral leaders), and the MictlanTeuctli complex (concerned with the cult of death).

Although heuristically useful, these categories do not separate the gods into discrete, non-overlapping categories. Rather, the gods may share in all of them to varying degrees. And there are several gods, such as Quetzalcoatl and Yahcateuctli, who do not easily fit into these larger assemblages. It is doubtful that an exclusive and exhaustive categorization of the gods is possible, since their various attributes trace from many different locales, times, and traditions. It is likely, however, that within a given locale the supernatural world was reasonably coherent and consistent.

In addition to their individual characteristics, the gods also possess a temporal significance that affects their relations with human beings and dictates the ritual cycle of Aztec society, tied to and reflected in the Aztec calendar. There were, in fact, two (concurrent) calendars, each based on a major cycle, one of 260 days and one of 365 days. In the 260-day cycle (the *tonalpohualli*—"the count of the days"), each day-name consists of a day-number and a day-sign. There are thirteen day-numbers and twenty day-signs, which run concurrently.

The twenty *tonalpohualli* day-signs, in conventional sequence, are as follows:

1. cipactli	alligator
2. ehehcatl	wind
3. calli	house
4. cuetzpalin	lizard
5. coatl	snake
6. miquiztli	death
7. mazatl	deer

8. tochtli	rabbit
9. atl	water
10. itzcuintli	dog
11. ozomahtli	monkey
12. malinalli	grass
13. acatl	reed
14. ocelotl	jaguar
15. cuauhtli	eagle
16. cozcacuauhtli	vulture
17. olin	(earth)quake
18. tecpatl	flint
19. quiahuitl	rain
20. xochitl	flower

Each of the thirteen day-numbers is accompanied by one of the thirteen Lords of the Day as follows:

1. Xiuhteuctli	Turquoise-lord
2. Tlalteuctli	Lord-of-the-land
3. Chalchihuitl Icue	Her-skirt Is Jade
4. Tonatiuh	He-goes-becoming-warm
5. Tlahzolteotl	Filth-goddess
6. MictlanTeuctli	Lord-in-Mictlan
7. Centeotl	Ear-of-maize-god
8. Tlaloc	Land-lier
9. Quetzalcoatl	Plumed-serpent
10. Tezcatl-Ihpoca	Smoking Mirror
11. Chalmecateuctli	Lord-who-is-a-resident-in-Chalman
12. TlahuizcalpanTeuctli	Lord-at-the-Dawn
13. Citlalli Icue	Her-skirt Is Stars

Since the lowest common multiple of 13 and 20 is 260, a given combination of day-number plus day-sign will recur only after as many days. Thus, with the 260-day period, the combination of the 13- and 20-day cycles will uniquely identify a day.

In the 365-day cycle, there are eighteen named "months" of twenty days each, totaling 360 days, plus five additional days, called *nen ontemi* [pronounced *nēmontēmi*] or *nentemi*, intercalated at the end of the eighteenth month (Sahagún 1951:152). The eighteen months of the 365-day calendar are as follows (Sahagún 1951:1–34):

1. Atl Cahualo	Water is abandoned
2. Tlacaxipehualiztli	Flaying of men
3. Tozoztontli	Short vigil
4. Huei Tozoztli	Long vigil
5. Toxcatl	Drought
6. Etzalcualiztli	Eating of bean porridge
7. Tecuilhuitontli	Small festival of the Lords
8. Huei Tecuilhuitl	Great festival of the Lords
9. Miccailhuitontli	Small festival of the dead
10. Huei Miccailhuitl	Great festival of the dead
11. Ochpaniztli	Sweeping of the road
12. Pachtontli	Small Spanish moss
13. Huei Pachtli	Great Spanish moss
14. Quecholli	Macaw

15. Panquetzaliztli	Raising of the flags
16. Atemoztli	Descent in the form of water
17. Tititl	Shrunk *or* Wrinkled thing
18. Izcalli	Sprout

Both the *tonalpohualli* and the 365-day calendar run simultaneously, in independent cycles. The multiples of the 20 day-names, 13 day-numbers, and 18 months (plus 5 days) generate unique combinations through 52 cycles of the 365-day calendar or 73 *tonalpohualli* cycles and constitute the Calendar Round, after which the entire cycle begins anew.

The years of the 365-day calendar are named for the day-name on which they begin. The cycle of 360 days, of 18 complete 20-day cycles, does not include the five *nen ontemi* days (the days that become full in vain, i.e., days of misfortune). Consequently, the years always begin on one of 4 days, known as the year-bearers, which are 5 days apart in the day-sign sequence and which occur in disproportionate frequency in indigenous chronicles (Davies 1977:171–72). These day-signs—*calli, tochtli, acatl,* and *tecpatl*—each accompanied by a number, designate a year thirteen times during the Calendar Round (Sahagún 1953:21–22).

An additional cycle of days, although by no means the only other one, is that of the nine Lords of the Night, the Yohualteuctin:

1. Xiuhteuctli	Turquoise-lord
2. Itztli *or* Tecpatl	Obsidian *or* Flint
3. Piltzinteuctli	Child-lord
4. Centeotl	Ear-of-maize-god
5. MictlanTeuctli	Lord-in-Mictlan
6. Chalchihuitl Icue	Her-skirt Is Jade
7. Tlahzolteotl	Filth-goddess
8. Tepeyollohtli	Heart-of-the-mountain(s)
9. Tlaloc	Land-lier

The calendar of central Mexico can be viewed as a series of different-sized cogs, each turning at its own rate but combining to create larger temporal units as the various cogs coincide. No recognized temporal unit was without its supernatural association: each "month" was dedicated to a god, and each day had simultaneous Lords of the Night and Lords of the Day, as well as a calendrical name, such as One Reed, with further supernatural associations (e.g., either representing a god or marking a divine event, such as the creation or birth of a god). Within the daily cycle time was further segmented and associated with various gods (Carrasco in Graulich 1981; Graulich 1981; Klein 1975), so that neither day nor "hour" was without multiple, overlapping supernatural associations.

The Aztecs saw themselves as the culmination of a supernatural developmental process and felt themselves to be located in supernatural space as well as in supernatural time. From the center of the earth, everything extended out to the four directions, each associated with an afterworld. In this concept of directionality, time and space merged. Directions all had characteristic colors and day-signs:

East	yellow	Cipactli, Coatl, Atl, Acatl, Olin
North	red	Ehehcatl, Miquiztli, Itzcuintli, Ocelotl, Tecpatl
West	blue-green	Calli, Mazatl, Ozomahtli, Cuauhtli, Quiahuitl
South	white	Cuetzpalin, Tochtli, Malinalli, Cozcacuauhtli, Xochitl

Even individual days were conceptualized both temporally and spatially (Graulich 1981; Klein 1975).

The earth was only one of many layers in the universe. The heavens were conceived as tiers above the earth, while the underworlds were tiers below the earth. The standard version of the heavens held that there were thirteen layers, with associated gods. There are, however, variant accounts of a nine-tiered heaven. The underworld was a nine-tiered structure. Thus in the Aztec world everyone was precisely located in supernatural space and time, and every referent had temporal-spatial implications and vice versa. Whatever the sophisticated theological speculations that may have concerned the religious elite, at the everyday level the gods were neither Aztec society writ large nor ethereal beings touching only tangentially on individuals' lives. Rather, the gods represented (*were?*) all the basic elements of Nahuatl existence—the physical world (sun, moon, stars, Milky Way, earth, water, and mountains), the elements (rain, lightning, clouds, wind), flora and fauna (maize, tobacco, maguey, peyote, deer, eagles, snakes, jaguars, pumas), and major cultural functions (fishing, hunting, war, sex, death) as well as evil forces (Tzitzimitl, Colelectli, ghosts). Not simply possessed of divine patrons, the Nahuatl world was suffused with the supernatural. The spiritual world infused the material, hence the multiple referents. Maize was *centli*, but it could also be addressed as the god Centeotl, or as Chicome-Coatl (Seven Snake), its day-name name. Everything possessed material, spiritual, temporal, and spatial aspects, with references to any one of these potentially invoking the others. Consequently, Nahuatl invocations were metaphorically complex and allusorily sophisticated.

Maintenance of this orthodoxy and attendance to the necessary rituals were the obligations of the priests. As one would expect, in view of the complexity implicit in the foregoing, the priestly organization of the Aztecs was highly elaborate and hierarchically organized. Highest of the priests were the two Quequetzalcoah (Quetzalcoatl ToTec Tlamacazqui and Quetzalcoatl Tlaloc Tlamacazqui) (Acosta Saignes 1946:149; Caso 1958:82–83; Nicholson 1971:436; Sahagún 1952:67). Of equal status, the former was dedicated to Tlaloc and the latter to Huitzilopochtli, the two gods who occupied dual temples atop the main temple in the Aztec capital, Tenochtitlan. Below these came the *cuacuilli*, the *papahhuah*, the *tlenamacac*, the *tlamacazqui*, and the *tlamacazton* (for a more elaborate discussion of the priestly hierarchy, see Acosta Saignes 1946).

Although priests of major centers may have exercised some control over those of subordinate centers, the priests of each community were essentially autonomous. Novitiates were largely recruited from among noble youths who were trained in religious schools—the *calmecac*—connected with the various temples. Despite the appearance of an integrated hierarchy, most priests were dedicated to specific gods and were organized around their respective temples (Sahagún 1951:161–62, 165–80, 193–201; Durán 1967, vol. 1). And much of what applies to the gods regarding their qualities, purposes, and so forth, applies to their respective priesthoods.

Simultaneously there existed a substratum of "folk" practitioners—magicians, diviners, and curers (the division between the official and unofficial practitioners is more easily drawn in theory than in practice, since they shared many functions and approaches). A major distinction lies in the societal (official) objectives of priests versus the individual (unofficial) objectives of the folk practitioners. Magicians, diviners, curers, and illusionists often overlapped the official priests in function but did not depend on the official hierarchical organizations for their existence (for a complete list of such practitioners found in Ruiz de Alarcón's *Treatise*, see Appendix C; for a more comprehensive account of these practitioners in the pre-Hispanic period, see Nicholson 1971:438-43; Sahagún 1961:31-32; Sahagún 1957:42-43, 192-93; Sahagún 1970:24).

As with the gods, there were various traditions in central Mexico concerning fundamental beliefs. A generalized account begins with the god Tonacateuctli and his spouse Tonacacihuatl, who gave birth to the four manifestations (or personifications) of Tezcatl-Ihpoca.

Next followed the creation sequences of the world. There were four prior worlds (Caso 1958:14-16; Nicholson 1971:398-99). The first world, presided over by Tezcatl-Ihpoca, was destroyed by jaguars in the year Four Jaguar. The second world, presided over by Quetzalcoatl, was destroyed by hurricanes in the year Four Wind. The third world, presided over by Tlaloc, was destroyed by fiery rain in the year Four Rain. The fourth world, presided over by Chalchihuitl Icue, was destroyed by floods in the year Four Water. The fifth world (our world), presided over by Tonatiuh, will be destroyed by earthquakes in the year Four Earthquake.

The present world was rebuilt by the gods, primarily by Tezcatl-Ihpoca and Huitzilopochtli, after which Quetzalcoatl retrieved some bones of the previous generation of humanity from MictlanTeuctli in the underworld, Mictlan. These bones were then finely ground, and the gods mixed them with their own blood, obtained through autosacrifice, and thence emerged the primal human pair, Oxomoco and Cipactonal, from whom all human beings descended. Although the versions vary, it is generally held that the gods then delivered to man the means of his subsistence—maize, beans, amaranth, chia, and other provisions. All this transpired in darkness. The present sun was created when Nanahuatzin and Tecciztecatl threw themselves into the bonfire to become the sun and moon, respectively. Thereupon, the remaining gods nourished the sun through autosacrifice. This voluntary sacrifice was, however, insufficient and therefore continued sacrifice was required by human beings to ensure the perpetuation of the world. Thus war was created to gather sacrifices for the gods.

Mesoamerican religion bore within itself a certain fatalism, offset only slightly by a concept of gods who were as dependent upon man for nourishment as men were dependent upon the gods. Although the Aztecs were enmeshed in the supernatural, their relationship to the gods was not one of divine punishment or reward that depended on the ethical quality of one's life but one in which the gods controlled the various social and natural aspects of man's life. The Aztecs were therefore forced to confront them. Certainly the gods could be provoked to wrath, and thus worship and sacrifice were designed for their propitiation. The ethical dimension was lacking, however. One's life in the afterworld was decided by the manner of one's death, not the manner of one's life (Caso 1958:58). The goal of Aztec life was prosperity and the avoidance of ill fortune: since bad fortune could be evaded, the system was not strictly determined (Lanczkowski 1970:123). The experience of worship, including human sacrifice, was community with the deities (Lanczkowski 1970). The goal was achievement of necessary ends, such as crop fertility. It was this pivotal role of transforming the desires of the people into rapprochement with the gods, by whatever means—autosacrifice, prayers, chanting, dancing, fasts, confession, and so forth—that the priests performed. Although individual idols and altars attest to considerable personal worship, the major celebrations—largely those tied to the 365-day and *tonalpohualli* calendar cycles—were vast, elaborate affairs requiring the services of priestly specialists to know the proper ritual, to determine the feast days, to coordinate the events, and even to act in the capacity of gods (cf. Durán 1967, vol. 1; Sahagún 1951).

SYNCRETISM

Having faced the problem of Christianizing the infidel throughout the centuries of the reconquest of their homeland from the Moslem invaders, the Spanish clergy were well prepared for their mission in the New World. Their main concern was that the natives of New Spain should turn away from their pagan practices and adopt Christianity:

> Ye who are natives in New Spain, ye Mexicans, ye Tlaxcalans, ye Cholulans, ye Michoaca, and all ye who are vassals dwelling in the land of the Indies—
>
> Very great was the darkness and the confusion, the unbelief, the idolatry in which your fathers, your grandfathers, your great-grandfathers left you, as is evident in your ancient picture writings.
>
> Hear and understand well. For now our Lord God hath willed, hath accorded, hath sent to you the brightness, the torch, the light to reveal the true God, the Creator Who seeth over all His creation.
>
> And confusion, in which you have lived in all past time, came to you. It hath misled and deluded you. But by means of the brightness, the light, you may attain the true faith. (Sahagún 1970:55)

While the differences in religions were vast to the Spanish priests, there were areas of similarity, if not compatibility.

In the earliest catechism printed in Mexico (1544), Pedro de Córdoba (1970:99-104) listed the Ten Commandments as the road to heaven. Durán (1967, 1:35-36), however, noted that the Aztec priests used exhortations that he considered similar:

> The ancient beliefs are still so numerous, so complex, so similar to our own in many cases that one overlaps the other. Occasionally we suspect that they are playing, adoring idols, casting lots regarding future events in our very presence—yet we do not fully understand these things. We believe they do (Christian) penance and practice certain abstentions. But (they) always had their own sacraments and a divine cult which in many ways coincides with our own religion. (Durán 1971:54-55)

Although, as Friar Sahagún (1970:66) stated, "By Thy words Thy preachers admonish sinners, and Thy priests give them the Sacraments that they may change their lives and that they may satisfy Thee," these sacraments—through which sinners can attain pardon of God (Córdoba 1970:105)—had remarkable parallels to Aztec practices:

> The first Sacrament is Baptism, through which God pardons all sins. Thus, the Indians were admonished that . . . if any small child who does not have the desire to be baptized should die without baptism, this child is lost to one of the divisions

of Hell which is called Limbo, where he shall remain forever, without ever going to Heaven or seeing God. You must, therefore, be very diligent to see that your children are baptized as soon as possible, so that they will not die without being baptized and their souls lost. (Córdoba 1970:106)

This practice had a parallel in the Aztec bathing ceremony. Four days after the birth of a child, he was bathed by the midwife in a solemn ceremony (Sahagún 1951:39; Sahagún 1969:201-202).

The second Sacrament is Confirmation, to strengthen the Christian's faith (Córdoba 1970:107), paralleled in the Aztec dedication of their children to temple schools to become priests (Sahagún 1969:213).

The third Sacrament is Penance, in which the sinner repents his sins, resolves not to commit them again, and confesses to the priests who will absolve him of his sins (Córdoba 1970:107-108). This too had an Aztec parallel in confession to the goddess Tlahzolteotl (Sahagún 1969:29-34; Sahagún 1970:24-27).

The fourth Sacrament is the Eucharist, in which priests, through transubstantiation, change bread and wine into the Body and Blood of Christ, to be consumed by Christians. They must participate in this Sacrament each year at Easter, and, by so doing, they receive Jesus Christ (Córdoba 1970:108-14). The Aztec parallel involved the fashioning and eating of amaranth idols of Huitzilopochtli and Omacatl (Sahagún 1952:5-6; Sahagún 1970:33).

The fifth Sacrament, Extreme Unction, was administered to the dying to pardon their sins (Córdoba 1970:114). Although the Aztec concept of the relationship between gods and man led to a different view of sin, there were ceremonial parallels (Sahagún 1952:39).

The sixth Sacrament, Holy Orders, is conferred on those who are to become ministers of the church, who will say mass and administer the other sacraments (Córdoba 1970:114). Aztec religion also had its sacred orders with specially trained priests (Sahagún 1969:209-18) dedicated to their respective gods (Sahagún 1951: 193-201).

The seventh Sacrament, Holy Matrimony, provides for the blessing of the church on monogamous marriages (Córdoba 1970:114-15). Aztec marriages contained considerable ceremony (Sahagún 1951:39-41; Sahagún 1969:114-15), and while the explicit role of the priests appears to have been slight, marriages were celebrated in relation to portentous days and festivals for gods, implying divine favor.

In short, there were many points of similarity, even without the more abstract issue of whether the Aztec elite had adopted or were approaching the concept of a single, nonanthropomorphic god (León-Portilla 1971:73-74). While the acceptance of foreign religious practices was a characteristic of Aztec religion, such was not the case with Roman Catholicism. As a messianic religion, Christianity could not tolerate such polytheism:

Since it is one, one Church, adoring one True God, it cannot coexist with any other religion or belief in other gods. Any other human belief opposed to the Faith loses the quality of the Faith itself, and though this [individual] believe in the Catholic Faith, he is deceived inasmuch as his belief is based not on Christian but on human faith. (Durán 1971:51; also see Appendix A.)

Despite assertions that Aztec paganism was to be completely uprooted and destroyed so that Catholicism could flourish (Durán 1967, 1:3), actual church practice did not follow this course.

While the religious syncretism that occurred in Mexico after the Conquest has been portrayed as the adaptation of Catholic parallels and traditions to native needs and attitudes, and the result of a long tradition of adapting to the religion of the conqueror (Madsen 1960:118), it was not simply a matter of natives accepting and altering those parts of Christianity that were most compatible with existing practices and beliefs. The process of syncretism was fostered by the Catholic priests themselves. This priest-led syncretism may be seen in their manner of instruction. Friar Pedro de Gante adapted traditional Aztec songs, dances, and folk drama to teach about Christian heroes (Madsen 1960:134–35). Confessions were written in the native glyph system (Motolinía 1973:146), to be recited before the priest confessor, and catechisms were produced by means of this system (see the examples in Cuevas 1946, 1:237; Robertson 1959:53–55, pl. 8). In an effort to teach the Indians the words of a prayer, the friars used the Aztec glyph system as a mnemonic device. For example, the Nahuatl word that sounds similar to *Pater* is *pantli* ("flag"), while *noster* resembles *nochtli* ("nopal cactus"). Thus *Pater noster* was represented by the glyphs for flag and nopal cactus (Mendieta 1971: 245–46).

All of these practices involved tacit syncretism promulgated by Catholic priests. The priests, however, also fostered a more active form of syncretism. Catholic doctrine did not unequivocally denounce the native religion as baseless and therefore to be discarded. Rather, it interpreted Aztec religion in a form compatible with the Catholic understanding of the world. Since the Aztec gods were not God, they were cast in the only other intelligible roles, that of devils (Sahagún 1970:68; Durán 1971:51; Motolinía 1973:131–32, 244–46), a practice that has its roots in 1 Corinthians 10:19–21:

19. What then? Do I say, that what is offered in sacrifice to idols, is any thing? Or, that the idol is any thing?
20. But the things which the heathens sacrifice, they sacrifice to devils, and not to God. And I would not that you should be made partakers with devils.
21. You cannot drink the chalice of the Lord, and the chalice of devils. You cannot be partakers of the table of the Lord, and of the table of devils.

The catechism, *Doctrina Cristiana*, that was used to initiate the Indians into Catholicism was sponsored by Juan de Zumárraga, the first bishop of Mexico, and reflects the officially accepted (though simplified) dogma of the period (Córdoba 1970:13). Throughout the *Doctrina*, which had been emended by Zumárraga, particular attention was placed on its relation to and relevance for the Indians who had previously practiced a different religion:

There is only one all-powerful God, and . . . there are not many gods, nor more than one single God. And this God is all-powerful. . . . God does not ask you to sacrifice your children, or kill your slaves, or any other living person, or cut your own flesh, or spill your own blood. He only wants you to love Him and honor Him as the true God, and not to consider any other as God, for there is no other God except Him. And those things that you worship as gods have no power. They cannot give you anything, because there is only one God. He is the one we preach to you, and He is very good. The gods you worship and honor as gods are only devils and evil enemies of the true God. The God whom we preach to you threw your gods from His house, . . . because they were evil, and they wished you ill. They ordered you to kill your children and your slaves and other persons, and they further ordered you to spill your own blood. But the real God of whom we preach, since He is good, loves Christians well, and will love you if you wish to be His friends. He does not want you to kill your children or your slaves, or any other person, nor does He want you to shed your blood unnecessarily. . . . so you will recognize the deception in which you have lived by believing that Huizilopochtli [*sic*] or Tezcatlipoca, and others whom you regarded as gods, were gods. They were not gods, but evil demons who deceived you, . . . since there is not in all the world or in Heaven or on earth or in the sea any god except the one and only God who rules and governs and sustains everything. (Córdoba 1970:57–61)

Córdoba continued, explaining such doctrines as the Trinity, Adam and Eve, and the expulsion of the Devil:

. . . the evil angels fell from Heaven because they did not wish to obey God. Some of them fell into the bottom of Hell, and others remained here on earth among us. And they all wish us ill, and they envy us because they know that God created us in order to fill the seats of Heaven that they lost. For this reason they desire to do all the ill to us that they can and to make us sin, so that we will not go to Heaven but, instead, go to Hell with them. . . . These evil angels who are devils are those who have deceived you and have caused you to believe that there were many gods. And they have influenced you to worship them and to build cues [i.e., pyramids] and teocallis [i.e., sacred places] and temples. And they have even arranged it so that the honor that you should render the true God, you have given to them. . . . You should see and know that all of those objects that you have worshiped and have regarded as gods are only devils who have deceived you. And, therefore, you should put aside and denounce Huizilopochtli [*sic*] and Tezcatlipoca and Quetzalcoatl, and all the others that you have considered to be gods, for they wish you ill, and they have deceived you. You must also put aside all their images and refrain from making sacrifices and performing all other acts that are connected with those idols. (Córdoba 1970:76–78)

By placing the Aztec gods within the Christian concepts of the supernatural, the priests gave them legitimate, albeit evil, roles. Their fundamental realities were not challenged, merely the interpretation of those realities. Their powers were not challenged, merely their proper place in the cosmology.

Thus many native actions were acceptable, but their motivations were not. Actions that would be acceptable among Christians were condemned when practiced by the natives because the priest perceived a difference in rationales:

The ancients worshiped Quetzalcoatl, who was ruler at Tula. And you named him Topiltzin. He was a common man; he was mortal. He died; his body corrupted. He is no god. And although a man of saintly life, who performed penances, he should not have been worshiped. What he did which was like miracles we know he did only through the command of the devil. He is a friend of the devils. Therefore he must needs be abhorred, abominated. Our Lord God hath thrust him into the land of the dead. . . . And his soul our Lord God damned and thrust into the land of the dead. There it is. It will forever suffer in the flames. (Sahagún 1970:69)

While, as mentioned, the Indians frequently accepted the Christian God, saints, and the Virgin Mary into their religious world views without thoroughly repudiating their original gods, so too did the Catholic priests accept the indigenous gods—not as gods, but as devils. And the ability of these devils actively to cause evil in the world was accepted by Indian and priest alike. While it is easy to understand the continuation of religious practices by the Indians on purely theological grounds (the fact that religion was inextricably interwoven with the fabric of their social life aside) since they accepted the powers of their gods, it is strange to see the complacence with which the Spanish clergy accepted it. This too, however, had a precedent. The same concept of the devil giving powers and participating in the world was an accepted way of explaining the power of paganism, which, in Spain, meant witchcraft.

The existence of devils was a fundamental tenet of Catholic faith (Ciruelo 1977:83), and the devil taught men all superstitions and witchcraft (Ciruelo 1977:91). The devil draws people into his power by offering them what they desire (Remy 1970:1). Their power depends on pacts with the devil, which are either explict (talking with the devil) or implicit (using vain ceremony and objects to achieve some purpose for which they do not have the natural power) (Ciruelo 1970:103, 108–109). Belief in the power of pagans to perform miraculous feats was not antithetical to Catholicism; it was the logical extension of a cosmology that demanded a devil.

When confronted with the religion, beliefs, and apparent powers of the various Mexican practitioners, the Catholic response was not skepticism at its possibility but ready acceptance, reinterpreting the foreign patterns along familiar lines and placing native religion, medicine, and magic in a familiar context that admitted their power but attributed their effectiveness to the Christian devil, not to the indigenous gods, rituals, or medical practices. Their basic approach, even when they sought to comprehend the native religion, was not understanding of the native beliefs per se but understanding so that the underlying reality—the devil—could be perceived.

SYNCRETISM IN THE *TREATISE*

Although it is relatively simple to discuss religious syncretism in Mexico by drawing on notorious examples from many disparate regions and historical sources, Ruiz de Alarcón's text offers an opportunity to assess the changes in one area and time. As seen in this corpus, a major dynamic of religious change was the pressure brought to bear on the natives—not only by a new religion but by Spanish cultural domination and, perhaps as important, the priestly exercise of judicial authority.

Many of the elements of classical native religion had either diminished or vanished in the hundred years since the Spanish conquest. But religious syncretism involves the selective retention of traditional elements, as well as additions from the introduced religion. Of the many gods, some are not mentioned in the *Treatise*, most notably Huitzilopochtli, although he was still worshiped elsewhere (see Appendix A), a phenomenon perhaps attributable to the relatively recent introduction of Huitzilopochtli into the Guerrero area during the Aztec expansion, so that he did not occupy a secure position in local worship.

Much of the god loss is attributable to the extinction of formal native priesthoods, whose members would have striven to maintain the position of their respective patrons. With the loss of these practitioners there was also a loss of elaborate rituals that had characterized pre-Columbian religion. Calendrically determined festivals were also undermined, both the movable festivals (tied to the *tonalpohualli*), and the annual festivals (tied to the 365-day calendar). Consequently, not only were festivals that had been directed to specific gods abandoned, but so too were the festivals with more utilitarian goals, such as praying for rain—a need still felt by the agrarian society, whatever its religion.

If we are to judge by Ruiz de Alarcón's *Treatise*, there was also a virtual absence of native rites of passage—birth, baptism, naming, marriage, death—that formed so prominent a part of pre-Columbian ritual. Many important elements of native religious life had dropped from their lives, or at least from public view.

Though much of native religion was lost, much was also added. Yet the true extent of this is not reflected in Ruiz de Alarcón's *Treatise*—a work compiled to show the Christianization yet to be done, not what had already been accomplished. The conversion of Mexico was swift and comprehensive, even though the depth of the converts' beliefs can be questioned. But since Ruiz de Alarcón was focusing on the unconverted, the apostate, and the syncretist, those Christian elements appear that were wrenched from their Roman Catholic contexts and turned to native uses and beliefs. Catholic saints often replaced indigenous gods, or were added to them, and were blamed for ills as would the native gods have been. Catholic ritual items, such as rosaries, also served in place of native items to effect cures and work wonders. And much of the Roman Catholic ritual—including Latin quotations—was inserted into otherwise traditional incantations. In short, from Ruiz de Alarcón's perspective, the most abused elements of Christianity were those that were easily transferred from one religious system to the other, because of either parallel usage or superficial similarity.

What was retained in the native religion was as important to the question of religious syncretism as the deletions and additions. As evidenced by Ruiz de Alarcón's *Treatise*, worship of many of the native gods persisted. Native rituals continued, but, for the most part, they appear to have been personal or individualistic rites. The native cosmological view also continued, if not completely, at least as part of the folk explanation of such phenomena as the names for animals and scorpions, and vividly enough to retain references to Chicomoztoc ("Seven-caves-place"), the mythical place of origin of the tribes of central Mexico (although it was used metaphorically in curing to refer to internal areas of the body).

The native view of the supernatural world persisted in the concepts of a celestial realm and an underworld. The celestial realm, Topan ("Above-us"), also called ChiucnauhTopan ("Nine-Topan") and Chiucnauhtlanepaniuhcan ("Nine-layering-place"), has nine levels, although these are not discussed separately, nor are internal distinctions drawn. However, in a separate incantation (II:12), references are made to green, yellow, and white Tlalocan—the eternally-spring paradise of Tlaloc (Sahagún 1952:45), identified with the south. Nicholson (1971:407) suggests that the nine-level celestial world is an earlier tradition than the thirteen-level view dominant in central Mexico at the time of the Spanish conquest, but whether, after a hundred years of missionization, the nine-level celestial world of Ruiz de Alarcón's *Treatise* reflects indigenous tradition or was a corruption is unknown (the fact that nine is the highest ritually used number found in the manuscript may be relevant here). The *Treatise* lacks more extensive discussion of this realm but associates Topan with Mictlan ("Deadman-land"), the underworld (II:2,3; V:2; VI:22), perhaps merely as a means of referring to the supernatural world as a whole. Mictlan, also called ChiucnauhMictlan ("Nine-Deadman-land"), likewise has nine levels, consistent with general Mexican tradition, although specific details regarding this place are also absent.

Despite the difficulties caused to the clergy in their conversion efforts by the syncretic replacement of native deities by Catholic ones, an even more telling difficulty lay in the contrasting views of the supernatural world. Native belief (at least at the folk level) differed markedly from the ideal Christian belief of the relationship between gods and people. In the Christian view God was the ultimate goal of man's strivings, whereas in the native view the gods were not goals themselves. Rather, they held power over many of the material goals of life. Thus, when the natives accepted Catholic deities, they incorporated them into their supernatural worlds in much the same capacity as their own gods, imbuing them with the same benevolent-malevolent ambiguity—exhorting them to material goals and blaming them for physical misfortunes.

A further distinction between Christianity and the native religion lay in their fundamental views of the physical world. The dominant Western view held the nonbiological world to be filled with lifeless objects. The native view held it to be full of animate beings—clouds, fire, and so forth. Consequently, two very different perspectives on causation were in contrast. To the natives, whatever had happened or would happen was the result of one's relationships to these entities. The world is seen not as random and accidental but as supremely ordered—supernatural involvement was the natural order. To the Westerner, however, the world lacked this comprehensive, supernatural flavor. Randomness and accidents are ordinary—the world is viewed mechanistically, supernatural intervention being extraordinary (Wax and Wax 1962:179–84; Wax and Wax 1963:500–501). Consequently, many of Ruiz de Alarcón's accusations of magic were leveled from a profound misapprehension of the native perspective, regardless of the degree to which his view enjoyed official support. When the natives invoked either their own gods or Catholic saints, angels, or God, they continued to seek their intervention in the world—frequently in an explicitly mechanistic manner. This, to the Catholic clergy, was magic (at best) and justifiably condemned, since God did not ordinarily operate in the world in this manner. That left only the devil; thus the Indians were ipso facto engaged in demonic acts, whether knowingly or not.

The task of changing the natives' religious orientation was eased by the Spaniards' destruction of the native religion's organizational base through the burning of native books, the razing of temples, and the elimination of indigenous priestly organizations. Religion as it had been practiced in Mexico could not continue without the sophisticated leaders, specialized training, and organization it had had or the societal economic support it had received. What remained were remnants, the folk religion and practices of the kind gathered by Ruiz de Alarcón. But the elimination of native religious competition did not ensure the success of Christianity. The struggle against religious survivals and folk practices depended on the ability of the church to compel their eradication. A major element in conversion was the exercise of judicial authority by priests. Repeatedly Ruiz de Alarcón yields examples of the use of ecclesiastical law against Indians for idolatry. Ecclesiastical law was directed largely at religious offenses, such as divination (*Treatise* I:6; V:1), and using incantations in otherwise acceptable healing practices (VI:12), and the means employed were often harsh. Physical coercion was used to extract confessions (I:2), guards were placed on homes and suspects (I:6), and priests exercised the power to arrest and punish both violators (I:2, 6; V:1; VI:12) and those who consulted them (V:1). Secular authorities also exercised jurisdiction over religious offenses, even to the extent of executing death penalties for sorcery (I:1)—the legal rationale for such a sentence may have been based on the death itself, rather than on the means. Despite the rhetoric of conversion and enlightenment, the spiritual battle in Mexico was often fought with corporeal means.

Although the Catholic clergy determinedly opposed many native religious practices, other aspects of the native system that did not directly oppose Catholic dogma were spared the brunt of this opposition. While the Catholic calendar of feast days opposed and supplanted many of the native ones, the much fuller native temporal association of gods lacked a Catholic equivalent and thus persisted. Colors, which were more richly symbolic of deities within the native tradition than within the Catholic, continued as well, as did the more extensive native spatial orientation. While both religions had concepts of ascendant and descendant afterworlds, the directional aspect of deities was exclusively Mexican and continued apparently without awareness of its significance by most of the Catholic clergy. Christianity was most successful in banning those aspects of worship which could be readily observed, such as hallucinogenic drugs, divination, and idols, and with which there was an obvious clash. This is particularly evident in the pattern of rituals that persisted. Those rituals on which Ruiz de Alarcón focuses are not the major rites of passage: these had been either replaced by equivalent Catholic rituals or incorporated into them in less obvious ways. What remains in the Ruiz de Alarcón manuscript are minor rituals—those, such as divination, curing, hunting, and agriculture, for which there were no immediate (or perhaps, sufficient) Catholic equivalents. Those parts of native religion (and medicine) that persisted and were officially opposed were not the syncretic elements (such as the substitution of Roman Catholic saints for native gods) which were covert but those elements which were either overtly syncretic, such as the placement of idols in crosses, or which persisted because Catholicism lacked equivalent elements with which either to replace or to submerge them. The more subtle forms of syncretism recognized by early priests, such as Durán, were not Ruiz de Alarcón's concern—either because he did not feel them to be dangerous or, more likely, because he simply failed to recognize them as syncretic owing to his lack of comprehension of the native system or lifelong immersion in the milieu.

Throughout his *Treatise*, Ruiz de Alarcón presents ample evidence regarding his own views of Indian religion, but the accuracy of his opinions is subject to considerable question, not only because of his Western, Catholic perspective but also because of his failure to grasp much that was happening around him. In a comparison with the much briefer report of Ponce (see Appendix A), many shortcomings become obvious. Not only did Ruiz de Alarcón miss the subtle religious elements, such as offering pulque in church, but also he overlooked the more obvious ones, such as major gods. Thus much of his interpretation is based on incomplete information. Moreover, even where he has adequate information, he occasionally errs in his interpretation, as when he rationalizes his mistranslation of Chicuetecpacihuatl (following III:1:2). He viewed many native actions as simply foolish, even when they were closely analogous to Roman Catholic practices. Catholicism was, to Ruiz de Alarcón, a religion: the native practices were at best superstition and at worst magic involving pacts with the devil.

Although early-seventeenth-century native religion did not approach the sophistication and elaboration it enjoyed a century earlier, it was not merely the remnants of the previous tradition. Much of the continuing practice was folk religion—involving pilgrimages, offerings at hilltop temples, sacred objects, and devotion to deities—that had existed before the Spanish conquest. This blend of orthodox and folk had long pre-Hispanic roots, with its own indigenous specialists. Many of the rituals were modified to incorporate elements from the Christian tradition, but the fundamental outlines were indigenous. There was tremendous continuity (see Sahagún 1951–75 for the pre-Columbian period and Appendix A for the seventeenth century).

It may be excessive to claim that early-seventeenth-century native religion formed a seamless whole, but major aspects that are incompletely covered in the *Treatise* are likely due to Ruiz de Alarcón's own inadequacy as an ethnographer, or to the way he collected and presented data—consistently and completely if one is trying to construct a case against paganism and syncretism, but inconsistently and only partially if one is trying to record a religious system.

With the introduction of Christianity, the religious world of the Indians underwent impoverishment. Many elements of the native system dropped out as they were replaced by or amalgamated with Catholic elements. The process of change was not a simple one of interchangeable parts, however. Very different concepts of the supernatural were involved. Whereas Christianity viewed God as the single locus of power (appealed to through many channels—Jesus, the Virgin Mary, and saints), the native view saw supernatural power everywhere. Not only were the gods powerful, but so too were all the elements, such as wind, rain, and fire, and power could be manifested anywhere, even in such mundane objects as beds (II:2:4). With the coming of Christianity, this broader view of the loci of power was challenged: appeals to these sources were now paganism. Consequently, the native supernatural world was severely curtailed. Not only was their ritual life reduced, but their perspectives on supernatural deities and power were sharply circumscribed. In comparison to the native religion, Christianity was ritually pauperized. And it was largely from those areas that were not compensated for by Catholism that Ruiz de Alarcón collected his heretical materials. Some syncretism that the church found repugnant did occur. Some paganism that directly opposed the church did occur. But much of the church's inquisitorial concern was directed toward those continuing rituals and beliefs for which it had no substitutes.

Roman Catholicism did, however, have an impact on this folk religion. Unlike the Catholic view of good and evil as opposing forces, native beliefs tended to regard good and evil as concomitants, existing simultaneously in all things, and varying in proportion. Consequently, while Ruiz de Alarcón saw native practices as opposed to Christianity—and therefore evil, in opposition to the Catholic good—the native perspective could incorporate the Roman Catholic pantheon of saints, devils, and the Trinity, without rejecting their own deities. Saints and angels were incorporated into the native supernatural world and used in the same way native deities were used. The circumstances of native life had changed, however, and so too did the emphases placed on the gods. While the Rain-Moisture-Agricultural Fertility cluster was still important in this agrarian society, and the Celestial Creativity-Divine Paternalism cluster was also significant, both to explain events and as supplicatory objects, the position of the gods of the War–Sacrifice–Sanguinary Nourishment cluster underwent considerable change. War was no longer a significant factor in the natives' lives, sacrifice was prohibited (though autosacrifice continued to some degree), and the world had continued despite the lapse in ceremonies and sacrifices. These gods continued to be important in the everyday affairs, but they were adapted to complementary, and different, ends. Instead of appealing to them in war and sacrifice, the Indians appealed to them in more mundane circumstances—against disease, invading insect and animal pests, and other dangers. The gods' aggressive powers were aimed not against human enemies but only against those threats that remained significant in the natives' lives. The role of the gods changed, adapting to the new social circumstances in which the Indians found themselves.

There are few sources that offer a firsthand view of the situation. Primary among these are the works of Ruiz de Alarcón and Ponce de León. The more extensive of these is that of Ruiz de Alarcón. While his *Treatise* is a work of major importance for the understanding of native belief systems as they were perceived a hundred years after the Conquest, it is not without shortcomings. One of the limitations of the corpus is that it does not present the cultural and performative matrices of the rituals accompanying the incantations. The text is presented without the context (for a general discussion of the text-context problem, see Dundes 1980). Among other unknowns in the context, we find no indications of the kinds of preparation that the speakers of these incantations must have undergone beyond the occasional description of several instances of initiatory sickness and dreams (for the incidence of such preparatory experiences in other cultures, see Eliade 1974:32–66). There are suggestions that the speakers must have undergone training or apprenticeship, since there is (as Ruiz de Alarcón claims) an accepted way of organizing the verbal aspects of the incantations and an accepted vocabulary and conventionalized formulas that had to be learned. On turning to the problem of the performance aspect of these incantations, one has no way of reconstructing the presentational facts. Nevertheless, it must be continually borne in mind that the incantations belong to a verbal-nonverbal complex. In certain of these incantations there are discontinuities and abrupt shifts on the verbal level that undoubtedly were accompanied by, or even required by, shifts on the activity level. In a number of instances it seems that the verbal is accommodated to nonverbal activity (i.e., to the core activity, not to the "theatrical" embellishments that "sell" the efficacy of the core activity to the patient or onlookers). As a consequence of the way Ruiz de Alarcón collected the data, we lack information concerning modes of delivery (manner, rate, cadence, intonation, gestures, body orientations, props and their manipulation, timing, the temporal enmeshing of words and actions, and the problem of pauses between sentences that are not merely silences because they are filled with manipulations of physical concomitants) and the interaction between the speaker and his audience. To focus solely on the verbal aspect, as we are forced to do, leaves the interpretation open to too many ambiguities that could be resolved by witnessing the events or by having an adequate account of the actions.

It was, apparently, precisely this verbal aspect that attracted Ruiz de Alarcón's attention to the incantations and motivated his collection of them. It was their communicational intent, the use of words to contact a spiritual entity, that seemed an abomination to him since, as he points out on several occasions, there is a resemblance between them and Christian prayer, a resemblance he believed was purposely created by the Devil, who out of pride and envy was constantly trying to ape the ceremonies and rituals of the Catholic church. Ruiz de Alarcón saw it as his personal obligation to disrupt and destroy the use of these false prayers, as well as any other lines of communication the Indians had with their supernatural world—and to that end he undertook the confiscation of idols, the destruction of offerings, and the denigration of *ololiuhqui*.

He was correct in seeing the incantations as prayers, because prayer is their governing mode, the communication of the speaker with a deity or power entity, but only for the purpose of presenting a petition or issuing a command, never for that of making a confession or expressing praise or thanksgiving. This may mean no more than that Ruiz de Alarcón lacked the opportunity to discover these other varieties of prayer since he was primarily interested in those incantational circumstances in which chance and uncertainty played a predominant role. Possibly as a consequence of his limited interest, the underlying situation in most of the incantations in the corpus involves the interplay of a benevolent agent against a malevolent one, seeking to superimpose benefit over harm, that is, to redress a harm or satisfy a need. A large number of these incantations thus have as their hypothetical starting point an "obligatory" initial essential motif of villainy-or-lack (Dundes 1964:61–72; Propp 1973:30–36). This is not surprising, since the incantations are part of a problem-solving situation; a disequilibrium (misfortune, need) has occurred and equilibrium must be reestablished. The help of a hero (shaman, doctor, etc.) would not be needed for problemless situations. The basic interaction between the forces of amelioration and those of detriment or lack takes place on a metaphysical level, but the result is to be reflected on the physical level. The basic presupposition is that the physical world is in direct contact with the spiritual world and is responsible for and responsive to it. The spiritual world envelopes the physical one, and entities in the spiritual world can be induced to change the events in the physical one, since they have pervasive power to manipulate it. Communication can be established; persuasion can be effective.

The meaning of the incantations, as well as their organization, is guided by their pragmatic, down-to-earth purpose: the enlistment of metaphysical powers in order to deal with a specific problem. These problems are confined to a rather narrow range of mundane concerns and interests and fall, for the most part, within two general categories: (1) the securing of information: the identification of the guilty (who stole something; who abducted someone; who brought misfortune to someone); the location of what is missing (where is the lost thing; where is the abducted or runaway person); the specification of the remedy (what medicine is required; what is the patient's chance of recovery) and (2) the attainment of a technical result (success in hunting, fishing, finding honey, lime-making, planting, protecting the fields, curing, and so forth).

The incantations tend, then, to become categorized and standardized. One finds not only formulaic phrasing, synonymy and appositional rewording, metaphorical or ritual renaming, but a repetition of the basic symbolic situations and rhetorical tactics. It is as if there were an inventory or stock supply of phrasings from which a speaker could draw expressions, images, and motifs whenever they might be applicable, even though the chosen phrasings might be used for different purposes and even with different meanings (as a minor example, the name White Woman can represent copal and salt even within the same incantation).

For analytical purposes, the incantations may be viewed as theatrical scripts. And as scripts designed for performance, the incantations have two dimensions: the dramatic and the theatrical. By "dramatic" we mean the "on-stage" action engaged in by the speaker in relation to the addressee and the "stage props"—in other words, the supernatural communication undertaken by the speaker. We can term this performance "drama" even though it is strictly monologic (even the "conversation" in II:8:18—a play within a play—is performed by the speaker alone). By "theatrical" we mean the indirect communication sent by the "on-stage" performance to the audience. This is an indirect relationship because at no point does the speaker break out of his supernatural enterprise to address his client or any other spectator directly. We can call this aspect "theatrical" even though in a few instances the "audience" (i.e., the client) is the speaker himself or a single other person. While reading these scripts, we should constantly attend to both of these dimensions, even while seeing them as manifestations of the more fundamental principle, rhetoric, that underlies every aspect of their performance.

One striking aspect of many of these incantations is their brevity, even to the point of consisting of only one or two sentences, so that one wonders at their effectiveness on either the dramatic (speaker-to-spirit) or theatrical (performer-to-audience) level. When one contrasts them with the curing ceremonies of, for example, the Navahos (as described by Kluckhohn and Leighton 1962), their brevity becomes even more startling. Was it the result of the Spanish destruction of the natives' official ceremonialism? Or was it due to the failure of Ruiz de Alarcón to collect fuller versions? Or was it due, rather, to an absolute faith in the efficacy of word power, so that under the proper circumstances only the briefest of utterances were considered necessary to bring about the desired result? It may be, of course, that the incantations, whether brief or not, could be expanded through repetition, although, except in IV:3 after the third segment ("This is all the cure, which they repeat as many times as it seems right to them") and possibly in VI:10, Ruiz de Alarcón does not mention such repetition.

Turning now to the problem of style, one finds a tense and laconic manner of speaking. There is a prosaic quality. In saying this, we are speaking in broad, general terms; these incantations come from a variety of sources and thus are not of a single texture or manner, either among themselves or necessarily within a given incantation. Furthermore, they undoubtedly represent a variety of time depths, some being apparently much older than others. It may be that some were originally poetry, but it would be difficult to single out incantations that have a consistent aesthetic quality (the only exception may be IV:2; see Appendix F). Although some images are certainly poetic and startlingly precise, their freshness is probably due more to our lack of familiarity with the expressive traditions than to the effect of the images on Nahuatl speakers. For instance, to us, the image of the fire god lying so that his mouth is beneath the fire in the fireplace (II:8:6) is a striking figure of speech in which myth and metaphor are intricately intertwined. But for the speaker it was probably a literal statement and probably a cliché. Despite these occasional poetic expressions, in style and tone all of the incantations in the manuscript are different from the work published by Garibay in *Poesía náhuatl* (1964, 1965, 1968). There is, moreover, not the slightest hint anywhere in Ruiz de Alarcón's commentary that any of these incantations were sung or that they were chanted. There is no mention of drumming in association with incantations (the drum music and singing referred to in I:3 has nothing to do with an incantatory situation), nor is there any mention of rattles or other musical instruments. It seems evident throughout that these incantations were spoken. This argues strongly against the possibility that they were poems. Since these incantations were used in a context of action, and, as we have suggested, since the verbal activity was constituted in response to a program of nonverbal activity, they may be said to be practical-minded rather than creative. The speaker is not allowing his imagination to range freely in a poematic fashion but rather is harnessing it to a problematic purpose. And although a commonplace physical activity (preparing for a hunt, fashioning a snare, pressing copal on a decayed tooth, massaging sore muscles) is lifted out of everyday reality by metaphorical and mythological transformations (with the verbal spiritualizing the nonverbal), the speaker cannot exercise poematic freedom. Even the metaphors and myths were conventional disguising; consequently, these magical utterances are constrained, and even directed, by two factors: nonverbal programs and verbal formulas. Activity and myth work together as determinants of the verbal expression.

This assessment of style is intended to be merely descriptive, not condemnatory, and to read it otherwise is to misread our purpose here. There are, indeed, from time to time, metaphors of poetic quality ("my turquoise mountains, my bracelet-like mountains"), but, generally speaking, they are tied to a pragmatic function (flattery, coercion, or cajolery) so that (still in general terms) the rhetorical dimension is everywhere predominant. There are no apparent formal poetic devices. The only possible exception is an occasional repetition of certain formulas and a rare repetition of segments, but even here there is nothing that could be considered a refrain or other special artistic sequencing. There is, for example, no parallelistic structure of the kind found in "singing for power" songs of the Papagos (Underhill 1976) or the ceremonial songs of the Navahos (Kluckhohn and Leighton 1962), although we do find distanced repetitions such as *Cuix ezzohqueh? Cuix tlapallohqueh?* (II:14:1; II:14:2) or parallel constructions such as *Teōātēntli īca tichuītequizqueh. Teōātēntli īca ticmōtlazqueh* (VI:4:1); such constructions are not, however, particularly noteworthy, given the fact that doubled, tripled, etc., expressions are among the most commonplace stylistic devices of Nahuatl prose (see Andrews 1975:343–45). Furthermore, a repetition such as *Iuhqui tiyez īn; iuhqui tiyez īn* (VI:33:2) is merely a verbal comment on a nonverbal repetition. There is certainly no use of the kinds of poetic devices or conventions one finds in classical Nahuatl poetry. We say this despite our awareness of rare faint reminders of the ceremonial songs collected by Sahagún (1951:231, 234, 240). If these incantations are poems, we have been unable to determine the parameters that define them as such. It is true that in the old man's speech to the penitent pilgrim-to-be (I:4:2) the format is short-lined as if it were poetry. But the reason for this is not evident, and, furthermore, that speech is not an incantation.

Garibay and Fellowes apparently believe that these incantations have been transferred from the temples to the villages and fields, that is, demoted from an originally grand purpose to a rather pedestrian one. We believe, however, that if they go back to pre-Conquest times (and some may well do this) they had substantially the same location and purpose then that they have in Ruiz de Alarcón's time.

NAHUATL MEDICINE

A major difficulty in dealing with indigenous New World medical practices lies with the available historical sources. With few exceptions, medical, herbal, and ritual treatises were written by Spaniards who usually shared the conceptual biases of their culture, despite some notable exceptions. Even among the latter, the information presented appears to have been consciously edited, e.g., Badianus (Guerra 1967:173; Pozo 1967:86) and Sahagún (López Austin 1974:217), possibly to avoid difficulties with secular or religious authorities. For example, the Badianus manuscript discusses 251 plants yet overlaps the medicinal plants of Sahagún's works (a total of 225 plants) only fifteen times—possibly reflecting a difference in the perspectives of the two chroniclers, Sahagún deals more with folk medicine, whereas Martín de la Cruz, the author of the Badianus manuscript, who was trained as a physician in the Spanish tradition, discusses the medicinal plants as used by a Spanish physician (Pozo 1967:71). Other significant sources include Clavijero (1979) and the *Relaciones geográficas* of 1579–80 (Paso y Troncoso 1905a–c, Paso y Troncoso 1906). A major source that clearly shows its European bias is the *Historia natural* of Francisco Hernández (1959a, b). This monumental sixteenth-century work lists many Mexican plants, animals, and minerals and their medicinal uses. Hernández also, however, lists their properties in accordance with the humoral concept of medicine and even comments on the Indians' use of plants that were inappropriate for the disease for which they were administered—according to their hot-cold, moist-dry properties. In any event, all the information available concerning medicinal practices has been influenced in varying degrees by the European medical perspective. Thus interpretations are necessarily made through this perceptual glaze.

Aztec medical practices diffused throughout much of central Mexico, probably as a consequence of the Aztecs' economic expansion and dominance (Aguirre Beltrán 1947:109). They have been regarded as relatively advanced, certainly in comparison with Old World medical practices (Emmart 1937:2, 42). The Aztec approach to medicine inextricably mixed religious and medical practices (Schendel 1968:24; Aguirre Beltrán 1947:110; Emmart 1940:42; Soustelle 1970:191; Pozo 1967:65). Various gods and goddesses were associated with both specific and generic diseases and with their remedies (Schendel 1968:24; Emmart 1940:42). Diseases were considered divine punishments, the result of some deviation in behavior (Pozo 1967:65), but the medicines also contained a rational element (i.e., they were organically effective, as seen from the Western perspective). While there is debate about the extent to which Aztec practices stemmed from rational and not merely religious beliefs (Guerra 1966:326; Soustelle 1970:191-92), the extensive Nahuatl terminology for body parts, ailments, and treatments, as well as the Aztecs' extensive herbal knowledge, indicates a well-versed and knowledgeable medical community.

Most members of Aztec society possessed some knowledge of medical arts (Aguirre Beltrán 1963:38), but there was also a separate medical profession. Medicine was practiced by both men and women (Guerra 1966:321) and, like most other professions in Aztec society, was passed down from father to son, mother to daughter, in hereditary fashion (Pérez Trejo 1959:211). The profession was jealously guarded, and charlatans were prosecuted. It is difficult, however, to separate secular medicine from religious practices, and, in effect, physicians also had priestly attributes (Aguirre Beltrán 1947:110).

While the secular and sacred aspects of curing were merged in the Aztec physicians and other specialists, for analytical purposes these two aspects will be severed to present a more easily understood overview of Aztec medicine.

We begin with the sacred or religious aspects of curing. Not only were a large number of gods and goddesses associated with the general field of curing (Schendel 1968:24), but deities were considered the causes of many diseases. The concept of disease was interwoven with that of the deities. Mesoamerican gods and goddesses had dual aspects concerning disease: they cured disease, but they also inflicted it (Emmart 1940:42; Schendel 1968:24). Disease was provoked by the ire of gods (Aguirre Beltrán 1947:110), and cure entailed a diagnosis involving the attributes of the responsible god (closely associated with the disease symptoms) and often linked to specific herbs (Schendel 1968:24). Thus diagnosis entailed not only identifying the symptoms of disease but also determining the underlying supernatural influences involved (Guerra 1966:324). While it is not feasible (if indeed it is even possible) to list here all the gods associated with specific diseases, the following are some of the major gods and goddesses involved with diseases and curing (for a complete list of the gods and goddesses in the *Treatise*, see Appendix B).

The goddess Tzapotlan Tenan cured itching and skin ailments (Sahagún 1970:17) and presided over medicines generally (Clavijero 1979, 1:431; Guerra 1966:320; Pérez Trejo 1959:211; Vargas Castelazo 1956:121; Schendel 1968:27). ToNantzin, the earth goddess, was goddess of herb medicines (Schendel 1968:28). Tlaloc, god of waters, both caused and cured rheumatic ailments, respiratory diseases, and other illnesses associated with dampness (Guerra 1966:320; Schendel 1968:26; Torquemada 1976:368–69). Xipe ToTec, Our Lord the Flayed One, both caused and cured exanthematic diseases, boils, skin infections, and common dermatoses (after the Conquest he also ruled over smallpox) (Guerra 1966:320; Schendel 1968:28; Aguirre Beltrán 1947:116; Sahagún 1970:39). Tezcatl-Ihpoca induced incurable and contagious diseases and buboes (Guerra 1966:320; Sahagún 1970:5, 1952:11–12; Torquemada 1976:71); Macuilxochitl inflicted hemorrhoids, boils, and venereal diseases (Guerra 1966:320; Sahagún 1970:31). Xochiquetzal was responsible for buboes, scabies, skin exanthemata, and other infections. Xolotl was responsible for twins, monstrosities, and malformed bodies. Nanahuatl was responsible for "leprosy" (Vargas Castalezo 1956:121).

Several gods and goddesses are most noted as patrons of various aspects of curing. Thus Xochiquetzal was patron of pregnant women, Macuilxochitl was invoked for normal births, and Centeotl was patron of therapeutic plants and the god of the *temazcalli* (Vargas Castalezo 1956:121). Teteoh Innan, Mother of the Gods, was worshiped by the physicians who cured hemorrhoids and eye ailments, as did midwives, those who cast auguries, and owners of sweathouses (Sahagún 1970:15; Torquemada 1976:369).

The importance of astrology in Mexican curing has been an accepted part of medical history (Guerra 1966:324-25; Emmart 1940:45; Dietschy 1944:122-24; Vargas Castelazo 1956:125), as indicated largely on a picture in the Codex Vaticanus A (Codex 3738), in which the twenty day-signs are associated with various parts of the body. Given the prominence of this form of medical astrology in Europe, however, both before and after the Conquest, and the similarities of the Vaticanus depiction to these European graphs, and the internal peculiarities, there is doubt about how close a parallel the New World astrology was to that of the Old World (for a more detailed analysis of New World medical astrology, see Andrews and Hassig, n.d.).

From the secular perspective, effectiveness of treatment can be examined, divorced from supernatural components. To judge by their linguistic designations (Sahagún 1961:95-138), the Aztecs had a complex understanding of the various parts of the body, even if their comprehension of it as a functioning whole was no better than that of the Spaniards. The Aztecs knew large numbers of herbs with medicinal value and associated many with specific illnesses (for a full list of medicinal herbs mentioned in the *Treatise*, see Appendix D). The area of herbal research that has attracted the most attention in Mexico concerns hallucinogenic drugs, with whose sources Mexico is abundantly supplied (Schultes and Hofmann 1979:26-30). Use of more mundane drugs by the Aztecs is equally impressive, however. Their botanical expertise was advanced, plants being grouped according to morphology, size, structure, fruits, and use (Pozo 1967:69). In addition, the Aztecs also employed direct physical treatments. The *temazcalli* (sweatbath) was used for various ailments, as well as for ritual purification (Guerra 1966:333; Durán 1967 1:175). Wounds were wrapped and sutured (Emmart 1937:44); phlebotomies were common, both in religious worship and in the treatment of diseases (Emmart 1940:47); and fractures were set.

Although sixteenth- and seventeenth-century Europe stood on the brink of major changes in medical outlook and treatment, the medicine the Spaniards brought to the New World remained a medieval art. It rested heavily on the medical precepts of Hippocrates, as elaborated and refined by Galen (Siegel 1968). Under this school, health was thought to be a balance of the four principal humors: yellow bile, black bile, blood, and phlegm. These resulted from the combination of the four contraries (hot, cold, moist, and dry) in the human body: blood was hot and moist and was associated with the element air and spring and summer; phlegm was cold and moist and was associated with the element water and winter; black bile was cold and dry and was associated with the element earth and autumn; and yellow bile was hot and dry and was associated with the element fire and summer and fall. Thus health was primarily a balance of these four humors within the body, and healing was the process of reestablishing the disrupted balance by the use of drugs possessing the opposite qualities (Siegel 1968:17-19). These prescriptions, however, were not absolutes, but were affected by the patient's nature—whether he was sanguine (blood-dominant), phlegmatic (phlegm-dominant), melancholic (black-bile-dominant), or choleric (yellow-bile-dominant). Furthermore, since seasons were also associated with humors, they too affected the type and quantity of medicine used. Diagnosis had to do not merely with determining the particular illness which had a corresponding remedy but with balancing the humoral disruption by the calculated introduction of correcting amounts of the contrary elements, the factors of essential personality and season being taken into account.

Spanish physicians entered the New World with Columbus (Guerra 1963:149). Like much else in New Spain, medicine was not an individual enterprise but an organized and centrally administered profession (Guerra 1963:150). A council, the Protomedicate (Protomedicato), presided over by a head physician, had the power to examine and regulate practitioners of medicine, surgery, obstetrics, pharmacy, and phlebotomy. The first Protomedicate of Mexico City was named by the *cabildo* (city council) in 1527 (Guerra 1953:118–19; Schendel 1968:99), and quickly extended its authority beyond Spanish physicians to include indigenous practitioners as well, controlling Indian midwives by 1540 (Schendel 1968:99). In most places, however, the Protomedicate had a negligible impact on the Indians (Guerra 1969: 179–80). In 1570 the local system was supplanted by the Royal Protomedicate, controlled directly by the crown (Guerra 1963:147–48).

The expansion of the Spanish medical tradition into the New World was rapid and pervasive. The first hospital in the New World was established in Santo Domingo in 1501 (Guerra 1963:151), and the first one in New Spain was established in Mexico City in 1524, with a leprosarium following in 1526, a venereal-disease hospital in 1534, and a mental hospital in 1566 (Schendel 1968:89–94). Founded in 1551, the Universidad Nacional de México began teaching medicine in 1553 (Guerra 1963:151; Schendel 1968:98). Medical publishing began at midcentury (Guerra 1963:152), though much of it was a rehash of European medical traditions (Jarcho 1957). While iron instruments and the Arab medical tradition granted the Spaniards superiority over indigenous practices in surgery (Guerra 1963:150), many Aztec herbs found their way into Spanish medical writings (Jarcho 1957:437).

While Spanish medicine may be treated as a distinct topic, both the motivation for its introduction into the New World (aside from its practical benefits to the colonists) and the means by which this was achieved were closely tied to religion. Many of the early medical practitioners were regular priests, and the motivation for the creation of hospitals was avowedly religious, based on the tradition of Christian charity (Guerra 1969:179–80). Furthermore, the distinction between religion and medicine was not always clear during the colonial period. Saints were patrons of various diseases, illness frequently took on moral tones, and medical books customarily included enormous numbers of prayers, novenas, and religious tracts for preventing and curing disease (Guerra 1969:183).

Until contact with the Spaniards, many common Old World diseases, such as smallpox, measles, mumps, scarlet fever, and chicken pox, were absent from the Americas. The natives had acquired some immunity to the indigenous diseases, but to the Old World introductions they had none (Newman 1976:671; Cook 1946: 335). The consequent depopulation of central Mexico owing to pestilence was drastic. Not only were the medical professionals ill-equipped to deal with these strange new diseases (for instance, one of the major indigenous treatments, the *temazcalli* [sweatbath], would have actually increased the infections and fostered their spread, rather than helping cure them), but the indigenous medical profession itself suffered most heavily in the highly urban depopulation. Thus Spanish medical competition, different concepts of treatment, and the general Indian depopulation, combined to undermine the status, numbers, and effectiveness of the native practitioners.

In the debate over pre-Columbian medical beliefs, the data are muddled by the apparent similarity between pre-Columbian practices and salient features of the Spanish system—notably the hot-cold division (López Austin 1975:16–31). Logan (1977:88–94) argues for the worldwide diffusion of the hot-cold theory of disease, originating in the Far East and spreading westward and on into the New World with the Spaniards. Humoral medicine did become an important element in folk medicine in New Spain, possibly owing to preexisting parallel conceptual patterns. The issue of independent origin versus diffusion of the hot-cold concept may be unresolvable, but later Aztec parallels with Spanish practice strongly suggest medical syncretism.

The different approaches to medicine taken by Spaniards and Aztecs inevitably led to clashes, particularly since the Spaniards were politically dominant and felt culturally superior as well. Many medical remedies and practices, particularly those with religious implications, were suppressed (Schultes and Hofmann 1979:144–45), but the utility of many herbs was recognized, and they were used in both the New World and the Old (Sauer 1976:818–19). Nevertheless, primarily those Aztec elements survived that were absorbed into the formal Spanish system; many of the remainder persisted, but as folk remedies.

While the religious elements in Aztec medicine have not been ignored, there is a strong tendency in the secondary literature to emphasize the rational, empirical aspects of the Indians' medicine, focusing on their pharmaceutical approach to curing (Emmart 1940:49) and their empiricism in establishing disease symptoms and pathologies (Guerra 1966:324; Vargas Castelazo 1956:126), although a comprehensive herbal approach to disease is either lacking or unrecorded. Concentrating on a pharmaceutical analysis, however, involves a fundamental distortion of Aztec medicine—probably as it was practiced before the Spanish conquest and certainly as it is presented in Ruiz de Alarcón's *Treatise*.

In dealing with "primitive" medicine, the constituent elements are of less concern than the medical "pattern" and the degree to which it is integrated into the cultural pattern (Ackerknecht 1971:53–54). In approaching non-Western medical systems, the main focal areas are what constitutes an illness, what illnesses are recognized, and what criteria are used in diagnosis. All medical systems are logical (i.e., consequences follow logically from premises), but not all are rational in the Western sense. That is, not all share basic premises about disease, tying it to physical and physiological bases. In analyzing a medical system in a different tradition, it is easy to yield to the temptation to assess practices in terms of Western concepts. The result is often an impressive list of effective procedures and medicines, but the list is just that, a disjointed assemblage lacking logical cohesion. While such an approach may be acceptable as a method for seeking effective remedies to be incorporated into Western medicine, it fails to comprehend the indigenous system on its own terms, deriving from its own premises. The partial mapping of indigenous practices onto Western medical theory inevitably leaves large areas that do not fit our perspective and cannot be analyzed by means of it.

It is the magical-religious and social aspects of the medical practice that are paramount, not the effectiveness of some of the cures, since these, even when effective, are suffused with the supernatural (Ackerknecht 1971:99). Many remedies are objectively effective (see Moerman 1979:526), but by stressing such criteria as effectiveness, indigenous medical practices are implicitly judged by the Western view of disease (Fabrega 1971:387), which distorts the conceptual basis and logic of the indigenous system. Only those aspects are seen that overlap the Western. Thus to place emphasis on the empirically effective remedies in the Aztec medical system confuses rather than elucidates the analysis.

Aztec medicine of the early seventeenth century included a number of effective herbal treatments. For instance, *tlacopahtli* has been shown to be an effective aphrodisiac, antispasmodic, and stimulant (Díaz 1977:13), and the use of copal for toothaches finds a modern continuation in the commercial tooth sealant copalite. The psychoactive medicines *ololiuhqui* and peyote clearly possess neurological agents (Díaz 1977:22, 26).

Many elements, however—herbs, treatments, gods, and sorcery—were not organically effective. To understand these as well as the more readily comprehended elements, the Aztec medical system must be seen as a subset of the religious system, and the whole as a part of the social system, involving the relation of self to others, norms, and gods (Fabrega 1971:387). To appreciate more fully the Aztec medical system, the treatment of illness must be examined—cause (who or what is responsible), diagnosis (how it is determined), and therapy (how to redress the situation). In all societies there are theories of illness (Fabrega 1978:15), but in most medical systems the concern is not with the pathological process but with the underlying cause (Glick 1967:34–35). Illness is explained not by natural causes but by supernatural ones (Ackerknecht 1971:19).

Aztec concepts of illness frequently, although not invariably, involved gods. Infirmities were often caused by gods (I:2; V:1)—or saints by the seventeenth century (VI:1)—or deified objects such as *ololiuhqui* (I:6; VI:1) or sorcerers (V:3).* Primitive medicine is primarily spiritual medicine, based on diseases of the soul, bodily diseases being symptoms of soul diseases (Ackerknecht 1971:20; Bidney 1963:144; Fabrega 1971:386). Thus concepts and practices of medicine are inextricably intertwined with the religious, the former being a lesser aspect of the latter (Glick 1967:32–33).

The cause of an ailment was suspected from the nature of the infirmity, but the correctness of the diagnosis was ascertained either by various forms of fortune-telling (V:1, 3, 4) or by the administering of psychoactive herb decoctions (V:3, 7). Although both methods were used for several purposes, such as finding lost objects, *ololiuhqui* or peyote was consulted to determine whether or not a sorcerer was involved and, if so, his identity. When gods were deemed the cause of the ailment, nonhallucinogenic fortune-telling was employed (V:1).

*Although the *Treatise* indicates natural causes for some infirmities (V:1), it is likely that this is Ruiz de Alarcón's interpretation, not an indigenous one.

Once the cause was determined, the same means were used to discover the appropriate treatment (V:1), but if a sorcerer was involved, he was confronted (I:9), whereas if a god was the cause, he was appeased by offerings (I:2), pilgrimages (I:4), and autosacrifice (I:4). The supernatural causes were identified and appeased while medical remedies and treatments were simultaneously applied.

Not all illnesses were treated the same way. Some infirmities, such as wounds or fractures, were obviously of natural causes, but that did not entirely remove the supernatural element. Rather, ultimate causes were sought (I:7). At the opposite extreme were those infirmities, such as loss of the *tonalli* (literally, "day-name," but signifying, loosely, the soul) or psychological disturbances, which were overwhelmingly supernatural in nature (IV:3; VI:1, 2, 3). Intermediate were the illnesses for which causes were attributable, but less so than such ills as fractures, fevers, swellings, and pain. Thus a range of infirmities was recognized and treated accordingly. The most patently organic ailments involved the fewest supernatural elements, although none were devoid of them. The intermediate ailments involved herbal treatments and supernatural assistance. The least obviously organic ailments involved the fewest medicinal potions and the greatest reliance on gods. The conceptual underpinnings of medical practices are much more difficult to deal with, however, than are techniques of treatment, on which emphasis is usually placed (Laughlin 1963:116). For the Aztecs, the supernatural was invariably involved. Medicine was one aspect of man's relation to the gods and his fellows, and it was in that context that medicine was applied.

There is substantial variation between the god-disease and god-curing relationships in classical Aztec religion and those evident in the Ruiz de Alarcón manuscript. For instance, many of the gods classically associated with curing, such as Tzapotlan Tenan, ToNantzin, Xipe ToTec, Teteoh Innan, and Macuilxochitl, do not appear in Ruiz de Alarcón's *Treatise*, and of those that do—Tlaloc, Tezcatl-Ihpoca, Xochiquetzal, and Nanahuatl—none bears the same relationship to disease that he or she did in classical times (at least not in the dominant tradition). Classically, Xochiquetzal was associated with buboes, scabies, skin exanthemata, and infections, while in Ruiz de Alarcón's *Treatise* the goddess's only association with medicine is with scorpion stings (VI:32) and attracting affection (IV:2). Others classically associated with disease, such as Nanahuatzin, are mentioned in the *Treatise*, but not in a curing context.

Not only is there no overlap between the Classic-period god-disease associations and those of the Ruiz de Alarcón manuscript, but the diseases mentioned reflect altogether different patrons. In the few instances in which divine responsibility for disease is recognized, the associations between the gods and diseases are not the same as those of Classic times. For example, instead of Teteoh Innan, midwives are associated with Tlahzolteteoh; instead of Tzapotlan Tenan, Xipe ToTec, or Xochiquetzal, rashes and impetigo are associated with Four Reed (i.e., Huehuehteotl); and, instead of Xochiquetzal, childbirth is associated with Caxxoch and Cuaton. Other ailments with classic patrons, such as Macuilxochitl, who is associated with hemorrhoids, appear to lack god patrons altogether in the Ruiz de Alarcón manuscript. Other illnesses appear to lack immediately identifiable causal gods, since one of the major questions posed in the diagnosis asks who is responsible. Other illnesses with known patrons or cures in Classic times, such as ToCih, the patron of sweatbaths, are not mentioned in the *Treatise* (the bath mentioned in IV:3, for example, is not a sweatbath).

The significance of these differences is difficult to determine. They may reflect either a divergent tradition, as with the nine-level versus the thirteen-level celestial world, or they may be the result of post-Conquest changes. The former explanation appears more likely, since native medicine, as reflected in Ruiz de Alarcón's *Treatise*, forms a logical and integrated system.

THE TREATISE

Al Illustrissimo S.ᵒʳ Don Francisco Manso de Çuniga, del consejo de su Mag.ᵈ en el de Indias. Arcobispo de Mexico.
El B.ᵉʳ Hernando Ruiz de Alarcon, Benef.ᵈᵒ de Atenanco.

Illu.ᵐᵒ S.ᵒʳ

Opening page of the prefatory letter, folio 2r of the Museo manuscript.

[PREFATORY LETTER]

To the Most Reverend Don Francisco Manso de Zúñiga,[1] of His Majesty's Council in the [Realm] of the Indies, Archbishop of Mexico. [From] Bachelor Hernando Ruiz de Alarcón, Beneficiado of Atenanco.

Most Reverend Sir:

Many days ago I was ordered to find out, as soon as I could, about the heathen customs, idolatries, and superstitions with tacit and express pacts [with the Devil] that today persist and are being continued and passed on from generation to generation among the Indians, since I have the commission of Ordinary to be able better to attend to this charge and to impose whatever remedy might seem most advisable. After having spent in this undertaking all the time during five years that I could spare from the duties of my parish, I have found many things toward the prevention of which every possible prosecution should be made. And even, as the saying goes, no effort should be spared in order to erase them, and even to scrape them, from the memory of men. But how much trouble I encountered from this enterprise is not for me to say. Although I think that it will not be held against me to speak of my opinions about why these heathen customs and superstitions have remained and have been continued for so long in these natives after baptism, and even some [now exist] that were not permitted to them in their heathen state, such as drunkenness—which, in their heathen state, had the penalty of death. And the others have a weak foundation, because a tradition of their false gods is hardly found among their stories, as much because they did not know how to write as because one has not been able to find absolute clarity even about how they have come to inhabit this land or by what route. Thus the religion and devotion to their gods had few or no roots, and the drunkenness which at present (for our sins) runs among them is so injurious and such a cruel enemy of Christian customs that it is today the worst of their vices. This is the cause of the total destruction of the health of their bodies, and consequently the sufficient and principal barrier to their preservation and increase. And although one offers me the objection that, since it has not been possible to prevent the lesser, neither will it be possible to remove the greater (which is idolatry relative to drunkenness), I answer that late or never will one who does not regret the manifest sin deal with the remedy for the hidden vice. And drunkenness is so clearly a manifest sin that it is self-evident, and it even proves and makes palpably obvious that it is and has been the total cause of the Indians' wasting away; so that in addition to removing the great harm to their souls, ministers are under the great obligation of remedying drunkenness for the conservation and increase of their bodies.

But to return to the subject: While the matter was in this state, Your Reverence came to this city to shepherd these mangy sheep, and with the pastoral vigilance of so great a prelate, taking the necessary steps for the improvement of your flock, you acquainted yourself with the dangers to it, and, finding that the one that was in my care was not among the least, you ordered me to record whatever I might have noticed concerning this matter, a thing that I could and even should have refused, not only because of the small surplus of time due to the excessive and difficult duties of my parish, but also because of my defective intellect and small or nonexistent experience with writing, especially about a subject concerning which I cannot find help from either the living or the dead—because today not a word is found written about it and those who are living cannot help me or else do not want to, because those who desire to help do not have sufficient information about this subject, and those who have it are offenders in it; either they do not want to reveal it or, already having been caught in the act, hide completely what they can. And that which is found written about the subject among the likes of these is all in a difficult and almost unintelligible language, both because the Devil, its inventor, influences his veneration and esteem by means of the difficulty of the language found in all the conjurations, invocations, and spells, and because the more figures and tropes the language has, the more difficult it is to understand—and the language I report is nothing but a continuous use of metaphors, not only in the verbs but also even in the nouns and adjectives and at times passes into being a sustained allegory.

All these difficulties—and even greater ones were experienced in the performance of my task—were overcome within me by considering, first, that whatever might be found wrong in this work carries with itself the certain and sufficient exoneration of having been done through obedience and, second, that although mistaken, it might be able to suffice for the goal that is sought by means of it. Because doubtless it hurts one to see that so numerous a race, which so easily lay aside heathenism and idolatry, may, before being sufficiently instructed in the Christian Religion, come almost completely to its end, the cause of which (taking into account that part due to the Indians' accustomed drunkenness and its results) I believe to be [first] that the ministers have entered late into their parishioners' languages due to their diversity and difficulty, since even today some are completely unknown. And, second, only much later were the Indians grouped into congregations[2] where their vices may be noticed more easily and where they might see and communicate to the parish priest more often that which, being permitted to them, they reject as much as they can. And finally, and most importantly, it is the limited communication, the brief presence, and easy reassignment of the parish priests, because the minister who is not perpetual, for whatever reason, is in much danger of being or seeming mercenary and not a pastor, and more so if such a one administers through a third person. If they are reassigned after two or three years, and if there have been three or more substitutes who at the end of those years leave the parish, neither the substitutes nor the one who assigns them have become acquainted with the customs and needs of their parishioners, or even their names.

I have been prolix, Reverend Sir; I have not been able to avoid it with one who, because of his holy zeal, desires it and whom, because of his office, it behooves to become acquainted with everything that can be beneficial in this matter, because the more it is understood, so much the better can the damage be remedied, since the principal thing for the cure is that one be acquainted with the sickness.

May Our Lord guard Your Reverence for the consolation and protection of this Kingdom.

[PROLOGUE]

Prologue to the Treatise on the Heathen Superstitions and Customs That Today Live Among the Indians, Native of This New Spain, Written in Mexico, in the Year 1629. By Bachelor Hernando Ruiz de Alarcón

My intent with this work is not to make a detailed inquiry into the customs of the natives of this land. This would require a very long work and many parts, and I do not know what use such an undertaking would have today. I seek only to open a path for the ministers of Indians so that in both laws[1] they may be able to become acquainted with this corruption in order that thus they may be better able to deal with its correction, if not with the remedy. Informed of what they will here find written, paying careful attention both to the words of the conjurations, invocations, and spells that are here reported and to the requirements that usually precede, accompany, and follow such works, they will be able to compare what they hear from the Indians, in both laws, in order to find the spool by following the thread, and discover land where the Enemy spreads out so many fogbanks and which, to their detriment, these unfortunate people sustain and preserve with so much care in order that such frauds will not be discovered. And although those who are not acquainted with the Mexican language will gain only small advantage from this work, I am not writing it for those who are not, or should not be, ministers of Indians. I beg those competent in the language who are engaged in this ministry to pardon what has been insufficiently corrected and what is erroneous when making use of whatever they find helpful here and right.

And if in the translation some clauses and expressions are discordant to readers, let them realize that in the translation I tried to conform as much as I could to the literal meaning and phrasing of the Indians, especially of those who were practitioners of these superstitions. May Our Lord be willing that this work be of benefit, as I desire, for His greater honor and glory. Amen.

y errado. Y si en la traduccion les dissonaren algunas clausulas, y el lenguage, advierten que en ellas procuro conformarme quanto pude a la letra, y frases de los indios en especial de aquellos, que eran executores destas supersticiones. Quiera nuestro Señor que esta sea aprouechosa como deseo para mayor honra y gloria suya. Amen.

Preambulo a este tratado.

Cap. 1.

Del fundam.to de las idolatrias de la Adoracion y culto de diferentes cosas. en especial del fuego. De los hechos naturales. y como puede ser.

Es tanta la ignorancia o simplicidad, de casi todos los indios. y no digo de todos, porque no he corrido toda la tierra, pero poca differencia creo deue de auer; que segun se entiende de todos son facilissimos en persuadirse lo que les quisieren dar a creer. Assi que por su ignorancia tenian, y tienen tan varios Dioses, y modos de adoracion tan differentes, que venido a averiguar el fundam.to, y lo que son todos, hallamos tan poco de que echar mano como si quisiessemos asir en el humo el humo o el viento.

Lo cierto es que las mas o casi todas las adoraciones actuales, o acciones idolatricas, que aora hallamos, y a lo que podemos juzgar, son las mesmas que acostumbraban sus antepassados, tienen su raiz y fundam.to en mal entender ellos, que las nubes son Angeles y dioses, capaces de adoracion, y lo

Page from First Treatise, chapter 1, folio 4r of the Museo manuscript.

[FIRST TREATISE]

PREAMBLE TO THIS TREATISE

CHAPTER 1

About the Basis for the Idolatries. About the Adoration of and Cult to Different Things, Especially Fire. About the *Nahuales*[1] and How It Can Be

THE ignorance or naïveté of almost all the Indians (and I do not say of all because I have not traveled through all the land, but there must be little difference) is so great that, according to general opinion, all are very easily persuaded of whatever one might want to lead them to believe. Thus, because of their ignorance, they had, and have, such a variety of gods and such different modes of adoration that, having resolved to ascertain the basis of their beliefs and what they all are, we find as little to get hold of as if we tried to squeeze smoke or wind in our fist.

What is certain is that the majority, or almost all, of the present-day adorations or idolatrous actions which we today find—and, from what we can judge, they are the same ones that their ancestors customarily used—have their root and formal basis in their belief that the clouds are angels and gods, worthy of being adored, and they think the same thing about the winds, because of which they believe gods live in all parts of the land, such as on the slopes and hills and in the valleys and ravines. They believe the same thing of the rivers, lakes, and springs, since to everything mentioned they offer wax and incense. And that to which they give most veneration—and almost all consider to be a god—is fire, as will be seen in the Treatise on idolatry.

It should be pointed out that almost every time they undertake to offer a sacrifice to their imagined gods, it originates from the fact that satraps—a doctor, a sorcerer, or a seer—of the Indians command it or order it thus. Most of them base their decisions on their spells or on what comes into their heads after having become deranged from drinking what they call *ololiuhqui*, peyote, or tobacco, as will be stated in its place.

For more clarity I shall enter into this Treatise by way of what they used to do with a person from the moment of his birth, continuing with him up to his end and death. The veneration and honor that all the Indians have here for fire is so excessive that at the moment they are born they become entangled in this superstition. They put the fire in the room of the woman lately delivered of a child, and there they encourage it, without an ember being removed from it until the fourth day because they believe that if they were to take some embers from the fire before that time a film would grow on the eyes of the newborn child. And the ancient Indians

Page from First Treatise, chapter 1, folio 4v of the Museo manuscript.

used to remove the newborn child from the room on the fourth day, and along with him the fire, and they circled his head with it four times. I have not succeeded in finding out whether this is done today.[2]

And when they were circling his head four times, making two circles in one direction and two in the other, they gave him the name he was to have, which was in accordance with that of the god of the day on which he was born, since the Devil seeks that his followers imitate in his service the manner of the Christians in that of God, Our Lord. They would take this name from some calendars, for I have found in those of this type that they have apportioned to the days the names of animals, such as *Ocēlotl,* Jaguar, *Quauhtli,*[3] Eagle, *Cuetzpalli,* Caiman, *Coatl,*[4] Snake, and inanimate things, such as *ātl,* Water, and *calli,* house. From this I have deduced that they were dedicated to the animal that the Devil assigned them in order that they might be what they call a *nāhualli,* as I will explain below, and in this manner the child turned out to be, as it were, baptized in their way, having that as his name. Others were different in that they performed this imitation of the baptism with water, washing the head of the child on the fourth day and giving him its name.[5]

All of this work of fire and water was entrusted to the sage who had it as a profession—ordinarily these sages have the name and profession of doctors. They are always deceitful and ceremoniatic and seek to persuade people that they are consummate in knowledge, since they profess to know what is absent and to foresee what is in the future, which, it may be, is revealed to them by the Devil, who can, through knowledge and conjecture, foresee many future events.

And because I have mentioned the *nāhualli,* I will say immediately what I feel, according to what I deduce from what I have seen and experienced.[6]

Trustworthy persons have told me that while they were with an Indian he began to shout, saying, "Oh, they are killing me! They are harassing me! They are killing me!" And when they asked him what he was talking about, he replied, "The cowhands of such-and-such a ranch are killing me!" Going out into the countryside, they went to the commons of the mentioned ranch and found that the cowhands of it had hunted and killed a fox, or vixen. And upon returning to see the Indian, they found him dead. And, if I remember correctly, with the same blows and wounds that the fox had.

They affirmed that the same thing had happened with another Indian and a caiman. The Indian, without anyone harming him, began to complain that they were killing him in the river. Going to the river, they found in it a dead caiman, and then they found the Indian dead in the same manner.

How this may happen I will tell below. But if we do not find these two cases convincing, because of the fact that the persons who told them were not fully qualified informants, I will recount others with witnesses who are flawless.

The Father Tutor Friar Andres Ximenez, of the Order of Saint Dominic, told me that, around nightfall, while two priests of this order were in a cell, a bat, much larger than the ordinary ones, entered by a window and that the two religious chased the bat, throwing their hats and other things at it until it got away from them and left. And on the next day an old Indian woman came to the gate of that convent, and, calling to one of the two religious, she asked him why he had mistreated her so, for he had almost killed her. And when the religious asked her if she was crazy, and where or how that could be, she answered by asking if it was true that, the night before, he and another religious had mistreated and knocked around a bat that had entered the cell by a window. And when the religious told her that it was so, the Indian woman said, "Well, that bat was I, and I have been left very tired." Upon hearing this with amazement, the religious tried to call his companion so that he might know the Indian. And in order to detain her, he told her to wait, that he was going in to get some alms. He entered, and, upon returning with his companion, he neither found the Indian woman nor could he find out who she was.

I have known many other cases like this, but in order not to drag on and bore with things of this kind, accepted as undoubtable in this land, I will tell very few of them.

Antonio Marques,[7] a Spaniard worthy of credence and who knows the Mexican language well, told me that on hearing a case of this kind recounted—one that had happened on the coast of Acapulco to a certain Simon Gomez, a Spaniard—he had doubted the truth of the happening, but on meeting the said Simon Gomez, he asked him if what had been told about him was true. In answer Simon Gomez replied that it was the truth. He said that while he was fishing on the Cachutepech River,[8] which is near Acapulco, one of two sons he had with him climbed up on a stony place that was in the river. A caiman came out and began to circle around the stony area, as if it intended to catch the boy, who, being frightened, shouted to his father, who, seeing what was happening, asked for the harquebus from his other son and shot the caiman and killed it. And, at the time the report of the harquebus was heard in his house, an old Indian woman, who was there weaving along with some others, fell over, saying, "Simon Gomez has killed me," a remark that the wife of Simon Gomez and all the others who were there spinning and weaving heard very clearly. The [news of the] happening spread in the town, whereupon the kinsmen of the dead Indian woman, like ignorant and blind people, complained of Simon Gomez to the magistrate of Acapulco, and he was imprisoned because of the complaint. The truth was ascertained, namely, that, while Simon Gomez was absent, the Indian woman said that he was killing her, and he confessed that he had killed the caiman. When the magistrate saw the bad proof of the complaint, he released Simon Gomez, who, at the time he told it, had just got out of jail.

A similar thing was testified to me by Father Andres Giron, a priest who knows the Mexican language very well, a minister and friend of Indians, and worthy of all credence, and who at present resides and administers in the region of the Mines of Taxco.[9] The priest said that while he was going with others to hear mass in a town near the city of Guatemala, they had to cross a river near the town and upon seeing a caiman in it, one of the companions fired two harquebus shots at it and killed it, one shot entering through an eye and the other in the jaw so that on its way it broke the mouth. And afterwards they dragged it along, and, pulling it from the river, they singed it with the bulrush that they found dry there and continued on their way to hear mass. And upon arriving at the church of the town, they found a great noise and uproar, because an Indian woman who, being among the other women in the catechism, had fallen down dead at the time that they had shot the caiman in the river, without any other ailment or accident supervening. The strangers came up, then, to the Indian woman, and they found in her the wounds that the two shots of the harquebus had made in the caiman. The Indian woman had one eye broken and her mouth torn. In order to verify the truth even more, they took off her *huipil* and found all her back singed, which was the part they had singed on the caiman with chamisa or bulrush.

Thereupon all those of the town said that the old woman had always been considered a *nāhualli* witch. And in witness of the event, what had always been understood about her was proved to be true. And the Devil paid her in his coin with the last of evils, making her experience in her body the fire that was prepared for her soul forever in Hell.

I have heard many cases similar to what I have told, and therefore supposing them to be certain—although extraordinary and outside of what is known of other nations and peoples who are accustomed to having a pact with the Devil—we will examine how this may be, noticing first the astuteness of Satan, who exercises it on this kind of people, so that, once captives of this sin, correction seems impossible, because, although they are accused and convicted, they deny it perversely, until they die impenitent.

It is the same with the sorcerers whom they call *Tēxōxmî* or *Téyollòquāni* or *tētlàchihuiani,*[10] all of which are practically the same thing. They never confess, even though there is information against them. I have had such information concerning these kinds of sorcerers in different provinces and have never been able to make them confess and thus bring it entirely into the light, although in the secular law it was proved against some Indians of the town of Coyuca, in the province of Acapulco, that, by means of some ashes that they had placed a span beneath the ground in a hermitage of the said town, near an altar where those of that settlement ordinarily prayed, they had killed many people with a furious illness in a very short period. And they confessed to having received these ashes from some owls or cuckoos that had brought them in their claws from many leagues away wrapped up in some rags, while it seemed to them that they themselves were also in the form of owls when they received them. I judge that on this last point they were deceived because of what I have reported above. By remission of the magistrate of Acapulco this case was decided by Dr. Juan Cano, most worthy senior professor of law in this city of Mexico, condemning some of the aggressors to death.

From all the cases that I have become acquainted with of this kind of *nahualles*[11] and witches—who are different from the witches of Spain—I deduce, first, that when a child is born, the Devil, by the express or tacit pact that its parents have with him, dedicates or subjects it to the animal which the child is to have as a *nahual*—which is like saying, as owner of his birth and master of his actions, or what the gentiles used to call fate. And [second] by virtue of this pact the child remains subject to all the dangers and travails that the animal may suffer until its death. And on the other hand the Devil makes the animal always obey the command of the child, or else the Devil himself carries it out, using the animal as instrument. And in this way the impossible, thought-up transformations and other difficulties are not needed [to explain what happens]. I infer this from many cases of this kind, as I said above, in which, when one of these Indians, thought to be a *Nahualli,* threatens another Indian or Spaniard, it has happened that such a threatened Indian or Spaniard has later had an encounter with some caiman in the river or with some other animal in the field; and when the animal comes out of the encounter wounded or hurt, they later find the Indian who made the threat with the same wounds that the caiman or animal got, with that Indian being absent at the time and occupied in other affairs.

This is what I have been able to find out, and I have not found a minister or other person who can give me a more reasonable explanation nor any other better solution for these cases, and therefore I leave it here, but not without first stating that I consider it doubtless that, after he reaches the age of reason, such a child for whom the parents made the pact with the Devil reiterates the pact or ratifies it tacitly or expressly. Without this condition it is not credible that the Devil has so much power, especially against a baptized person. For another thing, I observe that the name and meaning of the noun *Nahualli* can be derived from one of three roots: the first means "to command"; the second, "to speak with authority"; the third, "to hide oneself" or "to wrap oneself up in a cloak." And although there are conveniences for which the first two meanings apply, the third suits me better since it is from the verb *Nahualtia,* which is "to hide oneself by covering oneself with something," which comes to be the same thing as "to wrap oneself up in a cloak," and thus *Nahualli* probably means "a person wrapped up or disguised under the appearance of such or such an animal," as they commonly believe.[12]

CHAPTER 2

About the Idolatries and Superstitions and an Observation of Things to Which They Attribute Divinity, Especially *Ololiuhqui, Piciete,* and Peyote

With regard to that which concerns idolatries, although the majority have their beginning and root in the healers and sorcerers, as also has been seen in the provinces of Peru, in this Kingdom, others, although not many, are found that are as if established by law and are kept at the present.

From what I have been able to learn, it is like what in Peru they call *huacas,*[1] the places where they adore and the things that they adore indistinctly. Here for such *Huacas* the Indians have the hills or springs, rivers, fountains, or lakes where they put their offerings on appointed days, like that of Saint John, that of Saint Michael, and other similar ones, with the faith and belief that from those waters, fountains, or hills their good happenings and their health have their origin—or their sicknesses if by chance those waters, fountains, or hills, or the *ololiuhqui* are angry with them, although it be without their having given them occasion. They look upon and adore the aforementioned things as god. And the *ololiuhqui* is a kind of seed like lentils that is produced by a kind of ivy of this land. And when this seed is drunk, it deprives one of judgment because it is very powerful. And by this means they communicate with the Devil, because he usually talks to them when they are deprived of judgment with the said drink and deceives them with different appearances. And they attribute it to the deity that they say is in the seed, called *ololiuhqui* or *Cuexpalli,*[2] which is the same thing. More will be said about these later.

The idolaters also used to adore and now invoke, as I shall tell of later, a god whom they knew no more about than that they used to call him and today call him *Yāotl, tiytlacahuan,*[3] which can be translated "God of battles, whose servants (or slaves) we are." They also call him *Tlālticpaque,* which means "Owner (or lord) of the earth."

As a proof of what has been said, I have seen many things that have no evasion or answer because I have found in the hills many offerings of copal (which is the incense of this land), and skeins of thread, and little cloths of what they call *Poton,*[4] "badly woven material," and candles and bouquets, some very old and others new. And on the Day of Saint Michael[5] of this year of 1626, I found on a hill an offering that had just been made and the fresh track of him who made it. And although my men followed it, they could not overtake him because the roughness of the land did not show tracks well. The offering, then, was in a pile of rocks, off a long distance from the roads. A small cave had been made in it in which the offering was protected from the sun and the water. And although later I made many inquiries in the surrounding villages, I was never able to find the trail of the one who made the offering, because the Indians of this land, just like those of Peru, hide this very diligently, warned, as I see it, by the Devil on account of what is of interest [to him]. Here let the ministers observe that such piles of stone, which the Indians call *Teolocholli,*[6] are suspect because from many of them I have taken copal, candles, bouquets, and other things that they offer on appointed days, as has been said.

But most commonly they come from the healers and sorcerers, both those using maize—who are like those with beans in Spain—and those using the hands, whom they call *matlapouhqui;*[7] those using maize are called *tlaolxiniani.*[8] I will speak of this later.

There usually are in these piles of stone, and in the passes and crossroads, some idols or rocks that resemble faces, and to these is directed the intent of the ones who make the offering, seeking to get the deity who resides there to be favorable to them or that no evil will befall them on the trip they are making or in order to have a harvest or for similar things, especially the sick on the advice of their seer-doctors, who counsel them and even order them—as they have declared before me—to carry wax candles to the river. And, at times, on behalf of the sick, the doctor goes and throws the candles in the river or carries them to the hills.

Also they are perverse when they elect some youth as *gobernador.* The first time, in order to give him the post, the old people and *principales*[9] of the town take him at dawn to the river and bathe him[10] as if offering him to the river, in order that it be favorable to him so that in the future he be suitable in the post that he is beginning to exercise. And then they celebrate his wedding and, what is worse, the drunkenness, which is where it will end up, like all their meetings. And the respect they have for these things, as also is told in the mentioned book on Peru, is so much that I saw an Indian woman who had up to four little *tecomates*[11] in a locked *chicubite,* and they were inherited from her ancestors, who were from this town of Atenango, from the barrio of Tlālāpan. In passing, let it be noted that it is common to have these superstitions and idolatries in the barrios and villages that are in the hills and deserts remote from the main towns, as we have found them. I have seen that the mentioned Indian woman from whom I took away the four *tecomates* had so much respect for and fear of them that, after I had accused her of idolatrizing them, in order to keep her from hiding them, it was necessary for me to go to her house with a notary, a constable, and witnesses. And after I had made her confess by physical force that she had them and where, having reached the point of opening the *chicobite,* so great was the fear that beset her that she was unable to open the *chicobite* out of fright and agitation until I came up to help her. And after the *chicubite* was open, in no way did she dare to take the *tecomates* from it, since it seemed to her that she was committing sacrilege, until by dent of persuasion and threats, becoming pale and almost fainting with fear, she took them out. And afterward she seemed to have become undeceived of the error in which she was.

Here one should note the diligence and sagacity that are required in the judge who tries to find and punish these crimes and to extirpate them, because what diligent efforts the mentioned Indian woman and others like her would not make to hide what they so much esteem and venerate, since she almost died on taking the *tecomates* from the basket, or *chicubite,* in which she had them! And thus, when one finds out about such a thing, it will be good advice not to lose sight of it until an end is put to it, and to be in the place where it is kept, before the delinquent suspects that it is a matter of that thing. Without this, all the other diligent efforts will be useless, because if one does not find them with the stolen goods in their hands, as people say, they would rather let themselves be torn to pieces than confess the crime, with the result that they will be more obstinate and more cautious. Of the type told about above, I have found another Indian woman in a village called Cuetlaxxochitlan, who had *tecomates* like those spoken of, which she worshiped with a respect and fear equal to the one that has been reported, for the comprehension of which it should be observed that when some old man who is like the head of his lineage has accepted *ololiuhqui* or peyote or some idol as his advocate, he makes for it a small basket, the most unusual that he can, in which he keeps it. And inside of it he puts that which he offers to it, such as incense, some small embroidered handkerchiefs, little girls' dresses, and other things of this nature. And that is kept in such custody and veneration that no one dares to open the small case, and much less the offering that is inside, nor the *ololiuhqui,* peyote, or idol—although they venerate idols much more. The children and descendants are inheritors of this little basket along with what it has inside, without anyone of the lineage daring to be careless about it. This is so much the way things are that if it happens that the lineage of those who had the duty of guarding that little basket (whom they call in Mexican *ytlàpial,*[12] which means "those that have the obligation of guarding such a thing") should come to an end, then no one dares move it from the place where the owners kept it and the inheritors have left it, which usually is on the altar of their oratories that they call *Santòcalli,*[13] as I will explain later. And this is observed so punctually that in the last case that was mentioned, about the Indian woman of Cuetlaxxochitlan, it happened that, when it was ascertained that she had one of these little baskets, without her suspecting a thing I caught her in the church in order to make her confess the crime. And seeing that she denied everything, I took her to her house, and, entering the oratory, I had the little basket searched for, and it was in the oratory just as it had been for so long a time that the mats had turned to dirt, and the images had almost totally lost their colors, and no one dared to move or to touch anything of what was there, because the little case was in the oratory and we found it over a mat that served as the canopy of the oratory altar. In this little basket was the *ololiuhqui* and one of the little *tecomates*[14] that have been spoken of and some small pieces of fabric, and the Indian woman did not dare to touch the *ololiuhqui* with her hand. The Indian woman, when asked for what reason and for what purpose she had that there, answered, *Àmo notlàpial caçan ypan nehcoc*[15] (meaning "It does not belong to me through inheritance, but I found it here when I came to live in this house"). When asked for what reason she had denied it, she answered almost the same thing, saying *ypampa ca àmo notlàpial,*[16] as if to say, "Because it was not something I inherited," and thus if the woman had had a place to hide the basket, without doubt she would have, and therefore I did not let her out of my hands after she found out why she was summoned.

In order that there may be more success in these cases, let it be noted that, when the Indians find out that it is a matter of such an inquiry, those that have these things immediately hide them beneath the platform of the little altar in their oratories or behind the altarpiece or over the canopy or baldachin of the altar itself so that they will not be noticed. And I have taken them from these places when the delinquents do not have more time to hide them, but if they have somewhat more time, it is almost impossible to find what they hide, because easily they either bury[17] the basket or put it in a place it cannot be found, as has been seen in Peru, where they hide in small caves and beneath the earth the idols they call *Huacas* and the bodies of their ancestors whom they also adore.

Some have these little baskets inside boxes for better keeping and veneration, especially when they have some little idol to whom they attribute the increase of wealth. And if they attribute the increase of maize, wheat, and other seeds to it, they have it inside the granaries that they call *Cuezcomatl,*[18] as a certain Miguel Bernardino had them, a native of the village of Quauhchinalla[19] and an inhabitant of that of Tetelpan in the Amilpas in the region of Cuernavaca. This Miguel Bernardino had five little idols, and, after I had brought proceedings against him for a single idol, in order not to miss the mark, while following him, I summoned the secular justice for another purpose. I caught him outside his village, where, confronted with the proof, he confessed to having one single idol in the granary, where I sent posthaste three Spaniards. And having entered the granaries, they found five idols. Afterwards, when I asked Miguel Bernardino why he had denied the four, he said that only one was of his inheritance, which is what they call *ytlàpial,*[20] and he had the four in his keeping, but he had believed that it was his own that had increased the harvests.

I have found many people like this in other villages. And in order that it be understood how important this warning is, I will tell what happened to me in the village of Xoxouhtla, which is in the Amilpas, a region of Cuernavaca. I summoned an Indian, Don Miguel, a *principal* of the village of Teocaltzinco, a congregant there, who had been a *fiscal* in it. And after he was with me a short while, he confessed that he had an idol. And his wife had moved it, and I deduced this because immediately thereafter I went with the Indian to his house with a notary and witnesses to see in what place he had the idol, and with what veneration he held it, and so that he would hand it over to me. And the Indian went straight to the room and the locked basket where he had it, and, not finding it there, he went out to where the woman was and muttered to her that, since he had already declared to me that he had the idol, she should bring it out. And I compelled the Indian woman to tell where she had hidden it. She went to a large pile of gourds that she was dividing, and from the midst of them she took it out on a plate of black varnish and with it two other idols with many bracelets and toys, which are usually put on children as adornment, although the black varnish of the plate in which they were clearly showed the bad lodgings of those who were reverenced in those idols. An effect was attributed to each one of these three idols, such as increasing the sown lands, wealth, etc.

In the village of Tasmalaca it happened to me that, after I had caught unawares a certain Miguel de Escobar, a singer in the church choir, he confessed to me that he had in his house an idol, as I had already found out about him. I locked up the Indian immediately so that he would not give the order to hide the idol while people went to his house, where I went with all haste. And I made straight for his oratory, where, while I questioned his mother-in-law about the location of a white stone that her son had confessed to me that he had, Miguel de Escobar's wife removed three idols that she had, leaving only one white stone. The old woman referred me to the daughter, and the daughter denied [it] perversely. But God was served that in her gestures I noticed that she had on herself what she denied. I had the ministers search her, and the Indian woman had already covered them with her sash where they found them. She had separated them from the other white stone that the husband adored, because the husband had inherited only the said stone from his ancestors, and she the three idols.

From this the ministers will deduce the sagacity that is necessary [in dealing] with these people, because neither the fear of God nor an oath nor any other thing is of advantage [in getting them] to confess the truth, but rather they have to be persuaded to confess out of fear because no other path is found with them, or, as people say, they have to be caught with the theft in their hands so that they cannot deny it.

The superstition of the *tecomates*, which are the vessels they usually use for drinking, has its beginning and foundation in the use of them as a thing that is consecrated and dedicated for their idolatrous offerings and sacrifices. And it is the case that, when they make pulque (which is their wine) of new magueys, that is to say, when they use the vineyard for the first time, the first wine that they make in their way, the first fruit that is this kind of wine, is offered to the god they take a fancy to, such as fire or some idol, and this offering is made in the *tecomates.* Filling them with pulque and putting them on the altar with much veneration, they accompany them with incense and lighted candles, and, a little while after that, they spill a little there in sign of sacrifice. And then the owners and the guests give, as people say, good account of the remainder in the *tecomates* and of the contents of the pots—which are their barrels—or, to express it better, a bad account, and so bad that with it they lose account of their life and customs, with everyone ending up out of his wits and everything that usually happens after this, and especially where men and women attend such meetings together, from which so many offenses to our Lord and so many gains for the Devil, the author of all evil, usually follow one another. After this tempest, the said *tecomates,* which do not serve any other use, are put away. And these, along with the superstition, are inherited by the children and descendants, and they use them for a similar occasion, or, if for some other purpose or for the beginning of some work, they [use them to] make similar sacrifices.

CHAPTER 3

About the Adoration and Cult That They Give to *Huauhtli*

THE time when there is most manifestly formal idolatry is at the end of the rainy season with the first fruits of a seed smaller than mustard, which they call *huautli*,[1] because the Devil also wants them to offer him first fruits. This seed is, then, earlier than any other in hardening and becoming ripe, and thus they gather it when the maize which they call early or three-month maize[2] begins to produce ears—which happens in two months in the hot lands. From this seed they make a drink like porridge to drink cold, and they also make some cakes which in their language they call *tzoalli*, and these they eat cooked in the manner of their tortillas.

Idolatry is in whatever thanksgiving with which it may have been seasoned. From the first [*huauhtli*] that they gather, well ground and kneaded, they make some idols in the shape of a human figure and the size of a fourth of a *vara*,[3] a little more or less. They have a lot of their wine prepared for the day that they form them, and after the idols are made and cooked, they put them in their oratories, as if they are placing some [holy] image, and setting before them candles and incense, they offer them, along with their bouquets, some of the wine prepared for the dedication, either in the superstitious little *tecomates*[4] mentioned above or, if they do not have them, in other chosen ones, and for this all of those of the clique that is the brotherhood of Beelzebub get together, and, seated in a circle with much applause, having placed the *tecomates* and bouquets before the said idols, they begin in their honor and praise, and in that of the Devil, the music of the *teponaztli*,[5] which is a drum all of wood, and the soft singing of the old people is accompanied with it. And when they have already played and sung what they have [received] from tradition, the owners of the offering and the most illustrious ones arrive, and, as a sign of sacrifice, they pour out before the little idols of *Huauhtli* either a part or all of that wine which they had placed in the little *tecomates*,[6] and they call this action *tlatōtoyāhua*.[7] And then they all begin to drink what is left in the *tecomates* first, and then they relentlessly pursue the pots until finishing them, and their wits with them—and what is usual for idolatries and drunken sprees follows. But the owners of the little idols guard them with care for the following day, on which, after the participants of the festival have met together in the oratory, distributing pieces of the little idols as if for relics, they all eat them together.

This fact proves very well the very great anxieties and diligences of the Devil, in continuation of that first sin of his, the origin of all pride, of wanting to be like God, Our Lord, since he works so much to imitate Him even in the mysteries of our redemption, since in what I have just related one sees so vividly envied and imitated the most singular mystery of the very holy Sacrament of the altar, in which Our Lord, by summarizing the benefits of our redemption, disposed that we should most truly eat him. And the Devil, the ape, the enemy of all that is good, arranges for these unfortunate people to eat him, or let themselves be taken possession of by him in eating him in those little idols.

CHAPTER 4

About the Adoration and Sacrifice That They Made on the Hills to the Idols and Piles of Rocks Along the Roads That Are Prominent Even Today

THIS kind of idolatry I have ascertained to be so general that I consider it certain that no generation of Indians escapes from it, especially in the villages that are remote and isolated from the ministers of the doctrine and justice. It has become clear, and much more abundantly, that there are fewer [idolatrous] people [who are caught] because of having fewer to be afraid of, because if for some reason they know that there is someone who is not of the included ones, and especially if he is a stranger, they go around with care and alert, and they close themselves up and post guard so that he cannot arrive even at the door of their consultations so that he cannot inform us of them.

Another kind of idolatry, that of self-sacrifice,[1] used to be practiced and in some parts is still seen. And it is the one they performed on the peaks of the hills and on high slopes, whose roads we see today as prominent as if they were roads for coaches, because that is the way they must have made them in olden times, for they go straight up toward the top, stopping at some pile of rocks, or a hillock of them, where they used to make their adoration, sacrifice, and prayers. And I have found out now in great detail the way they performed them from Don Baltasar de Aquino, an old Indian cacique and the most ancient in all my parish. He related it thus.

There were in each village certain old people dedicated to the ministry of the sacrifices of penitents (whom they call *tlamàceuhque).*[2] And those old men used to be called *tlamacazque,* which means "priests." These used to summon whomever they wanted to from the village to send him as if on a pilgrimage, because even in this the Devil imitated the spiritual. And when the one summoned arrived in the presence of that old man, then the old man would command him to go swiftly to ask for favors. And it was the case that they believed that there where they were going (which was on the peaks of the mountains or on the high slopes where the circles or mounds of rocks were, where they had the idols of different shapes and names) in the same places was that supreme God, whom all call "Lord of the world," *Tlalticpaque;* "he whose captives we are," *Tiytlacahuan;* "God of battles," *Yaotl;* "the ticklish one," *Moquequeloatzin,* as if they might say "he who does not permit tickling" or "the jealous one."[3]

The old [a]*tlamacazqui,* [a]{priest}, would send the [b]*tlamaceuhqui,* [b]{penitent}, on the pilgrimage in the following manner.

There used to be in each village something like a large well-swept courtyard, delegated for such purposes, like a church. Everyone had the obligation of bringing green firewood to this courtyard for the old men, who were distinguished by a long lock of hair which they let grow on their heads, which also among the Indians was a mark of great captains and warriors called *tlacauhque.*[4]

This old man, being seated, then, on a low seat of stone, in such a way that he was as we say squatting, holding in his hands a large *tecomate* of the herb that mixed with lime they call *Tenex yhetl,*[5] which means "tobacco with lime,"[6] and having before him in the courtyard the *tlamàceuhq̃* who was to go on the pilgrimage, he made his speech to him and ordered him to the place that he designated for the adoration of the idols, to the one who was *Tlalticpaq̃,*[7] which means "Lord of the earth," and the words were:

[1] [a]Depart quickly, [b]you who share the same bowl with me, [c]my youngest child, [d]my only one. [e]Do not detain yourself in vain,[8] [f]for I remain waiting for you, [g]taking tobacco and lime and [h]hiccoughing with it and [i]watching what you do in my absence (as if he said "prophesying"). Look here at what I give you for food to carry.

[a]Xon ỳciuhtiuh [b]nocomìchic [c]Noxocoyo [d]nocenteuh [e]Maçan cana Timàahuiltitiuh. [f]Nimitzchixtiez. [g]Nican niyehtlacuitica [h]nitlacuepalotica [i]Nitlachixtica yzca nimitzqualtia tichuicaz.

Go hurrying away, my bowl-scrapings,[9] my youngest child, my only one. Beware of dallying somewhere! I will be waiting for you. Here I am taking tobacco; I am burping. I am watching. Here is what I am giving you to eat, which you will carry.

Xonihciuhtiuh, nocōmihchic, noxocoyo, nocenteuh. Mā zan canah timahāhuiltihtiyah![10] Nimitzchixtiyez. Nicān niyetlacuiticah; nitlacuepalohticah.[11] Nitlachixticah. Iz cah nimitzcualtia, tichuīcaz.

He said this last part because the old man used to give the penitent a small part of the *Tenex yetl*[12] which he had in the *tecomate* in order that the penitent might take [it][13] along the road, and the old man also took it in the courtyard, where he remained seated by the fire waiting for the pilgrim. And they say he did this in order not to fall asleep with the long wait for the pilgrim, because this pilgrimage was always made at night. And it should be noticed that the old man also gave the *Tenex yyetl* to the pilgrim, like a guardian angel for the road, because also they have a superstition about this herb, attributing divinity to it, so that the pilgrim carried it like a guardian angel. Having given him the *Tenex yyete,*[14] the old man would continue, and, giving him a staff, he would say:

[2] Take your staff on which you will go supporting yourself. If in some place you find your uncles, put your hands in their mouths; if they are sorcerers who want to make sport of you, put your hands quickly in their mouths, for if they are not sorcerers but wild deities, then you will know them in that they have slobbery mouths; they do not want to harm you. But if they are sorcerers, you will know them in that they have a wall of teeth. Kill such as these with sticks and bring a branch torn off some tree.

Izcà mochiquacel yctimotlaquechìtiaz yntlacanà tiquinnāmiquiz Motlàtlàhuan. Yntlanco timāyahuiz Yntla tlahcanahualli Moca mocàcayahuaznequi. Niman ytlanco ximāyahui. Auh yntlācan quauhtlà chanècācâ Tlanmahalactic àmo tle mitzchihuiliznequi, auh yntla tlacanahualli ytech tiquittaz, yntla çan tlantechinampol xicquahuihuītequi, xicmicti Tichualcuih yntlapoztectli acxoyatl.

Here is your staff; with it you will go supporting yourself. If somewhere you meet your various uncles, you will put your hand on their teeth. If he[15] is a person-*nahualli,* he wants to make

Iz cah mochicuahcol;[17] īc timotlaquechihtiyāz. In tlā canah tiquinnāmiquiz motlahtlahhuān,[18] īntlanco timāyahuiz.[19] In tlā tlācanāhualli,[20] moca mocahcayā-

fun of you. Immediately put your hand on his teeth. And if he is only a forest dweller, his teeth will be slick; he does not want to do anything to you. But if he is a person-*nahualli,* you will see it in him if he is just a big fence of teeth. Strike him severely on the head. Kill him. You will bring back a fir bough[16] that has been broken off.

huaznequi. Niman ītlanco ximāyahui. Auh in tlā zan cuauhtlah chānehcācah,[21] tlanahalactic;[22] ahmō tleh mitzchīhuilīznequi. Auh in tlā tlācanāhualli, ītech tiquittaz in tlā zan tlantechināmpōl. Xiccuāhuihhuītequi.[23] Xicmicti. Tichuālcuiz[24] in tlapoztectli[25] acxōyatl.

This branch which he asked him for was the sign that he had gone to the place where he was sent, because the trees that grew there were known, and because the branch could be compared later with where it had been taken from.[26]

This old man was so obeyed and feared that no one excused himself from going to the place assigned to him, no matter how difficult it might be. And if he [the summoned person] excused himself to him, they relate that he [the old man] would strike him with a stick, and the old man was not punished or molested in any way, even if he killed him, because all this business was considered and esteemed to be a divine thing and dedicated to the gods, and thus that old man used to speak and command like a man from a higher sphere, with revealed science and prophetic knowledge, and therefore he used to say to the pilgrims at the time of their departure that he remained behind watching all their happenings, steps, and deeds, and thus he used to say:

[3] Here I remain watching you, I, the one of superior science,[27] the dexterous ancient one, and we would almost say.[28]

Nican nitlachixtica nixomoconihuēhue nicipac nitonal. as if he said, *Ego Vir Videns.*[29]

Here I am watching. I am Ohxomoco, I am Old-man; I am Cipactonal, [I am Old-woman].[30]

Nicān nitlachixticah. NOhxomoco, niHuēhueh; niCipactōnal, [nIlamah].[31]

And they believed so firmly that it was true that he saw everything and that nothing escaped his knowledge that even those living today consider it true—and in order to deceive them more, it would be very possible for the Devil, their patron, to show them the absent events. Also, in conformity with the words of the old seer, they considered it certain that, if the ones he met on the road had teeth, those were sorcerers who, envious of his task, came out to hinder him and to prevent him from accomplishing it. The old man ordered the pilgrim to kill these and to continue his trip. The pilgrim was very contented with this and only replied:

[4] Let it be in a fruitful hour, my superior lord.

Caye qualli nihcauhtzine.

It is indeed good, my younger brother.[32]

Ca ye cualli, niccāuhtziné.[33]

He was very satisfied, for if he died on the quest he was going very well employed, as if he were offered up to martyrdom. With this he would leave on his trip, carrying for his first offering copal, which is the incense of this land, and some skeins of thick cotton thread poorly spun, like that from which a wick is made, or some small piece of cloth woven of that kind of thread, which for this reason they call *Poton;*[34] it means "loosely twisted," because in places the cotton shows, and I have found it like this in the offerings at the piles of stone, as I mention elsewhere. And they used to accompany the offering with that which they call *Quauhamatl*,[35] which is a kind of white paper like linen that is made in Tepoztlan from the soft bark of a tree. The offering used to be wrapped in this paper, and it served along with the cotton as something for the god or idol, to whom it was being offered, to wear, which is so that the angels who walk on the clouds or in the passes and crossroads can be dressed *Vt alibi.*[36]

Upon arriving at the place of the idol or at the pile of rocks, he prostrated himself where he was to place the offering, and, after having placed it, he sacrificed himself by spilling his blood, for which purpose he carried a sharp needle made of a little sliver of cane, and with it he pricked his ears in the parts where women put earrings until much blood was spilled. And he poured it into some little vessels that they made in the rocks like saltcellars. And thus they shredded the ears so that they became like big rings when they were old men, a thing which they called *Nacaztecòcoyacpol.*[37] They also pricked themselves below the lip above the chin until they made a hole in it like a nostril, and some also the tongue on the upper side. All this they used to do for sacrifice. And they say that some even fainted or fell asleep, and in this ecstasy they would hear, or thought they heard, words from their idol who spoke to them, of which they would become very proud and seemingly certain that they would be granted what they were requesting, which ordinarily was children, wealth, a long life, a family, or health.

After finishing bleeding himself, if he did not fall asleep, or after having come to himself from the ecstasy, he would tear a branch off the tree that was most particular and well known for that place, and he would hasten back until he set it down in front of the one who had dispatched him. And they call this branch [a]*Tlapoztec* [b]*acxōyatl* [c]*nēzcayotl*,[38] which means "the [a]torn-off [b]branch [c]of the testimony," as a proof of having arrived at that place. He would present it, then, to the old man, with which he convinced him that he had fulfilled and obeyed his command and had made that kind of pilgrimage. And if in it that god to whom he had made an offering of his blood had shown himself to him or had spoken to him, or if he thought that he had, he would be very happy, saying that he had now received grace and had obtained what he was seeking.

Those living today saw many like these, as stated by Don Baltasar de Aquino and Don Diego de San Matheo, inhabitants of this district of Atenanco. And surely we should be ashamed, we to whom the less hard and so much more advantageous works from which no difficulty ought to dissuade us seem to be so uphill.

CHAPTER 5

About the Penitential Pilgrimage Made by Those Who Used to Live on the Rivers and in the Fertile Valleys

THOSE who lived in the fertile valleys of the rivers used to make their pilgrimage in the water. They used to call them "penitents of the water," or "in the water," in their language, *Āyahualco tlamàceuhque.*[1] Such a one would go with his gourd upriver along the bank until [he reached] the backwater or whirlpool which they [the *tlamacazqueh*] determined for him. There the best and most happy outcome was for him to show himself to a crocodile—or lizard or caiman—which they call *Ācuetzpal chimalli nauhcompa tzontecome,*[2] which means "lizard-shield that has four heads." Upon seeing the caiman, the penitent would leap upon its neck, and it would take several turns around the whirlpool or backwater, where it would then dive while the penitent remained above with his gourd, with which he would then let himself float downriver until he arrived at his village or hut, from where he had left for the said pilgrimage, without even thinking about the danger of the caiman, the darkness of the night, or the cold of the water, even though the pilgrimage that was assigned to him might be very distant—because everything seemed worth suffering because it was, as he saw it, in penitence and for the sake of attaining favors, as if they were from one from whom he might really receive them, with everything being the work of the Devil, who, in the deed and in the circumstances of it, clearly showed everything to be the night and darkness of idolatry.

It seems somewhat difficult to believe that [story] about the caiman, but since everything was the work of the Devil, for whom this is easy, it can be believed, because this and much more would he do in order to gain, or, in better words, in order to lose, a soul for which he suffers so much yearning.

If, after having arrived at the backwater indicated, the caiman did not show itself to him, he contented himself with having arrived, and in fulfillment of his penitence he threw himself in the water with his gourd, letting himself float downriver to his village or post from where he had left for the said penitence.

I found out about these[3] pilgrimages and penitences because there is a *gobernador* of my district called Don Diego de Mendoza in the village of Cuetlaxxochitla, reared in my time, who, upon reprimanding those of his village because they were excusing themselves and becoming obstinate about coming to the church, for the doctrine, the mass, and the divine offices, in order to make them ashamed, said the following to them: *Caotiquincaquilìque tocolhuan, tocìhuan, l.*[4] *tocizhuan*[5] *ynhuehuetque, ynilamatque, yn que nin*[6] *tlahuenchihualoya tepeticpac, yntecolalco, ynteolocholco, ỹmanel yca yohuac, mixtecomac tlacomoni, yn quẽman chicahuac*[7] *quiahui, ye àmo quicahuaya yntlahuenchihualiztli huel conàxitiaya. Auh tlejn ỹ mācehual? caçan tētlapololtiliztli, caçan tlacatecolotl quitlátlauhtiaya. Auh ynaxcan caymahuizçotzin yxquich yteoyotzin tlacatl. tty*º. *D.*[8] *noyxquich tomàcehual,*[9] *auh çan canpa tiquittâ, auh çan nepa titotlahcali:*[10] *cahuel tétlapololti; catétequipacho, ca huey totlatlacol yxpantzinco ynDios.*

Translated, this says, "We heard from our forebears, the elders, the manner and care with which in their time the elders made their sacrifices and offerings on the heights of the hills, in the circles of stones, and on the piles of them, at night in deep darkness, even though it might be, as they say, pitch black,[11] even if thundering or even if raining very hard, and even so they did not fail to make their offerings and sacrifices; rather, they attended with every punctuality and complete observance. And let us find out: what did they get out of it? or what use was it to them? since it was all blindness, deceit, and adoration of the Devil.[12] But since now the excellence of the faith, honor, and treasure of the divinity of God is so much, so fully for our good that we almost stumble upon it, it seems that in order to flee from the good, we hurl ourselves over precipices knowingly—a thing that is worthy of surprise, astonishment, and of very great sorrow, because in truth I say to you that this fault and offense to God, in the presence of his divine majesty,[13] is very serious in us."[14]

These words edified me, and they stamped themselves on my soul *quasi stilo ferreo*,[15] and thus after more than a year they have come to my mind at this point, and I put them here so that the preachers of these peoples can take advantage of them.

Father Friar Agostin Guerra, of the Order of Saint Augustine, wrote to me that in the province of Tlapa, when he was going one morning to a *visita* to say mass, he saw an Indian who was climbing to the highest part of a hill, which is where these old roads go. Suspecting from the place the Indian was going that idolatry was involved, the religious, with those whom he took with him, set out in the direction of the Indian on the hill, at which spot when they arrived, although the Indian was already gone, they found his offering and lighted candles in front of a stone idol, and having seen this, they made vigorous efforts and sent trackers in search of the Indian, and they could not find him, not even a trace of him, about which they were quite amazed.

And it cannot be doubted that there is probably a lot of this where they have not made vigorous efforts in investigating, preventing, and punishing it. At least if this were dealt with as carefully as it should be, these pusillanimous people would stop out of fear of punishment, even if such offenses to God were not abandoned out of love and reverence for Him. And, with the difficulties and oppression they [would thus] suffer, it would be easily forgotten, and it would not be handed down to grandchildren.

CHAPTER 6

About the Superstition Concerning *Ololiuhqui*

THE so-called *ololiuhqui* is a seed like lentils or lentil vetch which, when drunk, deprives one of judgment. And the faith that these unhappy natives have in this seed is amazing, since, by drinking it, they consult it like an oracle for everything whatever that they want to know, even those things which are beyond human knowledge, such as knowing the cause of illnesses, because almost everyone among them who is consumptive, tubercular, with diarrhea, or with whatever other sickness of the persistent kind right away attributes it to sorcery. And in order to resolve this doubt and others like it, such as those about stolen things and of aggressors, they consult this seed by means of one of their deceitful doctors, some of whom have it as their job to drink this seed for such consultations, and this kind of doctor is called *Pàyni*,[1] because of the job, for which he is paid very well, and they bribe him with meals and drinks in their fashion. If this doctor either does not have this function or wishes to excuse himself from that torment, he advises the patient himself to drink that seed, or another person for whose services they also pay as they do the doctor, but the doctor indicates to him the day and the hour in which he is to drink it, and he tells him for what purpose he will drink it.

Finally, whether it is the doctor or another person in his place, in order to drink the seed, or peyote, which is another small root and for which they have the same faith as for that other seed,[2] he closes himself up alone in a room, which usually is his oratory, where no one is to enter throughout all the time that the consultation lasts, which is for as long as the consultant is out of his mind, for then they believe the *ololiuhqui* or peyote is revealing to them that which they want to know. As soon as the intoxication or deprivation of judgment passes from this person, he tells two thousand hoaxes, among which the Devil usually includes some truths, so that he has them deceived or duped absolutely.

It is the case that he who drinks the *ololiuhqui* very quickly loses his judgment because of the excessive potency of the seed. Then, his judgment having been transformed, there comes to his mind that conversation held with him about the problem at hand. And in it he passes the judgment to which the Devil—who has no lack of skill for such deceptions—inclines him. Perhaps he condemns an innocent person, perhaps he discovers the culprit, perhaps he comes out with such silly remarks that they could not have been dreamed up except by an addled mind. And the unfortunate people believe it all—whether the Devil reveals it to him, or whether it is just a representation of the imagination caused by the conversation—because they attribute it all to the divinity of the *ololiuhqui* or peyote, for which for this reason they have so much veneration and fear that they do however much they can [to conceal it], and they withdraw so that it will not come to the notice of the ecclesiastical ministers, especially if they are judges who can prohibit and punish it, as I said in the Treatise[3] on the idols and superstitious *tecomates,* and I will speak more at length of it in this Treatise.

An Indian woman of the village of Huitzoco had a little case or little basket with *ololiuhqui* with its incense and the rest that they usually have. She gave it to some *compadres* of hers to keep, telling them to hold it for her so that when I returned to the village I would not be able to find it. I arrived at the village, and without her being able to take precautions, I arrested the women and the male friend separately, without her knowing it.

After having been arrested, she was asked about the little basket, and she persistently denied [all knowledge of] it, although I asked her many and very tricky questions, and although I assured her that by revealing it she would not suffer because of it and that I already knew that she had the little basket and where. Nothing sufficed for her to confess. I proceeded to the male friend, and by questioning him with trickery about the little basket, like one who already knew that he had received it for safekeeping, he confessed, being stopped short and confused with the truth. I returned to the Indian woman, and I pressed the issue as much as I could to make her confess, and she refused. I set before her how the friend had already declared the truth. It was not enough. I left them detained separately, as I say, and I went to the house of the friend, heading for the oratory, where I found the little basket hidden in the little altar, and I got it and returned to the Indian woman, and she still denied it until I placed it before her.

The same thing happened with this Indian woman in regard to an idol that she had in a house. She never would confess it, although I came with questions that implied I knew she had it. I gave the address of the house in which it was, because the house was within my authority; nevertheless, she denied it. Finally I told her that the box was already in the house of the *vicario* of the place and that if she did not give up the key I would smash the box. Seeing that she had no way out, she confessed. She opened the box, from which she took out the idol, and handed it over to me, which the *vicario* Fr[ancis]co de la Cruz and Antonio Marques, my notary, and Christoval Hernandez, and others saw.

In order that it be realized how alert it is necessary to be in this matter, I will tell another case. In the village of Cuetlaxxōchitla, an Indian woman had a little basket with this superstition of the *ololiuhqui*. And she had some disagreement or other with the people of her house, and shortly thereafter I arrived in the village, which, because it was of my parish, was the reason for the Indian woman's apprehension. Immediately after I arrived, I found out about the little basket, because one of the women of the family told me about it. In order not to miss the target, I ordered her to search the place again, since she would be able to do so without being noticed because she was of the same house, and to see if the little basket still had the *ololiuhqui* inside and the other things that she had denounced. With this she went home and came back to me saying that the little case was no longer in the place it had been or anywhere in the oratory.

With all speed I then had the Indian woman who was the owner of the little basket brought before me, and I put guards on the house of a sister she had in the village. And I asked the delinquent such tricky questions, mentioning special and particular marks of the little basket, that she could not deny it, but she said that it did not have inside that which they asked about, or anything else of importance, and that the little basket had not been moved from its place. I sent immediately for it, and they found it where she stated, but now divested of the treasure, as she knew would be the case, because they had removed the *ololiuhqui* and a cloth of the kind that they offer to it—about which the denouncer had deposed—so that in the little basket there was only a very small amount of *ololiuhqui*. Considering the quantity of *ololiuhqui* that was missing and the cloth, I had the delinquent's sister arrested, and although I pressed her with the truth and a description so accurate that only a family witness could give, I spent all day in questions and answers in order to discover what she had taken out of the little basket, because in the short time it took me to summon the sister and to send guards to her house, she had time to remove all the *ololiuhqui* and the superstitious cloth and return the basket to the sister's oratory and to divide into many parts the quantity of *ololiuhqui* with which the little basket had been stuffed.

Being asked why she had perversely denied it, she answered the usual: *Oninomauhtiaya*,[4] which means, "Out of fear I did not dare." And here it should be carefully noticed that this fear is not of the ministers of justice for the punishment that they deserve but of the *ololiuhqui*, or of the deity who they believe lives in it, and they have this respect and veneration for it so firmly rooted that indeed the help of God is needed to rip it out. And so the dread and fear which prevents them from confessing is that of angering that false deity they pretend is in the *ololiuhqui*, in order not to fall into his ire and indignation, and thus they say, *àço nechtlahueliz*,[5] "Let it not be that he become irate and angry with me," as I experienced it myself in the following case.

Having known of the blindness in which these unfortunate people were, in order to take away from them such a great stumbling block and such a strong impediment to their health, immediately after I arrived at the *beneficiado* of Atenanco, where I am today, I began to seek ways of uprooting from their hearts their harmful superstition, preaching urgently against it and removing from their oratories a large quantity and throwing it in the fire in the presence of its owners and of many others, and commanding them to clear a large quantity of bushes that produce the fruit—and there are abundant growths of them on the banks of the river. At this time Our Lord was served that I contract an illness, as usually happens to those new and unaccustomed to a hot climate, because very few escape. In spite of the experience of what happens to all those newly come to a hot climate, when the blind superstitious people saw me sick, they spread it about that the sickness which I had had been given to me by *ololiuhqui,* for my not having revered it, but rather having angered it with what I had done against it. This is how far the blindness of these people reaches. But by the honor and grace of God, I recovered from my ailment, and I found out what had been spread around about the case. And in order to dissuade them anew, having urged as much as I could in sermons, I finally ordered a large bonfire made on a day of solemn festival on which all the *beneficio* gathered for the solemnity and, while everyone was watching, I had almost a *[f]anega*[6] of the seed that I had collected burned, and I ordered burned and cleared anew the bushes that might be found of that kind.

But the diligence of the Devil, who stays vigilant for our harm, is so great that, through his cunning, every day new stumbling blocks in this matter are found, and thus it is very necessary that the ministers of both laws be exceedingly diligent in investigating, extirpating, and punishing these results of the ancient idolatry and cult of the Devil. And in order to achieve it better, it is necessary to pay careful attention to the following:

First, the one suspected of having an idol or other thing that he worships should be seized before he can take precautions or warn his people at the time of the seizure, for which reason it will be opportune to catch him outside his village.

Second, on the one hand, when catching the delinquent and, on the other hand, when putting reliable guards at the house or places where it has been heard that such an idol or superstition is, everything should be done at one and the same time, and it will even be prudent to put a guard on at least the nearest relatives such as the wife, brothers, sisters, etc.

Third, the judge should be careful with regard to the ministers and not trust anyone of the village of the delinquent, because usually there is no one who is faithful.

Fourth, when it is possible, the judge in person should take out the idols or superstitious things that are sought, and, if this is not possible, his ministers[7] should, and only if it is unavoidable, the delinquent may take them out. Let the judge and the ministers keep their eyes open, because in such a case, if he can, the delinquent will swallow the idol in order to hide it even though he is already convicted and knows that if he swallows it he will surely die.

Fifth, also let it be noted that for concealment, when there is no other place, they usually put the idol in some old and dirty pot, and thus, in looking for it, no diligence is to be spared, because in Comala—which is a village in my district of Atenanco—it happened to me to arrest for that crime an Indian woman, the wife of

Francisco Diego, and, without letting it out of her hand, [even while] gripping it, she confessed to having had it but that now they had stolen it from her, and for proof she asked to be taken to her house so that all of it could be cleared. I went with her, and immediately after our arrival I went in, opening all the boxes and little baskets and searching through everything inside. While it did not actually show up in the house, she had an old, dirty pot covered with a potsherd in the courtyard of the house. The black pot was full up to the brim with *ololiuhqui,* and in the middle of it, in the depth of the pot, wrapped in a rag, was the little idol, which was a little black frog of stone.

Also they usually put the idols in the platforms of the crosses, especially those that are in deserted places, for two purposes: first, because no one would suspect the union (*quae conventio lucis adtenebras?);*[8] second, because with this dissimulation they frequently venerate and adore the idols by putting in front of them lighted candles, incense, bouquets, and other like things. This was found to be the case not long ago with the cross at Chilapa, the head of this district, which the Indians frequented with similar offerings because the platform was pregnant with this infernal pestilence.

Also I have found out that in many other places things of this kind have existed until God, Our Father, has made them manifest, as happened in the sierra of Meztitlan, under the jurisdiction of Augustine friars, where lightning struck the platform of a cross so many times that the religious, having been informed, had it torn up in their presence, and they found an idol inside. After it was taken away, never again has lightning struck from that day to this throughout more than twelve years.

From what has been said, it seems that one can infer that the [Christian] faith is in the Indians very imperfectly and that, since preaching has not sufficed, rigorous punishment is needed, because, being—as they are—children of terror, it may be that punishment may accomplish what reason has not been sufficient to, since the Apostle said, *compellite eos intrare.*[9]

CHAPTER 7

About the Use of and the Troubles That Follow from the Superstition Concerning *Ololiuhqui*

GIVEN the manner in which they use this drink, it remains to particularize for what purposes they drink it, and the great troubles that follow from it. For which let what was said above be noted: the ones suffering from protracted illnesses and from those which, being confirmed, are considered by the doctors to be incurable, such as are the consumptives and the tuberculars, etc., seeing that they do not improve with ordinary medicines, then attribute their illness and sickness to witchcraft and at the same time consider it certain that they will never become well if the one who bewitched them does not cure them or does not want them to get well. This is the most usual case in which they use to their advantage, or to their harm, the infernal superstition of *ololiuhqui*, because, having first consulted the one who among them has the job of doctor, whom they call *Ticitl* (and by the way, be advised that the said name should always be considered suspect because of what I have said). This doctor, to support his frauds and also not to confess that they [i.e., the doctors] do not know how to cure that sickness, immediately attributes it to witchcraft. And this is the same thing that the sick person persuaded himself of when he called him. And in order to agree about everything, the patient immediately recounts his suspicions and the reason why he thinks as he does. Then the false doctor orders that *ololiuhqui* be used to resolve the doubt, for which purpose the doctor's order is followed precisely, like the words of a prophet or the answer of an oracle, whereupon the *ololiuhqui* is taken by the doctor or the sick person or someone hired for this purpose, whom they first instruct in the method and in the suspicion with its circumstances.

After this there follows the intoxication of the drink, and in it, he condemns the one indicated[1] by the suspicion—either because the inebriate's fantasy brings to the fore those pieces of information that he previously learned about the suspicion, or else because the Devil speaks to him by virtue of the pact which is included in it on this occasion at least tacitly. He makes public his condemnation as soon as he comes out of his intoxicated state, which usually lasts one or two days—although he may perhaps remain dazed for many, or even become totally mad. With this sentence, war is declared between the kinspeople of the sick person and the one suspected of the sorcery and his kinspeople, and hatred and rancor become so firmly established upon this that, from experience, it seems to me that only God or His most particular aids will be enough to uproot it. And what is worse, the rancor passes along and the children and grandchildren inherit it, and it is an enormous impediment for the salvation of these miserable people.

Many cases of this kind have passed through my hands. In some of them the intervention of the Holy Office has been necessary, since other races—such as Spaniards, half-breeds, blacks, and mulattos—are involved, because in such suspicions they exempt no one. And also those who deal frequently with the Indians easily become infected with their customs and superstitions, especially if they are base people, as I witnessed in the district of Tepequaquilco[2] with Agustin de Alvarado, a mulatto who, suspecting that an Indian *alcalde* of Mayanala had bewitched him, made use of this superstition and [after coming out of the trance] made known his suspicion, and everything came to light, because—since they consider it established that the sick person cannot get well except through the will of the one who bewitched him—the mulatto requested the Indian *alcalde* to cure him, or else he would rouse the village against him and make him publicly known to be a sorcerer. The Indian *alcalde*, being ignorant of the case and surprised at the imputed blame, turned to the offices of the law, wherewith all the muddle and the superstition was discovered, and the Holy Office became informed and proceeded against the mulatto.

Also if in the presence of the sick person it is said that someone is a sorcerer, and the sick person has no particular cause for blaming his sickness on someone else, without more proof he assaults the presumed sorcerer and immediately makes him, and supposes him to be, the malefactor, and then he requests him to pacify his ire and anger and to cure him. If the one accused of the crime denies it, then the sick person takes refuge in the *ololiuhqui* in the manner described above. Thus it happened as a fact in the town of Tlaltizapan with an Indian woman who got sick there and not having reason on her own to blame anyone in particular, because of gossip of the village she suspected a certain Don Juan Bautista, with whom she had never had any enmity or clash. And because she confirmed her suspicion with the infernal superstition of the *ololiuhqui,* enmities, hatreds, and rancors have grown up between them that last today and will even endure, along with many other troubles that always accompany such angers.

Also they make use of this drink to find things that have been stolen, lost, or misplaced and in order to know who took or stole them. By going to the *ololiuhqui,* as in the first case, they affirm as very certain and evident what they turn over in their imaginations during the time of the intoxication, or what the Devil, the father and beginning of all deception, makes them believe and understand. And even though experience afterward shows them the deception, it is not enough to make them come out of that blindness—captives of the one single time out of a thousand in which the Devil made them be correct in the prognostication. We experience this every day because many thefts occur owing to the poor safekeeping of these miserable people's houses and property, the great inclination that base persons have for theft, and the strong incitement offered by the slight safekeeping combined with opportunity, because very frequently the houses remain totally empty. And they are so unfortunate that, no matter how worthless the things that are stolen from them may be, right away they consult *ololiuhqui.* And since the thefts are so many, the stolen things are found in the rarest instances; nevertheless they remain obstinate and blind in their error.

When the wife leaves the husband or the husband the wife, they also take advantage of *ololiuhqui,* and in this case the imagination and fantasy work also, and even better than in the case of sicknesses, because in this second case conjectures follow that are the cause of more vehement suspicion, and thus it works with greater strength at the time of the intoxication, since it is easily seen that one person will be persuaded that another carried off his wife or stole his property. Of this kind I will relate here a few cases, only for them to serve as examples, because I would never stop if I tried to relate even a tenth of the cases of this kind. Similar to the so-called doctors I have spoken of, among the Indians there is another kind whom they call *tlachixqui,*[3] which is equivalent to "prophet" or "fortune-teller." It is to these that those whose wife or husband is missing or whose property has been stolen go in order to find out where she or he is and who took the one or the other, as Saul went to the Pythoness {Kings 28},[4] being pressed by the Philistines, and with the same result.

Finally these prophets make use of *ololiuhqui* or of peyote to solve these riddles, in the way already described. Then they say that a venerable old man appears to them who says that he is the *ololiuhqui* or the peyote and that he has come at their call in order to help them in whatever way might be necessary. Then, being asked about the theft or about the absent wife, he answers where and how they will find it or her.

Thus it happened in the province of Chietla, of the bishopric of Tlaxcalan,[5] that, after his wife had run away, an Indian who was a native of Nauituchco,[6] having become tired of looking for the woman, went as a last refuge to the *ololiuhqui.* As he later declared before Father Friar Agustin Guerra, an Augustine religious and a good interpreter of the language, after he had drunk that evil drink, that old man appeared to him and said he was the *ololiuhqui* and had come to help him. The Indian told him that his difficulty was that he did not know about his wife or where he might find her. The old man answered; "Do not fret yourself, because you will soon find her. Go tomorrow to the village of Ocuylucã[7] and station yourself in front of the convent, at such and such an hour, and when you see a religious on a horse of such and such a color enter the convent, go immediately to such and such a house and without going beyond the entry hall of it, look behind the door, and there you will find her." After the Indian had come out of the consultation and the intoxication, he went to the village, which was ten leagues down the road. He stationed himself in front of the convent and what the Devil had told him happened to him. He found the woman behind the indicated door; he carried her to his house, where the miserable woman hanged herself that night. For this reason did the Enemy go along so solicitously and set up all his triangulations! And like such a great philosopher, he matched all the contingencies well for that disastrous outcome.

A similar thing happened to another person who had the same kind of problem. Upon being consulted, the *ololiuhqui*—and in truth the Devil—answered that in such and such a village at such and such a time of the fair that here they call *tianguez*,[8] he should place himself in such and such a spot and continually watch such and such a street, because along it he would see his wife. And it happened like that. And such as these are the answers, hitting the mark or missing it; and if they miss it, the unhappy people attribute the miss to their own fault, saying that because of this or that thing they angered the *ololiuhqui;* they did not sweep, or they did not incense the room well where they drank it, or some dog entered or barked, or whatever, so that the error is excused.

It is the same for lost or stolen things, as happened in the Amilpas with one of these false prophets, who said that they should go at such and such an hour to such and such a road, and they would find it in the shade of a tree of such and such a kind. And, in fact, it happened that way, since it was a mule about which the question was asked. The owner went to the tree and found it in the shade of it.

A success of this kind gets out and excuses two thousand errors, and these miserable people are so enticed by the success that no disproof is sufficient to make them come to their senses and lead them back to the knowledge of the truth. Rather, on the contrary, the Devil usually mixes something of our holy religion in those apparitions of his so that he whitewashes his malice and lends a color of goodness to such a great evil as will be seen in the next case.

In the village of Iguala, when I was investigating these crimes by order and command of the Most Reverend Don Juan de la Serna,[9] the Archbishop of Mexico, last year, 1617,[10] I arrested an Indian woman called Mariana, a seer, a liar, a healer of the type they call *Ticitl.* This Mariana declared that what she knew and used in her sorcery and frauds she had learned from another Indian woman, Mariana's sister, and that the sister had not learned it from any other person, but that it had been revealed to her, because when the sister was consulting the *ololiuhqui* about the cure of an old wound, having become intoxicated with the strength of the drink, she summoned the sick person and blew upon his wound over some embers, whereupon the wound healed immediately, and after the puff of breath there immediately appeared to her a youth whom she judged to be an angel, and he consoled her saying: "Do not be upset. Behold, God gives you a favor and a gift because you live in poverty and much misery, so that with this favor you will have chili pepper and salt, meaning 'sustenance'; you will cure wounds just by licking them and the rash and the smallpox. And if you do not respond to this, you will die." And after this the youth spent all night giving her a cross and crucifying her on it and driving nails into her hands, and while the Indian woman was on the cross, the youth taught her the ways she knew for curing, which were seven or more exorcisms and invocations. And they had light for fifteen continuous days where the person sick with the wound was. It must have been in veneration of the cure and of the portent.[11]

With these diabolical chimeras, fictions, and representations which the Devil puts into their imagination, they make themselves esteemed as almost divine, leading people to believe that they have the grace of the angels, for the dispensation of which they deserve the temporal things that they understand under the names of chili pepper and salt [i.e., food], and thus these liars do not live from anything else than these lies, usurping what the Gospel says: *dignus et.n. operarius mercedesua,*[12] because in this also the Devil seeks more glimmering light, or to put it better, he creates some shadows in the resplendent lights of the Gospel.

Here it should be carefully noted how much these miserable people hide this superstition of the *ololiuhqui* from us, and the reason is that, as they confess, the very one they consult orders them not to reveal it to us. He well knows that in this he puts in jeopardy the accomplishment of his aspirations to harm us, and the Indians themselves are so pusillanimous and so weak in the [Christian] faith that they believe that, if they should reveal it, the *ololiuhqui* himself would kill them or would do them other harm. And thus their excuse is *ipampa àmo nechtlahueliz,*[13] which is as if to say "in order that the *ololiuhqui* will not declare himself to be my enemy."

CHAPTER 8

About Other Superstitions of the Indians

SINCE in this land it is so necessary, so common, and so easy for every kind of people to ride horseback—because almost all the land is very rough, the settlements are very far apart, the roads lack provisions, and horses and other beasts exist in large quantity, and along with this, there are many herds of cattle where a large number of mulattos, mestizos, Indians, and base people are always occupied—the Devil, who stands vigil against the human race and who, to the fullest of his abilities, does not miss a chance to introduce a heathen superstition, [has caused] people such as these to believe that, by carrying with them a certain root, they will never fall from their mount, nor will they be wounded by bulls, though they expose themselves to great risks. And though the majority of those of this occupation of cattle herding are mestizos or mulattos, even so I make mention here of this because Indians also take part, and thus I say that the Devil has made these cowhands believe that the said root—whose name I intentionally do not mention[1]—has in itself such great virtue that it suffices to protect one from the great risks that are always suffered by those who have to make use indiscriminately of every kind of beast, and to enter on them among wild bulls and feel encouraged to wound them or anger them so that they attribute divine virtue to this root, and thus they venerate it like a holy thing, carrying it as if it were a relic, around the neck, in little pouches, decorated the best they can, that they call amulets. What I have said I managed to find out by deducing it, as they say, *a posteriori*. By noting the kinds of risks they expose themselves to, and by carrying out an examination of similar reckless acts, I came to ascertain the superstition about the root, and I made many charges about it because of the pact that it carries with it, at least implicitly, many of which I forwarded to the Holy Office.

And although they ordinarily carry it with them, fearful of being caught, they usually hide it in the pads, in the little cushions, the protective padding of the saddles on which they usually ride, and in other places.

CHAPTER 9

About Other Superstitions That in Spain Are Called *Agüeros* [Omens]

WHAT in Spain they call *agüeros* [omens] in Mexico they call *tetzahuitl*,[1] though the Mexican word means a little more than the Castilian one, because it means "augury, omen, portent, or prodigy that foretells some present or future evil." All this is included in the word *tetzahuitl*. And among all of them they make a great difference between ones and others, holding in most esteem the more extraordinary ones, although they may be unavoidable, for instance, an eclipse of the sun and, somewhat less, of the moon. And among the Indians the ones more remote from the Mexican civil society are the ones much more given to soothsaying.

They consider it an omen to see or find any extraordinary animal, like a puma, a jaguar, a bear, a wolf, and even a coyote. The same is true of a fox, even though it is such a common animal, and much more so in this land, where there are more than eight species. Among these species the one that upsets them the most is the one that has a very bad odor, and a very strong one, so that it seems that it is enough to infect with the plague.[2] And in Mexican it is called *èpatl*,[3] and if by chance this little animal urinates inside someone's house, he considers it a very bad sign.

They believe the same thing about extraordinary birds, for example, eagles. And among the ordinary ones, they fear the little feather bird[4] and the one they call *huactzin*, or *huacton*[5] (which is the same thing). And it is a little bigger than an eaglet, with a very good bill and claws. It feeds on snakes and vipers, killing them skillfully, because if it sees them coiled up, it perches on some high place nearby and from there it clamors until, frightened, the viper begins to flee, and then this eaglet follows it and, seizing it by the neck, carries it aloft and drops it. And after it is dead or stunned from the blow, it rips it up and eats it. The calls of this eaglet are considered by the Indians to be an omen, and many times they stubbornly affirm that it calls them by their names, without any reason whatever being sufficient to dissuade them, although from the eaglet one never hears anything but *huac huac*, from where it seems it got its name.

They feel the same thing about grubs and extraordinary worms, and especially about the one called *xiuhquiquimiltzin*,[6] the same about spiders, and especially about the one they call *tequantocatl*,[7] which is called *yerba* [i.e., poison] in Castilian, and the one called *tzintlatlauhqui*[8]—this second one still does not have a name in Castilian. Both kill with their poison. The first is as large as half an egg, and the second is like a chick-pea, and it has a tawny tail end or posterior, and from there it ejects its poison.

They consider all snakes as omens, and more so the vipers. And it is a worse omen if this snake or viper crosses the road in front of them when they are walking, because, they say, *Coatl onechòhuiltequi*,[9] as if to say, "It cut the thread of my life," and it is to be noted that there are in this land more than ten known kinds of vipers, and the snakes are infinite. Among the snakes they fear most the one called *maçacoatl*,[10] which means "snake of beasts," "a snake that can swallow a beast," and it is so because they have been seen seven or more *varas* long. And among the vipers they fear most is the one called *metlapilcoatl*[11] or *çelcoatl*,[12] for the reason I just mentioned.[13]

From this variety of animals they take omens not only about their sicknesses but even about their enmities and hatreds. And if it is the case that some fox, bat, barn owl, owl, or any other animal of those they consider to be omens has entered their house, they say, *tlenquìtoa? tleinquinequi ĩ? àço nech yaochihua, àço nechmiquitlani intlacanahualli*,[14] which means "What does the animal (or bird) mean, or what does it want? It must be a sorcerer, my enemy, or who wants—or prepares—my death." With this, there having occurred an annoyance or a quarrel, where with the continual drunken sprees they are most unavoidable, immediately they cast judgment upon whoever threatened them in the quarrel, and there result enmities and continuing hatreds. But if the omen is from fire, or better from the fact that the sun or moon has eclipsed, since they used to adore such things, there is greater danger in them because, as has been said, bad habits of heathendom remain in them. And thus if, because of the omen of fire or an eclipse of the sun or the moon, any of their satraps, who are called *ticitl* or *tlachixqui*, should say to them that the sun, the moon, or the fire was angry, there is no doubt but that it would be enough to induce them to offer a sacrifice to them in whatever way that seer of theirs might order them to.

They fear exceedingly to find or see the viper *colcoatl*[15] or *metlapilcoatl*. This one never grows to be two *varas*[16] long. It is thick and flat-nosed, and it rises up straight on its blunt tail and jumps a full five or six *varas*. There is no Indian who believes this to be an animal, but rather an Indian *nahuri*[17] or demon, and thus they flee from it, and they consider it a most certain prognostic of very great evils, deaths, hungers, and plagues.

From what has been stated, the *doctrineros* can become informed in order to dissuade the Indians from such great deceptions and to teach them patiently, enlightening them about how there are no transformations, and how animals act naturally and not with free acts, and the demons cannot exceed what God, Our Lord, permits, advising them how comets are natural effects, and eclipses the same. And for this last point, before an eclipse occurs, it will be of great moment to prepare them by telling them about it, and praying to Our Lord that He open the eyes of their understanding in order to know very truthfully, and to embrace, the Catholic truths.

CHAPTER 10

About the Basis That the Indians Have for Adoring the Sun

In this New Spain, as in all the other heathen nations, they held and, for our sins, still today hold the sun in great veneration, doing so as if it were God.

The basis that they had for this was a tradition that was current among the Indians, namely that there used to be two worlds or two kinds of people.[1]

The first [world was one] in which the kind of men that it had were transformed into animals and into the sun and the moon [in the second one], and thus they attribute a rational soul to the sun and moon and animals, speaking to them for the purpose of their witchcraft as if they understood, calling to them and invoking them with other names for the purpose of their incantations, as will be told in more detail later. And in order to establish a basis for the adoration of the sun they tell a fable after the manner of those of Ovid's *Metamorphoses*, which they relate briefly.[2] They say that, since the transformation had to be according to the merits of each one, in order for those of that [first] age to transform themselves into the things that they were to be in the second [age], a very big bonfire was ordered to be made, so that, after it was burning strongly, by testing themselves in it, they might acquire merits for the said transformation, with the understanding that by means of the fire they would gain honor and excellence and would remain lords of what was superior in the second age.

This promise and hope of excellence and superiority and of becoming gods brought together in a short time a great number of people, especially *mandones* and potentates of that age, ambitious and desirous of commanding everything—as always happens in such people, since it always seems to them that everything is owed to them, even though it be against reason.

Now that a large number of *mandones* and potentates had gathered and the furnace or bonfire was burning strongly for the test, the potentates began the enterprise, preferring themselves over the humble people as they always do in such solicitations, although they [the potentates] may have many fewer merits [than the humble people]. But in this [endeavor], since the strength of favor or bribery was not involved in the business, they did not prevail because, even though the furor of ambition and desire to command incited and encouraged them, fear held them back, and the danger of the fire discouraged them. And thus, upon arriving at the test, some stopped at the first step, others at the second.

The most courageous did not pass beyond the first stairstep of the furnace. Many hours were spent on these without there being anyone who would dare enter the fire.

Suddenly, the then so-called God, in their language, *Centeotl ycnopiltzintli*,[3] which interpreted literally means, "Sole God, the child without a father," came out into the middle of all. He spoke to a sick man who was there, afflicted with pustules and having sores. And he said to him that, since he saw what was happening and that, although the prize was so great, none of those powerful magnates and rich people dared to face the test, he appointed him among all, and he should take away such a great prize from their hands by entering the fire before anyone else. The sick man excused himself, saying that the magnates themselves would not allow him to reach there. But the God insisted that he was talking to him, persuading him to rush through the middle of everyone and quickly throw himself into the fire. With this, the poor sick person—pustulous and scabby—resolved to undergo the rigorous test. And while he was passing toward it among those powerful people, they stopped him, affronting him and upbraiding him about such a vile person, a sick person, poor and with a bad odor, daring to undertake a venture fitting and proper only for persons such as they. But after they had stopped him in this way one and another time, he passed the third time without their being able to stop him or even to see him until he was at the mouth of the furnace, from where, because nobody dared approach, they did not remove him. Immediately the sick man courageously threw himself into the midst of the furious fire, with whose force and flames he purged and purified all his sickness and sores and became beautiful and shining and was converted into the sun, which is the most resplendent of the planets, and this as a prize for the test of his courage and suffering, for which he deserved the said transmutation and to climb to the sky and be adored as god. But immediately after he came out purified from the bonfire, he threw himself into a pool of very cold water, which was also prepared for a test, and having come out of it very clean, he passed immediately to the sky where he hid.

Seeing this event and ashamed of what had happened and of the fact that a sick and pustulous person (whom in their language they call *Nanāhuatzin*, and they give this name to the man converted into the sun) had attained such a great honor and had distinguished himself among so many, one of the healthy ones of that multitude who had assembled for the test, spurred by ambition and envy, did the same as the first. Passing with boldness through the midst of all, he threw himself into the furnace, where, finding it cooled with the test of the first one, from the moisture and corruption that had come from him, he could not arrive at such purity, although upon coming out of the furnace he also threw himself into the pool of water; but since [he could] not [be transformed] into the sun, he was transformed into the moon, with less light than the sun and with mutability in his brightness because of having found the furnace unequal in heat. Thereupon he climbed up to the sky like the sun.

This having been done, it only remained for the sun to show himself to them so that each one might fulfill his obligation by honoring him as a god, making a sacrifice to him and making an offering to him. And this had to be done while fasting, under penalty of a bad outcome in the transformation, because transforming all the rest of those people now belonged totally to the sun; therefore, in order to improve himself in the said transformation, each one tried to better his lot through his offering. And everyone, while fasting, waited for the sun to show himself to them in order to make their sacrifice and offering to him. While they were thus waiting, the sun showed himself to them toward the west but hid again so quickly that they did not have time to present offerings. The second time, he came out in the south, and the same thing happened as the first time. The third time, he came out in the north and hid as on the first two. With this, one of those prepared for the offering, tired of fasting and furious at the jokes, ate up his offering. Afterward, the sun came out in the east and continued his course to the west, so that all the prepared ones made their offerings and sacrifices. But the one who had eaten up the offering found himself a fool without anything to offer, and although he went for help to the others, no one would give anything to him, as happened with the foolish virgins in the Gospel.[4] Seeing himself pressed by necessity and the occasion, he sought indiscriminately for something to offer, laying hand now on a rock, now on a stick, now wanting to grasp shadows without substance, and in the end he found nothing to offer. For this crime they say the sun changed him into a bird called *huinaxcatl*[5] and condemned it to being perpetually hungry for not having fasted and to grasping at vain shadows for not having made an offering. And they confirm this by the fact that this bird appears at night and in that it is nothing but feathers and bones, and it seems that it is always hare-brained. As for the rest who fasted and made offerings, they say that the sun changed them into good animals and that they would always have something to eat.

Upon this fabulous story, or, in better words, storied fable, is based most of what the Indians do today in their idolatries to the sun, carrying offerings to it, at the moment of its rising, to the peaks of the mountains and hills and to the ponds of water.

Second, the custom and superstitious devotion of keeping the fire in the room of women who have given birth, without removing it for four continuous days, as will be described at more length later.

Third, their use of the number four in all their superstitions and idolatrous rites, such as in the insufflations that they make when the sorcerers and false doctors conjure or invoke the Devil, the cause of which I was never able to track down until I heard the story of the waiting for the sun. And for the same reason, the hunters, when they set their snares in order to catch deer, give four shouts toward the four parts of the world, asking for favor, and they put four crossed cords over a rock.

The bowmen call four times to the deer, repeating four times the word *Tahui*, which no one today understands,[6] and then they cry four times like a puma.

They put a lighted candle on the tomb for a dead person on four successive days, and others throw a pitcher of water on it for him on four successive days. And, finally, among them the number four is venerated.

[SECOND TREATISE]

[Untitled]

CHAPTER 1 OF THE SECOND TREATISE

[Untitled]

It is established and rooted among these miserable people that the words of their invocations, incantations, curses, and protestations—and all the other words that the Devil taught their ancestors—have an infallible effect according to their meaning. And if Our Lord permitted it to the Devil—the father and author of this invention and deception—it is even possible thus. But we see them innumberable times defrauded in their purpose, notwithstanding the fact that all the said invocations and incantations carry at least an implicit pact with the Devil; and it seems it would have been explicit with their ancestors, from whom those of our time inherited them. The worst thing is that they are so bound to these superstitions that, as people say, God and then some is needed to separate them from them, because, since this falls on ignorant and unreasoning people, neither arguments nor reasons move them, nor are they convinced by seeing that they [i.e., the incantations] very frequently fail to have any effect, since they are blind or overcome by the fact that on rare occasions they brought about the desired result. Thus it happened to me in Comala, a village of my parish, with an angler called Juan Matheo, after my having spent already almost twenty years preaching designedly against these superstitions and incantations. The said Juan Matheo used to throw his hook with certain invocations of the kind fishermen use, and, persuaded by my words, he left off the invocation and threw the hook. He caught a beautiful catfish. Later, on another occasion, he threw the hook and did not catch anything. And then he was troubled by the doubt about not having caught anything because of not having made the invocation that he used to make. And impugned by me because of the many times he had not caught a fish after having thrown the fishhook with the said invocations, he confessed that it was so. But he again stumbled over the fact that he had not caught anything when he did not make the invocation. Their dullness reaches this far, and their being so caught up in their superstitions blinds them this much.

Since I am to deal with the various kinds of spells and invocations, I will start with the first case of this kind that I handled in the year 1618, by commission of the Most Reverend Don Juan de la Serna, Archbishop of Mexico. The case was against Juan Vernal, an inhabitant since birth of the village of Yguala,[1] in the region of the Mines of Taxco, because he used certain words and a spell in order to fight, with which, he affirmed, he had always traveled safely along the roads and had never been overcome by enemies or highwaymen; rather, on the contrary, he had always come out victorious. Being arrested, the Indian confessed openly and said that he had proof of the truth and effect of the words because of the many times he had been delivered with them and that, recently, while carrying his Majesty's tribute,[2] highwaymen had come out against him on the road, and he had overcome and killed

27

Page from Second Treatise, chapter 1, folio 27r of the Museo manuscript.

them by virtue of his words and that, although the authorities had arrested him because of the deaths, they had finally set him free.

For the spell,[3] first he prepared himself with a weapon which was[4] a very good club that served him as a staff, which he conjured when he arrived at the places, saying:

[1] I myself, the god *Quetzalcoatl* or the crested snake; I the god called *Matl*, I who am the very war, and I make fun of everything, for I neither fear nor do I owe.

Nòmatca nèhuatl niquetzalcoatl nimatl ca nèhuatl niyaotl nimoquequeloatzin, àtle ipan nitlamati.

It is I in person. I am Quetzalcoatl. I am Matl. I indeed am Yaotl; I am Moquehqueloatzin. I consider things as nothing [i.e., I am afraid of nothing *or* I respect nothing].

Nohmatca nehhuātl.[5] NiQuetzalcōātl. NiMātl. Ca nehhuātl niYāōtl; niMoquehqueloatzin. Ahtleh īpan nitlamati.

[2] Now it has to be, for I am to make fun of my sisters {He calls his enemies this as an insult[6]}, the ones who are of my very nature, and in order to make fun of them,[7] come and join me, you quarrelsome and warrior gods, you who wound together, you who strike together, for now my sisters are coming, those similar to me in nature.[8] We are to make fun of them, for they come with blood and color[9] {i.e., with the fragility of flesh and blood}.

Ye axcã yez; niquin mà ahuíltiz nohueltihuan, nitlacaxillohuã, inic niquinmàahuiltiz tlaxihualhuian ollòque yaoyòque, in ĩhuan tlahuitequi, in ihuã tlatzòtzona; canicã huitze nohueltihuan notlacaxillohuã tiquinmàahuiltizque, yèhuantiz ezçotihuitze, tlapallòtihuitze.

It will be at this time [i.e., I am ready]. I will give pleasure to my older sisters, my human kinsmen [i.e., I will fight my weak enemies]. In order for me to give pleasure to them, come, Rubber-owners, *Iyauhtli*-owners,[10] you[11] who strike things in their company, you who pound things in their company [i.e., you gods]. Indeed here come my older sisters, my human kinsmen. We will give them pleasure. They come possessing blood; they come possessing color [i.e., they come being vulnerable].

Ye āxcān yez. Niquimahāhuiltīz nohuēltīhuān, notlācaxīlōhuān. In īc niquimahāhuiltīz, tlā xihuālhuiān, Ōllohqueh, Iyāuhyohqueh, in īnhuān tlahuītequih, in īnhuān tlatzohtzonah. Ca nicān huītzeh nohuēltīhuān, notlācaxīlōhuān. Tiquimahāhuiltīzqueh. Yehhuāntin ezzohtihuītzeh; tlapallohtihuītzeh.

[3] But I am as without blood or flesh (i.e., insensible) and I bring the priest {*Tlamacazq*+, priest of idols. He is probably referring to the Devil} with me, and the time or heat of a summer (i.e., the club). I bring the priest, unique death, one flint, who before anyone else is to be stained with blood, because unexpectedly the stone is to be stained (i.e., with the blood of the enemy), the stick is to become drunk, the land is to become drunk at the same time with me and with my arms.

Auh in nèhuatl àmo nezço àmo nitlapallo caonicualhuicac in tlamacazqui çe atl, itonal, intlamacazqui çe miquiztli, çe tecpatl, achtotipa ezçoaz, achtotipa tlapalloaz tetl ihuintíz quahuitl ihuintíz tlalli ihuintíz tonèhuã.[12]

But as for me, I do not have any blood, I do not have any color [i.e., I am not vulnerable]. I have brought the priest, His-*tonal* Is One Water [i.e., the staff], [or] the priest, One Death [i.e., rocks],

Auh in nehhuātl ahmō nezzoh, ahmō nitlapalloh. Ca ōnichuālhuīcac[14] in tlamacazqui, Cē-Ātl Ītōnal, in tlamacazqui, Cē-Miquiztli, Cē-Tecpatl. Achtotipa ez-

Page from Second Treatise, chapter 1, folio 27v of the Museo manuscript.

[or] One Flint [i.e., the knife]. First he will become covered with blood, first he will become covered with color. The stones will become drunk; the trees will become drunk; the land will become drunk[13] at my will.

zōhuaz, achtotipa tlapallōhuaz. Tetl īhuintiz, cuahuitl īhuintiz, tlālli īhuintiz [in] nonehuiyān.[15]

[4] For this purpose I bring my hands and my insensible body in order not to feel the hurts or jokes which my brothers,[16] men like me, want to do to me, for it is not possible for them to wound or offend me, for I am a priest and the god *Quetzalcoatl* or snake with a plume, and because nothing can make an impression on me: I am the priest, the very war, for whom everything is a joke and laughter. Come on, for already my sisters come, humans like me. One of them has already brought a bouquet or a bunch of roses, let it be[17] her breath; she brings her duster of cotton and her ball of yarn in order to offend me. {Downplaying the opponent's weapons; the rocks, balls of yarn; the clubs, canes.[18]}

onichualhuicac nomiccama, nomicca nacayo, inic àmo nicmatiz inic nech ahuiltizq⁺ in nohueltihuã innotlacaxillohuã; àmo nèhuatl innech huitequizque in nitlamacazqui niquetzalcoatl, àtleipan nitlamati nèhuatl nitlamacazqui, niyaotl, nimoquequeloatzin, ca ye no iz huitze nohueltihuã, notlacaxillohuã, ye quihualhuica in mohueltiuh in xochiquetzal quihualhuica in ìhiyo yez ini ichca tlahuitec ini icpateuh, inic nechàahuiltizque,

I have brought my dead-man [i.e., insensible] hands, my dead-man flesh, in order that I will not feel it when my older sisters, my human kinsmen [i.e., my weak enemies], give me pleasure [i.e., fight me]. I am not the one whom they will strike, for I am the priest, Quetzalcoatl. I consider things as nothing [i.e., I fear nothing *or* I respect nothing]. As for me, I am the priest, I am Yaotl, I am Moquehqueloatzin. Already also here come my older sisters, my human kinsmen. Already they are accompanying hither my older sister, Xochiquetzal [i.e., a person who is ineffectual in battle]. They are bringing that which will be her breath [i.e., gentle, loving attack], her cotton fluff [i.e., ineffectual clubs], and her ball of thread [i.e., ineffectual rocks], with which they will give me pleasure.

Ōnichuālhuīcac nomiccāmā, nomiccānacayo, in īc ahmō nicmatiz in īc nēchāhuiltīzqueh in nohuēltīhuān, in notlācaxīlōhuān. Ahmō nehhuātl in nēchhuītequizqueh, in nitlamacazqui, niQuetzalcōātl. Ahtleh īpan nitlamati. Nehhuātl nitlamacazqui, niYāōtl, niMoquehqueloatzin. Ca ye nō iz huītzeh nohuēltīhuān, notlācaxīlōhuān. Ye quihuālhuīcah in nohuēltīuh, in Xōchiquetzal. Quihuālhuīcah in iihīyo[19] yez, in īchcatlahuītec, in īcpateuh, in īc nēchahāhuiltīzqueh.

[5] Come, then, turmoil of people, come [a]thighs {Or some god of that name, i.e., devil}, come quarrelsome and warrior gods who together wound and strike. Come, priests of idols, those of the east and west, wherever you are. Come, animals and birds, and since I invoke you from the four parts of the world, for now it is to be.

Tlaxihuallauh tlaltetecuin, tlaxihuallauh [a]tonacametzin, tlaxihuallauh olloque, yaoyoque, inihuã tlahuitequi, inīhuã tlatzotzona, tlaxihualhuiã tlamacazque tonatiuh i quiçayan tonatiuh icalaquian in ixquichca nemi, inyolli, in patlantinemíin ic nauhcã niquintzàtzilia ycaxcãyez.

Come, Tlaltehtecuin [i.e., the road]. Come, Sustenance-thigh (H). Come, Rubber-owners, *Iyauhtli*-owners, you[20] who strike things in their company, you who pound things in their company

Tlā xihuāllauh, Tlāltehtecuīn. Tlā xihuāllauh, Tōnacāmetztzin.[22] Tlā xihuālhuiān,[23] Ōllohqueh, Iyāuhyohqueh, in īnhuān tlahuītequih, in īnhuān tlatzoh-

[i.e., you gods]. Come, priests [i.e., the speaker's spiritual allies], from the sun's setting place, from the sun's rising place, from as far as an animal or a flying thing lives. Throughout the four directions I am shouting to them,[21] in order that it will be now.

tzonah. Tlā xihuālhuiān, tlamacazqueh, tōnatiuh īquīzayān, tōnatiuh īcalaquiyān, in ixquichca nemi in yōlli in patlāntinemi. In īc nāuhcān niquintzahtzilia, īc āxcān yez.

[6] Come, one rabbit (metaphor, the land), you who are standing or face up. Throw yourself face downward.[24] Come, you, heat, one time of one summer,[25] be warned that you are to stain yourself and bloody yourself. Aim at the shins.[26] Watch out that you do not miss the target. Strike the very shins. Come on,[27] flint or rock, for you are to bloody yourself.[28] Come on, let the turmoil of people now sound in my favor.

Tlaxihuallauh çe tochtli àquetztimani, tlaximixtlapachtlaça, tlaxihuallauh çeatl itonal tezçoaaz, titlapalloaz, tlaimitzcalco, àmo çan canin tiaz huel itzcalco. Tlaxihuallauh çe tecpatl tezçoaz, titlapalloaz, tlaxihuallauh tlaltecuin.

Come, One Rabbit, She-is-supine [i.e., the land]. Throw yourself face down [i.e., remove any obstacles]. Come, His-*tonal* Is One Water [i.e., the club]. You will be covered with blood; you will be covered with color. Let it be at their sides [i.e., strike my enemies in the side]; it is not just anywhere that you will go, but right at his side.[29] Come, One Flint [i.e., the knife]. You will be covered with blood; you will be covered with color. Come, Tlaltecuin [i.e., the path].

Tlā xihuāllauh, Cē-Tōchtli, Ahquetztimani. Tlā ximīxtlahpachtlāza. Tlā xihuāllauh, Cē-Ātl Ītōnal. Tezzōhuaz, titlapallōhuaz. Tlā īmītzcalco; ahmō zan cān in tiyāz, huel īītzcalco. Tlā xihuāllauh, Cē-Tecpatl. Tezzōhuaz, titlapallōhuaz. Tlā xihuāllauh, Tlāltecuīn.

With this he ended his false incantation, and he remained very satisfied, considering the good outcome as very certain.

CHAPTER 2

About the Incantation That They Use to Induce Sleep

In the incantation to induce sleep, they affirm that the one under the spell remains in that state, that he can by no means awaken even though they do to him whatever they may want. And if they have experienced it as they certify, it is certain that this is the express work of the Devil, especially since it is always directed toward some reprehensible action, such as theft or adultery.[1] The words they use are:

[1] I myself, whose name is darkness, in order that I, in order that from nine parts,[2] in order that then; come now, enchanting sleep,[3] for the time when I went to bring my sister nine times. I, priest (or devil, a fable of antiq-

Nòmatca nèhuatl nino yoalito atzin, inic nèhuatl, inic chicnauhtopa, inìquac tlaxihualhuin intemic xoch, inìquac inic nicanato in nohueltiuh chicnauhtopa nitlamacazqui in nohueltiuh

uity}[4], whose sister is the goddess Xochiquetzal, even though the priests and the rest of the town, the prince and the most powerful ones[5] were guarding her, so that it was impossible to enter, for which purpose I invoked sleep in a loud voice, and therewith all went away to the nine depths {i.e., the guards fell into a profound sleep}. Because I am the youth, I whose joints creak and who foolishly shout to every direction.

xochiquetzal, inic çencaquipiaya in tlamacazque in mochintin in quahuili in oc celome in ayhehuel calaquia inic nictzàtzili in cochiztli inic chicnauhmictlã yàque, inic nèhuatl nixolotl nicapa nitli in çan tlalhuiz nouyan nitzàtzi.

It is I in person. I am Moyohualihtoatzin. Because I am I, throughout Nine-Topan, at that time [...]. Come [pl], Dream-flower [i.e., sleep]. At that time I went to seize my older sister [i.e., the woman being hypnotized] throughout Nine-Topan [i.e., the state of consciousness]. I am the priest whose older sister is Xochiquetzal [i.e., the woman who is to be taken sexual advantage of]. Because the priests and all of the eagles and the jaguars[6] were guarding her, so that no one could enter, therefore I shouted to sleep so that they went to Nine-Mictlan [i.e., into a trance state], because I am Xolotl, I am Capanilli, who just thoughtlessly shouts everywhere [i.e., I have no regard for propriety]

Nohmatca nehhuātl. NiMoyohualihtoatzin.[7] In īc nehhuātl, in īc ChiucnāuhTopan, in ihcuāc [...].[8] Tlā xihuālhuiān, in Tēmicxōch. In ihcuāc in īc nicānato in nohuēltīuh ChiucnāuhTopan. Nitlamacazqui in nohuēltīuh Xōchiquetzal. In īc cencah quipiayah in tlamacazqueh, in mochintin in cuāuhtin in ocēlōmeh, in ayāc huel[9] calaquiya, in īc nictzahtzilih in cochiztli, in īc ChiucnāuhMictlān yahqueh, in īc nehhuātl niXōlōtl, niCapānīlli in zan tlalhuiz nōhuiyān nitzahtzi.

[2] Come on, come now, priest or Devil, One Flint {This functions as an appositive or is the name of the summoned devil.}, go to find out whether my sister is already sleeping, because already I am going in order to remove her, in order that they do not covet me, a youth,[10] in order that none of her brothers covet me, in order that they do not covet me when already I am carrying her to the nine depths, for soon I am to carry [her] to the center of the earth, and it is in order to hand her over there to the darkness (i.e., to sleep) in order that, although I turn her throughout the four directions, she will not be aware, I who am the very war, for whom everything is a joke and who already set up jokes on everyone, changing them into others, making them remain insensible, I who am the war itself, the mocker of everyone, because I want to hand them over now in order that they become drunk, lost in (or with) darkness,[11] i.e., with sleep.

Tla xihuallauh tlamacazqui çe tecpatl tla xoconmatiti in nohueltiuh, cuix ococh ye niquixtitiuh, inic àmo nechelehuizq+ yèhuantinixquichtin ioquichtihuan àmo nech elehuizq+, inic ye nichuicaz inchicnauh mictlan, inoncan nichuicaz tlalli innepantlà, inic oncã nic macatiuh in moyohuallitoatzin, inic naucan nic cuepaz, inic àmo quimatíz nèhuatl niyaotl ninoquequeloatzin inic ye níc à ahuiltiz, inic ye niquincuepaz niquin micacuepaz in niyaotl ninoquequeloatzin, inic ye niquinmacaz, inic ye huallahuanizq+.

Come, priest, One Flint.[12] Go in order to know whether my older sister [i.e., the woman being hypnotized] has gone to sleep. I am about to go in order to take her out; [even] therewith her older brothers will not covet [i.e., harm][13] me.

Tlā xihuāllauh, tlamacazqui, Cē-Tecpatl. Tlā xoconmatiti in nohuēltīuh cuix ōcoch. Ye nicquīxtītīuh, in īc ahmō nēchēlēhuīzqueh yehhuāntin ixquichtin īoquichtīhuān. Ahmō nēchēlēhuīzqueh in

They will not covet [i.e., harm] me when I will have carried her to Nine-Mictlan. I will carry her there to the middle of the earth in order to go to give her to Moyohualihtoatzin. When I turn her through the four directions[14] even so she will not know it. I am the one who is Yaotl, I am Moquehqueloatzin, therefore I will soon give her pleasure, therefore I will soon change them, I will change them into dead people [i.e., I will hypnotize them], I who am Yaotl, I who am Moquehqueloatzin, because I will soon give it [i.e., sleep] to them, in order that they will become inebriated in the night [i.e., they will fall asleep].

Īc ye nichuīcaz in ChiucnāuhMictlān. In oncān nichuīcaz tlālli īnepantlah, in īc oncān nicmacatīuh in Moyohualihtoatzin. In īc nāuhcān niccuepaz, in īc ahmō quimatiz. Nehhuātl niYāōtl, niMoquehqueloatzin, in īc ye nicahāhuiltīz, in īc ye niquincuepaz, niquinmiccācuepaz in niYāōtl, niMoquehqueloatzin, in īc ye niquinmacaz, in īc yohuallāhuānazqueh.[15]

With these words they state that not only do the conjured ones fall asleep, but they even appear insensible, and thus they do to them everything they take a notion to, picking them up and carrying them to other places.

They also state that they will not wake up if they do not disenchant them. And for the disenchantment they use other words in which they signify that what they said in the first spell was not the truth but rather sham and what they affirmed as perpetual was only temporary. The words are the following:

[3] In order to bring these from the center of the earth and from the four directions and in order that it not be true that I enchanted them and converted them into others and that they were sleeping and that they went to the nine depths, nor that sleep or darkness carried them away. Come on here, for already I return them, and I take away the spell of sleep, I who have something like a nocturnal drunkenness.

Inic ni quīmānatiuh tlalli ynepātla, ynic nauhcampa ynàmo nelli ỹ noniquincuepa yn àmo cochia ynàmo oyàcâ chiucnauh mictlã yn àmonelli oquinhuicac ỹ moyohualỳtoatzin. Ea yeniquincuepa ynyèhuatl yntēmicxoch, ỹ nèhuatl ỹ niyohuallahuantzin.

In order that I go to seize them from the middle of the earth and from throughout the four directions, [I state] that it is not true that I also change them, that they were not sleeping, that they did not go to Nine-Mictlan, that it is not true that Moyohualihtoatzin carried them. Come on! Already I who am Yohuallahuantzin change them [i.e., the ones in the trance] and the one who is Dream-flower [i.e., the trance itself].

In īc niquimānatīuh tlālli īnepantlah, in īc nāuhcāmpa, in ahmō nelli in nō niquincuepa,[16] in ahmō cochiyah, in ahmō ōyahcah ChiucnāuhMictlān, in ahmō nelli ōquinhuīcac in Moyohualihtoatzin. *Ea!*[17] Ye niquincuepa[18] in yehhuātl in Tēmicxōch in nehhuātl in niYohuallāhuāntzin.

With this they say that the spell becomes undone and the ones under the spell awake. And because the Devil does not forget his clever tricks, after these words we find on the page *in nomine domini,*[19] in which the Devil manifests his ambition.

ABOUT THE INCANTATION AND SPELL FOR THE MAT ON WHICH THEY SLEEP

In the same way that the Christian church uses compline in the divine office, the Devil introduced his kind of compline among these superstitions, and it is like a prayer at the time they lie down with which they conjure the miserable bed they use, which ordinarily is a mat which in this land they call a *petate*, and for a pillow they use a piece of timber hewn for a seat, which in their language they call *ycpallitl*,[20] and they use the said incantation for protection, in order that they not be put under a spell nor be done another similar harm.

I caught a very ancient old man using this superstition. The old man is from Temimiltzinco, which is in the Marquisate, and his name is Martin de Luna. The words of the incantation are as follows:

[4] Come on now, my mat marked like a jaguar's skin {Possibly because the palmleaf weaving resembles the spots of a jaguar.}, you who open your mouth toward four directions {Four mouths for the four corners.}. Yes, for you also are thirsty and hungry. Come on, for already the malignant one comes, he who mocks people and is of bad counsel. Why?[21] What is he to do to me? Am I not a wretched person who lives without anything and for nothing and with perpetual misery?. [*sic*]

Tlacuel no ocelopetlatzine ỹ nauhcanpa ticamachalòtoc Notà amiqui, notiteòcihui, Auh yehuitz yntlahueliloc yntecamocàcayāhua yollòpoliuhqui tleyn nechchihuiliz Cuix àmo nicnotlacatl? ninentlacatl? Àmo ninotolinìtinemi, yntlalticpac?

Let it be soon, O my jaguar mat (H), you who lie opening your mouth wide toward the four directions. You are very thirsty and also hungry. And already the villain who makes fun of people, the one who is a madman, is coming. What is it that he will do to me? Am I not a pauper? I am a worthless person. Do I not go around suffering poverty in the world?

Tlā cuēl, nocēlōpetlatziné, in nāuhcāmpa ticamachālohtoc. Nō tahāmiqui, nō titeohcihui. Auh ye huītz in tlahuēlilōc in tēca mocahcayāhua, yōllohpoliuhqui. Tleh in nēchchīhuiliz? Cuix ahmō nicnōtlācatl? Ninēntlācatl. Ahmō ninotolīnihtinemi in tlālticpac?

And it is as if he said, "My mat, similar to the jaguar ('to the jaguar': this is probably in order to attribute power to it or because of the similarity to the spots of the jaguar in the design of the palm leaf, from which their mats are usually made), for whom your four corners serve as four mouths, I conjure you in my favor, for you also have needs like everybody. Defend me if some wicked being comes to do me evil. Surely he has the wrong target, because what profit can he get from a wretched poor person whose life is of no importance, since I live on the earth in perpetual misery?"

And to the pillow, which, as I have said, is a poor seat from a piece of timber, he says something similar:

[5] Come on, my pillow who is like a jaguar. You have four mouths. You also are thirsty and hungry.[22]

Tlacuel no ocelo ycpalê nauhcampa camachaloque, yeno tà āmiqui notiteòcihui.

Let it be soon, O my jaguar seat, O you who are wide-mouthed toward the four directions. Already you are very thirsty and also hungry.

Tlā cuēl, nocēlōicpalé, nāuhcāmpa camachālohqué. Ye nō tahāmiqui, nō titeohcihui.

And so on, in the same manner and words with which in the preceding paragraph he conjured the mat. With this elegant exorcism they consider themselves safe against nocturnal fears *(Vt ita dicam)*[23] because, in every way he can, the Devil apes the Church.

And in order to imitate it in everything, he also gave them the prayer of prime, which they use at the time of getting up, and it is as follows.

WHEN THEY GET UP

[6] My little mat, similar to a jaguar, has it perhaps happened that some malicious being came to harm me? Or, on the other hand, perhaps not? Did he perhaps come to me absolutely, or to my clothing, and did he raise it?

No ocelopetlatzine àço ohuitza yntlahueliloc no ço àmo àço huel oàcico àço huel ytech oàcico àço oquehuac oca àcocuic ỹ notilmâ?

O my jaguar mat (H), did the villain perhaps come or not? Was he perhaps able to arrive? Was he perhaps able to arrive right up to my blanket? Did he perhaps raise it, lift it up?

Nocēlōpetlatziné, ahzo ōhuītza in tlahuēlilōc, nōzo ahmō? Ahzo huel ōahcico? Ahzo huel ītech ōahcico? Ahzo ōquēhuac, ōcahcocuic in notilmah?

Martin de Luna used to use this one and declared that, although the sorcerers and other enemies and wizards had come and attempted to harm him on his wretched bed and had even lifted the bed clothing of it in several places, they had never been able to do more, being stopped by the invocations. And it is very certain that the Devil persuaded him about the second in order to make him believe the first. To such blindness do these miserable people come!

This Martin de Luna used these incantations for this purpose and used very many others with different intents, and principally to cure different sicknesses, because of which he was discovered. And after I had arrested him for it and had imprisoned him in the village of Tlalticapan[24] {This will be spoken of later}, the Father Guardian of Xiuhtepec, where the old man was living, came to the village and was greatly surprised about the imprisonment of the old man, considering him to be innocent since he was so very old and not believing in any way that he used similar incantations, until he confessed them in his presence.

I tell this not in order to accuse the ministers of being not very diligent but in order to warn them and in order that they may know with how much diligence these superstitions are hidden among the Indians, since this Indian, Martin de Luna, possessed and used so many and was almost one hundred and ten years old, and had for more than fifty years taken recourse to them without them ever coming to the notice of the regular parish priest, and this in the Marquisate and Amilpas, where there are so many [members] of all the religious orders, and many of them very good translators, very good long-time ministers.

CHAPTER 3

About the Incantation, Spell, or Invocation for Cutting Wood

In almost all the work that these miserable people do, they use these incantations and invocations as will be seen in the course of this Treatise, and in this place enters the one that they use for cutting wood.

Among others it was used by Juan Mateo, a very old Indian of my district. He is the one I told about who used another for fishing with a hook in the village of Comala.

First, the woodcutter gets ready the *piciete,* which in this matter [of incantations] we can call the *sine qua non* [since it is inevitably present].[1] Then he conjures it, entrusting it with the work and with guarding him in order that no misfortune befall him, and for this end he uses the following words:

[1] Come on now,[2] come in my favor, you, the nine times beaten one, son of the one of the starry skirt, and engendered by her, you who know Hell and Heaven.

Tla xihuallauh chiucnauh tlatetzotzonalli citlal cueye ytlachihual mictlan mati, topan mati

Come, Nine-[times]-rock-pounded-one, Citlalcueyeh's creation, the one who is acquainted with Mictlan, the one who is acquainted with Topan [i.e., tobacco, here said to have transcendental knowledge].

Tlā xihuāllauh, Chiucnāuhtlatetzohtzonalli, Cītlalcuēyeh ītlachīhual, Mictlānmati, Topanmati.[3]

[2] What are you thinking about now? Amuse yourself for I have now finally come, I, the priest {or Devil}, the prince of wizards, I who am the god Quetzalcoatl {or snake with a plume or crest}, and I bring the Devil, the red Chichimec, the red mirror {*ut supra*[4] or the ax, because it is of copper and shines like a mirror}.

Tlè ticmati? Chama yequene onihualla nitlamacazqui ninahualteuctli niquetzalcoatl nichualhuica tlamacazqui tlatlauhqui chichimecatl tlatlauhqui tezcatl

What do you know? [I.e., Pay attention!] Amuse yourself! Finally I have come. I am the priest, I am the *nahualli*-lord, I am Quetzalcoatl. I bring the priest, Red Chichimec, Red Mirror [i.e., the ax].

Tleh ticmati? Ximahāhuilti![5] Yēquen eh ōnihuāllah. Nitlamacazqui, ninähualtēuctli, niQuetzalcōātl. Nichuālhuīca tlamacazqui, Tlātlāuhqui Chīchīmēcatl, Tlātlāuhqui Tezcatl.

[3] Do not covet me (i.e., do not wound me), Devil whose luck some waters are (he says this for the tree). What are you thinking about now? For already the time has arrived when I shall throw at your shins[6] from below the left side the minister who is the red Chichimec.

ma tinechelehuiliz tlamacazqui ceatl ytonal Tlè ticmati? nican mitzcac moopochcopa nocontecaz yntlamacazqui, tlatlauhqui chichimecatl.

You will not covet him [i.e., the ax] from me [i.e., you will not damage him], priest, His-*tonal* Is One Water [i.e., the tree]. What do you [i.e., the tree] know? [i.e., Pay attention!] It is here in your left side[7] that I will stretch out [i.e., use] the priest, Red Chichimec [i.e., the ax].

Ahmō[8] tinēchelēhuilīz,[9] tlamacazqui, Cē-Ātl Ītōnal. Tleh ticmati? Nicān mītzcac mopōchcopa nocontēcaz in tlamacazqui, Tlātlāuhqui Chīchīmēcatl.

The word "minister" means in this last part of this incantation the same thing that in others is meant by "priest,"[10] since the priest of idols that these people knew had as his job to sacrifice by wounding, and because of the effect of wounding he gives the same name of priest or minister of the sacrifice to the ax with which he is to cut.[11] And this word in the language is *tlamacazqui,* which has many meanings, but the most common ones are priest or minister of sacrifices or Devil who serves some idol or adorns it.[12] Let this be noticed for similar incantations.

CHAPTER 4

About the Incantations, Spells, and Words That They Use for Carrying Loads and for Traveling

At the time they set out from their houses for the purpose of making a trip with a load, they get ready with the *piciete* as a guardian angel and make their incantations directed toward preventing misfortune from overcoming them on the road. And it seems that it was a particular mercy of Our Lord that this should come to my notice, in view of the fact that in all these things these people are as circumspect as they are deluded by the Enemy.

It happened that, having come to the banks of the river of my parish, an Indian, called Francisco de Santiago, an inhabitant of the village of Santiago, came upon others who were taking a bath, and, passing by them, he saw on the road a written piece of paper and picked it up without being seen and, reading it, understood what it contained, because of having been reared in my house. And thus he brought the paper to me immediately and told me what it contained, how he found it, and whose it was, because it was signed by the owner, who was a sacristan of the village of Cuetlaxxochitla, who hardly knew how to write. But the Devil helped him in order that this spell would not be lost. When the author was brought, he confessed the crime and said that he had lost the original, about the author of which he could give no information. And thus the interpretation of the incantation which runs as follows was more difficult.

[1] Let no kind of pains offend me, green and dark dusky pain {for what they cause}. Busy yourselves and assail with the hands and feet of those that live with the Gods {For the animals that live on the mountains and hills,[1] which is where they think gods live}, and you, Lord, green beaten one, green mauled one, come to my help, for I am a famous enchanter and the God {or wizard}, Quetzalcoatl, for I am not just anybody whosoever.

Ayac nechelehuiz yayāhuic coàcihuiztli[2] ynxoxohuic coàcihuiztli yntlaỹ mactzinco ymicxictzinco xonmoteca, yayahuic coàcihuiztli ynteochamecan tlahual; tlaxihualmohuica xoxohuic tlatecapaniltzin xoxohuic tlatetzotzonaltzin. Ninahualteuctli. Ni quetzalcoatl àmo çan acâ,

No one will covet [i.e., harm] me, dusky palsy, green palsy [i.e., pain, sickness], if you lie stretched out, dusky palsy, at the hands (H) and at the feet (H) [i.e., if you prevent the approach] of my uncles [i.e., the wild animals] from the place of the temple owners [i.e., the forest or wasteland]. Come (H), Green Rock-slapped-one (H), Green Rock-pounded-one (H) [i.e., the tobacco]. I am the *nahualli*-lord, I am Quetzalcoatl. I am not just anybody!

Ayāc nēchēlēhuīz, yāyāhuic cōahcihuiztli, in xoxōhuic cōahcihuiztli, in tlā īmmāctzinco, īmicxictzinco xonmotēca, yāyāhuic cōahcihuiztli,[3] in teōchānehcān notlahhuān.[4] Tlā xihuālmohuīca, Xoxōhuic Tlatecapānīltzin, Xoxōhuic Tlatetzohtzonaltzin. Nināhualtēuctli, ni-Quetzalcōātl. Ahmō zan nacah!

[2] Come on, Sun or day {They call the sun *nānāhuatzin*, which means "pustulous," as in the mentioned fable.}, help me, in order that I may anticipate you and walk first the

Tlacuel tlaxihualmohuica Nanahuatzin achtopa niaz achtopa nòtlatocaz çātepantiaz çātēpan tòtlatocaz achtopa nictlamiltiz yz cē teotlalò ê yz cé como-

road that you will go later, and you will walk your road later because before you end it {i.e., before the sun sets}, I will have walked and passed the plains and gorges and ravines which I will soon find {tread on}[5], and I will not be harmed by the unevenness of the ground or earth—literally it says *its inane face*, which really is not inane land[6] {it also says becoming blind[7] in the land}[8]—because I am to go above the very sky, above the very sky am I to walk.

lihui e, cayeniquiçaz yn tlalli yxcapactzin àmo nechelehuiz ca àmo nelli tlelli yxcapactzin, ca çan ylhuicac ypan nonyaz ypan ninemiz.

Let it be soon! Come (H), Nanahuatzin [i.e., the sun]! First I will go; first I will follow the road. Then you will go; then you will follow the road. First I will finish the entire desert road, the entire uneven one. I will soon tread on Earth's Face-slapped-one (H)[9] [i.e., the road]. It will not covet [i.e., harm] me. Indeed it is not true that it is [upon] Earth's Face-slapped-one (H) [that I will go], it is indeed only upon the sky that I will go, upon it I will walk.

Tlā cuēl! Tlā xihuālmohuīca, Nānāhuatzin! Achtopa niyāz; achtopa nohtlatocaz. Zātēpan tiyāz; zātēpan tohtlatocaz. Achtopa nictlamīltīz in centeohtlālohtli,[10] in cencomōlihuic.[11] Ca ye niquiczaz[12] in Tlālli Īīxcapactzin. Ahmō nēchēlēhuīz. Ca ahmō nelli Tlālli Īīxcapactzin, ca zan ilhuicac īpan nonyāz, īpan ninemiz.[13]

Then he turns to speak to the [load] and says:[14]

[3] Come on, my load, I want to test you. I want to lift you in order to see how you are. Are you heavy?

Tlanimitzyèyeco tlanimitzàcocui quentami tietic?

Let me test you. Let me lift you up. How heavy are you?

Tlā nimitzyehyeco. Tlā nimitzahcocui. Quēn tamih tetic?[15]

Then he talks to the *piciete*[16] {when they pulverize it}:

[4] Come on, then, help me, Lord, green beaten one, green mauled one, for already I have come, I a Priest and the God, Quetzalcoatl or the snake with bunches of feathers {who was the said idol}, prince in the spells, for I wish to take up the burden soon of this little load, because, for this purpose here go four hundred priests {family devils} of the son of the Gods, who are to take up the burden of this little load and to carry it along the road. Note that I am as if I had no flesh and blood or color.

Tlacuel tlaxihualmohuica xoxohuic tlatēcapaniltzin xoxohuic tlatetetzotzonaltzin caonihualla nitlamacazqui niquetzalcoatl ninahualteuctli, ca yenicmāmaz ynìhuitlamāmalli canican yahui yn tēteo ypiltzin centzontlamacazque yn quimamazque yn còtlatoctizque ynìhuitlamamalli yn àmo nitlapallo.

Let it be soon! Come (H), Green Rock-slapped-one (H), Green Rock-pounded-one (H) [i.e., tobacco]. I have come. I am the priest, Quetzalcoatl; I am the *nahualli*-lord. Indeed I will soon carry the featherweight load. Indeed here go the child of the gods [i.e., the speaker] and the four hundred [i.e., many] priests [i.e., spirit helpers] who will carry the featherweight load, who

Tlā cuēl! Xihuālmohuīca, Xoxōhuic Tlatecapānīltzin, Xoxōhuic Tlatetzohtzonaltzin. Ca ōnihuāllah. Nitlamacazqui, niQuetzalcōātl; ninähualtēuctli. Ca ye nicmāmāz in ihhuitlamāmalli. Ca nicān yahuih in tēteoh īmpiltzin centzontlamacazqueh[17] in quimāmāzqueh, in cohtlatoctīzqueh in ihhuitlamāmalli, [in

will cause it to go along the road, since [I do not have blood,] I do not have color [i.e., I am supernatural].

ahmō nezzoh,][18] in ahmō nitlapalloh.

[5] Here go those who have blood and color, but I have neither blood nor color, because I am a Priest {or demon tlamacazqui}, I am the god Quetzalcoatl, for I am not just anybody, I am a prince of spells for I want soon to take up the burden of this apparent or enchanted hill.[19] Who formed it? Who made it? For I did not.[20]

Canicanyahui ynezçòque yn tlapallòque auh ỹ nehuatl àmo nezço àmo nitlapallo canèhuatl canitlamacazqui niquetzalcohuatl, àmo çan nacâ ninahualteuctli cayé nicmāmaz yn nahual tepèxitl aquin quichichiuh aquin quiyōliti? àmo nèhuatl?

Here go the ones having blood, the ones having color [i.e., the other carriers, who are mere human beings]. But as for me, I do not have any blood, I do not have any color [i.e., I am supernatural]. I am indeed the one. I am indeed the priest; I am Quetzalcoatl. I am not just anybody. I am the *nahualli*-lord. Soon I will carry the *nahualli*-crag [i.e., the load]. Who is the one who made it? Who is the one who gave it life? Was I not the one?

Ca nicān yahuih in ezzohqueh in tlapallohqueh. Auh in nehhuātl, ahmō nezzoh, ahmō nitlapalloh. Ca nehhuātl. Ca nitlamacazqui; niQuetzalcōātl. Ahmō zan nacah. Ninähualtēuctli. Ca ye nicmāmāz in nāhualtepehxitl. Āc in quichihchīuh? Āc in quiyōlītih? Ahmō nehhuātl?

[6] Come here, you, the one with leaves like wings {he is speaking to the *piciete*} for already I have come, for the hour has arrived for me to walk and carry those who have heads and a heart of flesh.

Tlacuel tla xihualmohuica xiuhpapatlantzin caonihualla caye nòtlatocaz caye nictlalloz ỹ nacayollo ỹ naca tzontecome,

Let it be soon! Come (H), Turquoise-flutterer (H) [i.e., tobacco]. I have come. I will soon follow the road. I will soon run with the meat-hearted one, the meat-headed one [i.e., the load].

Tlā cuēl! Tlā xihuālmohuīca, Xiuhpahpatlāntzin. Ca ōnihuāllah. Ca ye nohtlatocaz. Ca ye nictlalōz[21] in nacayōleh,[22] in nacatzontecomeh.

[7] And you, lady earth, face-beaten one {because they step on it}, do not offend me, do not hurt me, since you are a rabbit face-up {a metaphor in the language}, for here face-up rabbits are broken, here they are opened at the chests {he invokes the earth}.

tlacuel tlaxihual mohuica tlalli yxcapaniltzin àmo tinechelehuiz ce tochtli àquetztimani canicantzintlapan nican elpachi cé tochtli àquetztimani.

Let it be soon! Come (H), Earth's Face-slapped-one (H)[23] [i.e., the road]. You will not covet [i.e., harm] me, One Rabbit, She-is-supine [i.e., the land]. Here One Rabbit, She-is-supine, has broken open at the fundament, has caved in at the chest [i.e., the land will have no strength to hurt me].

Tlā cuēl! Tlā xihuālmohuīca, Tlālli Īīxcapānīltzin. Ahmō tinēchēlēhuīz, Cē-Tōchtli, Ahquetztimani. Ca nicān tzīntlapān, nicān ēlpachiuh Cē-Tōchtli, Ahquetztimani.

Chapter 5

About the Incantation and Spell of Those Who Rig Lime Kilns

The experts in making lime and rigging the kilns, in order that there be superstition in everything, cut the wood while using an incantation also, and they begin by speaking to the ax as follows:

[1] I say to you, red Chichimec, that here is the priest in order to burn[1] and consume this tree. What do you understand, red Chichimec? With this I am to give life to or engender my sister, the white woman {for the lime}.

Tlacuel tlaxihuallauh, tlatlāhuic chichimecatl, canican ỳcac tlamacazqui cēatl ytonal anquitlătizq̃ anquipòpolozque tleynticmati tlatlāhuic chichimecatl? canican nicyōlitiz ỹ nohueltiuh yztac cihuatl

Let it be soon! Come, Red Chichimec [i.e., the ax]. Here stands the priest, His-*tonal* Is One Water [i.e., the tree]. You [pl] [i.e., the hands and the ax] will hide him [i.e., kill him], you [pl] will destroy him. What is it that you know [i.e., Pay attention], Red Chichimec? I will give life to my elder sister, White Woman [i.e., the lime].

Tlā cuēl! Tlā xihuāllauh, Tlātlāhuic Chīchīmēcatl. Ca nicān ihcac tlamacazqui, Cē-Ātl Ītōnal. Anquitlātīzqueh; anquipohpolōzqueh. Tleh in ticmati, Tlātlāhuic Chīchīmēcatl? Ca nicān nicyōlītīz in nohuēltīuh, Iztāc-Cihuātl.

[2] You, ax,[2] are not to covet {for "to wound"} the priests that I bring with me {for "my hands and feet and fingers and toes"},[3] for they do not have blood or color. I am the one who commands it, the prince of the spells for "enchanter."

Àmo tiquimelehuiz yntlamacazque nican niquinhuicatinemi, àmo ezçòque àmo tlapallòque. nòmatca nèhuatl ninahual teuctli.

You [i.e., the ax] will not covet [i.e., hurt] the priests [i.e., the fingers and toes] whom I go bringing here. They have no blood, they have no color [i.e., they are supernatural]. It is I in person. I am the *nahualli*-lord.

Ahmō tiquimēlēhuīz in tlamacazqueh nicān niquinhuīcatinemi. Ahmō ezzohqueh, ahmō tlapallohqueh. Nohmatca nehhuātl. Ninābualtēuctli.

Having cut the wood, they begin to rig the kiln, putting as a base the firewood, which they conjure first, saying:

[3] Come here, genie,[4] whose happiness consists in the waters; stretch out in my enchanted lime kiln. There you are to change yourself into smoke and mist. With this my sister, the white woman {the lime}, will be engendered and will be born.

Tlacuel taxihuallauh tlamacazqui cé atl ytonal tlaximotecati ỹ nonahual texcalço oncan tipoctiz oncan tayauhtiz, oncan yoliz oncan tlācatiz ỹ nohueltiuh yztac cihuatl.

Let it be soon! Come, priest, His-*tonal* Is One Water [i.e., the wood]. Go in order to stretch out in my *nahualli*-kiln. There you will become smoke; there you will become mist. There my older sister, White Woman [i.e., the lime], will become alive; there she will be born.

Tlā cuēl! Tlā xihuāllauh, tlamacazqui, Cē-Ātl Ītōnal. Tlā ximotēcati in nonāhualtexcalco. Oncān tipōctiz; oncān tāyauhtiz. Oncān yōliz; oncān tlācatiz in nohuēltīuh, Iztāc-Cihuātl.

After having placed the first bed of firewood, they then conjure the rock in order to put it in place, saying:

[4] Come, you, my sister, Death, for here you are to revive and to be born. My servants will bring this about in you, drinking you and eating you (which means "burning you"). I order it thus, the prince of the spells.

Tlacuel xihuallauh nohueltiuh ce miquiztli canican tiyoliz nicã titlacatiz, càmo çan yuhtlamatizque ỹ nopilhuan nican cate mitzīzque mitzquazque, nòmatca nèhuatl ninahualteuctli.

Let it be soon! Come, my older sister, One Death [i.e., the limestone]. Here you will become alive; here you will be born. Indeed it is not merely that my sons [i.e., the flames] who are here will taste things. They will drink you; they will eat you. It is I in person. I am the *nahualli*-lord.

Tlā cuēl! Xihuāllauh, nohuēltīuh, Cē-Miquiztli. Ca nicān tiyōliz; nicān titlācatiz. Ca ahmō zan iuh tlamatizqueh in nopilhuān nicān cateh. Mitzīzqueh; mitzcuāzqueh. Nohmatca nehhuātl. Nināhualtēuctli.

Having thus rigged the kiln, the firewood and rocks being arranged for the lighting of the fire, they conjure the fire, commanding it, although with respect, to perform its office well.

[5] Come to my aid, you, my father, four reeds, burning with blond hair {for the flames}, you who are the mother and the father of the Gods.

Tlacuel tlaxihuallauh notâ nahui acatl milintica, tzoncoztli, teteo y nni non teteo yntâ.

Let it be soon! Come, my father, Four Reed, He-is-scintillating,[5] Yellow-hair,[6] Teteoh Innan, Teteoh Intah [i.e., the fire].

Tlā cuēl! Tlā xihuāllauh, notah, Nāhui-Ācatl, Milīnticah, Tzoncōztli, Tēteoh Īnnān, Tēteoh Īntah.

[6] Now you can come, because now I have brought my mat of Roses. Upon it you are to sit down, but not in order to be seated, for you are to pass [quickly],[7] and you are to eat and drink, and you are to return quickly in order that the white woman quickly be engendered and be born. For this purpose my servants await you. Not just anybody commands it; I the prince of the spells.

Tlaxihualhuian yeonicmanato noxochipetl yn ipan timotlalitiuh tel àmo tihuècahuatiuh, cantiỳciuhtiuh çantitlaquatiuh can ỳciuhca tihuallaz yoliz tlācatiz yniztaccihuatl canican mitzchixticate ỹ nopilhuan. àmo çan acâ nòmatca nèhuatl ninahualteuctli.

Come [pl]! I have already gone to lay out my flowery mat [i.e, the wood] on which you [sg] [i.e., the fire] will go to sit. But you will not go to linger. You will just go hurrying; you will just eat and go; you will just come quickly. White Woman [i.e., the lime] will become alive, she will be born. Here my sons [i.e., the firewood] are waiting for you [i.e., the fire]. I am not just anybody. It is I in person. I am the *nahualli*-lord.

Tlā xihuālhuiān! Ye ōnicmanato noxōchipetl, in īpan timotlālītīuh. Tēl ahmō tihuehcāhuatīuh. Zan tihciuhtiuh; zan titlacuahtiuh; zan ihciuhcā tihuāllāz. Yōliz, tlācatiz in Iztāc-Cihuātl. Ca nicān mitzchixticateh in nopilhuān. Ahmō zan nacah.[8] Nohmatca nehhuātl. Ninālhualtēuctli.

Upon lighting the fire, in order that it have the desired effect and not go out, but easily penetrate all the kiln to the top, they conjure the wind, saying:

[7] Come on, now come, my sister, the green woman, go to hasten in order that my

Tlacuel xihuallauh ỹ nohueltiuh xoxohuic cihuatl tla xictlaỳcihuiti mahual-

father, the four flaming reeds, will hurry fast.

ỳcihui notâ nahui acatl milinticâ.

Let it be soon! Come, my older sister, Green Woman [i.e., the wind]. Make my father, Four Reed, He-is-scintillating [i.e., the fire], hurry hither! If only he would hurry hither.

Tlā cuēl! Xihuāllauh, in nohuēltīuh, Xoxōhuic-Cihuātl. Tlā xichuālihcihuītī![9] Mā huālihcihui notah, Nāhui-Ācatl, Milīnticah.

[8] Come now, you, green wind, go to hasten my father, the four flaming reeds. In what are they indolent? Make him hurry in order that the white woman be engendered and be born and that we look upon her face.

Tlaxihuallauh xoxouhqui èhecatl tla xiqualìcihuititi notà nahui acatl tleaxtica mahuel ỳcihui yoliz tlācatiz yztac cihuatl yxco ycpac titlachiazque.

Come, Green Wind. Go in order to make my father, Four Reed [i.e., the fire], hurry hither. What is he doing? If only he would hurry hither. White Woman [i.e., the lime] will become alive; she will be born. We will look upon her face, upon her head-top [i.e., we will see her in person].

Tlā xihuāllauh, Xoxōuhqui-Ehehcatl. Tlā xichuālihcihuītīti[10] notah, Nāhui-Ācatl. Tleh āxticah? Mā huālihcihui. Yōliz, tlācatiz Iztāc-Cihuātl. Īīxco, Īcpac titlachiazqueh.

With this he goes on to set it afire. And in order to better compel and certify their incantations, they used to dance around the kiln and, along the way, to drink until, from being drunk or tired, they all were sleeping.

CHAPTER 6

About the Incantation or Witchcraft That They Use in Order to Hunt, Beginning with the Hunting of Fowls

ORDINARILY they hunt fowls with nets, setting them up and spreading them out on the bank of the streams and springs where the birds come to drink. And being convinced of their superstitions, they conjure the nets in order that they have the desired effect, and for greater force they start off by giving themselves authority, claiming unjustly and appropriating divine power, because they say:

[1] I myself, the son without a father {or orphan}, the only God, the one named Quetzalcoatl {a very important idol}, I have come to look for my uncles, the nobles of the sky. What am I saying? For already they are here; already I see my uncles, stretched out here, who have, as it were, distilled themselves or slipped to the ground.

Nòmatca nèhuatl nic nopiltzītli nicenteotl niquetzalcoatl onihualla niquintemoz ỹ notlàhuan tlamacazque ylhuicac pīpiltin. Tlacà yenican onoque y nnotlàhuan tlamacazque orchipinque orpeyauhque {Not Mexican words[1]}

It is I in person. I am Icnopiltzintli. I am Centeotl. I am Quetzalcoatl. I have come in order to seek

Nohmatca nehhuātl. NIcnōpiltzintli. NiCenteōtl. NiQuetzalcōātl. Ōnihuāllah ni-

my uncles, the priests, the nobles in the sky [i.e., the birds]. But lo! My uncles, the priests, Ones-dripping-with-rubber, Ones-overflowing-with-rubber [i.e., the birds], are already sitting here!

quintēmōz in notlahhuān, tlamacazqueh, ilhuicac pīpiltin. Tlacah! Ye nicān onoqueh in notlahhuān, tlamacazqueh, Ōlchipīnqueh, Ōlpeyāuhqueh!

[2] Here the house and clothing of my mother {the net} has been brought. Here I will set a stake upright, driving it into the throat, into the belly, into the sides of my mother, the one of the skirt like precious stones {the earth because of the flowers}. Here I will wait for my uncles, the genies who descend. By distilling, they slide to the ground.

nicã niqualhuica[2] ỹ nonan ycal yhuipil, nican nic ehualtiz yntlamacazqui ceatl ytonal ytozcatlan yxillan yciacatlan noconaquiz ỹ nonan chalchiuhcueyê nican niquimōchiaz yn notlahuan tlamacazque orchipenque orpeyauhque.

Here I bring my mother's house's *huipil*[3] [i.e., the net]. Here I will erect the priest, His-*tonal* Is One Water [i.e., the stakes]. I will cause him to enter into the throat, the belly, the armpits [i.e., the body] of my mother, Chalchiuhcueyeh [i.e., the water]. Here I will wait for my uncles, the priests, Ones-dripping-with-rubber, Ones-overflowing-with-rubber.

Nicān nichuālhuīca in nonān īcal īhuīpīl. Nicān niquēhualtīz in tlamacazqui, Cē-Ātl Ītōnal. Ītozcatlan, īxīllan, īciacatlan noconaquīz in nonān, Chālchiuhcuēyeh. Nicān niquimonchiaz in notlahhuān, tlamacazqueh, Ōlchipīnqueh, Ōlpeyāuhqueh.[4]

CHAPTER 7

About the Method of Witchcraft for Seeking Beehives and Bees, Which Is with Spells and Incantations

SINCE among the Indians it is so common to look for beehives for the benefit of the honey and wax, and [because of its] being a fruit that is gathered without being cultivated, I judged it would be certain that, in this exercise as in the rest, the superstitions, incantations, and spells would be involved as in the other things, and even in this one much more because of the uncertainty of attaining the goal. Motivated by this thought, I reflected on how I would bring the truth to light, and, thanks be to God, a scheme came to my mind, the success of which proved to be good. Having found out that in my village there was an Indian, a stranger called Miguel, a native of the village of Xicòtlan,[1] who looked for beehives as a profession, I set to spy on him an old Indian man, trustworthy and respected in the village, to whom I entrusted the business, in order that by using a stratagem he might bring that superstition to light, as he did, because by any other way it would have been impossible. The good old man cunningly flattered the stranger and stood him treat, and after having regaled him and cajoled him, he set before him his request [saying] that he was old and with obligations, with a large family and without a means of being able to support it, and because the husbanding of honey and wax, which the said Miguel had for an occupation and job, was so profitable and not expensive, he wanted to know the method by which he found the beehives so easily. With this, the stranger, obligated and overcome by the courtesy and gifts of the old man, made known to him and dictated a long incantation and spell, which the astute old man wrote down, making it seem that he was very grateful and obliged to him. And with this the paper came into my hands.

Then, for another purpose, I had the stranger, Miguel, summoned. And after he had come, I commenced the work by way of what he could not deny, because he was of the number of the deceitful doctors which I have spoken of, called in the language *ticitl tlamatini*[2], which means "very wise doctor." I propounded to him his manner of curing, the herbs which he used and what they promised and prognosticated, and the words which he used in these exercises. And, although it was certain, for there were infinite witnesses, even all this was not enough to make him confess, until, after I had made a pressing argument about so public a thing, he, having come to the point of not being able to deny it, confessed.

Then I relentlessly pursued the business of the search for beehives, asking him what diligence and words he made use of in order to find them so easily. He denied everything stubbornly, because there were few witnesses of this case or perhaps only one, without whom it would be impossible to verify the superstition, which is among the greatest of this kind. Having seen that no diligence was sufficient to make him confess, I availed myself of the same paper that he had dictated to the old man, pretending that I only wanted to compare [and see] if he knew more than what that paper contained, for the cloaking and dissimulation of which I began to read him some beginnings of other incantations of the kind, and turning the pages of a book, I read the incantation of the beehives. Incited by the very words that he knew from memory much better than the Ave Maria, and thinking that it would not be a crime, since I had those words, he confessed them and continued, without changing nor missing a single word of the ones that he had dictated earlier to the old man who gave me the paper in which he had written them. And with this he gave his deposition about the incantation and spell, which is as follows:

[1] Come on, now come here, beaten ones on the land, for we are to make a trip and to travel; come on, come here, red Chichimec, for we are to go and to travel. Come here, you genie, Seven Jaguars, fruit and flower of the earth or flower of wine.[3] Come on, bring with you what was put and guarded within you, the green spirit, the green genie, for presently I am to carry you where all is forest and density of trees and grass; we are going to look for our uncles, the genies, the ones who among the genies are like Gods or superiors, who live many together and are yellow and have yellow wings, people who inhabit gardens and live on high and in company.

Tlacuel tla xihuallauh tla xilcapan tontiazque tonòtlatocazque tlaxihuallauh tlatlahuic chichimecatl tonyāzque tonòtlatocazque tlacuel tla xihuallauh tlamacazqui chicomocelotl, tlalocxochitl. Tla xiqualcui[4] ỹ mìtic tlaliloc ynxoxohuic tzitzimitl yn xoxohuic colelectli yenimitzonhuicaz yz cenquauhtla yz cençacatla tiquintètemozque yntotlàtlàhuan tlamacazq̃, tēteo tlamacazque yntollantzinca yn coçauhqueme yn coçauhmàtlapalèque yn xochimilpan tlāca, yn àco calpaneca yntollantzinca

Let it be soon! Come, Earth-face-slapper [i.e., the sandals]! We will go; we will follow the road.

Tlā cuēl! Tlā xihuāllauh, Tlālīxcapān![9] Tonyāzqueh;[10] tonohtlatocazqueh. Tlā

Come, Red Chichimec [i.e., the ax]! We will go; we will follow the road. Let it be soon! Come, priest, Seven-jaguar,[5] Land-wine-flower [i.e., maguey-fiber net-sack]![6] Come get Green Air-spirit, Green Demon,[7] who has been placed in your stomach! I will soon carry you through the entire forest, through the entire grassland. We will diligently seek our various uncles, the priests, the gods, the priests who are Tollantzinco[8] people, who are owners of yellow clothing, who are owners of yellow wings, the people from the flower fields, the attic dwellers, the people from Tollantzinco [i.e., the bees].

xihuāllauh, Tlātlāhuic Chīchīmēcatl! Tonyāzqueh; tonohtlatocazqueh. Tlā cuēl! Tlā xihuāllauh, tlamacazqui, Chicōmocēlōtl, Tlālocxōchitl! Tlā xichuālcui in mihtic tlālilōc in Xoxōhuic Tzitzimitl, in Xoxōhuic Cōlēlectli! Ye nimitzonhuīcaz in cencuauhtlah, in cenzacatlah. Tiquintehtēmōzqueh in totlahtlahhuān, tlamacazqueh, tēteoh, tlamacazqueh in Tōllāntzincah, in cōzauhquēmehqueh,[11] in cōzauhāmaahtlapalehqueh, in xōchimīlpan tlācah, in ahcocalpanēcah, in Tōllāntzincah.

[2] And you, deity, snake of stone or of wood, who have me at your disposal, my twisted sister, upon you am I to go, upon you am I to walk alone, the war itself or the warrior, I to whom the slaves belong, the one who mocks all, I myself have come, the enemy, I who come for my uncles, the superiors among other spirits, and I am to bring them[12] from my gardens and from my woods and groves.

Tlaxihualhuian tlamacazqui tecoatl. quauhcoatl tleynticmati? nohueltiuh cenmalinalli mopāniaz, mopan nòtlatocaz nicel yatl niicelti ytlacahuan ninoquequeloatzin nòmatca nèhuatl onihualla ỹ niyaotzin niquīmānaco ỹ notlàhuan yn teteo tlamacazque ynnoxichimilpan ynnoquauhmilpan

Come [pl], priest, Stone-snake [i.e., rocky road], Wood-snake [i.e., mountain road]. What is it that you [sg] know? [I.e., Pay attention!] My older sister, One-grass[13] [i.e., the sandals], upon you I will go; upon you I will follow the road. I am Yaotl's solitary one, I am Titlacahuan's solitary one. I am Moquehqueloatzin. It is I in person who have come. I, who am Yaotzin, have come to get my uncles, the gods, the priests [i.e., the bees], in my flower fields, in my tree fields.

Tlā xihuālhuiān, tlamacazqui, Tecōātl, Cuauhcōātl.[14] Tleh in ticmati? Nohuēltīuh, Cemmalīnalli, mopan niyāz; mopan nohtlatocaz. Nīcēl Yāōtl, nīcēl Tītlācahuān.[15] NiMoquehqueloatzin. Nohmatca nehhuātl ōnihuāllah. In niYāōtzin niquimānaco in notlahhuān, in tēteoh, tlamacazqueh, in noxōchimīlpan, in nocuauhmīlpan.

[3] And it is certain that I am not to go far, not to travel on a long trip, for near here, from my gardens and groves I am to turn around and to return, for I am to do no more than arrive and gather my buzzing princesses from the spirits and gods who live in company and inhabit the gardens of roses {They believe that the gods dwell in the forests and ravines.}. For this purpose I have brought the red Chichimec {the ax to cut the stick of the beehive}, who comes to drink and to eat, I myself, the possessed one or divine one, an idol, snake {appositives}.

cuix huèca nonyaz? cuex huèca nonòtlatocaz? çan nechca noxochimilpan, çan nechca noquauhmilpan çan nechca nihualylotiz nihualnocuepaz çan niquinmonanti heetzico ynnò chitzipihuã teteo tlamacazque tullantzinca xochi milpan chanèque. Onichualhuicac yntlatlahuic chichimēcatl, onātlico ontlaquāco nòmatca nèhuatl nitlamacazqui cecoatl.

Will I go far away? Will I follow the road far away? Only right over there to my flower field; only right over there to my tree field. From right over there I will return, I will come back. I have only come in order to seize swiftly my various lisping [i.e., buzzing] ones, the gods, the priests, the Tol-

Cuix huehca nonyāz? Cuix huehca nohtlatocaz? Zan nechca noxōchimīlpan; zan nechca nocuauhmīlpan. Zan nechca nihuālīlōtiz, nihuālnocuepaz. Zan niquimonāntihuetzico in notzihtzīpihuān,[16] tēteoh, tlamacazqueh, Tōllāntzincah,

lantzinco people, the dwellers in the flower fields [i.e., the bees]. I have brought Red Chichimec [i.e., the ax]. He has come to drink; he has come to eat. It is I in person. I am the priest, One Snake.

xōchimīlpan chānehqueh. Ōnichuālhuīcac in Tlātlāhuic Chīchīmēcatl. Onātlīco; ontlacuāco. Nohmatca nehhuātl. Nitlamacazqui, niCē-Cōātl.[17]

He then conjures the impediments and obstructions in order that, if there is none to impede his attempt, he may easily achieve his desire. And for this he says:

[4] Come on, withdraw and do not be an obstruction for me, white, dark, and yellow spiders,[18] nor you, white, dusky, or yellow little doves, do not be an obstruction for me. White, dusky, or yellow lizards, let there be nothing that hides or conceals my uncles from me, those who live in company and dwell on high.

Tlaximehuacan yztac tocatl yayahuic tocatl coçahuic tocatl yztac pāpālotl yahuic pāpālotl coçahuic pāpālotl yztac cuetzpalli yayahuic cuetzpalli coçahuic cuetzpalli, ma ayac quimmianti, ma ayac quintlapacho ỹ motlàtlàhuan yntollantzīca yn àcocalpan chanèque.

Depart, white spider, dusky spider, yellow spider, white butterfly, dusky butterfly, yellow butterfly, white lizard, dusky lizard, yellow lizard. Let anyone beware of hiding [i.e., let no one hide] my various uncles, the Tollantzinco people, the attic dwellers [i.e., the bees]; let anyone beware of covering [i.e., let no one cover] them up.

Tlā ximēhuacān, iztāc tocatl, yāyāuhqui tocatl, cōzahuic tocatl, iztāc pāpālōtl, yāyāhuic pāpālōtl, cōzahuic pāpālōtl, iztāc cuetzpalli, yāyāhuic cuetzpalli, cōzahuic cuetzpalli. Mā acah quimihyānti[19]; mā acah quintlapachoh in notlahtlahhuān, in Tōllāntzincah, in ahcocalpan chānehqueh.

Then he sets forth his merits, saying:[20]

[5] I who come to do this enmity to you come driven by necessity, for I am poor and wretched.

Ynnèhuatl onihualla niycnoyaotzin ninotolinìcatzintli

As for me who have come, I am IcnoYaotzin. I am Motolinihcatzintli.

In nehhuātl ōnihuāllah, nIcnōYāōtzin. NiMotolīnihcātzintli.[21]

[6] And thus I only come to look for my sustenance, because of which let no one be frightened or be afraid of me, for I will only carry you to see my sister, the goddess *Xochiquetzal,* the so-called precious bouquet.

Nictēmoco ỹ noneuhca ynnocochcâ mayaca nechinmacìti, mayaca nechmauhcahuati niquinhuicaz quithuatihui (l.[22] quittatihui) nohueltiuh xochiquetzal.

I have come to seek my means of rising [i.e., my morning meal] and my means of sleeping [i.e., my evening meal ("morning meal, evening meal" is a metaphor for "livelihood")]. Let anyone beware of fearing [i.e., let no one fear] me. Let anyone beware of looking [i.e., let no one look] upon me with fear. I will carry them[23] so that they go and see my older sister, Xochiquetzal [i.e., my wife].

Nictēmōco in nonēuhca in nocochca. Mā acah nēchīmacazti.[24] Mā acah nēchmauhcāithuahti.[25] Niquinhuīcaz quithuatīhuih (*or* quittatīhuih) nohuēltīuh, Xōchiquetzal.

Or possibly this may mean the wife of the one who makes the incantation. And it seems that he is praising the beauty of his wife to the bees in order to inspire affection in them so that they will go to live with her.

And both the fishermen and these men who look for honeycombs and honey have their established superstition, that, in order to have a good outcome, they are not to engage in the said enterprises while being upset by annoyances or quarrels; rather, they are to carry them out with much peace and pleasure, because with this they will find with great ease that which they desire. And concerning the bees, they give two reasons, which are as follow:[26]

[7] They are divine for they seek food for us and are enemies of troubles.	Catéteo mochiuhticate ca tetlayecoltia auh àmonetequipachtli quinequi.
Indeed they are making themselves into gods. Indeed they serve people. And they do not want worries.	Ca tēteoh mochīuhticateh. Ca tētlayecōltiah. Auh ahmō netequipachtli quinequih.
[8] Second, they say that, because they make the wax that is to burn before God, they deserve to be treated with reverence, because of the great degree to which they are esteemed and enhanced.	Ypampa ca xicò cuitlatl quichichihua cayxpantzinco tlatlaz yntty° Dios yèhuatl yca motlaçòtlatoque mohuey nectoque.
Because they make the wax that will burn before Our Lord, God, for that reason they are loved and are held in esteem.	Īpampa ca xīcohcuitlatl quichihchīhuah, ca īīxpantzinco tlatlaz in ToTēucyo,[27] *Dios,* yehhuātl īca motlazohtlatoqueh, mohuēinectoqueh.[28]

With this they attribute divinity to the bees and similarly to other animals, so that we should be universally warned in order to pay careful attention to any kind of suspicious language.

CHAPTER 8

About the Spell and Incantation That They Use for Hunting Deer with Snares and the Great Superstitions That They Involve in This

Before all else they suppose that whoever is to engage in this occupation must be free of all kinds of unpleasantness, both of distressing cares and of quarrels, so that he may be what in Latin is described as *Omni modis peca animas.*[1]

Next there enters the disposition of the house,[2] in which the first order of business is to prepare the house for the good outcome—setting it in order, and sweeping it, and then setting into place its three rocks that they call *tenamaztli*[3] (which is the trivet of the Indians). This being done, the preparation for the departure follows, which is to collect the *piciete,* fire, and snares, I mean, the ropes with which they are to be rigged.

The invocations, incantations, and spells enter in three places. They are made by speaking to many things, which, in order not to break the thread of the incantation, will be noted in the margin,[4] because in the incantation they speak to the *piciete,* the common ferment of these brews,[5] and to the fire, to the earth, to the ropes, to the forests and grassy places, to those whom they believe to be forest gods, even to the deer themselves. In the interpretation of the incantation I shall try to keep close to the letter, as long as in doing so the result will not be totally unintelligible in our language, and even as a remedy for this I will take recourse to putting explications of the expressions in the margin.[6] Now then, in order to do his work, the house having been swept and the fire laid and the three stones [set in place], he picks up the *piciete*, the fire, and the ropes and commences by conjuring the *piciete*, saying:

[1] Come or favor me now, spirit seven times pounded, seven times beaten. How inattentive you are since now I am to take you away.

Tlaxohuiqui tlamacazqui chiucnauh tlatetzotzonalli, chiucnauh tlatecapanilli tlèticmati yetihuicoz.

Come, priest, Nine-[times]-pounded-one, Nine-[times]-slapped-one [i.e., tobacco]. What do you know? [I.e., Pay attention!] You will soon be accompanied.

Tlā xihuiqui,[7] tlamacazqui, Chiucnāuhtlatetzohtzonalli, Chiucnāuhtlatecapānīlli. Tleh ticmati? Ye tihuīcōz.

[2] Come, you, my mother, din of the earth, and you, my father, one rabbit, shining stone that smokes, and you my sister twisted in one direction, you, my mother earth,[8] does it not anger you, does it not annoy you to see yourself wounded in as many places as the possessed ones, the owners of seven roses {the deer because of the points of their antlers}[9] and who inhabit the lands of the gods {because they walk in the forests and ravines} walk along digging you?[10] For those lands are the place of amusement of my sister, the goddess, snake with the face of a puma {the idol}.

Tlaxihuiqui nonan tlaltecuintli,[11] notà ce tochtli tezcatl yncan hualpopōcatimani, nohueltiuh cenmalinalli, nonan tlaltecuintli ayocac ynmoqualan? ayocac ỹ motlahuel yncan titatacacpol mitznemītia yntlamacazq̃, chicomexochitl, teo tlālhua ỹ nohueltiuh ỹ mizcoacihuatl ynaca xoch.

Come [sg], my mother, Tlaltecuin, my father, One Rabbit, Mirror that is just smoking hither [i.e., the earth], my older sister, One-grass [i.e., the rope (this seems to be here in error; see II:8: 4)]. My mother, Tlaltecuin [i.e., the earth], is there no longer anyone who is your [sg] anger? Is there no longer anyone who is your [sg] hatred at the place where the priest, Seven Flower, Desert-owner [i.e., the male deer], and my older sister, Mixcoacihuatl [i.e., the female deer], and Acaxoch [i.e, the deer][12] make you live as a miserable hole-scarred one?

Tlā xihuiqui, nonān, Tlāltecuīn, notah, Cē-Tōchtli, Tezcatl in zan huālpopōcatimani, nohuēltīuh, Cemmalīnalli. Nonān, Tlāltecuīn, ayoc āc in mocualān? Ayoc āc in motlahuēl in cān titlatatatacpōl[13] mitznemītiah in tlamacazqui, Chicōme-Xōchitl, Teohtlālhuah, in nohuēltīuh, in Mixcōācihuātl,[14] in Ācaxōch?

[3] Already, already I see their houses, their lands where they walk in herds. Here is where I am to set up, where I am to rig entrances {snares} for the muzzles, entrances made with stakes through which they will enter in herds. I spirit,[15] the God of the first age,[16] orphan son {without any man who can be found

Yenican ychan ye nican ytexòtlalpan yntollan ye nican nicchichihuaz ye nican nic yolitiz yn tĕnan quiahuatl quauhquiahuatl yntullan òtli ynnitlamacazqui niycnopiltzintli ỹ niceteotl téteo niypiltzin téteo niytlachihual.

to be his father}, son of the Gods and a creation of theirs.

Right here is his home. It is right here in the desert, which is Tollan. Right here I will make the wall-doorway, the wood-doorway, the road to Tollan [i.e., the snare]; here I will cause it to come into being. I am the priest. I am Icnopiltzin. I, Centeotl, am the child of the gods, am the creation of the gods.

Ye nicān īchān. Ye nicān in teohtlālpan,[17] in Tōllān. Ye nicān nicchihchīhuaz; ye nicān nicyōlītīz in tenānquiāhuatl, cuauhquiāhuatl, in Tōllān ohtli. Nitlamacazqui. NIcnōpiltzin. In niCenteōtl tēteoh nīmpiltzin, tēteoh nīntlachīhual.

[4] Sister, twisted in one direction {he speaks to the ropes when the deer chafe or break them}, how it irritates you and angers you to see yourself raveled, and how ignominiously and uglily the possessed one of seven roses {the deer because of its horns}, the dweller of the lands of the gods or of the rugged ground, makes raveled-out threads hang from you.

Nohueltiuh cenmalinalli ayocac ỹ mo qualan? ayocac? yncantiquāpachpol yncan àhuicpa mitztzontia yntlamacazqui chicome xochitl ynteo tlālhua.

My older sister, One-grass [i.e., the rope], is there no longer anyone who is your anger? Is there no longer anyone [who is your hatred] at the place where you are unkempt headed, at the place where the priest, Seven Flower, Desert-owner [i.e., the deer], causes your hair to grow this direction and that [i.e., causes you to become raveled]?

Nohuēltīuh, Cemmalīnalli, ayoc āc in mocualān? Ayoc āc [in motlahuēl][18] in cān ticuāpachpōl, in cān ahhuīcpa mitztzontia in tlamacazqui, Chicōme-Xōchitl, in Teohtlālhuah?

[5] And you, possessed one {to the *piciete*}, nine times beaten one, how are you demarcating yourself?[19] Let the instruments of the snares be taken away and hidden and be concealed. Let the rest of the stakes and enchanted wood[20] be taken away and hidden and burned.[21] Let it not be that anything of this offend me. Be informed that I am not a living being. I do not have blood nor any other humor.[22] And you, possessed one, green deity, how inattentive you are, since you are to go with me. And you, divine sun, you who before were pustulous, great prince, show me the seven [*sic*] times beaten one, the nine times pounded one.

Tlaxihuallauh tlamacazqui chiuc nauh tlatetzotzonalli, tlèticmati? maon èhehualo[23] maon nitlatilo yc omochiuhqui yn yahualiuhqui, maon mehua maon motlāti yntlaco quau tli, manechelehuìti ca àmo niyollo[24] ca àmo nezço ca àmo nitlapallo tlamacazqui xoxouhqui tlamacazqui tlèticmati yetehuan tiaz? tlaxihuiqui tlamacazqui nānāhuatzin xiuhpilli can mach yn tictlalia yn chiucnauhtlatecapānilli chiuhnauhtlatlatetzotzonalli.

Come, priest, Nine-[times]-pounded-one [i.e., tobacco]. What do you know? [I.e., Pay attention!] Let them be taken away, let them be hidden—the things with which the circle [i.e., the snare] has been made. Let the stick-eagle [i.e., the trigger of the snare(?)] be taken away; let it be hidden. Let it beware of coveting [i.e., hurting] me. I do not have life; I do not have any blood; I have no color [i.e., I am supernatural]. Priest, Green Priest [i.e., tobacco], what do you

Tlā xihuāllauh, tlamacazqui, Chiucnāuhtlatetzohtzonalli. Tleh ticmati? Mā onehēhualo, mā ontlātilo[25] īc ōmochīuhqui in yahualiuhqui. Mā onmēhua, mā onmotlāti in tlacōcuāuhtli.[26] Mā nēchēlēhuihti.[27] Ca ahmō niyōlloh; ca ahmō nezzoh; ca ahmō nitlapalloh. Tlamacazqui, Xoxōuhqui Tlamacazqui, tleh ticmati? Ye tēhuān tiyāz. Tlā xihuiqui, tlamacazqui, Nānāhuatzin, Xiuhpilli. Cān mach in tic-

know? [I.e., Pay attention!] You will soon go with people. Come, priest, Nanahuatzin, Xiuhpilli [i.e., the fire]. Where ever is it that you are putting Nine-[times]-rock-slapped-one, Nine-[times]-rock-pounded-one?

tlālia in Chiucnāuhtlatecapānīlli, Chiucnāuhtlahtlatetzohtzonalli?

[6] Come on, since we are now going; we will go following the four flaming reeds. Come, you, my father, the four reeds that throw flames[28] and a red [*sic*] comet, Father and mother of the Gods, you who, covered with sparkles,[29] breathe through four parts, whose body[30] is made of many steps, through whose mouth a thick stream of black water flows forth, who is accompanied by the leftovers[31] of those of badly adorned heads, his proclaimers, who have never had contentment nor pleasure but rather are with much sorrow and tears.

Tla huiyan tlatictocaca nahui acatl milinticâ. Tlaxihuiqui ynnotâ nahui acatl milintica xiuhtli coçauhqui milintica tēteo ynan téteo yntâ, nauhcampa tle muchitl ycatlatlalpitztica centzonmamatlatl yca tlacçatica tlilātl yca tenpatlahuatica yniqua onoque ynquahuac cacauhtin ynte te epoyo ỹ àquenmanpāqui àquenman àhahuia ỹ nican ycho quiz ye ymixayo quimātentoque.

Let us go![32] Let us follow Four Reed, He-is-scintillating [i.e., the fire]. Come, my father, Four Reed, He-is-scintillating, Yellow Comet, He-is-scintillating, Teteoh Innan, Teteoh Intah [i.e., the fire]. Toward the four directions he is repeatedly blowing on things by means of sparks. He is treading on things by means of four hundred [i.e., many] stairsteps. He is being wide-lipped by means of black water.[33] At his head the emaciated derelicts, the proclaimers who are never happy, who never make merry, lie there; here they already lie pouring out their weeping and their tears.[34]

Tlā [ti]huiān! Tlā tictocacān Nāhui-Ācatl, Milīnticah. Tlā xihuiqui, in notah, Nāhui-Ācatl, Milīnticah, Xīhuitl[35] Cōzauhqui, Milīnticah, Tēteoh Īnnān, Tēteoh Īntah. Nāuhcāmpa tlemōyōtl[36] īca tlahtlalpītzticah. Centzontlamamatlatl īca tlaczaticah. Tlīlātl īca tēmpatlāhuaticah. In īcuāc[37] onoqueh in cuahuāccācāuhtin,[38] in tētecpoyoh in ahquēmman pāquih, ahquēmman ahāhuiyah; in nicān īnchōquiz, ye īmīxāyo quimātēntoqueh.

[7] My father, the four flaming reeds, it is certain that I am not to receive gratification and pleasure first, because in this you are to be preferred, because from the prey before all things I am to offer you the warm blood, the fragrant blood, the heart, and the head of the possessed one of seven roses {of the deer because of the points of its horns}, who lives in the land of the Gods: he is yours.

Notâ nahuiacatl milintica cuix nè nàhahuiaz? cuix nè nihuellamatiz achtotipa tipaquiz achtotipa tiquittaz yn eztli totonic yn eztli àhuiac yni yol ynitzontecon ynticcuiz yntlamacazqui chicome xochitl ynteotlalhuia

My father, Four Reed, He-is-scintillating [i.e., the fire], am I perchance the one who will make merry? Am I perchance the one who will be content? First you will be happy. First you will see the warm blood, the fragrant blood, his heart, his head, when you will get the priest, Seven Flower, Desert-owner [i.e., the male deer].

Notah, Nāhui-Ācatl, Milīnticah, cuix neh nahāhuiyaz? Cuix neh nihuellamatiz? Achtopa tipāquiz. Achtopa tiquittaz in eztli totōnic,[39] in eztli ahhuiyāc, in īyōl,[40] in ītzontecon, in ticcuiz in tlamacazqui, Chicōme-Xōchitl, in Teohtlālhuah.

[8] Now I am leaving. Presently I will seek, presently I will call and find what yesterday and the day before cost tears and sorrow to my sister the goddess Xochiquetzal and what also yesterday and the day before caused tears

yeniyauh ye nictemoz, yenicanaz. Yenic notzaz ynyalhua yehuiptla ynica choca ynica nētlamati? Ỹ nohueltiuh ynxochiquetzal, y nyalhua yehuiptla yca nichocaya yca ninentlamati ỹ nitla-

and painful concern to me, who am a possessed one who suffers much need, many hardships, and fatigue, for I have neither chili pepper nor salt. Already I am leaving, and soon I will find and will gather that which I seek, which is not to be tomorrow or the following day, but right away. Now I carry my sister, the female snake, the one who performs the offices of a woman. Presently I will follow the wide road and the one that divides into two which has neither beginning nor middle. Come on, raise up your spinning and your weaving. Let not some misfortune befall me with the snares and [let it not happen] that I cut them like a fool!

macazqui ninotolinia niquiỳyohuia niciahui. Polihui ỹ nochil polihui ỹ noztauh, ye niyauh yenic anaz Cuix moztla? Cuix huiptla? niman axcan. Yenic huicaz ỹ nohueltiuh yz cihuacoatl yz cihua tequihuâ. Yenictŏcaz y nòtli patlahuac y nòtli maxalihuic yn àcan yole ynahua tzontecome, Maon tla èhehualo yn anmotzahual ỹ an mìquit macana nitlaycxihui manitlacoco tōnti.

Now I go. Soon I will seek him. Soon I will seize him. Soon I will call the one for whom since yesterday and even the day before [i.e., for some time] my older sister, Xochiquetzal [i.e., my wife], has been crying, because of whom she has been sad. Since yesterday and even the day before, I, the priest, have been crying for him, I have been sad because of him. I am poor, I suffer poverty. I am tired. My chili pepper is becoming ruined; my salt is becoming ruined [i.e., my food is becoming ruined].[41] Already I am going. Soon I will seize him. Will it be tomorrow? Will it be the day after? It will be immediately today. Soon I will carry my older sister, Cihuacoatl, the female warrior [i.e., the rope]. Soon I will follow the wide road, the bifurcating road which at no place has a heart, and which at no place has a head. If only people would lift things up, such as your [pl] weavings and your [pl] woven material. Let me beware of stepping on things somewhere. Let me beware of tearing things to pieces.

Ye niyauh. Ye nictēmōz. Ye nicānaz. Ye nicnōtzaz in yālhua ye huīptla in īca chōca, in īca nēntlamati in nohuēltīuh, in Xōchiquetzal. In yālhua ye huīptla, īca nichōca, īca ninēntlamati in nitlamacazqui. Ninotolīnia, niquihīyōhuia. Niciyahui. Polihui in nochīl; polihui in noztauh. Ye niyauh. Ye nicānaz. Cuix mōztla? Cuix huīptla? Niman āxcān. Ye nichuīcaz in nohuēltīuh, in Cihuācōātl, in cihuātequihuah.[42] Ye nictocaz in ohtli patlāhuac, in ohtli māxalihuic in ahcān[43] yōleh, in ahcān tzontecomeh. Mā ontlaehēhualo in amotzāhual, in amihquit. Mā canah nitlacxihuih. Mā nitlacohcotōnti.[44]

[9] Come on now, come now, my sisters, the lesser goddesses, remain on guard of my house. In case someone brings causes for annoyance and sorrows, you can remove them from it. You can detain them, in order that they not be a hindrance to me. In what are you amused?

Tla xihuiqui nohueltiuh, yn antlàçotēteo; tlanican xoconpixti nemican yn noquiahuac. Yehuitz yn quihualcuiz yn çomalli yntlahuelli. Nican ancanilizque anqui cuilizque tlè anquimati.

Come, my older sister [i.e., my wife]. You who are Beloved-goddesses [i.e., household gods], continue guarding my doorway here. Soon the one who will fetch anger and hatred is coming. Here you will take them from him; you will seize them from him [i.e., you will preserve peace and serenity in the house]. What do you know? [I.e., Pay attention!]

Tlā xihuiqui, nohuēltīuh. In anTlazohtēteoh,[45] tlā nicān xocompixtinemicān in noquiāhuac. Ye huītz in quihuālcuiz in zōmalli, in tlahuēlli. Nicān ancānilīzqueh; anquicuīlīzqueh. Tleh anquimatih?

When the aforesaid was finished, as a last farewell to the house, the Devil ordered him to incense the ropes or cords with which to set up the snares, like someone adding one more blessing or power, and, having done the incensing, to depart immediately for the forest and rough terrain, where, after he arrived, he commanded him to make a salute to the place. For this he should choose a round rock, and, after having set it down in a swept place, he should put over it the four ropes with which he is to set up the snares. And after they have been placed, the incantation begins:

[10] Come on, now come, my mother, lady {or goddess} of the earth; come, my father, one rabbit, mirror that smokes, make me not offend your face {A metaphor for the land because he who falls puts his hands on the ground and, figura[tively,] slaps it}, I who am a priest or enchanter, one of the gods. It will be better for you[46] to humble yourself to me, which means, by acquiescing,[47] in order that he not stumble and fall.

Tlaxihuiqui nonan tlalteuctli notâ cé tochtli tezcatl, çan huel popōcatimani. Mamixco non mayauh nitlamacazqui ni ce teotl maxihualmixtlàpachmana.

Come, my mother, Tlalteuctli, my father, One Rabbit, Mirror that is just smoking hither [i.e., the land]. Let me beware of putting my hand on your face [i.e., let me not stumble and fall]. I am the priest. I am Centeotl. Come and place yourself face down [i.e., remove any obstacles in my way].

Tlā xihuiqui, nonān, Tlāltēuctli, notah, Cē-Tōchtli, Tezcatl [in] zan huālpopōcatimani.[48] Mā mīxco nonmāyauh.[49] Nitlamacazqui. NiCenteōtl. Mā xihuālmīxtlahpachmana.

[11] Come on, come to my help, spirits, owners of the earth, you who are present toward the four winds and there you are supporting the skies *(appositive)*;[50] with your consent and pleasure, I have come here; you well saw and knew about my coming and arrival at this place,[51] for I am an orphan possessed one, one of the Gods, you being hills with bracelets and precious stones {For the rivers that circle them} as if [you were] made of turquoises {For the greenness of the grass}. On your shins[52] and sides {For the hills and slopes} I have come along, stopping out of tiredness and suffering need and travail and fatigue.

Tlaxihuiqui yn antlamacazqui yn antlalloque yn nauhcanpa an onoque yn nauhcampa ancate yn amylhuicatl quitzquìtoque anmixpan anmotlamatian yn onihualla yn onechcoc ỹ nitlamacazqui, ni ycnopiltzintli ni ce teotl y nican anmaquiztetepe yn anxiuhtetepe ynimitzcac ynimopochcopa ynonihuallàtia ỹ onihualnoquèquetztia ỹ ninotolinia ỹ niqui ỳyohuia niciyahui

Come, you who are priests, you who are Tlalocs, you who are lying there toward the four directions, you who are toward the four directions, you who lie gripping the sky [i.e., the mountains]. It is before your eyes, before your knowing place [i.e., into your perceiving presence], that I, who am the priest, Icnopiltzintli, Centeotl, have come, that I have arrived, here where you are bracelet-like mountains, where you are turquoise mountains, on whose left side I went along coming, came along whiling away the time, I who am poor, I who suffer poverty, I who am tired.

Tlā xihuiquih, in antlamacazqueh, in anTlāloqueh,[53] in nāuhcāmpa amonoqueh, in nāuhcāmpa ancateh, in amilhuicaquītzquihtoqueh.[54] Amīxpan, amotlamatiyān in ōnihuāllah, in ōnehcōc in nitlamacazqui, nIcnōpiltzintli, niCenteōtl, in nicān ammāquīztētepeh, in anxiuhtētepeh in amītzcac in amopōchcopa[55] in ōnihuāllahtiyah, in ōnihuālnoquehquetztiyah, in ninotolīnia, in niquihīyōhuia, niciyahui.

[12] Let your hearts that you have in your entrails feel this compassion, owners and lords of the earth, because the most [part] is already done, for already I have arrived at the town, at the fertile land.[56] Truly here is the house and dwelling of the spirit[57] of the seven Roses because the meat is fat and tasty for my sister, the snake who has a face of a puma, and for the said meat yesterday and the day before my sister, the goddess, Xochiquetzal, which means "feather-bunch of roses," has cried, and I also for that very reason have cried and have suffered anxieties yesterday and the day before.

Matlaocoya yn amoyollo ỹ amìtic onca ỹ Antlalloque yeonechcoc ỹ tollan ynteo tlalpan ye nican ynchan ye nican ycalìtic yntlamacazqui yn chicome xochitl ỹ nohueltiuh ỹ mizcoacihuatl ynacaxoch yny alhua yehuiptla yca choca yca nentlamati ỹ nohueltiuh yn xochiquetzal. ynyalhua yehuiptla yca nichoca yca ni nentlamati

Let your hearts which are within you be sad, you Tlalocs [i.e., mountains]. Already I have arrived at Tollan, at the desert. Right here is his home, right here is the inside of the house of the priest, Seven Flower [i.e., the male deer], my older sister, Mixcoacihuatl [i.e., the female deer], Acaxoch [i.e., the deer]. For him, since yesterday and even the day before [i.e., for some time], my older sister, Xochiquetzal [i.e., my wife], has been crying, because of him she has been sad. For him since yesterday and even the day before I have been crying, because of him I have been sad.

Mā tlaōcoya in amoyōlloh in amihtic oncah, in anTlāloqueh.[58] Ye ōnehcōc[59] in Tōllān, in teohtlālpan. Ye nicān īchān, ye nicān īcalihtic in tlamacazqui, in Chicōme-Xōchitl, in nohuēltīuh, in Mixcōācihuātl, in Ācaxōch. In yālhua ye huīptla īca chōca, īca nēntlamati in nohuēltīuh, in Xōchiquetzal. In yālhua ye huīptla īca nichōca, īca ninēntlamati.

[13] It has already arrived at the point where I come to catch her, by calling her. Already I have made and rigged for them an entrance and door for their muzzles and heads, through where they may enter by herds, for through there they are to go, through there my sheep, whose mother and father, grandfather and grandmother I am, are to pass.

ye aman niquīmanaco, niquīnotzaco yeonicchìchiuh onicyoliti yntĕnan quiahuatl yn quauhquiahuatl yntollan òtli, yn on can yazque yn oncan quicazq̃ yn no ychcahuan ỹ ni ỹ nan ỹ ni yntâ, ynni yncîyn ni yncol.

Already at this instant I have come to seize them,[60] I have come to call them. Already I have created, have brought to life the wall-doorway, the wood-doorway, the road to Tollan [i.e., the snare], through where my sheep [i.e., the deer] will go, from where they will come out, for I am their mother, I am their father, I am their grandmother, I am their grandfather.

Ye āman niquimānaco, niquinnōtzaco. Ye ōnicchihchīuh, ōnicyōlītih in tenānquiāhuatl in cuauhquiāhuatl, in Tōllān ohtli, in oncān yāzqueh, in oncān quīzazqueh in nochcahuān, in nīnnān, in nīntah, in nīncih, in nīncōl.

[14] Let it in no way happen that they go through another place. Already I see them come through here. Let them come through here, let them pass through here. Here their only leader and governor, the spirit,[61] Lord God of the earth,[62] will find his blanket of roses and his necklace of them [i.e., of roses].

Manepa yaz necti nican huitz nican yaz nican quiçaz nican quicuiz yni xochiàpan yni xochicozqui ynin tla ce ya canal yntlamacazqui teotlalhua

Let him beware of wanting to go over there. It is here that he is coming. It is here that he will go. It is here that he will leave. It is here that their totally-guided-one, the priest, Desert-owner [i.e., the male deer], will get his flower-mantle, his flower-necklace [i.e., the noose of the snare].

Mā nēpa yāznecti.[63] Nicān huītz. Nicān yāz. Nicān quīzaz. Nicān quicuiz in īxōchiahpān, in īxōchicōzqui, in īntlacenyacānal,[64] in tlamacazqui, Teohtlālhuah.

[15] Here my sisters will dress him in it and will put it on him,[65] the goddesses, worthy of esteem {the nets} stand guard on the royal and much traveled road that never ends and which dust {for desire}[66] never covers, where they may walk at night or during the day.

nican macoz nican conaquiltizque ynnohueltihuan yntlaçòtēteo nicã quipixtimani yntollan òtli, yn àquenman cahui yn àquēman teuh yohuâ yz cemilhuitl yz ceyohual yntŏcô.

Here he will be given it. Here my older sisters, Beloved-goddesses [i.e., the hands], will cause him to put it on. Here they will be guarding the road to Tollan [i.e., the snare], which at no time becomes abandoned, which at no time is covered with dust, which all day and all night is followed.

Nicān macōz. Nicān conaquīltīzqueh in nohuēltīhuān, in Tlazohtēteoh. Nicān quipixtimanih in Tōllān ohtli, in ahquēmman cāhui, in ahquēmman teuhyōhua,[67] in cemilhuitl, in cenyohual in toco.[68]

[16] And you, my sister, snake[69] {to the ropes}, female that performs the office of a woman, what do you feel about this? Here you will be established in a sure place, as in our house and abode, for we are slaves, and we work for others {Because he must offer the head, the heart, and the blood of the game [killed].}. Here you will amuse yourself. Here you will take pleasure, for soon you will turn around, and one with another like one who embraces himself you will become entangled with the stake and the branches[70] {with which it is rigged and covered}, for already I have constructed you, already I have given you being, and I have finished you perfectly.

Tlaxihuiqui nohueltiuh cihuacoatl cihua tequihua tlè ticmati yè tehuatiez nican tochan nican tocalìtic titétlácahuan titétlayecoltìcahuan. Nican tipáquiz nican tàhahuiaz yenican timòhuimolloz ynehuan timoquechnāhuaz (q.n. quechnahuàtequiz) yntlamacazqui ce atl ytonal yhuan y xoxōuhq̃ tlamacazqui, yeonimitzchìchiuh yeonimitzyoliti yeonimitztlāca tlamili.

Come, my older sister, Cihuacoatl, the female warrior [i.e., the rope]. What do you know? [I.e., Pay attention!] Soon you will be sitting here in our home, here inside the house of us slaves, of us servants [i.e., of us human beings]. Here you will be happy, here you will have pleasure. Soon here you will join perilously with the priest, His *tonal* Is One Water [i.e., the stakes], and Green Priest [i.e., the branches], and you [sg] will hug (which means that you will embrace) him. Already I have made you. Already I have given you life. Already I have perfected you.

Tlā xihuiqui, nohuēltīuh, Cihuācōātl, cihuātequihuah. Tleh ticmati? Ye tēhuatiyez nicān tochān, nicān tocalihtic titētlācahuān, titētētlayecōltihcāhuān.[71] Nicān tipāquiz, nicān tahāhuiyaz. Ye nicān [īhuān] timohhuimōlōz,[72] īhuān[73] timoquechnāhuāz (quihtōznequi [timo]quechnāhuahtequiz)[74] in tlamacazqui, Cē-Ātl Ītōnal, īhuān in Xoxōuhqui Tlamacazqui. Ye ōnimitzchihchīuh. Ye ōnimitzyōlītih. Ye ōnimitztlācatlamilih.

[17] Help, you, also, my sister {For the hand.} and the five solar beings {For the fingers

Tla xihuiqui nohueltiuh macuiltonelleque,[77] tlàçotéteo tlanican xonmani-

with which they count the five days.[75]}; and you, lesser gods and goddesses,[76] attend to this work, for it will not last, nor will it be greatly protracted, for already the possessed one or foreigner comes, the one who inhabits the land of the gods. Immediately you will encounter him there, and you will rise up to meet him, and you will throw over him this garment of thin or enchanted ribbons {for the woven net}, your festival garment, because when he arrives here, he will not bring sight, and he will come foolishly, here will be your pleasure and joy.

can, yehuitz yntlamacazqui ynteotlālhua nimã nechca anconnamiquizque anconnamictehuazque anconaquiltizque an motlaxochhuipil yn anmotlaihuitzanal ỹ nicã ècoz cuix oc ytztihuitz? cuix oc tlachixtihuitz? nican anpáquizque amàhahuiazque.

Come, my older sister. Five-*tonal*s-owners, Beloved-goddesses [i.e., the hands], settle down here. Already the priest, Desert-owner [i.e., the male deer], is coming. Immediately you will meet him there; you will quickly meet him. You will dress him in your *huipil* of ribbons, your holiday-fabric [i.e., the net]. When he arrives here, will he still come seeing? Will he still come looking? [i.e., No, he will not see the snare.] Here is where you [pl] will be happy, you will be joyful.

Tlā xihuiqui, nohuēltīuh. Mācuīltōnalehqueh, Tlazohtēteoh,[78] tlā nicān xonmanicān. Ye huītz in tlamacazqui, in Teohtlālhuah. Niman nechca anconnāmiquizqueh; anconnāmictēhuazqueh. Anconaquīltīzqueh amotlaxōchhuīpīl, in amotlailhuitzāhual.[79] In nicān ehcōz, cuix oc itztihuītz? Cuix oc tlachixtihuītz? Nicān ampāquizqueh, amahāhuiyazqueh.

It then says on the paper: *Otlamic: Nauhcanpa toyohuaz. Tic yehecoz*,[80] which means, "Having finished the spell, you will shout toward the four winds energetically," as is explained in what follows.

With this, the incantation and spell of the net and snares ends, and then the Devil ordered him to call the deer—shouting and howling toward the four winds, imitating a wild beast—and for him to do this very well. And then he starts the incantation to the deer in the form of an argument as follows:

[18] Possessed one or foreigner, he of the seven roses, dweller of the forests, your fight is over. Suddenly night has caught you. He of the seven Roses,[81] what has become of him? Did he run, or did he suffer adverse fortune? Ha ha ha {laughter}! They caught him in the net. With this, his fight is over.

Tlamacazqui chicomexochitl teotlalhua ye yuhqui otitetlani huac yohualli, cayn xochitl cācâ, caopatōloc, ho, ho, tlamaloc ye yuhqui.

Priest, Seven Flower, Desert-owner [i.e., the male deer], it is already over with. You have been dispatched [i.e., sent as a messenger to the gods].[82] It is night.[83] Where is [Seven]-Flower? Where is he? A game of fortune has been played. Ha ha! People have captured things [i.e., a captive has been taken]. It is already over with.

Tlamacazqui, Chicōme-Xōchitl, Teohtlālhuah, ye iuhqui. Ōtitītlanīhuac. Yohualli. Cān in [Chicōme]-Xōchitl?[84] Cān cah? Ca ōpatōlōc. Ho ho! Tlamalōc. Ye iuhqui.[85]

Then it says *toyohuaz*,[86] which means, "he will shout many times like a wild beast."

Immediately after this speech, the Devil's rule commands him to shout and howl again, as stated above. And quieting down because of waiting for the game, he makes a speech, recapitulating almost all of the incantation and adding a few words as follows:

[19] Be alert, my sister, female snake {he speaks to the ropes}, you who work like a woman {because it works while being still}. Do not become distracted, for I have already put you together. I have already formed you. I have already finished you perfectly. Here will be your joys, here your pleasures, here your happiness. Here with care you will attend to the entrance and gateway and royal road of the one who is presently coming and is to enter through here, the possessed one of the seven roses {for the deer}, dweller of the land of the gods. Here the possessed one, the dweller of the forests, is to put on and don his showy garb and his necklace of roses.

Tlaxihuiqui nohueltiuh cihuacoatl cihuatequihua, tlè ticmati yconimitzchìchiuh yc onimitzyoliti yc onimitztlácatlamili. nican tipaquiz nican tàhahuiaz nicã tihuellamatiz. Ye nican ticpixtiez yntĕnanquiāhuatl yn quăuhquiāhuatl, yn tollan òtli, nizhuitz nican quiçaz yn tlamacazqui chicome xochitl yn teotlalhuâ, ye nican quicuiz yn yxochiàpan yn ixochicozqui yn tlamacazqui ynteotlalhua.

Come, my older sister, Cihuacoatl, woman-warrior [i.e., the rope]. What do you know? [I.e., Pay attention!] For this purpose I have made you. For this purpose I have given you life. For this purpose I have perfected you. Here you will be happy. Here you will have fun. Here you will be contented. Soon here you will be guarding the wall-doorway, the wood-doorway, the road to Tollan [i.e., the snare]. Here is where the priest, Seven Flower, Desert-owner [i.e., the male deer], is coming; through here is where he will leave. Soon here the priest, Desert-owner, will get his flower-mantle, his flower-necklace [i.e., the noose].

Tlā xihuiqui, nohuēltīuh, Cihuācōātl, cihuātequihuah. Tleh ticmati? Īc ōnimitzchihchīuh. Īc ōnimitzyōlītih. Īc ōnimitztlācatlamilih. Nicān tipāquiz. Nicān tahāhuiyaz. Nicān tihuellamatiz. Ye nicān ticpixtiyez in tenānquiāhuatl, in cuauhquiāhuatl, in Tōllān ohtli. Niz huītz; nicān quīzaz in tlamacazqui, Chicōme-Xōchitl, in Teohtlālhuah. Ye nicān quicuiz in īxōchiahpān, in īxōchicōzqui in tlamacazqui, in Teohtlālhuah.

[20] Hail, sister, female snake {for the snare}, you who work like a woman {to the ropes}, do not let it act up on you and do not ruin or spoil this work out of impatience. Also do not let it happen that you fail because of fear, and for this reason do not pay attention to the faces and heads[87] of the possessed one, the dweller of the forests, whose fat meat delights the snake that has the face of a puma.

Nohueltiuh cihuacoatl cihuatequihua mate tihuexcapehuaz necti, ma tihuexcatlatlacoznecti; ma timomauhti, mayxco ma ycpac titlachiaznecti yn tlamacazqui teotlalhua y nacaxoch mixoacihuatl.

My older sister, Cihuacoatl, woman-warrior [i.e., the rope], you be the one to beware of wanting to begin in ill humor. Beware of wanting to spoil things in ill humor. Beware of being afraid. Beware of wanting to look at the face, at the head-top [i.e., the physical presence] of the priest, Desert-owner [i.e., the male deer], Acaxoch [i.e., the deer], Mixcoacihuatl [i.e., the female deer] [i.e., beware of frightening him off by being too obvious *or* beware of looking at him and becoming flustered].

Nohuēltīuh, Cihuācōātl, cihuātequihuah, mā teh tihuēxcāpēhuaznecti.[88] Mā tihuēxcātlahtlacōznecti. Mā timomauhtih. Mā īīxco, mā īcpac titlachiaznecti in tlamacazqui, Teohtlālhuah, in Ācaxōch, Mixcōācihuātl.

[21] Gods who inhabit and dwell in the four parts of the world, with your pleasure and consent I have come and arrived at this place, I who am one of the gods and an orphan. Already I have walked and passed my field of irrigated land and my fertile hills full of bracelets {for the beauty of the countryside}. Along its sides and slopes I have come little by little with great effort, since I am one of the Gods, a son and creation of theirs.

Ynantlamacazque ỹ nauhcāpa amonoque ỹ nahuianpa yn ancate an mixpan an momatian ynonihualla ynonècoc yn nitlamacazqui ỹ niyc nopiltzintli niceteotl yeonicnemili yn nāmil ỹ nochiauhtepec ỹ nomáquiztetepe ynin mitzcac ỹ moopochcopa ynonihuallàtia ninotolinia ỹ ni ce teotl teteo niypiltzin téteo niytlaca chihual.

You who are priests who lie facing the four directions, you who are toward the four directions, it is before your eyes, before your knowing-place [i.e., into your perceiving presence] that I, who am the priest, Icnopiltzintli, Centeotl, have come, that I have arrived. I have walked over my irrigated fields, which are my turquoise mountains, my braceletlike mountains, on whose left side I went along coming. I, who am Centeotl, I, who am the child of the gods, I, who am the creation of the gods, suffer poverty.

In antlamacazqueh in nāuhcāmpa amonoqueh, in nāuhcāmpa[89] in ancateh, amīxpan amotlamatiyān in ōnihuāllah in ōnehcōc in nitlamacazqui in nIcnōpiltzintli, niCenteōtl. Ye ōnicnemilih in nāmīl, in noxiuhtepēhuān,[90] in nomāquīztepēhuān[91] in īmītzcac in īmopōchcopa[92] in ōnihuāllahtiyah. Ninotolīnia in niCenteōtl, tēteoh nīmpiltzin, tēteoh nīntlachīhual.[93]

[22] Come on, come to my aid, my mother and my father, the earth[94] and the water and the starry sky, and my father, the one of the rays {to the sun}, God, you who were formerly loathsome and [now] seem produced of emeralds. My sister, the one twisted in one direction {for the grassy place},[95] and the trees, all of you, keep my secret. Let no one make it known nor say it to the possessed one of the seven roses {to the deer}, who lives in the forests. Already he is coming; presently he will arrive here. With that you will have fun and you will be happy. Here is where you are to hold him and to catch him.

Tla xihuiqui, nonan tlaltecuintli, notâ ce tochtli tezcatl cahuālpopócatimani, nonan citlalcueye, notâ totonametli tlamacazqui nánáhuatzin, xiuhpiltzintli. Nohueltiuh cenmalinalli, tlamacazqui ceatl ytonal Ayac quilhuiz, ayac quinonotzaz yn tlamacazqui chicome xochitl ynteo tlalhua, yehuitz yehuallaz nican ỹ câ anpáquizque anmàhahuiazque, nican anquitzitzquizque ancanazque.

Come, my mother, Tlaltecuin, my father, One Rabbit, Mirror that just lies smoking hither [i.e., the earth], my mother, Citlalcueyeh [i.e., the Milky Way], my father, Tohtonametl, priest, Nanahuatzin, Xiuhpiltzintli [i.e., the fire], my older sister, One-grass [i.e., the rope], priest, His-*tonal* Is One Water [i.e., the stakes]. No one will speak of it to the priest, Seven Flower, Desert-owner [i.e., the male deer]; no one will warn him. Already he is coming. Soon he will come. Here is the place where you [pl] will be happy, you will be content. Here you will grasp him; here you will seize him.

Tlā xihuiquih, nonān, Tlāltecuīn,[96] notah, Cē-Tōchtli, Tezcatl [in][97] zan huālpopōcatimani, nonān, Cītlalcuēyeh, notah, Tohtōnamētl, tlamacazqui, Nānāhuatzin, Xiuhpiltzintli, nohuēltīuh, Cemmalīnalli, tlamacazqui, Cē-Ātl Ītōnal. Ayāc quilhuīz; ayāc quinōnōtzaz in tlamacazqui, Chicōme-Xōchitl, in Teohtlālhuah. Ye huītz. Ye huāllāz. Nicān in cān ampāquizqueh, amahāhuiyazqueh. Nicān anquitzītzquīzqueh; ancānazqueh.

Then he continues or ends by shouting toward the four parts of the world, as has been said, pronouncing the word *tahui* four times,[98] with which the Devil has made these people understand that the deer will come at their call so blindly that they will enter the nets as quickly as they would enter the waters after having been wounded. And how much more blind are they who believe in such illusions! And how fully without contemplation do they use and praise them! May Our Lord, through his infinite compassion, enlighten them in such blindness.

CHAPTER 9

About the Superstition of the Bowmen and the Incantations That They Use

THOSE who habitually hunt with bow and arrow also have their incantations and spells to which they entrust their good fortune, both in finding game and in killing it after having found it. In view of this they need an incantation for the one and for the other, and thus part of the incantation is directed toward and intended for the bow and arrows, and the other part toward the deer, which are the game that they usually seek. The incantation is as follows:

[1] Already I am leaving, I the orphan, the one god, and I carry the bow,[1] the bow and its arrows, which my mother, the goddess *Tōnacācihuatl* {Ceres}, and the one called *Xochiquetzal* {Venus} made and devised.[2] And on the arrow there goes inserted and adapted a point of wide flint, which I am also to carry, and with this I come to catch and I am to carry my father, the one of the seven roses, a noble and a lord, for my mother, the goddess Xochiquetzal {Venus}, is awaiting him. I come to look for him wherever he may be, whether it be in the ravines or on the slopes, or whether he walks on the hillocks. I have come to look for the noble and the *principal*[3] of the seven roses, and no less the one who is delicious or enchanted meat. I am to carry it to the goddess Snake.

Yenonehua nèhuatl niycnópiltzintli nicenteotl yenichuica ceatl ytonal yèhuatl yhuan y ācayo yno qui chìchiuh ỹ nonan *tōnacácihuatl xochiq̃tzal* cihuatl ompa ỳcatiuh *ytzpāpálotl* yequenè nichuicaz notâ chicome xochitl piltzin teuctli, nicanaco, nichuicaz, yequi chixcācâ nonan xochiquetzal nictemoco canin comolihuic tepeiecatl campa teliuhqui qui to catinemi Piltzin tecutli chico me xochitl nictemoco can man ihuan nic temoco Miz co aci uatl inacaxotzin nichuicaz.

Already I am departing, I who am Icnopiltzintli, Centeotl. Already I am carrying His-*tonal* Is One Water [i.e., the bow]. It is he [i.e., the bow] and his reed [i.e., the arrow shaft] that my mother, Tonacacihuatl, Xochiquetzal [i.e., my wife], who is a woman, made. Itzpapalotl [i.e., the arrowhead] goes standing there [i.e., I have Itzpapalotl with me].[4] At last I will carry my father, Seven Flower, Piltzinteuctli [i.e., the male deer]. I have come to seize him. I will carry him. Already my mother, Xochiquetzal [i.e., my wife], is waiting

Ye nonēhua nehhuātl, nIcnōpiltzintli, niCenteōtl. Ye nichuīca Cē-Ātl Ītōnal. Yehhuātl īhuān īācayo in ōquichihchīuh in nonān, Tōnacācihuātl, Xōchiquetzal, cihuātl.[5] Ōmpa ihcatiuh Ītzpāpālōtl. Yēquen eh nichuīcaz notah, Chicōme-Xōchitl, Piltzintēuctli. Nicānaco. Nichuīcaz. Ye quichixcācah nonān, Xōchiquetzal. Nictēmōco cān in comōlihuic tepēyacatl, cāmpa teliuhqui quitocatinemi. Piltzintēuctli, Chicōme-Xōchitl, nictēmō-

for him. I have come to seek him in the place where the mountain spur is ravine-filled, in the place where he goes following the rough terrain. It is Piltzinteuctli, Seven Flower, whom I have come to seek wherever he may be. And with it I have come to seek Mixcoacihuatl [i.e., the female deer], Acaxoch (H) [i.e., the deer]. I will carry him.

co cān mani. Īhuān nictēmōco Mixcōācihuātl, in Ācaxōchtzin. Nichuīcaz.

If with this they did not see [a deer] they are ordered yoyohuaz coyotzatziz quitoz *that he bellow a lot and say* tahui *or* Mixcoacihuatl,[6] *vsia fra.*[7]

They state that the deer obey this incantation without any objection and that they not only show themselves but wait for the shot, which is also on target, and it does not miss by virtue of the incantation made to the bow and arrow.

But in case the game is somewhat slow in appearing, he follows the sequence of the incantation, bellowing four times toward the four parts of the world, repeating an equal number of times that barbaric word *Tahui,*[8] thus rounding up the deer in order that it will stop, commanding it to return and to await him. And if it is a female, he changes the name of *Tahui, Tahui* to another, which is *Mixcoacihuatl,* and says to it, "Turn toward me," *xi hual mi lacatzo.*[9] This spell and incantation was used by, among others, a certain Augustin Jacobo, of the district of Hoapan. And he used to state that with it he infallibly found game and killed it, although after having trained with a certain Baltazar Hernandez, a Spaniard, a great sharpshooter and huntsman, and in this kind [of hunting] the most famous of New Spain, Augustin Jacobo used to say that he did not need any incantation.

Augustin Jacobo having come into my hands, I commanded him not to use such incantations, giving him to understand that they included a pact with the Devil. He promised to quit, but as time went by, it was necessary for him to hide out away from populated places because of other crimes that he had committed—because seldom do such people abstain from other equal or greater sins, according to what the Orator said: *nonpotest ea natura quae tantum façinus semel admi serit, eo,* only this one satisfies, *necese est semper aliquid huius modi moliatur,*[10] and thus it happened in [the case of] this Augustin Jacobo. And having withdrawn from populated places to the forests, he went back to continuing his depraved custom of his incantations, as he ultimately confessed—having been arrested for those other crimes—in my presence and in that of the Licentiate Juan Gonzalez del Cotero, a *beneficiado* who is at present of the said district of Hoapan.

This case shows well the little constancy of these miserable people and the great vigilance that their ministers must exercise and the care that they are to take in order to banish such infernal superstitions, because it is not enough to explain to them the disguised poison that these superstitions bring with themselves, nor to arrest them and punish them for them, but it is furthermore necessary [to exercise] a perpetual vigilance, and, as the saying goes, to be ever alert.

CHAPTER 10

About the Incantations and Words That They Use to Hunt Animals of Other Kinds

ALTHOUGH those who are entangled in these superstitions use different incantations for each different kind of bird and animal that they attempt to hunt, nevertheless, I shall not put them down, because they differ only in the names of the animals or birds, because the tenor of all the said incantations is almost one and the same, and the one presented here will suffice to give information about the style of all. The order that they have is, first, to get ready with fire and copal, which is the incense of this land, and with the instruments proper to the kind of game they have in mind. And with this they go to the place proper to that kind of bird or animal, and having arrived at it, they say:

[1] I myself in person, the warrior, who come sent by the gods, come to seek my uncles, the possessed ones stained with ink {wild pigs}, whom immediately I am to find, for it is not to be put off until tomorrow or until the day after tomorrow. Here I bring my enchanted mirror {this probably stands for the water}, whose surface smokes, and also I bring the five solar beings that look toward a single direction, which are to intercept and prevent the flight of my uncles, the possessed ones stained with ink {enchanted pigs}.

Nomatca nehual, niyaotl niititlan, Niicahuan, nican niquin temos in no tlahuan tlamacazque tlilpotonqui niman axcan niquimittaz, àmo quinmoztla àmo quinhuiptla nican nichualhuicac nonahualtezcauh inixcehual popocatimani. yhuan niquinmonhuica in macuiltonallèque cemithuallèque quimontzatzauctiazq^{+} in motlahuan tlamacazque tlilpotonque.

It is I in person. I am Yaotl. I am his messenger, his celebrity.[1] I am here searching for my uncles,[2] the priests, the black-stinkers[3] [i.e., the peccaries]. Right away I will see them, not by-and-by tomorrow, not by-and-by the day after tomorrow. I have brought here my *nahualli*-mirror whose surface just lies smoking hither [i.e., magic earth], and along with it I am bringing Five-*tonal*s-owners, One-courtyard-owners [i.e., the hands]. They will go blocking the way of my uncles, the priests, the black-stinkers.

Nohmatca nehhuātl. NiYāōtl. Nītītlan, nīcahuān. Nicān niquintēmoa[4] in notlahhuān, tlamacazqueh, tlīlpotōnqueh. Niman āxcān niquimittaz, ahmō quin mōztla, ahmō quin huīptla. Nicān nichuālhuīcac nonāhualtezcauh in īīx zan[5] huālpopōcatimani, īhuān niquimonhuīca in Mācuīltōnalehqueh, Cemithualehqueh. Quimontzahtzauctiyāzqueh in notlahhuān, tlamacazqueh, tlīlpotōnqueh.

Of this tenor are all the incantations which they use when hunting, with dogs, all kinds of animals, that differ only in the names; for instance, pigs are called "possessed ones stained with ink," *tlamacazque tlilpotonque*;[6] others are called "dusky possessed oncs," *tlamacazque yayauhque*;[7] or "yellow ones," *tlamacazq^{+} cococauhq^{+}*.[8] These same people who hunt with dogs, as if for an occupation, also come to the defense of the sown fields and the orchards, in order that the large number of animals that abound in this land not graze on them and destroy them, for which they use the incantation [given in the next chapter].[9]

CHAPTER 11

Incantation and Spell in Order That Animals Not Eat or Do Damage to the Sown Fields

For this purpose, they get ready with fire and incense, and as soon as they arrive at the edges of the sown fields, first of all they remove the broken stalks or mangled ears of corn or spikes of grain or fallen fruit which such animals have damaged or begun to eat, and then, burning his incense as if for an offering to the one from whom succour and help is requested, he begins by saying:

[1] I myself in person, the wizard jaguar, have come to look for my uncles, the possessed ones, the yellow possessed ones, the dusky possessed ones. What am I saying? For already here is the trail. They came through here. They entered through here. They left through here.

nomatca nèhuatl ninahualocelotl onihualla niquimittaz notlahuan tlamacazque cocauhque tlamacazque, yayauhque tlamacazque. tlaca nican ohuallaque tlaca nican ocallaque ye no nican quizque

It is I in person. I am *Nahualli*-jaguar. I have come to see my uncles, the priests, the yellow priests, the dusky priests [i.e., the destructive animals]. But wait! They have come here! But wait! They have entered here! They have also already left through here!

Nohmatca nehhuātl. NiNāhualocēlōtl. Ōnihuāllah niquimittaz notlahhuān, tlamacazqueh, cōzauhqueh tlamacazqueh, yāyāuhqueh tlamacazqueh. Tlacah! Nicān ōhuāllahqueh. Tlacah! Nicān ōcalacqueh. Ye nō nicān quīzqueh.

[2] Well, already I have come to chase them and drive them away, and no longer are they to do any more damage here, for I command them to go and to dwell very far from here, for already I bring the white and dusky[1] and yellow incense, with whose power I intercept them, and I prevent those uncles of mine, the possessed ones or the foreigners, the dusky or yellow possessed ones, from being able to pass.

nican nihualla niquintotocaz aocmo nican tlaquazq^{+}. Hueca niquintitlani hueca nemizq^{+}, nican nichualhuica in iztac copalli, coçauhqui copalli, ic niquintlacuiliz in notlahuan tlamacazq^{+}, cocauhque tlamacazque yayauhque tlamacazque.

I have come here to pursue them. No longer will they eat here. I am sending them far away. They will dwell far away. I am bringing here the white copal, the yellow copal. With it I will take things away from my uncles, the priests, the yellow priests, the dusky priests [i.e., I will prevent them from entering the field].

Nicān nihuāllah niquintohtocaz. Ahocmō nicān tlacuāzqueh. Huehca niquintītlani. Huehca nemizqueh. Nicān nichuālhuīca in iztāc copalli, cōzauhqui copalli. Īc niquintlacuīlīz in notlahhuān, tlamacazqueh, cōzauhqueh tlamacazqueh, yāyāuhqueh tlamacazqueh.

With this they continue their burning of incense and to the above words some add:

[3] My father, the four reeds that give off flames.[2]

Nota nahui acatl milintica.

He is my father, Four Reed, He-is-scintillating [i.e., the fire].

Notah, Nāhui-Ācatl, Milīnticah.

With which they let it be understood that they are invoking the fire and that it is to help them in that task.

CHAPTER 12

An Invocation That They Use Against Coatis in Order That They Not Come Around or Eat the Sown Fields

HAVING carried incense and *piçiete* with them, as soon as they have arrived at the sown field, they go around it all, as if they were erecting a fence or wall. Then they pick up and take away from it all that the coatis have ruined, because, they say, this will attract them again and will keep the door open for them to enter the sown field again. After they have taken away what was ruined, the incantation begins:

[1] Come on, you my sister, the woman bred in the mountain, what are the possessed ones, the owners of the caves,[1] doing? Or why are they damaging this unfortunate sown field,[2] for already they are finishing it off. Back! Let them go through those wide valleys. There they will find the *jicamilla*[3] and the *camotillo*,[4] the food and drink with which old and young will nourish themselves. With this, let none appear here. Let none remain here, because the gods of the earth[5] will be guarding. The green deity, the white one, and the yellow one are to be guards. Because of that, let them look out for themselves, because the one who falls will not have anyone to complain about.

Tlacuele nohueltiuh tepetlauhca cihuatl tlencaitia tlamacazq+ tlalloca teuctli itzicamil ye contlamilia tla nechca huicoa teo ixtlahuacan nepantla onpan catqui intlacimatl in tlanelhuatl in ihualoni quicenca huaz in illamatzin in huehuentzin Ayac nican neciz ayac nican mocahuaz quipiazque intlamacazque xoxohuic tlallocan, iztac tlallocan coçahuic tlallocan quipiezque, aquic nican temac huetziz çan teyollo tlama yehuan quimati.

Let it be soon, my older sister, Woman-from-Tepetlauhco [i.e., the magic earth for a magic barrier]! What is it that the priests [i.e., the coatis] are doing to Tlalocateuctli's antfield [i.e., the client's garden]? Already they are consuming it to his harm. Let them be carried there to the middle of the dangerous plains. It is there that the small *cimate*[6] is, the root that is drinkable; it will refresh Old-woman and Old-man. No one will appear here; no one will stop off here. The priests from Green Tlalocan, from White Tlalocan, from Yellow Tlalocan will guard it. They will guard it. He who falls here into someone's hands [does so] just voluntarily [i.e., it is his own fault]. They know it [i.e., They have been warned].

Tlā cuēl eh, nohuēltīuh, Tepētlāuhcacihuātl![7] Tleh in cāītiah[8] tlamacazqueh Tlālocātēuctli ītzīcamīl? Ye contlamiliah.[9] Tlā nechca huīcōcān[10] teohixtlāhuacān nepantlah. Ōmpa in catqui in tlālcimatl, in tlanelhuatl in īhualōni; quincencāhuaz[11] in Ilamatzin in Huēhuēntzin. Ayāc nicān nēciz; ayāc nicān mocāhuaz. Quipiazqueh in tlamacazqueh Xoxōhuic Tlālocān, Iztāc Tlālocān, Cōzahuic Tlālocān. Quipiezqueh. Āc in[12] nicān tēmac huetziz, zan teyollo tlamah. Yehhuān quimatih.

His fate is in his own hands as we put it; and in Latin *sibi imputet.*[13]

CHAPTER 13

Against Ants

In another Treatise[1] I mentioned a certain Martin de Luna, a native of Temimiltzinco, in the Amilpas, who was one hundred and ten years old, and was held in high repute and to be of consummate wisdom among the Indians. I think that he had gained this reputation with these infernal spells, as will be seen in this and in other Treatises, where I will quote him for his evil skills. He used to use the preceding incantation or exorcism against coatis and the one that follows against ants. I came to know the latter from Captain Pedro de Ochoa, an inhabitant of the Amilpas. After I had gotten my hands on the incantation and on Martin de Luna, who was arrested on account of this superstition, he denied it, even though it was proved against him, and he had on other occasions fallen into prison for these causes and had been convicted for similar superstitions. Even so, this time, arrested and convicted, he denied it stubbornly, until I began his wicked and superstitious incantation, which is:

[1] Come on now, uncles, possessed ones or foreigners, for you are all similar one to another,[2] with your veiled {or wizard-owned} eyes or faces, and with teeth like sharp points. Why are you doing harm to your sister, the white woman {the sown field}, and [why] have you lost respect for her? Is that sweeping her? Is that cleaning her? And weeding her? Is that honoring her and respecting her? If you do not do it, I will tear down your dwelling and lodgings if you do not obey me.

Tlacuel tlatlahuane tlamacazque, puputecatle, nahual ixeque, nahual itztlameque tle ancaítia in ammohueltiuh iztac cihuatl in ixco in icpac annemi cuix anquitlacuicuilizq+, cuix anquitlachpanizq+, anquimahuiztilizq+, intlacamo anquihuicazq nicxitiniz inic ancate, intlacamo annechtlacamatizq+.

Let it be soon! Oh my various uncles, priests, oh people from Popotlan,[3] *Nahualli*-eyes-owners, *Nahualli*-obsidian-teeth-owners [i.e., the ants], what are you doing to your older sister, White Woman [i.e., the sown field], before whose face, before whose head-top [i.e., in whose presence] you live? Will you tidy up the floor for her? Will you sweep for her, will you respect her? If you will not accompany her [i.e., do her honor], I will tear down that by means of which you are [i.e., the ant hill]. If you do not obey me [you will regret it].[4]

Tlā cuēl! Notlahtlahhuāné, tlamacazqueh, Popōtēcatlé,[5] Nāhualīxehqueh, Nāhualītztlanehqueh, tleh ancāītiah[6] in amohuēltīuh, Iztāc-Cihuātl, in īīxco in īcpac annemih? Cuix anquitlacuihcuīlīzqueh? Cuix anquitlachpānīzqueh, anquimahuiztilīzqueh? In tlācamō anquihuīcazqueh, nicxitīnīz in īc ancateh. In tlācamō annēchtlācamatizqueh.

With this he claimed that the ants would not again do harm to the grove or sown field. But if at times they overstepped, not showing they had understood, in that case he carried out his threat, going ahead with the destruction of their house, which he also did by conjuring a certain quantity of water and throwing it on the anthill and sprinkling the outer edge and circumference of the anthill with his so-venerated *pisiete*. And in order to conjure the water he used the following words:

[2] Come on now, the one of the skirts of precious stones, for what the ones similar among themselves {the ants} do cannot be tolerated. Go lay waste to them, for they do not obey me. Do they perchance have roots? Well, even if they had them, you know well how to pull up trees and carry them instantly and leave them in the midst of wide or uncultivated plains! [I am amazed] that you {suple[7]} ants persist! Do you perchance have roots?

Tlacuel chalchiuhcueye tlein ay in puputecatl Tlaxiquinpopoloti àmo nechtlacamati cuix nelhuayo ticate, ye quahuitl tichuica, tictlalochtitiquiça, in hueca ixtlahuacan, teo ixtlahuacan nepantla toconxica Cuix annelhuayoticate.

Let it be soon! Chalchiuhcueyeh [i.e., water], what is it that the people from Popotlan [i.e., the ants] are doing? Go in order to destroy them. They do not obey me. Are they perhaps rooted? You [sg] already carry trees [i.e., If they are indeed rooted, that should be no problem for you, Water, since you have the power to uproot and wash away trees]; you quickly rush them away to the far-off plains; in the middle of the dangerous plains you go to abandon them. Are you [pl] perhaps rooted?[8]

Tlā cuēl! Chālchiuhcuēyeh, tleh in āi in Popōtēcatl? Tlā xiquimpohpolōti. Ahmō nēchtlācamatih. Cuix nelhuayohticateh? Ye cuahuitl tichuīca; tictlalōchtihtiquīza in huehca ixtlāhuacān; teohixtlāhuacān nepantlah toconxiccāhua.[9] Cuix annelhuayohticateh?[10]

Having made this incantation, he used to pour one or two pitchers of conjured water into the mouth and entrance of the anthill where earlier he had spread his venerated *pisiete*. And with this he claimed that either the anthill would totally collapse or the ants would move their dwelling very far from there. For an infallible effect (in his judgment) he conjures the *piçiete* also, saying:

[3] Come on now, green possessed one of wide leaves. What persistence is this? Go immediately. Throw out and run off the ants from where they are.

Tlacuel xoxouhqui tlamacazqui, xiuhpapatlantzin tleaxtica? tlaxocon totocati in puputecatl.

Let it be soon! Green Priest, Turquoise-flutterer [i.e., tobacco], what is he doing? Go in order to pursue the person from Popotlan [i.e., the ant (sg for pl)].

Tlā cuēl! Xoxōuhqui Tlamacazqui, Xiuhpahpatlāntzin, tleh āxticah? Tlā xocontohtocati in Popōtēcatl.

CHAPTER 14

About the Spell and Incantation That the Fish-Trap Fishermen Use

I HAVE already said elsewhere how these wretched people use these diabolical incantations in almost every profession they exercise. But much more so in those whose good profit seems to depend on luck or, as others say, on chance. And one of these is fishing. Those who practice it with fish traps enter their blind superstition from the first step they take for this purpose, which is when they go to cut the cane from which they are to form the fish trap, which in their language they call *Pitzotl*, which means "pig," because of the similarity to the shape of the body. They also call it *chiquiuitl*,[1] which means "large basket,"[2] which it also resembles. In order to cut the cane they say:

[1] Come on, come quickly, green Devil, for I have come for you. And for this purpose I bring the five solar beings,[3] whose ends terminate in shells. They are as if they do not have blood or color.

Tla xicihui xoxouhqui tzitzimitl, ca nimitzanaco, oniquinhualhuicac in macuiltonaleq^{+}, cuexcochepyoque. Cuix ezcoque, cuix tlapallo que.

Hurry, Green Air-spirit [i.e., the cane]. I have come to capture you. I have brought here Five-*tonal*s-owners [i.e., the hands] and Owners-of-nacre-at-the-occiput [i.e., the fingers]. Do they have blood? Do they have color? [i.e., No! They are supernatural; i.e., they cannot be hurt while cutting the cane.]

Tlā xihcihui, Xoxōuhqui Tzitzimitl. Ca nimitzānaco. Ōniquinhuālhuīcac in Mācuīltōnalehqueh, Cuexcochepyohqueh. Cuix ezzohqueh? Cuix tlapallohqueh?[4]

As if he said, "They cannot be hurt or harmed," and more clearly, "I bring my enchanted hands." Having cut the cane, they immediately try to make the fish trap, for the good effect of which they make another incantation:

[2] Come on, obey me now, green devil, for now I am starting, and I want to construct the chest of the prince's son {the fish trap because of its shape}. I in person, the orphan son, the one god. Do not hurt the five solar beings. Note that they do not have blood, nor do they have color.

Tla xihualhuia xoxouhqui tzitzimitl, ca ye nicyollalitiz yenicchichihuaz, in ipiltzin teuctli yelchiquiuh, nomatcanèhuatl ni icnopiltzintli niceteotl matiquimelehuiti in macuiltonalleq^{+}, cuix ezçoq^{+}, cuix tlapalloq^{+}.

Come [pl], Green Air-spirit [i.e., the cane]. I will soon give it life, I will soon make Piltzinteuctli's chest [i.e., the fish trap]. It is I in person. I am Icnopiltzintli; I am Centeotl. Beware of coveting [i.e., hurting] Five-*tonal*s-owners [i.e., the hands]. Do they have blood? Do they have color? [I.e., No! They are supernatural.]

Tlā xihuālhuiān, Xoxōuhqui Tzitzimitl. Ca ye nicyōlītīz,[5] ye nicchihchīhuaz in Piltzintēuctli[6] īēlchiquiuh. Nohmatca nehhuātl. NIcnōpiltzintli; niCenteōtl. Mā tiquimēlēhuihti[7] in Mācuīltōnalehqueh. Cuix ezzohqueh? Cuix tlapallohqueh?

Having made the fish trap, they hang it, and they set the bait, conjuring the one and the other, and they say:

[3] Come on, come quickly, you who are the hair of my sister, the goddess Xochiquetzal. Come on, do not be lazy, possessed chest of the prince's son, because now I put in you and I hang from you the food of all kinds of fish, a food as delicious as fruit. Be attentive toward all directions. Stretch out in all directions. From all four directions let them come to enter through this door. From all four

Tlacuele tlaxihualhuia nohueltiuh xochiquetzal iquetzon tlaxicihui tlamacazqui piltzinteuctli y elchiquiuh, yeni mitzontlalilia, ye nimitzonpilhuilia in nepapan tlaqualiztli, xochitlaqualiztli cemanahuac yaz timotecaz, yaz timopiloz nauhcacohuic yquiahuac matizque, nauca cohuic in quihualquazque ica paquizque, ica àahuiazq^{+} in no-

directions let them come to eat, and with that let my uncles, the possessed ones, the ones with seven fins, the ones who have shining eyes, the ones who have beards like divided plumes, the white possessed ones, take pleasure and be glad.[8]

tlahuan tlamacazq⁺, chiconatlapalleq⁺, tezcaixeque, quetzal tentzon maxaliuhque iztaque tlamacazque.

Let it be soon! Come [pl], nape-hair of my older sister, Xochiquetzal [i.e., of my wife] [Xochiquetzal's nape-hair is the cord used to fasten the fish trap]. Hurry, chest [i.e., the fish trap] of the priest, Piltzinteuctli. I am setting down for you, I am suspending for you[9] various kinds of food, which is flowery [i.e., delicious] food.[10] It will go throughout the world where you will stretch out, it will go where you will hang. It is from the four directions that they will be knowledgeable about its doorway. It is from the four directions that they will come to eat it. With it my uncles, the priests, Seven-fins-owners, Mirror-eyes-owners, Those-with-divided-plume-beards, White Priests [i.e., the fish], will be happy; with it they will have pleasure.

Tlā cuēl eh! Tlā xihuālhuiān, nohuēltīuh, Xōchiquetzal īquechtzon.[11] Tlā xihcihui, tlamacazqui, Piltzintēuctli īēlchiquiuh. Ye nimitzontlālilia, ye nimitzonpilhuilia in nepāpan tlacuāliztli, [in][12] xōchitlacuāliztli. Cemānāhuac yāz timotēcaz, yāz timopilōz.[13] Nāuhcācohuīc īquiāhuac matizqueh. Nāuhcācohuīc in quihuālcuāzqueh. Īca pāquizqueh; īca ahāhuiyazqueh in notlahhuān, tlamacazqueh, Chicōmahtlapalehqueh, Tezcaīxehqueh, Quetzaltēntzonmāxaliuhqueh, Iztāqueh Tlamacazqueh.

[4] Hail, do not grumble. Let it not be that this work is harmed because of your grumbling. Come very well on your behalf, because before anyone else you will amuse yourself enjoying their yellow hearts and their warm blood.

Maçan notetonhuexca pehuaz necti ton huexca tlatlacoz necti. Achtocopa taàhuiaz achtocopa tiquittaz in yyollotli coçahuic ineztli totonic.

You yourself be the one to beware of wanting to start off grumbling, of wanting to spoil things by grumbling. Before anyone else you will have pleasure; before anyone else you will see the yellow heart, the warm blood.

Mā zan nō teh tonhuēxcāpēhuaznecti, tonhuēxcātlahtlacōznecti.[14] Achtocopa tahāhuiyaz; achtocopa tiquittaz in yōllohtli cōzahuic, in eztli totōnic.[15]

After having finished hanging the fish trap and putting the bait inside, as in way of a farewell, they make an uproar of happiness, and finally they counsel it, warning it to be ready in every way for the good effect with the following words:

[5] My flowery gourd[16] {to the fish trap}, now leaving you I will cross the river. Aluala! Aaa, eee! {shouting and yelling for joy}

Noxoch ayouh ye moca nipanoz ayaohuiaoh Ayaye oa, Aye oa.

My flower-turtle [i.e., the flotation gourd], soon I will cross over[17] by means of you. *Ayaohuia oh, ayaye oa, aye oa!* [a shout for joy].

Noxōchāyōuh, ye moca nipanoz. Ayaohuia oh, ayaye oa, aye oa![18]

[6] I who suffer needs, being an orphan, the one God {they give this name to the God of the first age, a fable}. Sister of mine, the one of the womanly dress, reside here, stay hidden here.

ninotolinia ni icnopiltzintli, nice teotl nohueltiuh tecihuatlaqueme oc xime ehuati, oc ximotlatiti,

I suffer poverty. I am Icnopiltzintli. I am Centeotl. My older sister, Stone-woman-attire-owner [i.e., the caiman], for yet a while go in order to remain seated; for yet a while go in order to hide.

Ninotolīnia. NIcnōpiltzintli. NiCenteōtl. Nohuēltīuh, Tecihuātlaquēmeh,[19] oc ximehēhuati; oc ximotlātīti.

[7] Let me not see you elsewhere. Let me not find you elsewhere {he commands it not to become loose and to act in such a way that the fish will not see it}. Rocks and sticks, be like drunks lost to my will, for I am the orphan, the one god or traitor.

àmo campa nimitzittaz àmo campa nimitznamiquiz tetl ihuinti quahuitl ihuinti innonehuian niicnopiltzintli ni ce teotl.

It is not anywhere that I will see you [i.e., the caiman] [i.e., Do not let me see you anywhere!]. It is not anywhere that I will meet you [i.e., Do not let me come across you anywhere!]. Rocks become drunk, trees become drunk at my will [i.e., Otherwise you will be sorry]. I am Icnopiltzintli. I am Centeotl.

Ahmō cāmpa nimitzittaz. Ahmō cāmpa nimitznāmiquiz. Tetl īhuinti, cuahuitl īhuinti in nonehuiyān. NIcnōpiltzintli. NiCenteōtl.

With this, this infernal work ends.

Chapter 15

About the Incantation of Those Who Fish with Fishhooks

Those who fish with fishhooks, preparing themselves in their home with *piçiete* and canes, conjure the one and the other as protection against a bad outcome and help for a good one, with the following words:

[1] Come on! Come and help me, nine times beaten one, nine times cudgeled one, the son of the one of the starry skirt and perfect creature of hers, for already I am leaving, I the orphan, the one god, for already my father and my mother, the goddess Xochiquetzal, sends me myself,[1] the orphan, the one God.

Tla xihualhuia chicnauhtlatetzotzonalli chicnauhtla tecapanilli citlalcueyo iconeuh citlalcueyo itlaca cihuatl ye niauh niicnopiltzintli niceteotl, ye nechtitlani in nota in nonan in xichiquetzal in nomatca nèhuatl ni icnopiltzintli nice teotl

Come [pl], Nine-[times]-rock-pounded-one, Nine-[times]-rock-slapped-one, Citlalcueyeh's child, Citlalcueyeh's creation [i.e., tobacco]. Already I, who am Icnopiltzintli, I, who am Centeotl, am going. Already my father, my mother [i.e., my mainstay], Xochiquetzal [i.e., my wife], is sending me. I, who am in person, am Icnopiltzintli; I am Centeotl.

Tlā xihuālhuiān, Chiucnāuhtlatetzohtzonalli, Chiucnāuhtlatecapānīlli, Cītlalcuēyeh īconēuh, Cītlalcuēyeh ītlachīhual.[2] Ye niyauh, nIcnōpiltzintli, niCenteōtl. Ye nēchtītlani in notah, in nonān, in Xōchiquetzal. In nohmatca nehhuātl, nIcnōpiltzintli; niCenteōtl.

[2] Come on! Come now, lesser gods, and placate now any anger and sorrow.

tlaxihualhuian tlacolteteo,[3] ye nican anquicehuizq⁺, inçumalli in tequipachtli.

Come, Tlahzolteteoh [i.e., household gods]. Soon you will here cool off any anger or worry [i.e., you will preserve peace and serenity in the house].

Tlā xihuālhuiān, Tlahzoltēteoh. Ye nicān anquicēhuīzqueh in zōmalli in netequipachtli.[4]

[3] Come on! Come now, yellow possessed one, for already I am leaving, I, the orphan, the one God.

Tla xihualhuia cocauhqui tlamacazqui ye niauh ni icnopiltzintli nice teotl.

Come [pl], Yellow Priest [i.e, the fishing cane]. Already I, who am Icnopiltzintli, I, who am Centeotl, am going.

Tlā xihuālhuiān, Cōzauhqui Tlamacazqui. Ye niyauh nIcnōpiltzintli, niCenteōtl.

[4] Come on! Come now, gods like roses. Let the obstacles be removed now from my house. Let them be hidden, let them be burned.[5] Let them not cause me to cut the cloth for anyone. Through where do I have to go? This is my father's road. Well then, it will be well for me to go along it. Through where do I have to go? This is certainly my father's road, my mother's road. Along it I am to go, because it is smoking.[6]

Tla xihualhuia xochiteteo tla ontlaeheualo, tla ontlatlatillo ma ce tlacatl nocontlaxio cotonilitiquizti catli nictlalloz cayèhuatl nota yohui, ma yè huatl notlallo, catlehuatl nictlalloz yè ye huatl nota iohui in nonan yohui in xate popotocatoc in yhui popotocatoc.

Come, Xochiteteoh [i.e., the broom (?)]. Let people lift up everything. Let people hide everything away.[7] Let me beware of abruptly cutting things like warp-threads for a person. Which is the one [i.e., the road] I will travel over? It is indeed the one that is my father's road. Let that one be the one I travel over. Which is the one I will travel over? It is that very one that is my father's road, my mother's road, the one that lies coated with pebbles, the one that lies coated with feathers [i.e., the river].[8]

Tlā xihuālhuiān, Xōchitēteoh. Tlā ontlaehēhualo. Tlā ontlatlātilo. Mā cē tlācatl nocontlaxiyōcotōnilihtiquīzti.[9] Cātlih nictlalōz?[10] Ca yehhuātl notah īohhui. Mā yehhuātl nictlalo.[11] Cātl ehhuātl nictlalōz? Yeh yehhuātl notah īohhui, in nonān īohhui, in xāltepopotocatoc, in ihhuipopotocatoc.

Then he conjures the earthworms and says:

[5] Come on now, white enchanted one or *possessed one,* for now here you are to embrace the red Chichimec. And note that I do not call only one kind of fish. I have called all: the new ones, the old males, the old females, and those who dwell in the bends of the river.

Tla xihualhuia in iztac tlamacazqui ye nican ihuan timonahua tequiz in tlatlauhqui chichimecatl cuix çan cenicnotza ca çan mochi nicnotza in piltontli, in huehuentzin, illamatzin in Anenecuilcan chaneque.

Come [pl], White Priest [i.e., the earthworm]. Soon here you will embrace the Red Chichimec [i.e., the fishhook]. Am I perchance calling just one? Indeed I am calling just everybody[12]—the

Tlā xihuālhuiān, in Iztāc Tlamacazqui. Ye nicān īhuān timonāhuahtequiz[13] in Tlātlāuhqui Chīchīmēcatl. Cuix zan cē nicnōtza? Ca zan mochi nicnōtza—in pil-

child, the old man, the old woman, the dwellers in the places where the river wanders back and forth.

tōntli, in huēhuēntzin, ilamatzin, in āneh-necuilcān chānehqueh.

With this they end the superstitious incantation by throwing their fishhooks under its protection, with them [i.e., the fishermen] being [caught] rather on [the hook] of our Enemy, who so easily deceives them and entangles them in these superstitions.

CHAPTER 16

Another Incantation That They Use for the Same Purpose of Fishing with a Hook

I HAVE chosen not to pass over in silence this incantation because, although being for the same purpose [as the preceding one], it is different. This one was used by, among others, a very ancient old man, Juan Matheo, of the village of Comallan, of this district of Atenango, and it is as follows:

[1] Come on! Come, my mother, the one of the skirt[1] of precious stones {to the water because of the shores full of little drops} because here I come to seek my uncles, the possessed ones of seven fins, those of the dark[2] {for enchanted}[3] eyes, those of the beards like plumes, those that have the sides with specks {for the scales}. Hello! already the ones sought throughout all the world walk through here.[4]

Tlaxi hualhuia nonan chalchicueye nican ni quin temoz notlatlahuan tlamacazque, chicoca atlapalleque ayauhixeque quetzaltentzoneq+, olchipinque tlaca nican xintinemi, çemanahuac quitlatemolitinemi

Come [pl], my mother, Chalchiuhcueyeh [i.e., the water]. Here I will seek my various uncles, the priests, Owners-of-fins-located-in-seven-places, Mist-eyes-owners, Plume-beard-owners, Ones-dripping-with-rubber [i.e., the fish]. But wait! Here they go capitulating,[5] through the world [i.e., everywhere] they go seeking things for her [i.e., my wife].[6]

Tlā xihuālhuiān, nonān, Chālchiuhcuēyeh. Nicān niquintēmōz notlahtlahhuān, tlamacazqueh, Chicoccān-ahtlapalehqueh, Āyauhīxehqueh, Quetzaltēntzonehqueh, Ōlchipīnqueh. Tlacah! Nicān xīntinemih, cemānāhuac quitlatēmolihtinemih.

[2] Note that I come sent by my sister, the resplendent woman,[7] the goddess Xochiquetzal, and that I bring, in order to catch them, every kind of food. With it I come here to assemble my uncles, the possessed ones {enchanted ones}. And I am to carry them immediately with me, for already my sister, the resplendent woman {or the goddess Ceres}, is waiting for them. Already their mother's rug of grass is completely made and finished.[8] Come on, uncles! Approach here.

onech hualtitlan no hueltiuh Tonaca çihuatl, xochiquetzal onichualhuicac in nepapan tlaqualiztli, nican niquinnamictico notlatlahuan tlamacazque nican niquinhuicaz ye quinhualchixtica nohueltiuh tonaca cihuatl ontlayehecauh innan xiuh petlatzin ompa ammaaxitizque

My older sister, Tonacacihuatl, Xochiquetzal [i.e., my wife], has sent me hither. I have brought a variety of foods. Here I have come to cause my various uncles, the priests [i.e., the fish], to meet her. I will carry them from here. Already my older sister, Tonacacihuatl [i.e., my wife], is expecting them. Their mother, Turquoise-mat (H) [i.e., the riverbank], has done everything possible. There you [pl] [i.e., the fish] will arrive (H).

Ōnēchhuāltītlan nohuēltīuh, Tōnacācihuātl, Xōchiquetzal. Ōnichuālhuīcac in nepāpan tlacuāliztli. Nicān niquinnāmictīco notlahtlahhuān, tlamacazqueh. Nicān niquinhuīcaz. Ye quinhuālchixticah nohuēltīuh, Tōnacācihuātl. Ontlayehēcauh īnnān, Xiuhpetlatzin. Ōmpa ammahahxītīzqueh.

[3] Come on! Come already, nine times beaten one, son of the one of the starry skirt. Let nothing move you to animosity or do not grumble,[9] because before all things I shall offer you their warm blood, their yellow hearts.

tla xihualhuia chicnauhtlatetzotzonalli ỹ citlalcueye iconeuh mate tihuexcapeuhti tipatiquittaz eztli totonqui yollòtli cocauhqui.

Come [pl], Nine-[times]-rock-pounded-one, Citlalcueyeh's child [i.e., tobacco]. You be the one to beware of starting with grumbling. First you will see the warm blood, the yellow hearts.

Tlā xihuālhuiān, Chiucnāuhtlatetzohtzonalli, in Cītlalcuēyeh īconēuh. Mā teh tihuēxcāpēuhti.[10] Achtotipa[11] tiquittaz eztli totōnqui, yōllohtli cōzauhqui.

Quite clearly one sees in what manner a formal idolatry is found in all these incantations, since in all of them an offering and sacrifice is offered to the fire, or to *piçiete*, or to one of the idols of their heathenism, such as Quetzalcoatl or Xochiquetzal, etc., so that to what extent the [Christian] faith among the barbarians is in its beginning is proved. And as I have related about this Juan Matheo contained in this chapter, many years after I had commanded him not to use the said incantation and had put a penalty on his doing so, at the end of them I found him as attached to superstition as if I had not prohibited it to him, wherefrom I am convinced that the way to make oneself understood by these people is that of the second Psalm: *Reges eos in virga ferrea.*[12]

CHAPTER 17

About the Invocation That Is Used by Fishermen Who Use Fences and Weirs

THESE people, like almost all superstitious people, prepare themselves with their venerated *piçiete*, and they leave with it for the river where they start by conjuring the fish, saying:

[1] My uncles, painted and spot-stained ones, you who have your beards, horns, and fins like beautiful plumes or like turquoises, come here and be quick about coming, for I here call you. Here I in person seek you, I, the orphan, the one God. You have understood.[1] Here I

Notlatlahuane olpeyauhque, olchipinque, quetzalitentzon quetzal iquaquauh, quetzalimatlapal tlaxihualhuian tlaxicihuican ca nican nammechnotza canican nammechtēmoa nomatcanèhuatl ni icnopiltzintli nicenteotl o nican nam-

have come to [...][2] for you, because I have come to prepare for you a beautiful gallery, an elegant and multicolored fence within which you are to amuse yourselves and take many pleasures, where with good benefit you will seek all kinds of food and the most choice of it.

mechmanilico [...][3] anmechtequili inammoçaquan cihual, in ammoçaquan chinan in ìtic ampaquizque ìtic ammàahuiazq^{+}, ìtic anquihualtemozq^{+}, nepapan tlaqualiztli in xochitlaqualiztli.

O my various uncles, Ones-overflowing-with-rubber, Ones-dripping-with-rubber, Their-beards Are Plumes, Their-horns Are Plumes, Their-fins Are Plumes [i.e., the fish], come! Hurry! Indeed I call you here. Indeed I seek you here. It is I in person. I am Icnopiltzintli. I am Centeotl. Here I have come to lay down for you your troupial-courtyard,[4] your troupial-fence [i.e., the weir]; I have come to stretch it out for you. Inside of it you will be happy; inside of it you will have pleasure; inside of it you will find a variety of foods, which are flowery [i.e., delicious] foods.

Notlahtlahhuāné, Ōlpeyāuhqueh, Olchipīnqueh, Quetzalli Īntēntzon, Quetzalli Īncuācuauh, Quetzalli Īmahtlapal, tlā xihuālhuiān! Tlā xihcihuicān! Ca nicān namēchnōtza. Ca nicān namēchtēmoa. Nohmatca nehhuātl. NIcnōpiltzintli. NiCenteōtl. Ōnicān namēchmanilīco, ōnamēchtēquilih in amozacuānithual,[5] in amozacuānchinān. In iihtic[6] ampāquizqueh; iihtic amahāhuiyazqueh; iihtic anquihuāltēmōzqueh nepāpan tlacuāliztli, in xōchitlacuāliztli.

[2] Come on, make haste to come, for this command of mine is not meant for tomorrow or the day after. It is for right now, for I have come on your account. I am to carry you away, because my sister, the goddess Xochiquetzal,[7] my sister, the goddess of sustenance, is waiting for you. When I came, I had already spread out your beautiful and multicolored rug for you and your beautiful and mottled seat where you may sit, where you may lie down after arriving. And she is waiting for you to give you some of her drink[8] and the leftovers of her food, which you are to [...][9] in her company.

Tla xicihuican cuix quinmoztla, cuix quinhuiptla nitlàtoa niman Aman ca nammech annaco, ca nammechhuicaz, ca ammech chixtica nohueltiuh in tonacacihuatl in onihualla oammechhual tlaçocohuilli in ammoçaquanpetl in ammoçaquan icpal inipan ammotlallitacizq^{+}, ipan ammotecatacizque, ca ammech hualchialtitica iniatolauh in itlapan cauqui[10] in ihuan, anconquatacizq^{+}, anconitacizq^{+}.

Hurry! Will it be by-and-by tomorrow? Will it be by-and-by the day after tomorrow? I speak; it will be right away. Indeed I have come to get you. Indeed I will accompany you. Indeed my older sister, Tonacacihuatl [i.e., my wife], is awaiting you. When I came, I unfolded things for you. Upon your troupial-mat, your troupial-seat [i.e., the weir] you will sit upon arriving; upon it you will stretch out upon arriving. Indeed she is causing you to wait for her atole-water and her broken things [i.e., crumbs] which she drinks. In her company you will eat them upon arriving, you will drink it upon arriving.

Tlā xihcihuicān! Cuix quin mōztla? Cuix quin huīptla? Nitlahtoa; niman āman. Ca namēchānaco. Ca namēchhuīcaz. Ca amēchchixticah nohuēltīuh, in Tōnacācihuātl. In ōnihuāllah, ōamēchhuāllazohzōhuilih. In amozacuāmpetl, in amozacuānicpal in īpan ammotlālihtahcizqueh, īpan ammotēcatahcizqueh. Ca amēchhuālchialtihticah in īātōlāuh in ītlapāncāuh qui.[11] In īhuān anconcuahtahcizqueh, anconītahcizqueh.

[3] Do I perchance call only one? Perchance to only one do I shout? I call to every one there: the very old males as well as the very old females, the youths and the most famous ones. I call all of them jointly, I who am the orphan, the One God or Enemy.

Cuix çan ce nicnotza cuix çan ce nictzàtzilia ixquich nicnotza inicnohuehue inicnoillama intelpochtli intlamacazqui in çaço ixquich nictēmoa in ni icnopiltzintli nicenteotl.

Is it perchance only one that I am calling? Is it perchance only one that I am shouting to? I am calling all—the pitiable old man, the pitiable old woman, the youth, the priest. I who am Icnopiltzintli, who am Centeotl, seek all whomsoever.

Cuix zan cē nicnōtza? Cuix zan cē nictzahtzilia? Ixquich nicnōtza in icnōhuēhueh, in icnōilamah, in tēlpōchtli, in tlamacazqui. In zāzo ixquich nictēmoa, in nIcnōpiltzintli, niCenteōtl.

Having made this incantation to the useful fish, he starts immediately the incantation against the useless, harmful ones that usually break the partitions so that they will not enter instead of the useful ones.

[4] You my sister, flower of heat,[12] of the ash-colored dress,[13] beware of coming here, for if I see you here, I shall kill you and finish you off. Come on, let everyone go away and let the dusky harmful ones[14] hide, and let the green otters not come here. Let them not appear here, for even the rocks are to become mentally deranged for the sake of obeying me, for I am the orphan, the One God. Now I summon here, now I seek here my uncles, the possessed ones, the ones painted and besplattered with spots.

nohueltiuh xochtonaltecihuatlaqueme. Manican tihualyati intlanican nimitzittaz nimitzmictiz nimitzpòpoloz ma ocneyahualoti, ma oc netlatiloti ya yauhqui conotli xoxouhqui conotli Ayac nican huallaz Ayac nican niquittaz tetl ihuintiz innonehuian niicnopiltzintli, nicenteotl. ye oc nican niquinnotza niquintēmoa in notlatlahuan tlamacazq⁺, olpeyauhq⁺, olchipinque.

My older sister, Xochitonal, Stone-woman-attire-owner [i.e., the caiman], beware of coming here. If I see you here, I will kill you, I will destroy you. Let everyone who is a dusky otter, a green otter, beware for a while of being self-coiled [i.e., of being publicly self-shamed], let everyone beware for awhile of being self-hidden [i.e., of committing suicide]. No one will come here. I will see no one here. The stones [will get drunk, the trees] will get drunk at my will [i.e., You will regret the consequences of disobeying me.]. I am Icnopiltzintli. I am Centeotl. Already still I call here, I seek my various uncles, the priests, Ones-overflowing-with-rubber, Ones-dripping-with-rubber [i.e., the fish].

Nohuēltīuh, Xōchitōnal, Tecihuātlaquēmeh, mā nicān tihuālyahti.[15] In tlā nicān nimitzittaz, nimitzmictīz, nimitzpohpolōz. Mā oc neyahualōlohti,[16] mā oc netlātilohti yāyāuhqui conohtli, xoxōuhqui conohtli. Ayāc nicān huāllāz. Ayāc nicān niquittaz. Tetl [īhuintiz, cuahuitl][17] īhuintiz in nonehuiyān. NIcnōpiltzintli. NiCenteōtl. Ye oc nicān niquinnōtza, niquintēmoa in notlahtlahhuān, tlamacazqueh, Ōlpeyāuhqueh, Ōlchipīnqueh.

Having made this incantation, he continues [finally with][18] the entrusting of all the work to the *piciete* or tobacco as they usually do, because it seems to them that with its help everything will turn out for them very much to their liking. They say, then:

[5] Come on, nine times beaten one, nine times cudgeled one, come with speed in my favor, for you are the guide and the owner of all this work which is to be done in the water, for they are my palaces, for which purpose I carry you with me on the side of my heart.

Tla xicihui chicna uhtlatetzotzonalli, chicnauhtla te capanilli, caye te tinech onyacanaz in na Amoxco in na Atecpan, nican noopo chco pa tonyetiaz.

Hurry, Nine-[times]-pounded-one, Nine-[times]-slapped-one [i.e., the tobacco]. Indeed already

Tlā xihcihui, Chiucnāuhtlatetzohtzonalli, Chiucnāuhtlatecapānīlli. Ca ye teh tinē-

you are the one who will lead me away to my water-book-place, to my water-palaces. Here you will go being toward my left side [i.e., I have you on my left].

chonyacānaz in nahāmoxco, in nahātēcpan.[19] Nicān nopōchcopa tonyetiyāz.

In these last words with which they conclude the incantation, it is very well seen and it is proved how much they adore it [i.e., the *piciete*], since they rely on it, they ask for its help, and they entrust the work to it. May God free us through his compassion from the one who for our perdition disguises and veils his frauds and pride with the cover and disguise of *piçiete.* Amen.

[THIRD TREATISE]

SUPERSTITIONS OF FARMERS AND THEIR INCANTATIONS

CHAPTER 1[1]

[Incantation] for Planting Maguey

OUR Enemy is vigilant, and he does not neglect any effort for acting in any business from which our harm can result, no matter how small it may be. From here it follows that he takes great pains with our small harms[2] from which the greater ones come. There he aims all his strength. There lie the stratagems, finesse, and watchfulness. And the more [he acts] with greater cunning and care, the more his experience increases his confidence in the certainty of a good profit in such business. I say this because, having tried to put himself [into] the actions and occupations of these wretched people—not only into the neutral ones but also into those which are in themselves good—how much more he will have been attracted to those affairs that are open to being twisted or are easily twisted to sinister ends and to the perdition of souls. It is thus that he established among the farmers the superstition of the incantation and the idolatry of asking him for, and availing themselves of, his favor for good success in the sowing of, and good profit in the harvest of, any kind of seed. But he did his best and put all he had into it, in dealing with a thing through which he seeks[3] the perdition of infinite souls and numberless bodies: that is, through the sowing and cultivation of maguey the astute Enemy has introduced and set ever so firmly in place among these Indians the vice of drunkenness and, by means of it, [has caused] ever so many abominations in them and in all manner of people, with ever so much havoc on their bodies and perpetual perdition of their souls. The perdition of the souls is publicly evident in and of itself alone. The havoc on the bodies is well proved by the very great reduction to which these people have come in so few years, a people who were found without number in this land at the time of the Conquest, when drunkenness was prohibited to them with a penalty of death, this drunkenness being, in the judgment of wise and experienced men, the principal cause of this reduction, although other causes may also be involved.

Coming, then, to our purpose, when undertaking the cultivation of this plant which they call "maguey,"[4] from the first step that the Indians take, the superstition of the incantation accompanies it in this manner. When they transplant the magueys, which they remove from the uncultivated place in order to transfer them to the cultivated vineyards, they prepare themselves with *piçiete,* as with the guardian angel or with the deity to whom they entrust the work. And next they pick up a sharp stick with which they are to dig up the small magueys and start by conjuring the stick, getting it ready to do its duty well, and thus they say:

[1] Come on, for already it is time, possessed one[5] whose happiness is in the waters, let us go for we are to dig up and lift out the worthy woman, the one of eight in order,[6] for I am to	tla cuele, tlaxihualmohuica tlamacazqui ceatl ytonal tic teco pehuazque, tic quetztehuazque in chi cuetecpa ciuatzin nictlallitiuh nictlallitiuh incāpa

go to plant her. I have to put her in a very fitting and very fertile place that I have cleared off for her. There I have to put her where she will be very much at her pleasure—as if he entices her with the improvement of the new site.[7]

qualcan yeccã nictlachpani, oncã no cõ notlaliliz on cãme hui titiez.

Let it be soon! Come (H), priest, His-*tonal* Is One Water [i.e., the digging stick]. We will begin rooting out Eight-flint-woman (H) [i.e., the maguey], we will begin to set her upright. I am going in order to set her down. I am going in order to set her down in a place which is good, which is fine, where I have swept for her. There I will set her down; there she will be sitting.

Tlā cuēl eh! Tlā xihuālmohuīca, tlamacazqui, Cē-Ātl Ītōnal. Tictecopīntēhuazqueh,[8] ticquetztēhuazqueh in Chicuētecpacihuātzin. Nictlālītīuh. Nictlālītīuh in cāmpa cualcān, yēccān, nictlachpānih. Oncān noconnotlālilīz; oncān mēhuītihtiyez.

Having said this, they dig up the small magueys that they are to transplant, and having carried them to the place where they have tilled and cultivated for the new vineyard, they speak to the maguey, as if welcoming it, and they say:

[2] Be welcome now, noble woman of eight in a row, for here it is very fitting and a very good place. Here I have tilled and cultivated in order for you to be very much at your pleasure.

tlacueli xi hualmohuica chi cue tecpacihuatzin canican qualcã yeccan onimitztlachpani, nican timehui ti tiez.

Let it be soon! Come (H), Eight-flint-woman (H) [i.e., the maguey]. Indeed here is the good place, the fine place that I have swept for you. Here you will be sitting.

Tlā cuēl eh! Xihuālmohuīca, Chicuētecpacihuātzin. Ca nicān cualcān yēccān ōnimitztlachpānih. Nicān timēhuītihtiyez.

Having said this, they plant them—and note that they call them "women of eight in order or in a row" because usually they put them in a checkered pattern in rows of eight by eight. With this they go away very happy with having left their vineyard planted and the infernal recommendation made.[9]

When the magueys have grown and matured, after they are pruned, they exude the aguamiel, from which these unfortunate people make pulque and [celebrate] their usual drunken sprees. In order to prune them, they conjure the instrument, which is a hard stick with the point tapering like a chisel. And, taking it in their hands, they say to it:

[3] Come here, possessed one whose happiness is in the waters {stick}. Now is the time, for you are already ripe, woman of eight in order {maguey}. Be informed that the possessed one, whose happiness the rains are {stick}, is to enter to the hollow of your heart.

Tlaxi hualmo huica tlamacazqui ceatl itonal, caye ax can caotihueiac chi cuetecpa ciuatzin çamoyolcaltzinco no conaquiz tlamacazqui çeatl itonal.

Come (H), priest, His-*tonal* Is One Water [i.e., the pruning stick]. Indeed already it is now [i.e., the time has come]. Indeed you have become big, Eight-flint-woman (H) [i.e., the maguey]. I will just insert the priest, His-*tonal* Is One Water, into your heart chamber (H).

Tlā xihuālmohuīca, tlamacazqui, Cē-Ātl Ītōnal. Ca ye āxcān. Ca ōtihuēiyac, Chicuētecpacihuātzin. Zā moyōlcaltzinco noconaquīz tlamacazqui, Cē-Ātl Ītōnal.

Speaking and acting, he pushes the sharp stick to the center of the maguey and removes the heart. Then the next step is to make the small pan or little basin in the center where the aguamiel, which is the product of the maguey, is secreted and is collected. For this purpose they conjure the instrument, which is a copper spoon with a cutting edge, to which they say:

[4] Come on, for now it is time, do your duty, red Chichimec {to the spoon}. Come on, already now scrape and clean your work. It is to be within the seat of the heart of the woman, the one of eight in a row. You are to leave her complexion very clean, and you are to make her then cry and be sad and shed many tears and sweat in such a way that a stream flows from the female, the one of eight in a row.

tlacuele tlaxihualmo huica tlatlauhqui chichimecatl, tla axcan tlaxicpopoa chicuetecpan ciuatzin iyollo calco tinemiz tic mixqualtiliz caye axcan tic ixayotiz tic choctiz, tictlao coltiz, tic itonaltiz tiquix memeyallotiz in chi cuetecpa cihuatzin.

Let it be soon! Come (H), Red Chichimec [i.e., the spoon]. Let it be now. Clean Eight-flint-woman (H) [i.e., the maguey] in her heart chamber where you will live, where you will clean off her face. Indeed already it is now that you will make Eight-flint-woman (H) shed tears, you will make her weep, you will make her sad, you will make her sweat, you will make her flow at the eyes [i.e., exude aguamiel].

Tlā cuēl eh! Tlā xihuālmohuīca, Tlātlāuhqui Chīchīmēcatl. Tlā āxcān. Tlā xicpohpōhua Chicuētecpacihuātzin īyōllōcalco tinemiz, tiquīxcualtilīz.[10] Ca ye āxcān tiquīxāyōtīz, ticchōctīz, tictlaōcoltīz, tiquītōnaltīz, tiquīxmehmēyallōtīz in Chicuētecpacihuātzin.

With this, the work by hand starts, scraping and smoothing with the copper spoon that hollow or concavity which remains in the center of the maguey after the heart has been removed, at which time, in the incantation, he asks—speaking metaphorically—that those lamentations and sweatings and streams be made, signifying that a large quantity of aguamiel should occur there, so that his harvest will be more abundant[11] and the harvest of the Devil no less, since all of it comes to end up in their excessive and pernicious drunken sprees.

Others use another manner of incantation for the same purpose, the words of which are:

[5] Be attentive to me, my mother and lady, Earth, for already I hand over to you my sister, the one of eight in a row. Take her and embrace her strongly, because I will not delay long in again requesting good profit from the plant, for within five instants I will return to visit her and to see her good profit.[12]

Tlaxihualhuia nonan tlalteuctli ca ye momac nocontlallia in nohueltiuh chi cuetecpa cihuatl huel xicnapalo, huel xicnahuatequi àmo quexquich cahuitl in nichualittaz ca çan macuil aman nichualittaz ixco, icpactzinco nitlachiaz.

Come [pl], my mother, Tlalteuctli [i.e., the earth]. Indeed it is already in your hands that I place my older sister, Eight-flint-woman [i.e., the maguey]. Carry her in your arms well. Embrace her well. It will not be a long time before I come to see her. Indeed it will be only five instants before I will come to see her, before I will look upon her face, upon her headtop [i.e., before I come into her presence].

Tlā xihuālhuiān, nonān, Tlāltēuctli. Ca ye momāc nocontlālia in nohuēltīuh, Chicuētecpacihuātl. Huel xicnāpalo. Huel xicnāhuahtequi. Ahmō quēxquich cāhuitl in nichuālittaz. Ca zan mācuīlāman nichuālittaz, īīxco, īcpactzinco nitlachiaz.

With this he makes known his recommendation to the deity whom they attribute to the earth, in order that the maguey take root and become easily and well rooted and in order that it very quickly become ripe. In the rest it is almost the same as the preceding incantation, and so I leave it.

CHAPTER 2

About the Incantations for the Sowing of Other Seeds

ABOUT MAIZE

FOR the sowing of [various kinds of] seeds the incantation is almost one and the same because, except for the name of the seed—which they always name with a metaphor—in all the rest they almost do not change a word. In the metaphor of the names, they follow the metaphor of the color or the manner of the plant in the branch or in the fruit or something else, according to the idiom of the language, and for this reason, having given the incantation for the sowing of maize, I will put down for the rest only the metaphorical names which they use because of the difference of the seeds, and they call these metaphorical names *nahualtocaitl*[1], which is equivalent to "muffled-up name" or "name that the wizards use," and thus let the ministers be warned that they should consider suspicious the Indians whom they hear use such names, and let them live warily with them as suspected of being superstitious or wizards, for in a short time they will know their game.

For the sowing of maize, they make themselves ready with a *coa*[2] or implement of a hard and well-hewn stick with which they are to dig in order to sow the maize. And at the same time they get the palm-leaf basket where they keep the ears of maize that are to serve as seed. And this means that, although they have to sow a large quantity, they always start the sowing with a few select ears upon which the incantation falls as if including the rest. These they save at the end of the harvests, tying them first in bunches, using for this a cord of the same shucks that cover the ear, and hanging them in the wind. And when they are completely dry, they put them in the palm-leaf basket that they carry in order to start the sowing with it.

Having got, then, the basket and the implement, he starts the incantation by speaking to the implement:

[1] Come on, possessed one, whose happiness is in the rains {stick}, do your duty, for the possessed ones, or the gods {clouds}, have already arrived. Now I am going in order to leave the possessed prince {maize} among others for he is seven snakes.

Tlaxihualmohuica, tlamacazqui ce atl itonal ca ye axcan oyecoque tlamacazque, axcan niccahuaco tlamacazqui tlaçòpilli chicome coatl

Come (H), priest, His-*tonal* Is One Water [i.e., the digging stick]. Indeed already it is now that the priests [i.e., the clouds] have arrived. Now I have come to carry away[3] the priest, Tlazohpilli, Seven Snake [i.e., the maize].

Tlā xihuālmohuīca, tlamacazqui, Cē-Ātl Ītōnal. Ca ye āxcān ōehcōqueh[4] tlamacazqueh. Āxcān niccāhuaco tlamacazqui, Tlazohpilli, Chicōme-Cōātl.

[2] Come on, let us go, for here is the basket of the goddess of bread,[5] who will carry you along the road, for your mother {the Goddess Ceres or the wife of the one who is speaking} has kept you in it a long time, and now the possessed ones, her brothers, have come.

tiuian ça nican ca tonaca chiquiuhtli mitzòtlatoctiz ca ye ixquich cahuitl mitzpixticatca in monantzin oyecoque tlamacazque yoquichtihuan.

Let us go. Right here is Sustenance-basket [i.e., the harvest basket]. She will cause you to follow the road [i.e., you will be carried in the basket]. Indeed already for all this time your mother [i.e., my wife[6]] has been guarding you. The priests, her older brothers [i.e., the clouds], have arrived.

Tihuiān. Zā nicān cah Tōnacāchiquihuitl.[7] Mitzohtlatoctīz. Ca ye ixquich cāhuitl mitzpixticatca in monāntzin. Ōehcōqueh[8] tlamacazqueh, īoquichtīhuān.

After having said this, he starts off with the equipment toward the readied field, and upon arriving, he starts another incantation, saying:

[3] Come on, bear a hand, possessed one whose happiness the waters are, for here is where we are to put the possessed one, seven snakes, beneath the ground.

Tlaxihualmohuica tlamacazqui ceatl itonal ca nican tictlallanhuizq⁺, in tlamacazqui chicomecoatl.

Come (H), priest, His-*tonal* Is One Water [i.e., the digging stick]. Indeed here we will put the priest, Seven Snake [i.e., the maize], beneath the ground.

Tlā xihuālmohuīca, tlamacazqui Cē-Ātl Ītōnal. Ca nicān tictlāllanhuīzqueh in tlamacazqui, Chicōme-Cōātl.

This metaphor of the seven snakes is always used in these incantations for the maize, and it is either because[9] of the tied bunches of the ears or because of the stalks on which it is produced, for usually they sow them and they are born seven by seven or because of the rows of kernels on the same ear which usually resemble the snakes stretched out in different colors.

After this second incantation he speaks to the land, letting it know what is going to happen and conjuring it for the benefit of his sowing. And he says:

[4] Come on, now on your part do what you should, Face-worked[10] Mirror that steams, for presently I am to hand the noble man seven[11] snakes over to you because here it is very fitting for his residence, for already the possessed ones {the clouds} have arrived.

Tlacuele xihualhuia tezcatl yxahual poztocatimani ca ye mopan nictlalliz intlaçòpilli chicome coatl ca nican qualca Mahuititiez, caye omecahuiq⁺ tlamacazque.

Let it be soon! Come [pl], Mirror whose surface just lies smoking hither [i.e., the earth]. Indeed I will set down upon you Tlazohpilli, Seven Snake [i.e., the maize]. Indeed here is the good place where he will be sitting. Indeed already the priests [i.e., the clouds] have arrived (H).

Tlā cuēl eh! Xihuālhuiān, Tezcatl [in] īīx zan huālpopōcatimani.[12] Ca ye mopan nictlālīz in Tlazohpilli, Chicōme-Cōātl. Ca nicān cualcān mēhuītihtiyez. Ca ye ōmehcahuihqueh tlamacazqueh.

Saying this, he makes the holes that they are accustomed to making with the implement, and he sows the maize with his badly founded hope.

Chapter 3

For Other Sowings

I have already said above that the incantations for the sowings are all almost one and the same, with the name of the seed changed. And thus they call the squash seeds *tlamacazqui chicome quauhtzin,*[1] which means "possessed one of seven branches" because of the many arms that it puts forth, that are like horns, which in Mexican they call *iquaquauh.*[2] They call the bean *tlamacazqui tlaçòpilli tlilpotonqui,*[3] which means "possessed one, prince of much esteem caparisoned[4] in black." This manner of speaking must be because of how much they respect this seed, which in this land is for them one of the most common foods. They go on like this in their metaphors and manners of speaking, and therefore I will not put down any more to avoid prolixity.

CHAPTER 4

About Another Incantation for the Sowing of Maize

For the same purpose of sowing maize they use another manner of conjuring, and this second kind used to be used by, among others, an Indian of Chillapa, considered and esteemed among the rest for his consummate knowledge, and the reason was that there was not any superstition in which he was not involved and about which he was not an expert,[1] as I will talk about in the scorpion cure. This Indian's name is Don Martin Sebastian y Ceron. This incantation is, then, as follows. Picking up the maize to sow it, he says:

[1] I, in person, the priest or possessed one or enchanter. Pay attention, Sister seed who are sustenance.[2] Pay attention, princess earth, for I now entrust into your hands my sister, the one who gives us, or the one who is, our subsistence.[3] Do not bring upon yourself an ignominious accident by falling into fault.[4] Do not do like the angry and grumbling peevish people do. Note that what I command you is not something for you to carry out at leisure, because I am[5] again to see my Sister, Our Sus-

nomatca nèhuatl nitlamacazqui tlaxihualhuia nohueltiuh tonaca cihuatl tlaxihualhuia tlalteuctli ye momacpalco nocontlallia in nohueltiuh tonacacihuatl àmo timopinauhtiz, àmo tihuexcapehuaz, àmo tihuexcatlàtlacoz, cuíx quinmoztla, cuix quinhuiptla in ixco icpac nitlachíaz in nohueltiuh, in tonaca cihuatl niman ìciuhca in tlalticpac hualquiçaz in nicmahuiçoz in nictlapaloz in nohueltiuh tonaca cihuatl.

tenance (the corn that he goes along burying). Immediately, very soon, it is to come out above ground. I want to see with pleasure[6] and to congratulate my sister, our sustenance, on her birth.

It is I in person. I am the priest. Come [pl], my older sister, Tonacacihuatl [i.e., the seed]. Come [pl], Tlalteuctli [i.e., the earth]. Already I am setting down my older sister, Tonacacihuatl, in the palm of your hand. You will not bring shame upon yourself. You will not begin by grumbling. You will not ruin things by grumbling. Will it be later tomorrow, will it be later the day after tomorrow that I will look upon the face, upon the headtop of [i.e., I will see in person] my older sister, Tonacacihuatl? It is immediately, quickly, that she will come out above the ground, that I will honor, that I will greet my older sister, Tonacacihuatl.

Nohmatca nehhuātl. Nitlamacazqui. Tlā xihuālhuiān, nohuēltīuh, Tōnacācihuātl. Tlā xihuālhuiān, Tlāltēuctli. Ye momācpalco nocontlālia in nohuēltīuh, Tōnacācihuātl. Ahmō timopīnāuhtīz. Ahmō tihuēxcāpēhuaz. Ahmō tihuēxcātlahtlacōz. Cuix quin mōztla, cuix quin huīptla in īīxco īcpac nitlachiaz in nohuēltīuh, in Tōnacācihuātl? Niman ihciuhcā in tlālticpac huālquīzaz, in nicmahuizōz, in nictlahpalōz in nohuēltīuh, Tōnacācihuātl.

With this he continues his sowing until finished. And in this incantation for the sowing of other seeds they also change the names according to the one that they sow, as has been said in the preceding incantation.

CHAPTER 5

About the Incantation for Garnering Maize or Seeds in the Harvest

YET to be spoken of is the incantation that they use, when the seed has already been gathered, for the preservation of it, both against vermin and against spoilage, and in order that it not run out quickly; I mean, in order that in the granary it multiply like the flour and oil of the widow.[1] At the time of garnering it, they say:

[1] I, in person, the possessed one and priest of idols and enchanter, I am the one who commands it. I say to you, sister, our sustenance,[2] that now I want to deposit you in my precious granary.[3] Keep yourself well, and defend yourself from all four directions {because the granary is square}.[4] Do not fall into insult by failing me, for from you I am to take inspiration. From you I am to take comfort, I who am the orphan, the one God. To you, my sister, I say that you are my[5] sustenance.

nomatca nèhuatl nitlamacazqui tla xihualhuia nohueltiuh tonaca cihuatl ye nimitzoncahuaz in nochalchiuh contzinco nauhcampa xitlaquitzqui àmo timopinauhtiz motech nihìyocuiz, motech niceceyaz in ni icnopiltzintli in ni centeotl in tinohueltiuh titvnaca cíhuatl.

It is I in person. I am the priest. Come [pl], my older sister, Tonacacihuatl [i.e., the seed]. Soon

Nohmatca nehhuātl. Nitlamacazqui. Tlā xihuālhuiān, nohuēltīuh, Tōnacācihuātl.

I will leave you in my jade pot (H) [i.e., the granary]. Hold on to things from the four directions [i.e., remain inside the granary]. You will not bring shame upon yourself [i.e., You will do your duty properly.]. I, who am Icnopiltzintli, Centeotl, will take a breath [i.e., breathe easily] because of you, I will cool off [i.e., rest] because of you, my older sister, Tonacacihuatl.

Ye nimitzoncāhuaz in nochālchiuhcōntzinco. Nāuhcāmpa xitlaquītzqui. Ahmō timopīnāuhtīz. Motech nihīyōcuiz, motech nicecēyaz, in nIcnōpiltzintli, in niCenteōtl, in tinohuēltīuh, tiTōnacācihuātl.

With this it seems to him that he makes sure that he will have sustenance for a long time and that the garnered maize will not be harmed.

CHAPTER 6

Another Incantation for the Sowing of Squash

For the sowing of squash that in this land they call *tamalayòtli*[1]—and it is the one that in this kind excels the rest in size—they use the following incantation when placing the seed:

[1] I speak to you, my mother, the Princess Earth, who are face up. And I speak to you, my father, One Rabbit. In the palms of your[2] hands I put a piece of flint {the squash seed}. Cover it well and clutch it firmly in your hands. Let not its uncles, those who live in the houses of those who sting or bite {the ants}, who are the red Chichimecs, covet it.

Tlaxihualhuia nonan tlalteuctli aquetztimani nota ce tochtli momacpalco nocontlallia cetecpatl, ma huel xicmapiqui xicmatzollo àmo quellehuizque in itlatlahuan tequan chamecan tlatlauhque chichimeca.

Come [pl], my mother, Tlalteuctli, She-is-supine, my father, One Rabbit [i.e., the earth]. I am placing One Flint [i.e., a knife, *metaphor for* the squash seed][3] in the palm of your hand. Grasp him well in your fist, hold him in your fist. His various uncles from the place of the dwellers who sting [*lit.*, who eat people], the Red Chichimecs [i.e., the ants], will not covet [i.e., harm] him.

Tlā xihuālhuiān, nonān, Tlāltēuctli, Ahquetztimani, notah, Cē-Tōchtli. Momācpalco nocontlālia Cē-Tecpatl. Mā huel xicmāpīqui, xicmātzolo. Ahmō quēlēhuīzqueh in ītlahtlahhuān tēcuānchānehcān,[4] Tlātlāuhqueh Chīchīmēcah.

[2] Its fertility is to astonish the possessed ones. They are to be amazed on seeing their feet entangled at each step with the cords which are the enchanted intestines of that which is our sustenance[5] and on seeing that at each moment they stumble over the enchanted heads. And you, Lady Earth, finally now I admonish you that you not shame yourself by falling into fault.[6] Do not begin to grumble and, by grumbling, to fail to fulfill your obligation.

Nican motetzahuizque in tlamacazq⁺, ycmotetzahuizque yc moximecaniznazque in tonaca me catlal in nahual cuetlaxcolli, yc moxitepo tlaminazq⁺ in nahualtzonteconmeme xihualauh tlaltectli, aman yequene amo timo pinauhtiz amo tihuexcapehuaz amo tihuexca tlatlacoz.

Here the priests will be amazed; because of it they will be amazed. They will go entangling their feet in the sustenance ropes, the *nahualli*-guts [i.e., the vines]. They will go stumbling upon the *nahualli*-head-carriers [i.e., the vines]. Come, Tlalteuctli [i.e., the earth]. It is at this instant at last [i.e., Now is the time for action.]. You will not bring shame upon yourself. You will not begin grumblingly. You will not spoil things by grumbling.

Nicān motētzāhuīzqueh in tlamacazqueh; īc motētzāhuīzqueh. Īc mocximecanihtiyāzqueh[7] in tōnacāmecatl,[8] in nāhualcuitlaxcolli. Īc mocxitepōtlamihtiyāzqueh[9] in nāhualtzontecommēmeh.[10] Xihuāllauh, Tlāltēuctli. Āman yē quen eh. Ahmō timopīnāuhtīz. Ahmō tihuēxcāpēhuaz. Ahmō tihuēxcātlahtlacōz.

He means that on its part the earth should respond well by obeying what he commands and by not doing like the obstinate people, who, acting obtusely in obedience, grumble and mutter and finally do not do what they have been ordered to; and *Huexca tlatlacoz*[11] means that.

CHAPTER 7

About the Incantation for the Sowing of *Camotes*

HAVING cut into segments the roots or cuttings that they are to sow, he starts the incantation by speaking to the sun.

[1] I in person, the orphan, the one or only God, I am the one who speaks to you, my uncle, possessed one, you who used to be pustulous. Look here, I tie my thigh, and I sow it {He shows the cutting or root he is to sow to the sun}. I speak to you my uncle, you who once were pustulous. Look here, I tie my head, for I tie it with my sister, the flower, mouth-biter, the clasping flower[1] {Because one uses another[2]}. With her help I am to breathe; with her I am to remedy all my needs, I who am a poor and unhappy man.

Nomatca nehuatl niicnopiltzin tli nicenteotl {Name of the god of the first age.}, tla xi hualhuia notlatla, tlamacazqui nanahuatzin {It was his name before the transformation.}, cani can niquilpia no metzquauhyo nictoca. tlaxihualhuia notlatla nanahuatzin cani ca niquilpia notzontecon caica noconigria in nohueltiuh in teten quaquaxochitl, temaco chihuia xochitl itetzinco nihiouiz, itetzinco nipahtiz ni icno tlacatzintli.

It is I in person. I am Icnopiltzintli. I am Centeotl. Come [pl], my uncle, the priest, Nanahuatzin [i.e., the sun]. Indeed here I am tying my thigh. I am burying it. Come [pl], my uncle, Nanahuatzin. Indeed here I am tying my head. Indeed I tie it by means of my older sister, Flower That-chews-people-at-the-lips, Flower That-embraces-people [i.e., the earth]. Because of it I will breathe [i.e., I will rest easy]; because of it I who am a poor person will get well [i.e., I will survive].

Nohmatca nehhuātl. NIcnōpiltzintli. Ni-Centeōtl. Tlā xihuālhuiān, notlah,[3] tlamacazqui, Nānāhuatzin. Ca nicān niquilpia nometzcuauhyo. Nictōca. Tlā xihuālhuiān, notlah, Nānāhuatzin. Ca nicān niquilpia notzontecon. Ca īca noconilpia[4] in nohuēltīuh, in Tētēncuacuah Xōchitl, Tēmācochihuia[5] Xōchitl. Ītechtzinco nihīyōcuiz;[6] ītechtzinco nipahtiz nicnōtlācatzintli.

[FOURTH TREATISE][1]

[Untitled]

CHAPTER 1

About the Incantation and Words That They Use to Placate Anger

HAVING dealt with the incantations that these natives use in their occupations and actions pertaining to inanimate things or directed toward things not free,[2] it seemed to me [that I should put] next[3] the incantations and words that they use in the occupations and things that, by their nature, are directed to human communication and to him who uses reason and free will. They attempt to have access to this and even dominion over it by virtue of the words they use for different purposes—and among these, the purpose we are to deal with in the present chapter, which is to direct a person's condition and even his state of will, seeking that the angry person be pacified or that the one who is naturally fractious and quick to anger not be so, and, alternatively, that the pacific person not be so, and that the one at present in love hate and become ill-willed toward the person he formerly loved. This could, of course, be directed toward a good end, as would be the case if the unhappily married woman were to try to get her husband to abandon and hate the women responsible for her unhappy marriage or if a man who is hated by his wife were to seek her friendship according to the law of matrimony. Even so it would never be right to use such means, according to the common axiom: *non sunt facienda mala, vt inde eueniãt bona.*[4] But the harm is much greater, because he who guides this dance [i.e., the Devil] always contrives things in such a way that some evils become linked, joined, and addressed to others. And thus he has established among these wretched and blind people that they use the superstition of incantation and that they invoke him in their favor, and this [is] at the service and means of other sins, because ordinarily they use them for the brokerage of bad friendships and adulteries, trying to get the husband to suppress his love and affection for his own wife and to transfer it to another woman, or to get the wife to hate her legitimate husband, or to get the husband to be, as it were, insensible to the offenses against the matrimonial vow, passing through them as if they did not pass through him. For this purpose they use a means that includes two things: a philter and words. And although the two things included in this means customarily are of many kinds, I will put down only one kind, because those who are to deal with this remedy will have sufficient information with what I will say here, and putting down all the variations is not necessary and could be a hindrance and an opportunity for greater sins for the evil people.[5] Now then, one of the things they use for medicine to which they attribute part of the effect is some maize kernels that are located at the commencement and birth of the spike or ear, and these kernels have their points contrary at birth—backwards and in a contrary direction to the rest on the said ear—and to this contrariety they attribute the contrary effect on the inclination and will with regard to affection or hatred. To these kernels of maize they apply the second part of this means, which are the words with which, in their judgment, by conjuring the maize kernels, they give them added strength and power in order to obtain the effect of the change they seek. The words, then, are:

[1] Come here, illustrious and esteemed man, one god, you who are to placate the heart inflamed {with anger},[6] you who are to banish from him the green anger.

tla xihualhuiatlaçopilli çenteotl, ticçehuiz coçauhqui yollotli quiçaz xoxouhqui tlauelli, coçauhqui tlauelli.

Come [pl], Tlazohpilli, Centeotl. You [sg] will calm down the yellow heart. The green wrath, the yellow wrath will come out.

Tlā xihuālhuiān, Tlazohpilli, Centeōtl. Ticcēhuīz cōzauhqui yōllohtli. Quīzaz xoxōuhqui tlahuēlli, cōzauhqui tlahuēlli.

[2] I am to banish the yellow wrath and to put it to flight, for I am the priest, the Prince of spells, I who am to give the medicinal possessed one, heart-changer {for "conjured one"}, to him to drink.

nic quixtiz, nictotocaz nitlamacazqui Ninahualtecutli niquihtiz tlamacazqui pahtecatl, yollo cuepcatzin, *vel* yolcuepcatzin.

I will make it come out; I will pursue it. I am the priest; I am the *nahualli*-lord. I will cause it [i.e., the wrath] to drink the priest, Pahtecatl, Yollohcuepcatzin (*or* Yolcuepcatzin).

Nicquīxtīz; nictohtocaz. Nitlamacazqui; nināhualtēuctli. Niquītīz tlamacazqui, Pahtēcatl, Yōllohcuepcātzin (*or* Yōlcuepcātzin).

Having made this incantation, in order to apply the medicine, by grinding up the conjured maize, they make some drink such as atole or chocolate from it, according to the custom of this land. And they have the one whose will or affect they are attempting to change drink it. And thus, in order to introduce discord, they use contrary words and give the drink in the manner I have just related.

The deceit and superstition are easily seen, as is the fact that they would never attain their intent by these means if an express or at least tacit pact [with the Devil] does not intervene.

Chapter 2

About Another Incantation to Attract or Inspire Affection

Of the type described is the superstition of attracting another's will to affection, used by people in love, who avail themselves of it if it is to their advantage—and thus it comes in here as in its proper place. And this superstition is based only on words, to which they attribute the power to deliver whomever they fancy to their will. The words of the incantation say, then:

[1] On the crystalline hill where the wills appear,[1] I seek a woman, and I sing love songs to her, fatigued by the solicitude that love for her brings me, and thus I do all that

Tezcatepec nenamicoyã niçihua notza niçihua cuica non nentlamati, nihualnentlamati yeno cõhuica in nohueltiuh inxochiquetzal, ce coatl ica apan tiuitz

is possible on my part. Now I bring to my aid my sister, the goddess Xochiquetzal {Venus}, who comes elegantly encircled by one snake and girdled with another, and wears her hair caught up in her ribbon. This loving concern has made me tired and tearful, yesterday and the day before. This has me sad and anxious.

cecoatl ica cui tlal pitiuitz tzonil pi tihuitz ye yalhua ye huiptla ica nichoca ica ninentlamati

On Mirror Mountain at the place where people meet I am summoning a woman, I am singing because of a woman. I am sad there; I am sad here. Already I accompany my older sister, Xochiquetzal [i.e., my beloved]. She comes mantling herself with One Snake;[2] with One Snake she comes girding up her loins, she comes tying up her hair. Since yesterday, and since the day before [i.e., for some time], I have been crying because of her, I have been sad because of her.

Tezcatepēc nenāmicōyān nicihuānōtza, nicihuācuīca. Nonnēntlamati; nihuālnēntlamati. Ye noconhuīca in nohuēltīuh, in Xōchiquetzal. Cē-Cōātl īca mahpāntihuītz;[3] Cē-Cōātl īca mocuitlalpihtihuītz, motzonilpihtihuītz. Ye yālhua, ye huīptla,[4] īca nichōca, īca ninēntlamati.

[2] I think that she is truly a goddess; truly she is most beautiful and consummate. I am to acquire her not tomorrow or the day after but right this very moment. Because I in person am the one who thus orders and commands it, I the youth, the warrior, I who shine like the sun and have the beauty of the dawn. Perchance am I just any common man? Or am I of humble birth? I came and was born for the sake of the elegant and transparent feminine sex,[5] etc.

camach nelli teotl camach nelli mahuiztic cuix quin moztla cuix quin huiptla niman aman nòmatca nehuatl, nitelpochtli, ni yaotl no nitonac, nonitlathuic cuix çan cana onihualla cuix çanca na oni hual quiz ompa oni hualla ompa oni hual quiz, etc.

Indeed people say that in truth she is a goddess. Indeed people say that in truth she is a marvelous being. Will it perchance be by-and-by tomorrow, or will it perchance be by-and-by the day after tomorrow [that I will see her]? It will be immediately at this instant. It is I in person. I am Telpochtli. I am Yaotl. I have sunshined and also I have dawned.[6] Have I perchance come from just anywhere? Have I perchance come out from just anywhere? It is from there[7] that I have come. It is from there that I have come out, etc.

Ca mach nelli teōtl. Ca mach nelli mahuiztic. Cuix quin mōztla, cuix quin huīptla [niquittaz]?[8] Niman āman. Nohmatca nehhuātl. NiTēlpōchtli. NiYāōtl. Nō nitōnac, nō nitlathuic. Cuix zan canah ōnihuāllah? Cuix zan canah ōnihuālquīz? Ōmpa ōnihuāllah. Ōmpa ōnihuālquīz, etc.

The rest of the words are such that, although somewhat disguised, they are not put down out of concern for modesty and for chaste ears. Finally, by way of conclusion, they say:

[3] Truly she is worthy of being considered a goddess for she is among the most beautiful women in the world. I am not to acquire her tomorrow or the next day but immediately right now, for I in person command it, the warrior youth. Perchance do I bring war? War is not mine but the conquest of women.

Ca mach nelli teotl?[9] ca mach nelli mahuiztic cuix quin moztla cuix quin huiptla niquitaz Nyman Aman, Tomatla nehual nitelpochtli niyaotl cuix nelli niyaotl? ahmo nelli niyaotl çan ni cihuayotl.

Indeed people say that in truth she is a goddess. Indeed people say that in truth she is a marvelous being. Will it perchance be by-and-by tomorrow, or will it perchance be by-and-by the day after tomorrow that I will see her? It will be immediately at this instant. It is I in person. I am Telpochtli. I am Yaotl. Is it perchance true that I am Yaotl? It is not true that I am Yaotl. I am only Womanizer.[10]

Ca mach nelli teōtl. Ca mach nelli mahuiztic. Cuix quin mōztla, cuix quin huīptla niquittaz? Niman āman. Nohmatca nehhuātl. NiTēlpōchtli. NiYāōtl. Cuix nelli niYāōtl? Ahmō nelli niYāōtl. Zan niCihuāyōtl.

CHAPTER 3

About the Diseases and Sicknesses That Come from Illicit Love Affairs

Among the heathen superstitions that have remained among the Indians, not the least pernicious one is the fiction that there are sicknesses caused by illicit love and forbidden desires—a matter which is contained in this chapter—and although the feigned cure of these illnesses appears to belong in the "Treatise on the Superstitious Doctors and Their Frauds" [the Sixth Treatise], nevertheless, I decided to put it here because this fraud is based on the affects of free will, as will be seen.

This chapter has two parts. The first contains the fiction of the illnesses and diseases that they call or entitle "of love affairs and illicit desires," and their cause, or the manner of falling into these illnesses; the second part contains the superstition of the cure and remedy of the said illnesses and injuries. With regard to the first part, the artifice of the Enemy is such that, for the sake of profiting—given the occasions to our harm—he has introduced and established that many illnesses come from love affairs and illicit desires; for instance, because of some third person being in a bad state. And although the proper conclusion to draw from this opinion should be that, because of that, it would be best for everyone to live well, the Enemy—changing everything into evil and manufacturing and preparing poison even out of good doctrine—has drawn two harms from there: the first is that there are many who desire this profession because of the advantage that those impostors who pretend that they are doctors—diviners who know and are able to remedy these illnesses and diseases—have in the course of the feigned cure of them. The second and more serious harm is that, with this opportunity, he introduces and persuades that it is good to sin, because, carefully considered, if on the surface and crust of this superstition, illnesses and diseases caused by the sins are disclosed, by looking with care on the inside of it we see the wicked intention of the Enemy. He only feigns this corporal and temporal harm in the persons attendant and present[1] because of their participation, not paying attention to those spiritual and eternal harms in the delinquents; and what is more, wishing to establish as a doubtless fact that such illnesses and hurts have as a cure and remedy the committing of other similar or greater crimes, sins which match or surpass the feigned cause of them. And in order that this be better understood:

First, let it be noted—and this is the first part of this chapter—that the illnesses and harms that are contained in this chapter are three: the first one, the sickness of the children who habitually become frightened and cry out as if they have seen something dreadful—when they wake up screaming and crying as if frightened, or when, without any apparent cause, they are subject to fainting and remaining as if dead, and others injure [themselves];[2] and these illnesses are usually called falling sickness and epilepsy. The second one is when someone gradually becomes thin and wastes away—either because of advanced age or because of being naturally sickly or because of a weakness of the stomach or because of being consumptive or phthisical. The third kind has more latitude, and the Enemy takes more advantage of it for the second intent, which is to induce diseases of guilt rather than[3] those of pain so that in order to remedy temporal diseases, they bring upon themselves eternal punishments with harm and death of the soul.

And thus, whatever sickness or indispositions our doctors commonly judge to be incurable, these impostors say that they come from an excess of crimes by the consort, whether it be his wife or her husband, or whether it be her friend or friends. And they include and add to this kind of illness those which we are accustomed to calling misfortunes and tribulations, such as poverty and failures, for instance, the freezing of the sown fields, the seeds becoming mildewed, the animals damaging the maize and wheat, the animals becoming lost or falling down a ravine, not finding an outlet for the merchandise, and not prospering from the contracts, and even their meals and drinks not being well prepared—things, from one or another of which, there is no person who escapes. These are what they call illnesses and harms caused by an excess of transgressions of the consort, as has been said, which in the Mexican language they call *tlàcolmiquiztli,*[4] which means, "harm caused by love or desire." They put this same name to the children's sicknesses mentioned above, although they usually call epilepsy *tlacolmimiquiliztli,*[5] which means almost the same thing, except that it denotes at the same time the lack of sense; the second kind of illnesses, of thinness and wasting away, they call *netepalhuiliztli,*[6] which probably means "dependence on another," and more strictly interpreted, "harm because of dependence on another."

Now it remains to say how they feign that these harms and illnesses are caused and then we will deal with their feigned cure, which is the second part[7] of this chapter.

These impostors pretend that two kinds of persons are subject to these illnesses, and these are children or those already adult, both men and women. They affirm that the children incur these above-mentioned illnesses because at their[8] birth some person given to dissipation and lewdness assisted or was present or because such a person came into the mother's presence while the infant was still in her belly or in her arms after its birth.

In the adults, they give as a cause—if they are married or living in concubinage—excess adulteries or concubinages in the consort. And they call the illnesses contracted due to this cause, in their opinion, and the illnesses of the children of the preceding section[9] *tlacolmiquitztli.*[10] But if the sick adults are neither married nor keeping bad company, in such a case they say that they got sick from one of two causes: the first one [is] because, while the sick person was in the company of others, some other person of dissipated living or who was keeping bad company and concubinages came into their presence or mingled with them. The second cause, they say, is because, while the sick person was in the company of others, some person of the group wished to obtain some woman or coveted something belonging to another, and because that third person does not get his desire, it usually causes in him much melancholy and sadness. They say that, as the philosophers affirm, through sympathy and superfluity they infect the companion and they cause in him the disease of gradually becoming thin and drying up. And this they call *netepalhuiliztli,*[11] as was said above.

Let us now turn to the fraud of the cure of these illnesses, which is the second part of this chapter. To all these sicknesses they apply a single remedy, which is the one they call *tetlacolaltiloni,*[12] as if we might say "bath for the sickness caused by love affairs or by affection." But although they consider this to be the sole remedy, even so, they do not exclude the remedy that they bring in against the harm due to the excess of transgressions, namely, to equal them or to surpass them. And this is pure heathen blindness.

The baths—a fraud and general cure for these diseases—are customarily as follows: the impostor gets ready with fire,[13] copal, and water. And, stretching out a clean cloth over a mat, he places the sick person on his feet near it. Then he talks to the fire, and then to the water, saying:

[1] Come here, you who have hairs like smoke and like fog, and you, my mother, the one of the precious skirts. And you, white woman. And come, you gods of love; for instance, Cupid, Venus, etc.

tla xihualhuia ayauhtli ytzon pctli, tzon Nonã chal chicueye istac cihuatl tlaxihualhuiã in antlaçolteteo intiquato, in ticaxoch, intitlahui, in tixapel. xi[14]

Come, Her-hair Is Mist, Her-hair Is Smoke [i.e., the fire], my mother, Chalchiuhcueyeh [i.e., the water], White Woman [i.e., the copal]. Come, you Tlahzolteteoh, Cuaton, Caxxoch, Tlahui, Xapel.[15]

Tlā xihuālhuiān, Āyahuitl Ītzon, Pōctli Ītzon, nonān, Chālchiuhcuēyeh, Iztāc-Cihuātl. Tlā xihuālhuiān in anTlahzoltēteoh, in tiCuātōn, in tiCaxxōch, in tiTlāhui, in tiXāpel.

And immediately after naming them he picks up the fire and throws the copal into it and incenses the sick person, as if he were offering him to those gods[16] that he has named. And then he bathes him with the prepared water and immediately passes him over the cloth that is over the mat in as much as he is now clean of the disease that he had, or at least in a better disposition. And while he is doing all these frauds and fictions, he does not cease the incantation, but continues what is above by saying:

[2] Named goddesses, help me, and you, dusky, white, and green sicknesses of love, notice that I have come, I the priest, the prince of spells, green and white terrestrity,[17] do not rise up against me nor attack me on the rebound, I in person am the one who commands it, the priest, the prince of spells.

Xinech itztimamaniqui yayauhqui tlaçolli iztac tlaçolli xoxouhqui tlaçolli onihualla nitlamacazqui ninahualtecutli xoxouhqui tlaloc iztac tlaloc ma noca techuat, ma noca timilacatzoti nomatca nehuatl nitlamacazqui ninahualtecutli.

Come in order to be seeing me, dusky filth, white filth, green filth [i.e., illness provoked by sexual misconduct].[18] I have come. I am the priest; I am the *nahualli*-lord. Green Tlaloc, White Tlaloc [i.e., the force behind the sickness], beware of rising up against me. Beware of turning against me. It is I in person. I am the priest; I am the *nahualli*-lord.

Xinēchitztimahmaniqui, yāyāuhqui tlahzolli, iztāc tlahzolli, xoxōuhqui tlahzolli. Ōnihuāllah. Nitlamacazqui; ninähualtēuctli. Xoxōuhqui Tlāloc, Iztāc Tlāloc, mā noca tēhuahti.[19] Mā noca timīlacatzohti.[20] Nohmatca nehhuātl. Nitlamacazqui; ninähualtēuctli.

It seems that the impostor says this last part in order that they value the cure more and that they pay him better for it, since he lets it be known that, by his curing the sick person, his casting out those illnesses from the patient can be a sufficient cause for all the sickness to pass into the doctor, as if the Devil, being thrown out of a body, would take possession of the same one that threw him out. That is what the last words, "green and white terrestrity, do not rise up against me, etc.," say, and thus he ends them with those others, "I in person command it, the priest, the prince of spells," as if he said, "You do not have power against me because of the great power that I have against you."

Upon having concluded this incantation, with the sick person being now on the cloth that is extended on the mat, this impostor shifts the address to the sky, commending the sick person to the Milky Way, which we [Spaniards] call "the Road of Saint James," in order that the sick man may be entrusted to it, as people say, under its protection and help. And in order to put it under more obligation, he acknowledges it as his maker and creator, and thus he says:

[3] Mother of mine, the one of the starry skirt, you made this one. You gave him life. How, then, are you also against him? How have you turned against him? It is certain that you made life for him. It is certain that in your hands he received being.

Nonançitlal cueye oticmochi huili? oticmo yo litili? cano tehuatl ica tehua? ica timilacatzoa? O tic mochihuilli? O ticmo yo litili mixpantzinco oyecauhqui.

My mother, Citlalcueyeh [i.e., the Milky Way], did you make (H) him? Did you give (H) him life? Is it indeed also you who rise up against him? Do you turn against him? You made (H) him. You gave (H) him life. He became finished in your presence (H).

Nonān, Cītlalcuēyeh, ōticmochīhuilih? Ōticmoyōlītilih? Ca nō tehhuātl īca tēhua? Īca timīlacatzoa? Ōticmochīhuilih. Ōticmoyōlītilih. Mīxpantzinco ōyēcauhqui.

With this the healer ends the cure by fanning the sick man with the *huipil*, if the healer is a woman, and if he is a man he fans him with the blanket with which they usually cover themselves, like one who blows on him in order to remove the exterior dust from him, and in order to impart to him good and healthful air and free him of the infected air[21] in which he is enveloped.

This is all the cure, which they repeat as many times as it seems right to them. And if by chance the sick person gets well, the impostor is accredited for being the best doctor and diviner in the world, but if the sick man either does not improve or dies—which is the more usual thing—the healer excuses himself by inventing another fraud for their imagination or [by saying] that the sick man either did not take care of himself or did not have faith in the cure or that he communicated with another person of dissipated living or that he was keeping bad company, and this is sufficient in order to satisfy such barbarous and blind people.

Others use another manner of incantation for the beginning of this cure and fraud—although in the rest they conform to what has been related, both in the actions as well as in the continuation of the incantation. And thus I shall put down only the first part which is where they differ.

Having got ready, then, with fire and copal and water, and having stretched the cloth out over the mat, and having placed the sick person on his feet next to it as has been said, he begins the incantation by saying:

[4] Come on, come here, the five solar beings,[22] and you, goddesses of love, Cuato and Caxoch, help me. And let us bring here our little god of precious stone. Come also you, my mother {to the water}, the one of the skirt of precious stones. Let us bathe and let us purify here the one entrusted to us, who because of you, goddesses Cuato and Caxoch, has being and life. I in person am the author of this work, the prince of spells, for we are to throw out this sickness of love affairs immediately, right away. Will it last, perchance, until tomorrow or the day after? No, for immediately, in this instant, it is to leave.

tla xihualhuian macuiltonaleque intiquato in ticaxoch tlaxihualhuian tla nican tocotquican tochalchiuhteũtzin tla xihualhuia nonan chalchi cueye tlanican toconaltican, in tomaçehual, in tiquato, ynticaxoch anmo tla chihual an mo yo litil no matca nehuatl ninahualtecutli Toconquixtizque in xoxouhqui tlaçolli niman aman cuix moztla? cuix huiptla? cã niman Aman.

Come, Five-*tonal*s-owners [i.e., the hands]. You who are Cuaton, and you who are Caxxoch, come. Let us now[23] carry thither our Jade-god (H) [i.e., the sick person]. Come [pl], my mother, Chalchiuhcueyeh [i.e., the water]. Let us now go, O Cuaton, O Caxxoch, and bathe our vassal, your creation, the one you two caused to have life. It is I in person. I am the *nahualli*-lord. We will cause the green filth to leave immediately at this instant. Will it be tomorrow? Will it be the day after? Indeed it will be immediately at this instant.

Tlā xihuālhuiān, Mācuīltōnalehqueh. In tiCuātōn, in tiCaxxōch, tlā xihuālhuiān. Tlā nicān tocotquicān[24] toChālchiuhteōtzin. Tlā xihuālhuiān, nonān, Chālchiuhcuēyeh. Tlā nicān toconāltīcān in tomācēhual, in tiCuātōn, in tiCaxxōch, amotlachīhual, amoyōlītīl. Nohmatca nehhuātl. Nināhualtēuctli. Toconquīxtīzqueh in xoxōuhqui tlahzolli niman āman. Cuix mōztla? Cuix huīptla? Ca niman āman.

Then he makes the bath, first incensing the sick person as has been said, and continuing, in the rest, the incantation and actions, as has been said.

This is the general cure that these wretched people use for all these diseases that they say to be "of love affairs" or because of superfluity and excess of transgressions by the consort. Although as has been noted, for these indispositions and misfortunes that they feign to happen because of excess of transgressions in the consort, whether it be licitly or illicitly, in addition to this bath, they give as a remedy, the matching or surpassing of the transgressions of the consort. Thereby they commit an equal number, many more, and greater transgressions—a remedy that only could come out of Hell and its republicans, from where all these figments and idolatrous superstitions originate.

Finally, it occurs to me that in this bath our Enemy has intended to imitate the Holy Sacrament of the baptism since (as we Christians believe that by this means we attain the purity of the soul and the remedy against all the harms of faults and their results) this old and astute Enemy seeks that these unfortunate people, blind in their heathen errors, believe and persuade themselves that by these feigned baths they can attain cleanliness of the body and free themselves of the diseases of temporal pains and harms. May God, through his mercy, disillusion them and bring them to a true knowledge, by inspiring in the ministers new fervors for the teaching of such a blind and barbarous people, in order that everything be converted into His greater power and glory. Amen.

[FIFTH TREATISE][1]

ABOUT THE SEERS AND SUPERSTITIONS OF THE INDIANS AS REGARDS DIVINATION

[Preamble]

IT has been common among all kinds of peoples and nations since the beginning of the world to use divination, and they have availed themselves of it for different ends, although the most common has been in being uncertain about the choice of persons for offices, in the resolution of difficulties, and for discovering delinquents. Of all these instances we find examples in profane and sacred writings, as is seen in chapter 16 of Leviticus; in Numbers, chapters 26, 33, 34, and 36; in Deuteronomy, first chapter; and throughout the book of Joshua; in First Kings, in the public election of Saul; in First Jonas,[2] whereby he was found at fault. And in the New Testament we find it expressed in the election of Saint Matthias as an apostle, Acts 26.[3] The books of the gentiles are full of this, from where the superstition of auguries and haruspices came. But it should be noted that every time the use of divination is found in Divine Scripture it was by the order of the Lord,[4] whom it pleased at that time to declare thus his will, without which requisite the use of divination would not be licit. Because, being by essence a pure contingency—to which Cicero, in 2 *De dicin,*[5] applied the name of temerity—it would be a manifest lack of prudence and even of judgment to attribute to, and depend on, temerity for the resolution of cases which are serious and which by their nature ask for attentive consideration and very mature judgment. And because the words of Cicero will be of use for the intent of this Treatise, I will put them down here. He says, then, *quid enim sors est? Idem prope modum quod micare, quid talos iacere, quod tesseras, quibus inrebus te meritas, et casus, non ratio, nec consili vn valet. Tota res einuenta fallacijs aut ad questum aut ad superstiçionem aut ad errorem.*[6] And if a gentile knew the uncertainty and deceit of the contingency of divination, there will be little [reason] to doubt how little credit should be given to it among Christians. And this is well proved when those who depend on it for their resolutions or persuade themselves that through its contingency they can arrive at a knowledge of occult things, as Saint Thomas, in 2.2.c.95, ar. 8,[7] says. And it should be noted that the sacrilege with which we are dealing here is this one in which one seeks the knowledge of occult and future things, a thing which should be completely avoided. And [avoidance of divination] is a common doctrine of the saints; even when mentioning the places of the Scripture in which the licit use of divination is found, [they condemn it,] since they tell us it has been a privilege, and elsewhere [the use was] licit, having been a divine disposition. But all agree that it should not be imitated, and therefore Saint Jerome says, *super sonam non debemus sub exemplo sonae sortibus credere, vel illud de actibus apostolorum huius testimonio copulare vbi sorte Mathias in Apostolatum eligit.*[8] And Bede [says] about the Acts of the Apostles, *non exemplo Matiae, vel qd. Ionas propheta sorte de prehensus sit indifferenter sortibus est cre dendum cum priuilegia singulorum communem legem omnino-facere non possint,*[9] etc., so those who, looking for excuses for their perversity, wishing to make use of a thing so forbidden among Christians, are convicted of being hypocrites and superstitious people. Under the cloak of religion they avail themselves of sorcery, claiming it is a thing of the Apostles with the end of foretelling future events, as Saint Isidore, in book 4, *Etymol.*, says: *sortilegij sunt, qui sub nomine fictae religionis per quasdam, quas sanctorum, seu Apostolorum vocant sortes diuinat*[*ion*]*is, scientiam profitentur.*[10] This pestiferous superstition stands so [firmly] introduced among these Indians that there are many who live from it alone and support themselves as with a profession, to whom the needy ones come with their doubts and difficulties as to an oracle, thinking to find in them a remedy for their travails and a resolution of their doubts. These people are consulted by those sick with troublesome afflictions in order to know their cause and remedy, by those who have sustained a loss of possessions, by those whose wives, children, or slaves have left them, and by those who have been robbed in order to see where they will find what was taken from them and who was the aggressor—things possible to conjecture and impossible to know in the manner that these profess unless a pact with the Devil intervenes, because of which Saint Isidore, in book 4, *Etymolo.*, said, *sortilegium est quoddam genus culturae idolorun ex Daemonum consultationibus futura praedicendo.*[11] Unless it is what Saint Augustine, in *Lib. de nat. Daemonum*, said: *diuinitate enim se esse plenos assimulant, et astutia quadam fraudulenta hominibus futura coniectant,*[12] because, by feigning to be divine, with diabolic astuteness and sagacity, by conjecturing some things from others, they deceive and defraud the people, pretending to know the future, as will be seen in its place.

The thing that surprises me most is that, while, as has been said, contingency is the precise essence of fortune—and this is so well established that there is no one who can be ignorant of it no matter how barbaric he may be—the ignorance of the Indians is so great, they have such dull intellects and such darkened natural light, that they consider things that in themselves depend on free will to be by chance, remitting to its contingency the resolution of their doubts, which is the limit to which blindness can reach. And to this blindness they add that they consider it to be evident that the fortune told without an invocation will not have the desired effect, nor will it have its proper effect, so that they attribute the greatest part of the prediction to the incantation. They are persuaded that the instruments take on their proper disposition because of the words.

The first of this is evident because, in order to prophesy using the hands, they do not do it by the lines—a custom and superstition of gypsies—but by measuring the left forearm from the elbow to the tips of the fingers with the right hand, extending the palm along the forearm. And it is the rule for prophesying that the measure come out long or short—as if whether the measure comes out unequal or equal were not dependent on the will alone of the fortune-teller who is measuring, shortening or lengthening the palm at his will, or by measuring along a straight line or a more or less crooked one as will be told in the next chapter. The same thing happens in the fortune they tell with pebbles or maize kernels, which they throw upon a cloth that they spread out in front of themselves on the flat floor. And they judge the fortune according to whether the pebbles or kernels have fallen near or far from themselves, not noticing that by throwing them hard they will go far and they will remain near if they are thrown gently, with the one or the other depending on the will of the one who does the throwing.

For another thing, in these two kinds of sorcery (as in the rest) they have their incantations, invocations, and spells with which they conjure and cast spells on the instruments of the divination, such as the hands or the fingers, by invoking their heathen gods, and by casting a spell on the pebbles or maize kernels that they throw, as will be told in more detail in its place; in which it can easily be seen how much they are in the beginnings of the true Christian religion, which so much abhors such superstitions, because of which Saint Augustine, in *Book of Christian Doctrine,* said, *omnes igit artes huiusmodi l. nugatoriae l. noxiae superstitionis ex quadam pestifera societate hominum e Daemonum quasi pacta infidelis, et dolosae amicitiae constituta penitus ff. repudiandae et fugiendae Xpiano,*[13] and Saint Gregory, *Contra idolorum cultores et haruspices, atq⁺ sortilegos fraternitatem tuam vehementius pastorali hortamur inuigilare custodia,*[14] where the saint paired and put idolatry and fortune-telling in the same class. And truly it is the same thing, since in fortune-telling they avail themselves of the favor of the Devil, and frequently they invoke him, or at least the gods of their heathenism, so one should put much greater care than that which there is today in extirpating such an evil custom. Let us come, then, to the deed.

CHAPTER 1

About Fortune-telling with the Hands

I AM putting in first place this kind of fortune-telling, which I mentioned in the preceding paragraph, because it is the one most used by the Indians. In order to understand this fortune-telling, one should be aware of the fact that they make use of it for all kinds of difficulties, be they present doubts or past ignorances, or be they future events or nonfuture ones. By this fortune-telling they determine what the cause of illnesses may be, what the medicine will be, or whether none will be of any help, who did the stealing, where a missing person will be found, for what cause or because of whom and where he went, or whether he will return and show up. So that, considered carefully, with this alone all troubles would have a remedy if it were not a pernicious deception of Satan, against which Saint Augustine, {[in] *De ciuitate Dei*}, said, *proinde omnis inquisitio, et omnis curatio, quae adiuinis, et magicis artibus l. ab ipsis Daemonibus in idolorum cultura expetitur mors potius est dicendae, quam vita.*[1] All is death and perdition without God, whom, without faith, one can neither possess nor please. But these unfortunate people, lacking it, look for the remedy where it is impossible to find. They go, then, with these doubts to the fortune-tellers and seers, which in their language they call *ticitl,*[2] which almost always coincides with doctor, and therefore I have warned that this name should be considered suspicious.

They propound to such a person their doubt and the cause that they know or the circumstances of it, and the very learned and astute one asks all that can be of use to him for a proper conjecture. After becoming well informed of the case and the circumstances of it, he does his fortune-telling, for which he gets ready with the *piçiete* or *tenexiete,* which is the same thing with the addition of lime. Picking it up with his right hand, he puts it in his left palm, and there he breaks it up with his thumb. And then he adjusts his clothes like a person who is preparing for some business of importance. Then, gathering up his belongings, he sits down neatly,[3] and then, rubbing between his two palms the *piçiete* or *tenexiete* which he previously put in one of them, he begins his invocation and incantation in order to tell the fortune, saying:

[1] Help, for now it is time, you the possessed one, nine times beaten and nine times rubbed between my hands (or nine times cudgeled one), green possessed one, mother and father of mine, son of the Milky Way, my mother, Supine Rabbit, you who are resplendent, Mirror that is Smoking, I warn you that no one fail in his obligation, no one resist grumblingly.

Tlacuele, tla xihualhuia tlamacazqui chiucnauhtlatecapanilli chiucnauhtlatlamatellolli (others say chiucnauhtla tlatetzotzontli), xoxouhqui tlamacazqui nonan, nota citlalcueye ipiltzin nonan cetochtli àquetztimani titzotzotlacatoc tezcatl in çan hualpopocatimani ayac tlàtlacoz ayac tlahuexcapehuaz

Let it be soon! Come [pl], priest, Nine-[times]-rock-slapped-one, Nine-[times]-crumbled-in-the-hands-one (*others say:* Nine-[times]-rock-pounded-one), Green Priest, my mother, my father [i.e., my mainstay], Citlalcueyeh's child [i.e., the tobacco], and my mother, One Rabbit, She-is-supine, She-lies-glittering, Mirror that is just smoking hither [i.e., the earth]. No one will ruin things. No one will start by grumbling.

Tlā cuēl eh! Tlā xihuālhuiān, tlamacazqui, Chiucnāuhtlatecapānīlli,[4] Chiucnāuhtlahtlamātelōlli (*others say:* Chiucnāuhtlahtlatetzohtzontli), Xoxōuhqui Tlamacazqui, nonān, notah, Cītlalcuēyeh īpiltzin, nonān, Cē-Tōchtli, Ahquetztimani, Tzotzotlacatoc,[5] Tezcatl in zan huālpopōcatimani. Ayāc tlahtlacōz. Ayāc huēxcāpēhuaz.[6]

[2] Now I kiss the five solar beings[7] that I brought for this purpose.

Ca nic tenamiqui macuiltonale ca oniquinhualhuicac.

Indeed I kiss Five-*tonal*s-owner [i.e., one hand].[8] Indeed I brought it and the other one[9] hither.

Ca nictēnnāmiqui Mācuīltōnaleh. Ca ōniquinhuālhuīcac.

Here he kisses his two thumbs, crossed one over the other with his hands together as if for praying, and continues:

[3] Come on, come here, my brothers, the five solar beings {the fingers},[10] who all look, and have your faces, toward one side {because all have their surfaces toward one side}, and end in shells of pearls {for the fingernails}. Come and let us examine our enchanted mirror {here he begins to measure the forearm by palm lengths}, in order that we may see what god, which powerful one, now breaks, now destroys, and totally consumes our precious stone {for the sick person}, our jewel, our rich emerald or rich plume.

Tla xihualhuian nooquichtihuan in macuiltonallèq⁺ cemithuallèq⁺ (and others cemixeque) tzonepitzitzime tlatocon itacan tonahualtezcauh ac teotl, ac mahuiztli ictlapoztequi ic tlaxaxamania, yc quixpoloa in tochalchiuh intocozqui, intoquetzal

Come, my older brothers, Five-*tonal*s-owners, One-courtyard-owners [i.e., the hands] (*and others:* One-face-owners [i.e., the fingers]),[11] Nacre-as-hair (H) [pl] [i.e., the fingers]. Let us go see our *nahualli*-mirror [i.e., the patient's

Tlā xihuālhuiān, noquichtīhuān, in Mācuīltōnalehqueh, Cemithualehqueh (*and others:* Cemīxehqueh), Tzoneptzitzinmeh.[13] Tlā toconittacān tonāhualtezcauh. Āc teōtl, āc mahuiztli īc tlapozte-

forearm]. Who is the god, who is the marvelous being who thus breaks things, who thus shatters things, who thus destroys our jade, our jewel, our *quetzal*-feather [i.e., the sick person]?[12]

qui, īc tlaxahxamānia, īc quīxpoloa in tochālchiuh, in tocōzqui, in toquetzal?

[4] Come on, come and let us go up our precious ladder {because he measures the forearm upwards}, for it is not to be for tomorrow or the next day, but now, right away, we are to see who is the one who kills the son of the gods.

tlaxi hualhuian tlatotocon ecahuican tochalchiuh ecahuaz, amo quimoztla, ahmo quin huiptla, çaniman axcan toconitazque ac yequimictia in teteo ipiltzin

Come. Let us climb up our jade ladder [i.e., the forearm]. It will not be by-and-by tomorrow, it will not be by-and-by the day after tomorrow, but it will be immediately now that we will see who is the one who is killing the child of the gods [i.e., the sick person].

Tlā xihuālhuiān. Tlā tocontlehcahuīcān[14] tochālchiuhehcahuāz. Ahmō quin mōztla, ahmō quin huīptla, zan niman āxcān toconittazqueh āc yeh quimictia in tēteoh īmpiltzin.

[5] Note that I command it, I, the knowing priest or doctor or seer, consummate in wisdom.

nomatca nehuatl nitlamacazqui, nitlamatini, nimimatca tiçitl.

It is I in person. I am the priest. I am the sage. I am the skillful doctor.

Nohmatca nehhuātl. Nitlamacazqui. Nitlamatini. Ninihmatcātīcitl.[15]

This is the common incantation with which they tell fortunes, and as they recite it, they measure the left forearm with the right palm, as I have said. And if the fortune-telling dealt with whether some sick person would recover or die, and the last palm ended by matching the measuring fingers with the ones being measured,[16] they prognosticate that he will die right away and that there is no longer any remedy that can help him. In the last measuring, if a lot is left over on the measured arm, for example, the fingers or half a hand on the forearm measured, they say that the sickness still has a lot left to run. And thus they say, *oc huetztoc*,[17] which means, "He will be lying down for a long time yet," as if he said, "He will not get up so quickly," or "They will not carry him off to be buried so quickly." In the incantation given for this fortune-telling with the hands, it is to be noticed that some [seers] change some of the words, expressing more the invocation to the Devil and his power, because where the incantation given above says at the beginning, "Help, for now is the time," etc., they prefix:

"I am the one who commands it, the prince of Hell, the priest or possessed one." *Nomat ca ne huatl ni mictlantecutli nitlamacazqui.*[18]

{And others:}[19] "I the Prince of the spells." *Ninahualtecutli.*[20]

{Others:} "I command it in person, the page." *Nomatca nehuatl nixollotl.*[21]

And it is as if he said "The Servant of the Devil," for the same name of *xollotl* is also applied to the Devil, and thus it will translate, "I the Devil command it."

In the incantation, where it says "Our precious ladder," *Tochalchiuh ecahuaz*,[22] {they say,} "Our infernal ladder," *To mictlan ecahuaz.*[23]

Others conclude the incantation, saying:

[6] I in person, the prince of Hell, I want him to know[24] the state of this sick person. Will he perchance die soon? or not? Is he to last rather for some time?

Nomatca nehuatl ni mictlantecutli quenye quitlamachtia cuix quitlanahuitiz? ca. cuix achicatiz.

It is I in person. I am MictlanTeuctli. How does it [i.e., the medicine] already make him prosper? [i.e., Is it helping him?] Will it perchance make him worse? Or on the contrary, will he last a while longer?

Nohmatca nehhuātl. NiMictlānTēuctli. Quēn ye quitlamachtia? Cuix quitlanahuītīz? Cah,[25] cuix achicatiz?

With what has been reported, the express pact with the Devil can hardly be denied, especially seeing that by this means they say and foresee things impossible to reach by human reason, and more so since it is evident that the measurement's coming out equal or unequal [depends on the will of the seer].[26] And when I make this objection to some of these seers, they answer that it is not thus but that, without their being able to avoid or prevent it, the hand becomes longer or shorter and goes straight or twists in the measurement. And if they are speaking the truth in the answer, therewith it is well proved to be the express work of the Devil. Also I observe that by the same measuring of the forearm to tell one's fortune, they prognosticate the remedy of an illness and likewise whether any remedy exists, and also whether the sickness is caused naturally, which they call, *Dios onechmomaquili*,[27] which means "God gave it to me," or else whether it is by means of some bewitchment, a thing which they believe easily, or whether it was caused by only the will of some enemy of the sick person or some person whom he has angered. And in this last case their folly reaches so far as for them to put the blame of illnesses on the saints and even on the Virgin, Our Lady, giving as a reason that they have angered her or another saint because of having done some discourtesy to their images, such as when boys urinate in the oratory or do some other such thing, or not having celebrated their holy day. If by chance he prognosticates the anger of some saint to be the cause of the sickness, they immediately seek to find out through fortune-telling about the means of placating the angered saint, because that will be the cure of the illness. And usually they prognosticate that they will placate them by making some image for them, or, if they already have one, by making it some clothing or a veil, and by adding some ornament to it and by making some feast for them. And none of the said things is to take place without banquets and drunken sprees and many offenses to God, Our Lord, and consequently to the saint that they name, so that the sick people would get worse if the cause and remedy of the illness were the one which the false seers say. But since they have their reputation so firmly established, [it does not matter whether] the sick person dies or gets well.[28] If he gets well, the fame and credence of the seer remains more fixed. If he dies, there is no one to enter an action against him for the error. And thus the frauds and deceptions and the perdition of the souls of these wretched people continue, and more so when the seer says that the cause of the sickness is such and such a person. Because of the enmity that they have for him [i.e., the person named], the hatred becomes established for generation after generation, and the rancor lasts for many years without lessening, and no reason whatever is sufficient to dissuade or placate them, not even denying them absolution in confessions, because the credence of the false seer is established and fixed in them more than that of the preachers of the Gospel.

Even if no further harm resulted from these fortune-tellings than the one that I have just reported, such as the use of *ololiuqui*[29] and peyote which I spoke of in the Treatise about them, one should use all possible diligence in totally extirpating such a pernicious thing from among Christians, whose life and improvement consists in love and charity, because it is certainly a very great pity to see the perdition of souls caused by these hatreds and rancors born from these false predictions, and more so if one considers that no diligence can avail to wrest from the heart what has once entered by this means.

It is the same when they foretell about thefts or when they divine who carried off someone's daughter or wife because, if they place the blame on Juan, and the wife does not appear, there is no satisfaction that suffices, and the credulous accuser lives in perpetual affliction, and the offended persons in perpetual hatred of him.

In order to use this fortune-telling with the hands in cases of thefts or absences and in cases of remedies for sickness, the same reported incantation serves, with some changes of words that refer to the case about which the fortune is told; for instance, if the fortune is told concerning what remedy the sickness will have, where in the incantation it said,[30] "Immediately, right away, we are to see who is the one who is killing," etc., *Tla tiquitilican toconitazq̄, ac ye quimictia,*[31] etc., they say "We are to see what remedy will be useful to the son of the gods. Will he perchance do as well with the medicine called white woman?" *Tla tiquitilican teteo ipiltzin ahço quinamiquiz ahço quihuelmatiz inpahtzintli iztac atlinan çihuatzintli,*[32] etc. {Daughter of the water-herb[33]}. "Perchance he will be well with the yellow possessed one or with the green possessed one," etc. *Aco quihuelmatiz incozauhqui tlamacazqui* {*tlacopati*[34]}, *ahnoço xoxoqui tlamacazqui*[35] {the herb *piciete*}.

And as they say these words, they measure the forearm until the fortune comes out to their will. And if it comes out good, they apply the medicine which the fortune indicated.[36]

For theft [*lit.*, smoke eye] in the same place they say:

[7] Let us see[37] the son of the gods. Who carried away (or who smoked) his maize or his little animal (if the stolen thing is an animal)?	tla tiquitilican teteo ipiltzin aquin oqui huicac, ac oquichtequili ytonacayotzin anoço y yolcatzin.
Let us see for the child of the gods who is the one who has taken, who has stolen his maize (or perhaps his animal) from him.	Tlā tiquittilīcān tēteoh īmpiltzin āc in ōquihuīcac, āc ōquichtequilih ītōnacāyōtzin (ahnōzo īyōlcātzin).

If it is a wife or a daughter who is missing, they say:

[8] Let us find out where she is or where she went *(the wife or the daughter)*.[38] Did she perchance go very far? Or is it not so, but rather that this unhappy man's wife has not absented herself, but remains quiet?	tlatiquitilican campa catqui campa oya àço hueca oya, ahço ayocmo neçiz? °ca?[39] yeoc onca inamitzin icnotlacatl.
Let us see for him where she is, where she went. Did she perhaps go far away? Will she perhaps no longer appear? Or on the contrary, is the poor man's wife still there?	Tlā tiquittilīcān cāmpa catqui, cāmpa ōyah? Ahzo huehca ōyah? Ahzo ayocmō nēciz? Cah, ye oc oncān īnāmictzin icnōtlācatl?

In all these incantations where they put the word *ca,* it is an adversative particle and contradicts the entire preceding clause.[40] In order to know who carried them away, they say:

[9] Who carried them off or who kidnapped them?	A aquin oquihuicac aquin oquichtec
Who is the one who took her? Who is the one who stole her?	Āc in ōquihuīcac? Āc in ōquichtec?

As above in the thefts [*lit.,* smokes] of things, in order for the incantation to serve for everything, they change only the words that refer to the case about which it is said, although they always try to disguise things with metaphorical words—the ones that they call *nahualtocaitl,*[41] which means "language or name that wizards use."

I have arrested and punished many Indian men and women for this crime, although, having made a calculation, there have been more women than men. And these fortune-tellers are found in many provinces, because, on account of the name of seers, they are highly respected and highly cherished and very well provided with necessities. And since the profession does not cost them any money—but only memorizing the fortune-telling incantation and, along with that, saying they know a lot and that there is nothing that can hide from their knowledge—they easily enter into the profession and, with a greater facility in the performance, they are certain to profit. If, for our sins, he has got the prediction right once—a thing which frequently happens for anyone who has good reasoning—he becomes so reputed that not only Indians but Spaniards as well consult him, as I found out in the village of Yautepec[42] of the Marquisate, where a woman went to consult a seer of this kind about some clothing that had been stolen from her, and Our Lord willed that the one who had been right at other times should err this time by putting the blame on a person who was blameless, so that the case came to my attention, and the Holy Office punished the consulting woman.[43] For better success in their fraud, some of these fortune-tellers[44] drink the *ololiuqui*[45] in addition, and with this they more frequently hit the mark, because the Devil answers their doubts, by virtue of the pact that intervenes through the drinking of the *ololiuqui,*[46] as has been said in its place, and they disguise it by saying that they foretold it through divination. And because in this chapter I have made mention of how sometimes such fortune-tellers say that the sickness is caused by the anger of some saint, it will be necessary to extend myself more on this point in order that it be better understood and because also they add to those saints the ones they consider to be gods, such as clouds, hills, rivers, the air, and fire, and other things like this, since, when the fortune-teller finds himself obstructed, not finding a cause to which to attribute the sickness of the patient, in order to find a way out for his fraud, he says in his fortune-telling, in the place where it fits consistent with what has been reported above, the following:

[10] Here I must see in the mirror of my spell[47] who is the one who harms him, who is the one who is angry. Is he perhaps some saint? And for this, come, the nine times beaten one, the nine times crushed one, etc.	Nican nitlachiaz inamoxco, aquin on in quitlauelia aquin moqualanaltia ahço Santo tlaxihualhuia chicnautlatetzontli, chicnautlamateloli &.

Here I will look in my book [i.e., the patient's forearm]. Who is that person who hates him? Who is the one who is angry (H)? Is it perchance a Saint? Come [pl], Nine-[times]-rock-pounded-one, Nine-[times]-crumbled-in-the-hands-one [i.e., the tobacco], *etc.*

Nicān nitlachiaz in nāmoxco. Āc in ōn in quitlahuēlia? Āc in mocualānaltia? Ahzo santoh? Tlā xihuālhuiān, Chiucnāuhtlatetzohtzontli, Chiucnāuhtlamātelōlli, *etc.*

And he continues as has been reported above until, by making his measurements by palms, he foretells that it is some saint who causes the sickness. After having foretold that some saint is the causer of the sickness, it remains to foretell who that saint is, and thus, by making their measurements, they again tell the fortune, grafting onto the incantation, in the place where they fit, the following words:

[11] Let us find out who you are, you saint who are angry. Are you perchance Our Lady? Or perhaps are you Saint Gaspar or perhaps Saint John,[48] etc.[49]

Ac tehuatl y timoqualanaltia? ahço totlaçonātzin Ahço san gaspartzin Ahço san Juantzin, &c.

Who are you who are angry (H)? Is it perhaps Our Beloved-Mother (H) [i.e., the Virgin Mary]? Is it perhaps Saint Gaspar (H)? Is it perhaps Saint John (H)? *etc.*

Āc tehhuātl in timocualānaltia? Ahzo ToTlazohNāntzin? Ahzo SanGaspartzin? Ahzo SanJuantzin, *etc.*[50]

In this manner they speak and measure with their palms until it comes out to their purpose, and then they say that such and such a saint is the one who is causing the sickness. When the fortune-teller[51] has not found a saint, he goes on with his incantation and his measurements, submitting other gods and things that they adore, saying:

[12] Who is the angry one? Are they perhaps the owners of the earth,[52] the angels of God (for they call the clouds this)?

ac moqualanaltia acoahuaque Dios iAngelo tzitzihuan

Who is angry (H)? Are they perhaps Water-owners, God's angels [i.e., the clouds]?

Āc mocualānaltia? Ahzo Āhuahqueh, Dios īangelohtzitzinhuān?

And if the fortune has not emerged, they continue:

[13] Let us find out if the angry ones are the forest gods and he fell into their hands, or if he is One Rabbit face-up (for the earth), or is he the one who is my Father and mother, the four reeds that sparkle (for the fire).

Àco ohuican chaneque inmac ohuetz, ànoço cetochtli aquetztimani ànoco nota no nonan[53] nahui acatl milintica &

Did he perhaps fall into the hands of the Dwellers in Dangerous Places [i.e., the forest gods]? Or is it perhaps One Rabbit, She-is-supine [i.e., the earth]? Or is it perhaps our father, our mother [i.e., our mainstay], Four Reed, He-is-scintillating [i.e., the fire]? *etc.*

Ahzo Ohhuihcān Chānehqueh īmmāc ōhuetz? Ahnōzo Cē-Tōchtli, Ahquetztimani? Ahnōzo notah, nonān, Nāhui-Ācatl, Milīnticah? *etc.*

Finally they foretell who is the angry one, and then, in order to appease his anger, they begin the divination of the remedy in which the principal thing that one should note is that they give a formal idolatry as a remedy. If they foretell the angry one to be the fire, the water, the earth, the winds, the clouds, or the forest gods, which are like the fauns and satyrs of ancient paganism, they give as a means of pacifying them the offering of a sacrifice, and thus they order the sick person to offer incense, candles, bouquets, pieces of cloth, and other things, and even food and drink for the angered god. For example, if the patient became sick in the forest, they order that he put, in the place where he felt himself afflicted with the sickness, an offering of incense, etc., to the forest gods in order to placate them; if it was beside a river, they order that he put his offering next to it, and if at some crossroad, that he sacrifice there to the god of that passage, where there usually is some rock that they adore or a pile of rocks where they sacrifice, or by adoring the very pile of rocks or the god that they think is present in it; if they say that the angry one is the fire, to which they give the same veneration as to the saints, they command the sick person to make the sacrifice to the fire by putting it in a peculiar brasier over the altar and throwing on a lot of incense (for which copal serves) and putting next to it many bouquets and candles. And although perhaps they do not put the brasier of fire over the altar but over the platform, the cause is not less veneration but a fear that the oratory and even the house might burn up on them through their careless and drunken acts which usually accompany such sacrifices, with their circumstances, where in the one and in the other the Devil is so interested. Of all the instances mentioned, I have sentenced cases from many Indian villages where it has been proved by means of the accomplices themselves, and by means of other witnesses, that such sacrifices have been made, and many times the offerings themselves have been brought from the places where they have put them, as happened to me with a woman fortune-teller from Atenango who commanded a sick person to make his sacrifice to a rock in a pass where the illness had occurred. And thus they brought from that place the candles and incense, cotton and tortillas of the sacrifice, with the rock to which it had been made, all of which the Most Reverend Don Juan de la Serna, the Archbishop of Mexico, saw. And every day cases like this happen.

CHAPTER 2

About Another Incantation for Telling Fortunes

For the fortune-telling with the hands, others change the focus, making fire—which they adore—the master of all the work, and thus they enter into the incantation by invoking its favor, saying:

[1] Come here, my Father, the four reeds that throws[1] forth flames {the fire}, the one with blond hair, Prince of the dawn {because at dawn all provide [themselves] with fire}, Father and mother of the gods, for here I have brought my gods of the spell {he seems to say this in reference to the fingers}, my white gods {for the fingernails}. Come on, come on your behalf,

tlaxihual huia nota nahui acatl milintica, tzoncoztli, tlahuizcalpan tecutli, teteo inta teteo innan, caoniquinhualhuicac, no nahuatl teteo huan, noztac teteohuan, tlaxihualhuian ma cuiltonaleque tzoneptzitzime incançe imithual çançe inchayanacauh, tla tocon itancanto nahualtezcauh &.

the five solar beings,[2] you who end in shells of pearls and are on a single balcony and in a single railing-work {because they are together on the hand}, let us see now our mirror of spells, etc.

Come [pl], my father, Four Reed, He-is-scintillating, Yellow-hair, TlahuizcalpanTeuctli, Teteoh Intah, Teteoh Innan [i.e., the fire]. Indeed I have brought my *nahualli*-gods [i.e., the hands], my white-gods [i.e., the fingers]. Come, Five-*tonal*s-owners [i.e., the hands], Nacre-as-hair (H) [pl] [i.e., the fingers], whose-courtyard is only one [i.e., the hands], whose-balustrade is only one [i.e., the hands]. Let us look at our *nahualli*-mirror [i.e., the patient's forearm], *etc.*

Tlā xihuālhuiān, notah, Nāhui-Ācatl, Milīnticah, Tzoncōztli, TlāhuizcalpanTēuctli, Tēteoh Īntah, Tēteoh Īnnān. Ca ōniquinhuālhuīcac nonāhualteōhuān, noztācteōhuān.[3] Tlā xihuālhuiān, Mācuīltōnalehqueh, Tzoneptzitzinmeh, in zan cē īmithual, zan cē īnchayāhuacāuh.[4] Tlā toconittacān tonāhualtezcauh, *etc.*

And in the rest it is almost the same as the first of this type, although some put in its ending and conclusion that which follows:

[2] Immediately now[5] I am to see it, I in person, I who walk it all,[6] in whom the splendor and whiteness of the snow is,[7] a wise experienced old man or a wise experienced old woman, who knows even what there is in Hell and in the heights[8] {as if he said "in Heaven"}, I in person, the priest, prince of the spells.

Ça niman aman nomatcanehuatl, *nihocomoniz* {It is a word invented by the Devil; there is no such word in the Mexican language.[9]} nicepactonal, nicmati huehueel,[10] nicmati illama {if it is a woman}.[11] Nimictlan mati, ni topanmati, nomatca nehuatl nitlamacazqui ninahualtecutli.

It will indeed be immediately at this moment. It is I in person. I am Ohxomoco. I am Cipactonal. I know Old-man [or] I know Old-woman[12] (if it is a woman). I am knowledgeable about Mictlan, I am knowledgeable about Topan [i.e., I have transcendental knowledge.]. It is I in person. I am the priest. I am the *nahualli*-lord.

Ca niman āman. Nohmatca nehhuātl. NOhxōmoco. NiCipactōnal. Nicmati Huēhueh [*or*] nicmati Ilamah (if it is a woman). NiMictlānmati, niTopanmati. Nohmatca nehhuātl. Nitlamacazqui. Nināhualtēuctli.

Another Indian woman, called Maria Madalena, a native of Ozomatlan, the widow of Don Diego de la Cruz, used to add to the fortune-telling these words:

[3] Come on, come on your behalf, you who have skirts of different colors painted[13] like snakes. The five solar beings.[14] Come on, let us ascend my infernal ladder.

tlaxihualhuian nochparcueyeque[15] coa cueyeque macuil tonalleque &. tla toconecauican nomictlan ecauaz &.

Come, Nochpalcueyehqueh,[16] Coacueyehqueh, Five-*tonal*s-owners [i.e., the hands], *etc.* Let us climb my Mictlan ladder [i.e., the patient's forearm], *etc.*

Tlā xihuālhuiān, Nōchpalcuēyehqueh, Cōācuēyehqueh, Mācuīltōnalehqueh, *etc.* Tlā tocontlehcahuīcān[17] noMictlānehcahuāz, *etc.*

It is to be noted that I am fully aware that artificial words are inserted in all these incantations and that they are never heard in everyday language. The Devil must have put them in, perhaps in order for the ignorant people to respect more the words they do not understand—a condition of fools[18]—and because usually those that have a pact with the Devil use such language as not to be understood, because the pact is included in it, and in these incantations those words *Socomoniz*[19] and *nochpar cueyeque*,[20] which not only have no meaning in the Mexican language but cannot even be found in it, because they have letters which the Mexicans do not use, which are *s* and *r*, and thus it is seen that they are put in by artifice of the Devil for this purpose.[21] And the fortune-tellers themselves, when asked about the meaning of these words, answer that they do not know but that they heard them from their forefathers. And thus it passes from hand to hand. Finally, their blindness is so great that they go so far as to claim that the special gift of seers is limited to their locales, I mean, to the villages or cities where they live, or at least that they have it there more strongly than in other places. They give no reason whatever for this other than that it serves as an excuse for them when they make mistakes with fortune-telling in other places and the divination turns out false. But the certain fact about it is that, since, in order to tell fortunes, they first inform themselves of all the circumstances of the case and of the persons who are suspected (and this is[22] limited to the matter of thefts, because in the rest it is impossible to convince them of the error, in keeping with their low mental capacity), they will more easily and certainly hit the mark when acquainted with persons and places than when they have to foretell directly without any other help. This happened precisely this way in the village of Comala, of this district of Atenango, where Maria Madalena [*sic*], the wife of Baltesar [*sic*] Melchor, an inhabitant of Tazmalaca, had come. The said Maria Magdalena told the fortune about a theft, and through it she imputed the theft to one who knew nothing about it, which resulted in all of it coming to my notice. And the fortune-teller, being arrested and being harassed in the interrogation, confessed the deed. And concerning her having cast the blame on someone who was not guilty, she said that, if she erred, it was not because of a defect in the fortune-telling but because of her having done it outside her village. And she proved it with the fact that she had been right in her village in a fortune-telling that she had performed about some scissors, in another about money, and in others about other stolen things, and likewise about illnesses of children and their cures. And she did not note that she had been arrested before for the same crime, and, without being questioned, she confessed to having relapsed into vice, just to endorse the accuracy of fortune-telling. Cross-examined about why she had hit the mark more in her village than outside of it, she did not know the reason. She only said that now she would not tell fortunes outside her village unless she were importuned. Antonio Marques,[23] an inhabitant of Tamazcala,[24] and Antonio Ramirez, Spaniards, were witnesses of all of the aforesaid.

This fraud that outside their village they lack the gift of foretelling the future also extends to the fortune-telling with pebbles and dry or wet maize. And the reason is obvious, because, since in these kinds of fortune-telling there is no mystery other than the conjecture that the seer makes, according to how he informs himself about the circumstances, the details of which are greater among the people of whom he has knowledge, it is certain that he will err less where he has more informants and better bases for conjecture.

I only remark that this happens solely in those who do not have a pact with the Devil, because those who have one are not tied to a place, since they avail themselves of what is revealed to them by the Devil, whose knowledge is the same in any place. And thus by this alone we have a means for testing those who, by dint of fraud, pretend to be seers.

CHAPTER 3

About Fortune-telling Using Maize

FORTUNE-TELLING with maize is the second most important [kind of fortune-telling]. They use it in all the cases which have been mentioned in the fortune-telling with the hands, so that they feign it to be the general remedy for things stolen, for missing persons, for sicknesses and their causes, for their cures and healings.[1] They use this fortune-telling in the following manner. From an ear of maize or from among a lot of maize, the fortune-teller selects the most outstanding and beautiful kernels. He chooses sometimes nineteen kernels and sometimes twenty-five; this difference depends on the different ways they place them on the cloth on which the fortune is told. Having chosen the said kernels, the seer bites off their nibs with his teeth. Then he spreads out in front of himself a cloth doubled and well stretched out so that it does not wrinkle; then he puts on it one part of the kernels according to the quantity that he chose. The one who chose nineteen puts on the right side four very similar kernels, face up and with points toward the left side. He puts an equal number with the same order [on the left side] and then four others without order in front of himself and keeps seven kernels in his hand. Others put four each in each corner and keep nine in their hand, which add up to twenty-five in all. Others put seven in each corner and toss two in front without order and keep nine in the hand, which add up to thirty-nine in all.

Without our lingering on the number, which is not to the point, and coming to the execution, the seer, after having arranged the kernels on the said cloth, begins his fraud with those that remain in his hand, shaking them in it and tossing them in the air and catching them again many times. And then he begins the following invocation:[2]

[1] Welcome, precious man, seven snakes, come also, the five solar beings,[3] all of you who look toward one side. Now is the time when immediately we will see the cause of the pain and affliction of this one. And this is not to be put off until tomorrow or the day after, but immediately, at this moment, are we to see it and know it. I command it thus, the powerful one, I who am the light, the Old Man, I who have to see in my book and in my enchanted mirror which medicine will do him good or whether he is continuing on his way.[4]

tlaxihualmohuica tlahçopilli chicome coatl, tlaxihualuian macuiltonalleque, çe mithualleque, Aman yequene tlatiquitati ynincamanal yni netequipachol, cuix quin moztla? cuix quin huiptla? caniman aman, nomatca nehuatl nicipatl nitonal, nihuehue ye itic non tlachias in namoch, in no tezcauh, intlaquinamiqui pahtzintli, ahnoço motlana huitia.

Come (H), Tlazohpilli, Seven Snake [i.e., the maize kernels]. Come, Five-*tonals*-owners, One-courtyard-owners [i.e., the hands]. It is the instant at last [i.e., now is the time to act]. Let us go in order to see their joke that is his worry. Will it perhaps be by-and-by tomorrow? Will it perhaps be by-and-by the day after tomorrow? It will indeed be immediately at this instant. It is I in person. I am Cipactonal. I am Old-Man. Soon I will look inside my book, my mirror [i.e., the thrown maize kernels], [to see] if a medicine will match him [i.e., be appropriate to him] or if he will get worse.

Tlā xihuālmohuīca, Tlazohpilli, Chicōme-Cōātl. Tlā xihuālhuiān, Mācuīltōnalehqueh, Cemithualehqueh. Āman yēquen eh. Tlā tiquittatih in īncamanāl in īnetequipachōl. Cuix quin mōztla? Cuix quin huīptla? Ca niman āman. Nohmatca nehhuātl. NiCipactōnal.[5] NiHuēhueh. Ye iihtic[6] nontlachiaz in nāmox, in notezcauh, in tlā quināmiqui pahtzintli, ahnōzo motlanahuītia.

And at the time that he says the invocation he traverses the space that he has created with the stretched-out cloth at full speed with the hand in which he holds the kernels, moving his hand along the edge of the cloth over the maize kernels that he placed on it. And the invocation is addressed to the maize kernels and to the fingers of his hands, as if attributing divinity to them. After finishing the words of the incantation, he tosses the maize that he had in his hand into the middle of the cloth, and he judges the fortune according to how the maize kernels fall. The rule that they usually have in judging it is that, if the maize kernels fall face up, the fortune is good—for example, the medicine about which he is consulted will be good, or the lost person or thing that is being sought will show up—and the contrary if the maize kernels fall face down. This kind of fortune-telling, among others, was used with high repute in the village of Oapan[7] by Magdalena Juana, the wife of Don Melchor Gutierrez.

When they use this fortune-telling for other purposes, they change the words, accommodating them to the end they seek; for instance, if it is because of a woman who has run away or because nothing is heard from her, he says:

[2] I have to see in my book and enchanted mirror the worry and trouble of this poor son of the gods. Where did his wife go or in what place does she walk? Is she perchance very far from here? On the contrary, no? On the contrary,[8] is she among us?

Itic non tlachiaz in namox in notezcauh in tlein quitequi pachoa in icnotlacatl teteo ipiltzin, campa oya campa nemi ini na mictzin ahço hueca oya? ca ye oc onca.

I will look inside my book, my mirror [i.e., the thrown maize kernels], [to see] what it is that is troubling the poor man, the child of the gods [i.e., the client]. Where did his wife go? Where is she living? Did she perhaps go far away? Or on the contrary, is she still there?

Iihtic[9] nontlachiaz in nāmox, in notezcauh, in tleh in quitequipachoa in icnōtlācatl tēteoh īmpiltzin. Cāmpa ōyah? Cāmpa nemi in īnāmictzin? Ahzo huehca ōyah? Cah,[10] ye oc oncān?

If the fortune is told for a lost beast or for lost things, he says:

[3] I am to see where the small animal of the son of the gods went. Did they perchance steal it from him and carry it far away? Or, on the contrary, for it is perhaps nearby.

campa oya teteo ipiltzin y yolcaton ahço oquichtequilique, ahço hueca oquihuicaque? ca? çan cana nemi.

Where did the little animal of the child of the gods [i.e., the client] go? Did they perhaps steal it from him? Did they perhaps carry it far away? Or on the contrary, is it living just somewhere?	Cāmpa ōyah tēteoh īmpiltzin īyōlcātōn? Ahzo ōquichtequilihqueh? Ahzo huehca ōquihuīcaqueh? Cah,[11] zan canah nemi?

And in this manner they change the words in all cases where they use fortune-telling, as has been described in the one with the hands. Note that the ignorance and blindness of these wretched people reaches so far that they consult such fortune-tellers in order to know who is a wizard or sorcerer,[12] as they do with the *ololiuqui.*[13] And these fortune-tellers are so audacious and without fear of God that they venture to judge that they are one. And they are believed like prophets—to the very great detriment to the peace and the health of their souls and those of other people—with all the basis for success being in whether the maize kernels fall face up or face down, and also in falling far from or near to the one who throws them. The first is chance, and the second the fortune-teller freely[14] executes, throwing the maize kernels with more force or with less—less if he wants them to remain nearer.

CHAPTER 4

About Fortune-telling Using Maize in Water

OTHERS tell fortunes with maize by throwing it into water, preceded by the incantations and invocations in almost the same way as has been described above, except that they conjure the water, as if warning it to show and reveal what they are in doubt about, as I will speak of in another place with regard to the women impostors that they call *tetonaltia,*[1] who show the face of the sick child to the water, conjuring it in order that it show or find the child's fate, which in the language they call *tonalli,*[2] and return it to the child. The ones who use this fortune-telling make great gestures during the performance, preparing themselves as if for some very arduous business. Dressing in their best, they place in front of themselves a somewhat deep vessel of clean water and then pick up the grains of maize with the hand, and with great energy they say the incantation, and at the end of it they throw the kernels into the water, and very quickly they lean down to see the result in order to judge it. They consider it a happy omen if the maize falls fully to the bottom of the vessel and, on the contrary, as unhappy if it floats at the surface or remains somewhere in the middle. And thus they judge it.

It is to be noted that the outcome of this fortune-telling depends totally on the will of the fortune-teller, because if he wants the maize to sink, he chooses sound, fresh, and firm kernels, and if he wants it to float, he seeks very old and worm-eaten kernels.

This fortune-telling was used among others by Ana Maria, the wife of Gaspar de Morales, in the Marquisate, in the village of Xoxouhtla. And I shall not write at more length about it because it is completely consistent with the preceding ones although of less substance—all being of none.

partera se dize en esta lengua temixiuitiani y de este
postrer nombre q̃ es mas proprio vsan mui raras vezes y no carece
de misterio.

Auiendo de llegar las tales a la execución de su officio hacen
un conjuro en q̃ hablan a sus dedos y juntam.te con la tierra y es
como se sigue.

Acudid aqui los cinco solares, o	Tlaxihualhuian macuil
los de cinco hados, y tu mi madre	tonalleque Nonan cetochtli
un conejo boca arriba aqui has	Aquetztimani, ye nican
de dar principio a un verde dolor	ticyocoyaz xoxouhqui coaci-
veamos quien es la persona q̃ o	huiztli. Tlaquiltacan acmach
de rosa q̃ ya nos viene destru-	tlacatl in yanican techixpolo-
yendo. Cauen, caya el nueue	huitz. tlaxihuallauh tlacuel
veces golpeado, caya echemos	tihuatl tlamacazqui chicnauh-
de aqui al amarillo dolor, al	tlatecapanilli. Tlanican ticpehuican
verde dolor	in cocauhqui coacihuiztli xoxouhqui
	coacihuiztli

Con esto pone el paciente, y pone a parir su preñada
Pero si q̃ el buen sucesso del parto se pretende valer de fuego
y sahumerios q̃ comunm.te son con copal, o con la yerba llamada yauhtli
y en castellano yerba anis: donde dize en el conjuro nueue
veces golpeado chicnauhtlatecapanilli: dize

Mi padre las quatro cañas	Nota nahui acatl milintica	al fuego
q̃ echan llamas con cabellos rubios	Iconcotli iztac cihuatzin	al copal
O. muger blanca	coçauhqui tlamacazqui	a la yerba
o. amarillo espiritado		

Dicho el conjuro, y cogido, o preparado aquello de q̃ se piensa
valer al tiempo del parto, q̃ para facilitarlo pone a parir la
paciente

Page from Sixth Treatise, chapter 1, folio 79r of the Museo manuscript.

[SIXTH TREATISE]

[Untitled][1]

CHAPTER 1

About Those Whom They Call in Their Language *Ticitl*,[2] Which Means Doctor or Seer

IN the preceding Treatises I have pointed out the suspicion that this noun, *ticitl* in the Mexican language, gives rise to. And now, by the grace of God, we have arrived at its proper place, where we will deal more completely with the deceptions that this noun involves, there being concealed in it things that in no way are licit to the faithful and that should be banished with great care.

So I will begin this Treatise with the explication of the noun *tiçitl*. Commonly it is used for what is expressed by our word "doctor," but entering more deeply into it, [we find that] it is accepted among the natives as meaning sage, doctor, seer, and sorcerer, or, perhaps, one who has a pact with the Devil. From this arises the fact that it is taken for granted among the Indians that one of these people called *ticitl* is sufficient as a remedy for any need and trouble, no matter how large it may be, because, if it is a matter of sickness, they attribute to him a knowledge of medicine; if of having angered God, Our Lord, or the Most Holy Virgin, or one of the saints, they make him powerful enough to pacify him or her. Consequently, if he answers that the trouble or the sickness is [due to] the angered *ololiuhqui*, the peyote, or the forest gods (whom they call *ouican chaneque*),[3] or any such thing, the petitions and gifts start flowing to the *tiçitl* in order that he pacify and placate them or provide a remedy. And thus, from an infidelity an idolatry commonly results, because the usual advice is that the patient make a sacrifice to the sun, the fire, the *ololiuhqui*, or to whoever it has struck his [i.e., the *ticitl*'s] fancy to say was the angry one.

If the consultation is about something lost or stolen, or on account of a woman who has run away from her husband, or something similar, here enters the faculty of the false prophecy and divining, as has been pointed out in the preceding Treatises. And the divination is made in one of two ways: either through fortune-telling or by drinking peyote or *ololiuhqui* or tobacco for this purpose, or by ordering that another person drink it, and by giving the sequence that should be followed in it. And in all of this there is an implicit pact with the Devil, who, by means of the said drinks, frequently appears to them and speaks to them, making them understand that the one who is talking to them is the *ololiuhqui* or peyote or whatever other potion they will have drunk for that purpose. And the pity is that many believe both him [i.e., the Devil] and the impostors better than [they believe] the evangelical preachers.

Coming now in particular to the frauds and tricks with which these whom they call *ticitl* delude and confuse almost all of these people like apes of Simon Magus, we will start where a man does, at the entrance and miseries of life, which is at childbirth.

Page from Sixth Treatise, chapter 1, folio 79v of the Museo manuscript.

Because of the circumstances of midwifery, its exercise by means of women is accepted in all nations, and the same thing occurs in this nation of the Indians, and the said noun *ticitl* includes women. And also they call them *tepalehuiani*,[4] which means "male helper or female helper," because that which is expressed by "midwife" is called in this language *temixiuitiani*,[5] and this latter word, which is more proper, is seldom used—a thing that is not without mystery.

When these women come to the performance of their profession, they make an incantation in which they speak to their fingers and at the same time to the earth, and it is as follows:

[1] Come here, the five solar beings[6] or those of five fates, and you, my mother, one rabbit face up. Here you [sg] are to start a green pain. Let us see who is the powerful person who already comes destroying us. Come on, come. Come on already, the nine-times beaten one. Come on already, let us throw out of here the yellow pain, the green pain.

Tla xihualhuian macuil tonalleque nonan cetochtli Àquetztimani, ye nican ticyocoyaz xoxouhqui coacihuiztli, tla tiquittacan ac mach tlacatl in ya nican techixpolotiuitz, tlaxihuallauh, tlacuel tèhuatl tlamacazqui chicnauhtlatecapinilli, tla nican ticpehuican in coçauhqui coacihuiztli xoxouhqui coaçihuiztli.

Come, Five-*tonal*s-owners [i.e., the hands]. My mother, One Rabbit, She-is-supine [i.e., the earth], soon you will create here the green palsy [i.e, the labor pains]. Let us see whoever is the person who already comes destroying us here. Come. Let it be you soon, priest, Nine-[times]-rock-slapped-one [i.e., the tobacco]. Let us shoo away from here the yellow palsy, the green palsy.

Tlā xihuālhuiān, Mācuīltōnalehqueh. Nonān, Cē-Tōchtli, Ahquetztimani, ye nicān ticyōcoyaz[7] xoxōuhqui cōahcihuiztli. Tlā tiquittacān āc mach tlācatl in ye nicān tēchīxpolohtihuītz. Tlā xihuāllauh. Tlā cuēl tehhuātl, tlamacazqui, Chiucnāuhtlatecapānīlli. Tlā nicān ticpēhuīcān in cōzauhqui cōahcihuiztli, xoxōuhqui cōahcihuiztli.

With this she puts down the *piçiete*[8] and sets her pregnant one to giving birth.

But if for the good outcome of the childbirth she intends to avail herself of fire and incensings, which commonly are with copal or with the herb called *yauhtli*—that is, anise—where she says in the incantation "nine-times beaten one," *chicnauhtlatecapanilli*, she says:

[2] My father, the four reeds that throw off flames, with blond hair, or white woman, or yellow possessed one.

Nota nahui acatl milintica tzoncoztli {to the fire} iztac cihuatzin {to the copal} coçauhqui tlamacazqui {to the herb}.

My father, Four Reed, He-is-scintillating, Yellow-hair [i.e., the fire], White Woman (H) [i.e., the copal], Yellow Priest [i.e., the *iyauhtli*].

Notah, Nāhui-Ācatl, Milīnticah, Tzoncōztli, Iztāc-Cihuātzin, Cōzauhqui Tlamacazqui.

Having said the incantation and chosen or prepared that of which she intends to avail herself at the time of the childbirth, and in order to facilitate it—she sets the patient to giving birth.

In place of what has been related, other women use the manner and incantation that follows. They pick up the *piçiete* in the hand and crush it, and then they move the hand with the *piçiete* over the belly of the pregnant woman, especially over the fetus, and say:

[3] Come on, come, the nine-times beaten one, the nine-times cudgeled one. You goddesses, Cuato and Caxoch {proper names}, come to make this childbirth easy, opening up the fountain. And you, possessed ones, the ones of the five fates {the fingers}[9] and who all look toward one direction, all of you,[10] help me in order that we catch and hinder whosoever is the one who is causing this harm, for he now wishes totally to destroy the daughter of the Gods, or better, the one who will be giving birth, &.

Tlacuel tla xihuallauh chinauhtlatetzotzontli chicnauhtlatecapantli, tlacuel xichualquetzati in ammaapan in tiquato, inticaxoch, tlacuel tla xihualhuian tlamacazq+ macuiltonallèq+, cemithualleque tlatoconquitzquican in ac mach tlacatl, in ye nican ye techixpoloa teteoipiltzin.

Let it be soon! Come, Nine-[times]-rock-pounded-one, Nine-[times]-rock-slapped-one [i.e., the tobacco]. Let it be soon! Come, you who are Cuaton and you who are Caxxoch,[11] in order to open up your channel [i.e., the vaginal passage]. Let it be soon! Come, priests, Five-*tonal*s-owners, One-courtyard-owners [i.e., the hands]. Let us seize whoever is the person who already here already is destroying us and the child of the gods [i.e., the woman in labor].

Tlā cuēl! Tlā xihuāllauh, Chiucnāuhtlatetzohtzontli, Chiucnāuhtlatecapāntli. Tlā cuēl! Xichuālquetzatih in amāpan,[12] in tiCuātōn, in tiCaxxōch. Tlā cuēl! Tlā xihuālhuiān, tlamacazqueh, Mācuīltōnalehqueh, Cemithualehqueh. Tlā toconquītzquīcān in āc mach tlācatl in ye nicān ye tēchīxpoloa tēteoh īmpiltzin.[13]

After the birth has taken place, the superstition concerning the infant begins immediately and, in order to wash it, she makes an incantation to the vessel and to the water, and it is thus:

[4] Come on, come here, you, my precious cup, and also you who have precious stones for a skirt {the water, because of the vegetation[14]}, for the hour has now arrived when you are to wash and clean here the one who had life because of you and was born in your hands.

Tlaxihualhuian nochalchiuhxical nona chalchicueye, ye nican ticaltiz ye nican ticpòpoaz in momac tlacat in momac oyol.

Come, my jade vessel [i.e, the basin] and my mother, Chalchiuhcueyeh [i.e., the water]. Here you [sg] [i.e., the water] will soon bathe the one who was born into your hands, the one who became alive in your hands; you will soon make him clean.

Tlā xihuālhuiān, nochālchiuhxīcal, nonān, Chālchiuhcuēyeh. Ye nicān ticāltīz, ye nicān ticpohpōhuaz in momāc tlācat, in momāc ōyōl.

This last they say because, in their judgment, the first thing that comes into contact with the infant is water, because immediately after being born they bathe it.

But when the childbirth is difficult, one must find out to what or to whom the difficulty of the childbirth is to be attributed and what remedies are to be used in that danger.

When there is a difficulty in the childbirth, a well-known remedy, and one common in all New Spain, is the tail of a little animal called *tlaquatzin.*[15] And all kinds of people use it in this way. It is administered by having the tail ground into a powder (up to a half an ounce at the most) and given as a drink. In this well-known remedy they mix superstition by making an incantation to it which says:

[5] Come on, come here now, black possessed one. Go to remove the infant, since the daughter of the gods is now tired. Come [sg] here, you, Goddess Cuato, and you, Caxoch.

tlacuel, tlaxihualhuia tliliuhqui tlamacazqui tla xoconquixtiti in piltzintli inye quitequipachoa teteo ypiltzin tla xihualhuiā in tiquato, inti caxoch.

Let it be soon! Come [pl], Black Priest [i.e., the ground-up tail of the opossum]. Go in order to make the child go out, for it [i.e., the unborn child] is already troubling the child of the gods [i.e., the woman in labor]. Come, you who are Cuaton and you who are Caxxoch.

Tlā cuēl! Tlā xihuālhuiān, Tlīliuhqui Tlamacazqui. Tlā xoconquīxtīti in piltzintli, in ye quitequipachoa tēteoh īmpiltzin. Tlā xihuālhuiān, in tiCuātōn, in tiCaxxōch.

Finally, they use fortune-telling to judge the cause of the difficulty of the childbirth, and although they usually attribute it to various causes, the most usual thing is to say that the patient has committed adultery. And they say that the remedy for this is for her to receive her own saliva by means of a clyster.[16] And thus they do it, in which is easily seen the little respect for honor, the temerity of the judgment, and the faultiness[17] of the remedy.

CHAPTER 2

About the Cure for Children Who Get Sick

THE Devil is so diligent in our harm and so skillful in his art that no opportunity arises that he does not take advantage of, and he increases even the smallest opportunities in such a way that he usually obtains great effects. This is clearly seen in the subject matter of this chapter, since all that is needed to introduce a million superstitions among the Indians is for children to get sick. If they do not know the sickness and its cause—a thing that occurs quite commonly even in very learned doctors because it happens to subjects who neither know how nor are able to say what they feel, and necessarily this knowledge is even more lacking in the Indians because of their scanty reasoning and total ignorance of medicine—on seeing the child sick, they attribute the sickness to some superstitious cause, being unaware of their ignorance and stupidity. They immediately consult some female fortune-telling healer of the ones they call *ticitl*, who almost always answers that the cause of the child's sickness is that he lacks his fate or fortune or star,[1] for these three things are included under the noun *tonalli* in the Mexican language. Then this healer, seer, impostor, and, frequently, witch deals with the remedy by stating that the child has been abandoned by his fortune, etc., and that, if it is not returned to him and if his fate is not again favorable to him, he will never get well. These female healers are called *tetonaltique*,[2] which means "the women who return the fate or the fortune to its place."

Let us come now to the specifics and see by what means they give authority to their fraud. Immediately after they are called for this purpose, making great displays regarding the child's sickness, they use one of two methods for diagnosing the sickness and its cause. The first is the common one, which is fortune-telling with the hands or with maize, either dry or in water, as has been said. And having cast the fortune, they foretell whatever appeals to their fancy with regard to the sickness and its cause. And for its remedy, they tell the fortune once more, always using the invocations and incantations in the process. And in conformity with the result of the fortune-telling, they apply the remedy.

The second method is another great fraud because to gain this knowledge they put on the floor a deep vessel with water, and over it they hold the child in order to judge according to what shows up [reflected] in the water. The women who use this second method are called *atlan tlachixque,*[3] which means "diviners who know the secret through looking (or by looking at it) in the water." And for this purpose they conjure the water, saying:

[1] Come on, come now, my Mother, precious stone or the one of the skirts and *huipil* of precious stones, the one of the green skirts and *huipil,* the white woman. Let us see for this troubled child whether he suffers because his star, his fate, or his fortune has abandoned him.

Tlacuel tla xihuallauh nonan chalchiuhe, ochalchiuhtli[4] ycue chalchiuhtli ihuipil xoxouhqui ycue, xoxouhqui yhuipil iztac cihuatl tla tocon itilican in icnopiltzintli, àço oquicauh ytonaltzin.

Let it be soon! Come, my mother, Chalchiuhcueyeh, *or* Chalchihuitl Icue, Chalchihuitl Ihuipil, Xoxouhqui Icue, Xoxouhqui Ihuipil, White Woman [i.e., the water]. Let us go and see for Icnopiltzintli[5] [i.e., the child] whether perhaps his *tonal* has abandoned him.

Tlā cuēl! Tlā xihuāllauh, nonān, Chālchiuhcuēyeh,[6] *or* Chālchihuitl Īcuē,[7] Chālchihuitl Īhuīpīl, Xoxōuhqui Īcue, Xoxōuhqui Īhuīpīl, Iztāc-Cihuātl. Tlā toconittilīcān in Icnōpiltzintli ahzo ōquicāuh ītōnaltzin.

With this they place the child over the water, and if they see the child's face dark in it, as if covered by some shadow, they judge as certain the contrariety and absence of his fate and fortune, and if the child's face appears light in the water, they say that the child is not ill, or that the indisposition is very slight and he will get well without a cure, or they only incense him. In this action the deception is quite clearly seen, since the judgment consists in the mere free will of the judge because, whenever she wants to judge the child sick, when putting his face over the water, she will put his back to the light so that the face, remaining in the shadow, will appear dark in the water. And whenever she wants to judge the child well, his face will be put toward the light, and thus it will appear light in the water. And thus there is no more mystery in this judgment than the will of the judge, although, if a pact with the Devil intervenes, he will be able—if the Lord permits it—to show in the water the contrary of what should appear as a natural consequence. But assuming that the pact does not intervene,[8] it is quite clearly seen that the appearance of the child's face as light and dark in the water is not a basis for judging that he be healthy or sick, and much less for knowing what indisposition he suffers or what may be the cause of the sickness.

Having already made the judgment and said that the child is sick, next this impostor says his star has absented itself from him, *oquicauh itonal,*[9] as if she said, "His fate is contrary to him, does not favor him, or has left him," a thing which is understood neither by those who hear it nor by those who say it. With this they deal immediately with the remedy, which is to restore the fate to him or to reconcile him with it. However, they do not understand by this fate that which the ancient pagans used to call *genius*[10]—and among these people it may be that they understand it to be one of their heathen gods, to whose care they attribute the good or bad outcome of the infant, as can be inferred from the incantation and invocation that they make for that reconciliation or restitution.

CHAPTER 3

About the Remedy That They Use for What They Call "Reconciling"

HAVING diagnosed the sickness, one must now deal with the remedy, and although they use different means for this, I shall reduce them to one chapter because they coincide in intent and in manner. And almost all of it is reduced to the force of words and incantations. Taking it for granted that water always comes in as a principal agent and a *sine qua non,* to this they add at times fire and at times *piçiete* or *tenexiete,* all of which they conjure. And in the invocation they always start by speaking to the water and, at times, to the earth, because they attribute the principal agent in the child's birth to water because of its being the first thing he touches (in their opinion) immediately after being born, because with it they wash from him the blood that he takes from the womb, and to the earth because in being born he falls on it.

She starts, then, the invocation and incantation, which is as follows:

[1] {She speaks to the water} Come on already. Come to my aid, my Mother, the one of the skirt of jewels {because of the vegetation that always accompanies it}, the white woman. And you, dusky fate, white fate, what is detaining you [pl] {she supposes the absence of the fate}: the white or yellow hindrance or anger?[1] {the causes of its having absented itself.}

tlacuel tla xihuallauh nonan chal chicueye iztac çihuatl yayauhqui tonalli iztac tonalli, iztactlaelpan, yocauhqui tlaelpan

Let it be soon! Come, my mother, Chalchiuhcueyeh, White Woman [i.e., the water]. The dusky *tonal,* the white *tonal* is in the white filth, in the yellow filth.

Tlā cuēl! Tlā xihuāllauh, nonān, Chālchiuhcuēyeh, Iztāc-Cihuātl. Yāyāuhqui tōnalli, iztāc tōnalli, iztāc tlahēlpan, cōzauhqui tlahēlpan.

[2] For I have now come to put here the yellow conjured one and the white conjured one {the medicines that they use, *piciete* and water}. I in person have come for this, the priest, prince of spells {I understand here the medicine *piciete* and water.}. I have already devised you, and I have given you life.

cayenican oniquesaco[2] cocauhqui tla macazqui iztac tlamacazqui nehuatl onihualla nitlamacazqui ninahualtecutli ye onimitzchichiuh, onimitz yolliti

Already I have come here in order to set up Yellow Priest [i.e., the *piciyete*] or White Priest [i.e., the water]. It is I who have come. I am the priest; I am the *nahualli*-lord. I have already made you, I have caused you to live.

Ca ye nicān ōnicquetzaco Cōzauhqui Tlamacazqui, Iztāc Tlamacazqui. Nehhuātl ōnihuāllah. Nitlamacazqui; nināhualtēuctli. Ye ōnimitzchihchīuh, ōnimitzyōlītih.

[3] You my mother, the one of the starry skirt {to the Milky Way, which they consider a Goddess}, you also show yourself to be contrary to the one you made and to the one to whom you gave life {for the sick child} and you turn against him.

Nonan acitlal cueye in otic chiuh in oticmoyollitili, çan no tehuatl ica tehua ica timilacatzoa

My mother, Citlalcueyeh [i.e., the Milky Way], are you the very one who rises up against, who turns against the one whom you made, the one whom you caused to live [i.e., the sick child]?

Nonān, Cītlalcuēyeh,[3] in ōticchīuh, in ōticmoyōlītilih, zan nō tehhuātl īca tehēhua, īca timīlacatzoa?

[4] Adverse fate {she shifts the address to the fate}, dark star, in the greatness of the waters {she means the sea} and in its extensiveness I will deposit you. I say it in person, the priest, prince of the spells.

yayauhquitonalli atl ihueican atlipatlahuaca nimitzoncahuaz nomatca nehua nitlamacazqui ninahual tecutli

Dusky *tonal,* I will carry[4] you to the water's big place, in the water's wide place [i.e., the sea]. It is I in person. I am the priest. I am the *nahualli*-lord.

Yāyāuhqui tōnalli, ātl īhuēicān, ātl īpatlāhuacān nimitzoncāhuaz. Nohmatca nehhuātl. Nitlamacazqui. Ninahualtēuctli.

[5] Come on, come now, my mother, the one of the skirt of precious stones. Come on now, walk, go to seek and to see the shining possessed one who inhabits the house of light in order that we may know what God or what powerful one is now destroying[5] and is turning into dust, this unfortunate one.

tla xihualhuia nonan chalchicueye tlaxihuia tlaxictemoti, tla xiquitati tlamacazqui tlauhtzin tlauhcalco onca acteotl ac mahuiztli, in yequipolocayotia in yequiteuhyotia

Come [pl], my mother, Chalchiuhcueyeh [i.e., the water]! Go [pl]! Go in order to seek the priest, Tlauhtzin[6] [i.e., the bright reflection of the child's face], who is there in Tlauhcalco[7] [i.e., the reflective surface of the water in the basin]; go in order to see him. Who is the god, who is the illustrious being who already fills him with chaff, who already fills him with dust?

Tlā xihuālhuiān, nonān, Chālchiuhcuēyeh! Tlā xihuiān! Tlā xictēmōti; tlā xiquittati tlamacazqui, Tlāuhtzin, Tlāuhcalco oncah. Āc teōtl, āc mahuiztli in ye quipolōcayōtia, in ye quiteuhyōtia?

[6] Green sickness, dark green sickness, leave here for anywhere and consume yourself any way you like. And you, shining possessed one, you are to clean and purify him. And you, green fate or yellow one, who have walked like an outcast through the mountain ranges and deserts, come, for I seek you. I miss you, and I want you. Here I ask for you, O fate.

xoxoqui cocoliztli yayauhqui cocoliztli çan can tiaz çan can tipolihuiz, ticpahpacaz tic yectiliz in tlamacazqui tlautzin, tlaxihualhuia xxoqui tonalli yayauhqui tonalli centepetl cemixtlahuatl tinemia, nican nimitztemoa nicanimitz itlani Tonallie

Green sickness, dusky sickness, it is just anywhere that you will go, it is just anywhere that you will become destroyed [i.e., I do not care where you go or what happens to you as long as you leave here]. You [i.e., the water] will thoroughly wash the priest, Tlauhtzin[8] [i.e., the bright reflection of the child's face]; you will purify him.[9] Come, green *tonal,* dusky *tonal.* It was on a whole mountain, it was on a whole plain [i.e., a once-healthy body] that you used to live. I am seeking you here, I am asking about you here, O *tonal.*

Xoxōuhqui cocoliztli, yāyāuhqui cocoliztli, zan cān tiyāz, zan cān tipolihuiz. Ticpahpācaz, ticyēctilīz in tlamacazqui, Tlāuhtzin. Tlā xihuālhuiān, xoxōuhqui tōnalli, yāyāuhqui tōnalli. Centepētl, cemixtlāhuatl [in īpan][10] tinemiya. Nicān nimitztēmoa, nicān nimitzihtlani, tōnallié.

[7] And you, nine-times cudgeled one, nine-times crushed one, see that you do not shame yourself by falling into failure.

tla xihualauh chicnauhpa tlatzotzonalli chicnauhpa tlatemateloli ma timopinauhti,

Come, Nine-times-beaten-one, Nine-times-crumbled-in-the-hands-one [i.e., the tobacco]. Beware of bringing shame upon yourself [i.e., do your duty properly].

Tlā xihuāllauh, Chiucnāuhpatlatetzohtzonalli, Chiucnāuhpatlamātelōlli. Mā timopīnāuhtih.[11]

[8] Come on already, come, my mother, the one of the skirt of precious stones, one water (or the sea), two reeds, one rabbit, two rabbits, one deer, two deer, one flint, two flints, one caiman, two caimans. Hail, my mother, the one of the precious skirt. In what are you entertained and idle? Carry the one entrusted to me to be washed. Go to put him in some spring or pool of water or in some fountain, prince of the earth.[12]

tla xihuallauh nonan chalchicueye *ceatl,* ome acatl, cetochtli ome tochtli cemaçatl ome maçatl çetecpatl ome tecpatl cequetzpalli, omequetzpallin no nan chalchicueye tle chicaz? xocōpopoan nomacehual tlacana axicco ayahualco, macana amoloncã xoconcahuati tlallocatecutli

Come [sg], my mother, Chalchiuhcueyeh [i.e., the water]! He is One Water, [Two Water, One Reed,] Two Reed, One Rabbit, Two Rabbit, One Deer, Two Deer, One Flint, Two Flint, One Lizard, Two Lizard.[13] My mother, Chalchiuhcueyeh, what do you know? [I.e., Pay attention!] Go and wash my vassal. Go, Tlalocateuctli [i.e., the water], in order to carry[14] him to some whirlpool, to some eddy, to some gushing water.

Tlā xihuāllauh, nonān, Chālchiuhcuēyeh! Cē-Ātl, [Ōme-Ātl, Cē-Ācatl,][15] Ōme-Ācatl, Cē-Tōchtli, Ōme-Tōchtli, Cē-Mazātl, Ōme-Mazātl, Cē-Tecpatl, Ōme-Tecpatl, Cē-Cuetzpalin, Ōme-Cuetzpalin.[16] Nonān, Chālchiuhcuēyeh, tleh ticmati?[17] Xocompohpōhua in nomācēhual. Tlā canah āxīcco, āyahualco, mā canah āmolōncān xoconcāhuati, Tlālocātēuctli.

[9] I in person have come for this, the furious one, I who make noise, the one who does not have anyone to respect. I am the one whom even the sticks and stones tremble at and obey. Tie [pl] me here for I am as much as another.

Onihualla innixolotl in nicapanilli cuix tle ipan nitlamati? in tetl ihuinti inquahuitl ihuinti in nicã nẽnemi no tehuan no nehua

I have come, I who am Xolotl, I who am Capanilli. What perchance do I consider things as?[18] [i.e., I fear nothing *or* I regret nothing.] The rocks become drunk, the trees become drunk if he is a vagrant here [i.e., I am a force to be reckoned with if my orders are not obeyed]. Also I go off

Ōnihuāllah in niXōlōtl, in niCapānīlli. Cuix tleh īpan nitlamati? In tetl īhuinti, in cuahuitl īhuinti in nicān nēnnemi. Nō tēhuān nonēhua.[19]

with others [i.e., I am allied with other powerful forces].

[10] Well, let us see now which God or which powerful one wishes already to destroy the son of the Goddesses and Gods. I have come to seek his *tonalli* (fortune, fate, or star) whichever it may be.[20] I wonder where it has gone. Where does it tarry? Whither? To the nine-times?[21] Whither? To the nine unions or matchings? Did it go away to stay? Wherever it may be, I call it and I am to bring it, because you are to cure and to clean this heart and this head.

ac teotl ac mahuiztli yequipoloznequi teteo inconeuh teteo inpiltzin, nicanaco xoxoqui tonalli iztac tonalli camach on oya? camach in omotecato, can mach in chic nautopa chicnauhtlanepaniuhcan omotecato? nicanaco, nictzatzilico ticqualtiliz, ticyectiliz in yollotzin tzontecomatl.

Who is the god, who is the illustrious being who already wishes to destroy the child of the goddesses, the child of the gods?[22] I have come to get the green *tonal,* the white *tonal.* Wherever is it that he [i.e., the lost *tonal*] has gone? Wherever is it that he has gone to settle down? Wherever in Nine-Topan, in Nine-layering-place [i.e., the celestial realm], has he gone to settle down? I have come to get him. I have come to call to him. You [i.e., the *tonal*] will restore, you will make right the heart, the head.

Āc teōtl, āc mahuiztli ye quipolōznequi tēteoh īnconēuh, tēteoh īmpiltzin? Nicānaco xoxōuhqui tōnalli, iztāc tōnalli. Cān mach in ōyah? Cān mach in ōmotēcato? Cān mach in ChiucnāuhTopan, Chiucnāuhtlanepaniuhcān ōmotēcato? Nicānaco. Nictzahtzilīco. Ticcualtilīz, ticyēctilīz[23] in yōllohtzintli,[24] tzontecomatl.

Having finished this spell and incantation, boasting that they have now found the *tonal,*[25] they try to restore it to the child, which they commonly do by taking into their mouth some of the conjured water and putting it on the top of the child's head, or, having placed themselves face to face with the child, they spray him with it, startling him with the spray. Other women also put some of the water between his shoulder blades. And with these empty ceremonies they say that they have restored to him his *tonal* or fate and that he is now well. And then some prove it by placing the face over the vessel of water where they see it, and by means of the light face, the maize kernels, or the measurement with the hands, they say that it comes out favorable to him—all being manifest frauds but sufficient to dazzle such simple people, since up until now they have not noticed that the outcomes of such divinations are always at the will of the one who tells them. Others, after having judged the sickness and made the preceding incantation or another similar one, change the manner of the cure, which they make by an incensing, for which they conjure the fire, the smoke, and the copal, with which the incensing is to be made, and it is as follows:

[11] Come on now, old man and old woman {fire and smoke}, go to pacify the bracelet and emerald {the sick child}, for I do not know what is wrong with him, because he wants to break himself into pieces. Come on now, come, white woman {a metaphor to the stone of the copal}, pacify now this bracelet and this emerald

tlaxihualauh yntihuehue in ti illama tlaxocōyamaniliti in cozcatl in quetzalli quen mochihua? inyexamaniznequi. tlaxihuallauh iztac çihuatl tlaxic yamanili in cozcatl inquetzalli. tlaxihualauh xoxoqui cochcamachal,[27] yayauhqui cochcamachal.

or precious stone. Come on, come, green and yellow snares of sleep.[26]

Come [sg], you who are Old-man [i.e., the fire] or you who are Old-woman [i.e., the smoke]. Go in order to soften the jewel, the quetzal-feather[28] [i.e., the child]. How can it be done when he already wishes to become smashed? Come, White Woman [i.e., the copal]. Soften the jewel, the quetzal-feather. Come, Green Sleep-[opened]-jaw, Dusky Sleep-[opened]-jaw [i.e., yawn].

Tlā xihuāllauh, in tiHuēhueh, in tllamah. Tlā xoconyamānilīti in cōzcatl, in quetzalli. Quēn mochīhua in ye xamāniznequi? Tlā xihuāllauh, Iztāc-Cihuātl. Tlā xicyamānili in cōzcatl, in quetzalli. Tlā xihuāllauh, Xoxōuhqui Cochcamachāl, Yāyāuhqui Cochcamachāl.

This used to be used by, among others, Francisca Juana, the wife of Juan Baptista, of the village of Mescaltepec. Having said this incantation, she incenses the child with the conjured copal and fire, and with this they state that his *tonal* and *genius*[29] has returned to him and that he is perfectly well. And the worst thing is that they believe it.

CHAPTER 4

About the Treatise[1] About Superstitious Cures, Beginning with the Head

SINCE the Indians are totally ignorant of the science of medicine, they reduce all of it to superstition, and whether it belongs to surgery or to medicine, they include all of it in more or less one kind of superstition. And having to deal with this subject matter, it seemed to me that it would have more clarity and precision if I kept the order of the members of the human body in it, starting with the head and continuing through the eyes, ears, and the rest, and afterward [turning to] the cures that pertain to the illnesses of all the body, such as fevers, etc.

Considering what I have already said in other places about the name of *tiçitl*—which is suspect—these [doctors] use their manners of superstition. And frequently it passes into witchcraft and a pact with the Devil—under the pretext that they know how to cure. Summoned for a headache, what they do is press the aching head with their hands—and this they do for all kinds of pain—and, pressing it, they say this incantation:

[1] Come on, come, those of the five fates {the fingers},[2] all of whom look toward one side,[3] and you goddesses, Cuato and Caxoch. Who is the powerful one and the one worthy of veneration who now destroys our vassal? I am the one who speaks, the priest, the prince of spells, therefore we are to hit him (or it)[4] against the shore of the ocean and we are to throw him into it.

tla cuel tlaxihualhuian macuiltonalleque, çemithualeque in tiquato in ti caxoch ac tlacatl, ac mahuiztli in ye quitlacohua into maçehual no matcanehuatl nitlamacazqui ni nahual tecutli teo atentli, ica tichuitequizque teo atentli ica ticmo tlazque.

Let it be soon! Come, Five-*tonal*s-owners, One-courtyard-owners [i.e., the hands]. You who are Cuaton, and you who are Caxxoch, who is the person, who is the illustrious being who already is ruining our vassal? It is I in person [i.e., I have the authority to ask the question]. I am the priest. I am the *nahualli*-lord. We will strike him against the seashore [*lit.*, the shore of the god water]. We will hurl him against the seashore.

Tlā cuēl! Tlā xihuālhuiān, Mācuīltōnalehqueh, Cemithualehqueh. In tiCuātōn, in tiCaxxōch,[5] āc tlācatl, āc mahuiztli in ye quihtlacoa in tomācēhual? Nohmatca nehhuātl. Nitlamacazqui. Ninahualtēuctli. Teōātēntli īca tichuīltequizqueh. Teōātēntli īca ticmōtlazqueh.

While saying this incantation, he continually presses the patient's temples, and upon finishing the incantation, he blows his breath on the head in the manner of applying a nostrum. And with this he says that the cure has been accomplished.

But after the incantation has been said and this cleverness or activity has been performed, if the sick person does not feel relieved, he addresses an incantation to the water and says:

[2] Pay attention to what I say to you, mother of mine, the one of the skirt of jewels. Come here and revive the vassal of our Lord.

tlaxihualhuian nonan chalchicueye tlanican xocon iz caliti ynto tecuiyo imacehual.

Come [pl], my mother, Chalchiuhcueyeh [i.e., the water]. Please go from here in order to revive our lord's vassal!

Tlā xihuālhuiān, nonān, Chālchiuhcuēyeh. Tlā nicān xoconizcalīti in totēucyo[6] īmācēhual!

Saying this, he sprinkles his face with the water and, owing to the surprise and astonishment, or rather, owing to the coolness of the water, the sick person says he has been relieved. This manner of cure and incantation was used by a certain Catharina Juana, a native of Tequaquilco,[7] of the district of Atenango. But others, in place of the sprinkling of water, incense the head with the herb *yautli*,[8] which we call anise. When the head is swollen, they apply *piçiete* [mixed] with the root of the *chalalatli*[9] to it, with this incantation accompanying it:

[3] I the priest, Prince of the spells. I ask in what place is that which now wishes to destroy my enchanted head. Come on, come, you, nine-times beaten one, nine-times crushed one, for we are to placate my conjured head because the red medicine {this is the root *chalalatli*} is to cure it.

nehua nitlamacazqui ninahualtecutli, campamoquetza in ye quixpoloznequi no nahualtzontecon tlaxihualhuia chicnauhpa tlatetzotzon chicnauh tlamatelolli ic quiçehuiz no nahualtzontecon quipatiz in tlatlauhqui pahtecatl

It is I [in person]. I am the priest. I am the *nahualli*-lord. Where does the one who already wishes to destroy my *nahualli*-head stand up? [i.e., Where has he established himself?] Come [pl], Nine-times-rock-pounded-one, Nine-[times]-crumbled-in-the-hands-one [i.e., the tobacco]. Thereby the Red Pahtecatl [i.e., the root *chalalahtli*] will cool off my *nahualli*-head, he will cure it.

[Nohmatca] nehhuātl.[10] Nitlamacazqui. Ninahualtēuctli. Cāmpa moquetza in ye quīxpolōznequi nonāhualtzontecon? Tlā xihuālhuiān, Chiucnāuhpatlatetzohtzon, Chiucnāuhtlamātelōlli. Īc quicēhuīz nonāhualtzontecon, quipahtīz in Tlātlāuhqui Pahtēcatl.

[4] For I shout to and invoke the cool wind in order that it placate my enchanted head. To you, winds,[11] I ask, "Have you

nictzatzilia in cecec in eecatl in quicehuiz nonahualtzontecon. Inti chicnauh eecatl otiqualcuic[12] in quipatiz no na-

brought that which is to cure my enchanted head?" I wonder where it has gone. I wonder where it is hidden.

hualtzontecon? campa nel in oya? campa motlillia?

I call out to the cold wind so that it will cool off my *nahualli*-head. You who are Nine Wind [i.e., the *ticitl*'s breath], have you come to get the one who will cure my *nahualli*-head? Where is it really that he has gone? Where is he sitting down?

Nictzahtzilia in cecēc in ehehcatl in quicēhuīz nonāhualtzontecon. In ti-Chiucnāuhehehcatl, ōtichuālcuic in quipahtīz nonāhualtzontecon? Cāmpa nel in ōyah? Cāmpa motlālia?

Having said this incantation, he blows on the head with his breath four times as quacks are accustomed to do in Castile, in which let it be noted, first, how much the Devil tries to imitate the ceremonies of the Church; second, how the number four is superstitious among the Indians, alluding to their heathen tradition of the fable of the sun, either because the Devil is imitating the Holy Scripture in the number four—because of the generality that is contained in it—or because, on account of his pride, he adds one to the number three, so mysterious among the Christians. Be that as it may, they always observe this number four in their superstitions.

Having made the four insufflations, they consider the cure finished whether the patient gets well or not, because, deceived by the fraud of the incantation owing to the strategy of the Devil, they do not even know how to decide whether he has or not.

CHAPTER 5

Superstitious Cure of the Eyes

For afflicted and bloodshot eyes they commonly use cold water together with the exorcism and superstition of the spell, which was used by, among others, a certain Maria Salome, the wife of Gaspar Rodriguez, of the village of Tetelpan, in the jurisdiction of Cuernavaca, and it says:

[1] I ask you, one snake {to the veins}, two snakes, three, four snakes, why are you mistreating thus the enchanted mirror {the eyes} and its enchanted surface or complexion. Go where you will. Leave for wherever you like. And if you do not obey me, I shall call the one of the skirts and *huipil* of precious stones, for she will scatter you and turn you aside. She will throw you, scattering you. And she will leave you scattered throughout those deserts.

Tlacuele, tlaxihualhuia ce coatl, omecoatl, yey coatl nahui coatl tlen ticaitia in nahualtezcatl, o[1] in nahual ixtli, achcan ximoteca, achcan ximiquani, auh intlacamo tinechtlacamatiz noconnotzaz in chalchiuhtli ycue in chalchiuhtli ihuipil, ca yèhuatl mitzmomoyahuaz yèhuatl mitz cecenmanaz ixtlahuatl ipan mitz cecenmantiquiçaz.

Let it be soon. Come [pl], One Snake, Two Snake, Three Snake, Four Snake [i.e., the veins]. What

Tlā cuēl eh! Tlā xihuālhuiān, Cē-Cōātl, Ōme-Cōātl, Yēi-Cōātl, Nāhui-Cōātl. Tleh

is it that you [sg] are doing to the *nahualli*-mirror, the *nahualli*-eyes [i.e., the eyes]? Settle down, it does not matter where; move, it does not matter where [i.e., quit harming the eyes]. And if you will not obey me, I will call Chalchihuitl Icue, Chalchihuitl Ihuipil [i.e., the water]. Indeed she will dissipate you, she will strew you. Upon the plains she will quickly strew you.

in ticāītia[2] in nāhualtezcatl, nāhualīxtli? Ach cān ximotēca; ach cān ximihcuani. Auh in tlācamō tinēchtlācamatiz, noconnōtzaz in Chālchihuitl[3] Īcuē, in Chālchihuitl Īhuīpīl. Ca yehhuātl mitzmohmoyāhuaz, yehhuātl mitzcēcemmanaz. Ixtlāhuatl īpan mitzcēcemmantiquīzaz.

Having said this incantation, she throws the cold water in his eyes, and, since those who suffer usually have their eyes on fire, they feel relief owing to the cold of the water but attribute the effect to the false spell—[being] brutish and without understanding of the mercifulnesses of the Lord.

CHAPTER 6

Other Methods of Curing the Eyes

THEY also use another method of curing with its exorcism and spell. Among others, Marta Monica, an inhabitant of Teteltzinco, a barrio of Ohuapan, was mistress of this second method. They use, then, the sap of the bark of the tree called *mezquite,* which is harsh. When the bark of the tree is struck, that liquid comes out. They collect this with the head of a pin or something similar, and they rub the patient's eye with it until it bleeds, while saying this incantation:

[1] I, the offerer of sacrifices and the prince of spells, have brought you, head of pearl {pin or index finger}. Go seek the green, or dusky, or yellow[1] pain, you, the one with the head of pearl, seek and find out which God or which powerful one now wishes to destroy my conjured mirror {the eyes}. Also do your duty, you conjured medicine, green medicine.

Nitlamacazqui, ni nahualteuctli[2] nimitzhualhuicac in titzonepitzin[3] xictēmo xoxouhqui coacihuiztli xictemo tzonecptzin ac teotl, ac mahuiztli in ye quixpoloznequi nonahualtezcauh tla xihualhuia tlamacazqui pàtecatl xoxouhqui pàtecatl.

I am the priest. I am the *nahualli*-lord. I brought you who are Nacre-as-hair (H) [sg] [i.e., the finger]. Seek the green palsy [i.e., the eye pain]. Find out, Nacre-as-hair (H) [sg], who is the god, who is the illustrious being who already wishes to destroy my *nahualli*-mirror [i.e., the eyes]. Come [pl], priest, Pahtecatl, Green Pahtecatl [i.e., the mesquite sap].

Nitlamacazqui. Ninābualtēuctli. Nimitzhuālhuīcac in tiTzoneptzin. Xictēmo xoxōuhqui cōahcihuiztli. Xictēmo, Tzoneptzin,[4] āc teōtl, āc mahuiztli in ye quīxpolōznequi nonāhualtezcauh. Tlā xihuālhuiān, tlamacazqui, Pahtēcatl, Xoxōuhqui Pahtēcatl.

After rubbing the eyes with the sap, while saying the foregoing incantation, she then turns to the *piçiete* or *tenexiete* and says:

[2] Come here, you, the nine-times beaten one. Come here, conjured medicine. Let

Tlaxihuallauh chicnauhtlatetzotzonalli tlaxihuallauh tlamacazqui patècatl ac us find out who is the God, or who is the powerful one who wishes now to destroy our enchanted mirror.

teotl acteotl,[5] ac mahuiztli in ye quixpoloznequi in tonahualtezcauh.

Come, Nine-[times]-rock-pounded-one [i.e., the tobacco]. Come, priest, Pahtecatl [i.e., the tobacco]. Who is the god, who is the illustrious being who wants to destroy our *nahualli*-mirror [i.e., the eyes]?

Tlā xihuāllauh, Chiucnāuhtlatetzohtzonalli. Tlā xihuāllauh, tlamacazqui, Pahtēcatl. Āc teōtl, āc mahuiztli in ye quīxpolōznequi in tonāhualtezcauh?

Saying this incantation, she anoints the eyelids and parts of the forehead above the patient's eyebrows with the said *piçiete,* and she throws into the eyes the blood from the quills of chicken feathers which have just been pulled out, which is likewise a tested medicine for afflicted and bloodshot eyes.

Others use the herb called *texixiuhtli*[6] in place of the *mezquite* sap, and in the incantation, instead of *xoxouhqui pàtecatl,*[7] which means "green medicine,"[8] they say *iztac cihuatl,*[9] "white woman." In the rest it is the same.

Others cure this affliction of the eyes in the same way impetigo is usually cured, [which is] by pricking or rubbing it, excoriating it or making it bleed, and then putting a plaster on it. Thus they rub the eyes with a strong herb, called *tlachichinoa,*[10] which means "incendiary," until making them bleed, with their incantation accompanying this, and when that is finished, the blood that now runs freely over the eye is wiped away with copal, to which they have added a little *tequixquite* and salt. The incantation says:

[3] Come here, you, the ashen herb. Come to clean the dust and superfluities that obstruct my conjured crystal. Come on already, come, my uncles, the enchanted one of five fates who all look toward one side. Accompany the ashen or dark-colored herb.[11]

Tlaxihualhuia ayauh xihuitl tla xocon tlalteuhyo cuicuiliti tla xoconpopoloca cuicuiliti in tonahual tezcauh tlaxihualhuian intotlahuan tlamacazq⁺ macuiltonalleque cemithualleq⁺ tla ammoneoncahuil in ayauh xihuitl.

Come [pl], Mist-herb. Go and remove the dust from our *nahualli*-mirror [i.e., the eyes], go and remove the chaff from it. Come, our uncles, the priests, Five-*tonal*s-owners, One-courtyard-owners [i.e., the hands]. Let Mist-herb be the one whom you accompany to its dwelling.

Tlā xihuālhuiān, Āyauhxihuitl. Tlā xocontlālteuhyōcuihcuīlīti, tlā xocompohpolōcacuihcuīlīti[12] in tonāhualtezcauh. Tlā xihuālhuiān, in totlahhuān, tlamacazqueh, Mācuīltōnalehqueh, Cemithualehqueh. Tlā amoneoncāhuīl[13] in Āyauhxihuitl.

Having rubbed the eye, they make use of the copal and with it they clean the eye saying:

[4] Come you, white woman, and clean our conjured or enchanted mirror.

Tla xihualhuia iztac cihuatl xictlacuicuiliti intonahualtezcauh.

Come [pl], White Woman. Go in order to remove things from our *nahualli*-mirror.

Tlā xihuālhuiān, Iztāc-Cihuātl. Xictlacuihcuīlīti in tonāhualtezcauh.

And with this they consider the cure finished.

CHAPTER 7

The Cure for Earache

To cure an earache, they usually use the juice of the *tenexiete,* instilling some drops into the ear, accompanying them with the following incantation:

[1] Come on now, come you, the nine-times crudgeled one, the nine times beaten one, go in after the green pain. Who is that so-powerful one who wants now to destroy the one entrusted to my care? Beware that you do not do anything that you will be ashamed of, for now I blow here into my nine caves in order that my puff and breath may follow the green pain, which means that it may pursue it and throw it out.

tlaxihualauh chicnauhtlatetzotzonal chicnauhtlatecapanil tlaxictocaticalaqui in xoxoqui coaçihuiztli actlacatl ac mahuiztli inye quixpoloa nomaçehual maçan tlen ticchiuhti, ye nican non tlalpitza ihtic nochicnauh oztoc quitoticalaquiz in xoxoqui co acihuiztli.

Come, Nine-[times]-rock-beaten-one, Nine-[times]-rock-slapped-one [i.e., the tobacco]. Enter following the green palsy [i.e., the earache]. Who is the personage, who is the illustrious one who is already destroying my vassal? Beware of doing just anything whatever [i.e., do specifically what it is your duty to do]. Already here I am blowing to the inside of my Seven-caves-place [i.e., the ear]. It [i.e., my breath] will enter following the green palsy [i.e., in order to expel it].

Tlā xihuāllauh, Chiucnāuhtlatetzohtzonal, Chiucnāuhtlatecapānīl. Tlā xictocaticalaqui in xoxōuhqui cōahcihuiztli. Āc tlācatl, āc mahuiztli in ye quīxpoloa nomācēhual? Mā zan tleh in ticchīuhti.[1] Ye nicān nontlalpītza iihtic[2] noChicōmōztōc.[3] Quitocaticalaquiz[4] in xoxōuhqui cōahcihuiztli.

With this they consider the cure terminated, attributing the power of it to the incantation and to their breath, as they do in the rest.

CHAPTER 8

Cure for Pain in the Teeth or Molars

For tooth- or molar-ache they usually use copal alone, with *piçiete* or *tenexiete*[1]—which in these cases is[2] the same thing—going before as a precursor. And she starts the incantation, addressed first to the *piçiete.*

[1] Come to my help, *piciete,* nine-times beaten, nine-times crushed one. And you, dusky pain of molars, what are you doing? Come here, the female one of my sex, the white woman {since the one talking to the copal is a woman}. Enter in pursuit of the green

tlaxihualauh yetzintli chicnauh tla tetzotzonali chicnauh tla ma telolli tlaxihualhuia yayauhque tlanqualoliztli tla xihualauh noçihuapo iztac çihuatl tlaxitocaticalaqui xoxoqui co açihuiztli ma ti mo pinauhtiti maçan tlen tic

pain. Look out that you do not fall into an affront. Do not do anything that is not fitting. What you are to do is to remove and take away the green pain that now wishes to destroy the one entrusted to me, four small reeds[3] {here she is talking to the gum[4]}.

chiuh ticquixtiz in xoxoqui coaçihuiztli in ye quix po loz nequi in nomacehual[5]

Come, Tobacco (H), Nine-[times]-rock-pounded-one, Nine-[times]-crumbled-in-the-hand-one. Come [pl], dusky tooth-decay. Come, woman like me, White Woman [i.e., the copal]. Enter following the green palsy [i.e., the toothache]. Beware of bringing shame upon yourself [i.e., do your duty properly]. Beware of doing just anything whatever [i.e., do specifically what it is your duty to do]. You will cause the green palsy who already wants to destroy my vassal to come out.

Tlā xihuāllauh, Iyetzintli, Chiucnāuhtlatetzohtzonalli, Chiucnāuhtlamātelōlli. Tlā xihuālhuiān, yāyāuhqui tlancualōliztli. Tlā xihuāllauh, nocihuāpoh, Iztāc-Cihuātl. Tlā xictocaticalaqui[6] xoxōuhqui cōahcihuiztli. Mā timopīnāuhtihti.[7] Mā zan tleh in ticchīuh.[8] Ticquīxtīz in xoxōuhqui cōahcihuiztli in ye quīxpolōznequi in nomācēhual.

She stabs [the gum], draws blood, and goes on [talking] to the fingers:[9]

[2] Come, you also, the ones of five fates, for we are to take away the green pain. Why[10] is it now ruining my enchanted mill {the teeth or molars, because with them food is ground up} in their labor? or Why is it causing the wall made for war or defense to become soft?

tlaxihualhuian ma cuil to nalleque tic quixtizque inxoxoqui coaçihuiztli tlen ye quiixpoloa in nonahual metl yne tlayecolayan[11] {tlayecoltiayan} *(vel[12])* nonahual yao tepan mitl quihuehueloa.

Come, Five-*tonal*s-owners [i.e., the hands]. We will cause this green palsy [i.e., the toothache] to leave. What is it that is already destroying my *nahualli*-quern's[13] [i.e., the teeth's] food-getting-place [i.e., the mouth]? *or* [What is it that] is tearing down my *nahualli*-war-wall-quern [i.e., the teeth].

Tlā xihuālhuiān, Mācuīltōnalehqueh. Ticquīxtīzqueh in xoxōuhqui cōahcihuiztli. Tleh in ye quīxpoloa in nonāhualmetl īnetlayecōltiāyān?[14] *or* [Tleh in] nonāhualyāōtepānmetl[15] quihuehhueloa?

With this they burn the molar or the tooth that is hurting with a burning drop of the copal, which by its nature together with the activity of the fire is enough to deaden the pain, and they attribute it to the words.

CHAPTER 9

Cure for the Pain Beneath the Ear or in the Jaw

For this kind of pain they apply *tenexiete* with the following incantation:

[1] Let everyone be alert, for I am the one who speaks, the priest, prince of spells, and I am sent by my sister, the one of the starry

tlaxihualhuia. Nomatca nehuatl nitlamacazqui ninahualtecutli onech hualtitlanqui nohueltiuh çitlalcueye ni-

skirt {Milky Way, Road of Saint James}, and I bring the prince, dark-colored spirit,[1] and his pages, and the possessed one, nine-times beaten one. The prince or lord, the one who serves the idols, has already come with me. Well now, you [sg] green pain, dusky pain, whom do you [pl] consider lord and worthy of being obeyed? Already I have come to destroy them and to burn them, I the priest, the prince of the spells.

quinhualhuicac intlacatl intlamacazqui yayauhqui coconectin yhuan in tlamacazqui chicnau tlatetzotzontli. ya onichualhuicac in tlacatl, intlamacazqui, xoxouhtli coacihuiztli, ac tlacatl ac mahuiztli,[2] ye onihualla nicpòpoloco, nictlàtico[3] nitlamacazqui, ninahualteuctli.

Come [pl]. It is I in person. I am the priest. I am the *nahualli*-lord. My older sister, Citlalcueyeh [i.e., the Milky Way], has sent me hither. I have brought the lord, the priest, Dusky Nacre-as-hair (H) [sg] [i.e., the finger], and the priest, Nine-[times]-rock-pounded-one [i.e., the tobacco]. Already I have brought the lord, the priest, [Dusky Nacre-as-hair (H) [sg]. Soon here he will shoo away the] green palsy [i.e., the ache]. Who is the lord, who is the illustrious being [that is already destroying my vassal]? Already I have come; I have come in order to destroy it [i.e., the pain]; I have come in order to kill it [*lit.,* to hide it]. I am the priest. I am the *nahualli*-lord.

Tlā xihuālhuiān. Nohmatca nehhuātl. Nitlamacazqui. Nināhualtēuctli. Ōnēchhuāltītlanqui nohuēltīuh, Cītlalcuēyeh. Niquinhuālhuīcac in tlācatl, in tlamacazqui, Yāyāuhqui Tzoneptzin,[4] Īhuān in tlamacazqui, Chiucnāuhtlatetzohtzontli. Ye ōnichuālhuīcac in tlācatl, in tlamacazqui, [Yāyāuhqui Tzoneptzin. Ye nicān quipēhuīz in] xoxōuhtli[5] cōahcihuiztli. Āc tlācatl, āc mahuiztli [in ye quīxpoloa nomācēhual]?[6] Ye ōnihuāllah nicpohpolōco; nictlātīco. Nitlamacazqui. Nināhualtēuctli.

While saying the aforesaid incantation, they have the *piçiete* put on the ache and the hands[7] on top, rubbing the *piçiete* on the affected part with them. And with this they say that the cure is finished.

CHAPTER 10

About the Swollen Throat

THESE miserable people reduce this cure to two things: the first, in pressing the swollen part with hands smeared with what I shall soon say; the second is in the power and strength that they attribute to their superstitious incantations.

When the cure must be performed, the false doctor anoints the index and middle fingers with a medicine of this land called *tzopillotl,*[1] which is the fruit of a tree, or with the juice of ground up *tomate,* with a little salt or *tequixquite,* which is almost the same thing, added. He then puts his fingers into the patient's mouth until he reaches the swelling, and then, pressing down on it with his fingers, he says this incantation:

[1] Pay attention to what I command you, those of the five fates {the fingers}[2] who all look toward one side. Go quickly and take away the green pain, the dusky pain, for it is not right that it should want now to kill or

tlaxihualhuia macuiltonalleque çemithualleque tlaxoconpehuiti in xoxoqui coaçihuiztli, yayauhqui coaçihuiztli tlen ye qui mictia nocozqui noquetzal. tlaxihualhuia iztac çihuatl.

destroy my jewel, my precious stone. {He speaks to the medicine.} Come on, white woman, do your duty.

Come, Five-*tonal*s-owners, One-courtyard-owners [i.e., the hands]. Go in order to shoo away the green palsy, the dusky palsy [i.e., the throat pain]. What is it that already is killing my jewel, my quetzal-plume [i.e., the patient]?[3] Come [pl], White Woman [i.e., the salt].

Tlā xihuālhuiān, Mācuīltōnalehqueh, Cemithualehqueh. Tlā xocompēhuītih in xoxōuhqui cōahcihuiztli, yāyāuhqui cōahcihuiztli. Tleh in ye quimictia nocōzqui, noquetzal? Tlā xihuālhuiān, Iztāc-Cihuātl.

While saying this incantation, he presses down on and rubs the swelling until it seems to him that it has burst or gone down. And with this he considers the cure completed.

CHAPTER 11

Another Incantation for the Purpose of Curing a Swollen Throat

THEY anoint the fingers with a medicine called *achiote*[1] in order to press down on the swelling, as was said in the preceding paragraph, and when they are ready to press down, they say the following incantation:

[1] I, the priest, prince of spells, am to placate my conjured neck, and I am to cure it. Come here, you, fiery colored possessed one {to the *achiotl*}, for you are to placate the green pain in all the rest, etc.[2]

Nitla macazqui ninahualtecutli nicçehuiz nonahual coco nicpatiz tlaxihuallauh tlatlauhqui tlamacazqui ticcehuiz xoxoqui coaçihuiztli. &.

I am the priest. I am the *nahualli*-lord. I will cool off my *nahualli*-gullet. I will cure it. Come, Red Priest [i.e., the *achiotl*]. You will cool off the green palsy [i.e., the throat pain], *etc.*

Nitlamacazqui. Ninâhualtēuctli. Niccēhuīz nonāhualcocōuh.[3] Nicpahtīz. Tlā xihuāllauh, Tlātlāuhqui Tlamacazqui. Ticcēhuīz xoxōuhqui cōahcihuiztli, *etc.*

CHAPTER 12

About the Superstition in Applying Cupping Glasses with the Magic Incantation

ALL of the reported incantations in the cures before this one are manifestly involved in heathenism, but much more clearly so the one that will be described in this section about applying cupping glasses, as will be seen in it. This was the cause for a healer accused of this crime—having confessed it when she was arrested for it—to turn around and deny it after she perceived how full it was of heathenism, so that carefully applied diligence was necessary in order that she correct herself in her confession, which was in the village of Mayanalã,[1] in the district of Tepequaquilco,[2] which lies on the road that goes from the city of Mexico to the port of Acapulco. The case was that in that village a healer was denounced for applying cupping glasses[3] with certain incantations and superstitious words. The healer was arrested because of the accusation, and at that moment her confession was taken; she declared that in order to apply cupping glasses she used the following incantation to invoke the instruments with which she applied them, which are the cotton that serves them as tow and the fire with which it is lighted for this effect, and the bleeder says:

[1] Come on now, come, you, the white woman, and mingle here with my father, the four reeds from where tongues and flames come out. Come here, my father, the four reeds who throw off flames, whose hair has a reddish color, yellow possessed one, also you, combine with the white woman in order that thus you suck and attract the green pain, the yellow pain, the black pain (i.e., every sickness).

tlacuel tla xihualauh iztac cihuatzin tla nican yhuan ximohui molo in nota[4] nahui acatl milintica tlacuel tlaxihualauh nota nahui acatl milintica tzonco çahuiztica coztic tlamacazqui tlaihuan ximohui molo iniztac cihuatzin tic chichinaz tichio anaz xoxoqui co açihuiztli co çauhqui co acihuiztli, tlilliuhqui coacihuiztli.

Let it be soon! Come, White Woman (H) [i.e., the cotton]. Join (H) here perilously with my father, Four Reed, He-is-scintillating [i.e., the fire]. Let it be soon! Come, my father, Four Reed, He-is-scintillating, He-is-becoming-yellow-haired, Yellow Priest [i.e., the fire]. Join (H) perilously with White Woman (H). You will suck out, you will inhale the green palsy, the yellow palsy, the black palsy [i.e., the pain].

Tlā cuēl! Tlā xihuāllauh, Iztāc-Cihuātzin. Tlā nicān īhuān ximohhuimōlo[5] in notah, Nāhui-Ācatl, Milīnticah. Tlā cuēl! Tlā xihuāllauh, notah, Nāhui-Ācatl, Milīnticah, Tzoncōzahuixticah,[6] Cōztic Tlamacazqui. Tlā īhuān ximohhuimōlo in Iztāc-Cihuātzin. Ticchichīnaz, tiquihīyōānaz xoxōuhqui cōahcihuiztli, cōzauhqui cōahcihuiztli, tlīliuhqui cōahcihuiztli.

Upon reaching these words, she lights the cotton and applies the cupping glass, and then, to scarify, she conjures the lancet and bleeder, saying:

[2] Come here, conjured point similar to the wing of the butterfly, for I am to send you to the seven caves from where we are to remove and take away the green pain, the yellow pain which now wants to kill the son of the Gods.

tlaxihualauh tlamacazqui ico papallotzin oncã nimitztitlaniz chico moztococ, Ticquixtizque tic topehuazque xoxouhqui coaçihuiztli coçauhqui coaçihuiztli ynye quimictia teteo ypiltzin.

Come, priest, Itzpapalotzin [i.e., the obsidian blade]. I shall send you there to Seven-caves-place [i.e., into the body]. We will cause the green palsy, the yellow palsy [i.e., the pain], which is already killing the child of the gods, to leave, we will push it out.

Tlā xihuāllauh, tlamacazqui, Ītzpāpālōtzin.[7] Oncān nimitztītlaniz Chicōmōztōc.[8] Ticquīxtīzqueh, tictopēhuazqueh xoxōuhqui cōahcihuiztli, cōzauhqui cōahcihuiztli, in ye quimictia tēteoh īmpiltzin.

Having said this, she performs it by sending the bleeder to the the caves, inserting it in the back in such a way that usually caves remain, and the false doctor [remains] very happy with the butchery that she has made. After this healer or witch had confessed that she did and said everything reported, when it was necessary later that the confession be confirmed, I sent a notary with a commission for it. But no diligence sufficed, because she denied it perversely and, deceiving her *beneficiado*, made him believe that they were raising false testimony against her, so that she obligated him to write me to cease persecuting that Indian woman, because she was innocent. With this it was necessary for me to carry out the judicial formalities personally.

I went then to the village, and I had the witch brought before me. I began to examine and she to deny. I used the stratagem which is much more useful with these people than taking an oath from them, and that is to represent the fact to them as it happens,[9] and therefore I said to her: "So that when you apply cupping glasses you conjure the cotton and the fire and the bleeder, saying *tlacueltla xihuallauh iztac cihuatzin*[10] *&c.*," as is reported above. Then, with this procedure, the Indian woman again confessed and said that she had denied it before out of fear. I have reported all this story in order to warn the ministers and those who may have the duty of inquiring into similar crimes that they should bear two things in mind: the first one, that the Indians are stubborn in denying any crime, and much more if it smells of heathenism. The second thing, that [one should] abstain from taking an oath from them in a proper court because they are people with such small mental capacity that it seems to them that the oath does not indicate[11] a new obligation. Lastly, in the case now reported, and in the ones where an invocation to the fire or to the *ololiuhqui* intervenes, they are more circumspect and fearful and more stubborn in denying use of them, not only because they attribute divinity to these things but also because they fear that they will anger them if they confess, and they fear vengeance.

CHAPTER 13

Cure for Chest Pain Because of an Accident or Because of Fatigue

FOR chest pain they apply the powder from the cortex of the root of the *coanenepilli*,[1] approved for fever and sunstroke. They apply this and have a person drink it in water slightly thickened with dough of ground maize, pressing down on the chest of the patient with their hands, saying this incantation at the same time:

[1] Be at my command, the five solar beings,[2] or better, of different fates, for I am the priest, prince of the spells, and I am seeking the green pain, the dusky pain. Where is it hiding?[3] Where does it habitually go? I the priest, the prince of the spells, warn you, enchanted medicine, that I am to placate my sick flesh. You will enter for that purpose into the seven caves. Leave the yellow heart, possessed medicine. I throw out of here the green pain, the dusky

Tla xihualhuian tlamacazque macuiltonalleque nitlamacazqui ninahualteuctli, nictemoa xoxouhqui coacihuiztli, yayauhqui coacihuiztli, coa[5] campa motlātia? campa yani? nitlamacazqui, ninahualteuctli, tla xihualhuia, tlamacazqui, pàtecatl niccehuiz nonacayotzin ticalaquiz, chicomoztoc, xicmotlalcahuili coçauhqui xollòtli intitlamacazqui, pàtecal xoxouhqui coa-

pain. Come here, you, the nine winds. Throw out of here the green pain.[4]

cihuiztli yayauhqui coacihuiztli nictotoca tla xihuallauh in ticchicnauhècatl,[6] tla xihualtotocati &.

Come, priests, Five-*tonal*s-owners [i.e., the hands]. I am the priest. I am the *nahualli*-lord. I seek the green palsy, the dusky palsy [i.e., the chest pain]. Where is it hiding? Where does it habitually go? I am the priest. I am the *nahualli*-lord. Come [pl], priest, Pahtecatl [i.e., the medicine made from the *coanenepilli*]. I will cool off my dear flesh. You will enter Seven-caves-place [i.e., the stomach]. Step aside (H) for the yellow heart, you who are the priest, Pahtecatl [i.e., the atole-medicine]. I am pursuing the green palsy, the dusky palsy. Come, you who are Nine-wind [i.e., the *ticitl*'s breath]. Go in order to pursue it hither, *etc.*

Tlā xihuālhuiān, tlamacazqueh, Mācuīltōnalehqueh. Nitlamacazqui. Nināhualtēuctli. Nictēmoa xoxōuhqui cōahcihuiztli, yāyāuhqui cōahcihuiztli. Cāmpa motlātia? Cāmpa yāni? Nitlamacazqui. Nināhualtēuctli. Tlā xihuālhuiān, tlamacazqui, Pahtēcatl. Niccēhuīz nonacayōtzin. Ticalaquiz Chicōmōztōc. Xicmotlālcāhuili cōzauhqui yōllohtli, in titlamacazqui, tiPahtēcatl.[7] Xoxōuhqui cōahcihuiztli, yāyāuhqui cōahcihuiztli nictohtoca. Tlā xihuāllauh, in tiChiucnāuhehehcatl. Tlā xichuāltohtocati.[8] *etc.*

With this ends all the mystery of this cure, in which, in addition to the common superstition, one notices how this number four is superstitious among the Indians. This cure used to be used by Marta Monica, the wife of Juan Matheo, the *alcalde* of Teteltzinco, in Ohuapan, and the same one, with the change of a few words, by Catalina Maria, the wife of Agustin Bartolome, in that village.

CHAPTER 14

What They Use with Patients Open at the Chest

THERE is another affliction of the chest [which is] when it opens up. And this affliction comes from working too much with the arms, as is seen in those who dig in the mines. For this affliction, as for the rest, they apply—with the same folly—some herbs, with the incantation added. The herbs are *piciete* and *yauhtli* (which is the herb anise). The incantation is:

[1] Come here, the nine-times cudgeled one, the nine-times beaten one {to the *piciete*}, and you, the green pain, dusky pain. Who is so powerful that now he destroys and finishes off the one entrusted to me? Come on, you who are worthy of esteem. Go and throw him out of there. I wonder where he is. I wonder if he is inside my enchanted coffer of ribs {the chest} and in the spine.[1] Go in after the enchanted head, you, the one of the five fates; with the dusky woman do your duty. Do not fall into dishonor.

Tlaxihuallauh chicnauh tlatetzotzon chicnauhtlatecapanil yayauhqui coacihuiztli, xoxouhqui coacihuiztli, ac tlacatl, ac mahuiztli inye quixpoloanomacehual tlaxictotoca, tlaxihuia tlàcotli campa in omotecato, ìtic in nonahual tzontecomatl[2] tictocaticalaquiz tlamacazque macuiltonalleque ma ammopinauhtiti coçauhqui cihuatl.

Come, Nine-[times]-rock-pounded-one, Nine-[times]-rock-slapped-one [i.e., the tobacco]. [You will shoo away the] dusky palsy, green palsy [i.e., the chest pain]. Who is the person, who is the illustrious being who is already destroying my vassal? Pursue him. Go [pl], precious-one. Where is it that he [i.e., the pain] has gone to settle down? [He has gone to settle down] on the inside of my *nahualli*-[rib-box]. You will enter following [after the *nahualli*]-head. Priests, Five-*tonal*s-owners [i.e., the hands], beware of bringing shame on yourselves [i.e., do your duty properly], you and Yellow Woman [i.e., the *iyauhtli*].[3]

Tlā xihuāllauh, Chiucnāuhtlatetzohtzon, Chiucnāuhtlatecapānīl. [Ticpēhuīz][4] yāyāuhqui cōahcihuiztli, xoxōuhqui cōahcihuiztli. Āc tlācatl, āc mahuiztli in ye quīxpoloa nomācēhual? Tlā xictohtoca. Tlā xihuiān, tlazohtli.[5] Cāmpa in ōmotēcato? Iihtic[6] in nonāhual[omicicuilpetlacal ōmotēcato. Ītepotzco nāhual]tzontecomatl[7] tictocaticalaquiz. Tlamacazqueh, Mācuīltōnalehqueh, mā ammopīnāuhtihtin, Cōzauhqui-Cihuātl.

Saying this nonsense, they apply the ground-up herbs to his chest and consider the cure finished.

CHAPTER 15

The Same Chest Pain in Children

Because they use a different incantation with children, I shall make a separate chapter here, since the chest is still being discussed. They call it in their language *pachollizitli*,[1] which means "improvement of the chest by pressing it." And it is thus because they apply no more medication to the children than pressing down on them with their hands. For this she starts the incantation to the fingers contained in other chapters, and then she says:

[1] Hail, you [sg], green butterfly, yellow and white butterfly. What harm is this that you are doing to the son of the Gods? In no way are you welcome here. You will be better in the large sloughs (or in the pretty green fields).

Tlahuel xoxohuic papalotl, coçahuic papalotl iztac papalotl tlen ye tictoctia in teteo ipiltzin, àmo nican timonequi nechcan timonequi teochiahuitl ipan.

Let it be soon! Green butterfly, yellow butterfly, white butterfly [i.e., the chest pain], what is it that you are already causing the child of the gods to follow? You are not wanted here. It is over there that you are wanted, upon the dangerous marshes.[2]

Tlā cuēl! Xoxōhuic pāpālōtl, cōzahuic pāpālōtl, iztāc pāpālōtl, tleh in ye tictoctia in tēteoh īmpiltzin? Ahmō nicān timonequi. Nechca in timonequi teohchiahuitl īpan.

With this she presses down on his chest gently, attributing [to herself] a power to cure by means of *manus impositi*,[3] a fraud of Satan. Thus it used to be done by, among other women, Doña Catalina Paula, an inhabitant of Huitzuco.[4]

CHAPTER 16

About the Incantation and Spell for Bleeding

ALTHOUGH bleeding is not an illness in the arms but a remedy for other illnesses [I will nevertheless write of it here], since they use superstition in this more excessively than in the other remedies, availing themselves of a long incantation full of unused words and others very difficult to understand, together with other symbols[1] that probably have any meaning that the Devil, their author, may wish to give to them. In their interpretation, I will follow the meaning most acceptable among the very ones who have used this incantation, not greatly tying myself down to the rules of grammar, and much less to the neatness of the Mexican language, since any person who understands it well will notice how much affect the Enemy causes in these people [by using obscure language]. The unpolished quality of the language [in this incantation] and the unusualness perhaps [are] for the sake of making it more respected,[2] as usually happens more commonly among people of scanty intellect who consider divine what they do not understand, [this] frequently being a defect of the one who speaks and not of the one who hears. This being granted, the one who is to do the bleeding speaks as follows:

[1] I, the priest and prince of spells, am going now in pursuit of the ones of the four heads. Come on, our sisters, with your skirts tucked up, lay hold of and gather up your disheveled hair,[3] and your heddles, loom treadles, and [...?...].[4] I am speaking to you, my sisters, the ones who have skirts of color and like snakes. And you, possessed one, who are like a jaguar, come, for finally you will drink without restraint until you lose yourself. But look [pl] very well at where what all are seeking—which is *chilli* and seeds[5]—will be able to come from. Look at the misfortune that this poor man is suffering. Look at his need and misery. Your hopes, diligencies, have come out empty. In vain you [pl] have become despondent looking for your goods, your property, because order will be able to be found, since now I wish to find your property and your goods for you, for then you will be able to carry them. Wait, for I want to look for them everywhere, within the bones of the precious stones where the red woman {the blood} is established.

Nehuatl tlamacazqui {A}[6] ninahualteuctli ya niauh ya nictocaz {B} naucantzontecome ye tohueltihuan {C} tla xontlaeheuacan in ammoquentzon in ammoxiouh in annohueltihuan {D} nochparcueyeque coacueyeque {E} tlamacazqui ce ocelotl tla xihuallauh yequene tiyohuallahuaniz {F} Tlaxitlatlachiacan can huitz inanquitetemoa, chilli ayohuachtli, notolinia macehualli quiihiyohuia quiteopoa {G} oammonenchiuhqui oammoteopouhque in anquitetemoa in ammaxca in ammotlatqui? can huitz? {H} tla oc nictetemo in ammaxca in ammotlatqui anquihualcuizq⁺, oc nohuian nictetemo in chalchiuh omitl itic, campa moquetza in tlatlauhqui cihuatl

It is I [in person]. I am the priest. {A} I am the *nahualli*-lord. I am already going. I will soon follow {B} Four-places-heads-owner [i.e., the veins (?)]. Already, my older sisters [i.e., the hands]. {C} Lift things up in the manner of your warp and your heddle [i.e., as an example], you who are my older sisters, {D} Nochpalcueyeh-

[Nohmatca][7] nehhuātl. Nitlamacazqui.[8] {A} Nināhualtēuctli. Ye niyauh. Ye nictocaz {B} Nāuhcāntzontecomeh. Ye,[9] nohuēltīhuān.[10] {C} Tlā xontlaehēhuacān in amocuahtzon, in amoxiyōuh, in annohuēltīhuān, {D} anNōchpalcuēyehqueh,[11] anCōācuēyehqueh.[12] {E} Tla-

queh and Coacueyehqueh [i.e., the hands; the sentence means: Hands, do your job properly]. {E} Priest, One Jaguar [i.e., the lancet], come. At last you will become drunk in the night. {F} Look [pl] [speaking to the hands and the lancet] diligently at the place where the chili peppers and squash seeds [i.e., food, *here,* the blood] that you are seeking are coming from. The vassal is poor; he is struggling to make a living; he is suffering. {G} You have exerted yourselves in vain; you have suffered, you who diligently seek your property and your goods [i.e., the blood]. Where are they coming from? {H} Let me still diligently seek your property and your goods. You will come and take them. Let me still diligently seek everywhere on the inside of the jade bones, where Red Woman [i.e., the blood] stands.

macazqui, Cē-Ocēlōtl, tlā xihuāllauh. Yēquen eh tiyohuallāhuānaz. {F} Tlā xitlahtlachiacān cān huītz in anquitehtēmoah chīlli ayohhuachtli. Motolīnia mācēhualli; quihīyōhuia; quiteohpōhua. {G} Ōammonēnchīuhqueh; ōammoteohpōuhqueh in anquitehtēmoah in amāxcā in amotlatqui. Cān huītz? {H} Tlā oc nictehtēmo in amāxcā in amotlatqui. Anquihuālcuizqueh. [Tlā] oc nōhuiyān nictehtēmo in chālchiuhomitl iihtic, cāmpa moquetza in Tlātlāuhqui-Cihuātl.

[2] Mother of mine, the one of the skirt of precious stones {water}, now is the time for you to seek with care that which harms and wants now to destroy this unfortunate one; for this purpose, I carry you with me. Come on now, draw back, forest Gods or lesser green [gods].[13] Come on, hide, green spiders. Do not let it happen that I destroy you by mistake. Get out of the way, you also, spider, *xochua.*

{Q}[14] Nonanchalchicueye ye tictetemoliz macehualli ye quixpoloa, ye mitzhuicaz[15] {R} tla oc ximiquanican xoxouhqui tlacolteyotl tla ximotlatican xoxouhqui tocatl {S} manan mechixpoloti {T} tlaximiquani xochhua.

{Q} My mother, Chalchiuhcueyeh [i.e., the water], soon you will diligently seek for the vassal the one who is already destroying him. Soon he will accompany you. {R} Move aside [pl] for a little while, you and green filth-spider.[16] Hide [pl], you and green spider. {S} Let me be careful not to destroy you [pl]. {T} Move [sg] aside, flower-owner [i.e., a kind of spider].

{Q} Nonān, Chālchiuhcuēyeh, ye tictehtēmolīz[17] mācēhualli ye quīxpoloa. Ye mitzhuīcaz. {R} Tlā oc ximihcuanīcān, xoxōuhqui tlahzoltocatl.[18] Tlā ximotlātīcān, xoxōuhqui tocatl. {S} Mā namēchīxpolohti.[19] {T} Tlā ximihcuani, xōchhuah.

(All [these words] are [expressions resulting from] the very great drunken revelries of these people. For that reason it is understandable that it [i.e., the incantation] is so badly written.)

All this incantation is full of many difficulties, both in the interpretation of the language and in superstitious traditions, and thus it will be necessary to add to it some explanation in order that it be better understood, and because of this the letters have been included [in the Nahuatl text] so that each thing may be put in its proper place.

First, he starts by giving solidity to his authority in order that no one doubt the benefit of the work, and thus he says {A} "I the prince," in which he expresses the pact with the Enemy. Then he speaks to the veins and calls them {B} "the ones of the four heads," because it seems that all end in the arms and legs. He orders them to be prepared and ready for anything and {C} "that they gather up their disheveled hair," and it is a metaphor as if he said "gather up the blood that is scattered in you [pl]." He says that {D} "you have skirts of color and like snakes," because of the appearance of the blood and because of the resemblance with the snake.

Then he talks to the lancet and calls it {E} "possessed one" and "jaguar" as if to convince [people] of the strength of the incantation. Inasmuch as he had given feeling to the iron, to say to it that it talks[20] until getting lost is a metaphor of drunkenness, and he tells it to take out so much blood that, when imbibed, it will be enough to confound one.

When he says, {F} "Look very well at where the sustenance will be able to come from," it seems that he is talking to the veins and lancet. {G} "They have come out empty," etc., [is appropriately said] to[21] the veins, because, since the sick person is as he is, he will not be able to look for sustenance.

{H} "Since now I," with this it seems he wants to obligate the veins to gratitude. The rest that follows are metaphors used by sorcerers.

{Q} "Mother of mine," etc., can be accommodated to two things: the first one, to water which they call thus; the second thing, to the lancet.

{R} "Come on now, draw back, forest gods," etc., where they put the symbol "X"—and by it they understand the Enemy or Beelzebub—in order that, since he is superior to the others whom they call forest gods or lesser ones, he [the Devil] may take them [the forest gods] away from where they are hurting the sick person, and thus he [the sorcerer] calls them green, and then green spiders, and he puts there another symbol for the sake of calling the devils spiders, and because they [i.e., the natives] signify the sickness with colors. It seems that he makes it known that these enemies are the cause of the sickness, and when he says, {S} "Do not let it happen that I destroy you by mistake" and {T} "Get out of the way, you also, Spider, *xochua,*" it seems he captures our enemies' benevolence, as if he said that his intention is not to throw them from there to their harm, but that they depart agreeably.

The very ones who say that they use this do not know how to explain it. One should not be surprised that such an ancient thing—and a thing that has passed through so many hands and such rude traditions—should have come to be not totally understood, especially when the Devil mixes difficult words and rare phrases in order to make what is useless and evil in itself be respected and extolled. But although absolutely no coherent sense is found in the incantation, one sees manifestly that all of it is substantiated from superstition and magic and, consequently, that one should proceed in this matter with much care and prudence.

CHAPTER 17

In Order to Stop the Blood That Comes out of the Mouth or Some Other Place

For this the medicine that they ordinarily use is only copal or salt, putting the power of the remedy in this incantation:

[1] Come here, you, my mother, the white woman. Understand what I say, for you now are to destroy the green pain and the black pain. White woman, mother of mine, understand what I say to you for you are to enter into the seven caves, and there you will pacify the red woman (which is the blood), and you will hold strongly and with a steady hand the bird that is the spirit, for dust now covers it and it now swoons.[1] Perform this immediately, and not tomorrow or the next day.

Tla xihualhuia iztac cihuatl nonan, tle ticma, caye axcan ticpopoloz in xoxouhqui coacihuiztli yayauhqui coacihuiztli, iztac cihuatl nonan tle ticma? yetonmocalaquiz chicomoztoc tictlamachtlaliz tlatlauhqui cihuatl (eztli)[2] titlamachtzitzquiz in tototl in Spiritu[3] inye tlateuhyotia inye tlapolocayotia, niman axcan àmo quinmoztla Àmo quinhuiptla.

Come [pl], White Woman [i.e., copal or salt], my mother. What do you know? [i.e., Pay attention!] Indeed soon now you will destroy the green palsy, the dusky palsy [i.e., the pain]. White Woman, my mother, what do you know? [i.e., Pay attention!] Soon you will enter Seven-caves-place [i.e., the mouth]. You will carefully seat Red Woman (it is the blood). You will carefully seize the bird which is the Spirit which is filling things with dust, is filling things with chaff. It will be immediately today. It will not be by-and-by tomorrow; it will not be by-and-by the day after tomorrow.

Tlā xihuālhuiān, Iztāc-Cihuātl, nonān. Tleh ticmati?[4] Ca ye āxcān ticpohpolōz in xoxōuhqui cōahcihuiztli, yāyāuhqui cōahcihuiztli. Iztāc-Cihuātl, nonān, tleh ticmati? Ye tonmocalaquīz Chicōmōztōc. Tictlamachtlālīz Tlātlāuhqui-Cihuātl (eztli). Tictlamachtzītzquīz[5] in tōtōtl in *Spiritu,* in ye tlateuhyōtia, in ye tlapalōcayōtia. Niman āxcān. Ahmō quin mōztla; ahmō quin huīptla.

Having said this, he has him drink the said copal or injects it into him by means of an enema, and he is very happy and the sick person very confident—such is their wretchedness and scanty intellect.

CHAPTER 18

About Belly or Stomach Pain

THE general medicine is the one they call *atlinan,*[1] which means "the water procreates it," and it is thus because it is usually found in the water or in very damp places. This is administered by means of an enema, and they say:

[1] Come here, green possessed one, here I apply you to the seven caves in order that you throw the green, black pain out of them, &.

Tlaxihualhuia xoxouhqui tlamacazqui nican nimitzonteca chicomoztoc xocontotoca xoxouhqui coacihuiztli yayauhqui coacihuiztli.

Come [pl], Green Priest [i.e., the *atl inan*]. Here I am stretching you out [i.e., injecting you] there in Seven-caves-place [i.e., the rectum]. Pursue the green palsy, the dusky palsy [i.e., the stomach ache].

Tlā xihuālhuiān, Xoxōuhqui Tlamacazqui. Nicān nimitzontēca Chicōmōztōc. Xocontohtoca xoxōuhqui cōahcihuiztli, yāyāuhqui cōahcihuiztli.

And if the herb is *tzopilotl*,[2] they say:[3]

[2] Come here, white possessed one.[4]	iztac tlamacazqui.
[Come [pl],] White Priest [i.e., the *tzopilotl*].	[Tlā xihuālhuiān,] Iztāc Tlamacazqui.

Others incense the sick person, conjuring for this the fire and the fingers with which they massage his stomach or belly.

CHAPTER 19

About One Indian's Fiction Concerning the Cure of the Belly

WHEN I was visiting the region and district of what they call the Marquisate, whose head is Cuernavaca, I found widespread the fame of a venerable old man who was considered a saint in all that land, because he had a power from Heaven to cure sicknesses. This Indian was called Domingo Hernandez, and for many years he had deceived all the people with his fictions. This impostor lived in the village of Tlaltiçapan, and thus in it, as in all those he had entered and his fame had reached, he was considered divine, because he had told a lie about himself which, although tedious, deserves to be told in order to see the stratagem of Satan.

For many years this impostor had told about himself that, while he lay near death from a serious illness, two persons dressed in white tunics appeared to him, and they carried him very far from that place to another, where another sick person was, and there they fanned him,[1] and then they carried him to another place, where, having found another sick person, they again fanned him, and then they said, "Let us return to your house for already they are weeping for you. Rest now, because the day after tomorrow we will return for you." And at this time, upon recovering consciousness, he found that those of his house were already weeping for him as if he were dead. And then, on the third day, the two dressed in white returned and carried him off like the first time, and having seen the two sick people and having blown on him as before, they said to him: "Hurry if you want to see your parents and grandparents and the rest of your kin, but if they happen upon you, in no way may you answer them because [if you do] you will remain with them and never again return to the world." And then he saw two roads: one very wide, which many were following because it was of the condemned; the other very narrow, rough, and full of bushes, rushes, and thorns. And they told him that that was the one of our Redeemer. And he saw that few were going along it while many were going along the wide road.

Then those of the white tunics told him to follow them. And following them, they arrived at the houses of marvels, where, after having arrived, they said to him, *xitlamahuico*[2] &c., which means, "Look and take notice of whatever you see. Consider what happens to those who got drunk. Beware, do not drink again" (and [they said] many other things like this) "because you are to suffer the same torments. Immediately abstain from pulque, and three days from now you are to return here.

Let us go now to your house, because they are already weeping for you. Let it not be that they dig your grave." And then they said to him, "Listen, you who are poor and wretched, you see here the means by which you will have food and drink in the world." And then they taught him the words (which I will give later), so that from that day on he had always cured and been right in the cures no matter how difficult they were, and with this they returned him to his house, where, having recovered consciousness, he found that they were weeping for him as if he were dead.

Then he used to tell that on that very night three ladies, marvelously dressed in white, without a tinge of any other color, visited him. And he would relate some conversations that passed among the three—who according to this tale were Our Lady, the Virgin Mary, and Saint Veronica, and another whom he did not know—and [saying] that Our Lady said that Christ, Our Lord, had imprisoned that sick man and that she wished to protect him, and for that purpose she summoned Saint Veronica and commanded her to protect him. And Saint Veronica, obeying, fanned him with a cloth, and with this he regained consciousness and the following morning was well. And then they brought him a sick child on whom he tried out the words, and the child recovered, whereby he proved the power of the words, and from that day on he has healed all those whom he has tried to cure with them. And [he said] that he has moved to compassion, and caused amazement in, all those to whom he has told this occurrence.

With this false story he had firmly established his reputation, as has been said, and thus having had him brought before me so that he might give an account of himself, [I questioned him, and] when he was asked about the profession that he was using and the words that he uttered and the herbs that he applied to sick people, he answered that he had learned them not from men but from people of the other life. Asked about the words that he uttered and about the medicine, he answered that the medicine was to prick all the belly with a needle, and the words were:

[1] Come on, then, white snake, black snake, yellow snake, be advised that you are now going too far and are hurting the ropes of meat which are the guts in the coffer or little basket, but already the white eagle, the black eagle {the needle} is going there, but it is not my intention to hurt you or destroy you, because I only intend to stop the harm you are doing, by compelling you to put yourself in a corner and by constraining your powerful hands and feet there, but in case of rebellion, I will summon to my aid the spirit or conjured one, *huactzin,* and at the same time I will summon the black Chichimec {the needle}, who also is hungry and thirsty and is dragging his guts {the threaded thread} in order that he go in after you. Also I will summon my Sister, the one of the skirt of precious stones, who bewilders rocks and trees, in whose company will go the dusky conjured one who will go making noise in the place of the precious stones and of the bracelets. Also the green and dusky possessed one will accom-

Tlacuel iztac coatl yayauhqui coatl coçahuic coatl ye titlàtlacoa in topco in petlacalco yetiquitlacoa intonaca me catl intonacacuetlacoxcolli[3] In axcan ic ompa yauh in iztac quauhtli, yayahuic quauhtli in axcan àmo mocan onihualla, àmo onimitzpòpoloco çan çomolli, çan caltechtli nocontoctiz in moma in mocxitzin. Auh intlacamo tinechtlacamatiz noconnotzaz tlamacazqui huactzin, noconnotzaz yayahuic chichimecatl noamiqui, noteocihui quihuilana in icuitlaxcol ompa yaz, noconnotzaz in nohueltiuh chalchicueye, tetl ihuinti, quahuitl ihuinti contocataz in coçahuic tlamacazqui, quetzalcalco, maquizcalco içahuacatoc, contocataz in xoxohuic tlamacazqui in yayahuic tlamacazqui in nom[in]e Patris et Filij e[t] Sp[irit]us S[anct]i

pany him. In the name of the Father and of the Son and of the Holy Ghost.

Let it be soon! White snake, dusky snake, yellow snake [i.e., the stomach pains], already you are ruining things in a kit and in a case [*metaphor for* secretly]. Already you are ruining the abundant ropes, the abundant guts. Now for that reason the white eagle, the dusky eagle [i.e., the needle], is going there. At the present it is not against you that I have come. I have not come to destroy you. It is only the corners and the wall surfaces that I will cause your hands and feet to follow [i.e., I will make you hide]. And if you do not obey me, I will call thither the priest, Laughing-falcon [i.e., the needle].[4] I will call thither the Dusky Chichimec [i.e., the needle]. He is both thirsty and hungry. He is dragging his guts [i.e., the thread]. He will go there. I will call thither my older sister, Chalchiuhcueyeh [i.e., the water]. The rocks are drunk, the trees are drunk [i.e., the consequences will be unpleasant if I am not obeyed]. Yellow Priest [i.e., the *piciete*[5]] will go following the one who lies making noise in the quetzal-plume house, in the bracelet-house [i.e., in the precious and beautiful house, i.e., the stomach]. Green Priest [i.e., *atl inan*[6]], Dusky Priest [i.e., *iyauhtli*[7]] will go following it. *In nomine Patris et Filii et Spiritus Sancti.*

Tlā cuēl! Iztāc cōātl, yāyāuhqui cōātl, cōzahuic cōātl, ye titlahtlacoa in tōpco in petlacalco. Ye tiquihtlacoa in tōnacāmecatl, in tōnacācuitlaxcolli. In āxcān īc ōmpa yauh in iztāc cuāuhtli, yāyāhuic cuāuhtli. In āxcān ahmō moca in ōnihuāllah. Ahmō ōnimitzpohpolōco. Zan xomolli,[8] zan caltechtli nocontoctīz in momā, in mocxitzin. Auh in tlācamō tinēchtlācamatiz, noconnōtzaz tlamacazqui, Huāctzin. Noconnōtzaz Yāyāhuic Chīchīmēcatl. Nō āmiqui, nō teohcihui. Quihuilāna in īcuitlaxcol. Ōmpa yāz. Noconnōtzaz in nohuēltīuh, Chālchiuhcuēyeh. Tetl īhuinti, cuahuitl īhuinti. Contocatiyāz[9] in Cōzahuic Tlamacazqui quetzalcalco, māquīzcalco ihzahuacatoc. Contocatiyāz[10] in Xoxōhuic Tlamacazqui, in Yāyāhuic Tlamacazqui. *In nomine Patris et Filii et Spiritus Sancti.*

One can very clearly see from the context of this incantation how full all of it is with superstitions and how much its author made a show of obscurity in the language, since all of it is artificial, although reasonable, metaphors. And in order to end his fraud and to give it more color of holiness, he adds to it as a close, "in nom[in]e P[atr]is et filij esp[irit]us S[ancti]."

Who would believe such a strange pedantry in such ignorant people? In order to better recommend his deception, he made use of such a high name, accommodating his excommunicated incantation with the manner and order of the benedictions of the Church, in order totally to persuade the ignorant people that all those words had been communicated to him by sovereign and divine command.

His cunning had been achieved so well that there was no one who doubted the truth of the reported story. After being brought before me, and having stated the said incantation, when he was questioned and harassed by me [to reveal] from whom he had learned it, he continued his fraud by answering me what he had answered everyone else. I warned him of his error and of my disillusionment because, from a long time back, I had those words dictated by others. And I exhorted him to confess the truth, but no artifice or diligence was enough.

At this point I had him put under custody, and, before a day of his prison passed, a large number of Indians met. Bringing me a gift, they asked me very earnestly to let him go because he was their remedy and consolation of all their illnesses. I tried as much as I could to undeceive them, showing them that the words he said were known by many others, and from whom those others had learned them, and how full they were of superstition, so that, although they abandoned their petition, I do not know whether they were dissuaded from their misapprehension, since their intellect is so scanty.

I made another effort with the impostor, and he, persisting in his belief, always said that he had learned it by command of Heaven, so that I was forced to avail myself of the vicarial religious of that place, who made the old man understand how I knew as a fact that what he was saying was a lie and a fraud, and that therefore I would not let him go, and that I would take him with me as a prisoner until he confessed the truth. Seeing himself harassed, the old man confessed his fraud publicly in the church, telling when he had learned those words and from whom—another fellow like him, [who was] already dead. And with this I put an end to the story of this old man, Domingo Hernandez, and I destroyed the fraud that had so much authority in that region.

CHAPTER 20

About Another Fraud Similar to the Foregoing One

LAST year, in 1627, I spoke in the village of Tlaltiçapan[1] to another impostor, a blind healer, who also related about himself another fraud similar to the last one. [He said] that, being near death and having gone into a sleeplike state, he went down to Hell, where he had seen many Indians and other kinds of people, and that there, up high, was the majesty of God, the Father, and many other extravagant remarks like this, and that there they told him to return to the world and to carry with him that medicine and to drink it, because with it he would heal himself and others, and that they gave him two balls of medicinal herbs, and they taught him how he was to apply them, and to some he had said that he recognized the herbs here and to others that [he did] not. Also he had those of the region persuaded that he had knowledge and power from Heaven, and thus they brought him to find out whether a religious who had died there—who was Father Friar Luis Lorenzo, the *vicario* of that house—had been bewitched. This blind man put on a great affectation of gravity. He used to carry a black and white rosary almost two *varas* long. On the end of the staff he carried a dangling cross. He begged alms, and to the one who gave him something, he would throw the rosary around his neck and, holding him in his grip, he would make a prayer to the saint to whom he commended himself. This one's specialty was to cure hemorrhoids by applying *colopatli*,[2] which, to them, is the pyrethrum of the pharmacies. It seemed profitable to me to prohibit this one from curing by means of the fraud that he carried with him, and so I did it.

CHAPTER 21

The Incantation and Superstition That They Use for Pain in the Loins

EXPERIENCE has well proved that those who suffer body pain because of an excess of tiredness feel relief when their body is pressed on, especially those parts that hurt the most, and this kind of pressing they call *tepàpacholiztli.*[1] Concerning this, the false and superstitious doctors have introduced a deception with their excommunicated spells, attributing to words that which the act brings by itself. It is the case, then, that when someone is overly tired from walking or work or gets a chill while he is sweating from the excess of work and heat, and his spine has become stiff and taut, with pain in the loins, which also accompanies these troubles, in such a case these false doctors apply the cure that they call *tetleiccaliztli,*[2] all of which consists in imparting warmth to the pained part with pressure, warming first a rock or a comal. Then they stretch the patient face downwards on the floor, with all the back naked; then the false doctor with the staff in his hand thoroughly wets one foot, the calluses of which are like the knees of a camel because of the excessive use. With the foot being thus wet, he places it on the very hot bowl or rock. He leaves it there until the heat penetrates the calluses to the live flesh. As soon as he feels that the heat has penetrated, he settles the foot, which is thus very hot, on the loins and spine of the patient, and, when he presses down, the pain abates. The words are:

[1] Come on, now come here, you, the four reeds that emit flame and have blond hair. Come on, now come, and watch out that you do not covet me. Here I bring my spongy heel or callus.[3] Do not be employed in it[4] because with you and with it I intend to dislodge and take away the green pain, the dusky pain from where it is, which now wishes to destroy the son of the Gods, and on the contrary I am to destroy and burn you.

Tlacuele xihualhuia, nahui acatl milintica in tzoncoçahuiztica, tlacuele xihualhuia, àmo tinechelehuiz, nican nichualhuican nopoçoloac (àmo tinechelehuiz) ica noconpehuiz xoxouhqui coacihuiztli, yayauhqui coacihuiztli in ye quipopoloznequi in teteo inpiltzin, ye nimitzpopoloz nimitztlàtlatiz.

Let it be soon! Come [pl], Four Reed, He-is-scintillating, He-is-becoming-yellow-haired [i.e., the fire]. Let it be soon! Come [pl]. You [sg] will not covet [i.e., harm] me. I am bringing here my foam sandal [i.e., the calloused sole of the foot]. (You will not covet [i.e., harm] me.) With it I will shoo away the green palsy, the dusky palsy [i.e., the loin pain] that wishes to destroy the child of the gods [i.e., the patient]. Soon I will destroy you, I will thoroughly hide you [i.e., I will really kill you].[5]

Tlā cuēl eh! Xihuālhuiān, Nāhui-Ācatl, Milīnticah, in Tzoncōzahuixticah.[6] Tlā cuēl eh! Xihuālhuiān. Ahmō tinēchēlēhuīz. Nicān nichuālhuīca in nopozolcac. (Ahmō tinēchēlēhuīz.) Īca nocompēhuīz xoxōuhqui cōahcihuiztli, yāyāuhqui cōahcihuiztli in ye quipohpolōznequi in tēteoh īmpiltzin. Ye nimitzpohpolōz, nimitztlahtlātīz.

To this incantation some add:

[2] I have brought my dragnet, etc. Where has it gone? Where has it settled? Perchance inside the bed or table of pearls or of flesh?

onichualhuicac noçalitilma &c. can mach in oya ó[7] can mach in omotecato, cuix ìtic in chalchiuh pèpechtli in tonaca pepechtli

I have brought my house's blanket [i.e., idiomatically, the net; metaphorically, the foot as an instrument to capture pain], *etc.* Wherever is it that he [i.e., the pain] went? Wherever is it that he went in order to stretch out? Is he perchance inside the jade bed, the abundant bed [i.e., the back]?

Ōnichuālhuīcac nocal ītilmah,[8] *etc.* Cān mach in ōyah? Cān mach in ōmotēcato? Cuix iihtic[9] in chālchiuhpehpechtli, in tōnacāpehpechtli?

They continually press down with the heel until, feeling somewhat alleviated, the patient canonizes the miracle of the cure. And they are very proud, attributing the relief of the sick person to their secret power and to the incantation.

CHAPTER 22

For Bone Fracture

For the break in a bone they usually plaster the affected part with an herb of this land called *poztecpatli*,[1] which means "medicine for breaks." This they reduce to a very soft plaster, and on applying it to the part, they add this incantation:

[1] Come, for I speak to you, white conjured one, embrace my enchanted thigh because the green pain, the dusky pain, the yellow pain is now destroying it, and help the vassal of God who suffers miserably. You, conjured one {to the boards with which they splint it}, whose happiness is in the rains, embrace my enchanted thigh.

tlaxihualhuia iztac tlamacazqui tlaxicnapalo nonahual metz quauh yo in ye quixpoloa xoxouhqui co aci huiztli, yayahuic coaçihuiztli coçahuic coaçihuiztli ini macehualtzin dios tic mopalehuiliz mo tolinia. tlamacazqui ceatl itonal ticnapaloz nonahualmezquauhyo.

Come [pl], White Priest [i.e., the plaster made from *poztecpahtli*]. Carry in your arms my *nahualli*-thigh which already the green palsy, the dusky palsy, the yellow palsy [i.e., the pain of the broken bone], is destroying. God's vassal [i.e., the patient] whom you will help (H) is poor. Priest, His-*tonal* Is One Water [i.e., the splints], you will carry in your arms my *nahualli*-thigh.

Tlā xihuālhuiān, Iztāc Tlamacazqui. Tlā xicnāpalo nonāhualmetzcuauhyo, in ye quīxpoloa xoxōuhqui cōahcihuiztli, yāyāhuic cōahcihuiztli, cōzahuic cōahcihuiztli. In īmācēhualtzin *Dios* ticmopalēhuilīz, motolīnia. Tlamacazqui, Cē-Ātl Ītōnal, ticnāpalōz nonāhualmetzcuauhyo.

With this they splint and tie the broken part, although badly, and they consider the cure finished. And if it comes out crooked, they put the blame on the sick person—for an excuse is never lacking, such as, he was restless, or someone entered who wished him ill, or some other similar superstition, because they never wish to confess there is a flaw in the efficacy of their incantations and spells.

ANOTHER

I found in the Marquisate, in the village of Tlalticapan, another incantation for the purpose of a break in a bone, which is the one that follows:

[2] Hail, you, *male* quail, the causer of crackling[2] *or* [of] *noise* or *uproar*, what is this that you have done with the bone of Hell because you broke or crushed it? And now I have come to fix it and to set it in its place by stretching the bone that is amidst the flesh.

tlacuel tecuçoline[3] comontecatle tlen tic aitia in mictlan omitl in oticpoztec, in otic xamani, ca axcan nic yectecaco in tonacaomitl nictilitzaco, in omitl ytic ca in nacatl.

Let it be soon! O Lordly-quail, O person from Comontlan,[4] what is it that you are doing to the Mictlan-bone that you broke, that you crushed? Indeed I have come now in order to set right the abundant bone.[5] I have come in order to tighten the bone that is inside the flesh.

Tlā cuēl! Tēuczōliné, Comōntēcatlé, tleh in ticāītia[6] in Mictlānomitl in ōticpoztec, in ōticxamānih? Ca āxcān nicyēctēcaco in tōnacaomitl. Nictitilitzaco[7] in omitl iihtic cah in nacatl.

Having said this, he plasters, splints, and binds it and considers the cure done. I point out, for clarity, that he calls the pain, the annoyance, and the misfortune that the break of the bone caused a "male quail" because this quail, upon any disturbance, makes a certain noise with which, as if it disturbs the rest of its covey, all fly up suddenly; and thus he calls it a "causer of noise." The "bone of Hell" can be understood either because of being inside the flesh as in a center or because, by means of the pact of these black arts, they dedicate it to the Devil, whose kingdom is in Hell. With this, this incantation is explained.[8]

ANOTHER INCANTATION FOR THE SAME PURPOSE

In other places I have made mention of a certain Martin de Luna, of the village of Temimiltzinco, in the Marquisate, in all of which [region] this impostor had established the fame of being a miraculous doctor with the fraud of incantations and spells. In order to cure a break in a bone, this man, among others, used the one that follows. It says:

[3] What is this that my sister, the eight in order, the woman like a macaw,[9] has done? They have caught and detained the son of the gods. But I am the priest, the god Quetzalcoatl, I who know how to descend[10] to Hell and to ascend[11] to the upper [region][12] and even to the nine hells. From there I will remove the infernal bone. The possessed ones, the many birds, have done badly, [they have] cracked it, they have broken it.[13] But now we will unite it, and we will cure it.

tleo ax nohueltiuh in chicuetecpaçihuatl[14] tlalo çiuatl? oma naloque oma co choque teteo ipiltzin, canehuatl nitlamacazqui ni quetzalcoatl, niani mictlan niani topan, niani chicnauhmictlan ompa nic cuiz in mictlan omitl otlatlacoq+ intlamacazque in teuhtotome otlaxaxamaniq+ otlapoztecque auh in axcan tic çaça lozque, ticpatizque.

What did my older sister, Eight-flint-woman, Land-wine-woman [i.e., maguey; *and, by extension,* pulque], do? She and the child of the gods have embraced one another [i.e., my client became drunk], they have hugged one another. Indeed it is I. I am the priest. I am Quetzalcoatl. I am the traveler to Mictlan; I am the traveler to Topan; I am the traveler to Nine-Mictlan. There I will get the Mictlan-bone. The priests, the dust-

Tleh ōāx nohuēltīuh, in Chicuētecpacihuātl, Tlāloccihuātl?[15] Ōmonāpalohqueh, ōmomācochohqueh[16] tēteoh īmpiltzin. Ca nehhuātl. Nitlamacazqui. NiQuetzalcōātl. Niyāni Mictlān; niyāni Topan; niyāni ChiucnāuhMictlān. Ōmpa niccuiz in Mictlānomitl. Ōtlahtlacohqueh in tlamacazqueh, in teuhtōtōmeh.[17] Ōtlaxahxamānihqueh, ōtlapoz-

birds, have ruined things. They have crushed things, they have broken things. But now we will glue it back together; we will cure it.

tecqueh. Auh in āxcān ticzahzālōzqueh; ticpahtīzqueh.

Then he speaks to the cord tying up the break and says:

[4] Come on, you my cord, who are like the snake *maçacoatl.* Serve here as guard and do your duty well. Do not be careless, because tomorrow I will be with you.

tla cuel no maça coa mecatzin tlanican xontlapixto ma nentontlatlaco mopan nehcoz inmoztla.

Let it be soon! My deersnake [i.e., powerful] rope (H), lie here guarding things. Beware of ruining things. I will visit you tomorrow.

Tlā cuēl! Nomazācōāmecatzin, tlā nicān xontlapixto.[18] Mā nēn tontlahtlacoh.[19] Mopan nehcōz in mōztla.

Concerning this incantation one should note, first, that—as a thing established and undoubted among the Indians—he starts by laying the blame, loading it all on the magueys and the pulque, which is understood beneath the metaphor of "my sister, the eight in order, the woman like a macaw."[20] He calls them "the eight in order" because, as has been said in another place, they are always planted and cultivated set eight by eight in a chessboard pattern.[21] "Woman like a macaw," I understand to stand for the different colors and effects that it causes in those who drink it, or else because like a macaw it is a bird so vociferous and clamorous that there is no one who can put up with it. In the same way the pulque and drunkenness cause shouts, outcries, and tumults.[22] From this I deduce that, even if the pulque and drunken sprees of the Indians were not to cause more trouble than those disputes, hard feelings, enmities, and strife of the Indians, along with the many misfortunes which result from them that this infernal incantation supposes, one should apply an efficacious remedy and use absolute power in prohibiting them and extirpating them totally. Since, in addition to what has been said, we see that they are the total cause of the diminution of this nation, [and] if they are not taken away totally, they will be the cause of the total end of it. And no one of all those who have experience with these miserable people has any doubt about this, especially if they have dealt with them familiarly. Let us return to our purpose.

Then he represents the harm done as impersonal. This is another mystery. "They have caught," he says, "and detained the son of the gods";[23] he does not say who, in the first place, because he already has supposed that the harm was caused by the magueys and the pulque and, in the second place, because these misfortunes usually happen without anyone knowing who caused or performed them because, since those who come together in the drunken sprees are many, they easily become angry. When they come to blows, they move around in such a way that it usually happens that the first one to lay hands on the father is his own son, as I have seen through experience. After sobering up, no one can judge who did the damage, since all are out of their minds, and although there may be someone who says that it was the son, the son denies it, and no one believes it. Because of this, the incantation speaks in an impersonal manner, keeping the custom of the case, but "I am the priest and god," etc., speaks in the name of the Devil. Quetzalcoatl was an idol much celebrated during the heathen days of these barbarians.

He says "infernal bone" because the bone is inside the flesh as in a hidden center or else because he dedicates it to the Devil.[24]

"The possessed ones, the many birds, have done badly" [are] the drunks, because they are out of their minds, like demonized people. He calls them "possessed ones" and "many birds," because they usually get drunk in groups. With this, this incantation is explained.

CHAPTER 23

For Pains in the Bones of the Back

THE curing of diverse illnesses and pains by pricking the affected part with a needle or with a viper tooth is much used among the Indians, adding the incantation that accompanies it for perfection and certainty of the good outcome. And this method was used by a certain Martin de Luna, an inhabitant of Temimiltzinco, who for a long time earned his living by pretending to be a doctor, depending on the fraud of the spells. And among his spells he used one for pain in the back or in the bones of the spine, of which I became informed because this Martin de Luna, being summoned by a man to cure him, left him without money and much worse than before, having taken four *pesos* from him and increased his pain with some cruel punctures. This sick man made the entire case known to me, and after it was verified by those who were present, the old man was arrested and confessed the following to be the incantation:

[1] Hail, you, green, yellow, red, or white snake. Cease,[1] for the white strong pricker has arrived, and he is to walk over it all, mountains and hills. Unhappy he whom he finds, for he is to destroy him and swallow him down.

Tlacuel xoxohuic coatl, coçahuic coatl, tlatlauic coatl iztac coatl, ye huitz iztacquauh tzotzopitżal, nohuian nemiz intetl ìtic, inquahuitl ìtic, auh in aquin ipan àçiz quiquaz, quipopoloz

Let it be soon! Green snake, yellow snake, red snake, white snake [i.e., the back pain], soon Strong-puncturer-like-a-white-eagle [i.e., the needle] is coming. He will live everywhere, inside the rocks, inside the trees [i.e., in all affected parts of the body]. And he will eat, he will destroy the one whom he catches up with.

Tlā cuēl! Xoxōhuic cōātl, cōzahuic cōātl, tlātlāhuic cōātl, iztāc cōātl, ye huītz Iztāc Cuāuhtlatzotzopitzqui.[2] Nōhuiyān nemiz, in tetl iihtic,[3] in cuahuitl iihtic. Auh in āc in īpan ahciz, quicuāz, quipohpolōz.

He accompanied this with cruel prickings and sold his cure as dearly as he could.

CHAPTER 24

Another Incantation That Usually Accompanies Needle Prickings

HAVING received information about an old woman, Isabel Maria, an inhabitant of Temimiltzinco, who uses spells and incantations, I took measures to get my hands on her. And she was so careful that for more than a year I was not able to discover her. Finally she was found and brought before me. Among other superstitions, she confessed an incantation with which she accompanied needle prickings, with which she was accustomed to curing all kinds of illnesses. And it goes thus:

[1] Hail, what are you doing? You are killing the land and the mud (which means, the body). Already I come to examine you and no less comes the Chichimec {the needle}, the foreigner, the one who has white tripe similar to ours. [I promise] that I[1] will not leave a corner that I will not visit. And being between rocks or harquebuses will not defend you, for there it will destroy you.

Tle cuel ticmictia tlalli çoquitl, nihualla, nimitzicxitocaco, nimitz ittaco, Auh tel ye huitz chichimecatl in chontalli, ye huitz intonacayo cuetlax coliztac nohuian nemiz intetl ìtic in quahuitl ìtic mitzpopoloz.

Let it be soon! You are killing the earth and the mud [i.e., the body]. I have come. I have come in order to follow your footprints. I have come in order to see you. But also the Chichimec, the stranger [i.e., the needle], is already coming. Already White-sustenance-guts [i.e., the needle and thread] is coming. He will live everywhere, inside of rocks, inside of trees [i.e., in all affected parts of the body]. He will destroy you.

Tlā cuēl! Ticmictia tlālli zoquitl. Nihuāllah. Nimitzicxitocaco. Nimitzittaco. Auh tēl ye huītz Chīchīmēcatl, in chontalli. Ye huītz in Tōnacāyōcuitlaxcoliztāc.[2] Nōhuiyān nemiz, in tetl iihtic, in cuahuitl iihtic. Mitzpohpolōz.

[2] You will be better somewhere else where there is the shelter of a good house,[3] where there are cotton and maize. In truth, like an abundant house,[4] there will be rugs and chairs of authority. There will be bouquets and aromatic smoke.[5] Why are we stopping here, where, at the most, we will be able to stay only three days? We will be much better off where I say and much at our ease. I go following you, for I also suffer from thirst and hunger.

Nech can tiaz chanecapan qualcan on canca ich catl on can ca tlaolli cha necapan qualcan onca yntopetl onca yn to tetzon, to xochiuh topo quieuh, tle nenica nican tonyezque yeitonatiuhtzin? nech can to pactiezque nimitztepotz tocatiuh nò namiqui no ni teo cihui.

It is there that you will go, to the dweller's-place that is good. There is cotton there. There is shelled maize there. In the dweller's-place that is good are our mats, are our hoard,[6] our flowers, and our smoke-tobacco.[7] Why should we futilely stay here for three little suns [i.e., for three short days]? It is there that we will be happy. I will go along following behind you. I am also thirsty; I am also hungry.

Nechca in tiyāz chānehcāpan cualcān. Oncān cah ichcatl. Oncān cah tlaōlli. Chānehcāpan cualcān oncah in topetl, oncah in totetzon, toxōchiuh, topōquiyeuh. Tleh nēn īca nicān tonyezqueh yēi tōnatiuhtzin? Nechca in tompāctiyezqueh.[8] Nimitztepotztocatiuh. Nō nāmiqui; nō niteohcihui.

[3] But with what will you sustain yourself in the house of an unhappy person, where the air enters and leaves without anyone to prevent it and because of that it is freezing, where there is nothing on which to stumble?

Auh tlen ticquaz ic notlacatl ichan oticalaquico ehecatl calacticac tlaizcaltiticac atlehuetztoc

But what is it that you will eat in the poor man's home, where you have come in order to enter? The wind is steadily entering; everything is

Auh tleh in ticcuāz icnōtlācatl īchān ōticalaquico? Ehehcatl calactihcac; tlaītzcaltitihcac.[9] Ahtleh huetztoc.

steadily cold. Nothing lies fallen [i.e., nothing is at ease].

She says all this, cruelly pricking the painful part, with which she makes a very good, although dissembled, bleeding. And then she next avails herself of *piçiete,* and, rubbing it well on the punctured parts,[10] she says, speaking to the pain:

[4] The nine-times beaten one {the *piçiete*}, he who flies like nine will destroy you and will take away from you all your strength.

chicnauh tla tetzotzonal chicnauhpapa tlan tzin mitz poloc, mitz cecehuiz mitz quixtilis mochi mo chicahualis

Nine-[times]-rock-pounded-one, Nine-flutterer (H) [i.e., the tobacco],[11] will destroy you. He will chill you. He will cause all of your strength to leave you.

Chiucnāuhtlatetzohtzonal, Chiucnāuhpahpatlāntzin mitzpolōz. Mitzcehcēhuīz. Mitzquīxtilīz mochi mochicāhualiz.

This is all the mystery of the cure, and all the other incantations that this old woman used to use are the same that are reported in other places, or they differ so little that it seemed to me unnecessary to lengthen this Treatise by including them. I only observe that this old woman was so pleased {note!}[12] with the strength of this false incantation, that she said she had unburdened her conscience with having made it known, not hiding any of the things that God had communicated to her for the benefit of man. So one sees clearly how far she was from considering it evil and how much further from leaving the use and exercise of it, and it all proves how superficially these miserable people hold the [Christian] faith and how little instructed in it they are.

CHAPTER 25

For Rash, Impetigo, and Sicknesses of This Kind

To the sicknesses which are included under the names of rash and impetigo they apply the same medicines, which are, above all, to sprinkle the sick part with conjured water, accompanied with its incantation and spell, and then they apply other herbs such as *tlacopatli, piciete,* and *axin,* saying also their share of incantations to these medicines or to others, depending on who applies them. They say the incantation, speaking to the water:

[1] Come here, you, green woman, who are to go against my Father, the comet that sparkles, against the four reeds of the blond hair. [Part of the Nahuatl is not translated.][1] You are to quench it. Now you carry the green woman, mother, the one of the skirt of precious stones. Quench his fire where he has set it {note!}.[2] Come here, yellow possessed one, and you, nine-times beaten one, nine-times cudgeled one, who now accompany her and

tla xihualauh xoxouhqui cihuatl, ye yhuicpa tiauh nota xiuhtli milintica nahui acatl tzoncoztli campa oquitlalli ini tleuh nota xiuhtli milintica nahui acatl tzoncoztli, tic çehuiz yetichuica xoxouhqui çihuatl nonan chalchicueye ticçehuiz ini tleuh campa oqui tlalli tlaxihualhuia coçauhqui tla ma caz quichicnauh tlatecapanilli, chicnauh tlatetzotzonalli ye yhuan tiauh yhuan

go wrapped with her. Also the yellow +flying one {the *axin*}, accompanies you. Understand what I tell you, my mother, the one of the precious skirts {the water}. Now is the time, come with what I say. Go to destroy my father, the reeds that emit flames {the fire, a metaphor}, his breathing and voice. When he shines the most, when he is the clearest, he would want to make fun of you, but he grows weak and loses strength in you. Now finally you are to destroy, darken, and remove him from our presence.

timo moliuh tiuh yetichuica coçauhqui +tlapapalacatl tlaxihualhuia nonan chalchicueye aman yeque ne tla xihualhuia tla xicpopoliti nota nahui acatl milintica ihio, ytlatol iniquac in tlanez quimo camahahuiltizquia mopan ceceuhqui mopan popoliuhqui aman yequene ticpopoloz tic tlatiz tic quixtiz.

Come, Green Woman [i.e., the *atl inan*]. Already you are going against my father, Comet, He-is-scintillating, Four Reed, Yellow-hair[3] [i.e., the rash]. There where my father, Comet, He-is-scintillating, Four Reed, Yellow-hair, has set his fire [i.e., inflammation], you will extinguish it. Already you are carrying Green Woman [i.e., the *atl inan*], [O] my mother, Chalchiuhcueyeh [i.e., the water]. You will extinguish his fire there where he has set it. Come [pl], Yellow Priest, Nine-[times]-rock-slapped-one, Nine-[times]-rock-pounded-one [i.e., the tobacco]. Already you are going with her; you go thoroughly joining with her.[4] Already you bring Yellow Striped-reed [i.e., the *axin*]. Come [pl], my mother, Chalchiuhcueyeh. It is at this instant at last [i.e., the time to strike has come]. Come [pl]. Go in order to destroy the breath, the word [*idiomatically,* the speech; *metaphorically,* the burning itch] of my father, Four Reed, He-is-scintillating. At the time when it has dawned, he [i.e., the rash] would make fun of [i.e., irritate] him [i.e., the patient]. Because of you he [i.e., the rash] is one who has become cold; because of you he is one who has become destroyed. At this instant at last you will destroy him; you will hide him [i.e., you will kill him]; you will cause him to leave.

Tlā xihuāllauh, Xoxōuhqui-Cihuātl. Ye īhuīcpa tiyauh notah, Xīhuitl, Milīnticah, Nāhui-Ācatl, Tzoncōztli. Cāmpa ōquitlālih in ītleuh notah, Xīhuitl, Milīnticah, Nāhui-Ācatl, Tzoncōztli, ticcēhuīz. Ye tichuīca Xoxōuhqui-Cihuātl, nonān, Chālchiuhcuēyeh. Ticcēhuīz in ītleuh cāmpa ōquitlālih. Tlā xihuālhuiān, Cōzauhqui Tlamacazqui, Chiucnāuhtlatecapānīlli, Chiucnāuhtlatetzohtzonalli. Ye īhuān tiyauh; īhuān timohmōliuhtiuh. Ye tichuīca Cōzauhqui Tlapahpalācatl. Tlā xihuālhuiān, nonān, Chālchiuhcuēyeh. Āman yēquen eh. Tlā xihuālhuiān. Tlā xicpohpolōti notah, Nāhui-Ācatl, Milīnticah, iihīyo[5] ītlahtōl. In ihcuāc in tlanēz, quimocamanālhuīltīzquiya.[6] Mopan cehcēuhqui; mopan pohpoliuhqui. Āman yēquen eh ticpohpolōz; tictlātīz; ticquīxtīz.

When she invokes the water, she sprinkles the affected part with it, and when she reaches this part of the incantation,[7] she blows on the inflamed part as the priests do on an infant during the baptism. Having sprinkled and blown on that which is broken out in a rash or is inflamed, she then prepares the ointment that is usually made with a medicinal herb called *Axin,* and for this purpose she says:

[2] Come on, come, ruddy or bright-red flyer,[8] who now without hesitation or delay are to take away and destroy this sickness. I have come[9] to let you drink the yellow heat, the green heat, the dusky heat, the yellow heat,[10] the white heat {medicinal herbs that they use}, with which to throw you out of here {*coanenepilli*}[11] and for that I bring my ninth reed[12] {*coanenepilli*} (here he applies the *coanenepilli*).

tla xihuallauh tlauhqui tlapapalacatl, Aman yequene tic quixtiz ticpopoloz O nihuala nican nimitzitiz cacauhqui totonqui, xoxouhqui totonqui yayauhqui totonqui, iztac totonqui nican ni mitzpehuiz nican nic hualhuicac nochicnauh acatl (coa nenepilli quitequilia)

Come, Red Striped-reed [i.e., the *axin*]. At this instant at last you will cause him [i.e., the rash] to leave, you will destroy him. I came here in order to cause you, yellow heat, green heat, dusky heat, white heat [i.e., the inflamed rash], to drink it [i.e., the *axin*].[13] I will shoo you [i.e., the rash] from here. I have brought also Nine-reed [i.e., the *coanenepilli*] (he pours *coanenepilli* on it).

Tlā xihuāllauh, Tlātlāuhqui Tlapahpalācatl. Āman yēquen eh ticquīxtīz, ticpohpolōz. Ōnihuāllah nicān nimitzītīz, cōzauhqui totōnqui, xoxōuhqui totōnqui, yāyāuhqui totōnqui, iztāc totōnqui. Nicān nimitzpēhuīz. Nicān nichuālhuīcac nō Chiucnāuhācatl (cōānenepilli quitēquilia).[14]

And she puts on top of it a kind of grass that becomes reddish colored when it dries[15] {because of the internodes that the plant produces}.

[3] Come, you, my companion, the bright-red woman {*coanenepilli*}, follow the precious one, and watch what you do. Do not fall into shame, for if this does not have the desired effect, it will not be any shame of mine but of yours.

tlaxihuallauh no cihuapo tlatlauqui çihuatl tla xoc toca tlahçotli, Maçan tlen tic chiuh, mati mopinauhti cuix ne ninopinauhtiz? catehuatl.

Come, woman like me, Red Woman [i.e., the *coanenepilli*]. Follow the precious one [i.e., the *axin*]. Beware of doing just anything [i.e., do specifically what it is your duty to do]. Beware of bringing shame upon yourself [i.e., do your duty properly]. Am I the one who will become ashamed [i.e., if this procedure fails]? Indeed you are the one.

Tlā xihuāllauh, nocihuāpoh, Tlātlāuhqui-Cihuātl. Tlā xictoca tlazohtli.[16] Mā zan tleh in ticchīuh. Mā timopīnāuhtih.[17] Cuix neh ninopīnāuhtīz? Ca tehhuātl.

She continues by talking to the copal, which is an incense of this land.[18]

[4] Come on, come, white woman, go and eradicate—*suple*[19] this ill or sickness. Do the same thing, you, white woman {the salt}. Come here, you bright-red woman {the rash}. For what purpose are you here and why are you doing this harm to an unfortunate one? Come on now, come, you, Yellow-Earth, and obstruct the steps of the spider called *tlatlauhqui.*

tla xihualauh iztac çihuatl tla xinelhuayo cotonati, no teiztac çihuatl. tlaxihuallauh tlatlauhqui ciuatl tle in tic chihua nican? Tlein ticaitia in in tlacatl motilinia tla xihuallauh tlalcoçahuitl nican tic yacatzacuiliz tocatlatlauhqui

Come, White Woman [i.e., the copal]. Go in order to cut it [i.e., the rash] at the root. Also you are the one [i.e., it is your turn], White Woman [i.e., the salt]. Come, Red Woman [i.e., the rash]. What is it that you are doing here? What is it that you are doing to this person who is poor? Come, Yellow-earth.[20] Here you will intercept the red spider[21] [i.e., the rash].

Tlā xihuāllauh, Iztāc-Cihuātl. Tlā xicnelhuayōcotōnati.[22] Nō teh, Iztāc-Cihuātl. Tlā xihuāllauh, Tlātlāuhqui-Cihuātl. Tleh in ticchīhua nicān? Tleh in ticāītia[23] in īn tlācatl motolīnia? Tlā xihuāllauh, Tlālcōzahuitl. Nicān ticyacatzacuilīz tocatlātlāuhqui.

Having encircled the inflamed place with the yellow earth, in order that it obstruct the inflammation, she continues her incantation, directing it against the sickness itself, and she says:

[5] Hail, you, ruddy Chichimec, what are you doing? In what are you busying yourself? &c.[24]

Tlaxihuallauh tlatlauhqui chichimecatl, tlein ic tay?

Come, Red Chichimec [i.e., the rash]. Why are you doing it?

Tlā xihuāllauh, Tlātlāuhqui Chīchīmēcatl. Tleh in īc tāi?

And it continues as [in] the others, and she spreads *huauhtli* over all of the inflammation and considers the cure concluded.

CHAPTER 26

About the Method of Curing Other Inflammations and Swellings

THE most common medicine they use for these afflictions is copal. And having dissolved it in water, they apply it in the form of a plaster or poultice to the affected part with the same incantation as has been said in other sicknesses, changing only one word or another. While saying the incantation, they slap on the plaster that they put over the swollen part, with which both the fraudulent doctor and the sick person remain very pleased.[1]

CHAPTER 27

The Cure for Tertian Fever

THEY commonly cure this sickness by pricking the patient's spine with a good needle. Others incense the sick person with the herb called *yauhtli*, which is anise, using this incantation:

[1] Come on, now come, yellow conjured one or consecrated one, go to destroy and finish off the green humor, the dusky humor, the yellow humor that causes this tertian fever and wishes presently to kill this horrible son of mine because they are bringing him wrapped in dust, his head all disheveled.

tlaxihualhuia coçauhqui tlamacazqui Tla xoconpopoloti xoxouhqui atonahuiztli yayauhqui atonahuiztli cocahuic atonahuiztli in ye quimictia notetzauhpiltzin in ça qua tecuhpol in ça quapachpol quinemictia.

Come [pl], Yellow Priest [i.e., the *iyauhtli*]. Go in order to destroy the green chills-and-fever, dusky chills-and-fever, yellow chills-and-fever, who is already killing my omen-child [i.e., the patient] since he causes him to live just dust-headed and just disheveled-headed.

Tlā xihuālhuiān, Cōzauhqui Tlamacazqui. Tlā xoconpohpolōti xoxōuhqui ātōnahuiztli, yāyāuhqui ātōnahuiztli, cōzahuic ātōnahuiztli in ye quimictia notētzāuhpiltzin, in zā cuāteuhpōl,[1] in zā cuāpachpōl quinemītia.

With this they incense him and consider the cure concluded.[2]

For tertian fever, an Indian woman, Petronilla, of the village of Tlayacapan, used to have a person drink a medicinal potion which was *coanenepilli* and rue, dissolved in water, and she added to them [i.e., the herbs] another incantation similar to the others which, on the paper where she had it written, began with *ica motlatlauhtia in atl,*[3] which means "With this prayer a request is made to the water," with which it is clearly proved that they venerate this element and they attribute divinity to it, as to fire. The false prayer, then, says:

[2] Come on, now come, you, my mother, the one of the skirts and *huipil* of precious stones, and deign to come down to the belly of this creature of God, in order that there you subdue the ire of Heaven, justice.[4]

Tla cuel tla xihualhuia nonan chalchiuhtli ycue, chalchiuhtli yhuipil tla xomotemohui Dios itlachihualtzin itictzinco, tla xoconmoyamanili in ilhuicac Justicia.[5]

Let it be soon! Come [pl], my mother, Chalchihuitl Icue, Chalchihuitl Ihuipil [i.e., the water]. Go down to the stomach of God's creature [i.e., the patient]. Go soften the justice that is in Heaven [i.e., the pain].

Tlā cuēl! Tlā xihuālhuiān, nonān, Chālchihuitl Īcuē, Chālchihuitl Īhuīpīl. Tlā xonmotemohui *Dios* ītlachīhualtzin iihtictzinco.[6] Tlā xoconmoyamānili in ilhuicac *justicia.*

With this she had the patient drink the medicinal potion, etc.

CHAPTER 28

A Fraud for Urinary Sickness

THE mental resources of these Indians are so scanty that they do not distinguish the causes of the sickness and they do not know, for example, that the remedy that took away the abdominal pain for one person might make it worse for another person. It happens like that in the cure that they use for urinary sickness, since it is a single cure, no matter whether it [the sickness] comes from proud flesh, or from a stone or a wound or a rupture, although I am convinced that they attribute the principal power to the spell. Coming now to the cure, they prepare a medicinal potion from a yellow root,[1] as I found it used in the village of Tepequaquilco, by a certain Magdalena Juana, the wife of Pedro Mayor. And they accompany the potion with this incantation:

[1] Come here, minister of the Gods, yellow minister, a dweller in paradise. Go push away, go take away and placate the green pain. What God or which powerful being is now breaking and shattering my gem, jewel, and rich emerald?[2]

Tlaxihuallauh tlamacazqui, coçahuic tlamacazqui, teotlalpan chane, tla xicpehuiti tla xicquixtiti, tla xiccehuiti, ac teotl ac mahuiztli inye quixamania in yequipoztequi noquetzal &c.

Come, priest, Yellow Priest, Dweller on the desert-area [i.e., the *tlacopahtli*]. Go in order to shoo it away. Go in order to make it leave. Go in order to cool it off. Who is the god, who is the illustrious being who already crushes my quetzal-plume [i.e., the patient], who already breaks it, *etc.*

Tlā xihuāllauh, tlamacazqui, Cōzahuic Tlamacazqui, Teohtlālpan Chāneh. Tlā xicpēhuīti. Tlā xicquīxtīti. Tlā xiccēhuīti. Āc teōtl, āc mahuiztli in ye quixamānia, in ye quipoztequi noquetzal, *etc.*

Having said this incantation, she gives [him] her medicinal potion that is from the root they call *tlacopàtli*,[3] although perhaps they avail themselves of the tail of the *tlaquatzi*,[4] the unmatched remedy for obstructions to urine and to the other fluxes of the body, and even for difficulty in childbirth, and for this purpose it is used by all the midwives of this land, with which one could make an argument against these impostors that in such a case their spell or incantation does not accomplish anything.

CHAPTER 29

About the Cure and Frauds for Fevers

For the cure of fevers they use many remedies, all wrapped up in superstition and frauds. I shall put down here the most common ones. The most common remedy that they use is a medicinal potion of a compound of four herbs of those of this land. They call the compound *tlanechchilcopàtli*.[1] The four herbs are (1) *hueinacoztli*, (2) *xochimecatl*, (3) *coanenepilli*, (4) *xiuhcocòlin*.[2] They grind up these four herbs and mix them in plain water. And in order for the sick person to drink it, they prepare it with the following incantation:

[1] Come here, you, yellow possessed one, to banish the green pain or sickness, the dusky pain that now wants to take away the life of the son of the Gods.

Tlaxihualhuia coçahuic tlamacazqui xocontotoca xoxouhqui coacihuiztli, yayahuic coacihuiztli in ye quimictia teteo inpiltzin &c.

Come [pl], Yellow Priest [i.e., the herbs]. Pursue the green palsy, the dusky palsy [i.e., the fever], which is already killing the child of the gods [i.e., the patient], *etc.*

Tlā xihuālhuiān, Cōzahuic Tlamacazqui. Xocontohtoca xoxōuhqui cōahcihuiztli, yāyāhuic cōahcihuiztli in ye quimictia tēteoh īmpiltzin, *etc.*

Others use the superstitious *ololiuhqui*, and not only for fevers but also for all kinds of sickness. And granted the so accepted and established superstition[3] among these barbaric people, I am not surprised, because almost all of them adore this seed, and by attributing divinity to it, they consequently attribute power against all sickness to it, and at the same time they believe that, in addition to curing them, it will reveal the cause of the sickness to them.

Among others, Isabel Luisa, of the Mazatec nation, used this remedy, and she used to administer it dissolved as a drink. And the incantation that accompanied it is made in the fashion of a prayer to the *ololiuhqui*, and it goes like this:

[2] Come here, you, cold possessed one, for you are to take away this fever and are to console your servant who, perhaps for one day or perhaps for two days, will serve you and sweep the place where they venerate you.

tlaxihuallauh tlamacazqui cecec ticquixtiz totonqui ticmoyollaliliz momacehual, àco oc cemilhuitl, àço oc omilhuitl mitztequipanoz, mitztlatlachpaniz.

Come, Cold Priest [i.e., the *ololiuhqui*]. You will cause the heat to leave. You will console your vassal [i.e., the patient]. Perhaps for one day more, perhaps for two more days [i.e., for a short

Tlā xihuāllauh, Tlamacazqui Cecēc. Ticquīxtīz totōnqui. Ticmoyōllālilīz momācēhual. Ahzo oc cemilhuitl, ahzo oc ōmilhuitl mitztequipanōz, mitztlahtlachpānīz.

while, i.e., during the rest of his life that you permit him to live after curing him now] he will work for you, he will sweep diligently for you.

All this incantation is based on the opinion—so established among the Indians which almost all of them believe—that the *ololiuhqui* is a divine thing. As a consequence of this, in this incantation she refers to the custom of the veneration which they pay it among the Indians, which is to have it on their altars in the best little boxes or little baskets that they can afford, and to offer incense and bouquets of flowers to it there, and to sweep the room and, with great care, sprinkle it with water. And because of this the incantation says "perhaps he will serve you or sweep for you one or two days more." And with the same veneration they drink the seed, closing themselves up in the places like someone who might be in the *sancta sanctorum*,[4] with many other superstitions. And the excess with which these barbarians venerate this seed is so great that they even, as out of devotion, are accustomed to sweeping and sprinkling with water the places where the bushes—which are some very thick vines—that produce it are found. And [they do] this even though they may be [growing] in wastelands or ground covered with brambles.

In order to give authority to her fraud, this Indian woman, Lucia,[5] a Mazatec by nation, related that, upon her giving *ololiuhqui* to a patient, a strange person had appeared to him, saying that he was the *ololiuhqui*, and he had consoled him, saying to him, "Do not be troubled, for soon you will get well, for you have sought me. You were not looking for me yesterday or the day before." With this story this Indian woman had given as much authority to her fraud as if it had been based on some divine revelation.

Everything reported in this chapter about the root [*sic*] of the *ololiuhqui* holds likewise for the root [*sic*] called peyote,[6] which they venerate to an equal degree.

Others for the illness of fevers use enemas, using at times *ololiuhqui* or peyote for herbs, and at times *atlinan* or other herbs: and whether it be the one of the other, the method is to grind it up and dilute it in cold water and to inject it as an enema, accompanied with the following spell and incantation:

[3] Come on, come now, green woman, go and take away the green heat, the dusky heat, the inflamed heat, the yellow heat, because for this purpose I send you to the seven caves. Do not put off for tomorrow or the next day that which I command you. You are to do it immediately, at this moment. Who is the God or the one so powerful who now destroys the work of your hands? I command it, I, the prince of the spells.

tlacuel tlaxihuallauh xoxouhqui cihuatl tla xicpehuiti xoxouhqui tvtonqui yayauhqui tvtonqui, tlatlauhqui totonqui, cocauhqui tvtonqui ye oncan nimitztlitan, chicomoztoc àmo quin moztla, àmo quin huiptla niman axcan ticquixtiz, ac teotl, ac mahuiztli in ye quixpolloa motlachihualtzin, nomatca nèhuatl ninahualteuctli.

Let it be soon! Come, Green Woman [i.e., the *atl inan*]. Go in order to shoo away the green heat, the dusky heat, the red heat, the yellow heat [i.e., the fever]. I have already sent you there to the Seven-caves-place [i.e., the rectum]. It will not be by-and-by tomorrow. It will not be by-and-by the day after tomorrow. It will be immediately

Tlā cuēl! Tlā xihuāllauh, Xoxōuhqui-Cihuātl. Tlā xicpēhuīti xoxōuhqui totōnqui, yāyāuhqui totōnqui, tlātlāuhqui totōnqui, cōzauhqui totōnqui. Ye oncān nimitztītlan Chicōmōztōc. Ahmō quin mōztla. Ahmō quin huīptla. Niman āxcān ticquīxtīz. Āc teōtl, āc mahuiztli in

today that you will cause it to leave. Who is the god, who is the illustrious being who is already destroying your creature? It is I in person.[7] I am the *nahualli*-lord.

ye quīxpoloa motlachīhualtzin? Nohmatca nehhuātl. Nināhualtēuctli.

CHAPTER 30

For Fever Sickness and Other Illnesses

FOR fevers and other illnesses, a certain Don Martin Sebastian y Ceron, an inhabitant of Chilapa,[1] famous for his frauds and superstitions, used a fraud somewhat different from the ones reported, one single thing serving or trying to serve as a cure for many sicknesses, based on the incantations with which he used to accompany them. The medicine was water in which he had thrown, with his incantations, twelve maize kernels and mixed the juice of the herb called *atlinan*. He would pick up a vessel of water and conjure it, saying:

[1] I invoke you, my mother, the one of the precious skirts. Who is the God, or who is the so powerful one who wants now to destroy and bury the one entrusted to me?

tlaxihualhuia nonan chalchi cueye acteotl, Acmahuiztli in yequixpoloa nomaçehual inyequi tlatlatiznequi.

Come [pl], my mother, Chalchiuhcueyeh [i.e., the water]. Who is the god, who is the illustrious being that is already destroying my vassal [i.e., the patient], that already wants to hide him thoroughly [i.e., wants to really kill him]?[2]

Tlā xihuālhuiān, nonān, Chālchiuhcuēyeh. Āc teōtl, āc mahuiztli in ye quīxpoloa nomācēhual, in ye quitlahtlātīznequi?

Then he continues by invoking the medicine.

[2] Come on, now come, you, my sister, the green woman, for I want to go to leave you in the seven caves {in the belly}. I wonder where the green pain, the dusky pain, etc., is or is hiding. Go rub with your hands the enchanted guts, so that you bring about the desired effect. Let it not be that you fall into shame.

tlaxihualhuia nohueltiuh xoxouhqui çihuatl tla nimitzon cahuati chicomoztoc can mach in meeua in mo tlatia inxoxouhqui coaciuiztli? inyayauhqui coaçihuiztli &. tlaxo con matlalloti in nahual cuetlaxcolli, amo timo pinauhtiz.

Come [pl], my sister, Green Woman [i.e., the *atl inan*]. Let me go in order to take[3] you to Seven-caves-place [i.e., the stomach]. Wherever is it that the green palsy, the dusky palsy [i.e., the pain], *etc.*, is sitting, where is he hiding? Go in order to rub the *nahualli*-guts with your hands. You will not bring shame on yourself [i.e., do your duty properly].

Tlā xihuālhuiān, nohuēltīuh, Xoxōuhqui-Cihuātl. Tlā nimitzoncāhuati Chicōmōztōc. Cān mach in mehēhua, in motlātia in xoxōuhqui cōahcihuiztli, in yāyāuhqui cōahcihuiztli, *etc.* Tlā xoconmātelōti[4] in nāhualcuitlaxcolli. Ahmō timopīnāuhtīz.

Having said this, he shifts the address to the twelve maize kernels and says:

[3] I in person am the one who speaks, the priest. Come here, my mother, the one of the skirt of precious stones, for I am in person the priest. Come you also, my sister, sustaining woman. And because now is the time, because now, at last.

nomatca nehuatl nitlamacazqui tlaxihualauh nonan chalchi cueye nomatca nehuatl nitlamacazqui tlaxihualhuia nohueltiuh tonacaçiuatl ye aman yequene,

It is I in person. I am the priest. Come, my mother, Chalchiuhcueyeh [i.e., the water]. It is I in person. I am the priest. Come [pl], my older sister, Tonacacihuatl [i.e., the maize kernels]. Already it is at this moment at last [i.e., now is the time for action].

Nohmatca nehhuātl. Nitlamacazqui. Tlā xihuāllauh, nonān, Chālchiuhcuēyeh. Nohmatca nehhuātl. Nitlamacazqui. Tlā xihuālhuiān, nohuēltīuh, Tōnacācihuātl. Ye āman yēquen eh.

[4] Who is the god or the so powerful one who now destroys my vassal or the one entrusted to me? It will be best for what is harming him to come out and go away in peace and leave me, because there is probably no lack of places where they are waiting for it and where they will give it a better reception, where there are many gifts and an abundance of riches. Let it now leave this unfortunate one in peace. What does he have in him to be coveted? Let it go away immediately, at this moment. Will it perhaps leave tomorrow or the following day? No indeed, but rather immediately. And if it does not come out, the exemplary punishment that I will carry out on it is in my charge.

Ac teotl,[5] ac mahuiztli in yequixpoloa nomaçehualma çan yhuian quiça, ma çan yhuian nech tlalcahui, cayenepa inchialo caye nepe in te machilo netlacamachoyã, tlatquihuacapan, maquitlalcahui in icno tlacatzintli macamo quelehui maniman quiça cuix quinmoztla cuix quin huiptla in yaz? ca niman aman intlacamayaz, intlacamo quiçaz canehual nicmati intle ypan nicchihuaz.

Who is the god, who is the illustrious being that already is destroying my vassal [i.e., the patient]? Let him just quietly leave. Let him just quietly move aside for me. Indeed already it is over there that he is being awaited. Indeed already it is over there that he is expected, at a place where people are prosperous, in a place of property owners. Let him move aside for the poor man [i.e., the patient]. Let him not covet [i.e., harm] him. Let him leave immediately. Will it be by-and-by tomorrow, will it be by-and-by the day after tomorrow that he will go? Indeed it will be immediately at this moment. If he will not go, if he will not leave, I am indeed the one who knows what I will do to him.

Āc teōtl, āc mahuiztli in ye quīxpoloa nomācēhual? Mā zan īhuiyān quīza. Mā zan īhuiyān nēchtlālcāhui. Ca ye nēpa in chialo.[6] Ca ye nēpa in tēmmachīlo, netlācamachōyān, tlatquihuahcāpan. Mā quitlālcāhui in icnōtlācatzintli. Mācamō quēlēhui. Mā niman quīza. Cuix quin mōztla, cuix quin huīptla in yāz? Ca niman āman. In tlācamō yāz, in tlācamō quīzaz, ca nehhuātl nicmati in tleh īpan nicchīhuaz.

Having said this, he throws the twelve maize kernels in the water and then he squeezes the herb *atl inan* into the water and gives it to the patient to drink. And this is all the cure, and it is general for all the sicknesses, because they are so defective in intellect.

CHAPTER 31

For Body Fatigue and Pain

FOR the fatigue that they call *quaquauhtiliztli*[1] and for body pain, the cure is brief and [so is] the incantation. The cure is to provoke an evacuation with the help of an enema or clyster, or with something like it, or some similar method.

First, they massage the body from the kidneys and groin down to the heels, as has been said about the ones who do this cure by heating the soles of their feet and their heels, which they call *y tetleiça*,[2] and they add this incantation:

[1] Come here, dusky and green yawn or stretching, for we are to seek the dusky or green stiffness or pain of the body—that is, in order to get rid of it.

tlaxihualauh cocahuic ne aa nalli xoxouhqui nea analli, nican tictemozque inco cauhqui quaquauhtiliztli xoxohuic quauhtiliztli.

Come, yellow relaxed one, green relaxed one [i.e., the sphincter muscle]. Here we [i.e., the speaker and the enema] seek the yellow stiffness, the green stiffness.

Tlā xihuāllauh, cōzahuic neahānalli, xoxōuhqui neahānalli. Nicān tictēmōzqueh in cōzauhqui cuahcuauhtiliztli, xoxōhuic cuahcuauhtiliztli.[3]

With this incantation and with massaging the body or provoking it to evacuate with an enema or otherwise, they consider[4] the cure finished. Magdalena Petronilla Xochiquetzal, an old blind woman from Huitzoco,[5] used to use this fraud. Another woman called Justina, from the same village, used to use the herb that they call *tzopillotl*,[6] applied by an enema, with this incantation:

[2] Come here you, the white woman {to the herb}, go to consume the green and dusky pain—that is, to take away the fatigue.

tla xihuallauh iztac çihuatl, tlaxoconpopoloti in xoxouhqui coaçihuiztli, yayauic coaçihuiztli, q. n. quauhtiliztli.

Come, White Woman [i.e., the *tzopilotl*]. Go in order to destroy the green palsy, the dusky palsy (which means the stiffness).

Tlā xihuāllauh, Iztāc-Cihuātl. Tlā xocompohpolōti in xoxōuhqui cōahcihuiztli, yāyāhuic cōahcihuiztli (quihtōznequi cuauhtiliztli[7]).

With this they consider the cure finished without making any other effort.

NOTE

At this point, it seemed to me that I should speak of something that should be of interest to any person in whose charge the management and customs of these Indians may be—a thing, as established and accepted among them as it is pernicious, which the Enemy, who is vigilant for our harm, has introduced, taking advantage of their natural weakness and inclination, and it is that [they give themselves over to drunkenness] at the same time that they are compelled to personal service, both in the fields and in the mines, where they usually experience so much damage to their corporal health because of the excessive work. This labor, if borne for the love of God, would be of much spiritual profit, but the Devil has established his league against it by persuading them that, if they were to get excessively drunk before going to work, they would acquire so much strength and vigor that they would easily be able to bear any whatever of the tasks and [that] after these tasks they would regain their lost strength with drunkenness. They call these harmful drunken sprees *necehualiztli,*[8] so that, with the drunkenness and the intolerable work that they have, they end up getting sick and dying, without the continual deaths that every day come from their drunken sprees teaching them anything. And thus the ministers and curates of these wretched people should try to persuade them of the grave harm that comes to their bodies and souls from this, and also the secular authorities *invirga ferrea,*[9] since experience shows that no gentle means is of use in extirpating this infernal vice at whose hands such a multitude die, with this miserable race being totally finished off and consumed, taking death in their hands.

CHAPTER 32

Against the Wound and Poison of the Scorpion

FOR the understanding of this chapter it is necessary to tell an old fable and story which is well established among these barbarians and so well accepted that I believe few escape believing it. The fable is that when they feigned that, in the first age, those that now are animals were men, there was one whose name was Yappan.[1] For the sake of improving his condition in the transmutation that he felt near, in order to placate the gods and capture their benevolence, this man went off alone to do penance in abstinence and chastity, and he lived on a rock called *tehuehuetl.*[2] While Yappan persevered in his aim, they assigned to him as a guard another man, called Yaotl.[3] During this time Yappan was tempted by some women but not overcome. This being the situation, the two sister goddesses, Citlalcueye[4] and Chalchicueye[5] (who are the Milky Way and Water), foresaw that Yappan was to be converted into a scorpion and that, if he persisted in his purpose, after being converted into a scorpion, he would kill all those he stung. Seeking a remedy to this damage, they decided that their sister, the goddess Xochiquetzal, should go down to tempt Yappan. She descended to the place where Yappan was and said to him:

[1] Brother,[6] I have come, I, your sister, Xochiquetzal, to greet you and to give you solace and pleasure.	nooquichtiuh yappan onihualla nimohueltiuh nixochiquetzal nimitz tlapaloco, nimitzciauhquetzaco
"My older Brother, Yappan, I have come. I, your older sister, Xochiquetzal, have come to greet you. I have come to give you greetings."	"Noquichtīuh, Yāppān, ōnihuāllah. Nimohuēltīuh, niXōchiquetzal, nimitztlahpalōco. Nimitzciauhquetzaco."

To this Yappan replied:[7]

[2] You have come, sister of mine, Goddess Xochiquetzal.	otihuallauh nohueltiuhe, xochiquetzale
"You have come [i.e., welcome], O my older sister, O Xochiquetzal."	"Otihuāllauh, nohuēltīuhé, Xōchiquetzalé."

She answered:

[3] Yes, I have come, but where will I ascend?	onihualla, campa ye nitlècoz
"I have come. Where will I soon climb up?"	"Ōnihuāllah. Cāmpa ye nitlehcoz?"

To which he answered:

[4] Wait, for I am now going for you.	xicchie ye ompa niauh.
"Wait [a moment]. I am already going there."	"[Oc] xicchie.[8] Ye ōmpa niyauh."

With this the goddess Xochiquetzal climbed up and, covering him with her *huipil,* caused him to fail in his purpose [of chastity]. And the cause of this fall was Xochiquetzal's being a stranger and a goddess who came from the heavens, which they call *chicnauhtopan,*[9] which means "from the nine places." With the reported outcome, the spy Yaotl, who was not sleeping, said to Yappan:

[5] Are you not ashamed, bound-by-an-oath Yappan, of having sinned? Because of that, as long as you live upon the land, you will be of no benefit; you will not be able to serve for anything. Men will call you scorpion, and I now know you by this name. Realize that you are to remain like that.	àmo tipinahua tlamacazqui yappan otitlàtlaco? in quexquich cahuitl timonemitiz in tlalticpac àmo tle huel ticchihuaz intlalticpac àmo tle huel tictequipanoz mitztocayotizque in maçehualtin ticolotl, ca nican nimitztocayotia nimitztocamàti colotl xihualhuia yuhqui tiez
"Are you not ashamed, priest, Yappan, because you have ruined things? For however long you will live (H) upon the earth, you will be able to do nothing upon the earth, you will be able to achieve nothing. The vassals [i.e., the commoners] will call you 'Scorpion.' Indeed I here call you, I name you 'Scorpion.' Come [pl]. Thus you will be."	"Ahmō tipīnāhua, tlamacazqui, Yāppān, ōtitlahtlacoh? In quēxquich cāhuitl timonemītīz in tlālticpac, ahmō tleh huel ticchīhuaz in tlālticpac, ahmō tleh huel tictequipanōz. Mitztōcāyōtīzqueh in mācēhualtin 'tiCōlōtl.' Ca nicān nimitztōcāyōtia, nimitztōcāmati 'tiCōlōtl.'[10] Xihuālhuiān. Iuhqui tiyez."
[6] Accompanying his words with deeds, he knocked his head from his shoulders and threw it on his back, and because of this he is today called "head carrier."[11]	oquiquechcoton, oquiquechpano itzontecon, yèhuatl ica itoca tzonteconmama.
He cut off his head. He [i.e., Yaotl] carried it on his shoulders. It is for that reason that his [i.e., Yaotl's] name is "Head-carrier."	Ōquiquechcotōn. Ōquiquechpanoh ītzontecon. Yehhuātl īca ītōcā, "Tzontecommāmah."[12]

After being beheaded, Yappan was changed immediately into a scorpion, and Yaotl went after Yappan's wife and cut off her head and changed her into a scorpion. She was called Tlahuitzin.[13] And because of Yappan's having sinned,[14] the goddess Citlalcueye decided that all those who were stung by a scorpion would not die. And Yaotl was changed into a locust, which they call *Ahuaca chapullin,*[15] and by another name, *tzonteconmamama.*[16]

Given this false story, one will easily understand what I will now say about the cure and fraud involving the incantation that they use for wounds from a scorpion.

They apply very few medicines to those wounded by a scorpion. The entire cure consists in tying off the wounded part so that the poison will not pass further and in rubbing *piciete* or ground-up earth on the place of the sting. And to the one and the other they add this incantation:

[7] Come here, possessed one, Yappan of the curved thorn.[17] Where have you wounded us? In the most esteemed place, but you will not pass my boundaries.

tlaxihualhuian, tlamacazqui yappan huizcol[18] canin otitech min huel ompa tonecoyan ahmo ticpanahuiz in no quaxoch.

Come [pl], priest, Yappan, Thorn-curve. Where is it that you have stung us? It is right there in our needed place. You will not pass my boundary.

Tlā xihuālhuiān, tlamacazqui, Yāppān, Huitzcōl. Cān in ōtitēchmīn? Huel ōmpa tonecōyān. Ahmō ticpanahuīz in nocuāxōch.

This is all the cure of this incantation, and he means by "boundaries" the cord with which he ties off the wounded part in order to stop the poison. Others, considered as more wise [change this cure somewhat],[19] and among them a certain Don Martin Sebastian y Ceron, from Chillapan,[20] very respected among the natives as a sage, and who proclaimed himself a diviner and seer, a knower of intentions and who knew who was a wizard and sorcerer, of whom I have made mention elsewhere. This man, then, along with the rest, further enhanced the cure of scorpion wounds by lengthening the reported incantation and spell, and by touching in it more extensively on all the reported fable and adding the circumstances that I will soon speak of. First, in this second incantation, it seems that he suggests that, according to his heathen tradition, the one that is now a deer was called Piltzinteuctli[21] in the first age, and he had some superiority over the one called Yappan, who is the one changed into a scorpion, now called *colotl.*[22] They now call the deer *chicomexochitl.*[23] Well, when one of these feigned doctors is called for some scorpion wound, if it is shortly after the wound has occurred, he starts by saying the following incantation:

[8] I in person, the possessed one (or the one consecrated to the gods), the one of the seven roses {the deer}, I call you, the priest Yappan, you who are now the one of the curved sting, to an audience for you to explain why you offend people. Do you not already know, and have you no remorse about the fact that my sister, the goddess Xochiquetzal, made you break your fast and continence[24] there on that ancient rock[25] where you deceived her {metaphorical allusion to the fable}? Nothing, nothing can you do now. Your labor can no longer be of any profit to you. Go very far away from here to do wrongs. Go very far away from here to make fun of people.

Nomat ca nehuatl nitlamacazqui chicomexochitl tlaxihualhuia tlamacazqui yappan Huitzcol tle ica in teca ti mo cacayaua? cuix ah mo yetic mati ahmo yemo yollo quimati, in omitznecahualpoztequito nohueltiuh xochiquetzatl in ompa Tehuehueticpac in ompa ini ca otimo cacayauh ah mo tle tlein huel tic chihuaz ahmo tleinhuel tic tequipanoz nepahueca teca ximo cacayahuati nepa hueca teca ximahuiltiti.

It is I in person. I am the priest, Seven Flower [i.e., the male deer]. Come [pl], priest, Yappan, Thorn-curve. Why is it that you are making fun of people? Do you not already know, does your heart not already know that, in order to make

Nohmatca nehhuātl. Nitlamacazqui, ni-Chicōme-Xōchitl.[26] Tlā xihuālhuiān, tlamacazqui, Yāppān, Huitzcōl. Tleh īca in tēca timocahcayāhua? Cuix ahmō ye ticmati, ahmō ye moyōllo quimati in

you break your fast, my older sister, Xochiquetzal, went there on top of Stone-drum, there where you mocked her? There is nothing that you can do. There is nothing that you can accomplish. Go over there far away in order to make fun of people. Go over there far away to amuse yourself with people.

ōmitznezahualpoztequito nohuēltīuh, Xōchiquetzal, in ōmpa Tehuēhuēticpac, in ōmpa in īca ōtimocahcayāuh? Ahmō tleh in[27] huel ticchīhuaz. Ahmō tleh in huel tictequipanōz. Nēpa huehca tēca ximocahcayāhuati. Nēpa huehca tēca ximāhuiltīti.

[9] Come here, you, my mother, Princess Earth, placate willingly the one dedicated to the gods, Yappan, the curve-faced one, in order that he go away for good and leave you in peace (he applies earth while rubbing the wound). And I make him know that his going away and leaving you is not to take place tomorrow or the next day but right away, and if he does not come out and go away, it remains in my charge to punish him as he deserves.

tla xihualhuianonan tlaltecutli çany huiyan xictla cahualti intlamacazqui yappan Pelxayaque,[28] ma can ihuian quiça, macan ihuian mitztlalcahui, cuix quin moztla çuix huiptla yaz? ca niman aman intla camo quiçaz intla camo yaz caoc nehuatl nicmati yntle ipan nic chihuaz.

Come [pl], my mother, Tlalteuctli [i.e., the ground-up dirt]. Cause the priest Yappan, Pelxayaqueh, to leave things just quietly. Let him leave just quietly. Let him step aside for you just quietly. Will it perchance be by-and-by tomorrow, will it perchance be by-and-by the day after tomorrow that he will go? Indeed it will be immediately at this instant. If he will not leave, if he will not go, indeed I am still the one who knows what I will do to him.

Tlā xihuālhuiān, nonān, Tlāltēuctli. Zan īhuiyān xictlacāhualti in tlamacazqui, Yāppān, Pelxāyaqueh. Mā zan īhuiyān quīza. Mā zan īhuiyān mitztlālcāhui. Cuix quin mōztla, cuix quin huīptla[29] yāz? Ca niman āman. In tlācamō quīzaz, in tlācamō yāz, ca oc nehhuātl nicmati in tleh īpan nicchīhuaz.

With having done and said what has been reported, they consider the cure finished, and they want it to be esteemed as superior and of superhuman power. But after the scorpion's having stung someone, if perchance they delay in summoning the impostor so that when he arrives the poison has possession of the patient, in order to feign a more quick-acting and a more imperious authority over the scorpion and its poison, he begins by rebuking it in the person of the goddess Xochiquetzal, and therefore he says:

[10] Brother of mine, shaved-faced one, are you not ashamed? Why do you do wrongs and why do you make sport of people? Perchance do you not already know, perchance do you not already have remorse about the fact that I came[30] to make you interrupt your penance there on the rock of antiquity[31] (I who am the goddess Xochiquetzal), where you slept with me? Well, now I come again. I, the same one, your sister Xochiquetzal, to greet you and console you in order that willingly and without resistence you leave this vassal of mine alone. Look here, for already I cover you with my *huipil* or blouse; now I circle around you and I wrap you up in it. Sleep in peace, for now I put my head between your arms. Now I embrace you and kiss you.

No oquichtiuh pelxayaq⁺, ah mo tipinahua tleica in teca timo cacayahua? tle ica in teca ti mahuiltia? cuix amo yeticmati ahmo qui ma tica yn moyollo in onimitz necahualpoztequito in ompa tehuehueticpac in ni xochiquetzal in nompa nohuan oticoch, onihualla in nimohueltiuh ni xochiquetzal nimitz tlapaloco nimitz ciauhquetzaco çan yhuian xictlalcahui in no macehual tla nimitz huipil tepoya, tla nimitzhuipil lapacho tlanimitz huipil quimilo çan yhuian xicochi tla nimitz maco chiui tla ni mitz napalo tla nimitz nahuatequi.

My older brother, Pelxayaqueh, are you not ashamed? Why is it that you are making fun of people? Why is it that you are amusing yourself with people? Do you not already know, does your heart not already know that, in order to cause you to break your fast, I went there on top of Stone-drum, where you slept with me, who am Xochiquetzal? I, who am your older sister, Xochiquetzal, have come. I have come in order to greet you, I have come in order to give you greetings. Just step aside quietly for my vassal. Let me drape my *huipil* over you. Let me cover you with my *huipil*. Let me wrap you in my *huipil*. Just sleep quietly. Let me embrace you. Let me take you in my arms. Let me hug you.

Noquichtīuh, Pelxāyaqueh, ahmō tipīnāhua? Tleh īca in tēca timocahcayāhua? Tleh īca in tēca timāhuiltia? Cuix ahmō ye ticmati, ahmō quimatticah in moyōllo in ōnimitznezahualpoztequito in ōmpa Tehuēhuēticpac, in niXōchiquetzal, in ōmpa nohuān ōticoch? Ōnihuāllah in nimohuēltīuh, niXōchiquetzal. Nimitztlahpalōco, nimitzciauhquetzaco. Zan īhuiyān xictlālcāhui in nomācēhual. Tlā nimitzhuīpīltepoya. Tlā nimitzhuīpīllapacho. Tlā nimitzhuīpīlquimilo. Zan īhuiyān xicochi. Tlā nimitzmācochihui.[32] Tlā nimitznāpalo. Tlā nimitznāhuahtequi.

When he says, "Look here, for I already cover you with my *huipil,*" etc., if the one who is speaking is a man, he removes his blanket from his neck and throws it over the sick person. He covers him with it and pretends that he is embracing him and caresses him in other ways. But if the healer or impostor is a woman, she makes the gesture with her *huipil,* and, in order to tie off his wounded part, she removes the ribbon or small cord which is called *icxitl*[33] or *tzonipilhuaztli,*[34] with which women tie up their hair, and after having tied him with it, she says:

[11] Brother of mine, are you not ashamed of hurting people?

No oquichtiuh ahmo tipinahua, titeeleuia?

My older brother, are you not ashamed that you covet [i.e., harm] people?

Noquichtīuh, ahmō tipīnāhua titēēlēhuia?

Then she tightens the cord and makes this symbol as is painted[35] in the margin,[36] and says:[37]

[12] You are to be like this, thus are you to be like this figure,[38] because I have come to tie you and to block your steps. Here your power ends. You will not pass beyond here.

Yuhqui tiez inyuh qui tiez in nican nimitzilpico, nimitztzacuilico çan ni can tlantica in mo ne mac ah mo tipanoz

You will be like this one [i.e., the symbol]; [and] you will be like this one [i.e., the symbol repeated]. I have come here to tie you up, I have come to intercept you. Just here your gift is ending. You will not pass.

Iuhqui tiyez īn; iuhqui tiyez īn. Nicān nimitzilpīco, nimitztzacuilīco. Zan nicān tlanticah in monemac. Ahmō tipanoz.

With this they finish this cure and fiction based on the falseness of the heathen fable related at the beginning of this chapter, and I with it this Treatise.

APPENDICES

APPENDIX A

Brief Relation of the Gods and Rites of Heathenism

by Don Pedro Ponce
Beneficiado of the District of Tzumpahuacan[1]

[The following text is based on Paso y Troncoso's edition in the *Anales del Museo Nacional de México* VI:4–11.]

Satan has at all times attempted to usurp the reverence and adoration that is due to Our True Lord, God, seeking it for himself, attributing to himself the created things and asking that because of them man submit to him. And thus, in past times as in present ones, he has had, and has, people who make sacrifices to him in honor of the benefits that man receives from God, Our Lord, benefits that he attributes to himself. And among the natives of this New Spain [there are] believers who invoke him in their activities, seeking his favor in the things that they do. They have not forgotten the names of their Gods, for old people, youths, and children still remember them.

I shall put here the names of the Indians' Gods in order to speak of some that are renowned among them and whom they invoke, depending on how they have attributed powers to each one.

Ome-Tochtli,[2] Ome Cihuatl, who, they used to say, lived above the twelve heavens. Tezcatl-Ihpoca, also known as Titlacahuan, Telpochtli, Yaotl. Yohualli-Ehehcatl, Ipal-Nemohuani, the giver of great riches and seigniories.

Huitzilopochtli. Taras,[3] the God of those of Mechoacan.[4] Quetzalcoatl, Yahcateuctli, the god of the merchants and also known as Yacacoliuhqui, and Amihmitl, another god. Piltzinteuctli. And the sun Tonatiuh, also known as Cuauhtl-Ehuanitl, and Xippilli.[5]

They also canonized fire as God and they called him Xiuhteuctli, and, by other names given him in our times, Huehuentzin and Xoxeptzin, Ximeontzin.[6] They also call him Tocentah,[7] "everyone's father," because, among the Indians, all are born in the presence of fire, and after their death it accompanies them to their burial, burning in candles.

They also considered some women as Gods, and today they [still] venerate them. Chicome-Coatl, the goddess of cereals. And the goddess of waters, Chalchihuitl Icue or Chalchiuhcueyeh. Cihuacoatl for Eve. Tlahzolcoatl[8] [*sic*] for Venus.

They also revere the clouds, and they call them Ahuahqueh[9] and the God who governs them, Tlaloqueh[10] [*sic*], and they call the mountains where the clouds are engendered Tlaloqueh Tlamacazqueh.[11]

Among all these gods they put Christ, Our Lord and Redeemer, for they received Him as the last God, and in certain paintings about how sacrifices are to be made to their Gods, one finds the cross, nails, and scourge tied to the column and crucified and the priests saying mass. And at this time their dogmatizers make their sacrifices according to their ancient custom.

They have and make three kinds of idols: some small stone ones for inside their granaries; they make others of copal or of *tzoal*[12] dough, and these they send to the peaks of the hills where the altars they call *momoztli* are. From this *tzoal* dough was made the body of Huitzilopochtli, which was kept for the period of a year, after which it was distributed in small portions *vxcucoeyotia (sic).*[13]

CELEBRATION OF THE HOLIDAYS

Most of the Indians' sacrifices are made after midnight or at dawn, and thus on the holidays of their evocations of saints, before daybreak they have already eaten. And this is the way they cut off the heads of the chickens before the fire,[14] which is the God Xiuhteuctli. This they call in their language *tlaquechcotonaliztli.*[15] This sacrifice is made in the headman's house.

Having prepared these fowls according to their way and having made tamales, after having readied pulque, *poquietes,*[16] and roses with chocolate, they divide it into two parts, one of which they offer to the fire, and they pour out some of the pulque before the fire; the other half they carry to offer at the church, putting it in *xicaras*[17] before the altar. And in a standing *xicara* they pour out a little of the pulque, and they put it in the middle of the altar, and after it has been there a while they remove it and give it to the *teopan tlacas*[18] to eat. And the same thing is done with the part offered to the fire, which is for the headman.

THE MIDWIVES

The midwives who come to help in childbirths use the ceremonies of their heathenism. They are the following:

At the time when the children are born, they order that they wait for them [i.e., the midwives] until one day before the children receive the Holy Baptism in order to remove the fire from them, which in their language is called *itleuh quiçaz in piltzintli.*[19]

One day before the infant is baptized, the midwife comes to the house of the woman delivered of child where on the day of the childbirth she had ordered that they have pulque, tamales, and a fowl prepared for her and that they invite the neighbors and have a fire burning, all of which they have ready. The midwife takes the fowl, pulque, and tamales and offers them to the fire.

Then she takes a *xicara* of water and carries it out to the patio, and after placing it in the middle [of it], she returns to the room where the fire is and takes some of it in a pot. She goes to where the woman who has given birth is, and, taking the infant in her arms, she carries it out with the fire to where she left the *xicara* of water, and, having placed the fire very close to the water, she bathes the infant, and, with the water that she goes along splashing, she gradually kills the fire, and at this point she asks those present how the infant is to be called, and they answer a name from those of their heathenism or of their parents like *Ehcatl* or *Coatl,* and if it is a girl, *Xicoh* or *Xoco,*[20] and others like them. It is ascertained that these names are of certain spirits like angels that they call Tlaloques and *tlamacazques.* And after the ablution has ended, the midwife returns the infant to its mother and again takes fire in the pot, and, having returned to the woman who has given birth, she puts a cloth around its head, and with the fire she describes a circle around its head. Having finished, she returns to the fire where the pulque has been offered and pours some of it in a *xicara* and spills some of it before the fire; and she distributes to the guests some of what has been offered and [some of the] pulque.

In the valley of Toluca they then send the children to a hill. If it is a boy, he carries a digging stick to offer, and, if it is a girl, a spindle and cotton.

THE DOCTORS

The doctors of the Indians are very superstitious and carry along with them the hearts of the innocent people. When the doctor is called to see a sick person, he asks him about his illness and in what place and spot the sickness came upon him. And after the sick person has said what has happened to him, the doctor answers *qualani in Sancto*[21] or *qualani in Huehuentzin,*[22] attributing [the illness] to the fact that the saint of his village is angered, or that the fire is, and he tells them, for a remedy to the sickness, to seek for him a hen to sacrifice, pulque, roses, and *poquietes,* and that he will return the following day. Some order that the hens be beheaded before the fire and that they have the food [already] cooked; others do it themselves. When all of this has been prepared, the doctor comes and takes the blood of the sacrifice and anoints the three rocks that are like a trivet, which they call *tenamastles.*[23] And then he takes the tamales and the dressed fowl, the roses, and *poquietes* and divides them into two parts. One he offers to the fire, and the other he sends to be offered before the image or to the church, where he lights a wax candle. He makes his speech and petition to the fire and then pours out a little of the pulque before it. This they call *motençiahuaz in Huehuentzin.*[24] And after this has been finished, the doctor and the persons present eat the fowl and drink the pulque, and the poor sick person waits for the fire to make him well.

If other sick people say that they took sick near a stream, a spring, or a river, they make them carry everything mentioned to some spring and offer it to the goddess of waters, whom they call Matlalcueyeque[25] [*sic*] or Chalchihuitl Icue, and carry their wax candle and light it.

To others they say *qualani in tonacayotl,*[26] by which they mean the goddess Chicome-Coatl, the goddess of cereals. They make great sacrifices to this goddess when they or one of their children are sick. And the way they do it is for the doctor to take a hen and go to where they have the maize drying in their small enclosures or in front of the granaries, and there they behead the hen and order it to be dressed and tamales to be made and to have pulque. And when this is done, he offers one half to the fire and sends the other half to be offered before the small enclosures or granaries where the maize is. And there he burns a little copal, which is their incense.

Several cures are performed on children by some doctors whom they call *tetonal-macani,*[27] who are the ones who return the fortune [i.e., the soul] to the children who have lost it. And they say certain words while putting a certain root which they call *tlacopatli*[28] on their crowns.

Others, having sacrificed the hen to the fire, and while pouring out the pulque, palpate the child with *piciete,* which is tobacco, and invoke Quetzalcoatl, addressing their prayer to him.

They also attribute the sicknesses of children to the winds and clouds, and they say *qualani in èecame, cualani in ahuaque*[29] and blow on the winds, while making their incantation to them.

Those who are surgeons who cure broken bones invoke, and seek the favor of, the *quatlapanques*,[30] by which is meant the hills that are between ravines, in order that they help their cure.

The fire in the house of the Indians is never to be extinguished, nor is firewood to be lacking. And if by chance it were lacking and some misfortune befalls the tenant, when he reaches home he asks pardon of the fire, attributing the misfortune that befell him to the fact that the fire was not burning or to the fact that firewood was lacking. And thus in the Valley and in other places the Indians put some timbers from the ceiling, securing them to the wall, and beneath they put the fire, and over these timbers they put the firewood in order, so that one who sees it thinks they have it there to dry it out. Others put the firewood around or near the fire.

THE FARMERS

At the time when they are to prepare their fields for sowing, they first make a prayer to the land, telling it that it is their mother and that they want to open her and put the plow or the digging stick into her back. At this time they seek the favor of Quetzalcoatl in order that he give them strength to be able to till the land.

Having prepared the ground, and when the time for planting has arrived, they go to the prepared fields, and there first they invoke certain spirits whom they call Tlaloques and *tlamacazques*, imploring them to take care of the sown field, protecting it from small animals like coatis, squirrels, and rats so that they will not harm it. Then they sow it.

Seven or eight days after the maize has already sprouted, they carry a wax candle and copal to the field in honor of those spirits. And they light [it] and burn the copal in the middle of the field and again ask them [i.e., the spirits] to free their fields from the said little animals.

When the maize is ready for the first weeding, they again carry a wax candle and a hen to be sacrificed at the edge of the field. Putting the lighted candle in the middle of the field, they then prepare the sacrificed fowl. With tamales they carry it to where the candle is in the middle, and there they offer it to the Goddess Chicome-Coatl, the goddess of cereals, who they say dwells in the Mountains of Tlaxcala [Sierra de Tlaxcala], and they make their prayer and petition. And after the offering has been there for a while, they take it away and eat it with the rest, and then they burn copal.

Before starting the weeding, they invoke Quetzalcoatl, asking him for his favor and help with certain words that they use at this time, after the weeding is finished.

Those who are superstitious among the natives do not permit any leaf to be removed from the maize until the *xilotes*[31] start to come out. And after they have come out, they take some of the leaves of the maize and the first *xilotes* with the first flowers and the first *miahuatl*[32] and the first things that the land produces at that time, and they carry them to be offered before the granaries with a fowl, tamales, copal, and a wax candle and pulque in order to pour out a sufficient amount before the granaries.

At the time of the first *elotes*[33] that the fields produce, they make another offering to that which they call *tlaxquiztli*,[34] which [...],[35] having prepared the things necessary for this sacrifice, which are *ule*[36] [rubber], paper which they call *texamatl,*[37] and something like little blanket shirts that they call *xicoli,*[38] copal, pulque, a wax candle, and a hen for sacrifice.

They take the first *elotes* and go away to the little hills where they have their little pyramids that they call *teteli,*[39] which are like altars. It is a precept that the children should not go to these little hills so that they not find out what is done. And after arriving there, they make a fire at the foot of the little pyramid or in the middle of it in honor of the God Xiuhteuctli. And the wisest man takes some of this fire in a pot and throws some copal on it and incenses all the place of the sacrifice. And then he lights the wax candle and puts it in the middle of the little pyramid, and, when this has been done, he takes the offering, which is the *uli,* copal, pulque, and the little shirts and *xicaras* [and] paper and offers them in front of the little pyramid and the fire.

After this is finished, they set the *elotes* to roasting and take some of the offered pulque. They pour some of it in front of the little pyramid and the fire and sprinkle the *elotes* with the pulque. Some draw blood from their ears and sprinkle the *elotes* and the place with the blood.

Then he takes the hen that was carried for the sacrifice, and they decapitate it before the fire and little pyramid. They order this fowl to be dressed, and with tamales they offer it before the fire and the pyramid. And as for the little shirts, they dress some rocks that they put there with them. When this is finished, they eat the *elotes* and the rest of what was offered, while drinking the pulque. And in this way they pay the offering of the new fruits.

Now that the maize is ready for harvest, in the field where there is a stalk that bears two or three ears, which they call Xolotl,[40] the owner immediately informs the one who is the master of ceremonies, who usually is an old man, and tells him how there has been a good season[41] in his field. The master comes and, having seen the stalk with the two or three ears, orders that two kinds of tamales be made for the following day, white tamales and *tequixquitamales.*[42] And when he comes, he goes to the field and uproots that stalk with two ears, and he and the owner of the field take the made tamales and the stalk and go away outside the settlement to some place where two roads divide, one toward one direction and the other toward another, and there the master offers the two kinds of tamales and the stalk with the two ears, with the ends of the ears pointing toward the Sierra of Tlaxcala to the east, which is where the goddess Chicome-Coatl, the goddess of cereals, dwells, making a speech and sending a message with the ears, saying *yn tiXolotl ximohuicatiuh maxicmonahuatiliti in iztacçihuatl ca in mochihua motequipanoa in quimonequiltia.*[43] And as for these offered tamales, no one can take them, unless it be some poor person who passes by; and, when one does not pass by, they bring them back and give them to one of the poor people of the village. This, they say, is the knapsack of the Xolotl which goes with the message as a messenger.

At the time of the harvesting of the field they make an invocation to the goddess Chicome-Coatl and say *chicomemecatle* [sic] *caonihualla yn tiquetzal in titeçencozqui ca onic vatquic* [sic] *in noteocuitlachiquiuh in noteocuitlamacpal.*[44]

After the maize is harvested, since they are to throw it on the ground, they greet it and say *tla xihualauh tlaltechtli* [sic] *nican mopan nocontema in chicomecoatl amo çe tocon elehuiz.*[45]

THORN OR THE PLACING-OF-THE-THORN (NEW WINE)

The manner that the Indians have for pruning the new magueys and paying the offering of the first fruits to the fire is as follows. When the time for pruning them and drawing off the honey has arrived, they call an old man or master who is designated for that. He orders that, after the honey has been drawn off, they put it in their tubs or pitchers in order to make pulque. And first he pours out a very small amount of the honey where the new magueys are. And after having left the command that the pulque be made, he comes on the next day to the house of the owner of the vineyard where some neighbors have been invited. They have prepared for him the heart of the maguey, which in their language they call *ciotl.* He pours some of the new pulque into a *xicara* or tumbler, and with a pitcher of it he offers it to the fire. It sits there offered for a while. Then he takes the point of the heart of the maguey and puts it in a *xicara,* striking it with his finger so that it splatters the fire. And then he talks to it softly and goes outside and speaks, saying the words in the margin—*nican catqui in antlamacazque achitzin neuctzintli iconmohuellamachtizque.*[46] He gives himself a severe spank with the heart of the maguey, and then he drinks his little *xicara* and returns again and pours out some of the offered pulque and gives it to the first guest, giving him a severe spank, and he drinks. And he continues in this manner until the circle is finished. In this tasting of the new pulque people are not to get drunk. In the said manner is made and tasted the new wine, which they call *huitztli*[47] or *huitzmanaliztli.*[48]

FOR INAUGURATING NEW HOUSES, WHICH THEY CALL *NICALCHALIA*[49]

After having built the house and put in its four corners some little idol or some rocks with a good color and a very small quantity of *piciete,* the owner of the house calls the masters, or old men, and, after they have seen the house, they order a hen to be prepared for the following day and tamales to be made. And on the following day they come, and, standing in the middle of the house, they light a new fire with some sticks. And when it is burning well, they take the hen and cut off its head in front of the fire, spilling the blood, and they take some of it and anoint the four corners or four walls and then the andirons[50] of the hut or roofing and the lintels and sides of the door of the house. After this has been done, they order the fowl to be plucked outside the house, and they prepare it in their way, and, after it is prepared, they take it with tamales and again offer it to the fire. Having divided it into two parts, they leave one before the fire and send the other one to be offered before the image of the church, and when not *(sic)*[51] where there is some of it with a lighted candle, and, after it has been offered for a while, the guests eat it. And this is called *calchalia,*[52] which means "to inaugurate the house."

THE LIME MAKERS

In most parts of this New Spain the idea that not all people but only some designated old men can burn lime has been introduced among the natives. These are summoned when people are to burn lime. And when they have arrived, they take a little *piciete* and put it over the four or five rocks upon which the kiln is to be rigged which they call *tenamaztli*, and inside the kiln on the floor and on the outside they make some X-shaped marks[53] and a prayer to Xiuhteuctli, which is the fire, in order that he will help with his flame. After the kiln has been rigged, they have their pulque prepared and a hen, and upon firing the kiln they spill some pulque above on the border of the kiln, and in the low mouth they sacrifice a hen by cutting off its head. They usually dance in front of the mouth through where the fire breathes, for all of which, each particular thing, they say their words which will be put in the margin. [The text omits the words.]

THOSE WHO CUT WOOD, WHOM THEY CALL *QUAUHTLATOQUE*[54]

It is very common for each village to have designated people so that, when they are to cut beams or other wood, they go to the hill or forest. And before entering it, they make a prayer to Quetzalcoatl, asking him for permission and asking him not to attribute disrespect to them for wanting to remove wood from his forest and to give them the ability to remove that wood from his side because they promise him to put it in a place where it will be venerated by men. And after the beam or beams have been cut and tied in order to be dragged away, they put on its front end a small quantity of *piciete* and in the middle and on the rear end and then strike it some blows with a board in the middle and invoke Quetzalcoatl in order that he will help them and in order that a mishap not happen to them on the road, so that no one gets hurt. And they do the same thing when they haul big rocks and they incense them with copal in honor of Quetzalcoatl.

THE TRAVELERS

They say certain words which they call *acxotlatolli*[55] at the time that they see some person coming, just in case he is a highwayman or a murderer, which they call a runaway.[56] They invoke Quetzalcoatl because of being a valiant god, and then they call and invoke the wolves and pumas and jaguars, the linxes and the whirlwinds to help and succor them against such people.

THOSE WHO CHASE AWAY CLOUDS AND HAIL

There are others whom they call *teçiuhpeuhque*,[57] for in most parts of the valley there are those who chase away the clouds, and they conjure them. And most villages have them appointed and free them from the *coatequitl*.[58] They make many signs with their hands and blow on the winds.

OTHERS WHO THEY SAY BRING BACK FORTUNE OR HEALTH, WHOM THEY CALL *TETONALMACANI*[59]

When some child, because of fright or because of having fallen sick [needs help], there are among the Indians some who have the job of restoring his health. They look at the child's hand and raise the hairs on his crown upward, and then they invoke the sun and say to him, "Our lord, I beg you and plead that you have pity on this child and that you give him and restore to him the health or lost fortune, since it is in your hand." And having said this invocation, he makes a mark on the child with a small amount of *piciete* from the point of the nose, rising upward to the commissure of the head, and they call these *tetonalmacani.*

THOSE WHOM THEY CALL *ATLAUTLACHIXQUE* [*sic*][60]

They take a *xicara* of water, and, having placed it in front of the fire, they toss seven maize kernels into it, and they place themselves as if in prayer for some time, after which they say what they want to know from them. Others do this in another way. They measure a straw with three and a half fists.[61] Others measure with a straw from the inside of the arm to the middle finger, and, after this is done, they say what they think, and, although it be a lie, they believe them.

IN ORDER TO FIND OUT ABOUT LOST THINGS AND OTHER THINGS THAT PEOPLE WANT TO KNOW

They drink *ololiuhque*[62] [*sic*], peyote, and a seed that they call *tlitliltzin.*[63] These are so strong that they deprive them of their senses and they say that one like a little black man appears to them and tells them all they want. Others say that Our Lord appears to them, others the angels. And when they do this, they enter a room and close themselves in and set a guard so that he may hear what they say, and people are not to speak to them until the delirium has left them because they become like madmen. And then they ask what they have said, and that is what is certain.

This small treatise was composed by Pedro Ponce, the past *beneficiado* of the district of Tzumpahuacan.

APPENDIX B

Ritual and Supernatural Names Mentioned in the *Treatise*

The following listing of names of gods and mythical persons, metaphorical allusions, and day-names presents the names in normalized spelling, their translations, and a brief discussion. Characterizations of the gods by basic complexes are drawn from Nicholson (1971).

Traditionally, the spelling of Nahuatl god names has been according to conventions that disregard their morphological and syntactical structure. We have chosen to use a spelling system that attempts to make the constituent elements of the names more evident. While this may entail some initial difficulty for the reader, we believe that it is outweighed by the long-term benefits. The changes involve the use of the glottal stop (represented by *h*), hyphens, and capitalization, as well as spellings of sounds according to the orthographic canon presented in the Guide to Pronunciation (e.g., *cua-* is used for what is ordinarily spelled *qua-* in conventional texts).

With regard to grammatical structure, Nahuatl names fall into one of two types:

1. Single-nucleus formations
   a. Simple (e.g., *Yaotl, Yaotzin*)
   b. Compound (e.g., *Xiuhpilli, Xapel, Cemmalinalli, Chalchiuhcueyeh*)
2. Multiple-nucleus formations
   a. Structures of modification (e.g., *Iztac-Cihuatl, Tezcatl-Ihpoca*)
   b. Structures of conjunction (e.g., *Yohualli Ehehcatl*)
   c. Structures of supplementation (e.g., *Teteoh Innan*)
   d. Sentences (e.g., *Coatl Icue*)

Either of these formations may participate in larger name constructions:

1. Structures of modification (e.g., *Iztac Tlaloc, Tezcatl in zan hualpopocatimani*) (in such structures, hyphens are not used)
2. Structures of apposition (e.g., *Nahui-Acatl, Milinticah*)

   Noun stems that take the number suffixes *-tli, -tl,* or *-in* permit an alternative name formation (a "name form") that replaces these suffixes with silence (-ø); e.g., *Xapelli* or *Xapel.*

An entity may have several names: a given name that memorializes a characteristic, a special circumstance, a deity, or a parent or grandparent, and one or more aliases, appellations, or nicknames that may be used either alone or in apposition with the given name (e.g., *Yaotl* is another name for *Tezcatl-Ihpoca*). A special type of such aliases is the "calendrical name," a name that is a day-name (i.e., "day-number-plus-day-sign" combination taken from the *tonalpohualli*) that memorializes the entity's birthday (or baptismal day). For example, an entity born (or baptized) on the day *Ce-Acatl* would be called *Ce-Acatl.* At times the calendrical name is used more frequently than the given name.

Note that in the following listing there are given names, calendrical names, ritual names, and metaphorical names. Frequently the metaphorical names possess a riddlelike quality; for example, "Her-hair Is Mist, Her-hair Is Smoke" represents fire, as if one had said, "What is it that has hair like mist and hair like smoke?" We have not included among the names the various kinship terms that are used for address, for example, *nohuēltīuh,* "my older sister"; *nonān,* "my mother"; *notah,* "my father"; *notlah,* "my uncle." Note that the names are listed without the first or second person prefix of the subject (i.e., *ni-, n-, ti-, t-, am-, an-*). [N.B. For technical terms used in the analysis of the names, see Glossary of Linguistic Terms.]

Acaxoch [i.e., *Ācaxōch*] (Reed-flower). A "name-form" of the compound noun (Ā-CA-XŌCHI)-TL: embed, (Ā-CA)-TL, "reed"; matrix, (XŌCHI)-TL, "flower." In classical times, and in the *Treatise,* this served as another name for the deer.
Ahquetztimani (He/She-lies-supine). A compound present agentive noun: embed, the preterit tense theme (AH-QUETZ-ø)-, "[he/she] has raised [his/her] head," which consists of AH-, an embedding form of (Ā)-TL, "head," and the verb TLA-(QUETZA), "to stand something upright"; matrix, the present tense form of (MANI), "to be (spread out)." In the *Treatise,* this is a metaphorical name for land.
Ahuahqueh [i.e., *Āhuahqueh*] (Water-owners). A plural preterit agentive noun of possession: embed, (Ā)-TL, "water"; matrix, a preterit tense form of *TLA-(HUA), "to own something." The *-queh* is the plural suffix. In the *Treatise,* it is a metaphorical name for clouds.
Air-spirit, see *Tzitzimitl.*
Amihmitl [i.e., *Āmihmītl*] (Water-gig). A compound noun: embed, (Ā)-TL, "water"; matrix, (MIH-MĪ)-TL, a reduplicative form of (MĪ)-TL, "arrow," where the reduplicative prefix indicates distributive plurality, suggesting the idea of "gig." Found in Ponce, not in Ruiz de Alarcón. In classical times, *Amihmitl* was the god of fishing (Clavijero 1979, 1:256; Torquemada 1976:96), patron of Cuitlahuac (Sahagún 1970:79), a War-Sacrifice-Sanguinary Nourishment god.
Ayahuitl Itzon [i.e., *Āyahuitl Ītzon*] (Her-hair Is Mist). A double-nucleus name; a sentence whose matrix clause is *Āyahuitl,* "It is mist," and whose embedded clause is *Ītzon,* "It is her hair," functioning as a supplementary subject. In the *Treatise,* this is a metaphorical name for fire. It is used in conjunction with *Poctli Itzon* (q.v.).
Beloved-goddesses, see *Tlazohteteoh.*
Black Priest, see *Tliliuhqui Tlamacazqui.*
Capanilli [i.e., *Capānīlli*] (One-who-has-emitted-a-slapping-[*or* popping]-sound). A patientive noun from the verb (CAPĀ-NI), "to emit a slapping or popping sound (e.g., when cracking one's knuckles)." In the *Treatise,* the name occurs only in apposition to *Xolotl* (q.v.).
Caxxoch [i.e., *Caxxōch*] (Bowl-flower). A "name form" of the compound noun (CAX-XŌCHI)-TL: embed, (CAXI)-TL, "bowl"; matrix, (XŌCHI)-TL, "flower." In the *Treatise,* the name is possibly a regional variant of one of the four filth goddesses, *Tlahzolteteoh.* See *Tlahzolteotl.*
Ce-Acatl [i.e., *Cē-Ācatl*] (One Reed). A calendrical name. Another name for *Quetzalcoatl* (q.v.), *Tepeyollohtli* (q.v.), and *Tlahuizcalpan Teuctli* (q.v.) (Caso 1959:90). In the *Treatise,* it serves only as an example of a *tonalli* that can be summoned.
Ce-Atl [i.e., *Cē-Ātl*] (One Water). A calendrical name. In the *Treatise,* it serves only as an example of a *tonalli* that can be summoned.
Ce-Atl Itonal [i.e., *Cē-Ātl Ītōnal*] (His-*tonal* Is One Water). This is a double-nucleus name, a sentence whose matrix clause is the calendrical name *Cē-Ātl,* "It is One Water," and whose embed clause is *Ītōnal,* "It is his day-name," functioning as a supplementary subject. In the *Treatise,* this is a ritual name for wood or things made of wood (such as bow, digging stick, and so forth).
Ce-Coatl [i.e., *Cē-Cōātl*] (One Snake). A calendrical name. In classical times, it was the name of the sorcerer who represented *Tezcatl-Ihpoca* (q.v.); possibly another name for *Xochiquetzal* (q.v.) and *Chalchihuitl Icue* (q.v.) (Caso 1959:83-84). In the *Treatise,* this is a ritual name for the veins in the eyes (VI:5:1), for the beehive hunter (II:7:3), and for feminine apparel (IV:2:1).
Ce-Cuetzpalin [i.e., *Cē-Cuetzpalin*] (One Lizard). A calendrical name. In classical times,

it was another name for *Itztlacoliuhqui* (q.v.) (Caso 1959:83). In the *Treatise,* it serves only as an example of a *tonalli* that can be summoned.

Ce-Mazatl [i.e., *Cē-Mazātl*] (One Deer). A calendrical name. In classical times, this was the name of a creator god, possibly being the calendrical name for *Xochiquetzal* (q.v.) (Caso 1959:85). In the *Treatise,* it serves only as an example of a *tonalli* that can be summoned.

Ce-Miquiztli [i.e., *Cē-Miquiztli*] (One Death). A calendrical name. In classical times, it was the calendrical name of *Tezcatl-Ihpoca* (q.v.) (Caso 1959:84). In the *Treatise,* it is the ritual name for a weapon, possibly a rock (II:1:3), and for limestone (II:5:4).

Cemithualehqueh (One-courtyard-owners; it is to be understood that each owner has one courtyard). A compound preterit agentive noun of possession: embed, (CEM-ITHUA-L)-LI, "one courtyard," from (CEN)-ø, "one," plus the patientive noun (ITHUA-L)-LI, "courtyard," from the verbstem TLA-(ITHUA), "to see something" [a variant of TLA-(ITTA)]; matrix, a preterit tense form of *TLA-(E), "to possess something." The *-queh* is a plural number suffix. In the *Treatise,* it is a ritual name for the hands.

Cemixehqueh [i.e., *Cemīxehqueh*] (One-face-owners; it is to be understood that each owner has one face). A compound preterit agentive noun of possession: embed, (CEM-ĪX)-TLI, "one-face," from (CEN)-ø, "one," plus the nounstem (ĪX)-TLI, "face, eye"; matrix, a preterit tense form of *TLA-(E), "to possess something." The *-queh* is a plural number suffix. In the *Treatise,* it is a ritual name for the fingers.

Centeotl [i.e., *Centeōtl*] (Ear-of-maize-god). A compound noun: embed, (CEN)-TLI, "dried ear of maize"; matrix, (TEŌ)-TL, "god." In classical times, *Centeotl* was a male god of maize; a Rain-Moisture-Agriculture-Fertility god, celebrated in festivals of *Huei Tozoztli* and *Ochpaniztli.* He was also known as *Tonacayohuah* (q.v.) (Torquemada 1976: 87). In the *Treatise,* Ruiz de Alarcón translates it as "the only god," a syncretistic misinterpretation that takes the embed to be (CEN)-ø, "one."

Ce-Ocelotl [i.e., *Cē-Ocēlōtl*] (One Jaguar). A calendrical name. In classical times, it was the calendrical name for *Tlatlauhqui Tezcatl-Ihpoca* (q.v.), *Xipe* (q.v.), *Quetzalcoatl* (q.v.), or *Tlahzolteotl* (q.v.) (Caso 1959:92). In the *Treatise,* this is a ritual name for the lancet.

Ce-Tecpatl [i.e., *Cē-Tecpatl*] (One Flint). A calendrical name. In classical times, it was the calendrical name for *Huitzilopochtli* (q.v.) (Caso 1959:78). In the *Treatise,* it is a ritual name for seeds (III:6:1), a knife (II:1:3; II:2:2), and as an example of a *tonalli* that can be summoned (VI:3:8).

Ce-Tochtli [i.e., *Cē-Tōchtli*] (One Rabbit). A calendrical name. In classical times, it was the calendrical name for *Mayahuel* (q.v.), *Xiuhteuctli* (q.v.), or *Tlalteuctli* (q.v.) (Caso 1959:86). In the *Treatise,* it is a ritual name for land.

Cemmalinalli [i.e., *Cemmalīnalli*] (One-grass). A compound noun: embed, (CEN)-ø, "one"; matrix, (MALĪ-N-A-L)-LI, "something that can be twisted or rolled on one's thigh," i.e., "grass," a patientive noun derived from TLA-(MALĪ-N-A), "to twist or roll something on the thigh." A calendrical name. In classical times, it was the calendrical name for *Tetzauhteotl (q.v.)* (Caso 1959:89). In the *Treatise,* it is a ritual name for sandals (II:7:2) and for rope (II:8:3).

Centzonhuitznahuah [i.e., *Centzonhuitznāhuah*] (Four-hundred-Huitznahuas). A plural compound noun: embed, (CEN-TZON)-TLI, "one-times-four-hundred," i.e., "four hundred" (this is an idiomatic way of saying "many"); matrix, (HUITZ-NĀHUA)-H, the plural of (HUITZ-NĀHUA)-TL, "thorn-Nahua," from (HUITZ)-TLI, "thorn," and (NĀHUA)-TL, "a Nahua" (refers to a member of the Nahua peoples?). In classical times, the *centzonhuitznahuah* were stars dispersed by their brother *Huitzilopochtli* (q.v.) (the sun) at the end of night.

Chalchihuitl Icue [i.e., *Chālchihuitl Īcuē*] (Her-skirt Is Jade). A double-nucleus name; a sentence whose matrix clause is *Chālchihuitl,* "It is jade," and whose embedded clause is *Īcuē,* "It is her skirt," functioning as a supplementary subject. In classical times,

Chalchihuitl Icue was a Rain-Moisture-Agriculture-Fertility goddess; she presided over the third level of *Topan* (q.v.) and was celebrated in festivals of *Atl Cahualo* and *Etzalcualiztli.* She was the goddess of the waters (Sahagún 1970:13). Also known as *Matlalcueyeh* (q.v.), *Xochiquetzal* (q.v.), and *Macuilxochiquetzal* (Clavijero 1979, 1:252). In the *Treatise,* it is the ritual name for water. The name is a variant form of *Chalchiuhcueyeh* (q.v.).

Chalchihuitl Ihuipil [i.e., *Chālchihuitl Īhuīpīl*] (Her-*huipil* Is Jade). A double-nucleus name; a sentence whose matrix clause is *Chālchihuitl,* "It is jade," and whose embedded clause is *Īhuīpīl,* "It is her *huipil,*" functioning as a supplementary subject. In the *Treatise,* it is a stylistic (or rhetorical) expansion for *Chalchihuitl Icue,* "Her-skirt Is Jade," so that the pair *Chalchihuitl Icue, Chalchihuitl Ihuipil* is a coordinate construction equivalent to "Her-garments Are Jade." In the *Treatise,* it is a ritual name for water. In the *Treatise, Chalchihuitl Ihuipil* occurs only in conjunction with *Chalchihuitl Icue* (q.v.).

Chalchiuhcihuatl [i.e., *Chālchiuhcihuātl*]. A compound noun: embed, (CHĀLCHIHUI)-TL, "jade"; matrix, (CIHUĀ)-TL, "woman." In classical times, *Chalchiuhcihuatl* was a goddess of the harvest.

Chalchiuhcueyeh [i.e., *Chālchiuhcuēyeh*] (Jade-skirt-owner). A preterit agentive noun of possession: the embed is the compound (CHĀLCHIUH-CUĒI)-TL, "jade-skirt," from (CHĀLCHIHUI)-TL, "jade," plus (CUĒI)-TL, "skirt"; matrix, a preterit tense form of *TLA-(E), "to possess something." In classical times, *Chalchiuhcueyeh* was the goddess of water (Durán 1967, 1:171), companion of *Tlaloc* (q.v.) (Torquemada 1976:80). In the *Treatise,* it is a ritual name for water. The name *Chalchihuitl Icue* (q.v.) is a double-nucleus variant.

Chalchiuhteotzin [i.e., *Chālchiuhteōtzin*] (Jade-god (H), i.e., Precious-god (H)). A "name form" of the honorific form (marked as such by the suffix *-tzin*) of the compound noun (CHĀLCHIUH-TEŌ)-TL: embed, (CHĀLCHIHUI)-TL, "jade," and by extension, "precious"; matrix, (TEŌ)-TL, "god." In the *Treatise,* this is a ritual name for the person sick with love-related illness (IV:3:4). The *-tzin* suffix here may signify affection or compassion ("dear Jade-god" or "little Jade-god") rather than honorableness; the suffix ranges over the semantic area of the two concepts.

Chalchiuhtli Icue, see *Chalchihuitl Icue.*

Chalchiuhtli Ihuipil, see *Chalchihuitl Ihuipil.*

Chalmecateuctli [i.e., *Chālmēcatēuctli*] (Lord-who-is-a-resident-in-Chalman). A compound noun: embed, the gentile noun (CHĀL-M-Ē-CA)-TL, "a dweller in Chalman," from the place noun (CHĀL-MĀN)-ø, "(?)-area," from (CHĀL)-LI, "(?)," and (MĀN)-ø, "area." In classical times, this was another name for *MictlanTeuctli* (q.v.).

Chichimec, see *Chichimecatl.*

Chichimecatl [i.e., *Chīchīmēcatl*] (Person from Milk(?)-area). A gentile noun derived from the place name (CHĪCHĪ-MĀN), "milk(?)-area," which is composed of *(CHĪCHĪ)-TL, "milk(?)," and (MĀN)-ø, "area." In classical times, the *Chichimecs* were barbaric tribes from the north. In the *Treatise,* the word *Chichimec* is a metaphor for any of several dangerous or harmful things.

Chicome-Coatl [i.e., *Chicōme-Cōātl*] (Seven Snake). A calendrical name. In classical times, this was the calendrical name for the goddess of maize (Caso 1959:78), or *Centeotl* (q.v.) (Torquemada 1976:370). A deity of harvests and of grain (Durán 1967, 1:135–36). Associated with *Chalchihuitl Icue* (q.v.), she represented maize and sustenance in general (Sahagún 1970:13). The name was also a calendrical name for *Chalchiuhcihuatl* (q.v.) (Durán 1967, 1:135). In the *Treatise, Chicome-Coatl* is the ritual name for maize and is used in appositive constructions with *Tlazohpilli* (q.v.).

Chicome-Xochitl [i.e., *Chicōme-Xōchitl*] (Seven Flower). A calendrical name. In the *Treatise,* it is a ritual name for the male deer. The name appears in a structure of apposition with *Teohtlalhuah* (q.v.), and sometimes with *Piltzinteuctli* (q.v.).

Chicomocelotl [i.e., *Chicōmocēlōtl*] (Seven-jaguar). A compound noun: embed, (CHIC-

ŌME)-ø, "five-plus-two," i.e., "seven"; matrix, (OCĒLŌ)-TL, "jaguar." The calendrical name for maguey fiber. In the *Treatise*, it is the metaphorical name for the carrying net (see note II:7:5).

Chicomoztoc [i.e., *Chicōmōztōc*] (Seven-caves-place). A compound noun: embed, (CHIC-ŌM-ŌZTŌ)-TL, "seven-caves," which consists of (CHIC-ŌME)-ø, "five-plus-two," i.e., "seven," and (ŌZTŌ)-TL, "cave"; matrix, (C)-ø, a locative stem meaning "place." In classical times, the name designated the seven caves from which the seven major central Mexican groups were said to have come. In the *Treatise*, it serves as a metaphor for cavities in the body: the ear canal, the belly, the mouth, the rectum, and so forth.

Chicuetecpacihuatl [i.e., *Chicuētecpacihuātl*] (Eight-flint-woman). A compound noun: embed, the calendrical name (CHICU-Ē-TECPA)-TL, "Eight-flint," consisting of (CHICU-ĒI)-ø, "five-plus-three," i.e., "eight," and (TECPA)-TL, "flint"; matrix, (CIHUĀ)-TL, "woman." In classical times, the calendrical name *Chicuētecpatl* referred to the maguey plant and, by extension, to pulque. In the *Treatise*, *Chicuētecpacihuātl* is the ritual name for the maguey plant. See note III:1:6 of the *Treatise*.

Chicuetecpacihuatzin, a "name form" of the honorific form of *Chicuetecpacihuatl* (q.v.).

Chimalman [i.e., *Chīmalman*] (One-who-has-sat-like-a-shield). A compound preterit noun: embed, (CHĪMAL)-LI, "shield"; matrix, the preterit agentive noun (MAN-ø)-ø, "one who has extended over an area," from the verb (MANI), "to extend, to be; to extend over a surface; to be sitting [said of flat-bottomed objects]." In this personal name *-man* is not the *-mān* of place names such as *Chālmān*. The usual translation, "Shield Hand," is unlikely because the word does not end in *ma* from (MĀI)-TL, "hand"; the word has a final *n* as attested in the *Leyenda de los Soles* (see Velázquez 1975:122 and facsimile p. 4). In classical times, she was the wife of *Mixcoatl* (q.v.) and the mother of *Quetzalcoatl* (q.v.).

Chiucnauhacatl [i.e., *Chiucnāuhācatl*] (Nine-reed). A compound noun: embed, (CHIUC-NĀHUI)-ø, "five-plus-four," i.e., "nine"; matrix, (Ā-CA)-TL, "reed." A calendrical name. In classical times, it was the calendrical name for *Tlahzolteotl* (q.v.) (Caso 1959:92). In the *Treatise*, it is a ritual name for the medicinal plant *coanenepilli*. See Appendix D.

Chiucnauhehehcatl [i.e., *Chiucnāuhehehcatl*] (Nine-wind). A compound noun: embed, (CHIUC-NĀHUI)-ø, "five-plus-four," i.e., "nine"; matrix, (EH-EHCA)-TL, "wind." A calendrical name. In classical times, it was the calendrical name for *Quetzalcoatl* (q.v.) (Caso 1959:78). In the *Treatise*, it is the ritual name for the breath of the curer (López Austin 1967:13). See note VI:4:11 of the *Treatise*.

ChiucnauhMictlan [i.e., *ChiucnāuhMictlān*] (Nine-Deadman-land). A compound noun: embed, (CHIUC-NĀHUI)-ø, "five-plus-four," i.e., "nine"; matrix, *(Mictlān)* (q.v.). In classical times, it was the underworld, which had nine levels. In the *Treatise*, Ruiz de Alarcón translates this as "nine depths" or "nine hells."

Chiucnauhoztoc [i.e., *Chiucnāuhōztōc*] (Nine-caves-place). A compound noun: embed, (CHIUC-NĀUH-ŌZTŌ)-TL, "nine caves," from (CHIUC-NĀHUI)-ø, "five-plus-four," i.e., "nine," and (ŌZTŌ)-TL, "cave"; matrix, (C)-ø, a locative stem meaning "place." In the *Treatise* (VI:7:1), this is an apparent error for *Chicomoztoc* ("Seven-caves-place") (q.v.).

Chiucnauhpahpatlantzin [i.e., *Chiucnāuhpahpatlāntzin*] (Nine-flutterer (H)). The honorific form of a compound preterit agentive noun: embed, (CHIUC-NĀHUI)-ø, "five-plus-four," i.e., "nine"; matrix, the preterit agentive noun (PAH-PATLĀN-ø)-ø, "one who has fluttered," i.e., "flutterer," from the frequentative verbstem (PAH-PATLĀNI), "to flutter," from the verbstem (PATLĀNI), "to fly." In the *Treatise*, this is a metaphorical name for tobacco (see Appendix D).

Chiucnauhpatlamatelolli [i.e., *Chiucnāuhpatlamātelōlli*] (Nine-times-crumbled-in-the-hands-one). A compound noun: embed, (CHIUC-NĀUH-PA)-ø, "nine times," which consists of (CHIUC-NĀHUI)-ø, "five-plus-four," i.e., "nine," and (-PA)-ø, "times"; matrix, (TLA-MĀ-TEL-Ō-L)-LI, "a thing that has been crumbled in the hands," from the verbstem TLA-(MĀ-TEL-OA), "to crumble something in the hands," from (MĀI)-TL, "hand," and the verbstem TLA-(TEL-OA), "to crumble something." In the *Treatise,* this is a metaphorical name for tobacco (see Appendix D).

Chiucnauhpatlatetzohtzon [i.e., *Chiucnāuhpatlatetzohtzon*] (Nine-times-rock-pounded-one). A variant of *Chiucnauhpatlatetzohtzonalli* (q.v.), but using as the matrix the "name form" of an alternative patientive nounstem, (TLA-TE-TZOH-TZON)-TLI, a past patientive instead of an impersonal patientive stem (see Andrews 1975:235–36, 240).

Chiucnauhpatlatetzohtzonalli [i.e., *Chiucnāuhpatlatetzohtzonalli*] (Nine-times-rock-pounded-one). A compound noun: embed, (CHIUC-NĀUH-PA)-ø, "nine times," which consists of (CHIUC-NĀHUI)-ø, "five-plus-four," i.e., "nine," and (-PA)-ø, "times"; matrix, (TLA-TE-TZOH-TZONA-L)-LI, "a rock pounded one," a patientive noun from the verbstem TLA-(TE-TZOH-TZONA), "to pound something with a rock," from (TE)-TL, "rock," and TLA-(TZOH-TZONA), "to pound something." In the *Treatise,* this is a metaphorical name for tobacco (see Appendix D).

Chiucnauhtlahtlamatelolli [i.e., *Chiucnāuhtlahtlamātelōlli*] (Nine-[times]-crumbled-in-the-hands-one). A variant of *Chiucnauhpatlamatelolli* (q.v.) that lacks the (-PA)-ø, "times," in the embed and has a reduplicative prefix on the matrix.

Chiucnauhtlahtlatetzohtzonalli [i.e., *Chiucnāuhtlahtlatetzohtzonalli*] (Nine-[times]-rock-pounded-one). A variant of *Chiucnauhtlatetzohtzonalli* (q.v.), but with a reduplicative prefix on the matrix.

Chiucnauhtlahtlatetzohtzontli [i.e., *Chiucnāuhtlahtlatetzohtzontli*] (Nine-[times]-rock-pounded-one). A variant of *Chiucnauhtlatetzohtzontli* (q.v.), but with a reduplicative prefix on the matrix.

Chiucnauhtlamatelolli [i.e., *Chiucnāuhtlamātelōlli*] (Nine-[times]-crumbled-in-the-hands-one). A variant of *Chiucnauhpatlamatelolli* (q.v.) that lacks the (-PA)-ø, "times," in the embed.

Chiucnauhtlanepaniuhcan [i.e., *Chiucnāuhtlanepaniuhcān*] (Nine-layering-place). A compound noun: embed, (CHIUC-NĀHUI)-ø, "five-plus-four," i.e., "nine"; matrix, (TLA-NE-PAN-IUH-ø-CĀ-N)-ø, "a place where things in general become layered or tiered," i.e., "place of general layering or tiering," a locative noun that has as an embed the combining form (TLA-NE-PAN-IUH-ø-CĀ)- of the preterit agentive noun (TLA-NE-PAN-IUH-ø)-QUI, "one that has become generally layered over another," i.e., "a generally-layering-one" [from (TLA-NE-PAN-IHUI), the "impersonal *tla-*" verbstem from (NE-PAN-IHUI), "to become a layer or tier"] combined with the locative noun (-N)-ø, "place." Ruiz de Alarcón mistranslates this as *a las nueve juntas o emparejamientos,* "to the nine unions or matchings." This is another name for *ChiucnauhTopan* (q.v.).

Chiucnauhtlatecapanil [i.e., *Chiucnāuhtlatecapānīl*] (Nine-[times]-rock-slapped-one). A "name form" of *Chiucnauhtlatecapanilli* (q.v.).

Chiucnauhtlatecapanilli [i.e., *Chiucnāuhtlatecapānīlli*] (Nine-[times]-rock-slapped-one). A compound noun: embed, (CHIUC-NĀHUI)-ø, "five-plus-four," i.e., "nine"; matrix, (TLA-TE-CAPĀ-NĪ-L)-LI, "a rock-slapped one," a patientive noun from the verbstem TLA-(TE-CAPĀ-NI-A), "to slap something with a rock," from (TE)-TL, "rock," and TLA-(CAPĀ-NI-A), "to cause something to emit a slapping (*or* popping) sound, to slap something." In the *Treatise,* this is a metaphorical name for tobacco (see Appendix D).

Chiucnauhtlatecapantli [i.e, *Chiucnāuhtlatecapāntli*] (Nine-[times]-rock-slapped-one). A variant of *Chiucnauhtlatecapanilli* (q.v.), but using as the matrix an alternative patientive nounstem, (TLA-TE-CAPĀ-N)-TLI, a past patientive instead of an impersonal patientive stem (see Andrews 1975:235–36, 240).

Chiucnauhtlatetzohtzon [i.e., *Chiucnāuhtlatetzohtzon*] (Nine-[times]-rock-pounded-one). The "name form" of *Chiucnauhtlatetzohtzontli* (q.v.).

Chiucnauhtlatetzohtzonal [i.e., *Chiucnāuhtlatetzohtzonal*] (Nine-[times]-rock-pounded-one). The "name form" of *Chiucnauhtlatetzohtzonalli* (q.v.).

Chiucnauhtlatetzohtzontli [i.e., *Chiucnāuhtlatetzohtzontli*] (Nine-[times]-rock-pounded-one). A variant of *Chiucnauhtlatetzohtzonalli* (q.v.), but using as the matrix an alternative patientive nounstem, (TLA-TE-TZOH-TZON)-TLI, a past patientive instead of an impersonal patientive stem (see Andrews 1975:235–36, 240).

Chiucnauhtlatetzohtzonalli [i.e., *Chiucnāuhtlatetzohtzonalli*] (Nine-[times]-rock-pounded-one). A variant of *Chiucnauhpatlatetzohtzonalli* (q.v.) that lacks the (-PA)-ø, "times," in the embed.

ChiucnauhTopan [i.e., *ChiucnāuhTopan*] (Nine-Above-us). A compound noun: embed, (CHIUC-NĀHUI)-ø, "five-plus-four," i.e., "nine"; matrix, *Topan* (q.v.). In classical times, this word designated the celestial realm. In the *Treatise,* Ruiz de Alarcón translates it as "heavens."

Cihuacoatl [i.e., *Cihuācōātl*] (Woman-snake). A compound noun: embed, (CIHUĀ)-TL, "woman"; matrix, (CŌĀ)-TL, "snake." A Rain-Moisture-Agricultural Fertility goddess; celebrated in the festival of *Huei Tecuilhuitl.* In classical times, she was a goddess who brought people misery; she appeared garbed in white (Sahagún 1970:11). She was the sister of *Huitzilopochtli* (q.v.) (Durán 1967, 1:131). In the *Treatise,* this is the ritual name for rope. It appears as the head of a structure of apposition with *cihuatequihuah,* "woman-warrior." See note II:8:42.

Cipactli (caiman). In classical times, this was the monster from which the earth issued and on whose back it rested. The word also names the first of the twenty day-signs; in combination with a prefixed number, it names a thirteen-intervaled selection of days in the *tonalpohualli.*

Cipactonal [i.e., *Cipactōnal*] (Caiman-*tonal*). A "name form" of the compound noun (CIPAC-TŌNA-L)-LI: embed, (CIPAC)-TLI, "caiman"; matrix, (TŌNA-L)-LI, "day-name." In classical times, *Cipactonal* was a Celestial Creativity-Divine Paternalism deity. *Cipactonal* (along with *Ohxomoco*) was the mythological inventor of the divinatory arts. In the *Treatise,* this is a female power entity in I:4:3 and V:2:2, but a male power entity in V:3:1.

Citlalcueyeh [i.e., *Cītlalcuēyeh*] (Star-skirt-owner). A preterit agentive noun of possession: the embed is the compound (CĪTLAL-CUĒI)-TL, "star-skirt," from (CĪTLAL)-IN, "star," plus (CUĒI)-TL, "skirt"; matrix, a preterit tense form of *TLA-(E), "to possess something." In classical times, this was another name for *Ome Cihuatl* (q.v.) (Torquemada 1976:66). In the *Treatise,* this is the name of the Milky Way. The name *Citlalli Icue* (q.v.) or *Citlalin Icue,* "Her-skirt Is Star(s)," is a double-nucleus variant.

Citlalcueyeh's child, see *Citlalcueyeh iconeuh.*

Citlalcueyeh's creation, see *Citlalcueyeh itlachihual.*

Citlalcueyeh iconeuh [i.e., *Cītlalcuēyeh īconēuh*] (Citlalcueyeh's child). A possessive phrase: head, ø-Ī(CONĒ)UH, "he is her child"; possessor, *Citlalcueyeh* (q.v.). In the *Treatise,* this represents tobacco (see Appendix D).

Citlalcueyeh itlachihual [i.e., *Cītlalcuēyeh ītlachīhual*] (Citlalcueyeh's creation). A possessive phrase: head, ø-Ī(TLA-CHĪHUA-L)ø, "he is her creation"; supplementary possessor, *Citlalcueyeh* (q.v.). In the *Treatise,* this represents tobacco (see Appendix D).

Citlallatonac [i.e., *Cītlallatōnac*] (There-has-been-a-shining-by-means-of-stars). A compound preterit agentive noun: embed, (CĪTLAL)-IN, "star"; matrix, the preterit agentive noun (TLA-TŌNA-ø)-C, "things in general have shone *or* become warm," from the doubly impersonal verb (TLA-TŌNA), "for things in general to shine *or* become warm," from the inherently impersonal verb (TŌNA), "to sunshine, to become warm." In classical times, *Citlallatonac* was a male Celestial Creativity-Divine Paternity deity. He was the co-creator of the stars. This was another name for *Ome Teuctli* (q.v.).

Citlalli Icue [i.e., *Cītlalli Īcuē*] (Her-skirt Is Stars). Also *Citlalin Icue.* A double-nucleus name; a sentence whose matrix clause is *Cītlalli,* "It is a star," and whose embedded clause is *Īcuē,* "It is her skirt," functioning as a supplementary subject. The name *Citlalcueyeh* (q.v.) is a single-nucleus variant. In classical times, *Citlalli Icue* was a female Celestial Creativity-Divine Paternity deity. She was the co-creator of the stars. This was another name for *Ome Cihuatl* (q.v.).

Coacueyeh [i.e., *Cōācuēyeh*] (Snake-skirt-owner). A preterit agentive noun of possession: embed, (CŌĀ-CUĒI)-TL, "snake-skirt," from (CŌĀ)-TL, "snake," plus (CUĒI)-TL, "skirt"; matrix, a preterit tense form of *TLA-(E), "to possess something." *Coacueyeh* is a single-nucleus variant of *Coatl Icue* (q.v.).

Coacueyehqueh [i.e., *Cōācuēyehqueh*] (Snake-skirt-owners). The plural form of *Coacueyeh* (q.v.). The *-queh* is a plural suffix. In the *Treatise,* only the plural form is found and always in a structure of apposition with *Nochpalcueyehqueh* (q.v.). It is a ritual name for the hands.

Coatl Icue [i.e., *Cōātl Īcuē*] (Her-skirt Is Snakes). A double-nucleus name; a sentence whose matrix clause is *Cōātl,* "It is a snake," and whose embedded clause is *Īcuē,* "It is her skirt," functioning as a supplementary subject. In classical times, *Coatl Icue* was a Rain-Moisture-Agricultural Fertility deity. *Coatl Icue* is a double-nucleus variant of *Coacueyeh.* In classical times, *Coatl Icue* was the mother of *Huitzilopochtli* (q.v.), *Coyolxauhqui* (q.v.), and the *Centzonhuitznahuah* (q.v.).

Cold Priest, see *Tlamacazqui Cecec.*

Colelectli [i.e., *Cōlēlectli*] (Demon). In classical times, it was a malevolent spirit.

Comet, see *Xihuitl.*

Coyolxauhqui [i.e., *Coyōlxāuhqui*] (One-who-has-become-face-decorated-with-bells). A compound preterit agentive noun: embed, (COYŌ-L)-LI, "bell"; matrix, (XĀUH-∅)-QUI, "one who has become decorated at the face," the preterit agentive nounstem from the verb (XĀHUA), "to apply facial decoration." In classical times, she was the daughter of *Coatl Icue* (q.v.), and the sister of *Huitzilopochtli* (q.v.) and the *Centzonhuitznahuah* (q.v.).

Cozahuic [i.e., *Cōzahuic*] (One-that-has-become-yellow). A preterit agentive noun, (CŌZ-AHUI-∅)-C, "one that has become yellow," i.e., "a yellow one," from the verbstem (CŌZ-AHUI), "to become yellow," treated as a class A verb. A color word that occurs frequently as a modifier in metaphorical usages in the *Treatise.* Although there were variant traditions, yellow was usually associated with the east. *Cozahuic* is a variant of *Cozauhqui* (q.v.).

Cozahuic Tlalocan [i.e., *Cōzahuic Tlālocān*] (Yellow Land-lier-place). A structure of modification: modifier, *Cozahuic* (q.v.); head, *Tlalocan* (q.v.).

Cozahuic Tlamacazqui [i.e., *Cōzahuic Tlamacazqui*] (Yellow Priest). A structure of modification: modifier, *Cozahuic* (q.v.); head, *Tlamacazqui* (q.v.). In the *Treatise,* this is the name for *tlacopahtli* (VI:28:1) and certain herbs (VI:29:1).

Cozauhqui [i.e., *Cōzauhqui*] (One-that-has-become-yellow). A preterit agentive noun, (CŌZ-AUH-∅)-QUI, "one that has become yellow," i.e., "a yellow one," from the verbstem (CŌZ-AHUI), "to become yellow," treated as a class B verb. A color word that occurs frequently as a modifier in metaphorical usages in the *Treatise.* Although there were variant traditions, yellow was usually associated with the east. *Cozauhqui* is a variant of *Cozahuic* (q.v.).

Cozauhqui Cihuatl [i.e., *Cōzauhqui Cihuātl*] (Yellow Woman). A structure of modification: modifier, *Cozauhqui* (q.v.); head, (CIHUĀ)-TL, "woman." In the *Treatise,* this is a metaphorical name for *iyauhtli* (see Appendix D).

Cozauhqui Tlamacazqui [i.e., *Cōzauhqui Tlamacazqui*] (Yellow Priest). A structure of modification: modifier, *Cozauhqui* (q.v.); head, *Tlamacazqui* (q.v.). In the *Treatise,* this is a ritual name for the fishing cane (II:15:3), *iyauhtli* (VI:1:2; VI:27:1), *piciete* (VI:3:2; VI:19:1), Laughing-falcon (VI:19:1), *tlacopahtli* root (VI:25:1; VI:28:1), and *tlanechicolpahtli* (VI:29:1) (see Appendix D).

Cozauhqui Tlapahpalacatl [i.e., *Cōzauhqui Tlapahpalācatl*] (Yellow Striped-reed). A structure of modification: modifier, *Cozauhqui* (q.v.); head, the compound noun (TLA-PAH-PA-L-Ā-CA)-TL, "striped reed," whose embed is the patientive noun (TLA-PAH-PA-L)-LI, "a striped thing," from the verbstem TLA-(PAH-PA), "to stripe something, to paint something in various colors," from the verbstem TLA-(PA), "to paint something, to dye something," and whose matrix is the nounstem (Ā-CA)-TL, "reed." In the *Treatise,* this is the ritual name for *axin* ointment (see Appendix D).

Coztic Tlamacazqui [i.e., *Cōztic Tlamacazqui*] (Yellow Priest). A structure of modification: embed, the preterit agentive noun (CŌZ-TI-ø)-C, "one that has become yellow," from the verbstem (CŌZ-TI-YA), "to become yellow"; head, *Tlamacazqui* (q.v.). In the *Treatise,* this is a metaphorical name for *iyauhtli* (see Appendix D).

Cuaton [i.e., *Cuātōn*] (Small-head). An affective "name form" of (CUĀ-TŌN)-TLI, "small head," from (CUĀI)-TL, "head." The suffix *-tōn* indicates smallness with overtones of contempt. This is probably a regional variant of one of the four filth goddesses *Tlahzolteteoh.* See *Tlahzolteotl.*

Cuauhtl-Ehuanitl [i.e., *Cuāuhtl-Ēhuanitl*] (Taking-off-Eagle). A structure of modification: head, (CUĀUH)-TLI, "eagle" [the supportive *i* of the absolutive singular-number suffix *-tli* has been deleted because of the vowel of the following word]; modifier, the customary-present agentive noun, (ĒHUA-NI)-TL, "one who customarily takes off," i.e., "a taking-off one," from the verbstem (ĒHUA), "to take off." Found in Ponce, not in Ruiz de Alarcón. In classical times, this was a metaphorical name for *Tonatiuh* (q.v.), as the rising sun.

Cuexcochepyohqueh (Owners-of-nacre-at-the-occiput). A compound preterit agentive noun of possession: embed, (CUEX-COCH-EP)-TLI, "nacre-at-the-occiput," which consists of (CUEX-COCH)-TLI, "occiput," and (EP)-TLI, "nacre"; matrix, a preterit tense form of *TLA-(YOA), "to possess something abundantly." The *-queh* is a plural suffix. In the *Treatise,* this is a metaphorical name for the fingers.

Desert-owner, see *Teohtlalhuah.*

Dream-flower, see *Temicxoch.*

Dusky Chichimec, see *Yayahuic Chichimecatl.*

Dusky Nacre-as-hair, see *Yayauhqui Tzoneptzin.*

Dusky Priest, see *Yayahuic Tlamacazqui.*

Dweller on the Desert-area, see *Teohtlalpan Chaneh.*

Dwellers in Dangerous-places, see *Ohhuihcan Chanehqueh.*

Earth-face-slapper, see *Tlalixcapan.*

Earth's Face-slapped-one, see *Tlalli Iixcapactzin.*

Ei-Coatl [i.e., *Ēi-Cōātl*] (Three Snake). A calendrical name. In the *Treatise,* it is a ritual name for the veins in the eyes (VI:5:1).

Eight-flint-woman, see *Chicuetecpacihuatl.*

Five-tonals-owners, see *Macuiltonalehqueh.*

Flower-tonal, see *Xochitonal.*

Four-places-heads-owner, see *Nauhcantzontecomeh.*

Four Reed, see *Nahui-Acatl.*

Four Snake, see *Nahui-Coatl.*

Green Air-spirit, see *Xoxohuic Tzitzimitl* and *Xoxouhqui Tzitzimitl.*

Green Demon, see *Xoxohuic Colelectli.*

Green Pahtecatl, see *Xoxouhqui Pahtecatl.*

Green Priest, see *Xoxohuic Tlamacazqui* and *Xoxouhqui Tlamacazqui.*

Green Rock-pounded-one, see *Xoxohuic Tlatetzohtzonaltzin.*

Green Rock-slapped-one, see *Xoxohuic Tlatecapaniltzin.*

Green Tlaloc, see *Xoxouhqui Tlaloc.*

Green Tlalocan, see *Xoxohuic Tlalocan* and *Xoxouhqui Tlalocan.*

Green Wind, see *Xoxouhqui Ehehcatl.*

Green Woman, see *Xoxohuic Cihuatl* and *Xoxouhqui Cihuatl.*

He-is-becoming-yellow-haired, see *Tzoncozahuixticah.*

He-is-scintillating, see *Milinticah.*

Her-hair Is Mist, see *Ayahuitl Itzon.*

Her-hair Is Smoke, see *Poctli Itzon.*
His-*tonal* Is One Water, see *Ce-Atl Itonal.*
Huehueh [i.e., *Huēhueh*] (Old-man). A preterit agentive noun meaning "one who has become old," from the verb (HUĒ-HUĒ-TI), "to become old (referring to a man)," from the noun *(HUĒ-HUĒ)-TL, "old man" [related to (HUĒ-I)-ø, "big"], and the element -TI, "to become like." The preterit is formed from the perfective stem, (HUĒ-HUE-H) [before a glottal stop a long vowel becomes short; concerning the /t/ to /h/ shift, see Andrews 1975:61, 64]. In this *Treatise,* it is sometimes a metaphor for fire. At other times, it is another name for *Ohxomoco* (q.v.) (I:4; V:2) and for *Cipactonal* (q.v.) (V:3).
Huehuentzin [i.e., *Huēhuēntzin*] (Old-man (H)). An affective form of (HUĒ-HUĒ-N)-TLI, "old man." Found in Ponce, not in Ruiz de Alarcón (the instance of *huēhuēntzin* in II:15 does not refer to the deity). In classical times, this was another name for *Xiuhteuctli* (q.v.) or *Huehuehteotl* (q.v.) (Sahagún 1970:29).
Huehuehteotl [i.e., *Huēhuehteōtl*] (Old-man-god). A compound noun: embed, (HUĒ-HUEH)-, the special combining form of *(HUĒ-HUĒ)-TL, "old man," [from which is formed the verbstem (HUĒ-HUĒ-TI), "to become like an old man, to become old," the source of the preterit agentive noun *huēhueh* (q.v.)]; the embed form (HUĒ-HUEH)- and the preterit agentive noun *huēhueh,* although superficially similar, are distinguished by different responses to distributional pressures; matrix, (TEŌ)-TL, "god." In classical times, this was the fire god.
Huitzcol [i.e., *Huitzcōl*] (Thorn-curve). "Name form" of the compound noun (HUITZ-CŌL)-LI, "thorn-curve," whose embed is (HUITZ)-TLI, "thorn," and whose matrix is (CŌL)-LI, "a bent-over or curved thing." In the *Treatise,* it is another name for *Yappan* (q.v.).
Huitzilopochtli [i.e., *Huitztzilopōchtli*] (Left-side/hand/foot-like-a-Hummingbird). A compound noun: embed, (HUITZ-TZIL)-IN, "hummingbird," which consists of the embed (HUITZ)-TLI, "thorn," and the matrix (TZIL)-IN, "small bell"; matrix, (OPŌCH)-TLI, "left side, left hand, left foot." N.B. This name does *not* mean "Hummingbird-on-the-Left" or "Hummingbird-from-the-South" (a misunderstanding that reverses embed and matrix), as it is commonly translated. The translation "Left-side/hand/foot-like-a-hummingbird" does not deny the fact that *Huitzilopochtli* had symbolic associations with the south, but it does help explain his depiction: *Auh cē pitzāhuac in īcxi īopōchcopa quipotōnih in īxocpal,* "And he had the sole of one of his thin feet, the left one, pasted with feathers" (Sahagún 1952:4). *Huitzilopochtli* is found in Ponce and mentioned by Serna (see note II:1:28 of the *Treatise*), not in Ruiz de Alarcón. In classical times, he was a war god (Sahagún 1970:1–2), worshiped especially by the peoples of the Valley of Mexico (Durán 1967, 1:17). A War-Sacrifice-Sanguinary Nourishment god, he was celebrated in festivals of *Toxcatl, Miccailhuitontli, Pachtontli, Panquetzaliztli,* paralleling the celebrations of *Tezcatl-Ihpoca* (q.v.).
Huixtohcihuatl [i.e., *Huixtohcihuātl*] (Turbulent-water(?)-woman). A compound noun: embed, (HUIXTOH)-TLI, "turbulent water(?)" [for a justification of the stem-final glottal stop, see *vixtotli* in Sahagún 1961:192]; matrix, (CIHUĀ)-TL, "woman." In classical times, she was the goddess of the salt makers.
Icnopiltzintli [i.e., *Icnōpiltzintli*] (Orphan-child). A compound noun: embed, (ICNŌ)-TL, "orphan"; matrix, (PIL-TZIN)-TLI, "child." This is another name for *Centeotl* (q.v.). In the *Treatise,* the name vacillates between being a god name (e.g., II:14:2) and simply a common noun (e.g., VI:2:1), where it may stand for "poor orphan."
IcnoYaotzin [i.e., *IcnōYāōtzin*] (Enemy-like-an-Orphan (H)). A "name form" of the compound nounstem (ICNŌ-YĀŌ-TZIN)-TLI: compound noun: embed, (ICNŌ)-TL, "orphan"; matrix, (YĀŌ-TZIN)-ø, an honorific form of (YĀŌ)-TL, "enemy." See *Yaotl.*
Ilamatzin (Old-woman (H)). An honorific "name form" of (ILAMA)-TL, "old woman." The instance of *ilamatzin* in II:15 of the *Treatise* does not refer to the deity. In the *Treatise,* it is sometimes a metaphor for smoke. At other times, it is another name for *Cipactonal* (I:4; V:2) and for *Ohxomoco* (I:4).

Ipal-Nemohuani [i.e., *Īpal-Nemohuani*] (He-by-whose-grace-Everyone-lives). A double-nucleus name; a sentence whose matrix clause, the customary-present impersonal verb-word ø(NEM-O-HUA)NI-ø, "everyone customarily lives," is modified by the adverbial embed, ø-Ī(PAL)ø, "it is by his grace." Found in Ponce, not in Ruiz de Alarcón. In classical times, the supreme, absolute, independent, and invisible god (Clavijero 1979, 1:241–42), a Celestial Creativity–Divine Paternalism god.

Itzpapalotl [i.e., *Ītzpāpālōtl*] (Obsidian-butterfly). A compound noun: embed, (ĪTZ)-TLI, "obsidian"; matrix, (PĀ-PĀL-Ō)-TL, "butterfly." In classical times, she was a Rain-Moisture-Agriculture Fertility goddess. In the *Treatise,* the name is a ritual name for a stone projectile point.

Itzpapalotzin, the honorific "name form" of *Itzpapalotl* (q.v.).

Itztlacoliuhqui [i.e., *Ītztlacōliuhqui*] (Everything-has-become-curved-by-means-of-obsidian; i.e., Everything-has-become-wilted-because-of-coldness). A compound impersonal preterit agentive noun: embed, (ĪTZ)-TLI, "obsidian," here a metaphor for coldness [compare (ĪTZ-TI), "to become like obsidian," i.e., "to become cold"]; matrix, the preterit agentive noun (TLA-CŌL-IUH-ø)-QUI, "things in general that have become curved," from the "impersonal *tla-*" verbstem (TLA-CŌL-IHUI), "for things in general to become curved," from the intransitive verbstem (CŌL-IHUI), "to become curved." The traditional translation of this name, "Curved obsidian knife," is not tenable and must be discarded since the name is not *Ītzcōliuhqui* [compare *Yacacōliuhqui* (q.v.)]. Another instance of an impersonal preterit agentive noun serving as a name is *Citlallatonac* (q.v.). In classical times, *Itztlacoliuhqui* was the god of cold and frost and was identified with *Tezcatl-Ihpoca* (q.v.).

Itztli [i.e., *Ītztli*] (Obsidian *or* Obsidian knife). In classical times, *Itztli* was another manifestation of *Tezcatl-Ihpoca* (q.v.) and one of the nine Lords of the Night, variantly represented by *Tecpatl* (q.v.).

Ixquitecatl [i.e., *Ixquitēcatl,* for *Īzquitēcatl*] (Person-from-Izquitlan). A gentile noun formed from the place name (ĪZQUI-TLĀN)-ø, "Popcorn-side" (in the sense of "beside the popcorn"), from (ĪZQUI)-TL, "popcorn," plus (TLAN)-ø, "side, vicinity." In classical times, he was the god of sorcerers (Caso 1959:78).

Ixtlilton [i.e., *Īxtlīltōn*] (Little-black-face). An affective "name form" of the compound nounstem (ĪX-TLĪL)-LI, "ink at the face," whose embed is (ĪX)-TLI, "face," and whose matrix is (TLĪL)-LI, "ink" (concerning the apparent reversal of embed and matrix in the translation "black face," see Andrews 1975:264). The affective element, -TŌN, indicates smallness with overtones of contempt. In classical times, *Ixtlilton* was a god of medicine. He was a Rain–Moisture–Agricultural Fertility deity.

Iyauhtli-owners, see *Iyauhyohqueh.*

Iyauhyohqueh [i.e., *Iyāuhyohqueh*] (*Iyauhtli*-owners). A plural preterit agentive noun of possession: embed, (IYĀUH)-TLI, "sweet scented marigold"; matrix, a preterit tense form of *TLA-(YOA), "to possess something abundantly." In the *Treatise,* this is a metaphorical name for the gods who are summoned to aid the traveler and is used in conjunction with *Ollohqueh* (q.v.).

Iztac [i.e., *Iztāc*] (A white one). A preterit agentive noun (IZTĀ-ø)-C, "one that has become white," i.e., "a white one," from the verb (IZTĀ-YA), "to become white." A color word that occurs frequently as a modifier in metaphorical usages in the *Treatise.* Although there were variant traditions, white was usually associated with the south.

Iztac-Cihuatl [i.e., *Iztāc-Cihuātl*] (White Woman). A structure of modification: modifier, *Iztāc* (q.v.); head, (CIHUĀ)-TL, "woman." In classical times, she was a goddess associated with the Sierra Nevada (Durán 1967, 1:159–62). In the *Treatise,* it is the ritual name for various medicines and white substances, such as cotton, water, salt, *copalli,* and *tzopilotl* (see Appendix D).

Iztac-Cihuatzin, the honorific "name form" of *Iztac-Cihuatl* (q.v.).

Iztac Mixcoatl [i.e., *Iztāc Mixcōātl*] (White Cloud-snake). A structure of modification:

modifier, *Iztāc* (q.v.); head, *Mixcōātl* (q.v.). In classical times, this was *Quetzalcoatl's* father.

Iztac Tlaloc [i.e., *Iztāc Tlāloc*] (White Land-lier). A structure of modification: modifier, *Īztāc* (q.v.); head, *Tlāloc* (q.v.).

Iztac Tlalocan [i.e., *Iztāc Tlālocān*] (White Land-lier-place). A structure of modification: modifier, *Īztāc* (q.v.); head, *Tlālocān* (q.v.).

Iztac Tlamacazqui [i.e., *Iztāc Tlamacazqui*] (White Priest). A structure of modification: modifier, *Īztāc* (q.v.); head, *Tlamacazqui* (q.v.). In the *Treatise*, this is the ritual name for the fishing worm, water, and the medicines called *poztecpahtli* and *tzopilotl*. In the plural form, *Iztāqueh Tlamacazqueh*, it is the name of the fish (II:14:3).

Jade-god, see *Chalchiuhteotzin*.

Land-wine-flower, see *Tlalocxochitl*.

Land-wine-woman, see *Tlaloccihuatl*.

Macuiltonaleh [i.e., *Mācuīltōnaleh*] (Five-*tonals*-owner). A compound preterit agentive noun of possession: embed, (MĀ-CUĪL-TŌNA-L)-LI, "five *tonals*, "from (MĀ-CUĪ-L)-LI, "five," plus the patientive noun (TŌNA-L)-LI, "a sun-heated thing," i.e., "heat of the sun; day," and, by extension, "day-sign, birthright," from the verb (TŌNA), "to be sunny; for the weather to be hot"; matrix, a preterit tense form of *TLA-(E), "to possess something." In the *Treatise*, it is a ritual name for a hand.

Macuiltonalehqueh [i.e., *Mācuīltōnalehqueh*] (Five-*tonals*-owners; it is to be understood that each owner has five *tonals*). The plural form of *Macuiltonaleh* (q.v.). In classical times, these were Rain–Moisture–Agricultural Fertility deities. In the *Treatise*, it is a ritual name for the hands (see note II:8:75 of the *Treatise*).

Macuilxochiquetzal [i.e., *Mācuīlxōchiquetzal*] (Five-flower-quetzal-plume). The "name form" of the compound noun (MĀ-CUĪ-L-XŌCHI-QUETZA-L)-LI; embed, the calendrical name (MĀ-CUĪ-L-XŌCHI)-TL, "five-flower," which consists of (MĀ-CUĪ-L)-LI, "five," plus (XŌCHI)-TL, "flower"; matrix, the patientive noun (QUETZA-L)-LI, "a thing that can be stood upright," i.e., "a quetzal tail feather," from the verbstem TLA-(QUETZA), "to stand something upright." In classical times, this was another name for *Chalchihuitl-Icue* (q.v.).

Macuilxochitl [i.e., *Mācuīlxōchitl*] (Five-flower). A compound noun: embed, (MĀ-CUĪ-L)-LI, "five"; matrix, (XŌCHI)-TL, "flower." A calendrical name. In classical times, *Macuilxochitl* was another name for *Xochipilli* (q.v.).

Matl [i.e., *Mātl*] (Hand). A variant of (MĀI)-TL, "hand." In the *Treatise*, this is considered a god and appears to be equated with *Quetzalcoatl* (q.v.).

Matlalcueyeh [i.e., *Matlalcuēyeh*] (Blue-skirt-owner). A preterit agentive noun of possession: embed, (MATLAL-CUĒI)-TL, "blue skirt," from (MATLAL)-IN, "dark green or dark blue color," and (CUĒI)-TL, "skirt"; matrix, a preterit tense form of *TLA-(E), "to possess something." Found in Ponce, not in Ruiz de Alarcón. In classical times, this was the Tlaxcallan name for *Chalchiuhcueyeh* (q.v.) (Clavijero 1979, 1:252; Torquemada 1976:78).

Mayahuel (?). Possibly the "name form" of (MĀ-YAHUAL)-LI, "round thing in the shape of a hand" or "round thing like a hand." In classical times, she was a goddess of pulque.

Mictlan [i.e., *Mictlān*] (Deadman-land). A locative compound noun: embed, (MIC)-TLI, "one who has become dead," i.e., "deadman," the past patientive noun from the verb (MIQUI), "to die"; matrix, (TLAN)-ø, a relational noun meaning "side." The word means literally "Deadman-side," in the sense of "beside the deadman." In classical times, this was the underworld and the northern region. In the *Treatise*, Ruiz de Alarcón translates this as "hell," as was general in colonial times.

MictlanTeuctli [i.e., *MictlānTēuctli*] (Lord-in-Mictlan). A compound noun: adverbial embed, *Mictlān* (q.v.); matrix, (TĒUC)-TLI, "lord." In classical times, he was Lord of *Mictlan* and was also associated with the sixth level of *Topan* (q.v.). In the *Treatise*, the name is translated syncretistically as "the prince of hell."

Milinticah [i.e., *Milīnticah*] (He-is-scintillating). A preterit-as-present agentive noun on the progressive verbstem (MILĪN-ø-TI-YE), "to be scintillating." See note II:5:5 of the

Treatise. In classical times, he was the god of fire (Sahagún 1951:148). In the *Treatise,* it is the ritual name for flames.

Mirror, see *Tezcatl.*

Mirror-mountain, see *Tezcatepec.*

Mixcoacihuatl [i.e., *Mixcōācihuātl*] (Mixcoatl's-woman *or* Woman-dedicated-to-Mixcoatl). A compound noun: embed, *Mixcoatl* (q.v.); matrix, (CIHUĀ)-TL, "woman." *Mixcoacihuatl* is the female deer. The name suggests that it is the preferred prey of *Mixcoatl,* the hunter. In the *Treatise,* Ruiz de Alarcón consistently mistranslates this as "goddess, snake with the face of a puma," but correctly recognized it as the name of the female deer.

Mixcoatl [i.e., *Mixcōātl*] (Cloud-snake). A compound noun: embed, (MIX)-TLI, "cloud"; matrix, (CŌĀ)-TL, "snake." In classical times, *Mixcoatl* was the god of the hunt, a War-Sacrifice–Sanguinary Nourishment of the Sun and Earth deity.

Moquehqueloatzin (Self-tickler *or* Self-derider). An honorific "name form" of the present agentive noun, (MO-QUEH-QUEL-OA-∅)-∅, "one who is tickling himself," "one who is making fun of himself," from the verb MO-(QUEH-QUEL-OA), "to tickle oneself," "to make fun of oneself." In classical times, this was one of the names given to *Tezcatl-Ihpoca.* In the *Treatise,* this is also taken to be another name for *Tezcatl-Ihpoca* (q.v.).

Motolinihcatzintli [i.e., *Motolīnihcātzintli*] (Poverty-Sufferer (H)). The honorific form of the preterit agentive noun (MO-TOLĪ-NI-H-∅)-∅, "one who has suffered poverty," i.e., "a poverty sufferer," from the verb MO-(TOLĪ-NI-A), "to suffer poverty." In the *Treatise,* the name appears in apposition with *IcnoYaotzin,* i.e., *Yaotl* (q.v.).

Moyohualihtoatzin (Night-volunteer (H)). An honorific form of the present agentive noun (MO-YOHUA-L-IHT-OA-∅)-∅, "one who volunteers in the night," from the compound verbstem MO-(YOHUA-L-IHT-OA), "to volunteer in the night," which has (YOHUA-L)-LI, "night," as an adverbial embed and M-(IHT-OA), "to volunteer," as the matrix. In classical times, this was another manifestation of *Xipe* (q.v.). In the *Treatise,* the name is a metaphor for sleep and is associated with *Mictlan* (q.v.).

Nacre-as-hair (H), see *Tzoneptzin,* and for the plural form, see *Tzoneptzitzinmeh.*

Nahualli-jaguar, see *Nahualocelotl.*

Nahualocelotl [i.e., *Nāhualocēlōtl*] (Nahualli-jaguar). A compound noun: embed, (NĀHUA-L)-LI, "sorcerer"; matrix, (OCĒLŌ)-TL, "jaguar." In the *Treatise,* the speaker becomes the jaguar in order to chastise the animals that have damaged the sown fields (II:11:1).

Nahui-Acatl [i.e., *Nāhui-Ācatl*] (Four Reed). A calendrical name. In classical times, it was another name for *NoTahtzin NoNantzin* (q.v.), *TlahuizcalpanTeuctli* (q.v.), *Citlalli Icue* (q.v.), *Tonatiuh* (q.v.), and *Tonacateuctli* (q.v.) (Caso 1959:91). In the *Treatise,* the name predominantly occurs as the head of a structure of apposition with *Milinticah* (q.v.) and is the ritual name for flames and for skin rash.

Nahui-Coatl [i.e., *Nāhui-Cōātl*] (Four Snake). A calendrical name. In the *Treatise,* this is a ritual name for the veins in the eyes (VI:5:1).

Nanahuatl [i.e., *Nānāhuatl*] (Pustulous-One). In classical times, this was a Rain-Moisture-Agricultural Fertility god. It was another name for the sun. In the *Treatise,* he is likewise the sun.

Nanahuatzin [i.e., Nānāhuatzin], the honorific "name form" of *Nanahuatl* (q.v.).

Nauhcantzontecomeh [i.e., *Nāuhcāntzontecomeh*] (Four-places-heads-owner). A compound preterit agentive noun of possession: embed, (NĀUH-CĀ-N-TZON-TE-COMA)-TL, "heads-in-four-places," from (NĀUH-CĀ-N)-∅, "four places," and (TZON-TE-COMA)-TL, "hair jar," i.e., "head," from (TZON)-TLI, "hair," and (TE-COMA)-TL, "jar"; matrix, a preterit tense form of *TLA-(E), "to possess something." In the *Treatise,* this is a metaphorical name for the veins (VI:16:1). Contrast the different meaning of *nāuhcāmpa tzontecomeh* mentioned in note I:5:2 of the *Treatise.*

Nine-caves-place, see *Chiucnauhoztoc.*

Nine-flutterer (H), see *Chiucnauhpahpatlantzin.*
Nine-layering-place, see *Chiucnauhtlanepaniuhcan.*
Nine-reed, see *Chiucnauhacatl.*
Nine-times-beaten-one, see *Chiucnauhpatlatzohtzonalli.*
Nine-[times]-crumbled-in-the-hands-one, see *Chiucnauhtlamatelolli* and variants.
Nine-[times]-pounded-one, see *Chiucnauhtlatzohtzonalli* and variants.
Nine-[times]-rock-pounded-one, see *Chiucnauhtlatetzohtzonalli* and variants.
Nine-[times]-rock-slapped-one, see *Chiucnauhtlatecapanilli* and variants.
Nine-[times]-slapped-one, see *Chiucnauhcapanilli* and variants.
Nine-Topan, see *ChiucnauhTopan.*
Nine-wind, see *Chiucnauhehehcatl.*
Nochpalcueyehqueh [i.e., *Nōchpalcuēyehqueh*] (Carmine-colored-skirt-owners, *or,* more literally, Prickly-pear-colored-skirt-owners). A preterit agentive noun of possession: embed, (NŌCH-PA-L-CUĒI)-TL, "prickly-pear colored skirt," from (NŌCH-PA-L)-LI, "a prickly-pear colored thing," a passive patientive noun from TLA-(NŌCH-PA), "to color something like a prickly-pear," a compound verb that has (NŌCH)-TLI, "prickly-pear," as an adverbial embed, and whose matrix is TLA-(PA), "to color something"; matrix, a preterit tense form of *TLA-(E), "to possess something." The *-queh* is a plural suffix. The singular form, *Nochpalcueyeh* (which has the double-nucleus variant *Nochpalli Icue,* "Her-skirt Is Prickly-pears"), was the name of a goddess in classical times. In the *Treatise,* the word is always found in a structure of apposition with *Coacueyehqueh* (q.v.). It is a metaphor for hands.
NoTahtzin NoNantzin [i.e., *NoTahtzin NoNāntzin*] (My Father (H) and My Mother (H), i.e., My Mainstay (H)). A coordinate phrase consisting of the two possessed nouns ∅-NO(TAH-TZIN)∅, "he is my father (H)" and ∅-NO(NĀN-TZIN)∅, "she is my mother (H)." In the *Treatise,* this is used in addressing the fire.
Ohhuihcan Chanehqueh [i.e., *Ohhuihcān Chānehqueh*] (Dwellers in Dangerous-places). A structure of modification: the adverbial modifier is a locative noun whose embed is the preterit agentive noun, (OH-HUI-H-∅)-∅, "a dangerous thing," in the combining form (OH-HUI-H-∅-CĀ)-, and whose matrix is the locative noun, (-N)-∅, "place" (concerning the glottal stop after the initial *o* of *ohhui-,* see note II:8:72); the head is the preterit agentive noun of possession (CHĀN-EH-∅)-QUEH, which is the plural form of (CHĀN-EH-∅)-∅, "home-owner," i.e., "dweller," whose embed is (CHĀN)-TLI, "home," and whose matrix is a preterit tense form of *TLA-(E), "to possess something." In the *Treatise,* this is a metaphor for forest gods.
Ohxomoco [i.e., *Ohxōmoco*] (Turpentine ointment-two-pine torches, i.e., two-pine torches smeared with turpentine ointment). A "name form" of the compound noun (OHX-ŌM-OCŌ)-TL: embed, (OHXI)-TL, "turpentine ointment"; matrix, (ŌM-OCŌ)-TL, "two-pine torches," from (ŌME)-∅, "two," plus (OCŌ)-TL, "pine torch, a stick of pine kindling." In classical times, this was a Celestial Creativity–Divine Paternalism deity. *Ohxomoco* (along with *Cipactonal*) was the inventor of the divinatory arts. *Ohxomoco* usually represents Old-man (q.v.) in the *Treatise.*
Olchipinqueh [i.e., *Ōlchipīnqueh*] (Ones-dripping-with-rubber). A compound preterit agentive noun: embed, (ŌL)-LI, "rubber"; matrix, the preterit agentive noun (CHIPĪ-N-∅)-QUEH, the plural of (CHIPĪ-N-∅)-QUI, "one that has dripped," from the verbstem (CHIPĪ-NI), "to drip." In the *Treatise,* this is a metaphor for birds and for fish.
Old-man, see *Huehueh.*
Old-woman, see *Ilamatzin.*
Ollohqueh [i.e., *Ōllohqueh*] (Rubber-owners). A preterit agentive noun of possession: embed, (ŌL)-LI, "rubber"; matrix, a preterit tense form of *TLA-(YOA), "to possess something abundantly." The *-queh* is a plural suffix. In the *Treatise,* this is a metaphor for the gods who are summoned to aid the traveler and is used in conjunction with *Iyauhyohqueh* (q.v.).

Olpeyauhqueh [i.e., *Ōlpeyāuhqueh*] (Ones-overflowing-with-rubber). A compound preterit agentive noun: embed, (ŌL)-LI, "rubber"; matrix, the preterit agentive noun (PEYĀ-UH-ø)-QUEH, the plural of (PEYĀ-UH-ø)-QUI, "one that has overflowed," from the verbstem (PEYĀ-HUA), "to overflow." In the *Treatise,* this is a metaphorical name for birds and for fish.

Omacatl [i.e., *Ōmācatl*] (Two-reed). A calendrical name; a compound noun: embed, (ŌME)-ø, "two"; matrix, (ĀCA)-TL, "reed." This is a single-nucleus variant of *Ome-Acatl* (q.v.).

Ome-Acatl [i.e., *Ōme-Ācatl*] (Two Reed). A calendrical name. In classical times, *Ome-Acatl* was the god of the barrio *Huitznahuac* in Tenochtitlan; he was the inventor of feasting (Sahagún 1970:33–34). This was the calendrical name for *Tezcatl-Ihpoca* (q.v.), *Yayauhqui Tezcatl-Ihpoca,* and *Xipe Totec* (Caso 1959:90–91). In the *Treatise,* it serves only as an example of a *tonalli* that can be summoned.

Ome Cihuatl [i.e., *Ōme Cihuātl*] (Woman Who-is-two). Found in Ponce, not in Ruiz de Alarcón. In classical times, this was another name for *Citlalli Icue* (Torquemada 1976:66). See *Citlalcueyeh.* Compare *Ome Teuctli.*

Ome-Coatl [i.e., *Ōme-Cōātl*] (Two Snake). A calendrical name. In the *Treatise,* this is a ritual name for the veins in the eyes (VI:5:1).

Ome-Cuetzpalin [i.e., *Ōme-Cuetzpalin*] (Two Lizard). A calendrical name. In the *Treatise,* it serves only as an example of a *tonalli* that can be summoned.

Ome-Mazatl [i.e., *Ōme-Mazātl*] (Two Deer). A calendrical name. In the *Treatise,* it serves only as an example of a *tonalli* that can be summoned.

Ome-Tecpatl [i.e., *Ōme-Tecpatl*] (Two Flint). A calendrical name. In the *Treatise,* it serves only as an example of a *tonalli* that can be summoned.

Ome Teotl [i.e., *Ōme Teōtl*] (God Who-is-two). In classical times, this was a Celestial Creativity-Divine Paternalism deity.

Ome Teuctli [i.e., *Ōme Tēuctli*] (Lord Who-is-two). Found in Ponce, not in Ruiz de Alarcón. In classical times, this was another name for *Citlallatonac* (q.v.) (Torquemada 1976:66). Compare *Ome Cihuatl.*

Ome-Tochtli [i.e., *Ōme-Tōchtli*] (Two Rabbit). A calendrical name. In classical times, this was the calendrical name for *Ixquitecatl* (q.v.). In the *Treatise,* it serves only as an example of a *tonalli* that can be summoned.

One-courtyard-owners, see *Cemithualehqueh.*

One Death, see *Ce-Miquiztli.*

One Deer, see *Ce-Mazatl.*

One-face-owners, see *Cemixehqueh.*

One Flint, see *Ce-Tecpatl.*

One-grass, see *Cemmalinalli.*

One Jaguar, see *Ce-Ocelotl.*

One Lizard, see *Ce-Cuetzpalin.*

One Rabbit, see *Ce-Tochtli.*

One Reed, see *Ce-Acatl.*

Ones-dripping-with-rubber, see *Olchipinqueh.*

One Snake, see *Ce-Coatl.*

Ones-overflowing-with-rubber, see *Olpeyauhqueh.*

One Water, see *Ce-Atl.*

Pahtecatl [i.e., *Pahtēcatl*] (Medicine-lander). A gentile noun from the locative noun (PAH-TLĀN)-ø, "Medicine-land," from (PAH)-TLI, "medicine," and the locative noun (TLAN)-ø, "side." The word *Pahtlan* means literally "Medicine-side," in the sense of "beside the medicine." In classical times, *Pahtecatl* was a Rain–Moisture–Agricultural Fertility god; he was the god of *octli* (pulque). In the *Treatise,* it is the ritual name for various medicines.

Pelxayaqueh [i.e., *Pelxāyaqueh*] (Bare-mask-owner). A preterit agentive noun of possession: the embed is the compound (PEL-XĀ-YACA)-TL, "bare-mask," from (PE-L)-LI, "a bare thing, smooth thing," plus (XĀ-YACA)-TL, "mask," which consists of (XĀ)-TL, "veneer," plus (YACA)-TL, "nose," in the combining form (YAQU-); matrix, a preterit tense form of *TLA-(E), "to possess something." In the *Treatise,* it is an abusive, contemptuous name for *Yappan* (q.v.), being a reference to the penile shape of the scorpion's tail. See note VI:32:28 of the *Treatise.*

Piltzinteuctli [i.e., *Piltzintēuctli*] (Child-lord). A compound noun: embed, (PIL-TZIN)-TLI, "child"; matrix, (TĒUC)-TLI, "lord." In classical times, *Piltzinteuctli* was a Rain-Moisture-Agricultural Fertility god. In the *Treatise,* this is the name of a person in the first age who metamorphosed into a deer (VI:32) and possibly the name of the god (II:14).

Poctli Itzon [i.e, *Pōctli Ītzon*] (Her-hair Is Smoke). A double-nucleus name; a sentence whose matrix clause is *Pōctli,* "It is smoke," and whose embedded clause is *Ītzon,* "It is her hair," functioning as a supplementary subject. In the *Treatise,* this is a metaphorical name for fire. In the *Treatise,* it is used in conjunction with *Ayahuitl Itzon* (q.v.).

Quetzalcoatl [i.e., *Quetzalcōātl*] (Snake-with-quetzal-plumes, *or* Plumed-serpent). A compound noun: embed, (QUETZA-L)-LI, "a thing that can be stood upright," i.e., "a quetzal tail feather," an impersonal patientive noun from TLA-(QUETZA), "to stand something upright"; matrix, (CŌĀ)-TL, "snake." In classical times, *Quetzalcoatl* was the wind who preceded the rains (Sahagún 1970:9). He governed the west (Spence 1923:59); he was celebrated at festivals of *Atl Cahualo, Huei Tozoztli, Etzalcualiztli,* and *Huei Tecuilhuitl.* In the *Treatise,* he is clearly recognized as a god.

Red Chichimec, see *Tlatlauhqui Chichimecatl* and *Tlatlahuic Chichimecatl.*

Red Mirror, see *Tlatlauhqui Tezcatl.*

Red Pahtecatl, see *Tlatlauhqui Pahtecatl.*

Red Priest, see *Tlatlauhqui Tlamacazqui.*

Red Striped-reed, see *Tlatlauhqui Tlapahpalacatl.*

Red Woman, see *Tlatlauhqui Cihuatl.*

Rock-pounded-one, see *Tlatetzohtzonaltzin.*

Rock-slapped-one, see *Tlatecapaniltzin.*

Rubber-owners, see *Ollohqueh.*

Seven-caves-place, see *Chicomoztoc.*

Seven Flower, see *Chicome-Xochitl.*

Seven-jaguar, see *Chicomocelotl.*

Seven Snake, see *Chicome-Coatl.*

She-is-supine, see *Ahquetztimani.*

She-lies-glittering, see *Tzotzotlacatoc.*

Sustenance-basket, see *Tonacachiquihuitl.*

Sustenance-thigh, see *Tonacametztzin.*

Tecciztecatl [i.e., *Tēcciztēcatl*] (Person-from-Tecciztlan). A gentile noun, (TĒC-CIZ-T-Ē-CA)-TL, from the place noun (TĒC-CIZ-TLĀN)-ø, "Conch-side" (in the sense of "beside the conch shell"), from (TĒC-CIZ)-TLI, "conch, conch shell," a variant of (TĒUC-CIZ)-TLI, plus the relational noun (TLAN)-ø, "side." In classical times, this was the moon.

Tecpatl (Flint). In classical times, this was one of the nine Lords of the Night, variantly represented by *Itztli* (q.v.). The word also names the eighteenth of the twenty day-signs; in combination with a prefixed number, it names a thirteen-intervaled selection of days in the *tonalpohualli.*

Telpochtli [i.e., *Tēlpōchtli*] (Youth). In classical times, it was another name for *Tezcatl-Ihpoca* (Torquemada 1976:71). In the *Treatise,* this is also another name for *Tezcatl-Ihpoca* (q.v.).

Temicxoch [i.e., *Tēmicxōch*] (Dream-flower). A "name form" of the compound noun-stem (TĒMIC-XŌCHI)-TL: embed, (TĒMIC)-TLI, "dream"; matrix, (XŌCHI)-TL, "flower." In the *Treatise,* this is a metaphor for sleep. See note II:2:3 of the *Treatise.*

Teohtlalhuah [i.e., *Teohtlālhuah*] (Desert-owner). A compound preterit agentive noun of possession: embed, (TEOH-TLĀL)-LI, "valley, plain, or deserted area," from (TEŌ)-TL, "god," plus (TLĀL)-LI, "land"; matrix, a preterit tense form of *TLA-(HUA), "to own something." In the *Treatise*, the name is found in apposition with *Chicome-Xochitl* (q.v.) and is a metaphorical name for the male deer.

Teohtlalpan Chaneh [i.e., *Teohtlālpan Chāneh*] (Dweller on the Desert-area). A structure of modification: the adverbial modifier is a locative noun whose embed is (TEOH-TLĀL)-LI, "valley, plain, or deserted area" from (TEŌ)-TL, "god," plus (TLĀL)-LI, "land," and whose matrix is the relational noun (PAN)-ø, "surface, area"; the head is the preterit agentive noun of possession (CHĀN-EH-ø)-ø, "home-owner," i.e., "dweller," whose embed is (CHĀN)-TLI, "home," and whose matrix is a preterit tense form of *TLA-(E), "to possess something." In the *Treatise*, this is a metaphorical name for *tlacopahtli*. See Appendix D.

Tepetlauhcacihuatl [i.e., *Tepētlāuhcacihuātl*] (Woman-from-Tepetlauhco). A compound noun: embed, the gentile noun (TEPĒ-TLĀUH-CA)-TL, "person from Tepetlauhco," from the place name (TEPĒ-TLĀUH-CO)-ø, "Mountain-ochre-place," from (TEPĒ)-TL, "mountain," plus (TLĀ-HUI)-TL, "ochre," plus the relational noun (-CO)-ø, "place"; matrix, (CIHUĀ)-TL, "woman." In the *Treatise*, this is the name for magic earth used to create or erect a magic barrier around a cultivated field. See note II:12:7 in the *Treatise*.

Tepeyollohtli [i.e., *Tepēyōllohtli*] (Heart-of-the-mountain(s)). A compound noun: embed, (TEPĒ)-TL, "mountain"; matrix, (YŌL-LOH)-TLI, "heart." In classical time, *Tepeyollohtli* was a Celestial Creativity-Divine Paternalism deity.

Teteoh Innan [i.e., *Tēteoh Īnnān*] (Mother of the Gods). A double-nucleus name: a possessive construction whose matrix is ø-ĪN(NĀN)ø, "she is their mother," and whose embed is ø-ø(TĒ-TEO)H, "they are gods," which functions as a supplementary possessor in cross reference with the basic possessor *īn-* in the matrix. In classical times, *Teteoh Innan* was the goddess worshiped by physicians and midwives and owners of sweathouses (Sahagún 1970:15-16). Also known as *Tlalli Iyollo* (q.v.) and *ToCih* (q.v.) (Sahagún 1970:15). In the *Treatise*, this is a ritual name for fire. *Teteoh Innan* occurs in conjunction with *Teteoh Intah* (q.v.) in the *Treatise*.

Teteoh Intah [i.e., *Tēteoh Īntah*] (Father of the Gods). A double-nucleus name: a possessive construction whose matrix is ø-ĪN(TAH)ø, "he is their father," and whose embed is ø-ø(TĒ-TEO)H, "they are gods," which functions as a supplementary possessor in cross reference with the basic possessor *īn-* in the matrix. In the *Treatise*, this is a ritual name for fire. *Teteoh Intah* occurs in conjunction with *Teteoh Innan* (q.v.) in the *Treatise*.

Tetzauhteotl [i.e., *Tētzāuhteōtl*] (Omen-god). A compound noun: embed, (TĒTZĀHUI)-TL, "omen, evil omen, portent"; matrix, (TEŌ)-TL, "god." In classical times, this was another name for *Huitzilopochtli* (q.v.).

Tezcatepec [i.e., *Tezcatepēc*] (Mirror-mountain-place). A locative noun: embed, (TEZ-CA-TEPĒ)-TL, "mirror mountain," from (TEZ-CA)-TL, "mirror," and (TEPĒ)-TL, "mountain"; matrix, the relational noun (-C)-ø, "place." In the *Treatise*, this is the place where lovers meet (IV:2:1).

Tezcatl (Mirror). In the *Treatise*, it is a metaphor for the eyes (VI:5, VI:6) and for an ax (II:3; possibly a remote reference to the Night Ax, a classical manifestation of *Tezcatl-Ihpoca* (Sahagún 1957:157)). Elsewhere, it is a metaphor for a divinatory device (e.g., the patient's arm in V:1:3). Also see *Tezcatl in zan hualpopocatimani*.

Tezcatl-Ihpoca [i.e., *Tezcatl-Ihpōca*] (Smoking Mirror). A double-nucleus name: a structure of modification in which the head is ø-ø(TEZ-CA)TL, "it is a mirror," and the adjectival modifier is ø(IH-PŌ-CA)ø-ø, "it emits smoke." N.B. This name does not mean "Mirror Smoke." Found in Ponce, not in Ruiz de Alarcón. In classical times, *Tezcatl-Ihpoca* was a major god whose abode was everywhere. He introduced vice, sin, anguish, and affliction. He also bestowed wealth, courage, nobility, and honor (Sahagún 1970:5). He was both a Celestial Creativity-Divine Paternalism and a Rain-Moisture-Agricultural

Fertility god; he presided over the tenth level of *Topan;* he was celebrated at festivals of *Toxcatl, Miccailhuitontli, Pachtontli,* and *Panquetzaliztli.*
Tezcatl in zan hualpopocatimani [i.e., *Tezcatl in zan huālpopōcatimani*] (Mirror that just lies smoking hither). In the *Treatise,* this is a metaphor for land. It vaguely implies *Tezcatl-Ihpoca* (q.v.) (II:8; II:10; III:2; V:1).
Thorn-curve, see *Huitzcol.*
Three Snake, see *Ei Coatl.*
Titlacahuan [i.e., *Tītlācahuān*] (We-are-his-slaves). A single-nucleus noun: a sentence in which the subject is T-...-HUĀN, "we," and the predicate is -Ī(TLĀCA)-, "his slaves." In classical times, this was another name for *Tezcatl-Ihpoca* (q.v.).
Tlahui [i.e, *Tlāhui*] (Red-ochre). A "name form" of (TLĀHUI)-TL, "red ochre." In the *Treatise,* she is probably one of the four filth goddesses, *Tlahzolteteoh* (q.v.). See *Tlahzolteotl.* This is also the name of *Yappan*'s wife in the myth about the creation of scorpions. She was transformed into a red scorpion (see VI:32).
TlahuizcalpanTeuctli [i.e., *TlāhuizcalpanTēuctli*] (Lord-at-the-Dawn). A compound noun: adverbial embed, (TLĀ-HUI-Z-CAL-PAN)-ø, "light-emitting-house-period," i.e., "at dawn," a compound whose embed is (TLĀ-HUI-Z-CAL)-LI, "light-emitting-house," i.e., "dawn," from (TLA-HUI-Z)-TLI, "act of emitting light," plus (CAL)-LI, "house," and whose matrix is the locative noun (PAN)-ø, "surface; area, period"; matrix, (TĒUC)-TLI, "lord." In classical times, *TlahuizcalpanTeuctli* was a War–Sacrifice–Sanguinary Nourishment god; he presided over the twelfth level of *Topan.* In the *Treatise,* this is a ritual name for fire.
Tlahzolteotl [i.e., *Tlahzolteōtl*] (Filth-goddess). A compound noun: embed, (TLAHZOL)-LI, "filth, trash"; matrix, (TEŌ)-TL, "god, goddess." In classical times, *Tlahzolteotl* was a goddess of evil and debauchery; she was also identified as the four sister goddesses, *Tiacapan, Teiuc, Tlahco,* and *Xocotzin* (Sahagún 1970:23–27). In the *Treatise,* she apparently is represented by *Caxxoch* (q.v.), *Cuaton* (q.v.), *Tlahui* (q.v.), and *Xapel* (q.v.). The singular form does not occur in Ruiz de Alarcón. See note VI:16:18 of the *Treatise.*
Tlahzolteteoh [i.e., *Tlahzoltēteoh*] (Filth-goddesses). The plural of *Tlahzolteotl* (q.v.). In the *Treatise, Tlahzolteteoh* refers to the goddesses and, at times, to the fingers.
Tlalcozahuitl [i.e., *Tlālcōzahuitl*] (Yellow-like-the-earth-thing, i.e., Yellow-earth). A compound noun: embed, (TLĀL)-LI, "land, earth"; matrix, (CŌZ-AHUI)-TL, "a yellow thing," a patientive noun from the verb (CŌZ-AHUI), "to become yellow." In the *Treatise,* this is a ritual name for *axin* ointment (see Appendix D).
Tlalixcapan [i.e., *Tlālīxcapān*] (Earth-face-slapper). A compound agentive noun: embed, (TLĀL)-LI, "land, earth"; matrix, (ĪX-CAPĀ-N-ø)-ø, "face slapper," which consists of the embed (ĪX)-TLI, "face," and the matrix (TLA-CAPĀ-N-ø)-ø, "one who has slapped something," the preterit agentive nounstem from the verb TLA-(CAPĀ-N-A), "to slap something." In the *Treatise,* this is a metaphorical name for sandals.
Tlalli Iixcapactzin [i.e., *Tlālli Īīxcapactzin*] (Earth's Face-slapped-one (H)). A double-nucleus name; a possessive construction whose matrix is the sentence ø-Ī (ĪX-CAPA-C-TZIN)ø, "he/she is an honorable face-slapped-one," built on compound noun (ĪX-CAPA-C)-TLI, "face-slapped-one," a patientive noun from the verb (ĪX-CAPĀ-N-A), "to cause a face to emit a slapping sound," i.e., "to slap a face," which consists of (ĪX)-TLI, "face," and the verb TLA-(CAPĀ-N-A), "to cause something to emit a slapping sound," i.e., "to slap something." The embed, which functions as supplementary possessor, is the sentence ø-ø(TLĀL)LI, "it is earth." In the *Treatise* this is a metaphorical name for the road (II:4:3).
Tlalli Iyollo [i.e., *Tlālli Īyōllo*] (Her-heart Is Land). A double-nucleus name; a sentence whose matrix clause is *Tlālli,* "It is land," and whose embedded clause is *Īyōllo,* "It is her heart," functioning as a supplementary subject. In classical times, *Tlalli Iyollo* was another name for *ToCih* (q.v.).
Tlaloc [i.e., *Tlāloc*] (Land-lier). A preterit-as-present agentive noun, (TLĀL-O-ø)-C, "one

who lies upon the land": adverbial embed, (TLĀL)-LI, "land"; matrix, the preterit-as-present agentive noun (O-ø)-C, "one who lies," from the verbstem (O), "to lie, to be recumbent." Note that in the name, the stem (TLĀL)-LI has taken over the adverbial function usually performed by ON-, "there" (the verbstem is usually listed with the adverb: (ON-O), "to lie there," but obviously this adverb is not an obligatory constituent of the verb; it is not present, for example, in "connective *ti-*" compounds). As its plural, *Tlāloqueh* (q.v.) proves, this god name does not mean "Land-wine" as some have maintained (compare *Tlaloccihuatl* and *Tlalocxochitl*). In classical times, *Tlaloc* was the provider; he created rain and caused things to grow (Sahagún 1970:7). He was a Rain-Moisture-Agricultural Fertility god who governed the east (Spence 1923:59); he presided over the eighth level of *Topan;* he was celebrated at the festivals of *Etzalcualiztli, Tecuilhuitontli,* and *Atemoztli.* Ruiz de Alarcón seems to have no knowledge of this god.

Tlalocan [i.e., *Tlālocān*] (Land-lier-place). A locative noun: embed, the preterit agentive noun *Tlaloc* (q.v.) in its combining form (TLĀL-O-ø-CĀ)-; matrix, the locative noun (-N)-ø, "place." In classical times, *Tlalocan* was the southern paradise to which went those who died by drowning, lightning, or any water-related illness. In the *Treatise* this this is the name of the place from which guardian spirits will come to protect the planted fields.

Tlalocateuctli [i.e., *Tlālocāteēuctli*] (Land-lier-lord). A compound noun: embed, the preterit agentive noun *Tlaloc* (q.v.) in its combining form (TLĀL-O-ø-CĀ)-; matrix, (TĒUC)-TLI, "lord." In classical times, this was another name for *Tlaloc* (Torquemada 1976:76-77). Another form of this name was *TlalocanTeuctli* [i.e., *TlālocānTēuctli*] (Lord-in-*Tlalocan*). In the *Treatise,* this is a metaphorical name for the owner of a sown field (II:12:1) and for water.

Tlaloccihuatl [i.e., *Tlāloccihuātl*] (Land-wine-woman). A compound noun: embed, (TLĀL-OC)-TLI, "land-wine," from (TLĀL)-LI, "land," and (OC)-TLI, "wine"; matrix, (CIHUĀ)-TL, "woman." The embed is not the preterit agentive noun *Tlāloc* ("Land-lier," i.e., the rain god), since to function as an embed, this word would have to be in the combining form, *Tlālocā-.* See note VI:22:15 of the *Treatise* for further discussion. In the *Treatise,* this name appears in apposition to *Chicuetecpacihuatl* (q.v.), a metaphorical name for maguey (see Appendix D).

Tlalocs, see *Tlaloqueh.*

Tlalocxochitl [i.e., *Tlālocxōchitl*] (Land-wine-flower). A compound noun: embed, the compound noun, (TLĀL-OC)-TLI, "land-wine," from (TLĀL)-LI, "land," and (OC)-TLI, "wine"; matrix, (XŌCHI)-TL, "flower." The embed is not the preterit agentive noun *Tlāloc* ("Land-lier," i.e., the rain god), since to function as an embed, this word would have to be in the combining form *Tlālocā-.* See note II:7:6 of the *Treatise* for further discussion. In the *Treatise,* it is the metaphorical name for a maguey-fiber carrying net and stands in apposition to *Chicomocelotl* (q.v.).

Tlaloqueh [i.e., *Tlāloqueh*] (Land-liers). A plural preterit agentive noun, (TLĀL-O-ø)-QUEH, "ones who lie upon the land," the plural of *Tlaloc* (q.v.). In classical times, these were the natural priests of *Tlaloc.* In the *Treatise,* as well as in Ponce's *Brief Relation* (see Appendix A), the word is a ritual name for mountains, where the clouds gather.

Tlaltecuin [i.e., *Tlāltecuīn*] (He-who-flames-up-on-the-land). A compound preterit agentive noun: embed, (TLĀL)-LI, "land"; matrix, the preterit agentive noun (TECUĪ-N-ø)-ø, "one who has flamed up," which is derived from the verbstem (TECUĪ-NI), "for the fire to catch, throwing up flames." In classical times, he was the god who presided over the curing of children. Another name for *Ixtlilton* (q.v.) (Sahagún 1970:35-36). In the *Treatise,* it is a ritual name for a pathway on the land. The name is also spelled *Tlaltecuintli* [i.e., *Tlāltecuīntli*] (II:8:2; II:8:22). In these spellings, it represents the earth. See note II:8:11 of the *Treatise.*

Tlaltehtecuin [i.e., *Tlāltehtecuīn*] (He-who-flares-up-on-the-land). A variant of *Tlaltecuin* (q.v.), using the frequentative verbstem (TEH-TECUĪ-NI), "to flare up."

Tlalteuctli [i.e., *Tlālteēuctli*] (Lord-of-the-land). A compound noun: embed, (TLĀL)-LI, "land"; matrix, (TĒUC)-TLI, "lord." In classical times, *Tlalteuctli* was an earth god (Durán 1967, 1:169). He was a War-Sacrifice-Sanguinary Nourishment god; he presided over the second level of *Topan* (q.v.). In the *Treatise*, this is a ritual name for the land. Ruiz de Alarcón treats *Tlalteuctli* as a feminine entity, addressing her as *nonan* ("my mother," i.e., "my lady").

Tlalticpaqueh [i.e., *Tlālticpaqueh*] (World-owner). A preterit agentive noun of possession: embed, (TLĀL-T-ICPA-C)-ø, "upon the land," i.e., "the world," a compound noun whose embed, (TLĀL)-LI, "land," is linked by means of a "connective *-ti-*" infix to the matrix, (ICPA-C)-ø, "on the top of, over the top of"; matrix, a preterit tense form of *TLA-(E), "to possess something." In the *Treatise*, this is another name for *Yaotl* (q.v.) or *Titlacahuan* (q.v.), i.e., *Tezcatl-Ihpoca* (q.v.).

Tlamacazqui (Priest). A future agentive noun, (TLA-MACA-Z)-QUI, "one who will give something," i.e., "a priest," from the verbstem TĒ-TLA-(MACA), "to give something to someone." In classical times, *tlamacazqui* was the title of one who was low in the priestly hierarchy (see our introductory remarks). In the *Treatise*, it is the term for any power entity.

Tlamacazqui Cecec [i.e., *Tlamacazqui Cecēc*] (Cold Priest). A structure of modification: head, *Tlamacazqui* (q.v.); modifier, the preterit agentive noun (CE-CĒ-ø)-C, "one that has become cold," from the verbstem (CE-CĒ-YA), "to become cold." In the *Treatise*, this is a ritual name for *ololiuhqui*, or possibly other medicines that lower one's fever (see Appendix D).

Tlatecapaniltzin [i.e., *Tlatecapānīltzin*] (Rock-slapped-one (H)). The honorific form of the patientive noun (TLA-TE-CAPĀ-NĪ-L)-LI, "a rock-slapped one," from the verbstem TLA-(TE-CAPĀ-NI-A), "to cause something to emit a slapping sound by means of a rock," a compound whose adverbial embed is (TE)-TL, "rock," and whose matrix is TLA-(CAPĀ-NI-A), "to cause something to emit a slapping (*or* popping) sound, to slap something." In the *Treatise*, this is a metaphorical name for tobacco (see Appendix D).

Tlatetzohtzonaltzin (Rock-pounded-one (H)). The honorific "name form" of the patientive noun (TLA-TE-TZOH-TZONA-L)-LI, "a rock-pounded one," from the verbstem TLA-(TE-TZOH-TZONA), "to pound something with a rock," a compound whose adverbial embed is (TE)-TL, "rock," and whose matrix is TLA-(TZOH-TZONA), "to pound something." In the *Treatise*, this is a metaphorical name for tobacco (see Appendix D).

Tlatlahuic [i.e., *Tlātlāhuic*] (One-that-has-become-red). A preterit agentive noun, (TLĀ-TLĀ-HUI-ø)-C, "one that has become red like ochre," i.e., "a red thing," from the verb (TLĀ-TLĀ-HUI), "to become like ochre," treated as a class A verb. This is a color word that occurs frequently as a modifier in metaphorical usages in the *Treatise*. Although there were variant traditions, red was usually associated with the north. *Tlatlahuic* is a variant of *tlatlauhqui* (q.v.).

Tlatlahuic Chichimecatl [i.e., *Tlātlāhuic Chīchīmēcatl*] (Red Chichimec). A structure of modification: modifier, *Tlātlāhuic* (q.v.); head, *Chīchīmēcatl* (q.v.). In the *Treatise*, this is a metaphorical name for an ax (II:5:1; II:7:1).

Tlatlauhqui [i.e., *Tlātlāuhqui*] (One-that-has-become-red). A preterit agentive noun (TLĀ-TLĀ-UH-ø)-QUI, "one that has become like red ochre," i.e., "a red thing," from the verb (TLĀ-TLĀ-HUI), "to become like red ochre," treated as a class B verb. This is a color word that occurs frequently as a modifier in metaphorical usages in the *Treatise*. Although there were variant traditions, red was usually associated with the north. *Tlatlauhqui* is a variant of *tlatlahuic* (q.v.).

Tlatlauhqui Chichimecatl [i.e., *Tlātlāuhqui Chīchīmēcatl*] (Red Chichimec). A structure of modification: modifier, *Tlātlāuhqui* (q.v.); head, *Chīchīmēcatl* (q.v.). In the *Treatise*, this is a metaphorical name for an ax (II:3:3; II:5:1) and for rash (VI:25:5).

Tlatlauhqui Cihuatl [i.e., *Tlātlāuhqui Cihuātl*] (Red Woman). A structure of modification: modifier, *Tlātlāuhqui* (q.v.); head, (CIHUĀ)-TL, "woman." In the *Treatise*, this is the ritual name for blood (VI:16:1; VI:17:1), a kind of grass that becomes reddish colored when dried (VI:25:3), and a rash (VI:25:4).

Tlatlauhqui Pahtecatl [i.e., *Tlātlāuhqui Pahtēcatl*] (Red Medicine-lander). A structure of modification: modifier, *Tlātlāuhqui* (q.v.); head, *Pahtecatl* (q.v.). In the *Treatise*, this is a ritual name for the root of the *chalalahtli* (see Appendix D).

Tlatlauhqui Tezcatl [i.e., *Tlātlāuhqui Tezcatl*] (Red Mirror). A structure of modification: modifier, *Tlātlāuhqui* (q.v.); head, *Tezcatl* (q.v.). In the *Treatise*, this is a ritual name for the ax.

Tlatlauhqui Tezcatl-Ihpoca [i.e., *Tlātlāuhqui Tezcatl-Ihpōca*] (Red Smoking Mirror). A triple-nucleus name: a structure of modification: modifier, *Tlātlāuhqui* (q.v.); head, *Tezcatl-Ihpōca* (q.v.). In classical times, this was another name for *Mixcoatl* (q.v.) or *Xipe* (q.v.).

Tlatlauhqui Tlamacazqui [i.e., *Tlātlāuhqui Tlamacazqui*] (Red Priest). A structure of modification; modifier, *Tlātlāuhqui* (q.v.); head, *Tlamacazqui* (q.v.). In the *Treatise*, this is the ritual name for *achiote* (see the Glossary of Nahuatlisms).

Tlatlauhqui Tlapahpalacatl [i.e., *Tlātlāuhqui Tlapahpalācatl*] (Red Striped-reed). A structure of modification: modifier, *Tlātlāuhqui* (q.v.); head, the compound noun (TLA-PAH-PA-L-Ā-CA)-TL, "striped reed," whose embed is the patientive nounstem (TLA-PAH-PA-L)-LI, "a striped thing," from the frequentative verbstem TLA-(PAH-PA), "to stripe something, to paint something in various colors," from the verbstem TLA-(PA), "to paint something, to dye something." In the *Treatise*, this is a metaphorical name for *axin* ointment (see Appendix D).

Tlauhcalco [i.e., *Tlāuhcalco*] (Red-ochre-house-place). A place name: embed, (TLĀUH-CAL)-LI, "red-ochre-house," from (TLĀ-HUI)-TL, "red ochre," and (CAL)-LI, "house"; matrix, the relational nounstem (CO)-ø, "place." In the *Treatise*, it is a metaphorical name for the reflective surface of the water in the basin used to see whether the child has his *tonal.*

Tlauhtzin [i.e., *Tlāuhtzin*] (Red-ochre (H)). The honorific "name form" of (TLĀ-HUI)-TL, "red ochre." The *-tzin* is an honorific suffix. In the *Treatise*, this is a metaphorical name for the bright reflection of the child's face in the water if he has his *tonal.*

Tlazohpilli (Beloved-princess). A compound noun: embed, (TLA-ZOH)-TLI, "a precious thing, a dear thing, a beloved thing"; matrix, (PIL)-LI, "nobleman, noblewoman." In the *Treatise*, this is found as the head of a structure of apposition with *Chicome-Coatl* (q.v.), and is thus a ritual name for maize.

Tlazohteteoh [i.e., *Tlazohtēteoh*] (Beloved-goddesses). A compound noun: embed, (TLA-ZOH)-TLI, "beloved, dear"; matrix, (TĒ-TEO)-H, "gods, goddesses," the plural of (TEŌ)-TL, "god, goddess." In the *Treatise*, these are household goddesses (II:8:9).

Tliliuhqui [i.e., *Tlīliuhqui*] (One-that-has-become-black). A preterit agentive noun, (TLĪL-IUH-ø)-QUI, "one that has become like ink," i.e., "a black thing," from the verb (TLĪL-IHUI), "to become like ink, to become black," treated as a class B verb. The verb is from the noun (TLĪL)-LI, "ink."

Tliliuhqui Tlamacazqui [i.e., *Tlīliuhqui Tlamacazqui*] (Black Priest). A structure of modification: modifier, *Tlīliuhqui* (q.v.); head, *Tlamacazqui* (q.v.). In the *Treatise*, this is the ritual name for the powdered tail of the opossum (see Appendix D).

ToCih (Our-Grandmother). A noun in the possessive state consisting of the possessive prefix *to-*, "our," and the nounstem (CIH)-TLI, "grandmother." In classical times, *ToCih* was another name for *Teteoh Innan* (q.v.).

Tohtonametl [i.e., *Tohtōnamētl*] (Sunrays). A compound noun with a reduplicative prefix, indicating distributive plurality, from the singular form (TŌNA-MĒ)-TL, "sunray," whose embed is the present patientive noun *(TŌNA)-TL, "that which has become hot," from the verb (TŌNA), "to be sunny, to become hot," and whose matrix is *(MĒ-TL), a variant of (MĪ)-TL, "arrow" [see the variant stem (TŌNA-L-MĪ)-TL, "sun ray," listed in Molina]. In the *Treatise*, this is a ritual name for the sun (II:8:22).

Tollan [i.e., *Tōllān*] (Reed-side). In classical times, this was a place of fabled wealth and skills. In the *Treatise*, it is the home of the deer.

Tonacachiquihuitl [i.e., *Tōnacāchiquihuitl*] (Sustenance-basket). A compound noun: embed, (TŌNA-ø-CĀ-YŌ)-TL, "sustenance"; matrix, (CHIQUIHUI)-TL, "basket." In the *Treatise*, this is a name for the harvest basket.

Tonacacihuatl [i.e., *Tōnacācihuātl*] (Sustenance-woman). A compound noun: embed, (TŌNA-CĀ-YŌ)-TL, "sustenance"; matrix, (CIHUĀ)-TL, "woman." In classical times, *Tonacacihuatl* was one of the two original creator gods and presided over the thirteenth level of *Topan* (q.v.). In the *Treatise*, this is another name for *Xochiquetzal* (q.v.).

Tonacametztzin [i.e., *Tōnacāmetztzin*] (Sustenance-thigh (H)). The honorific "name form" of the compound noun (TŌNA-ø-CĀ-METZ)-TLI, "sustenance thigh," whose embed is (TŌNA-ø-CĀ-YŌ)-TL, "sustenance," and whose matrix is (METZ)-TLI, "thigh." There is no reason to believe that the matrix is (ME)-TL, "maguey," since it violates the sense of the incantation (II:1:5). Ruiz de Alarcón also saw the word as referring to the thigh.

Tonacateuctli [i.e., *Tōnacātēuctli*] (Sustenance-lord). A compound noun: embed, (TŌNA-ø-CĀ-YŌ)-TL, "sustenance"; matrix, (TĒUC)-TLI, "lord." Found in Serna (see note II:1:25), not in Ruiz de Alarcón. In classical times, *Tonacateuctli* was one of the two original creator gods and presided over the thirteenth level of *Topan* (q.v.).

Tonacayohuah [i.e., *Tōnacāyōhuah*] (Sustenance-owner). A preterit agentive noun of possession: embed, (TŌNA-ø-CĀ-YŌ)-TL, "sustenance"; matrix, a preterit form of *TLA-(HUA), "to possess something." In classical times, this was another name for *Centeotl (q.v.)*.

ToNantzin [i.e., *ToNāntzin*] (Our-Mother (H)). The honorific form of the possessive-state noun *tonān*, "our mother," which consists of the possessive prefix *to-*, "our," and the nounstem (NĀN)-TLI, "mother." The element *-tzin* indicates an attitude of respect on the part of the speaker. In classical times, *ToNantzin* was another name for *Centeotl (q.v.)*.

Tonatiuh [i.e., *Tōnatiuh*] (He-goes-becoming-warm). A present agentive noun, (TŌNA-ø-TI-UH-ø)-ø, "a thing that goes along becoming or being hot," from the "connective *-ti-*" verbstem (TŌNA-ø-TI-UH), "to go along becoming or being hot," whose embed is the verbstem (TŌNA), "to be hot, to be sunny," and whose matrix is the verb (YA-UH), "to go." Found in Ponce, not in Ruiz de Alarcón; in VI:24:2, the word *tōnatiuhtzin* means nothing more than "sun" in the sense of "day." In classical times, *Tonatiuh* was the sun god (Torquemada 1976:91–92), a War–Sacrifice–Sanguinary Nourishment god.

Topan (Above-us). A possessive-state noun, ø-TO(PAN)ø, "it is our surface," i.e., "above us." In classical times, this was the celestial realm. In the *Treatise*, Ruiz de Alarcón translates it as "heaven."

Turquoise-flutterer, see *Xiuhpahpatlantzin.*

Turquoise-mat, see *Xiuhpetlatzin.*

Two Deer, see *Ome-Mazatl.*

Two Flint, see *Ome-Tecpatl.*

Two Lizard, see *Ome-Cuetzpalin.*

Two Rabbit, see *Ome-Tochtli.*

Two Reed, see *Ome-Acatl.*

Two Snake, see *Ome-Coatl.*

Tzapotlan Tenan [i.e., *Tzapotlan Tēnān*] (Someone's-mother in Tzapotlan). A structure of modification: modifier, the place name (TZAPO-TLĀN)-ø, "Sapote-side" (in the sense of "beside the Sapotes"), derived from (TZAPO)-TL, "sapote," plus the relational noun (TLAN)-ø, "side"; head, *tēnān*, "someone's mother," from (NĀN)-TLI, "mother." In classical times, she was the goddess who discovered the medicinal use of *ohxitl* (turpentine) (Sahagún 1970:17).

Tzitzimitl (Air-spirit). In classical times, it was a malevolent spirit.

Tzoncozahuixticah [i.e., *Tzoncōzahuixticah*] (He-is-becoming-yellow-haired). A compound present agentive noun: embed, the preterit tense theme (TZON-CŌZ-AHUI-X-ø)-, from the verbstem (TZON-CŌZ-AHUI-YA), "to become yellow at the hair," whose embed is (TZON)-TLI, "hair," and whose matrix is (CŌZ-AHUI-YA), "to become yellow"; matrix, the verbstem (YE), "to be." The embed and the matrix are joined by the "connective *-ti-*" infix. In the *Treatise,* this is a metaphorical name for fire. See note VI:12:6 in the *Treatise.*

Tzoncoztli [i.e., *Tzoncōztli*] (Yellow-hair). A compound noun: embed, (TZON)-TLI, "hair"; matrix, (CŌZ)-TLI, "a yellow one." The noun means literally "a yellow one at the hair." In the *Treatise,* this is another name for *Nahui-Acatl* (q.v.), *Milinticah* (q.v.), and *Xihuitl-Cozauhqui* (q.v.). This is one of the metaphorical names for fire.

Tzoneptzin (Nacre-as-hair (H)). The honorific "name form" of the compound nounstem (TZON-EP)-TLI, "nacre-as-hair," whose embed is (TZON)-TLI, "hair," and whose matrix is (EP)-TLI, "nacre." The *-tzin* is an honorific suffix. In the *Treatise,* this is a metaphorical name for a finger.

Tzoneptzitzinmeh (Ones-who-are-nacre-as-hair (H)). The plural form of *Tzoneptzin* (q.v.). In the *Treatise,* this is a metaphorical name for fingers.

Tzotzotlacatoc (She-lies-glittering). A compound preterit agentive noun: embed, the preterit tense theme (TZO-TZOTLA-CA-ø)-, from the frequentative verbstem (TZO-TZOTLA-CA), "to glitter," derived from the verbstem (TZOTLĀ-NI), "to glimmer, to shine"; matrix, the preterit-as-present tense form of the verbstem (O), "to lie, to be recumbent." The embed and the matrix are joined by the "connective *-ti-*" infix. In the *Treatise,* this is a metaphorical name for fire.

Water-owners, see *Ahuahqueh.*

White Priest, see *Iztac Tlamacazqui.*

White Tlaloc, see *Iztac Tlaloc.*

White Tlalocan, see *Iztac Tlalocan.*

White Woman, see *Iztac-Cihuatl.*

Woman-from-Tepetlauhco, see *Tepetlauhcacihuatl.*

Xapel [i.e., *Xāpel*] (Surface-smooth-one). A "name form" of (XĀ-PEL)-LI, a compound nounstem whose embed is (XĀ)-TL, "surface, veneer"; matrix, (PE-L)-LI, "a smooth one, a bare one" (see note VI:32:28). In the *Treatise,* she is probably one of the four filth goddesses, *Tlahzolteteotl.* See *Tlahzolteotl.*

Xihuitl [i.e., *Xīhuitl*] (Comet). In the *Treatise,* this is a metaphorical name for rash.

Xihuitl Cozauhqui [i.e., *Xīhuitl Cōzauhqui*] (Yellow Comet). A structure of modification: head, (XĪHUI)-TL, "comet"; modifier, *Cōzauhqui* (q.v.). In the *Treatise,* this is another name for *Tzoncoztli* (q.v.), *Nahui-Acatl* (q.v.), and *Milinticah* (q.v.). It is one of the ritual names for fire.

Xipe [i.e., *Xīpe*] (Flayed-one). A "name form" of the patientive noun (XĪP-E)-TL, "one who has become flayed," from the verb (XĪP-Ē-HUA), "to become flayed." The plural is (XĪP-E)-MEH, "flayed ones," a term that refers to the victims sacrificed to the god. In classical times, *Xipe* was a Rain-Moisture-Agricultural Fertility god. The title *ToTec* (i.e., *ToTēc* for *ToTēuc),* "Our-Lord," frequently stands in apposition to the name *Xipe,* creating the phrase *Xipe ToTec.*

Xiuhcoatl [i.e., *Xiuhcōātl*] (Turquoise-snake). A compound noun: embed, (XIHUI)-TL, "turquoise, grass"; matrix, (CŌĀ)-TL, "snake." In classical times, this was *Huitzilopochtli*'s atlatl (Nuttall 1891:21).

Xiuhpahpatlantzin [i.e., *Xiuhpahpatlāntzin*] (Turquoise-flutterer (H)). The honorific form of a compound preterit agentive noun: embed, (XIHUI)-TL, "turquoise, grass"; matrix, the preterit agentive noun (PAH-PATLĀ-N-ø)-ø, "one who has fluttered," i.e., "a flutterer," from the verb (PAH-PATLĀ-NI), "to flutter," the frequentative form of (PATLĀ-NI), "to fly." Since it is being used as a name, the preterit agentive noun here has the privilege of taking the honorific suffix *-tzin* directly, without a connective *-cā-*. In the *Treatise,* this is a ritual name for tobacco (see Appendix D).

Xiuhpetlatzin (Turquoise-mat (H)). An honorific "name form" of (XIUH-PETLA)-TL, "turquoise mat," a compound noun whose embed is (XIHUI)-TL, "turquoise, grass," and whose matrix is (PETLA)-TL, "mat." The *-tzin* is an honorific suffix. In the *Treatise,* according to Serna (see note II:16:8), this is the ritual name for the riverbank.

Xiuhpilli (Turquoise-noble). A compound noun: embed, (XIHUI)-TL, "turquoise, grass"; matrix, (PIL)-LI, "nobleman." In the *Treatise,* he is also known as *Nanahuatzin* (q.v.).

Xiuhteuctli [i.e., *Xiuhtēuctli*] (Turquoise-lord). A compound noun: embed, (XIHUI)-TL, "turquoise, grass"; matrix, (TĒUC)-TLI, "lord." Found in Ponce, not in Ruiz de Alarcón. In classical times, *Xiuhteuctli* was the god of fire, also known as *Huehuehteotl* (q.v.) (Sahagún 1970:29–30; Torquemada 1976:93). He presided over the first level of *Topan* and was a Celestial Creativity–Divine Paternalism god.

Xochipilli [i.e., *Xōchipilli*] (Flower-noble). A compound noun: embed, (XŌCHI)-TL, "flower"; matrix, (PIL)-LI, "noble, nobleman." In classical times, *Xochipilli* was the patron of festivities and symbol of summer. He was a Rain–Moisture–Agricultural Fertility deity.

Xochiquetzal [i.e., *Xōchiquetzal*] (Flower-plume). A "name form" of the compound stem (XŌCHI-QUETZA-L)-LI, "flower-quetzal tail feather," whose embed is (XŌCHI)-TL, "flower," and whose matrix is (QUETZA-L)-LI, "a thing that can be stood upright," i.e., "quetzal tail feather," the passive patientive noun from TLA-(QUETZA), "to stand something upright." In classical times, *Xochiquetzal* was the goddess of flowers, arts, and crafts (Durán 1967, 1:151–52). She was a Rain-Moisture-Agricultural Fertility goddess; she was also called *Tonacacihuatl* (q.v.); she was celebrated at the festival of *Huei Pachtli.* Also known as *Chalchihuitl Icue* (q.v.), *Matlalcueyeh* (q.v.), and *Macuilxochiquetzal* (q.v.) (Clavijero 1979, 1:252). In the *Treatise,* she is a goddess. When the speaker of the incantations impersonates a god, his wife is cast in the role of *Xochiquetzal.*

Xochiteteoh [i.e., *Xōchitēteoh*] (Flower-goddesses). A compound noun: embed, (XŌCHI)-TL, "flower"; matrix, the plural stem (TĒ-TEO)-H, "gods, goddesses," from (TEŌ)-TL, "god, goddess." López Austin (1967:24) suggests that, in the *Treatise* (II:15:4), it may represent the fishing poles. Serna (1892:441) says that it represents a broom.

Xochitonal [i.e., *Xōchitōnal*] (Flower-*tonal*). The "name form" of the compound noun (XŌCHI-TŌNA-L)-LI: embed, (XŌCHI)-TL, "flower"; matrix, (TŌNA-L)-LI, "day-name." The form in the manuscript (II:17:4), *Xochtonal* [i.e., *Xōchtōnal*], is a variant spelling. In classical times, this was a mythological caimanlike creature which guarded the approach to *Mictlan.* According to Serna (see note II:17:12 of the *Treatise*), this is the caiman.

Xolotl [i.e., *Xōlōtl*] (Double). In classical times, he was celebrated at the festival of *Etzalcualiztli.* In the *Treatise,* he is a god and sometimes stands in apposition to *Capanilli* (q.v.).

Xoxohuic [i.e., *Xoxōhuic*] (One-that-has-become-green). A preterit agentive noun, (XO-XŌ-HUI-ø)-C, "one that had become green," i.e., "a green one," from the verbstem (XO-XŌ-HUI), "to become green," treated as a class A verb. This is a color word that occurs frequently as a modifier in metaphorical usages in the *Treatise.* Although there were variant traditions, green was usually associated with the west. *Xoxohuic* is a variant of *xoxouhqui* (q.v.).

Xoxohuic Cihuatl [i.e., *Xoxōhuic Cihuātl*] (Green Woman). A structure of modification: modifier, *Xoxōhuic* (q.v.); head, (CIHUĀ)-TL, "woman." In the *Treatise,* this is a metaphor for wind (II:5:7; II:5:8) and for tobacco (see Appendix D). Also see *Xoxouhqui Cihuatl.*

Xoxohuic Colelectli [i.e., *Xoxōhuic Cōlēlectli*] (Green Demon). A structure of modification: modifier, *Xoxōhuic* (q.v.); head, *Cōlēlectli* (q.v.). In classical times, it was a malevolent spirit. In the *Treatise,* this is the ritual name for cane (II:14:1).

Xoxohuic Tlalocan [i.e., *Xoxōhuic Tlālocān*] (Green Land-lier-place). A structure of modification: modifier, *Xoxōhuic* (q.v.); head, *Tlālocān* (q.v.).

Xoxohuic Tlamacazqui [i.e., *Xoxōhuic Tlamacazqui*] (Green Priest). A structure of modification: modifier, *Xoxōhuic* (q.v.); head, *Tlamacazqui* (q.v.). In the *Treatise,* this is the ritual name for tobacco (see Appendix D). Also see *Xoxouhqui Tlamacazqui.*

Xoxohuic Tlatecapaniltzin [i.e., *Xoxōhuic Tlatecapānīltzin*] (Green Rock-slapped-one (H)). A structure of modification: modifier, *Xoxōhuic* (q.v.); head, (TLA-TE-CAPĀ-NĪ-L-TZIN)-∅, the honorific "name form" of the patientive nounstem (TLA-TE-CAPĀ-NĪ-L)-LI, "a rock-slapped thing," from the verbstem TLA-(TE-CAPĀ-NI-A), "to slap something with a rock," from (TE)-TL, "rock," and TLA-(CAPĀ-NI-A), "to cause something to emit a slapping (*or* popping) sound, to slap something." The *-tzin* is an honorific suffix. In the *Treatise,* this is a metaphorical name for tobacco (see Appendix D).

Xoxohuic Tlatetzohtzonaltzin [i.e., *Xoxōhuic Tlatetzohtzonaltzin*] (Green Rock-pounded-one (H)). A structure of modification: modifier, *Xoxōhuic* (q.v.); head, (TLA-TE-TZOH-TZONA-L-TZIN)-∅, the honorific "name form" of the patientive nounstem (TLA-TE-TZOH-TZONA-L)-LI, "a rock-pounded thing," from the verbstem TLA-(TE-TZOH-TZONA), "to pound something with a rock," from (TE)-TL, "rock," and the verbstem TLA-(TZOH-TZONA), "to pound something." The *-tzin* is an honorific suffix. In the *Treatise,* this is a metaphorical name for tobacco (see Appendix D).

Xoxohuic Tzitzimitl [i.e., *Xoxōhuic Tzitzimitl*] (Green Air-spirit). A structure of modification: modifier, *Xoxōhuic* (q.v.); head, *Tzitzimitl* (q.v.). In classical times, it was a malevolent spirit. In the *Treatise,* this might be a ritual name for tobacco (see Appendix D).

Xoxouhqui [i.e., *Xoxōuhqui*] (One-that-has-become-green). A patientive agentive noun, (XO-XŌ-UH-∅)-QUI, "one that has become green," i.e., "a green one," from the verb (XO-XŌ-HUI), "to become green," treated as a class B verb. This is a color word that occurs frequently as a modifier in metaphorical usages in the *Treatise.* Although there were variant traditions, green was usually associated with the west. *Xoxouhqui* is a variant of *xoxohuic* (q.v.).

Xoxouhqui Cihuatl [i.e., *Xoxōuhqui Cihuātl*] (Green Woman). A structure of modification: modifier, *Xoxōuhqui* (q.v.); head, (CIHUĀ)-TL, "woman." In the *Treatise,* this is a metaphor for tobacco and *atl inan* (see Appendix D). Also see *Xoxohuic Cihuatl.*

Xoxouhqui Ehehcatl [i.e., *Xoxōuhqui Ehehcatl*] (Green Wind). A structure of modification: modifier, *Xoxōuhqui* (q.v.); head, (EH-EHCA)-TL, "wind." In the *Treatise,* this is the draft of wind that makes the kiln burn stronger.

Xoxouhqui Icue [i.e., *Xoxōuhqui Īcuē*] (Her-skirt Is Green). A double-nucleus name; a sentence whose matrix clause is *Xoxōuhqui* (q.v.) and whose embed clause is the possessive-state noun ∅-Ī(CUĒ)∅, "it is her skirt." In the *Treatise,* this is another name for *Chalchihuitl Icue* (q.v.).

Xoxouhqui Ihuipil [i.e., *Xoxōuhqui Īhuīpīl*] (Her-*huipil* Is Green). A double-nucleus name; a sentence whose matrix clause is *Xoxōuhqui* (q.v.) and whose embed clause is the possessive-state noun ∅-Ī(HUĪPĪL)∅, "it is her *huipil.*" In the *Treatise,* the conjoined names *Xoxouhqui Icue, Xoxouhqui Ihuipil* are a rhetorical means of naming *Chalchihuitl Icue* (q.v.).

Xoxouhqui Pahtecatl [i.e., *Xoxōuhqui Pahtēcatl*] (Green Medicine-lander). A structure of modification: modifier, *Xoxōuhqui* (q.v.); head; *Pahtēcatl* (q.v.). See note VI:6:7 of the *Treatise.* In the *Treatise,* this is the ritual name for the sap of the *mizquitl* (see Appendix D).

Xoxouhqui Tlaloc [i.e., *Xoxōuhqui Tlāloc*] (Green Land-lier). A structure of modification: modifier, *Xoxōuhqui* (q.v.); head, *Tlāloc* (q.v.).

Xoxouhqui Tlalocan [i.e., *Xoxōuhqui Tlālocān*] (Green Land-lier-place). A structure of modification: modifier, *Xoxōuhqui* (q.v.); head, *Tlālocān* (q.v.).

Xoxouhqui Tlamacazqui [i.e., *Xoxōuhqui Tlamacazqui*] (Green Priest). A structure of modification: modifier, *Xoxōuhqui* (q.v.); head, *Tlamacazqui* (q.v.). In the *Treatise,* this is a ritual name for boughs used for making the deer snare (II:8:16), tobacco (II:8:5; II:13:3; V:1:1), and *atl inan* (VI:18:1; VI:19:1) (see Appendix D). See also *Xoxohuic Tlamacazqui.*

Xoxouhqui Tzitzimitl [i.e., *Xoxōuhqui Tzitzimitl*] (Green Air-spirit). A structure of modification: modifier, *Xoxōuhqui* (q.v.); matrix, *Tzitzimitl* (q.v.). In the *Treatise,* this is a metaphorical name for cane (II:14:1).

Yacacoliuhqui [i.e, *Yacacōliuhqui*] (Curved-nose). A compound noun: embed, (YACA)-TL, "nose"; matrix, the preterit agentive noun (CŌL-IUH-ø)-QUI, "one that has become curved," i.e., "a curved one," from the verb (CŌL-IHUI), "to become curved or bent." The name means literally "one who has become curved or bent at the nose." Found in Ponce, not in Ruiz de Alarcón. In classical times, this was another name for *Yahcateuctli* (q.v.) (Torquemada 1976:93).

Yahcateuctli [i.e., *Yahcātēuctli*] (Goer-lord). A compound noun: embed, the combining form (YAH-ø-CĀ)- of the preterit agentive noun (YAH-ø)-QUI, "one who has gone," i.e., "a going one, a goer"; matrix, (TĒUC)-TLI, "lord." Found in Ponce, not in Ruiz de Alarcón. In classical times, *Yahcateuctli* was the god of the merchants (Clavijero 1979, 1:256; Sahagún 1970:41–44; Torquemada 1976:93).

Yaotl [i.e., *Yāōtl*] (Enemy). In classical times, he was a War–Sacrifice–Sanguinary Nourishment god. This is another name for *Tezcatl-Ihpoca* (q.v.). In the *Treatise,* this appears to represent *Tezcatl-Ihpoca* and there is also a mythical person named *Yaotl* in the story about the creation of the scorpion in VI:32.

Yaotzin, the honorific "name form" of *Yaotl* (q.v.).

Yappan [i.e., *Yāppān*] (Black-maize-flag, i.e., Flag-having-the-color-of-black-maize). A "name form" of the compound noun (YĀP-PĀMI)-TL, "black maize flag," in the meaning of "flag having the color of black maize," whose matrix is (YĀ-HUI)-TL, "black maize," and whose matrix is (PĀMI)-TL, "flag." In the *Treatise,* this is the metaphorical name for the black scorpion. See note VI:32:1 of the *Treatise.*

Yayahuic [i.e., *Yāyāhuic*] (One-that-has-become-dusky). A preterit agentive noun, (YĀ-YĀ-HUI-ø)-C, "a thing that has become dusky," i.e., "a dusky thing," from the verbstem (YĀ-YĀ-HUI), "to become dusky," treated as a class A verb. This is a color word that occurs frequently as a modifier in metaphorical usages in the *Treatise. Yayahuic* is a variant of *Yayauhqui* (q.v.).

Yayahuic Chichimecatl [i.e., *Yāyāhuic Chīchīmēcatl*] (Dusky Chichimec). A structure of modification: modifier, *Yāyāhuic* (q.v.); head, *Chīchīmēcatl* (q.v.). In the *Treatise,* this is the ritual name for the needle.

Yayahuic Tlamacazqui [i.e., *Yāyāhuic Tlamacazqui*] (Dusky Priest). This is a structure of modification: modifier, *Yāyāhuic* (q.v.); head, *Tlamacazqui* (q.v.). In the *Treatise,* this is a ritual name for *iyauhtli* (VI:19:1).

Yayauhqui [i.e., *Yāyāuhqui*] (One-that-has-become-dusky). A preterit agentive noun, (YĀ-YĀ-UH-ø)-QUI, "a thing that has become dusky," i.e., "a dusky thing," from the verbstem (YĀ-YĀ-HUI), "to become dusky," treated as a class B verb. This is a color word that occurs frequently as a modifier in metaphorical usages in the *Treatise. Yayauhqui* is a variant of *Yayahuic* (q.v.).

Yayauhqui Tzoneptzin [i.e., *Yāyāuhqui Tzoneptzin*] (Dusky Nacre-as-hair (H)). A structure of modification: modifier, *Yāyāuhqui* (q.v.); head, *Tzoneptzin* (q.v.). In the *Treatise,* this represents the finger.

Yei-Coatl, see *Ei-Coatl.*

Yellow Comet, see *Xihuitl-Cozauhqui.*

Yellow-earth, see *Tlalcozahuitl.*

Yellow-haired-one, see *Tzoncoztli.*

Yellow Priest, see *Cozahuic Tlamacazqui, Cozauhqui Tlamacazqui,* and *Coztic Tlamacazqui.*

Yellow Striped-reed, see *Cozauhqui Tlapahpalacatl.*

Yellow Tlalocan, see *Cozahuic Tlalocan.*

Yellow Woman, see *Cozauhqui Cihuatl.*

Yohuallahuantzin [i.e., *Yohuallāhuāntzin*] (Inebriated-in-the-night (H)). The honorific "name form" of the compound preterit agentive noun (YOHUA-L-LĀHU-ĀN-ø)-QUI, "one who has become inebriated in the night": embed, (YOHUA-L)-LI, "night"; matrix, (TLĀHU-

ĀN-ø)-QUI, "one who has become inebriated," from the verb (TLĀHU-ĀNA), "to become inebriated," a compound verbstem whose embed is (TLĀHUI)-TL, "red ochre," and whose matrix is the transitive verb TLA-(ĀNA), "to get something." Since the preterit agentive noun is used as a name, it can take the honorific suffix *-tzin* directly, without the help of a connective *-cā-*. In classical times, *Yohuallahuantzin* was another name for *Xipe ToTec.* In the *Treatise* (II:2:3), the reference may also be to *Xipe.*

Yohualli Ehehcatl (Night-and-Wind). A structure of conjunction: first conjunct, (YOHUA-L)-LI, "night"; second conjunct, (EH-EHCA)-TL, "wind." Found in Ponce, not in Ruiz de Alarcón. In classical times, he was a Celestial Creativity–Divine Paternalism god.

Yollohcuepcatzin [i.e., *Yōllohcuepcātzin*] (Heart-changer (H)). An honorific form of the compound preterit agentive noun (YŌL-LOH-CUEP-ø)-QUI, "one who has changed the heart," the embed of which is (YŌL-LOH)-TLI, "heart," which functions as an incorporated verb object. The matrix is the preterit agentive noun (TLA-CUEP-ø)-QUI, "one who has changed something," i.e., "a changer," from the verb TLA-(CUEPA), "to change something." The *-tzin* is an honorific suffix. In the *Treatise,* it is found in apposition to *Pahtecatl* (q.v.). There is a variant form, *Yōlcuepcātzin,* which uses (YŌL)-LI, "living thing, heart," as the embed.

APPENDIX C

Medical Practitioners Mentioned in the *Treatise*

Atlan tlachixqui [i.e., *ātlan tlachixqui*]. A structure of modification consisting of the compound relational noun (Ā-TLAN)-ø, "water-side," i.e., "beside water," as modifier and *tlachixqui* (q.v.) as head. The combination can be translated as "a looker into water." A curer who attempts to ascertain the nature of a child's illness by studying the reflection of the child's face in a basin of water. The plural is *atlan tlachixqueh.*

Matlapouhqui [i.e., *mātlapōuhqui*]. A compound noun consisting of the adverbial embed (MĀI)-TL, "hand," and the matrix (TLA-PŌUH-ø)-QUI, a preterit agentive noun meaning "one who has counted things," i.e., "a counter," and by extension, "a sorcerer," "a diviner," from the verb TLA-(PŌHUA), "to count something." The word, therefore, means literally "one who has counted things by means of the hand" and, more freely, "a sorcerer who divines by using the hands." A curer who attempts to ascertain the outcome of an illness and the answer to other questions regarding the sickness by measuring the patient's forearm with the palm and fingers. The plural is *matlapouhqueh.*

Nahualli [i.e., *nāhualli*]. The word *nahualli* was discussed by Garibay (1946:170, note 2). He says: "The etymology of the word is problematic: the following ones can be proposed: (a) From *nahui* 'four,' . . . (b) From *nahuali, nahuala,* an archaic verb that we find in many compounds. Its meaning is in general to deceive, to dissemble." None of the examples Garibay gives in support of this second etymology is valid owing to an erroneous concept of Nahuatl morphology. He ends this section by saying: "It is doubtful, nevertheless, whether this verb is the primitive of *nahualli* or a derivative of it. This second one seems more acceptable." He continues: "(c) It might have been a Mayan loanword and might have meant 'the wise one,' from the Maya-Quiche root *Na, nao, naua,* which means 'wisdom, knowledge, magic.'" None of these three suggestions seems viable. Andrews (1975:455) suggests that (NĀHUA-L)-LI is a patientive noun derived from *TLA-(NĀHUA), "to interpose something (between self and public, skin and outer clothing, man and gods, the natural and the supernatural, and so forth)." The word would mean literally "an entity that can be interposed," i.e., "a mask, a disguise; a sorcerer." Molina translates it as "witch," and Siméon as "sorcerer, sorceress, magician, enchanter, necromancer." In the *Treatise,* it signifies "a sorcerer who has the power to transform himself into an animal" or "a sorcerer who has an animal as an alter ego." It has, then, to do with the idea of magic and magical powers but has such a different range of denotations and connotations that "magician" and "sorcerer" are inadequate to render it properly. The plural is *nanahualtin.*

Pahini [i.e., *pahīni*]. A customary-present agentive noun derived from the compound verbstem (PAH-I), "to drink medicine," consisting of the embed (PAH)-TLI, "medicine," which functions as an incorporated object in the compound, and having as the matrix the verbstem TLA-(I), "to drink something." The word, therefore, means literally "one who customarily drinks medicine," i.e., "a medicine drinker," and more freely "a diviner who drinks a hallucinogenic drug for the purpose of divining the nature of the patient's problem." The plural is *pahinih.*

Temixihuitiani [i.e., *tēmīxihuītiāni*]. A customary-present agentive noun derived from the verbstem TĒ-(MĪX-IHUĪ-TIA), "to cause someone to give birth," from the intransitive verbstem (MĪX-IHUI), "to give birth." The word, therefore, means literally "one who customarily causes someone to give birth," i.e., "a midwife." The plural is *temixihuitianih.*

Tepalehuiani [i.e., *tēpalēhuiāni*]. A customary-present agentive noun derived from the verbstem TĒ-(PAL-Ē-HU-IA), "to lift up favor with regard to someone," i.e., "to help someone." The word, therefore, means literally "one who customarily helps someone."

In Ruiz de Alarcón's *Treatise,* it is used in the meaning "midwife." The plural is *tepalehuianih.*

Tetlachihuiani [i.e., *tētlachīhuiāni*]. A customary-present agentive noun derived from the applicative verbstem TĒ-TLA-(CHĪHU-IA), "to do something to someone," from the verbstem TLA-(CHĪHUA), "to do something." The word, therefore, means literally "one who customarily does something to someone," i.e., "a sorcerer," "a soothsayer" (Sahagún 1957:41, 101). A malevolent sorcerer who bewitches people. The plural is *tetlachihuianih.*

Tetonaltih [i.e., *tētōnaltih*]. A preterit agentive noun derived from the verb TĒ-(TŌNA-L-TIA), "to provide someone with a *tonal* (*or* a soul)," a denominative verb from (TŌNA-L)-LI, "*tonal,*" and, by extension, "soul." A curer who attempts to bring about a cure by finding and retrieving a patient's truant soul. Compare *tetonalmacani* in note 27 of Appendix A. The plural is *tetonaltihqueh.*

Texoxqui [i.e., *tēxōxqui*]. A preterit agentive noun derived from the verb TĒ-(XŌXA), "to bewitch someone." The word, therefore, means literally "one who has bewitched someone," i.e., "a sorcerer," "a witch," "a wizard." A malevolent sorcerer who bewitches people. The plural is *texoxqueh.*

Teyollohcuani [i.e., *tēyōllohcuāni*]. A customary-present agentive noun derived from the compound verbstem TĒ-(YŌL-LOH-CUA), "to eat someone at the heart," consisting of the embed (YŌL-LOH)-TLI, "heart," which functions as an incorporated adverb in the compound, and having as the matrix the verb TĒ-(CUA), "to eat someone." The word, therefore, means literally "one who has eaten someone at the heart" and, more freely, "a sorcerer or sorceress who sucks blood." A malevolent sorcerer who brings about sickness. The plural is *teyollohcuanih.*

Ticitl [i.e., *tīcitl*]. A doctor, physician, or midwife. Molina defines it as "doctor or soothsayer and caster of lots." The plural is *titicih.*

Tlachixqui. A preterit agentive noun from the verbstem (TLA-CHIYA), "to look." The word, therefore, means literally, "one who has looked." According to Molina's entry, *veca ontlachiani* [i.e., *huehca ontlachiani*], the word should read *huehca ontlachixqui,* "one who has looked off in the distance," i.e., "a seer," "a prophet." The word is also used in *ātlan tlachixqui* (q.v.). The plural is *tlachixqueh.*

Tlamacazqui. A future agentive noun from the verbstem TĒ-TLA-(MACA), "to give something to someone" (the loss of the secondary object *tē-* ["someone"] is curious). The word, therefore, means literally "one who will give something" and, more freely, "a priest." In the *Treatise* the word is used to refer to any power entity. The plural is *tlamacazqueh.*

Tlaolxiniani [i.e., *tlaōlxīniāni*]. A customary-present agentive noun derived from the compound verbstem (TLA-Ō-L-XĪNI-A), "to cause shelled maize to collapse." The embed is the patientive noun (TLA-Ō-L)-LI, "something shelled (e.g., shelled maize)" [from the verb TLA-(Ō-YA), "to shell something (e.g., maize, beans)"], which functions as an incorporated object in the compound. The matrix is the verbstem TLA-(XĪNI-A), "to cause something to collapse," from the verbstem (XĪNI), "to collapse." The word, therefore, means literally "one who customarily causes shelled maize to collapse." A curer who attempts to answer questions concerning illness and other matters by reading the position of tossed maize kernels. The plural is *tlaolxinianih.*

APPENDIX D

Medicines Mentioned in the *Treatise*

Aguamiel (Spanish, *lit.*, waterhoney). The sap of the maguey, which, fermented, is pulque (III:1). See *maguey*.
Atl inan [i.e., *ātl īnān*] (Its-mother is water). A double-nucleus construction; a sentence whose matrix clause is *ātl*, "it is water," and whose embedded clause is *īnān*, "it is its mother," functioning as a supplementary subject. It is an herb, *Rumex pulcher* (Díaz 1976:117), commonly called fiddle dock. Use in the *Treatise:* a decoction is administered as an enema for stomach pain (VI:18) and fevers (VI:29), mixed with water and twelve maize kernels, then drunk for fevers (VI:30). Use in other sixteenth-century sources: *Atl inan* leaves are chewed in the morning to stop fevers and evacuate humors and bile (Hernández 1959a:26); its root and leaves are ground up into a powder to cure putrid ulcers; it is a natural astringent, stops diarrhea, dysentery, and flux (Hernández 1959a:26).
Atolli [i.e., *ātōlli*] (atole). A thick drink that is made with corn meal soaked in water and strained through a sieve and then boiled until it has the consistency of pap or porridge. There are many kinds, depending on the different flavors added to the basic recipe (fruits, honey, milk, and so forth). Use in the *Treatise:* it is frequently used as a base for medicines (IV:1). See *maize*.
Axin [i.e., *āxin*]. An oily, yellowish substance produced by a scale insect of the same name from the branches of *Jatropha curcas, Spondias,* and other trees (Standley 1920-26:641). These insects are cultivated in some locales. The bugs are boiled in water until they disintegrate and the wax rises to the surface, whereupon it is strained in a piece of cloth to extract all the wax possible. It is placed in containers and left to stand two hours or more, whereupon it coagulates and, when stirred, forms little balls, which are washed, put over a slow fire to remove moisture, and then strained and used when cold. Use in the *Treatise:* it is used as an ointment for rash or impetigo (VI:25). Use in other sixteenth-century sources: *axin* is used to treat the hair, and for ear ulcers and infections; it is boiled and used as an enema of last resort for diarrhea; and, mixed with *tzitzicaztli,* it is put on feet that go to sleep (Sahagún 1961:139–41, 158–59). It alleviates infirmities, cures tumors, eases pain, and increases agility (Hernández 1959a:91, 229, 255, 321, 387). Mixed with *piciyetl,* it is good for hernias (Hernández 1959b:385).
Cacao [probably from a Mayan source; the Nahuatl equivalent is (CACAHUA)-TL, "cacao bean"]. A seed produced in pods by cacao trees, of which there are numerous varieties: *Theobroma angustifolium, T. bicolor, T. cacao, T. leicarpum, T. pentagonum.* The medicinal variety is probably *Theobroma cacao* (Díaz 1976:123; Díaz 1977:119–20), a large-leafed flowering tree producing large, sessile, fleshy, five-celled fruit (Standley 1920, 26:805) cultivated in the tropics; it yields *cacao.* Chocolate is made from the cacao bean. Use in the *Treatise:* used primarily as a base in which other medicines are mixed (IV:1). Use in other sixteenth-century sources: *cacao* alleviates infirmities, cures dysentery, and stimulates the appetite (Hernández 1959a:305).
Chalalahtli [i.e., *chālalahtli*]. A tree with oblong leaves. Use in the *Treatise:* the root is mixed with *piciyetl* (q.v.) for swellings of the head (VI:4). Use in other sixteenth-century sources: it cures tumors (Hernández 1959a:336–37).
Coanenepilli [i.e., *cōānenepilli*] (snake-tongue). A compound noun: embed, (CŌĀ)-TL, "snake"; matrix, (NENE-PIL)-LI, "tongue," from (NENE)-TL, "doll, clitoris," plus (PIL)-LI, "child, appendage." *Passiflora jorullensis* (Díaz 1976:133) are usually scandent herbs, frequently woody at the base, with flowers. About forty species of this genus occur in Mexico, only two of which are shrubs (Standley 1920-26:849). However, Emmart (1940:

264, note 5) notes that the *coanenepilli* mentioned in the Badianus Manuscript appears to be *Dorstenia contrayerva,* a type of low herb (Standley 1920-26:202). It appears red because of its internodes. Use in the *Treatise:* the powdered cortex of the root is drunk in water thickened with ground maize for chest pain (VI:13), for tertian fever (VI:27), mixed with other herbs, for fevers (VI:29), and put on top of an *axin* potion for rash and impetigo (VI:25). Use in other sixteenth-century sources: the root is drunk as a medicine (Sahagún 1963:148), for urination of blood or pus (Sahagún 1963:156); it stimulates the appetite, causes evacuation of bile, cures fevers, coagulates the blood, eases pain (Hernández 1959a:198, 216; Paso y Troncoso 1905c:104), cures the spleen, restores impeded movement, combats snakebite (Hernández 1959b:229–30; Paso y Troncoso 1905c: 280; 1906:25). By 1580 it was also regarded as a cure for pestilence (Paso y Troncoso 1905b:76) and was widely regarded as a cure for *mal de frío*—presumably an adaptation to Spanish ideas of disease (Paso y Troncoso 1905b:63, 73, 76, 80, 92).

Chocolate, see *cacao.*

Colopahtli [i.e., *cōlōpahtli*] (scorpion-medicine). A compound noun: embed, (CŌLŌ)-TL, "scorpion"; matrix, (PAH)-TLI, "medicine." It comes from a tree. Use in the *Treatise:* a decoction is applied to hemorrhoids (VI:20). Use in other sixteenth-century sources: its ground root is used for scorpion stings and for stomach pain and to stop flatulence, cure colic, and evacuate urine (Hernández 1959a:327–33).

Copalli (copal). There are numerous varieties, most belonging to the genus *Bursera,* an aromatic unarmed tree or shrub with small flowers (Standley 1920-26:542). Martínez (1979:212–16) lists over forty species. *Copalli* is an aromatic resin obtained from the trunk of the *copalli* tree by spontaneous exudations or by means of incisions. Use in the *Treatise:* it was used in curings primarily as an incense (IV:3; V:1; VI:1, 3, 25) and an auxiliary to curing (IV:3; VI:6) or as an offering (I:2). It was also used for its curative properties, applied burning to teeth for toothaches (VI:8), mixed with salt to stop bleeding from the mouth (VI:17), as a drink or as an enema (VI:17), or used dissolved in water as a plaster or poultice for swellings and inflammations (VI:26). Use in other sixteenth-century sources: it is used for diarrhea when drunk with tepid water, or for swellings or fever as a poultice (Sahagún 1963:187), applied to the head for scabies (Emmart 1940:213) or for headaches or applied for strangulation of the uterus (Hernández 1959a: 177–79).

Cuexpalli. Use in the *Treatise:* it is either an intoxicant similar to *ololiuhqui* or a synonym for it. See note I:2:2 of the *Treatise.*

Huauhtli [i.e., *huāuhtli*]. *Amaranthus leucocarpus.* The plant is cultivated for its grain, a very small, dry fruit (Standley 1920-26:254). Sahagún (1963:286–87) distinguishes eight varieties of amaranth. Use in the *Treatise:* it is associated with the gods and ground into flour and made into dough, from which idols are made (I:3). It is also spread on top of swellings as the last part of a cure involving other herbs (VI:25). Use in other sixteenth-century sources: ground into a powder or used as a juice, it was a cure for the eyes. The root is eaten or the leaves are applied to the chest to relieve pain, and it cures old ulcers (Hernández 1959a:380).

Huei nacaztli [i.e., *huēi nacaztli*] (big ear). A structure of modification: modifier, (HUĒI)-ø, "big"; head, (NACAZ)-TLI, "ear." A large, unarmed tree, *Enterolobium cyclocarpum* (Díaz 1976:154; Martínez 1979:456), twelve to thirty meters high, with broad spreading crown, rough bark, and small white sessile flowers. The fruit is dark brown, flat, coiled, eight to eleven centimeters in diameter. The seeds are dark brown, about twelve millimeters long. Both fruit and bark are rich in tannin (Standley 1920-26:391). It is the yellow fruit of the *teonacaztli* tree (Sahagún 1963:120). Use in the *Treatise:* it is used with three other herbs as a drink to cure fevers (before VI:29:1). Use in other sixteenth-century sources: it is added to chocolate or to tobacco as a medicine. Excessive consumption was intoxicating (Sahagún 1963:120, 203). It was mixed with other herbs and washed on the body for fatigue and used as an amulet to safeguard travelers

(Emmart 1940:276-77, 314). It was noted as being produced in large quantities in Cuzcatlan, Puebla, in 1580 (Paso y Troncoso 1905b:52).

Iyauhtli [i.e., *iyāuhtli*] (an offered-up thing). A patientive noun from the verbstem TLA-(IYĀ-HUA), "to offer something in sacrifice to a deity; to incense." This word is frequently misleadingly spelled *yauhtli.* It is the herb *Tagetes lucida* (Díaz 1976:202), commonly called sweet-scented marigold. It has an odor reminiscent of anise and, because of this resemblance, Ruiz de Alarcón has translated it as "anise." Use in the *Treatise:* it is used as incense in place of *copalli* (VI:4, 27). Medicinally, it is mixed with *piciyetl* and used for chest pain (VI:14). Use in other sixteenth-century sources: it is drunk for chills and gout (Sahagún 1963:145-46). It cures fevers (Sahagún 1963:192) and is ground with other herbs to cure hiccups (Emmart 1940:238). It is also an incense (Sahagún 1963:146; Emmart 1940:302).

Iyetl (tobacco). The stem (IYE)-TL is related to root of the verb TLA-(IYĀ-HUA), "to offer something in sacrifice to a deity; to incense." The vowel *e* is occasionally a variant for *a;* the length on the *ā* of the verbstem results from the derivational process. See *piciyetl.*

Maguey [a Taino word; the Nahuatl equivalent is (ME)-TL]. There are numerous varieties, more than 200 species, most of the genus *Agave.* It is a cactus from which pulque and tequila are made. Its leaves contain an excellent fiber, and its sap is fermented to produce a drink (Standley 1920-26:107). Use in the *Treatise:* it is used as an intoxicant (VI:22). Use in other sixteenth-century sources: it is drunk before entering the sweathouse; it is used as a base for other medicines and as a poultice for gout (Sahagún 1963: 149, 179). The sap is used for skull wounds and fractures, and pulque is consumed for coughing (Sahagún 1961:140-41, 149-50). Pulque eases childbirth, induces lactation, is a diuretic, and prevents lice infestation (Emmart 1940:312-20). Maguey leaves cure ulcers; pulque provokes urine; the fruit cures mouth ulcers; and the juice cures fevers, as does the root, and stops flatulence (Sahagún 1963:41, 349-51; Sahagún 1961:38-39; 55-56). It is also used for snakebite (Motolinía 1973:198-99).

Maize [from Spanish, *maíz,* derived from the Taino word *mahiz;* the Nahuatl equivalent is (TLA-Ō-L)-LI, "dried, shelled maize," or (CEN)-TLI, "dried, unshelled maize"]. There are twenty-five recognized types of maize. The word generally refers to *Zea Mays* (Martínez 1979:545-46). Maize is a grain-producing, pod-bearing plant domesticated in Mexico. There are no wild varieties (Martínez 1979:545-46). Use in the *Treatise:* it is used primarily in divinatory aspects of curing (IV:1; VI:30), in fortune-telling (V:2, 3, 4), and as a base for other medicines (IV:1). Use in other sixteenth-century sources: the root is used for curing fevers, parts are used to cure impotence (Sahagún 1963:142, 281), and maize *atolli* is consumed for facial swelling (Sahagún 1961:141-42) and fatigue, irritated kidneys, and ulcers (Hernández 1959a:290).

Mizquitl (mesquite). There are numerous varieties; the one used for curing is probably *Prosopis juliflora.* Use in the *Treatise:* after the bark of the *mizquitl* tree is cut, the sap is collected on the head of a pin and is rubbed on the eyes as a cure (VI:6). Use in other sixteenth-century sources: *mizquitl* leaves are ground in woman's milk or dew or limpid water and put into painful eyes (Emmart 1940:218; Hernández 1959b:32). *Mizquitl* is also used for open wounds (Emmart 1940:220, note 7). Its leaves are used to wash the head to kill lice and restore hair. It alleviates chest pain, kills ringworm, cures dysentery, and cures fevers (Hernández 1959b:32-33).

Ololiuhqui (a thing that has become round like a ball). A preterit agentive noun from the verb (OLOL-IHUI), "to become round like a ball"; from the nounstem (OLOL)-LI, "ball, sphere." *Turbina corymbosa,* better known as *Rivea corymbosa* (Martínez 1979:637; Schultes and Hofmann 1979:58). The name refers to the fruit, which is a dry, spherical capsule containing seeds. It is a woody vine with long, ovate leaves and white flowers (Standley 1920-26:1208). A decoction is made from the ground seeds. Use in the *Treatise:* it is used as a narcotic intoxicant (I:1, 6), to which divinity was attributed (I:2, 6, 7; VI:1, 12,

29), which could also cause illness (VI:1), and which is consulted as an oracle (I:6, 7; V:1, 3; VI:12, 29). It is used medicinally in an enema for fever (VI:29). Use in other sixteenth-century sources: it is a narcotic (Sahagún 1963:129; Hernández 1959b:73), but it is also a cure for syphilis, constipation, pain, flatulence, tumors, and inflamed eyes (Hernández 1959a:287; 1959b:73; Paso y Troncoso 1905c:104). Mixed with resin, it alleviates broken bones and stimulates the appetite (Hernández 1959b:73). Its root is ground up and drunk for swollen stomach or nausea and for its laxative properties (Sahagún 1963:129, 165). The seeds cause hallucinations (Cárdenas 1945:243v–246v).

Peyotl [i.e., *peyōtl*] (peyote). A patientive nounstem, (PEYŌ)-TL, "a thing that glimmers, glows," from the verbstem (PEYŌ-NI), "to glimmer, glow." *Lophophora williamsii* (Anderson 1980:133–43; Díaz 1976:175; Martínez 1979:718–19). It is a dull bluish-green plant, somewhat flattened at top, five to eight centimeters broad, with a thickened taproot up to ten centimeters long, and with pale pink to white flowers (Standley 1920-26:932). It is a cactus, the fruit, or "button" of which is eaten for its narcotic, hallucinogenic properties. Use in the *Treatise:* it is used as a narcotic intoxicant (I:1), to which divinity is attributed (I:2, 6; VI:29), which could also cause illness (VI:1), and which is consulted as an oracle (I:6, 7; V:1; VI:1). It is used medicinally in an enema for fever (VI:29). Use in other sixteenth-century sources: it was a narcotic (Sahagún 1963:129; Hernández 1959b:92), but it was also a cure for fever (Sahagún 1963:147; Hernández 1959b:92). It causes hallucinations (Cárdenas 1945:243v–246v).

Piciyetl (piciete). A compound noun (PIC-IYE)-TL, "tiny tobacco": embed, (PIZ)-TLI, "a diminutive thing (?)" [cf. (PIC-Ī-L)-LI, "a granule"]; matrix, *iyetl* (q.v.). *Nicotiana rustica* (Robicsek 1978:45–46; Wasson 1966:330). It is an herbaceous species of tobacco (Standley 1920-26:1278). Use in the *Treatise:* it is treated as a deity (I:2; II:16) and used to conjure (II:3, 4, 8, 15, 17; III:1; VI:3, 8) and for fortune-telling (V:1). It is also used as a talisman to ward off animals and insects (II:12, 13). Medicinally, it is used in childbirth (VI:1), for pain (VI:8, 9, 14, 24), for toothache (VI:8), for swollen head (VI:4), and for rash and impetigo (VI:25). Use in other sixteenth-century sources: it is an intoxicant (Sahagún 1963:146). It is rubbed on for fatigue, and placed in the navel for a swollen stomach (Sahagún 1963:146). It is used for diarrhea (Emmart 1940:259), to alleviate asthma, produce sleep, cure afflictions of the uterus, headaches, inflammation of the spleen, toothaches, syphilis, snakebites, and arrow wounds (Hernández 1959a:81–82; 1959b:376). It is good for weak stomachs, asthma, and dropsy (Cárdenas 1945:164r; Paso y Troncoso 1905a:103); it also causes hallucinations (Cárdenas 1945:243v–246v); and it is used to alleviate pain (Paso y Troncoso 1905b:180–81; 1905c:320).

Rue. *Rutaceae.* One of several aromatic trees or shrubs, usually furnished with glands in the bark, leaves, and fruit. No herbaceous plants of the family are native to Mexico. The family includes the important tropical citrus fruits citron, lemon, lime, sour orange, sweet orange, grapefruit, and the limeberry (Standley 1920-26:524). Use in the *Treatise:* it is mixed with *coanenepilli* (q.v.) and drunk for tertian fever (VI:27).

Salt. Use in the *Treatise:* added to *copalli* and *tequixquitl,* it is used to cure the eyes (VI:6), and added to *tzopilotl* and *tomatl* juice, it is used for swollen throats (VI:10).

Tenexiyetl (tenexiete). A compound noun, (TE-NEX-IYE)-TL, "lime tobacco": embed, (TE-NEX)-TLI, "lime," from (TE)-TL, "rock," plus (NEX)-TLI, "ash"; matrix, *iyetl* (q.v.). It is ground *piciyetl,* mixed with lime, in the proportions of ten parts *piciyetl* to one part lime (Sahagún 1963:146; Hernández 1959a:82). Use in the *Treatise:* it is used as a talisman (I:4), and in fortune-telling (V:1), and it is conjured (VI:3). Medicinally, it is used as eardrops for earaches (VI:8), for pain in the jaw (VI:9), and for toothache (VI:8). Use in other sixteenth-century sources: it is used as a poultice for head abscesses, and is placed, with salt, in incisions for cysts (Sahagún 1961:140, 149). By 1580, it was also regarded as a cure for *mal de frío*—presumably an adaptation to Spanish ideas of disease (Paso y Troncoso 1905a:130).

Tequixquitl. Potassium nitrate (Emmart 1940:64). Use in the *Treatise:* added to *copalli* and salt, it is used to cure the eyes (VI:6), and, added to *tzopilotl, tomatl* juice, and salt, it is used to cure swollen throats (VI:10).

Texihxihuitl (rocks-grass). A compound noun: embed, (TE)-TL, "rock"; matrix, (XIH-XIHUI)-TL, a distributive plural stem of (XIHUI)-TL, "turquoise, grass." *Helitropium parviflorum* (Díaz 1976:190). One of several shrubs or trees with small flowers and dry fruit (Standley 1920-26:1233–34). Use in the *Treatise:* it is used in place of mesquite sap to rub on the eyes to cure them (VI:6). Use in other sixteenth-century sources: it cures ulcers, stops toothaches, dissolves tumors, and cures fevers, mange, and dysentery (Hernández 1959a:114).

Tlachihchinoa (over-the-fire-curer). A present agentive noun, (TLA-CHIH-CHIN-OA-ø)-ø, "one who dries something up, one who cures something over fire," from the verbstem TLA-(CHIH-CHIN-OA), "to dry something up, to cure something over fire," a reduplicative stem from TLA-(CHIN-OA), "to burn something (i.e., the fields"). There are numerous varieties: *Tournefortia capitata, T. mexicana, T. volubilis, Heliotropium parviflorum, Stevia linoides,* and *Plumbago scandens* (Díaz 1976:191), all shrubs or small trees, often scandent, with small, usually white, flowers and small drupaceous fruit (Standley 1920-26:1112–13, 1229–31, 1424). Use in the *Treatise:* it is used to cure eyes by rubbing it on them, with other herbs (VI:6). Use in other sixteenth-century sources: the leaves are ground up and drunk for fever in the mouth or abdomen (Sahagún 1963:176). It is applied to festering sores or itches (Sahagún 1963:176). It reduces swelling, stops fever chills, and cures itches and toothaches (Hernández 1959a:114).

Tlacopahtli [i.e., *tlacōpahtli*] (stick-medicine). A compound noun: embed, (TLACŌ)-TL, "stick"; matrix, (PAH)-TLI, "medicine." *Aristolochia mexicana* (Díaz 1976:191; Martínez 1979:872). Usually a scandent plant with capsule fruit (Standley 1920-26:238). Use in the *Treatise:* it is applied for rash or impetigo (VI:25), and the root is used as a potion for urine sickness (VI:28). Use in other sixteenth-century sources: it is used for fever (Emmart 1940:223, note 1, 284; Paso y Troncoso 1905c:142). The root cures deafness, and tumors, clears vision, heals broken bones, and cures infirmities of the eyes and spleen (Hernández 1959b:130–31). It also alleviates dysentery and stimulates the appetite; it is an astringent, and it cures worms (Hernández 1959b:131, 190). It was also used for pain (Paso y Troncoso 1905a:174; Paso y Troncoso 1905c:112).

Tlanechicolpahtli [i.e., *tlanechicōlpahtli*] (mixture-medicine). A compound noun: embed, (TLA-NECHIC-Ō-L)-LI, "things collected and accumulated or piled together," i.e., "a mixture," a patientive noun from the verbstem TLA-(NECHIC-OA), "to collect or accumulate things"; matrix, (PAH)-TLI, "medicine." Use in the *Treatise:* a concoction of four herbs *(huēi nacaztli, xōchimecatl, cōānenepilli, xiuhcohcōlin)* used for curing fevers (VI:29).

Tlaquatl [i.e., *tlacuātl*] (a thing that is eaten, i.e., an opossum). A patientive noun, (TLA-CUĀ)-TL, from the verb TLA-(CUA), "to eat something." Frequently used in the affective form *tlacuatzin. Didelphis marsupialis* (Leopold 1972:324). The opossum, a small, nocturnal, omnivorous marsupial (Leopold 1972:325–28). Use in the *Treatise:* the tail is ground into powder and drunk for difficult childbirths (VI:1) and to remove obstructions to urine (VI:28). Use in other sixteenth-century sources: the tail is used as medicine for expelling or extracting things from the body. It is used for difficult childbirths, as a laxative, to gather phlegm, and for constipation (Sahagún 1963:11).

Tlaquatzin [i.e., *tlacuātzin*], the honorific form of *tlaquatl* (q.v.).

Tobacco, see *piciyetl* and *iyetl.*

Tomate (*tomatl,* not to be confused with tomato, which is *jitomate*). A patientive noun, (TOMA)-TL, "a plump thing," from the verb (TOMĀ-HUA), "to become plump, to bulge." Use in the *Treatise:* added to *tequixquitl,* salt, and *tzopilotl,* it is used to cure swollen throats (VI:10).

Tzopilotl [i.e., *tzopilōtl*] (a thing hung over filth, i.e., a turkey vulture, but here referring to a plant). A compound noun: embed, (TZO)-TL, "filth, dirt, sweat"; matrix,

(PIL-Ō)-TL, "a hung thing," a patientive noun from TLA-(PIL-OA), "to hang something up." *Swietenia humilis* (Díaz 1976:197). A tree up to ten meters high, with poisonous seeds six to nine centimeters long. The family includes mahogany (Standley 1920-26: 559–60). Use in the *Treatise:* mixed with *tomatl* juice and *tequixquitl* or salt, *tzopilotl* is used for swollen throats (VI:10). It is used as an enema for stomach pain and body fatigue or pain (VI:31). Use in other sixteenth-century sources: it dissolves tumors, eases the chest, and alleviates ulcers (Hernández 1959a:144).

Xiuhcohcolin [i.e., *xiuhcohcōlin*] (turquoise-convoluted-thing). A compound noun: embed (XIHUI)-TL, "turquoise, grass"; matrix, (COH-CŌL)-IN, "a convoluted thing," from (CŌL)-LI, "a curved or bent thing." An herb. Use in the *Treatise:* mixed with three other herbs in water, it is used for fevers (VI:29). Use in other sixteenth-century sources: its root causes vomiting, and its juice cures ulcers of the mouth and cures the eyes (Hernández 1959b:215).

Xochimecatl [i.e., *xōchimecatl*] (flower-rope). A compound noun: embed, (XŌCHI)-TL, "flower"; matrix, (MECA)-TL, "rope." An herb. Use in the *Treatise:* mixed with three other herbs in water, it is used for fevers (VI:29).

Yauhtli, see *iyauhtli.*

Yellow root, see *tlacopahtli.*

Yetl, see *iyetl.*

APPENDIX E

Place-Names Mentioned in the *Treatise*

Acapulco (modern location: Acapulco de Juárez, Guerrero). Originally a subject of the Aztecs, it came under Spanish domination in the spring of 1523. It became a secular parish in the Archbishopric of Mexico sometime before 1569 (Gerhard 1972:39–41). Nahuatl etymology: *Ācapōlco,* "Place of the Large Reeds"; *lit.*, "Reed-large-place," from (ĀCA)-TL, "reed," plus -PŌL (affective suffix), "contemptibly large," plus -CO (relational noun), "place."

Amilpas (modern location: Cuautla Amilpas, Morelos). Originally a subject of the Aztecs, it came under Spanish domination in April, 1521. At first it was made up of settlements that were formerly subject to Oaxatepec. Dominicans established themselves there in the 1580s. Amilpas is in the Archbishopric of Mexico (Gerhard 1972:91–93; Riley 1973:133). Nahuatl etymology: *Āmīlpan,* "Area of Irrigated Fields," *lit.*, "Water-field-surface"; from (A)-TL, "water," plus (MĪL)-LI, "cultivated field," plus -PAN (relational noun), "surface."

Atenanco, see *Atenango.*

Atenango, in the precinct of Tlalapan (modern location: Atenango del Río, Guerrero). Perhaps independent of the Aztecs, it came under Spanish domination in September, 1520. From ca. 1600 a secular curate lived there. Atenango is in the Archbishopric of Mexico (Gerhard 1972:110–13). Nahuatl etymology: *Ātenānco,* "Place of the Eaves," *lit.*, "Water-wall-place"; from (Ā)-TL, "water," plus (TENĀMI)-TL, "wall" [(Ā-TENĀMI)-TL, "eaves overhang"], plus -CO (relational noun), "place."

Cacahuatepec (modern location: Cacahuatepec, Guerrero). One of four Yope states which were independent of the Aztec empire, it came under Spanish domination in the spring of 1523. A *vicario* was established in Cacahuatepec in 1611; it was in the Archbishopric of Mexico before 1569, then in the Bishopric of Tlaxcala (Gerhard 1972: 39–41). Nahuatl etymology: *Cacahuatepēc,* "Place of Cacao-bean Mountain," *lit.*, "Cacao-bean-mountain-place"; from (CACAHUA)-TL, "cacao bean," plus (TEPĒ)-TL, "mountain," plus -C (relational noun), "place."

Chietla, province of (modern location: Chietla, Puebla). Originally a subject of the Aztecs, it came under Spanish domination in September, 1520. A Franciscan monastery was built there in 1550; seventeen years later it was transferred to Augustinians. It was a Dominican *doctrina* in the seventeenth century. Chietla is in the Bishopric of Tlaxcala (Gerhard 1972:110; Mota y Escobar 1945:296). Nahuatl etymology: *Chietlān,* "Chia-seed-side"; from (CHIAN)-Ø, "chia seed," plus -TLAN (relational noun), "side."

Chilapa (modern location: Chilapa de Álvarez, Guerrero). Originally a subject of the Aztecs, it came under Spanish domination in the summer of 1521. Augustinians founded a *doctrina* there in 1533. It is in the Bishopric of Tlaxcala (Gerhard 1972:111–13; Mota y Escobar 1945:271). Nahuatl etymology: *Chīlāpan,* "Area of Red-pepper-water," *lit.*, "Red-pepper-water-surface," from (CHĪL)-LI, "red pepper" plus (Ā)-TL, "water," plus -PAN (relational noun), "surface."

Chilapan, see *Chilapa.*

Comala, in the district of Atenango, Guerrero. Originally a subject of the Aztecs, it came under Spanish domination in the summer of 1521. It is in the Archbishopric of Mexico (Gerhard 1972:111–12). Nahuatl etymology: *Comāllān,* "Griddle-side," from (COMĀL)-LI, "griddle (earthenware dish for baking maize tortillas)," plus -TLAN (relational noun), "side."

Comallan, see *Comala.*

Coyuca, in the province of Acapulco (modern location: Coyuca de Benítez, Guerrero).

Originally a subject of the Aztecs, it came under Spanish domination in the spring of 1523. Coyuca is in the Archbishopric of Mexico (Gerhard 1972:39–41). Nahuatl etymology: *Coyocāc,* "Hole-water-place," from (COYO-C)-TLI, "hole," plus (Ā)-TL, "water," plus -C (relational noun), "place."

Cuauhchimalla, near Tetelpan, in the Amilpas, Morelos. Originally a subject of the Aztecs, it came under Spanish domination in April, 1521. It is in the Archbishopric of Mexico (Gerhard 1972:94). Nahuatl etymology: *Cuauhchīmallān,* "Wood-shield-side," from (CUAHUI)-TL, "wood," plus (CHĪMAL)-LI, "shield," plus -TLAN (relational noun), "side."

Cuernavaca (originally Quauhnahuac, modern location, Cuernavaca, Morelos). Originally a subject of the Aztecs, it came under Spanish domination in 1521. Franciscans built a convent there in 1525 and were followed within a decade by Dominicans and Augustinians. It is in the Archbishopric of Mexico (Gerhard 1972:94–96; Riley 1973: 14–16). Nahuatl etymology: *Cuauhnāhuac,* "Place in the Vicinity of Trees," *lit.,* "Tree-vicinity-place," from (CUAHUI)-TL, "tree," plus (NĀHUA-C) (relational noun), "vicinity-place."

Cuetlaxxochitla (in modern Guerrero). Perhaps independent of the Aztecs, it came under Spanish domination in the summer of 1521. There was a secular curate at nearby Atenango. It is in the Archbishopric of Mexico (Gerhard 1972:111–13). Nahuatl etymology: *Cuetlaxxōchitlān,* "Leather-flower-side," from (CUETLAX)-TLI, "leather," plus (XŌCHI)-TL, "flower," plus -TLAN (relational noun), "side."

Cuetlaxxochitlan, see *Cuetlaxxochitla.*

Hoapan, see *Ohuapan.*

Huitzoco (modern location: Huitzuco de los Figueroa, Guerrero). Originally a subject of the Aztecs, it came under Spanish domination in 1521–22. At first it was probably an Augustinian area, but by 1570 a secular parish had been established there. Huitzoco is in the Archbishopric of Mexico (Gerhard 1972:146–47). Nahuatl etymology: *Huitzōcco,* "Footplow-place," from (HUITZŌC)-TLI, "footplow," plus -CO (relational suffix), "place."

Iguala, in the region of the Mines of Taxco (modern location: Iguala, Guerrero). Originally a subject of the Aztecs, it came under Spanish domination in 1521–22. By 1545 it was probably an Augustinian area, but by 1570 a secular parish had been established there. Iguala is in the Archbishopric of Mexico (Gerhard 1972:146–47). Nahuatl etymology: *Yohuallān,* "Night-side," from (YOHUA-L)-LI, "night," plus -TLAN (relational noun), "side."

Marquisate, landholdings of the Marquesado del Valle, originally belonging to Cortés. In the *Treatise,* this refers to the landholdings in Morelos, which encompassed virtually the entire state.

Mayanala, in the district of Tepecuacuilco (modern location: Mayanalan, Guerrero). Originally a subject of the Aztecs, it came under Spanish domination in 1521–22. It is in the Archbishopric of Mexico (Gerhard 1972:146–48). Nahuatl etymology: *Mayānallān,* "Starved-man-side," from (MAYĀNA-L)-LI, "starved man, hungry man," plus -TLAN (relational noun), "side."

Mescaltepec (modern location: in Guerrero). Originally a subject of the Aztecs, it came under Spanish domination in the spring of 1523. It was probably within the secular parish of Acapulco (Gerhard 1972:39–41). Nahuatl etymology: *Mexcaltepēc,* "Place of Cooked Maguey," *lit.,* "Cooked-maguey-place," from (ME-XCA-L)-LI, "cooked maguey," plus (TEPĒ)-TL, "mountain," plus -C (relational noun), "place."

Mexico (modern location: Mexico City, Federal District). Originally Tenochtitlan, the Aztec capital, it was conquered in August, 1521. It became the seat of the Archbishopric of Mexico (Gerhard 1972:180–81). Nahuatl etymology: *Mēxihco,* "Place of the Navel of the Moon," from (MĒX-XĪC)-TLI [from (MĒTZ)-TLI, "moon," plus (XĪC)-TLI, "navel," since /¢/ + /š/ > /šš/; the reason for the shift of *c* to *h* is not clear, but, given that shift, the replacement of *ī* by *i* is automatic since a long vowel followed by a glottal stop becomes short] "the navel of the moon," plus -co (relational noun), "place."

Meztitlan (modern location: Mestitlan de la Sierra, Hidalgo). A state independent of the Aztecs, it submitted to Cortés during the seige of Tenochtitlan, but rebelled until finally subdued in 1524. Augustinians were established in the area in 1536 and retained it until the 1750s. Meztitlan is in the Archbishopric of Mexico (Gerhard 1972:183–86). The location referred to in the text is the *Sierra de Meztitlan* (the Mountains of Meztitlan), where the town of Meztitlan is situated. Nahuatl etymology: *Mētztitlān*, "Moon-side," from (MĒTZ)-TLI, "moon," plus -TI- (connective infix), plus -TLAN (relational noun), "side."

Nahui-Tochco (modern location: Nahuituxco, Puebla). Originally a subject of the Aztecs, it came under Spanish domination in late 1520. It was a subject of Chiautla, which originally had a secular priest. An Augustinian monastery was founded in Chiautla in 1550. It is in the Bishopric of Tlaxcala (Gerhard 1972:108–109). Nahuatl etymology: *Nāhui-Tōchco*, "Place of Four Rabbit," which consists of the calendrical name *Nāhui-Tōchtli*, from (NĀHUI)-∅, "four," and (TŌCH)-TLI, "rabbit," plus -CO (relational noun), "place."

Ocuillohcan. A town located near Nahui-Tochco in the province of Chietla. Nahuatl etymology: *Ocuillohcān*, "a place characterized by worms," from the preterit agentive noun (OCUIL-LOH-∅)-∅, "one that has become covered with worms" [from (OCUIL)-IN, "worm," plus the preterit tense theme of *TLA-(YOA), "to own something in abundance"], plus (CĀ-N)-∅, "place."

Ohuapan, district of (modern location: San Agustín Oapan, Guerrero). Originally a subject of the Aztecs, it came under Spanish domination in the summer of 1521. Ohuapan was within the secular parish of Zumpango in 1570. A new *doctrina* was established in 1605 in connection with the *congregaciones*. It is in the Archbishopric of Mexico (Gerhard 1972:316–17). Nahuatl etymology: *Ohuapan*, "Area of the Green Maize Stalks," *lit.*, "Green-maize-stalk-surface," from (OHUA)-TL, "green maize stalk," plus -PAN (relational noun), "surface."

Ozomahtlan (modern location: Osomatlan, Guerrero). Originally a subject of the Aztecs, it came under Spanish domination in 1521. It may have been in the secular parish of Zumpango. It is in the Archbishopric of Mexico (Gerhard 1972:316–17). Nahuatl etymology: *Ozomahtlān*, "Monkey-side," from (OZOMAH)-TLI, "monkey," plus -TLAN (relational noun), "side."

Santiago (original Nahuatl name unknown), in the district of Atenango. Perhaps independent of the Aztecs, it came under Spanish domination in September, 1520. It is in the Archbishopric of Mexico (Gerhard 1972:110–13).

Tasmalaca (modern location: Santa Ana Tasmalaca, Guerrero). Originally a subject of the Aztecs, it came under Spanish domination in 1521–22. The first clergy at nearby Iguala were seculars, but Augustinians founded a monastery not far away at Tepecuacuilco in 1545. A secular parish was established in Tasmalaca in 1570. Tasmalaca is in the Archbishopric of Mexico (Gerhard 1972:146–47). Nahuatl etymology: *Tlachmalacac*, "Ballcourt-spindle-place," from (TLACH)-TLI, "ballcourt," plus (MALACA)-TL, "spindle," plus -c (relational noun), "place."

Taxco, Mines of (modern location: Taxco de Alarcón, Guerrero). Originally a subject of the Aztecs, it came under Spanish domination in 1521 or 1522. It was served by Franciscans; a secular priest was there from the 1530s on. Taxco is in the Archbishopric of Mexico (Gerhard 1972:252–54; Riley 1973:17). Nahuatl etymology: *Tlachco*, "Ballcourt-place," from (TLACH)-TLI, "ballcourt," plus -co (relational noun), "place."

Tecuaquilco, in the district of Atenango, Guerrero. Originally a subject of the Aztecs, it came under Spanish domination in the summer of 1521. Tecuaquilco is in the Archbishopric of Mexico (Gerhard 1972:111). Nahuatl etymology: *Tecuācuīlco*, "Statue-place," from (TE-CUĀ-CUĪ-L)-LI, "statue, idol, image" [from (TE)-TL, "rock," plus (CUĀI)-TL, "head," plus (CUĪ-L)-LI, "taken thing"], plus -co (relational noun), "place."

Temazcallan, near Huitzoco, Guerrero (?). Nahuatl etymology: *Temazcallān,* "Steam-bathing-house-side," from (TEMA-Z)-TLI, "steam-bathing," plus (CAL)-LI, "house," plus -TLAN (relational noun), "side."

Temimiltzinco, in the Amilpas, Morelos. Originally a subject of the Aztecs, it came under Spanish domination in April, 1521. A subject of Cuernavaca, it was probably under Franciscan control by 1525, and possibly Dominican after 1580 (Gerhard 1972: 94-97; Riley 1973:62). Nahuatl etymology: *Temimiltzinco,* "Stone-column-little-place," i.e., "little-stone-column-place," from (TE)-TL, "rock, stone," plus (MIMIL)-LI, "columnar thing," plus -TZIN (affective suffix), "little, dear," plus -CO (relational noun), "place."

Teocaltzinco (modern location: San Juan Teocalcingo, Guerrero). Originally a subject of the Aztecs, it came under Spanish domination in the summer of 1521. It was a secular parish from ca. 1600. Teocaltzinco is in the Archbishopric of Mexico (Gerhard 1972: 111-13). Nahuatl etymology: *Teōcaltzinco,* "God-house-little-place," i.e., "Little-temple-place," from (TEŌ)-TL, "god," plus (CAL)-LI, "house," plus -TZIN (affective suffix), "little, dear," plus -CO (relational noun), "place."

Tepecuacuilco (modern location: Tepecoacuilco de Trujano, Guerrero). Originally a subject of the Aztecs, it came under Spanish domination in 1521-22. Augustinians founded a monastery there in 1545, the monastery was secularized in 1563 or 1566. By 1570 it was a secular parish. Tepecuacuilco is in the Archbishopric of Mexico (Gerhard 1972:146-48). Nahuatl etymology: *Tepēcuācuīlco,* "Mountain-head-taken-place," from (TEPĒ)-TL, "mountain," plus (CUĀI)-TL, "head," plus (CUĪ-L)-LI, "taken thing," plus -CO (relational noun), "place." A *cuācuīlli* was an official who took charge of the sacrificed bodies and carried them to the place in the temple where they were dismembered.

Tepecuaquilco, see *Tepecuacuilco.*

Tepoztlan (modern location: Tepoztlan, Morelos). Originally a subject of the Aztecs, it came under Spanish domination in April, 1521. Dominicans built a monastery there in 1556. Tepoztlan is in the Archbishopric of Mexico (Gerhard 1972:94-96). Nahuatl etymology: *Tepoztlān,* "Copper-side," from (TEPOZ)-TLI, "copper," plus -TLAN (relational noun), "side."

Tetelpan, in the Amilpas, Morelos. Originally a subject of the Aztecs, it came under Spanish domination in April, 1521. It was a subject of Cuernavaca and thus probably was under Franciscan control by 1525 and probably Dominican after 1580. Tetelpan is in the Archbishopric of Mexico (Gerhard 1972:94-97; Riley 1973:62). Nahuatl etymology: *Tetelpan,* "Area of Rock-piles," *lit.,* "Rock-pile-surface," from (TE-TEL)-LI, "rock pile," plus -PAN (relational noun), "surface."

Teteltzinco, barrio of Ohuapan, Guerrero. Originally a subject of the Aztecs, it came under Spanish domination in April, 1521. At first it was in the jurisdiction of Iguala, but was transferred to Zumpango between 1582 and 1593, and to the jurisdiction of Acapulco ca. 1600; it was in the secular parish of Zumpango. A new *doctrina* was established in nearby Ohuapan in 1605. Teteltzinco is in the Archbishopric of Mexico (Gerhard 1972:316-17). Nahuatl etymology: *Teteltzinco,* "Rock-pile-little-place," i.e., "Little-rock-pile-place," from (TE-TEL)-LI, "rock pile," plus -TZIN (affective suffix), "little, dear," plus -CO (relational noun), "place."

Tlaltizapan (modern location: San Miguel Tlaltizapan, Morelos). Originally a subject of the Aztecs, it came under Spanish domination in April, 1521. A subject of Yautepec, it was probably served by the Dominicans, who were established there by 1550 and had founded a monastery there by 1591. Tlaltizapan is in the Archbishopric of Mexico (Gerhard 1972:96-98; Riley 1973:17, 84). Nahuatl etymology: *Tlāltīzapan,* "Area of Land Chalk," *lit.,* "Land-chalk-surface," from (TLĀL)-LI, "land," plus (TĪZA)-TL, "chalk, white clay," plus -PAN (relational noun), "surface."

Tlapa, province of (modern location: Tlapa de Comonfort, Guerrero). Originally a subject of the Aztecs, it came under Spanish domination in 1521 or 1522. It rebelled several times between 1523 and 1535. Secular priests were in this mining district by the early 1530s and probably earlier. Augustinians were established in Tlapa in 1535; it was an Augustinian *doctrina* in the seventeenth century. Tlapa is in the Bishopric of Tlaxcala (Gerhard 1972:321–23; Mota y Escobar 1945:263; Riley 1973:29). Nahuatl etymology: *Tlapahcān*, "Dyer's-place," from (TLA-PAH-ø)-QUI, "dyer" [from the verb TLA-(PA), "to dye something"], plus (CĀ-N)-ø, "place."

Tlayacapan (modern location: Tlayacapan, Morelos). Originally a subject of the Aztecs, it came under Spanish domination in April, 1521. Augustinians worked in the area, and Dominicans founded a monastery there in 1554. Tlayacapan is in the Archbishopric of Mexico (Gerhard 1972:102–105; Riley 1973:14). Nahuatl etymology: *Tlayacapan*, "Area of Something's Nose," *lit.*, "Something's-nose-surface," from TLA-, "something," plus (YACA)-TL, "nose," plus -PAN (relational noun), "surface."

Xicotlan (modern location: Xicotlan, Puebla). Originally a subject of the Aztecs, it came under Spanish domination in 1520. In 1550 an Augustinian monastery-parish was founded in Chiautla, from which Xicotlan was served until the eighteenth century. Xicotlan is in the Bishopric of Tlaxcala (Gerhard 1972:108–109). Nahuatl etymology: *Xīcohtlān*, "Bee-side," from (XĪCOH)-TLI, "bee," plus -TLAN (relational noun), "side."

Xiuhtepec (in modern Morelos). Originally a subject of the Aztecs, it came under Spanish domination in April, 1521. A Franciscan parish had been established there by the 1570s. Xiuhtepec is in the Archbishopric of Mexico (Gerhard 1972:94–96; Riley 1973:16). Nahuatl etymology: *Xiuhtepēc*, "Place of Turquoise Mountain," from (XI-HUI)-TL, "turquoise, grass," plus (TEPĒ)-TL, "mountain," plus -C (relational noun), "place."

Xoxouhtla, in the Amilpas, Morelos. Originally a subject of the Aztecs, it came under Spanish domination in April, 1521. It was a subject of Cuernavaca and was probably served by the Franciscans. Xoxouhtla is in the Archbishopric of Mexico (Gerhard 1972: 96–99). Nahuatl etymology: *Xoxōuhtlān*, "Green-side," from (XO-XŌ-UH)-TLI, "green thing," the past patientive noun from the verbstem (XO-XŌ-HUI), "to become green" [or possibly the embed is (XO-XŌ-HUI)-TL, "green thing," the present patientive noun from the same verbstem], plus -TLAN (relational noun), "side."

Yauhtepec (modern location: Yautepec, Morelos). Originally a subject of the Aztecs, it came under Spanish domination in April, 1521. A Dominican monastery was erected there ca. 1550. Yauhtepec is in the Archbishopric of Mexico (Gerhard 1972:94–96). Nahuatl etymology: *Iyāuhtepēc*, "Place of *Iyauhtli* Mountain," from (IYĀUH)-TLI, "sweet-scented marigold" [see *iyauhtli* in Appendix D], plus (TEPĒ)-TL, "mountain," plus -C (relational noun), "place."

APPENDIX F:

Paraphrases of the Incantations in the *Treatise*

There are a number of formulaic expressions that occur in the incantations in either similar or identical wording. The following eight are of noticeable importance:

1. Incitement: *Tlā cuēl!* ("Let it be soon!"). An incitement is used to mark a new unit in an incantation (a new addressee, a new motif, a new movement, a new phase). Such marking is optional.
2. Speaker-identification: *Nohmatca nehhūatl, ninābualtēuctli.* ("It is I in person. I am the *nahualli*-lord"). This kind of formula permits a number of further boastful items that establish the speaker's credentials for authority.
3. Summons: *Tlā xihuāllauh* ("Come"). Usually this is followed by a vocative, though in certain instances the pattern is reversed, and the vocative precedes. There are several versions of the formula: the plural, *Tlā xihuālhuiān;* the honorific, *Tlā xihuālmohuīca,* etc. Ordinarily a summons is followed by a command, a question, or simply a comment. Occasionally when this is not the case, the lack of a further address to the summoned entity signals that the speaker is engaged in physical activity with it. Incidentally, it should be understood that, when the speaker summons, for example, tobacco, he is not speaking to the material tobacco (which is in fact there at hand) but rather to its spiritual dimension.
4. Demand for attention: *Tleh ticmati?* ("What do you know?", i.e., "Pay attention!"). This may either follow or precede a related command, question, or comment.
5. A warning about shameful failure: *Mā timopīnāuhtihti* ("Beware of bringing shame upon yourself").
6. An announcement of presence: *Ca ōnihuāllah* ("I have come").
7. A warning not to bring hurt: *Ahmō tinēchēlēhuiz* ("You will not covet me"; i.e., "Do not hurt me"). Note that a future tense form can function as an equivalent of a command.
8. Rhetorical questions about immediate fulfillment of desires or purposes.

In addition to the formulaic expressions, there are less rigidly worded expressions that can be called rhetorical strategies, such as shaming tactics, flattery, promises, threats, warnings, admissions of poverty as a ploy for compassion, word magic including such things as the presentation of an imagined future success as if it were a present reality, the presentation of the speaker's project, rhetorical questions and answers, real questions, and many others.

In the following presentation of each incantation, the use of these formulas and these rhetorical strategies will be pointed out. The paraphrases should make the underlying structure apparent, showing the logical organization of the incantations and the careful phrasing, in which each step is a rhetorical maneuver with a specific purpose. For remarks on the nonverbal activity that accompanies the incantations, see Ruiz de Alarcón's commentary (not all incantations have such commentary). In the paraphrases, a notation such as "sentence 1:2" stands for "segment one, sentence two" of the Treatise and chapter indicated at the beginning of the paraphrase. The sentences are numbered from the sentence divisions established in our rewritten version and its translation (the rewritten Nahuatl and its English translation have identical sentence divisions). Also, a slash indicates the end of a segment, and two slashes mark the end of a phase in the development of the incantation. The number of incantations contained in each chapter is indicated at the beginning. It should be noted that at times there is a discrepancy between this number and the number of incantations indicated in the manuscript version.

II:1 (one incantation)

Structure: two phases (phase 1: segments 1–4; phase 2: segments 5–6). *Speaker:* a traveler (roles: Quetzalcoatl, Matl, Yaotl, Moquehqueloatzin). *Addressee:* self; various allies (gods, weapons, road, the speaker's legs). *Antagonist:* brigands. *Place:* lonely road. *Intention:* to inspire self-confidence. *Purpose:* to overcome brigands.

The speaker begins with a strong boastful self-identification (segment 1). / He next declares himself ready (sentence 2:1) and predicts that he will fight his assailants (sentence 2:2). He immediately summons the gods as allies to help him fight (sentence 2:3), explaining (with the implicit command "Notice that . . .") that his assailants are coming (sentence 2:4). He confidently predicts that the god-allies and he will fight them (sentence 2:5), since the assailants are only human (sentence 2:6). / He contrasts their mere humanity with his own supernatural nature (sentence 3:1) and explains that he has his weapons (staff, stones, knife) ready (sentence 3:2) and that the weapons will become bloody, a prediction that constitutes a command to the weapons (sentence 3:3). He immediately backs up the implicit command with a boastful threat of his power to the weapons (sentence 3:4). / He next turns to boast that his hands and body will be insensible to the pain inflicted by his assailants (sentence 4:1) and that these will not strike him since he is the god Quetzalcoatl (sentence 4:2), whereupon he repeats his boastful self-identification (sentence 4:3–4). He again contrasts his power to his enemies' weakness (sentence 4:5) and claims that their weapons are insignificant (sentence 4:6–7). // The second phase of the incantation begins with the speaker issuing a series of summons, first to the road (sentence 5:1), then to his legs (sentence 5:2), then, repeating an earlier summons, to the god-allies (sentence 5:3 repeats the summons part of sentence 2:3), then to all his spiritual allies (sentence 5:4), explaining that he summons them for the approaching fight (sentence 5:5). / He now summons the land (sentence 6:1) and commands her to make the way easy for him (sentence 6:2). He summons his staff (sentence 6:3) and predicts that it will draw blood (sentence 6:4). He commands it to strike his enemies' side (sentence 6:5). He next summons his knife (sentence 6:6) and predicts that it will draw blood (sentence 6:7). He ends the incantation with a summons to the road (sentence 6:8), thus indicating that he is now ready to move against his assailants.

This incantation exhibits faith in the power of words themselves since the speaker is not a "professional" sorcerer. He is using the incantation not to help someone else but to help himself (this is the same as in the *tlameme*'s incantation in II:4). Sentence 2:4 is logically prior to segment 1 since it announces the approach of the brigands, but the initiating event (the attack itself) has such pragmatic force that it does not require verbal recognition. When the approach is verbally recognized in sentence 2:4 (carrying the implicit command "Notice that . . ."), it functions as an argument to convince the summoned gods to intervene. Apparently the speaker begins by talking to himself, so that segment 1 sets the general intent of the incantation as a whole, the firming up of the speaker's courage and self-confidence. Since the entire incantation, on a secondary level, is self-oriented, it is appropriate that at no point does the speaker address his assailants. There is no indication that he says anything even in their hearing. The speech is apparently meant to be heard only by the power-entities that are summoned. A central element in the rhetoric of self-encouragement is the derogation of the enemy as both merely human and feminine (sentences 2:2, 2:4, 2:6, 4:1, 4:5, 4:6) in contrast to the praise of self as supernatural (segment 1 and sentences 3:1, 4:1-4); the contrast becomes explicit in 2:6 and 3:1. It is also evident in the contraposition of Yaotl (i.e., Tezcatl-Ihpoca) (segment 1 and sentence 4:4) and Xochiquetzal (sentence 4:6), where the aggressive male principle is contrasted to the coquettish female principle. The two phases of the incantation (segments 1-4 and segments 5-6) differ in tone. The first phase is an appraisal of the danger and consequently has a preparatory quality. Its only summons is that to the gods (sentence 2:3); the weapon-allies are not addressed but only spoken about (sentences 3:2-4). The second phase is more urgent since the physical action is more imminent. It contains eight summonses, the first four and the last one of which (sentences 5:1-4 and 6:8) are absolute (i.e., unaccompanied by a command, question, or comment), while those to the weapon-allies (i.e., land, staff, and knife—the crucial physical participants in the impending fight) are accompanied by specific instructions. The second phase is neatly demarcated by the fact that it opens and closes with the same summons (sentences 5:1 and 6:8). The two phases are effectively linked not only by the repetition of the summons to the gods (sentences 2:3 and 5:3) but also by the transformation of the third-person mention of the staff and the knife (sentence 3:2) to the second-person address (sentences 6:3-7), with a concomitant change in the phrasing of the "bloodying" motif.

II:2 (five incantations)

First incantation (segments 1-2). *Structure:* two phases (phase 1: segment 1; phase 2: segment 2). *Speaker:* hypnotist (roles: Moyohualihtoatzin, Xolotl, Capanilli). *Addressee:* the hypnotic trance, knife. *Victim:* woman victim and her guardians. *Place:* not specified, but presumably within the hearing of the victim. *Intention:* to put the woman into a hypnotic trance. *Purpose:* to take sexual advantage of the woman.

The speaker begins with a boastful self-identification (sentences 1:1-2) and states his project of hypnotizing his victim (sentence 1:3). He now summons the hypnotic trance (sentence 1:4) and immediately claims that he has attained his purpose (sentence 1:5) and boastfully identifies himself (sentence 1:6). He next reports on the difficulty that he had in abducting his victim from her protectors and that in order to succeed he also hypnotized them and ends the report with a boast about his disregard for propriety (sentence 1:7). // The speaker now begins the second phase of the incantation by summoning his knife (sentence 2:1) and ordering it to go test the depth of the trance (sentence 2:2), a test that is accomplished by the speaker pressing the knife point against the victim's skin. He now turns again to the problem of abducting the girl from her protectors and states that they will not harm him while he is hypnotizing her (sentences 2:3-4). He next predicts that he will take her into the deepest trance (sentences 2:5–6). He ends by boastfully identifying himself and predicting that he will hypnotize the protectors, then boasts yet again of his identity and predicts that he will take them into a deep trance (sentence 2:7).

It is rather strange that the person being hypnotized is never spoken to directly but that presumably both she and her protectors (who must also be put to sleep) are meant to overhear the incantation. The first phase of the incantation (segment 1) initiates the hypnosis; the second phase (segment 2) opens by testing for trance depth, after which the speaker proceeds to deepen the trance. In the first phase the speaker's strategy is to induce the trance by claiming that it has already happened. The speaker thus reinforces his stance of power, self-confidence, and swaggering pride by making his undertaking seem irresistible. The hypnosis is imaged as an abduction of mythological proportions, and the girl's protectors may or may not be real. In the second phase, after the testing for trance depth, there is a replay of what in the first phase was presented as accomplished fact, but now it is set forth as a project yet to be realized.

Second incantation (segment 3). *Speaker:* hypnotist (role: Yohuallahuantzin, i.e., the deepest trance state). *Addressee:* not specified. *Victim:* woman victim and her guardians. *Place:* not specified, but presumably within the hearing of the victim. *Intention:* to reverse the effect of the first incantation. *Purpose:* to awaken woman from trance.

The speaker begins by denying that he has hypnotized the people (sentence 3:1), and then, after an exclamatory call for arousal (sentence 3:2), he implicitly accepts the responsibility for having hypnotized them by declaring that he is returning them from the trance, boastfully identifying himself as the deepest trance (sentence 3:3).

The incantation is curiously split against itself, with the speaker first taking on a not-guilty pose (there are four occurrences of *ahmō,* "not," two of these participating in the clause *ahmō nelli,* "it is not true") and then surreptitiously accepting his responsibility by reassuming the earlier authoritarian stance of the first incantation. The first incantation is exceptional in the collection since its speaker is seeking a morally questionable goal of taking advantage of someone (that is, he is in the role of aggressor against another person), and the denial of guilt in the first sentence of this second incantation may be reflecting this situation.

Third incantation (segment 4). *Speaker:* person preparing for sleep. *Addressee:* sleeping mat. *Antagonist:* evil spirit. *Place:* inside house at night. *Intention:* to arouse protective stance of sleeping mat. *Purpose:* to ward off evil spirit during the night.

The speaker begins by summoning his mat (sentence 4:1) and, as an implicit command that it devour any attacker, reminds it of its hunger and thirst (sentence 4:2), warning that the evil spirit is coming (sentence 4:3). He next expresses his puzzlement about why the evil spirit would want to harm him who is only a poor nonentity (sentences 4:4–7).

The pose of weakness in this incantation is unusual. It is meant to discourage the evil spirit (whom the speaker apparently assumes is overhearing his speech to the sleeping mat) by pointing to the meaninglessness, the profitlessness, of the attack. The pose is as much a rhetorical ploy as the usual authoritative pose found in other incantations. It perhaps is justified by the fact that the speaker will be helpless while asleep and, at the same time that he discourages the attack, he appeals to the protective compassion of the bed to whom he entrusts himself. His vulnerability perhaps also prompts him to refrain from boastfully identifying himself.

Fourth incantation (segment 5). *Speaker:* person preparing for sleep. *Addressee:* pillow. *Antagonist:* evil spirit. *Place:* inside house at night. *Intention:* to arouse protective stance of pillow. *Purpose:* to ward off evil spirit during the night.

The speaker begins by summoning his pillow (sentence 5:1) and, as an implicit command that it devour any attacker, reminds it that it is hungry and thirsty (sentence 5:2).

Fifth incantation (segment 6). *Speaker:* person awakening from sleep. *Addressee:* sleeping mat. *Antagonist:* evil spirit. *Place:* inside house in the morning. *Intention:* to ascertain what happened during the night. *Purpose:* to gain peace of mind and to find out if countermeasures against an attack are needed.

The speaker begins by addressing his sleeping mat, asking it if the evil spirit has visited him during the night (sentence 6:1), and then asking more detailed questions about the possible visit (sentences 6:2-4). Presumably the questions would be accompanied by a careful inspection of the mat and the blankets in search for signs of a nocturnal attack.

II:3 (one incantation)

Structure: two phases (phase 1: segments 1–2; phase 2: segment 3). *Speaker:* woodcutter (role: *nahualli*-lord, Quetzalcoatl). *Addressee:* tobacco, tree. *Victim:* tree. *Place:* forest. *Intention:* to protect himself from getting hurt while cutting down a tree. *Purpose:* to cut down a tree.

The speaker begins with a summons to tobacco (segment 1), / followed by a demand for attention (sentence 2:1), followed in turn by a command inviting tobacco to enjoy itself (sentence 2:2). The announcement of the speaker's presence (sentence 2:3), coupled with the subsequent boasting self-identification (sentence 2:4), stands as a justification of the announcement of the possession of the ax (sentence 2:5). // The second phase begins abruptly with the speaker commanding the tree not to hurt his ax (sentence 3:1). He demands attention (sentence 3:2) and explains to the tree what he plans to do to it with the ax (sentence 3:3).

Phase 1 is concerned with the spiritual helper (tobacco), and phase 2 deals with the victim (the tree). The invitation to tobacco, seeking its spiritual assistance, seems to claim that what is going to happen is to be to its benefit, though the nature of this benefit is not explained. It is curious that there is no summons or address to the pragmatic helper (the ax); it is merely named and spoken about in the third person.

II:4 (one incantation)

Structure: four phases (phase 1: segments 1–2; phase 2: segments 3–5; phase 3: segment 6; phase 4: segment 7). *Speaker:* a *tlameme* (role: *nahualli*-lord, Quetzalcoatl). *Addressee:* sickness, tobacco, the sun, the load. *Place:* point of departure for the trip. *Intention:* to secure the cooperation of helper-allies and to render opponents ineffective. *Purpose:* to assure himself of a safe trip.

The speaker begins abruptly with an address to sickness, who is indirectly requested to rid the road of wild beasts (sentence 1:1). He then shifts abruptly and summons tobacco (sentence 1:2), and boastfully identifies himself (sentences 1:3–4). / There is another abrupt shift marked by an incitement (sentence 2:1) and a summons to the sun (sentence 2:2). In sentences 2:3–5, the speaker hints of a race between himself and the sun, a contest predicted to be won by the speaker. The speaker expresses his confidence in himself on the road (sentences 2:6–7) and then ends the first phase of the incantation with the symbolic apothesis of himself as the sun (sentence 2:8). // In the second phase, the speaker addresses his load, though there is no vocative to mark the shift, only the reference to testing and lifting (sentences 3:1–2) and the question to the load about its weight (sentence 3:3). / The speaker now again shifts abruptly and, after an incitement (sentence 4:1) again summons tobacco (sentence 4:2 is a repetition of sentence 1:2). This time, however, the speaker announces his presence (sentence 4:3) and boastfully identifies himself (sentence 4:4). He then boastfully predicts that he will carry the load, which is proclaimed to be as light as a feather (sentence 4:5). He then boasts of supernatural help and claims a supernatural nature (sentence 4:6). / He continues by contrasting the other carriers, who are merely human, with himself, who is supernatural (sentences 5:1–2), and by boastfully identifying himself (sentences 5:3–6). He ends this phase with a boast about his mythological strength and power (sentences 5:7–10). // The speaker begins the third phase of the incantation with an incitement (sentence 6:1), and again summons tobacco (sentence 6:2). He again announces his presence (sentence 6:3 repeats sentence 4:3) and vows to travel and carry the load (sentences 6:4–5). // The final phase of the incantation begins with an incitement (sentence 7:1) and a summons to the road (sentence 7:2), followed by a command to the land that it not harm the speaker (sentence 7:3). At this point, the speaker brings the incantation to an end by breaking off his address to the land and, shifting to a third-person reference to it, makes the gloating announcement that the land is no longer capable of acting against him (sentence 7:4).

The incantation is a fascinating study of the psychological defenses that the *tlameme* (porter) attempts to erect between himself and the dangers (wild animals) and hardships (heat of the sun, weight of the load, rough terrain) of his work. He pushes his insecurities into the background by creating a mythological image of himself that denies his own human frailty and enlists the aid of helpful allies, among the more important of which is tobacco, which is called on twice as a witness of the speaker's greatness. An important aspect of the *tlameme*'s struggle with his insecurity is the fragmented quality of the incantation, created by the speaker jumping from one addressee to another in seeking to bolster his courage. This does not mean, however, that the incantation lacks unity, since a compelling sense of urgency ties the whole together. The final sentence, which constitutes such an apt ending by presenting the subjugation of the terrain, is apparently addressed by the speaker to himself. It also constitutes an example of word magic in which the wished-for future is presented as an already accomplished fact.

II:5 (four incantations)

First incantation (segments 1–2). *Speaker:* lime maker (role: *nahualli*-lord). *Addressee:* the ax, the speaker's hands. *Victim:* the tree. *Place:* the forest. *Intention:* to secure the cooperation of the ax. *Purpose:* to obtain the tree for firewood without harm to self.

The speaker begins with an incitement (sentence 1:1) and then summons the ax (sentence 1:2), whom he introduces to the tree (sentence 1:3). The speaker shifts abruptly and addresses his hands, but without a vocative or summons to indicate the shift (the hands are named in sentence 2:1). The hands are commanded (by means of a future-tense statement) to cut down the tree (sentence 1:4). The speaker now again addresses the ax with a demand for attention (sentence 1:5), whereupon the speaker explains his intention of making lime (sentence 1:6), an explanation apparently intended to secure the ax's willing help. / In sentence 2:1, the ax is commanded not to hurt the fingers and toes or the hands and feet. To make the command compelling, the speaker boasts of their supernatural nature (sentence 2:2) and then boastfully identifies himself (sentences 2:3–4).

The incantation has a curious break after sentence 1:3, since the expected statement "whom you, ax, will hide [i.e., kill] and destroy" is not given. Instead, there is an abrupt shift to the hands (without naming them) and they are commanded to do what the ax should have been told to do, "hide [i.e., kill] [the tree], destroy it" (sentence 1:4). Possibly this sentence should have been in the second-person singular (with a continued reference to the ax), since sentence 1:5 returns to address the ax.

Second incantation (segment 3). *Speaker:* lime maker. *Addressee:* the firewood. *Victim:* the firewood. *Place:* the lime kiln. *Intention:* to secure the cooperation of the firewood. *Purpose:* to rig the lime kiln.

The speaker begins with an incitement (sentence 3:1) and a summons to the firewood (sentence 3:2). He commands it to place itself in the kiln (sentence 3:3) and explains what it will do there (sentence 3:4), promising the resultant creation of lime (sentence 3:5).

Third incantation (segment 4). *Addressee:* the limestone. *Victim:* the limestone. *Place:* the lime kiln. *Intention:* to secure the cooperation of the limestone. *Purpose:* to rig the lime kiln.

The speaker begins with an incitement (sentence 4:1) and summons the limestone (sentence 4:2). He explains what will happen (sentences 4:3–5) and, to compel compliance, he boastingly identifies himself (sentences 4:6–7), by which the explanation is converted into a command.

Fourth incantation (segments 5–8). *Speaker:* lime maker. *Addressee:* the fire, the wind. *Place:* the lime kiln. *Intention:* to secure the cooperation of the fire. *Purpose:* to produce the lime.

The speaker begins with an incitement (sentence 5:1) and a summons to the fire (sentence 5:2). / At this point, another summons is issued (sentence 6:1), but in the plural and to an unidentified addressee. In sentences 6:2–4, the fire is given an explanation of what is expected of it and in sentence 6:5 an explanation of the result. In sentence 6:6, the fire is indirectly urged to burn by being told that the firewood is awaiting it. This urging is backed up by a boasting self-identification (sentences 6:7–9). / The speaker's preoccupation with the fire is continued by his shifting to address the wind. He utters an incitement (sentence 7:1) and summons the wind (sentence 7:2), commanding it to hurry the fire (sentence 7:3). He expresses a nervous wish that the fire would hurry (sentence 7:4). / His nervousness is also evident in that he again summons the wind (sentence 8:1) and sends it to hurry the fire (sentence 8:2). The speaker's worried concern is expressed again in sentences 8:3–4, but then he ends the incantation neatly by confidently predicting that the lime will be produced (sentences 8:5–6).

There is probably an error in sentence 6:1 since at no other place in the collection is there an incitement sequence of specified summons in the singular plus an unspecified summons in the plural plus a sentence containing a reference to the entity specified in the first summons.

Notice that the division of the chapter into four separate incantations rests primarily on spatial and temporal considerations. The first incantation is clearly separate in that it occurs in the forest, and while the second, third, and fourth incantations all take place at the kiln, the activities, although occurring in a sequence, require more time than the words require for speaking.

II:6 (one incantation)

Structure: two phases (phase 1: segment 1; phase 2: segment 2). *Speaker* bird hunter (roles: Icnopiltzintli, Centeotl, Quetzalcoatl). *Addressee:* not specified. *Victim:* birds. *Place:* lakeshore or stream bank. *Intention:* to establish the speaker's justification and competence as a bird hunter. *Purpose:* to snare birds.

The speaker begins with a boasting self-identification (sentences 1:1–4). He then states his project of looking for birds (sentence 1:5). Immediately he exclaims that he has found them (sentences 1:6–7). // With this the second phase of the incantation begins with the speaker stating that he has brought the fowling net (sentence 2:1). He next sets forth his plan for erecting it (sentences 2:2–3) and states that he will wait for the birds (sentence 2:4).

The first phase deals with the establishment of authority and the explanation of why the speaker has come. The second phase presents the setting up of the net. In the first phase, sentences 1:6–7 may be word magic that seeks to assure success by claiming a future presence of the birds as a present reality. The last sentence (sentence 2:4) gives the actual present reality, one in which the birds are still being expected.

II:7 (three incantations)

First incantation (segment 1). *Speaker:* bee seeker. *Addressee:* sandals, maguey-fiber carrying sack. *Victim:* bees. *Place:* inside of house. *Intention:* to secure the cooperation of helper-allies. *Purpose:* to prepare for the bee-hunting expedition.

The speaker begins with an incitement (sentence 1:1) and then summons his sandals (sentence 1:2) and invites them to go with him on the road (sentence 1:3). The speaker now summons the ax (sentence 1:4) and invites it to go with him on the road (sentence 1:5). There now comes another incitement (sentence 1:6), after which the speaker summons the maguey-fiber carrying sack (sentence 1:7) and commands it to get ready (sentence 1:8), promising it that he will carry it into the woods and grasslands (sentence 1:9) and inviting it to seek the bees with him (sentence 1:10).

Second incantation (segments 2–3). *Speaker:* bee seeker (role: Ce-Coatl). *Addressee:* road, sandals. *Place:* on the road. *Intention:* to secure the cooperation of helper-allies. *Purpose:* to travel the right path in search of the bees.

The speaker begins by summoning the road (sentence 2:1), but says nothing more to it. Instead, he turns with a demand for attention to his sandals (sentence 2:2) and announces to them that he will use them in his travels (sentence 2:3). To give that announcement force, he next boastingly identifies himself and states his bee-hunting project (sentences 2:4-7). / This sentence develops into a rhetorical question-and-answer sequence about the distance to be traveled, with the answers serving as word magic that makes the distance short by emphatically (through repetition) stating it to be so (sentences 3:1–4). The speaker now states his project more expressively (sentence 3:5), saying that he has brought his ax which has come to do its duty (sentences 3:6–7). To make his statement more compelling, the speaker again boastfully identifies himself (sentences 3:8–9).

Third incantation (segments 4-6). *Speaker:* bee seeker (role: Icnopiltzintli, Motolinihcatzintli). *Addressee:* spiders, butterflies, lizards. *Victim:* the bees. *Place:* the bee hive. *Intention:* to convince the possible opponents not to interfere. *Purpose:* to get at the bees.

The speaker begins with a command that the obstacles (spiders, butterflies, lizards) get out of the way (sentence 4:1) and then issues a general warning for things not to side with the bees against him (sentence 4:2). / To give the warning a compelling force, he now announces his arrival and boastfully identifies himself (segment 5). / He next explains why he has come, mentioning his needs (sentence 6:1). This slight hint at a poverty motif permits him to end the incantation with a less authoritarian, more friendly tone. He suggests that he not be considered frightening (sentences 6: 2–3). He ends by using deception, stating in seeming innocence that he will carry the bees to see his wife (sentence 6:4).

At no point does the speaker speak directly to the bees. The closest he comes to direct address to them is in the general admonitions in sentences 6:2–3. Segments 7 and 8 are not incantatory and need no paraphrase.

II:8 (four incantations)

First incantation (segments 1–9). *Structure:* 3 phases (phase 1: segments 1–4; phase 2: segments 5–7; phase 3: segments 8–9). *Speaker:* deer hunter (roles: Icnopiltzintli, Centeotl). *Addressee:* tobacco, the land, the rope, the fire, the speaker's wife, household gods. *Victim:* deer. *Place:* inside the hunter's home. *Intention:* to enlist helper-allies. *Purpose:* to get things in order for the hunt.

The speaker begins with a summons to tobacco (sentence 1:1), a demand for attention (sentence 1:2), and a promise that the tobacco will soon be carried somewhere. / The speaker next summons the land (sentence 2:1) and undertakes a subversive campaign to irritate it against the deer and make it into an ally in the hunt (sentences

2:2-3). / The speaker next makes use of word magic, picturing the imagined distant hunting ground and the future erection of the snare as present inside his home (sentences 3:1-3). The image is given power by the speaker boastfully identifying himself (sentences 3:4-6). / The speaker now turns his attention to the rope and, without summoning it, undertakes the same kind of subversive campaign as he did earlier with the land, seeking to turn it against the deer to gain it as an ally (sentences 4:1–2). // Having set up the necessary alliances, the speaker now begins the second phase by turning his attention to cleaning up the house. He starts by summoning his spiritual ally, tobacco (sentence 5:1), thus returning to the position at the beginning of the incantation. This time after the demand for attention (sentence 5:2), the speaker issues general commands concerning cleaning up the house after the making of the snare (sentences 5:3-4), combined with a warning that he not be hurt (sentence 5:5), a warning justified by a claim to a supernatural nature (sentence 5:6). Addressing tobacco again and demanding attention (sentence 5:7), he advises it that it will soon be under way (sentence 5:8). He next summons the fire (sentence 5:9) and chidingly questions its treatment of the tobacco (sentence 5:10). / And having introduced the fire, he now turns his full attention to it. But first he invites tobacco to go with him and follow the fire (sentences 6:1–2), after which he issues a more expressive summons to the fire (sentence 6:3). But, surprisingly, at this point, he turns away from talking to the fire and talks instead about it, using highly descriptive, metaphorical language (sentences 6:4–7). / In sentences 7:1–2, however, he addresses it again by asking rhetorical questions, answering them in sentences 7:3-4 to assure it that it will be the first one to enjoy the success of the hunt. // The third phase begins in segment 8 as his preparations for departure near completion. He first reiterates his project and justifies his need to go hunting because of the wishes of both his wife and himself (sentences 8:1–5). He also points to his poverty and hunger (sentences 8: 6–8). And, having thus justified himself, he repeats his project (sentences 8:9–10 are repetitions of sentences 8:1 and 8:3), now strengthening it with rhetorical questions and answers about immediate fulfillment (sentences 8:11–13). In sentences 8:14–15, he states his intention to take his rope and set out, and in sentences 8:16–18, he again shows his concern for leaving the house clean and not upsetting anyone. / In sentence 9:1, he summons his wife, and in sentences 9:2–5, he ends the incantation by asking the household gods to protect the house and keep it peaceful and calm.

As the incantation develops, it becomes evident in the imagery that the house is a symbolic proxy for the hunting ground, since, while making preparations, the hunter imaginatively evokes the hunt and brings it into verbal existence; contrast the imaginary *nicān,* "here," in this incantation (sentences 3:1–3) with the real *nicān* in the third incantation (e.g., sentence 12:3). The importance of the hunter's concern for peace inside the house while he is away on the hunt thus becomes evident. Any disturbance in the place of the imaged hunt will automatically contaminate and disturb the real hunt. A concern for peace in the house is also found in II:15:2.

Second incantation (segment 10). *Speaker:* deer hunter (role: Centeotl). *Addressee:* land (i.e., terrain to be traveled over to reach the hunting ground). *Victim:* deer. *Place:* on the road to the hunting ground. *Intention:* to placate the land being traveled over. *Purpose:* to arrive safely at the hunting ground.

The speaker begins with a summons to the land (sentence 10:1), then expresses an aversion to offending it (sentence 10:2). Next, after boastingly identifying himself (sentences 10:3–4), he requests that the land make his travel easy (sentence 10:5).

Ruiz de Alarcón (in the commentary preceeding this segment) says that this incantation is spoken after the arrival at the hunting ground. This is *not* the case, however, since the incantation is addressed to the road, not to the hunting ground.

Third incantation (segments 11–18). *Speaker:* deer hunter (role: Icnopiltzintli, Centeotl). *Addressee:* mountains, the deer, the rope, the speaker's hands. *Victim:* the deer. *Place:* the hunting ground in the mountains. *Intention:* to create alliances and enlist the aid of the various helpers. *Purpose:* to capture the deer.

The speaker begins with a summons to the mountains (sentence 11:1), an announcement of arrival, a boastful self-identification, a description of his trip, and a plea for sympathy because of his suffering and tiredness (sentence 11:2). Notice that the last part of sentence 11:2 is a repetition of sentences 8:6-7. / The appeal for compassion is continued in sentence 12:1. But now the speaker begins to report the reality out in the field that matches the scenes imagined in his house. Sentence 12:2 (reporting his arrival) echoes sentence 3:2, the first part of sentence 12:3 (identifying the deer's home) repeats sentence 3:1 and the last part of it (naming the deer) echoes the last part of sentence 2:3, while sentences 12:4–5 (which explain his motives) replay sentences 8:4–5. / In sentence 13:1, the speaker reaffirms his purpose of capturing the deer, and in sentence 13:2 he reports on his setting up of the snare, combined with his claim to a parental right to the deer. / In sentence 14:1, the speaker begins a bit of word magic (seeking to talk the future into reality) by forbidding the deer to use another path, and, in sentences 14:2–5, he sets forth the contrary demand (couched in the future tense) that it will use the path where the snare is. / The word magic continues throughout segment 15 where the moment of capture is forecast. / At this point, the speaker turns to his helper-ally, the rope. He summons the rope (sentence 16:1), demands attention (sentence 16:2), commands it to stand ready (sentence 16:3), promises it pleasure (sentences 16:4), and commands it to cooperate with the stakes and branches (sentence 16:5). He now insistently obligates the rope to obedience by pointing out that he has made it (sentences 16:6–8). / The speaker summons the rope again (the singular form *nohuēltīuh,* "my older sister," may be an error for the plural form *nohuēltīhuān,* "my older sisters," in which case the summons would be directed to his hands) (sentence 17:1) and now turns his attention to his hands, commanding them to be ready (sentence 17:2) and, explaining the reason for the command, the coming of the deer (sentence 17:3), promises them they will encounter the deer (sentence 17:4) and capture it (sentence 17:5). Sentences 17:6–7 use rhetorical questions for word-magic purposes and are equivalent to denying that the deer will be aware of the trap. The speaker ends his address to his hands by predicting that they will be happy because of their successful capture of the deer (sentence 17:8). / And now that the preparation of the snare has been completed and his helper-allies have been properly counseled, the speaker turns to address the deer, telling it in sentences 18:1–2 that its fate has been decided. And as an ending to the incantation, the speaker adds a curious mock-dialogue of questions and answers that enacts the situation after the capture of the deer, thus coaxing reality to imitate the verbal representation (sentences 18:3–9).

Fourth incantation (segments 19–22). *Speaker:* deer hunter (role: Icnopiltzintli, Centeotl). *Addressee:* the rope, the mountains, the land, the Milky Way, the sun, the stakes. *Victim:* deer. *Place:* the hunting ground in the mountains. *Intention:* to create alliances and enlist the aid of the various helpers. *Purpose:* to capture the deer.

The fourth incantation is a fragment that presents a more fully developed variant of segment 16 (the address to the ropes) of the foregoing incantation (with segment 19 being almost completely merely a rearrangement of the elements found in segment 16). Sentences 19:1–2 are a repetition of sentences 16:1–2, and sentences 19:3–5 are a repetition of sentences 16:7–9, and sentences 19:6–7 are a repetition of sentences 16:4–5, while sentence 19:8 is an added synonymous expression. Sentence 19:9 reworks material found in sentence 13:2 (the shared words are *in tenānquiāhuatl, in cuauhquiāhuatl, in Tōllān ohtli,* "the wall-doorway, the wood-doorway, the road to Tollan"). Sentence 19:10 is a combination of sentence 14:2 and sentence 14:4 with the addition of the supplementary subject *in tlamacazqui Chicōme-Xōchitl, Teohtlālhuah* that was implicit in those sentences. Sentence 19:11 is a repetition of sentence 14:5. / The incantation now continues, however, with new material. In sentences 20:1–2, the speaker again addresses the rope and warns it against working unwillingly. In sentence 20:3, he warns it against fear and in sentence 20:4, he warns it about being concerned with the physical presence of the deer. / And having taken care of the advice to the rope, the speaker now turns his attention to the physical context. He addresses the mountains, so segment 21 is a reworking of segment 11. Sentence 21:1 is a reworking of sentence 11:1 and the first part of sentence 11:2. Sentence 21:2 is a variation on the middle part of sentence 11:2. And sentence 21:3 is a reworking of the last part of sentence 11:2. / The speaker now turns and summons the land, thus repeating in the first part of sentence 22:1 all of sentence 10:1, but then going on to include in his summons the Milky Way, the sun, the rope, and the stakes. He then issues a general command, warning all not to tell the deer (sentence 22:2). Sentences 22:3–4 present the arrival of the deer as imminent. And the incantation ends by promising all the allies happiness (sentence 22:5) and predicting their successful capture of the deer (sentence 22:6).

It is curious that at no point in any of these four incantations does the speaker identify himself with Mixcoatl, the god of the hunt, especially since the female deer is called Mixcoacihuatl, "Woman-associated-with-Mixcoatl" or "Woman-belonging-to-Mixcoatl." The speaker's identification of himself as Icnopiltzintli and Centeotl seems stereotyped and inappropriate.

II:9 (two incantations)

First incantation. *Speaker:* deer hunter (roles: Icnopiltzintli, Centeotl). *Addressee:* unspecified. *Victim:* deer. *Place:* at the hunter's home. *Intention:* to establish his credentials as a deer hunter. *Purpose:* to prepare for the hunt.

The speaker begins by announcing his departure with a boastful self-identification (sentence 1:1). He states that he has his bow and arrows ready (sentences 1:2–4).

Second incantation. *Speaker:* deer hunter. *Addressee:* unspecified. *Victim:* deer. *Place:* forest. *Intention:* to set forth his justification and competence as a deer hunter. *Purpose:* to kill the deer.

The speaker begins by stating his project (sentences 1:5–7). He justifies his hunt by the fact that his wife expects him to bring home the deer (sentence 1:8). He now states his determination to follow the deer over the difficult terrain (sentences 1:9–10) and ends the incantation by restating his project of capturing the deer (sentences 1:11–12; sentence 1:12 repeats sentence 1:7).

We have divided the single stretch of material in segment II:9 into two incantations according to internal evidence, namely the *on-* ("thither") of *nonēhua* (sentence 1:1) and the contrasting *-co* ("have come in order to") of *nicānaco* (sentence 1:6), *nictēmōco* (sentences 1:9, 1:10, and 1:11). It is, of course, entirely possible that what we have called the second incantation is spoken at the same time and place (the hunter's home) as the first one and that what seem to be indications of actual presence in the field (the past tense forms of the inbound purposive verbforms and the graphic description of the terrain) may be a particularly striking instance of word magic (anticipatory speech spoken in order to transform an imagined future into reality), but, if so, the obvious uses of that tactic within what we have called the second incantation (namely the future tense forms in sentences 1:7 and 1:12) would be anticipatory to a second degree.

These incantations are unusual in that there are no second-person indicators (no vocative, no summons), so that it is not clear to whom the speaker is talking. Again, as in the incantations in II:8, it is strange that the speaker does not identify himself with Mixcoatl, claiming instead to be Icnopiltzintli and Centeotl.

II:10 (one incantation)

Speaker: a field protector. *Addressee:* unspecified. *Antagonist:* peccaries. *Place:* a field damaged by peccaries. *Intention:* to erect a magic barrier around the field. *Purpose:* to prevent the entry of the peccaries into the field.

The speaker begins by boastfully identifying himself (sentences 1:1–3). He announces his project of seeking the peccaries (sentence 1:4) and predicts immediate success (sentence 1:5). He next reports on his preparedness, having brought magic earth and his hands (sentence 1:6). He ends by confidently predicting that these helpers will successfully protect the field (sentence 1:7).

The incantation is unusual in that it has no second person indicators (no vocative, no summons), so it is not clear to whom the speaker is talking. In sentence 1:6, it is not clear why the speaker shifts from *huāl-* ("hither") in *nichuālhuīca* to *on-* ("thither") in *niquimonhuīca,* when *huāl-* would have been expected in both words.

In the commentary preceeding this incantation, Ruiz de Alarcón implies that it is a hunting incantation like II:9. In the commentary that follows it, he strengthens this by an implied contrast when he points out that II:11 is for the protection of the cultivated field against marauding animals. But his classification of II:10 is in error, since, both in content and in organization, it is not for hunting like II:9 but for field protection like II:11.

II:11 (one incantation)

Structure: Two phases (phase 1: segment 1; phase 2: segment 2). *Speaker:* a field protector (role: *nahualli*-jaguar). *Addressee:* unspecified. *Antagonist:* animals that forage planted fields. *Place:* a field damaged by wild animals. *Intention:* to create a magic aura within the field. *Purpose:* to prevent the animals from entering the field.

The speaker begins by boastfully identifying himself (sentences 1:1–2), claiming to be in the particularly appropriate form of a jaguar. He announces his project of finding the animals (sentence 1:3) and to his surprise immediately discovers their tracks (sentences 1:4–8). // The second phase of the incantation begins with the speaker announcing his intention of driving the animals away (sentence 2:1), and predicting his success (sentence 2:2). He declares that he is banishing them (sentences 2:3–4). He next reports that he has brought his helper, copal (sentence 2:5), and predicts that because of it he will be successful in denying access to the animals (sentence 2:6).

The incantation is unusual in that it has no second-person indicators (no vocative, no summons), so it is not clear to whom the speaker is talking.

In segment 3 (consisting of only one sentence), a possible addition to the incantation is given. Since it is only a reference to the fire and has no grammatical connection with sentence 2:6, its exact function is not clear.

II:12 (one incantation)

Speaker: field protector. *Addressee:* the magic earth. *Antagonist:* coatis. *Place:* a field damaged by coatis. *Intention:* to create a magic barrier around the field with the magic earth. *Purpose:* to prevent the coatis from entering the field.

The speaker begins with an incitement and a vocative to the magic earth (sentence 1:1). He then asks an exasperated rhetorical question about what the coatis are doing to the field (sentence 1:2) followed by the disgusted answer that they are destroying it (sentence 1:3). At this point, he utters the wish that the culprits be banished to the middle of a desert where they can harm no one (sentences 1:4–5). He next forbids entry to the field (sentence 1:6) and explains that it will have magical guards (or, since Tlalocateuctli in sentence 1:2 represents the client, the field owner, the priests from Green, White, and Yellow Tlalocan may be metaphorical references to the client's kinsmen or field hands who will be posted to guard the field) (sentences 1:7–8). He ends the incantation by stating that those who get caught will be responsible for what happens to them since they have been duly warned (sentences 1:9–10).

This incantation is strange in that, although it has an initial incitement with a juxtaposed vocative (sentence 1:1), it has no further second person forms. Consequently, it would appear that the magic earth (the *tepētlāuhcacihuātl*) is being urged to listen to the rest of the incantation. Certainly sentences 1:2–3 are intended to appeal to her indignation against the evildoers to enlist her more willing participation in the work at hand. It seems strange, however, that the incantation does not contain a specific command to the earth to form the magic wall, since the speaker's physical act of erecting this magical protective barrier around the field is not verbalized in the incantation. Notice also that, for the end of the incantation to be valid, the speaker must assume that the coatis have heard his warning.

II:13 (three incantations)

First incantation (segment 1). *Speaker:* farmer. *Addressee:* ants. *Antagonist:* ants. *Place:*

an ant hill. *Intention:* to shame the ants into acting properly. *Purpose:* to get rid of the ants.

The speaker begins with an incitement (sentence 1:1) and then addresses the ants, reproachfully asking them what they are doing to the field (sentence 1:2). He intensifies his shaming tactic (sentences 1:3–4) and then ends by threatening to destroy the ant hill if the ants do not behave (sentence 1:5).

Second incantation (segment 2). *Speaker:* farmer. *Addressee:* water. *Antagonist:* ants. *Place:* an ant hill. *Intention:* to elicit water's cooperation. *Purpose:* to destroy the ant hill.

The speaker begins with an incitement (sentence 2:1), followed by an address to water and a question focusing on the problem of the ants' destructiveness and designed to elicit her (water's) indignation (sentence 2:2). The speaker then commands her to destroy the ants (sentence 2:3), explaining that they have refused to obey him (sentence 2:4). He asks a rhetorical question about their rootedness (with the question having an implicit negative answer), for the purpose of convincing water that she is capable of carrying out his order (sentence 2:5). He undertakes to further bolster up water's effectiveness by reminding her of her extraordinary strength even against rooted things (sentence 2:6). He ends the incantation by turning to address the ants, asking them the same rhetorical question earlier asked to water, perhaps exasperatedly, perhaps tauntingly reminding them that they are vulnerable to water's power (sentence 2:7).

Third incantation (segment 3). *Speaker:* farmer. *Addressee:* tobacco. *Antagonists:* ants. *Place:* ant hill. *Intention:* to elicit tobacco's help. *Purpose:* to destroy the ant hill.

The speaker begins with an incitement (sentence 3:1), followed by an address to tobacco and a question focusing on the problem of the ants and intended to elicit his (i.e., tobacco's) indignation (sentence 3:2). The speaker then commands tobacco to run the ants off (sentence 3:3).

II:14 (five incantations)

First incantation (segment 1). *Speaker:* a fisherman. *Addressee:* cane. *Victim:* the cane. *Place:* canebrake. *Intention:* to persuade the cane to cooperate and not hurt him. *Purpose:* to obtain cane to make a fishtrap.

The speaker begins abruptly (without an incitement or a summons) by commanding the cane to hurry (sentence 1:1) and explaining his project of getting it (sentence 1:2). He explains that he has brought his helpers, the hands and fingers, with him (sentence 1:3). He asks rhetorical questions about their vulnerability (sentences 1:4–5), the implicit answer being that they are supernatural and cannot be hurt during the cane cutting, an obvious bit of word magic.

Second incantation (segment 2). *Speaker:* a fisherman (role: Icnopiltzintli, Centeotl). *Addressee:* cane. *Victim:* cane. *Place:* at the fisherman's house or at the riverbank. *Intention:* to obtain the cooperation of the cane. *Purpose:* to construct the fishtrap.

The speaker begins by summoning the cane (sentence 2:1). He justifies the summons by explaining his project of making the fishtrap (sentence 2:2). And to justify his authority for carrying out his project, he now boastfully identifies himself (sentences 2:3–4), and, being who he is, he can therefore forbid the cane to hurt his hands and fingers (sentence 2:5). He ends by asking the same rhetorical questions as in the first incantation concerning the hand's vulnerability (sentences 2:6–7), again with the implicit answer being that they are supernatural.

Third incantation (segments 3 and 4). *Speaker:* fisherman. *Addressee:* the cord, the fishtrap. *Place:* riverbank. *Intention:* to convince the fishtrap to cooperate. *Purpose:* to set the fishtrap in place.

The speaker begins with an incitement (sentence 3:1) and then summons the cord with which the fishtrap is to be fastened in place (sentence 3:2). Without speaking further to the cord, he commands the fishtrap to hurry (sentence 3:3) and explains to it that he is hanging it in position and placing the bait inside (sentence 3:4), promising it that the bait will stay with it wherever it goes (sentence 3:5). The speaker now predicts that fish will come from everywhere to eat the bait and that they will enjoy it (sentences 3:6-8). / He next cautions the fishtrap to do its work willingly (sentence 4:1) and ends with the promise that it will have the privilege of enjoying the fish before anyone else (sentence 4:2).

Fourth incantation (segment 5). *Speaker:* fisherman. *Addressee:* flotation device used while setting the fishtrap in place. *Place:* riverbank. *Intention:* to secure the cooperation of the flotation device. *Purpose:* to leave the fishtrap successfully in place.

The speaker addresses the flotation device and advises it that he will cross the river by means of it (sentence 5:1). After this he gives a shout for joy at having finished his task (sentence 5:2).

As pointed out in note II:14:17, there is a slight possibility that this brief incantation is a dramatization of the fishtrap's acceptance of the fisherman's charge, so that the speaker would be the fishtrap itself rather than the fisherman. Also, the shout for joy would be over the prospect of catching the fish.

Fifth incantation (segments 6 and 7). *Speaker:* fisherman (roles: Icnopiltzintli, Centeotl). *Addressee:* the caiman. *Place:* riverbank. *Intention:* to intimidate the caiman. *Purpose:* to protect the fishtrap.

The speaker begins with the motif of poverty (sentence 6:1) but shifts immediately to a boasting self-identification (sentences 6:2–3). From this stance of authority he now commands the caiman to stay away from the fishtrap (sentence 6:4), forbidding it to come into his sight (sentences 7:1–2). He follows this with a threat of disaster if he is disobeyed (sentence 7:3) and, to back that up, ends with a repetition of the previous boasting self-identification (sentences 7:4–5 repeat sentences 6:2–3).

II:15 (two incantations)

First incantation (segments 1–4). *Structure:* two phases (phase 1: segments 1 and 2; phase 2: segments 3 and 4). *Speaker:* fisherman (role: Icnopiltzintli, Centeotl). *Addressee:* tobacco, Filth-goddesses, fishhooks, the broom(?). *Place:* inside fisherman's home. *Intention:* to enlist the cooperation of helper-allies and to set the house in order. *Purpose:* to get ready to go fishing.

The speaker begins by summoning tobacco (sentence 1:1) and announces, along with a boasting self-identification, that he is ready to go fishing (sentence 1:2), being sent by his wife (sentence 1:3). As if this diminishes his importance, he immediately seeks to reestablish his authority: he repeats his earlier boasting self-identification (sentence 1:4). / He now summons the Filth-goddesses (sentence 2:1), telling them that they will maintain peace and quiet in his home while he is away (sentence 2:2). // And having taken care of transcendental matters, he enters into the second phase of the incantation by summoning the fishing cane (sentence 3:1) and announcing, along with a repeat of his earlier boasting self-identification, that he is ready to go (sentence 3:2). / At this point, he summons the broom (?) (sentence 4:1) and gives a general command that the house be set in order (sentences 4:2–3) and expresses his apprehension about unintentionally irritating someone (sentence 4:4). He ends by turning to the problem of his destination, which he resolves by deciding to go to the river (sentences 4:5–9).

The involvement of Tlahzolteteoh (the goddesses concerned with sexual affairs) in the preservation of peace in the house (thus looking upon them as household goddesses) seems strange and suggests confusion, possibly with the Tlazohteteoh (Beloved-goddesses). See note II:8:45.

Second incantation (segment 5). *Structure:* two phases (phase 1: sentences 5:1–2; phase 2: sentences 5:3–4). *Speaker:* fisherman. *Addressee:* worm. *Victim:* the fish. *Place:* the riverbank. *Intention:* to bait the hook. *Purpose:* to catch fish.

The speaker begins by summoning the worm (sentence 5:1) and commands it to place itself on the hook (sentence 5:2). // The second phase begins with the speaker thinking about his prospective catch, asking a rhetorical question about which fish he wants to attract (sentence 5:3), his answer being equivalent to "any or all" (sentence 5:4).

II:16 (one incantation)

Speaker: fisherman. *Addressee:* water. *Victim:* fish. *Place:* riverbank. *Intention:* to enlist the aid of helper-allies and to persuade the fish to come forth. *Purpose:* to catch fish.

The speaker begins by summoning the water (sentence 1:1). He now informs it of his project in having come to the river, namely, to catch fish (sentence 1:2). In sentences 1:3–4, he excitedly points to the large number of fish which have come to please his wife (who is not named until sentence 2:1). This remarkable find is, of course, fabricated as magical rhetoric and is intended to persuade the possibility into reality. / In sentence 2:1, the speaker confesses that his wife has sent him, and in sentence 2:2, he reports that he has brought several kinds of bait. Next he explains his project of coming for the fish (sentences 2:3–4) and justifies it by the fact that his wife is expecting them (sentence 2:5). The speaker next announces that the riverbank is ready to receive the fish (sentence 2:6). At this point, he suddenly shifts from third-person report to second-person address; without a summons or a vocative, he speaks to the fish, indirectly ordering them to come out onto the bank by predicting that they will (sentence 2:7). / And now, coming near the end of the incantation, the speaker summons tobacco (sentence 3:1) and warns it not to act unwillingly (sentence 3:2), a warning he backs up by promising that it, as a bribe for its cooperation, will be the first to enjoy the catch (sentence 3:3).

This incantation, like II:6, presents an initial imaginary "discovery" of the sought-for game for the purpose of imposing that verbal image upon reality. The speaker later returns to a realistic assessment of the situation. This strategy is not, of course, to be confused with the initial actual discovery that we find in II:11 (where it is only the tracks of the game that are found).

II:17 (one incantation)

Structure: three phases (phase 1: segments 1–3; phase 2: segment 4; phase 3: segment 5). *Speaker:* fisherman. *Addressee:* fish, caiman, otter, tobacco. *Victim:* fish. *Antagonist:* caiman, otter. *Place:* riverbank. *Intention:* to invite the fish and to warn away undesirable guests. *Purpose:* to catch fish in a weir.

The speaker begins by summoning the fish (sentence 1:1), and then demanding that they hurry (sentence 1:2). The authoritarian stance is now supported by two imperious statements in which the speaker declares that he is calling for and seeking them (sentences 1:3–4). These statements in turn are backed up by a boasting self-identification (sentences 1:5–7). Having established himself as a person of authority, the speaker changes tactics, taking on a feigned graciousness, explaining to the fish that he has come to set up beautiful, enticing, pleasant places for them (sentences 1:8–9), seeking to lure the beguiled fish to their doom. / The imperious tone comes back in with a repetition of the demand that they hurry (sentence 2:1), followed by an unusually arrogant insistence that they come immediately (sentences 2:2–4). He again explains his project of capturing them (sentences 2:5–6), again stating that his wife is awaiting them (sentence 2:7). And again he shifts to a deceptive friendliness, saying now that his project has been to lay out beautiful resting places for them where they can find delicious food and drink (sentences 2:8–11). / At this point, the speaker shifts from talking to the fish to talking about them, asking rhetorically whether he is inviting only one (sentences 3:1–2). He rejects the idea outright, saying that his hospitality extends to all [notice how the embed *icnō-* ("orphan," i.e., "pitiable") pretends that he is doing the old men and old women a favor], and then reinforces this generosity by giving a boastful self-identification (sentence 3:3–4). // The speaker begins the second phase of the incantation by addressing the caiman and warning it not to approach (sentence 4:1). He becomes even more emphatic by next promising that if he sees it he will kill it (sentence 4:2). He next warns the otter that coming near will be like committing suicide (sentence 4:3) and issues a general negative command to any undesirables to stay away (sentences 4:4–5), threatening disastrous consequences to anyone who disobeys him (sentence 4:6). He backs his threat up with a boastful self-identification (sentences 4:7–8). And then he reiterates the positive aspect of his project by explaining that he is inviting the fish to come (sentence 4:9). // The third phase of the incantation begins with the speaker urging tobacco to hurry (sentence 5:1), explaining that it is his spiritual guide (sentence 5:2) and that it is something dear to him (sentence 5:3).

The first phase of the incantation (segments 1–3) is interesting because of the unusually forceful presentaion of its rhetoric and its almost schizophrenic oscillation between overbearing authority and friendly courtesy. The second phase is equally forceful in its negative stance in refusing admittance to and intimidating the caiman and the otter.

III:1 (four incantations)

First incantation (segment 1). *Speaker:* farmer. *Addressee:* the digging stick. *Place:* maguey field. *Intention:* to secure the digging stick's cooperation. *Purpose:* to dig up the young maguey plant for transplantation.

The speaker begins with an incitement (sentence 1:1) and then summons the digging stick (sentence 1:2). He invites it to join him in the task of transplanting the maguey (sentence 1:3), explaining that he plans to establish the plant in a chosen and prepared place where it will be well off (sentences 1:4–6).

The assumption behind the incantation is that the digging stick has a desire to benefit the maguey and consequently will be happy to cooperate with the speaker in his undertaking.

Second incantation (segment 2). *Speaker:* farmer. *Addressee:* maguey plant. *Place:* new location for maguey plant. *Intention:* to welcome the maguey plant to its new location. *Purpose:* to transplant the maguey plant successfully.

The speaker begins with an incitement (sentence 2:1) and summons the maguey plant (sentence 2:2), explaining to her that her new place will be pleasant and good for her (sentences 2:3–4).

Third incantation (segments 3 and 4). *Structure:* two phases (phase 1: segment 3; phase 2: segment 4). *Speaker:* farmer. *Addressee:* pruning stick, maguey plant, spoon. *Place:* the location of the now mature maguey plant. *Intention:* to get the maguey in the right frame of mind and to enlist the aid of a helper-ally. *Purpose:* to prepare the maguey plant for harvest.

The speaker begins phase 1 by summoning the pruning stick (sentence 3:1). He advises it that the time for action has arrived (sentence 3:2). He now turns and speaks to the maguey plant, telling her that she has become mature (sentence 3:3) and then announcing to her that he intends to cut into her heart (sentence 3:4), news that undoubtedly would make the plant sad and tearful, which is the hoped-for reaction. // The speaker immediately cuts out the center of the plant and begins phase 2 of the incantation by turning to the spoon, utters an incitement (sentence 4:1) and summons it (sentence 4:2), telling it that it is now time for it to act (sentence 4:3). He then commands it to clean out the hollowed-out center (sentence 4:4) so that the maguey will weep copiously (sentence 4:5).

What we have called two phases might be two separate incantations, depending on the degree of mismatch between activity time and utterance time.

Fourth incantation (segment 5). *Speaker:* farmer. *Addressee:* the land. *Place:* new location for maguey plant. *Intention:* to persuade the land to treat the maguey plant well. *Purpose:* to transplant the maguey plant successfully.

This is a variant of the second incantation. The speaker begins by summoning the land (sentence 5:1) and announces to her that he is planting the maguey (sentence 5:2). He commands her to embrace it (sentences 5:3–4) and ends by promising that very shortly he will return to inspect the plant (sentences 5:5–6).

III:2 (three incantations)

First incantation (segments 1 and 2). *Speaker:* farmer. *Addressee:* digging stick, the maize. *Place:* the granary. *Intention:* to persuade the implements and the maize to be cooperative. *Purpose:* to get ready to plant the maize.

The speaker begins by summoning the digging stick (sentence 1:1). He then informs it that the rainy season is at hand (sentence 1:2) and that it is time to get the seed maize (sentence 1:3). / The speaker abruptly turns and, without addressing it by name, invites the maize to go with him (sentence 2:1), pointing to the presence of the harvest basket (sentence 2:2) and telling it that she [the basket] will carry it [the maize] (sentence 2:3). He reminds the maize that his wife has been taking care of it (sentence 2:4) but that now the rainy season has arrived (sentence 2:5).

There may be an omission in the text after sentence 1:3 since, without summoning the maize and without naming it in a vocative phrase, the speaker invites the maize to go with him in sentence 2:1.

The speaker's reference to his wife's protection of the maize is a rhetorical ploy to induce feelings of obligation in the maize so it will produce more abundantly.

Second incantation (segment 3). *Speaker:* farmer. *Addressee:* the digging stick. *Place:* the field. *Intention:* to secure the cooperation of the digging stick. *Purpose:* to plant the maize.

The speaker begins by summoning the digging stick (sentence 3:1). He then tells it that he and it will plant the maize (sentence 3:2).

By presenting the planting as a cooperative matter, the speaker induces the digging stick to a more willing and effective action.

Third incantation (segment 4). *Speaker:* farmer. *Addressee:* the land. *Place:* the field after the ground has been prepared. *Intention:* to get the land into a receptive frame of mind. *Purpose:* to plant the maize successfully.

The speaker begins with an incitement (sentence 4:1). He then summons the land (sentence 4:2) and informs it that he is going to entrust the maize to her (sentence 4:3), stating that it is a good place where the maize is to be placed (sentence 4:4). He ends by explaining that it will rain shortly (sentence 4:5).

The prediction of rain with which the incantation ends, besides promising the land the blessing of the rain is a bit of word magic designed to bring about the effective arrival of the rain.

III:4 (one incantation)

Speaker: farmer. *Addressee:* the maize. *Place:* the field. *Intention:* to persuade the land to cooperate. *Purpose:* to plant the maize successfully.

The speaker begins with a rather mild boasting self-identification (sentences 1:1–2). He next summons the maize (sentence 1:3). Then, without saying anything else to the maize, he turns and summons the land (sentence 1:4) and informs her that he is entrusting the maize to her (sentence 1:5). At this point, he becomes more authoritarian, warning her not to bring shame on herself (sentence 1:6) and not to perform her work unwillingly (sentences 1:7–8). He continues his authoritative stance with rhetorical questions about how quickly the plants will appear (sentence 1:9) and demands their immediate and swift appearance (sentence 1:10).

III:5 (one incantation)

Speaker: farmer. *Addressee:* the maize. *Place:* outside the granary. *Intention:* to get the maize into a cooperative frame of mind. *Purpose:* to store the harvested maize successfully.

The speaker begins with a rather mild boasting self-identification (sentences 1:1–2). He then summons the maize (sentence 1:3) and announces that he will soon put her in the granary (sentence 1:4). He commands her to take care of herself (sentence 1:5) and warns her not to become spoiled (sentence 1:6). He then explains that he is depending on her, and ends with a boastful self-identification (sentence 1:7).

III:6 (one incantation)

Structure: two phases (phase 1: segment 1; phase 2: segment 2). *Speaker:* farmer. *Addressee:* the land. *Place:* the squash field. *Intention:* to secure the cooperation of the land. *Purpose:* to plant the squash successfully.

The speaker begins by summoning the land (sentence 1:1) and explaining to it that he is entrusting the squash seed to her (sentence 1:2). He now commands her to guard it well (sentence 1:3) and states that the ants will not harm it (sentence 1:4), as if placing the responsibility for this on the land. // He now begins the second phase by predicting that the vines will be so abundant that they will cause amazement and will be difficult to walk through (sentences 2:1–3). He comes out of his reverie and again summons the land (sentence 2:4) and urges her to action (sentence 2:5), warning her not to fail to produce (sentence 2:6) and to perform her work willingly (sentences 2:7–8).

The image of future success that serves as the center of this incantation has two functions. For one thing, it offers the land a picture of the goal she is to aim at in guarding the seed. For another, as a vision of the extraordinary results of the planting, it is an excellent example of word magic spoken with the purpose of inducing reality to copy the verbal model.

III:7 (one incantation)

Speaker: farmer. *Addressee:* sun. *Place:* camote field. *Intention:* to persuade the sun to have mercy on the farmer and help the camotes grow. *Purpose:* to plant the camotes successfully.

The speaker begins with a boasting self-identification (sentences 1:1–3). He then summons the sun (sentence 1:4), giving it no explicit command but implicitly asking it to witness the fact that he is sowing camotes (sentences 1:5–6). He now repeats his summons to the sun (sentence 1:7) and again only implicitly asks it to witness the planting of the camotes (sentences 1:8-9). He then explains that because of the camotes he, who is merely a poor person, will be able to get along (sentence 1:10).

The incantation is implicitly asking the sun to cause the camotes to grow well and seeks to win compliance by appealing to its sympathy. The humility motif that is explicit in the final sentence may be implicit in the metaphorical (and possibly mythological) images of sentences 1:2–6 and 1:8–9, where the act of planting is represented as an act of tying in combination with sacrificial-sounding metaphors (the identification of the camote slips with the speaker's body: *nometzcuauhyo*, "my thigh," *notzontecon*, "my head"). But even if this is not implicit humility, there is still a discrepancy between the initial boasting and the final humility. Notice that in spite of the initial boasting, the speaker never explicitly commands the sun to do anything.

IV:1 (one incantation)

Structure: two phases (phase 1: segment 1; phase 2: segment 2). *Speaker:* curer (role: *nahualli*-lord). *Addressee:* maize kernels. *Antagonist:* anger. *Place:* unspecified. *Intention:* to persuade the maize kernels to act against the anger. *Purpose:* to soothe the angry person.

The speaker begins by summoning the maize kernels (sentence 1:1). Using a future-tense form, he commands the maize to calm down the angry person (sentence 1:2). He next predicts the banishment of anger (sentence 1:3); that is, he expresses his confidence in the power of the maize to accomplish its task. // But now he begins the second phase by shifting the success to himself, claiming that he himself will banish and chase away the anger (sentence 2:1), and justifies this self-confidence by boasting of his power identity (sentence 2:2). He predicts that he will have the anger (synecdoche for the angry person) drink the concoction made from the maize (sentence 2:3).

IV:2 (one incantation)

Speaker: a man in love (role: Telpochtli, Yaotl, "Cihuayotl"). *Addressee:* unspecified (possibly the speaker's self). *Place:* an isolated place. *Intention:* to set in motion the forces that will bring the speaker the woman he loves. *Purpose:* to attract the affection of a woman loved by the speaker.

The speaker begins by imagining himself at the place where lovers meet on Mirror Mountain, where, he says, he is courting a woman (sentence 1:1). The image is a metaphorical way of confessing that he is in love. In sentence 1:2, he admits that he is wandering around (notice the use of the directional prefixes *-on-*, "thither," and *-huāl-*, "hither") filled with melancholy. And he consoles himself, first, by imagining that he is in his ladylove's company (sentence 1:3) and, second, by letting his mind call up her image (sentence 1:4). In sentence 1:5, he returns to the sadness motif. / He then breaks off to comment on the woman's divine beauty (sentences 2:1–2). And the thought of her beauty leads him to ask how soon he will see her (sentence 2:3), and he peremptorily answers that it will be immediately (sentence 2:4). His impatience now leads him to justify this answer with an extravagant boastful self-identification that occupies sentences 2:5–12. / At this point, Ruiz de Alarcón's prudish deletion of part of the text prevents us from knowing how the incantation develops, but if we are allowed to hypothesize, we can guess that it would continue as word magic, presenting a verbal image that is expected to become reality. Ruiz de Alarcón allows us to enter the incantation again at the point where it is winding down to a conclusion. This is accomplished very neatly with a repetition of sentences 2:1-7 in sentences 3:1-7, a sequence ending with the speaker's boast that he is Yaotl (the god of war). At this point, the speaker brings the incantation to a structurally neat close with three sentences, in the first of which he questions his earlier claimed identity (sentence 3:8) and in the second and third of which he denies it (sentence 3:9) and confesses that instead he is only a lover, a womanizer (sentence 3:10).

The incantation is remarkable for a number of reasons. It hardly seems an incantation at all; no powerful ally is summoned to help the speaker attain his goal, nor on the other hand is the beloved one appealed to. In fact, no one is addressed and the speaker seems to be talking to himself, so there is a lyriclike expression of feeling and a stating of desires that reminds one of a Renaissance love complaint, a similarity even more strikingly present in the war-versus-love motif, otherwise known as the Mars-versus-Venus (here, Yaotl-versus-Xochiquetzal) motif. The artistic skill shown here makes us even more exasperated with Ruiz de Alarcón's puritanical concerns for having deprived us of the opportunity to know the complete work. To judge from the parts that have been preserved, this incantation is among the better-structured works in the collection. The repeated segment, although exceptional because of its length, is handled well with regard both to placement and to refocusing of motifs. It leads easily and naturally into the surprise of the reversal presented in the last three sentences. We should not leave the incantation, however, without pointing out that it is indeed an incantation, although a subtle one, and not merely a lyrical outpouring of ardent desire. Its main thrust lies in magic persuasiveness, the endeavor to bring about the satisfaction of desires through verbal imaging, that is, the speaker is seeking a pragmatic result, with the unspecified addressee being, in fact, the supernatural powers that are expected to transform the verbal into the actual.

IV:3 (two incantations)

First incantation (segments 1-3). *Speaker:* curer (role: *nahualli*-lord). *Addressee:* fire, water, copal, the Tlahzolteteoh, Green or White Tlaloc, Citlalcueyeh. *Antagonist:* the illness. *Client:* person sick from a "love-related" illness. *Place:* in the sick person's presence. *Intention:* to persuade the illness to leave the sick person without harming the curer and to shame Citlalcueyeh into cooperation. *Purpose:* to heal the sick person.

The speaker begins by summoning fire, water, and copal (sentence 1:1). Without speaking further to them, he abruptly turns and summons the Tlahzolteteoh [the goddesses concerned with sexual affairs] (sentence 1:2). / Without speaking further to them, he abruptly addresses the illness, telling it to come and look at him (i.e., to become aware of him) (sentence 2:1). He announces his presence (sentence 2:2) and boastfully identifies himself (sentence 2:3). And having established his credentials, he now warns Green or White Tlaloc [i.e., the force behind the sickness] not to do anything against him (sentences 2:4–5). And to make the warning more effective, he again boastfully identifies himself (sentences 2:6–7). / He now turns to reproach Citlalcueyeh for having turned against one of her own creatures. The shaming tactic occupies all of segment 3 (seven sentences) and is the climax with which the incantation ends.

Second incantation (segment 4). *Speaker:* curer. *Addressee:* the curer's hands, Cuaton and Caxxoch, water. *Client:* person sick from a "love-related" illness. *Place:* in the sick person's presence. *Intention:* to seek the help of his hands and of the goddesses Cuaton and Caxxoch in dealing with the sickness. *Purpose:* to cure the sick person.

This is only a fragment that can serve as a variant beginning for the first incantation. The speaker here begins by summoning his hands (sentence 4:1). Without addressing them further, he abruptly turns and summons Cuaton and Caxxoch, two of the Tlahzolteteoh (sentence 4:2) and invites them to help him carry the patient to the bathing part of the ceremony (sentence 4:3). He now summons water (sentence 4:4) and turns again to Cuaton and Caxxoch and invites them to help him bathe the sickness off and out of the patient, who is called their creation more fully to assure their cooperation (sentence 4:5). And for the same purpose of assuring their help he boastfully identifies himself (sentences 4:6–7) and predicts that he and they working together will immediately banish the sickness (sentence 4:8). And to make certain that it will happen immediately, he imperiously asks when it will take place and demands that it be immediately (sentences 4:9–11).

Calling the patient Chalchiuhteotzin [*"Jade-god (H)"*] in sentence 4:3 is a rhetorical ploy designed to engage water's intervention more fully by suggesting its consubstantiality with the patient by the fact that their names share the embed (CHĀL-CHIHUI)-TL, "jade." Notice that water, Chalchiuhcueyeh, is summoned in the very next sentence.

V:1 (one basic incantation and alternatives to one segment)

Basic incantation. *Structure:* two phases (phase 1: segment 1; phase 2: segments 2–5). *Speaker:* diviner. *Addressee:* tobacco, the land; the curer's hands. *Antagonist:* an unknown agent of illness. *Client:* a sick person. *Place:* in the sick person's presence. *Intention:* to assure the cooperation of the diviner's hands. *Purpose:* to diagnose the client's sickness by identifying the being responsible.

The speaker begins with an incitement (sentence 1:1) and then summons tobacco and the land with an elaborate vocative sequence (sentence 1:2). He then issues two general commands about no one ruining things and starting off unwillingly (sentences 1:3–4). // He begins the second phase by reporting that he is kissing his hand (really, his crossed thumb) (sentence 2:1) and that he has brought his hands (sentence 2:2), an example of hysteron proteron that here serves to focus special attention on the hands since they are to be his pragmatic helpers in the divining ceremony. / And to do this even more insistently, he now summons his hands (sentence 3:1) and invites them to join him in looking into his divining device (i.e., the surface of the patient's arm) (sentence 3:2) to ascertain what power being has sickened his client (sentence 3:3). / He summons his hands again, though without naming them this time (sentence 4:1), and invites them to join him in the divining process (sentence 4:2). He imperiously states that he and they will find out immediately who is responsible for the patient's state (sentence 4:3). / To give strength to his command, he boastfully identifies himself (sentences 5:1–4), thus concluding the incantation.

The structure of the incantation resembles that found, for example, in II:3 and the first incantation of II:15. The two phases have to do with a division of labor in which the first phase is concerned with a spiritual helper (here, two: tobacco and the land) and the second with the pragmatic aspects (here, the pragmatic helpers, the hands).

First fragment (segment 6)

This is an alternative way of ending the incantation. After the speaker boastfully identifies himself, surprisingly, as being MictlanTeuctli (sentences 6:1–2), he asks about the effectiveness of the medicine (sentences 6:3–5).

Second fragment (segment 7)

This can be slipped into the first incantation in place of sentences 3:2–3 and segment 4 when the problem has to do with theft. In it the speaker invites his hands to join him in seeking to know who stole the client's maize (or his animal). The client here is not, of course, a sick person but one who is a victim of theft or loss.

Third fragment (segment 8)

This is another alternative for sentences 3:2–3 when the problem is a missing wife or child. The speaker asks his hands to join him in seeking to know where his client's wife or daughter went. The client is a person whose wife or child is missing.

Fourth fragment (segment 9)

This is another alternative for sentences 3:2–3, this time dealing with the kidnapping of the wife or daughter.

Fifth fragment (segment 10)

This is another alternative for sentences 3:2–3 when the problem is a sickness whose source is unknown. The speaker inquires about which power being has been angered (sentences 10:1–4). The speaker also strengthens the effectiveness of the search by summoning tobacco (sentence 10:5).

Sixth fragment (segment 11)

This is another alternative for sentences 3:2–3 when the problem is a sickness whose source is unknown. This is to be used if the suspected culprit is the Virgin Mary (sentences 11:1–2) or some saint (sentences 11:3–4).

Seventh fragment (segment 12)

This is another alternative for sentences 3:2–3 when the problem is a sickness whose source is unknown. The speaker asks whether the culprit is the clouds (sentences 12:1–2).

Eighth fragment (segment 13)

This is another alternative for sentences 3:2–3, asking whether the sick person is a victim of the forest gods (sentence 13:1), the earth (sentence 13:2), or the fire (sentence 13:3).

V:2 (fragments, possible variants of or additions to incantations in V:1)

First fragment (segment 1). *Speaker:* diviner. *Addressee:* fire, the speaker's hands.

This fragment contains an alternative beginning for the main incantation of V:1. In it, the speaker first summons fire (sentence 1:1) and then states that he has brought his hands and fingers (sentence 1:2), whereupon he gives them more prominence by summoning them (sentence 1:3). He next invites them to join him in looking into his divining device (sentence 1:4, which is the same as sentence 3:2 in V:1).

Second fragment (segment 2). *Speaker:* diviner (role: Ohxomoco or Cipactonal (depending on whether the speaker is a man or woman), *nahualli*-lord). *Addressee:* not specified.

This fragment can serve as an addition to the end of the main incantation of V:1. It contains a demand for immediate results (sentence 2:1) followed by an elaborate boastful self-identification (sentences 2:2–9).

The appropriateness of the speaker's self-identification as either Ohxomoco or Cipactonal rests on the fact that these two personages were the mythological inventors of divination.

Third fragment (segment 3). *Speaker:* diviner. *Addressee:* hands.

This fragment is a variant addition to the end of the main incantation in V:1. The speaker summons her fingers (sentence 3:1) and then invites them to join her in the divining task (sentence 3:2).

V:3 (one incantation with two fragments that can be inserted into it according to the circumstances)

Speaker: diviner (role: Cipactonal). *Addressee:* the maize kernels, the speaker's hands. *Client:* a person with a difficulty. *Place:* not specified. *Intention:* to secure the cooperation of the helper-allies. *Purpose:* to find out the nature of the client's difficulty and ascertain the remedy.

The speaker begins by summoning the maize kernels with which he will divine (sentence 1:1). Without speaking to them further, he now summons his hands (sentence 1:2) and imperiously states that the time for action has come (sentence 1:3). He then invites the hands to go with him in order to find out what the source of the client's trouble is (sentence 1:4). He now turns his attention to the speed with which this will be accomplished and demands that it will be immediately (sentences 1:5-7). To give weight to his demands, he boastfully identifies himself as Cipactonal, the mythological inventor of the divinatory art (sentences 1:8–10) and promises to read the maize kernels to ascertain what medicine is needed and whether the patient will get worse (sentence 1:11).

First fragment (segment 2)

This fragment gives the variant wording to be inserted in the main incantation when the problem has to do with finding a man's runaway wife. It consists primarily of questions concerning the whereabouts of the wife.

Second fragment (segment 3)
This fragment gives the variant wording to be inserted in the main incantation when the problem has to do with finding a lost animal. It consists of questions concerning what happened to the animal.

VI:1 (four incantations and a fragment)

First incantation (segment 1). *Speaker:* midwife. *Addressee:* the speaker's hands, earth, tobacco. *Patient:* woman in labor. *Place:* patient's bedside. *Intention:* to secure the cooperation of helper-allies. *Purpose:* to bring about a successful birthing.

The speaker begins by summoning her hands (sentence 1:1). Without saying anything else to the hands, she addresses the earth, informing it that it will create the birthing pains (sentence 1:2) and invites it to join her in finding out who is coming to destroy her and the birthing woman (sentence 1:3). She next issues another summons (sentence 1:4), which, although unspecified, is apparently directed to tobacco, since in sentence 1:5 she urges tobacco into action and ends the incantation by commanding it to frighten away the pain (sentence 1:6).

The incantation offers an interesting instance of the speaker claiming to be hurting along with the patient. This claim of shared suffering is a rhetorical ploy intended not primarily for its direct effect on the addressee (the earth) but for its indirect effect (comfort, encouragement) upon the patient (who is never addressed).

Fragment (segment 2). This vocative to the fire can serve as an alternative to the vocative to tobacco in sentence 1:5 above.

Second incantation (segment 3). *Speaker:* midwife. *Addressee:* tobacco, Cuaton and Caxxoch, the speaker's hands. *Patient:* woman in labor. *Place:* patient's bedside. *Intention:* to secure the cooperation of helper-allies. *Purpose:* to bring about a successful birthing.

This incantation is an alternative to the first one. The speaker begins with an incitement (sentence 3:1) and then summons tobacco (sentence 3:2) but says nothing else to it. There follows another incitement (sentence 3:3), followed by a command to Cuaton and Caxxoch to open the vaginal passage (sentence 3:4). There follows another incitement (sentence 3:5), and the speaker then summons the hands (sentence 3:6), whom she invites to join her in seizing whoever is causing the birthing woman pain (sentence 3:7).

Third incantation (segment 4). *Speaker:* midwife. *Addressee:* basin, water. *Client:* newborn baby. *Place:* birthing place. *Intention:* to secure cooperation of helper-allies in bathing the baby. *Purpose:* to bathe the baby.

The speaker summons the basin and the water (sentence 4:1), and then, without saying anything else to the basin, she commands the water to wash and bathe the child, putting it under an obligation by telling it that the child has been born into its hands (sentence 4:2).

Fourth incantation (segment 5). *Speaker:* midwife. *Addressee:* ground-up tail of the opossum, Cuaton and Caxxoch. *Patient:* woman in labor. *Intention:* to secure the cooperation of the medicine to get the child to be born. *Purpose:* to stop the difficulty that has occurred in the birthing.

The speaker starts with an incitement (sentence 5:1) and then summons the ground-up tail of the opossum, the medicine used to open up the vaginal passage (sentence 5:2). She commands it to cause the child who is troubling the woman to come out (sentence 5:3). And as an added help, she ends by summoning Cuaton and Caxxoch (sentence 5:4).

Note that none of these incantations contains a boastful self-identification.

VI:2 (one incantation)

Speaker: curer. *Addressee:* water. *Client:* sick child. *Place:* in the patient's presence. *Intention:* to secure water's cooperation in checking on the child's *tonal. Purpose:* to diagnose the condition of the child.

The speaker begins with an incitement (sentence 1:1) and then summons water (sentence 1:2), whom she invites to join her in finding out whether the child has lost its *tonal* (sentence 1:3) (at which point she holds the child's face over a basin of water and studies its reflection).

VI:3 (two incantations)

First incantation (segments 1-10). *Structure:* four phases (phase 1: segments 1-4; phase 2: segments 5-7; phase 3: segments 8-9; phase 4: segment 10). *Speaker:* curer (role: *nahualli*-lord, Xolotl, Capanilli). *Addressee:* water (?), the Milky Way, the truant *tonal,* the sickness, tobacco. *Antagonist:* the truant *tonal. Patient:* the sick child. *Place:* in the patient's presence. *Intention:* to secure the cooperation of water and other helper-allies in finding the truant *tonal. Purpose:* to restore the child's *tonal.*

The speaker begins with an incitement (sentence 1:1) and then summons the water (sentence 1:2). She then states the problem: the child's *tonal* is missing (sentence 1:3). / She reports that she has come to use the tobacco or water (sentence 2:1). She announces her arrival (sentence 2:2) and boastfully identifies herself as a power being (sentence 2:3) and, now speaking to the (tobacco or water), announces that she has created it (sentence 2:4). / In sentence 3:1 she now turns and addresses Citlalcueyeh (the Milky Way), reproaching her for having turned against the child after being the one responsible for its creation. / In sentence 4:1, the speaker now abruptly turns to the truant *tonal* and threatens to carry it to the ocean and, to support the threat, boastfully identifies herself as a power being (sentences 4:2-4). // At this point she begins the second phase by again summoning the water (sentence 5:1) and then repeats the summons, but without the vocative (sentence 5:2). She commands it to go seek the bright reflection of the child's face in the basin of water (sentence 5:3). And apparently upon looking again and still not seeing the bright reflection, she asks who is responsible for sickening the child (sentence 5:4). / In sentence 6:1, she addresses the sickness and commands it to leave. And now she addresses the water, although without naming it, and tells it to wash the bright image of the child's face clean (sentence 6:2). She turns now and summons the missing *tonal* (sentence 6:3), reminding it that it used to live in a pleasant place (sentence 6:4), and telling it that she is looking for it (sentence 6:5). / She turns now to summon tobacco (sentence 7:1) and admonishes it not to bring shame on itself for not doing its proper duty (sentence 7:2). // She now begins the third phase by summoning water for yet another time (sentence 8:1) and next identifies the *tonal* (giving a number of possible names) (sentence 8:2). And addressing water, she arouses its attention (sentence 8:3) and commands it to wash the child (sentence 8:4) and to take it to some place of rushing water (sentence 8:5) in order to intensify the cleansing action. / To give her command authority, she boastfully identifies herself as a power being (sentence 9:1) who knows how to face danger (sentence 9:2), and threatens dire consequences if her commands are not carried out (sentences 9:3–4). // And now she begins the fourth phase by again facing the question of who is responsible for sickening the child (sentence 10:1), saying that she has come to capture the missing *tonal* (sentence 10:2), asking where it has gone (sentences 10:3–5). She repeats her intention of seizing and calling forth the *tonal* (sentences 10:6–7), and now, as a conclusion to the incantation, she implies that she has succeeded by talking to the *tonal,* telling it that it will make the child well (sentence 10:8).

If the identity of the addressee in sentence 2:4 (tobacco or water) is correct (and the context suggests it is) the speaker's claim to having created one or the other of these power entities is exceptional in the incantations of the collection. Given the usual relationship of a speaker to either of these two beings, the claim seems to be exorbitant, although as a rhetorical ploy it stands behind the imperious tone of the commands given to tobacco and water in the rest of the incantation; as creations of the speaker, they would be obligated to obey.

Second incantation (segment 11). *Speaker:* curer. *Addressee:* fire, copal, sleep. *Client:* the sick child. *Place:* the child's house. *Intention:* to secure the cooperation of fire and copal. *Purpose:* to cure the sick child.

This is a variant that accompanies another way of curing and is spoken at the end of an incantation such as the foregoing. The speaker summons the fire (sentence 11:1) and commands it to heal the sick child (sentence 11:2) but then asks how such a healing is possible if the child itself does not want to be healed (sentence 11:3). She now summons the copal (sentence 11:4) and likewise commands it to heal the child (sentence 11:5). She ends the incantation by summoning sleep for the child (sentence 11:6).

VI:4 (three incantations)

First incantation (segment 1). *Speaker:* curer (role: *nahualli*-lord). *Addressee:* the speaker's hands, Cuaton, Caxxoch. *Antagonist:* the headache. *Client:* person with a headache. *Place:* in the client's presence. *Intention:* to secure helper-allies against the headache. *Purpose:* to cure the headache.

The speaker begins with an incitement (sentence 1:1) and summons the hands (sentence 1:2). Without saying anything else to them, he turns and addresses Cuaton and Caxxoch, asking who is responsible for the patient's sickness (sentence 1:3). And as if to assure their giving him an answer, he boastfully identifies himself as a power being (sentences 1:4–6). He ends by promising that he and they will destroy the culprit (sentences 1:7–8).

Second incantation (segment 2). Cast and circumstances are the same as in the first incantation but the addressee role is taken by water.

This incantation is used if the first one fails in its purpose. The speaker begins by summoning water (sentence 2:1) and commands it to give relief to the patient (sentence 2:2).

Third incantation (segments 3–4). *Speaker:* curer (role: *nahualli*-lord). *Addressee:* tobacco, the curer's breath. *Antagonist:* headache. *Client:* person with a headache. *Place:* in the client's presence. *Intention:* to engage the help of helper-allies in dealing with the headache pain. *Purpose:* to cure the headache.

The speaker begins by boastfully identifying himself as a power being (sentences 3:1–3), so that when he next asks where the head destroyer is (sentence 3:4), it is an indirect command for it to reveal itself. He now turns and summons tobacco (sentence 3:5) and states his conviction that the *chalalahtli* root will bring relief (sentence 3:6). / He next reports that he is calling on his breath to cool off the head (sentence 4:1) [this constitutes a summons], and upon its arrival he asks it whether it has brought that which will cure the headache (sentence 4:2). He ends the incantation by asking where the pain has gone (sentences 4:3–4), apparently suggesting that it is no longer in the head.

VI:5 (one incantation)

Speaker: curer. *Addressee:* the inflamed veins in the eyes. *Antagonist:* the pain in the eyes. *Client:* a person whose eyes are bloodshot. *Place:* in the client's presence. *Intention:* to convince the inflamed veins to leave under threat of destruction. *Purpose:* to cure the bloodshot eyes.

The speaker begins with an incitement (sentence 1:1) and then summons the veins in the eyes (sentence 1:2), demanding to know what they are doing to the eyes (sentence 1:3). She imperiously dismisses the troublemaker, sending it away (sentence 1:4) and then threatens to call forth the water if it refuses to obey her (sentence 1:5), predicting that it will dissipate it and scatter it on the distant plain (sentences 1:6–7).

VI:6 (four incantations)

First incantation (segment 1). *Speaker:* curer (role: *nahualli*-lord). *Addressee:* the curer's finger, the mesquite sap. *Antagonist:* the pain in the eye. *Client:* a person whose eyes are inflamed. *Place:* in the client's presence. *Intention:* to engage the services of helper-allies in attacking the pain. *Purpose:* to cure the eyes.

The speaker begins by boastfully identifying herself as a power being (sentences 1:1–2) and then announces to the finger that she has brought it (sentence 1:3), implying that she is its master. She commands it first to seek the pain (sentence 1:4) and then to find out who is causing the pain to the eyes (sentence 1:5). She now turns and summons the mesquite sap that is to serve as the medicine (sentence 1:6), but gives it no command.

It is, of course, to be understood that the speaker goes on and uses the mesquite medicine that she has summoned. The summoning itself, as in most other instances, is merely a metaphor for the act of taking up the summoned entity in the hands.

Second incantation (segment 2). Cast and circumstances are the same as in the first incantation but the addressee role is now filled by tobacco.

The speaker summons tobacco (sentence 2:1), then summons it again as a medicine (sentence 2:2) and asks who is the one responsible for the client's problem (sentence 2:3).

The first and second incantations form a single sequence and are separated by only an interval of nonverbal activity.

Third incantation (segment 3). Cast and circumstances are the same as in the first incantation, but the addressee role is now filled by the mist-herb and the speaker's hands.

The speaker begins by summoning the mist-herb (sentence 3:1) and commands it to clean off the eye (sentence 3:2). Next he summons his hands (sentence 3:3) and commands them to accompany the mist-herb to where it is going (sentence 3:4).

Fourth incantation (segment 4). Cast and circumstances are the same as in the third incantation except that the addressee role is now filled by the copal.

The speaker begins by summoning the copal (sentence 4:1) and commands it to go clean off the eyes (sentence 4:2).

The third and fourth incantations form a single sequence and are separated only by an interval of nonverbal activity.

VI:7 (one incantation)

Speaker: curer. *Addressee:* tobacco. *Antagonist:* earache. *Client:* person with an earache. *Place:* in the client's presence. *Intention:* to engage the services of a helper-ally to deal with the earache. *Purpose:* to cure the earache.

The speaker summons the tobacco (sentence 1:1) and commands it to go in the ear in pursuit of the earache (sentence 1:2), thus implicitly commanding it to find out who is responsible for the patient's trouble (sentence 1:3). He warns it to do its duty (sentence 1:4). He next reports that he is blowing into the ear (sentence 1:5) and that his breath is entering in pursuit of the earache (sentence 1:6).

VI:8 (two incantations)

First incantation (segment 1). *Speaker:* curer. *Addressee:* tobacco, toothache, copal. *Antagonist:* toothache. *Client:* person with a toothache. *Place:* in the client's presence. *Intention:* to engage the service of helper-allies in attacking the toothache. *Purpose:* to cure the toothache.

The speaker begins by summoning tobacco (sentence 1:1) but says nothing more to it. She now summons the toothache (sentence 1:2) but again says nothing more to it. Now she summons the copal (sentence 1:3) and commands it to go in the tooth in pursuit of the toothache (sentence 1:4), warning it not to bring shame on itself by not doing its duty (sentence 1:5) and also warning it to do precisely what it has been told (sentence 1:6). Using a future-tense form, she commands it to cause the toothache that is harming the client to leave (sentence 1:7).

Second incantation (segment 2). Cast and circumstances are the same as in the first incantation, but the addressee role is now filled by the curer's hands.

The speaker summons her hands (sentence 2:1) and promises them that she and they will make the pain leave (sentence 2:2). She ends by asking what it is that is harming the tooth or what it is that is weakening the teeth (sentences 2:3–4).

VI:9 (one incantation)

Speaker: curer (role: *nahualli*-lord). *Addressee:* unspecified. *Antagonist:* jaw pain and its perpetrator. *Client:* a person suffering from a pain in the jaw. *Place:* in the client's presence. *Intention:* to establish his authority and competence. *Purpose:* to cure the pain in the jaw

The speaker begins with an unspecified summons (sentence 1:1). He boastfully identifies himself as a power being (sentences 1:2–4) and says that he has been sent by Citlalcueyeh (sentence 1:5). He then reports that he has brought his finger and tobacco (sentence 1:6). He repeats that he has brought his finger (sentence 1:7) and promises that it will chase away the pain (sentence 1:8). At this point he asks who is the one responsible for the patient's condition (sentence 1:9) and announces that he has come to destroy and kill him (sentence 1:10). He ends the incantation by again boastfully identifying himself as a power being (sentences 1:11–12).

This incantation is peculiar in that the summons is to unspecified entities and no command is addressed to them. Since they are the only second-person participants, presumably the speaker is talking to them throughout the rest of the incantation, in which he attempts to impress them with his project.

VI:10 (one incantation)

Speaker: curer. *Addressee:* the curer's hands, salt. *Antagonist:* swollen throat. *Client:* a person suffering from a swollen throat. *Place:* in the client's presence. *Intention:* to enlist the service of helper-allies against the throat pain. *Purpose:* to cure the swollen throat.

The speaker begins with a summons to his hands (sentence 1:1) and commands them to frighten away the pain (sentence 1:2). He then asks what it is that is responsible for the patient's sickness (sentence 1:3). He ends by summoning salt (sentence 1:4).

The incantation ends abruptly with no command or comment to the salt after it has been summoned. As is obvious from the comment following the incantation, physical activity by the speaker continues without verbal accompaniment. For another instance of a summons not followed by other remarks to the summoned entity but similarly continued through unverbalized activity, see VI:6:1.

VI:11 (one incantation)

Speaker: curer (role: *nahualli*-lord). *Addressee:* unspecified entity and later the *achiote.*

Antagonist: the pain of the swollen throat. *Client:* person with a swollen throat. *Place:* in the client's presence. *Intention:* to present his credentials and to enlist the aid of his helper-ally. *Purpose:* to cure the swollen throat.

The speaker begins by boastfully identifying himself as a power being (sentences 1: 1-2). He then promises that he will cool off the throat and cure it (sentences 1:3-4). He then summons the *achiote* (sentence 1:5) and, with a future tense form, commands it to cool off the pain (sentence 1:6).

The incantation begins with the addressee unspecified. It is highly unlikely that the role was intended to be filled by the client, since the curer in these incantations never talks to the client directly since direct communication is always limited to the antagonist and the helper-allies. The likely candidate would be the throat pain.

VI:12 (two incantations)

First incantation (segment 1). *Speaker:* curer. *Addressee:* cotton, fire. *Antagonist:* a body pain. *Client:* a person suffering a body pain. *Place:* in the client's presence. *Intention:* to secure the cooperation of helper-allies. *Purpose:* to rid the body of the pain.

The speaker begins with an incitement (sentence 1:1). She then summons the cotton (sentence 1:2) and commands it to combine with the fire (sentence 1:3). The speaker again utters an incitement (sentence 1:4) and summons the fire (sentence 1:5), commands it to combine with the cotton (sentence 1:6), and predicts that it will draw out the pain (sentence 1:7) [the prediction serves as an implicit command].

Second incantation (segment 2). The cast and circumstances are the same as in the first incantation, but the addressee role is now filled by the obsidian blade that serves as a lancet.

The speaker summons the obsidian blade (sentence 2:1) and advises it that she intends to use it on the tumified flesh (sentence 2:2). She predicts that the blade will join her in getting rid of the pain that is troubling the patient (sentence 2:3).

These two incantations are part of a single sequence and are separated only by an interval of nonverbal activity.

VI:13 (one incantation)

Speaker: curer (role: *nahualli*-lord). *Addressee:* the speaker's hands, *coanenepilli* medicine, his speaker's breath. *Antagonist:* chest pain. *Client:* a person suffering from a chest pain. *Place:* in the client's presence. *Intention:* to engage the support of helper-allies in combatting the chest pain. *Purpose:* to cure the chest pain.

The speaker begins by summoning her hands (sentence 1:1), and, to give the summons more credence, she boastfully identifies herself as a power being (sentences 1: 2-3). She then states that she is seeking the pain (sentence 1:4) and asks where it is hiding (sentences 1:5-6). She again boastfully identifies herself (sentences 1:7-8). She now summons the medicine made from *coanenepilli* (sentence 1:9). She states her project to cool off the patient's body (sentence 1:10) and tells the medicine it will enter the body (sentence 1:11). She now tells the atole-medicine to step aside for the heart (sentence 1:12). In sentence 1:13 she states that she is pursuing the sickness and then turns to summon her breath (sentence 1:14), which she commands to go in pursuit of the sickness (sentence 1:15).

The *nonacayōtzin,* "my dear flesh," in sentence 1:10 is an instance of the curer's self-identification with the patient, a rhetorical strategy designed to convince the antagonist of the uselessness of his continued evil-doing (since the curer is such a powerful being, attack against her person is doomed to failure). Compare VI:22:1.

VI:14 (one incantation)

Speaker: curer. *Addressee:* tobacco, the curer's hands, *iyauhtli. Antagonist:* chest pain. *Client:* a person suffering from a chest pain. *Place:* in the client's presence. *Intention:* to enlist the aid of helper-allies. *Purpose:* to cure the chest pain.

The speaker begins by summoning tobacco (sentence 1:1), and predicts that it will (i.e., commands it to) frighten away the pain (sentence 1:2). He next asks who is responsible for the patient's trouble (sentence 1:3) and then commands the tobacco to pursue the pain (sentence 1:4). At this point, he commands it to go (sentence 1:5) and asks where the pain is residing (sentence 1:6) and then answers his question by saying it is in the patient's chest (sentence 1:7). He predicts that the tobacco will go (i.e., he orders it to go) following after the *nahualli*-head (the pain) (sentence 1:8). And as a conclusion to the incantation, he warns the hands and the *iyauhtli* not to bring shame upon themselves by not doing their duty properly (sentence 1:9).

VI:15 (one incantation)

Speaker: curer. *Addressee:* chest pain. *Antagonist:* chest pain. *Client:* child suffering from a chest pain. *Place:* in the client's presence. *Intention:* to persuade the chest pain to leave the child. *Purpose:* to cure the child of the chest pain.

The speaker begins with an incitement (sentence 1:1). He then addresses the chest pain and approaches it by asking what it is afflicting the patient with (sentence 1:2). He informs it that it is not needed here (sentence 1:3) but that, on the other hand, it is needed in some unpleasant place (sentence 1:4).

The final two sentences are equivalent to a command for the pain to leave. Contrast this consigning of pain to a disagreeable place with the invitation to it to go to a pleasurable place in VI:24.

VI:16 (one incantation)

Structure: Two phases (phase 1: segment 1; phase 2: segment 2). *Speaker:* curer (role: *nahualli*-lord). *Addressee:* the fingers, the curer's hands, the lancet; water, spiders. *Antagonist:* the blood. *Client:* a person who needs to be bled. *Place:* in the client's presence. *Intention:* to enlist helper-allies and to persuade the possible obstacles to get out of the way. *Purpose:* to bleed the client.

The speaker begins by identifying himself as a power being (sentences 1:1–3). He then announces that he is already going (sentence 1:4) and that he will follow the veins (sentence 1:5). He announces to his hands that the time has come for action (sentence 1:6), and then he commands them to act exemplarily (sentence 1:7). He now turns and summons the lancet (sentence 1:8) and promises that very shortly it will draw blood (sentence 1:9). Apparently addressing the hands (or the hands and lancet), he commands them to consider diligently the place where the blood is coming from (sentence 1:10) and next speaks of the poverty and suffering of the patient (sentence 1:11). He tells the hands (or the hands and the lancet) that they are wasting their time searching for their property [i.e., the blood] (sentence 1:12). In sentence 1:13, he wonders where it [their property] has come from. In sentence 1:14, he asks for a second chance to look for their property [i.e., the blood] and promises that they will come get it (sentence 1:15). In sentence 1:16, he repeats the request that he have a second chance to look for the blood even in the bone itself. // A new phase of the incantation begins when he turns and addresses water, commanding it (by means of a future-tense form) to look for the one who is harming the patient (sentence 2:1). He predicts that it will soon find it (sentence 2:2). He next addresses the various spiders, i.e., the obstacles, but instead of belligerently attacking them, he invites them to move out of the way and to hide (sentences 2:3–4) and says that he would like not to hurt them (sentence 2:5). He ends with another warning to the obstacles to move aside (sentence 2:6).

VI:17 (one incantation)

Speaker: curer. *Addressee:* copal or salt. *Antagonist:* the blood. *Client:* a person who is bleeding. *Place:* in the client's presence. *Intention:* to enlist the help of an ally in stopping the flow of blood. *Purpose:* to stop the bleeding.

The speaker begins by summoning the copal or salt (sentence 1:1) and then rouses it to attention (sentence 1:2) and tells it that soon it will destroy the pain (sentence 1:3). He again rouses the copal or salt to attention (sentence 1:4) and tells it that soon it will enter the body (sentence 1:5), that it will make the blood stop flowing (sentence 1:6), and that it will subdue the antagonistic "Spirit" (sentence 1:7). He ends the incantation with a strong demand that it will carry out the command immediately (sentences 1:8–9).

VI:18 (one incantation)

Speaker: curer. *Addressee: atl inan. Antagonist:* stomach pains. *Client:* a person suffering from stomach pains. *Place:* in the client's presence. *Intention:* to enlist the cooperation of the helper-ally in combating the stomach pains. *Purpose:* to cure the stomach pains.

The speaker begins by summoning the *atl inan* (sentence 1:1), then explains to it that he is injecting it into the client's rectum (sentence 1:2). He commands it to pursue the stomach pain (sentence 1:3).

The text indicates that in a variant, *tzopilotl* is summoned instead of *atl inan* (segment 2).

VI:19 (one incantation)

Speaker: curer. *Addressee:* belly pains. *Antagonist:* belly pains. *Client:* a person suffering from belly pains. *Place:* in the client's presence. *Intention:* to intimidate the belly pains into leaving. *Purpose:* to cure the belly pains.

The speaker begins with an incitement (sentence 1:1). He then addresses the belly pains and rebukes them for their secretive harm (sentence 1:2) and complains to them of their hurting the intestines (sentence 1:3). And, having stated his accusation, he now warns them that a needle is going to where they are (sentence 1:4). But he immediately explains that for the present he is not attacking them (sentence 1:5) (that is, the needle is just a messenger of warning), that he has not come to destroy them (sentence 1:6) (that is, as an honorable man he makes a conciliatory gesture of letting the pains act on their own in deciding to leave), and that he simply intends that they hide (that is, fade away and do no more harm) (sentence 1:7). But now he shows that this graciousness is not because of weakness on his part since he threatens that if they do not take the warning and obey him he will call his ally, the needle, their mortal enemy (sentences 1:8–9). He tells them that the needle is hungry and thus eager to attack them (sentence 1:10), and as a further threat he describes it as dragging its guts (i.e., the thread) (sentence 1:11). He promises that the needle will go against them (sentence 1:12). To intensify the threat, he further promises that he will summon water (sentence 1:13) and warns that dire consequences will follow if he is not obeyed (sentence 1:14). He predicts (i.e., threatens) that tobacco, *atl inan,* and *iyauhtli* will follow the pain into the belly (sentences 1:15–16). And he ends with Latin, placing the whole action in God's care (sentence 1:17).

This is one of the best organized incantations in the collection. It has a single vocative focus throughout. Also the personality of the speaker has a neat consistency in showing him to be a person of confident power. Starting off from an attitude of rebuke, he shows himself to be a reasonable and honorable man by first giving his enemies the option of leaving on their own. But like a prudent man, he then shows that this kindness is not the expression of weakness by laying out the alternative of force in a convincing display of the resources at his disposal. This image of the speaker as a person not to be trifled with is supported here by the lack of a boasting self-identification, since such confidence in one's power does not need such pronouncements. Note that, since the incantation presents only the initial parley, the helper-allies are only referred to, not summoned. The time for such a summons would come only after the failure of the enemies to respond properly to the verbal demands.

VI:21 (one incantation and a possible extension)

Speaker: curer. *Addressee:* fire, loin pain. *Antagonist:* loin pain. *Client:* person suffering from loin pain. *Place:* in the client's presence. *Intention:* to enlist the aid of a helper-ally in combating the loin pain. *Purpose:* to cure the loin pain.

The speaker begins with an incitement (sentence 1:1) and then summons the fire (sentence 1:2). There follows a repetition of the incitement (sentence 1:3) and another summons, apparently again to the fire, though it is not named (sentence 1:4). The speaker then commands it (using a future-tense form) not to hurt him (sentence 1:5) and tells it that he has brought his callused sole (sentence 1:6). Once again he commands it (with a future-tense form) not to hurt him (sentence 1:7). He then explains that by means of his sole he will chase away the pain that is hurting the patient (sentence 1:8). At this point, to end the incantation, he now directs his attention to the pain and, without naming it, tells it that he will destroy it (sentence 1:9).

In segment 2, the text gives a continuation added by some curers to the above.

The speaker continues talking to the pain, explaining that he has brought his sole, which will catch the pain with the efficiency of a net (sentence 2:1). [Presumably the *etc.* in the text means that this should hook into sentence 1:7.] After this, he apparently addresses his sole and asks where the pain has gone (sentences 2:2–3), whether perhaps it is inside the body (sentence 1:4). Apparently these questions, with which the incantation ends, are meant to suggest that the pain has gone away.

VI:22 (three incantations)

First incantation (segment 1). *Speaker:* curer. *Addressee:* plaster made from *poztecpahtli*, the splints. *Antagonist:* broken bone. *Client:* a person who has a broken bone. *Place:* in the client's presence. *Intention:* to enlist the cooperation of helper-allies. *Purpose:* to set the broken bone.

The speaker begins by summoning the plaster made from *poztecpahtli* (sentence 1:1). He commands it to carry the painful broken leg in its arms (sentence 1:2) and further commands it (by means of a future-tense form) to help the patient, who is suffering (sentence 1:3). He ends the incantation by addressing the splints, which he commands (by means of a future-tense form) to carry the broken leg in their arms (sentence 1:4).

Second incantation (segment 2). *Speaker:* curer. *Addressee:* the quail. *Antagonist:* the quail. *Client:* a person with a broken bone. *Place:* in the client's presence. *Intention:* to reproach the quail for breaking the bone. *Purpose:* to set the broken leg.

The speaker begins with an incitement (sentence 2:1) and then, speaking to the quail, asks it reproachfully what it is doing with the bone that it broke (sentence 2:2). He announces that he has arrived to set the broken bone (sentences 2:3–4).

The reproach to the quail shows the breaking of the bone to have a mythological transcendence; the present event is a manifestation of the mythological event (see note VI:22:8). But while the myth signifies human mortality (perishability rests on physical imperfection), its use here merely refers to physical fragility. The speaker of the incantation is not concerned with the myth logic of before and after (the etiological argument). A Mictlan bone is not now the potential for human creation, not the source of human vitality hedged with mortality found in the myth, but merely a synecdochic representative of a particular here-and-now bone. The speaker claims for himself the power of Quetzalcoatl not so that he might create life despite the marring of the bones but simply to restore the bone from a broken state to health, a claim that goes beyond any statement in the myth itself, since Quetzalcoatl made no effort to restore the bones to perfection, a task beyond his powers. He merely tearfully accepted and worked with their broken and marred condition. The curer, then, as on other occasions, is simply using myth as a warrant for entering into the spiritual world, that vital world in which changes in the physical world are generated. The curer transposes the metaphorical logic of the myth into the synecdochic logic of the incantation in order to take advantage of the spiritual presuppositions sanctioned by the myth.

Third incantation (segments 3–4). *Structure:* 2 phases (phase 1: segment 3; phase 2: segment 4). *Speaker:* curer (role: Quetzalcoatl). *Addressee:* an unspecified entity; the cord used to bind the splints. *Antagonist:* pulque. *Client:* a person with a broken bone. *Place:* in the client's presence. *Intention:* to criticize pulque for having harmed the client and to enlist the cooperation of the bindings on the splints. *Purpose:* to set the broken bone.

The speaker begins with a question to an unspecified entity, asking what pulque has done (sentence 3:1). He next states that pulque and his client have become involved with one another (sentence 3:2), with the implication that his client has been taken advantage of and pushed into harm by the pulque. He now boastfully identifies himself as a person of power with supernatural knowledge (sentences 3:3–6) and promises that he will get the bone from Mictlan (sentence 3:7) though it has been damaged (sentences 3:8–9). He ends the first phase of the incantation by promising that he and the unspecified entity initially addressed will heal the bone (sentence 3:10). // The second phase begins with an incitement (sentence 4:1). The speaker now addresses the cord used to bind the splints and commands it to remain guarding the bone (sentence 4:2). He warns it not to spoil things (sentence 4:3) and promises to return tomorrow (sentence 4:4).

This incantation refers more strongly to the marred-bones myth (the creation-of-man myth) (see note VI:22:8) than the second one, since the speaker identifies himself in the hero role of Quetzalcoatl. It seems that there has been a certain confusion in the informant since, logically, sentences 3:3–10 would seem to belong in the second incantation. As it is, there seems to be no overt and structurally satisfying connection between the accusations against pulque (sentences 3:1–2) and the speaker's entry into the role of Quetzalcoatl. It is true, of course, that Quetzalcoatl had reason to be antagonistic toward pulque since it was the main cause of his loss of Tollan (Tula) (see Sahagún 1952:15–16). Note that the unspecified entity addressed in sentence 3:1 should again not be thought to be the client; the latter is mentioned in the third person in sentence 3:2.

VI:23 (one incantation)

Speaker: curer. *Addressee:* the back pain. *Antagonist:* the back pain. *Client:* a person suffering from a back pain. *Place:* in the client's presence. *Intention:* to intimidate the back pain. *Purpose:* to cure the back pain.

The speaker begins with an incitement (sentence 1:1). He then addresses the back pain and tells it that the needle is coming (sentence 1:2) and that it will go throughout every part (sentence 1:3) and will eat and destroy anyone that it comes across (sentence 1:4).

Although Ruiz de Alarcón says that the words were accompanied by the pricking activity, the incantation is merely a promise of impending action and thus apparently serves only as a verbal introduction to the physical phase of the curing activity.

VI:24 (one incantation)

Structure: two phases (phase 1: segments 1–3; phase 2: segment 4). *Speaker:* curer. *Addressee:* illness. *Antagonist:* illness. *Client:* a person suffering from an illness. *Place:* in the client's presence. *Intention:* to persuade the pain to leave the body. *Purpose:* to cure the illness.

The speaker begins with an incitement (sentence 1:1). She then accuses the pain, without naming it, of trying to destroy the body (sentence 1:2). She announces her arrival (sentence 1:3), saying that she has come to track down and find the pain (sentences 1:4–5). She states that the needle is also coming (sentences 1:6–7) and promises that it will go throughout every part (sentence 1:8) and will destroy the pain (sentence 1:9). / After this threatening beginning, the speaker suddenly changes tactics. As if the thought of that destruction brings out her compassion, she now takes on a friendly stance, advising the pain to go to some place where there are good lodgings (sentence 2:1), where there is wealth (sentences 2:2–3). She takes now an even more comradely stance, using a first-person plural possessive to describe the various things of theirs that they will find in a good dwelling place (sentence 2:4). And then she asks why they (she and the pain) should bother staying where they are (sentence 2:5) while elsewhere they can live with pleasure (sentence 2:6). She urges the pain to go ahead of her and says that she will follow (sentence 2:7) since she is also hungry (sentence 2:8). / And having set forth the positive reasons for going elsewhere, she now stresses the negative ones for staying here, asking what can be found to eat here in the patient's body (sentence 3:1), where it is cold and windy (sentence 3:2) with no comforts (sentence 3:3). // The second phase of the incantation serves as its ending. The speaker utters a prediction that can be taken either as friendly advice or as a threat: tobacco will destroy the pain (sentence 4:1), will chill it (sentence 4:2), and will sap its strength (sentence 4:3).

This is another excellently structured incantation unified around a single addressee. The personality of the speaker is interesting because of her use of duplicity, attempting to persuade through friendly advice rather than through threats of violence. Even if sentence 4:1 is read as a threat, there is nothing to indicate that the tobacco will be acting on the speaker's behalf, so even here the integrity of the pretended friendly stance is maintained.

VI:25 (two incantations)

First incantation (segment 1). *Speaker:* curer. *Addressee: atl inan,* water, tobacco. *Antagonist:* skin rash. *Client:* a person suffering from skin rash. *Place:* in the client's presence. *Intention:* to enlist the cooperation of helper-allies. *Purpose:* to cure the rash.

The speaker summons the medicine *atl inan* (sentence 1:1) and tells it that it will counteract the rash (sentence 1:2), that it will extinguish the fire of the rash (sentence 1:3). She speaks now to water and informs it that it is now carrying (or accompanying) the *atl inan* (sentence 1:4) and repeats the statement that it will extinguish the fire of the rash (sentence 1:5). She turns now and summons tobacco (sentence 1:6) and tells it that it is going along mixing with the *axin* (sentence 1:7) and carrying it (sentence 1:8). She summons water again (sentence 1:9) and tells it that the time to strike has come (sentence 1:10). She summons it again (without naming it) (sentence 1:11) and commands it to go destroy the rash (sentence 1:12). She warns it against the mockery that at dawn the rash would make of the patient (sentence 1:13). And then, speaking of a future event as a past one, she declares that the water has destroyed the rash (sentence 1:14) and then shifts and predicts that now finally the water will destroy and banish the rash (sentence 1:15).

Second incantation (segments 2-5). The cast and circumstances are the same as those in the first incantation, but the addressee role is now filled by *axin*, the rash; *coanenepilli*, copal, salt, and yellow earth.

The speaker summons the *axin* (sentence 2:1) and predicts that finally it will banish and destroy the rash (sentence 2:2). The speaker now addresses the rash, explaining that she has come to make it swallow the medicine *axin* (sentence 2:3) and that she will drive it away (sentence 2:4). She also informs it that she has brought *coanenepilli* (sentence 2:5). / And at this point she turns and summons the *coanenepilli* (sentence 3:1) and commands it to follow the *axin* (sentence 3:2) and warns it about not doing what it is specifically told (sentence 3:3) and not to bring shame on itself for not doing its duty (sentence 3:4). She then points out that, if there is failure, it will not be her fault but the *coanenepilli*'s (sentences 3:5–6). / She now turns and summons copal (sentence 4:1) and commands it to go eradicate the rash (sentence 4:2). She then tells the salt that its turn has come (sentence 4:3). She now summons the rash (sentence 4:4) and reproaches it, asking what it is doing hurting a poor person (sentences 4:5–6). She turns and summons the yellow earth (sentence 4:7) and commands it (with a future-tense form) to block the spread of the rash (sentence 4:8). / And in conclusion, she again summons the rash (sentence 5:1) and reproaches it by asking what it is doing (sentence 5:2).

These two incantations are part of a single sequence but are separated by nonverbal activity.

VI:27 (two incantations)

First incantation (segment 1). *Speaker:* curer. *Addressee: iyauhtli. Antagonist:* tertian fever. *Client:* a person suffering from tertian fever. *Place:* in the client's presence. *Intention:* to enlist the cooperation of a helper-ally. *Purpose:* to cure the tertian fever.

The speaker begins by summoning the *iyauhtli* (sentence 1:1) and then commands it to go and destroy the chills and fever trying to destroy the patient (sentence 1:2).

Second incantation (segment 2). The cast and circumstances are the same as those in the first incantation, but the addressee role is now taken by water.

The speaker begins with an incitement (sentence 2:1) and then summons the water (sentence 2:2). He commands it to descend to the stomach of the patient (sentence 2:3) and to cure the sickness (sentence 2:4).

VI:28 (one incantation)

Speaker: curer. *Addressee: tlacopahtli. Antagonist:* urinary sickness. *Client:* a person suffering from urinary sickness. *Place:* in the client's presence. *Intention:* to enlist the cooperation of a helper-ally. *Purpose:* to cure the urinary sickness.

The speaker summons the medicine *tlacopahtli* (sentence 1:1) and commands it to drive away the sickness (sentence 1:2), to force it out (sentence 1:3), and to calm it down (sentence 1:4). He then asks who is responsible for the sickness that is harming the patient (sentence 1:5).

VI:29 (three incantations)

First incantation (segment 1). *Speaker:* curer. *Addressee:* herbs. *Antagonist:* the fever. *Client:* a person suffering from fever. *Place:* in the client's presence. *Intention:* to obtain the cooperation of the herbs in dealing with the fever. *Purpose:* to cure the fever.

The speaker summons the herbs (sentence 1:1) and commands them to pursue the fever that is troubling the patient (sentence 1:2).

Second incantation (segment 2). The cast and circumstances are the same as those in the first incantation, but the addressee role is now filled by *ololiuhqui.*

The speaker begins by summoning *ololiuhqui* (sentence 2:1) and commands it to force the fever to leave (sentence 2:2). He predicts that the *ololiuhqui* will console the patient (sentence 2:3); that is, he commands it to do so. He then promises that the patient will be grateful (sentence 2:4).

Third incantation (segment 3). The cast and circumstances are the same as those in the first incantation, but the addressee role is now filled by *atl inan.*

The speaker begins with an incitement (sentence 3:1). He summons the *atl inan* (sentence 3:2) and commands it to chase away the fever (sentence 3:3). He then informs it that he has injected it into the rectum (sentence 3:4) and demands that it not work later on (sentences 3:5–6) but immediately force the pain out (sentence 3:7). He then asks who is responsible for the sickness that is destroying the patient (sentence 3:8), speaking of the patient as if he belonged to the medicine (a rhetorical ploy to make the medicine more obligated to help). He then boastfully identifies himself as a power being (sentences 3:9–10).

VI:30 (one incantation)

Structure: two phases (phase 1: segments 1–3; phase 2: segment 4). *Speaker:* curer. *Addressee:* water, *atl inan. Antagonist:* fever. *Client:* a person suffering from fever. *Place:* in the client's presence. *Intention:* to discover and drive away the culprit. *Purpose:* to cure the fever.

The speaker begins by summoning water (sentence 1:1). He asks who is responsible for the sickness that is destroying the patient (sentence 1:2). / He now summons the medicine *atl inan* (sentence 2:1), saying that he plans to take it to the patient's stomach (sentence 2:2). He asks where the pain is (sentence 2:3) and then commands the medicine to go and tend to the guts (sentence 2:4), commanding (by means of a future-tense verbform) it not to bring shame on itself by not doing its duty (sentence 2:5). / He turns now and boastfully identifies himself as a power being (sentences 3:1–2). He summons the water (sentence 3:3) and, without saying anything else to it, again boastfully identifies himself (sentences 3:4–5). He now summons the maize kernels (sentence 3:6) and states that the time for action has arrived (sentence 3:7). // The speaker begins phase 2 by asking who is responsible for harming the patient (sentence 4:1). He issues an indirect command for the sickness to leave (sentence 4:2) and another for it to step aside for him (sentence 4:3). He states that the sickness is expected elsewhere (sentence 4:4), where things are more prosperous (sentence 4:5). He issues an indirect command for the sickness to leave the poor patient (sentence 4:6) and another for it not to harm him (sentence 4:7), and still another for it to go away immediately (sentence 4:8). He now demands that it happen immediately (sentences 4:9–10). And he ends the incantation by threatening punishment if it does not go away (sentence 4:11).

It is interesting to compare the indirect commands found here, where the speaker deals with the sickness only through intermediaries, with the direct commands found in VI:24.

VI:31 (two incantations)

First incantation (segment 1). *Speaker:* curer. *Addressee:* the relaxed sphincter muscle. *Antagonist:* the body stiffness. *Client:* a person suffering from stiffness. *Intention:* to convince the relaxed sphincter muscle and the enema to join in getting rid of the stiffness. *Purpose:* to get rid of the body stiffness.

The speaker begins by summoning the relaxed sphincter muscle (sentence 1:1) and then states that she and the clyster (which is not named) will find the stiffness (sentence 1:2).

Second incantation (segment 2). The cast and circumstances are the same as those in the first incantation, but the addressee role is now filled by the medicine *tzopilotl.*

The speaker begins by summoning the medicine *tzopilotl* (sentence 2:1) and then commands it to go destroy the body pain (sentence 2:2).

VI:32 (four incantations; the nonincantatory material, contained in segments 1–6, is not paraphrased here)

First incantation (segment 7). *Speaker:* curer. *Addressee:* the scorpion. *Antagonist:* the scorpion. *Client:* a person stung by a scorpion. *Place:* in the client's presence. *Intention:* to shame the scorpion. *Purpose:* to limit the effect of the scorpion sting.

The speaker begins by summoning the scorpion (sentence 7:1), asking it where it has stung the patient (sentence 7:2) and then finds the place (sentence 7:3). He then predicts that the poison will not go beyond the boundary he has set (sentence 7:4).

Second incantation (segments 8–9). *Structure:* two phases (phase 1: segment 8; phase 2: segment 9). The cast and circumstances are the same as those in the first incantation, but the addressee role is filled first by the scorpion and then by the ground-up dirt. The speaker takes the role of Chicome-Xochitl (the deer).

The speaker begins by boastfully identifying himself as a power being (sentence 8:1–2). He then summons the scorpion (sentence 8:3) and asks reproachfully why it mocks people (sentence 8:4). He asks whether it does not remember that it has been shamed by the goddess Xochiquetzal (sentence 8:5) and states categorically that the scorpion has no power and can do nothing (sentences 8:6–7). He now commands it to go elsewhere to make fun of people (sentences 8:8–9). // He now begins the second phase of the incantation by addressing the ground-up dirt that will serve as medicine (sentence 9:1) and commands it to cause the scorpion to depart (sentence 9:2) and then expresses the wish that the scorpion will leave (sentence 9:3) and that it will step aside for the medicine (sentence 9:4). He next demands that this happen immediately (sentences 9:5–6) and ends by threatening dire consequences if it does not leave (sentence 9:7).

Third incantation (segment 10). The cast and circumstances are the same as those in the first incantation. The speaker takes the role of Xochiquetzal.

The speaker begins by reproachfully asking the scorpion whether it is not ashamed of what it is doing (sentence 10:1). He reproachfully asks why it is making fun of people (sentences 10:2–3) and whether it does not remember that it has been shamed by Xochiquetzal, whom the speaker is pretending to be (sentence 10:4). The speaker, as Xochiquetzal, announces that he has arrived (sentence 10:5), having come to greet the scorpion (sentence 10:6). He commands it to leave his client (sentence 10:7). But he now changes tactics and begins seducing it and lulling it to sleep (sentences 10:8–14).

Fourth incantation (segments 11–12). Spoken by a woman. The cast and circumstances are the same as those in the third incantation.

The speaker, a woman in the role of Xochiquetzal, reproachfully asks the scorpion whether he is not ashamed of harming people (segment 11). Then, after fastening a tourniquet above the sting, she declares that the scorpion has been stopped (sentences 12:1–4).

The myth of Yappan is primarily concerned with the weakness of the scorpion's virulence, but the question the narrative logic undertakes to answer deals not only with the poison but also with the scorpion's appearance, its apparent headlessness and the phallic shape of its tail. The appropriateness of the myth's concern with the shape of the tail in a story about toxicity is founded in the fact that the stinger is in the tail. It is this preoccupation that allows the myth to exploit a metaphor based on the penile shape of the tail by developing an underlying proportion that holds that the tail is to a penis as the injection of poison is to the ejaculation of semen. The argument, therefore, is that Yappan's sexual abstinence, if maintained, would result in the scorpion's high toxicity while his sexual indulgence would result in the opposite. The presupposition is that sexual abstinence leads to physical power. Thus Xochiquetzal, by leading Yappan into sexual depletion, provides the narrative justification for the weakness of the scorpion's poison. The story thus moves from penile-shaped tail to sexual indulgence to weakened toxicity.

When we look at the three incantations used in curing a scorpion sting, we can distinguish three different modes of exploiting the myth, but all three rest on two basic synecdoches. The first maintains that the scorpion that stung the curer's patient is the mythical Yappan-become-scorpion. The second maintains that the poison itself is the scorpion.

In the first incantation there is a minimal degree of involvement with the myth.

The speaker does not go beyond the basic synecdoches and does not even identify himself. His power stance is simply assumed, as can be seen in his imperious command and in the very brevity of the incantation.

In the second incantation there is a much stronger involvement with the myth, though the speaker stands somewhat aloof from the version recounted in the *Treatise* since he identifies himself as Chicome-Xochitl, the deer, and thus the incantation presumably alludes to another myth in which Chicome-Xochitl would be shown to have power over Yappan. In sentences 8:5–7 the speaker taunts the poison with the shameful fact that it, as Yappan, broke its penance because of Xochiquetzal's seduction. Note that, because of the sexual implications of the verb phrases TĒ-(CA) MO-(CAYĀ-HUA), "to mock someone," and TĒ-(CA) M-(ĀHUI-L-TIA), "to frolic with someone" (in sentence 8:9), there is a hinted reference to the depletion-of-sexual-vigor motif. Furthermore, the taunting epithet, Pelxayaqueh, "Bare-mask-owner," refers to the phallic shape of the tail since it is a metaphor for penis. But the curer's tactic in attempting to make the poison abate is not to remind it of its weakness owing to Yappan's sexual indulgence; that is, he does not appeal to the real cause of the poison's ineffectiveness. He points instead to the shameful failure as a cause of impotence. That is, the curer is apparently more impressed with a reasoning that would justify physical weakness by moral weakness than in the original reasoning (i.e., in the myth) that located one kind of physical weakness in another kind of physical weakness.

It is in the third and fourth incantations, however, that one finds the fullest use of the myth. The speaker here identifies himself/herself as Xochiquetzal, and the relationship between the speaker and the poison is put on a personal plane. The shaming has now to do more fully with the sexual depletion of Yappan, as can be seen in sentences 10:4–14. The important point is that these sentences deal with the weakening of toxicity through sexual depletion, thus following the governing logic of the myth.

The fullness of the involvement of the third and fourth incantations with the myth shows the extent to which the two synecdoches are lived as a reality rather than merely exploited as a figure of speech. The interesting thing, however, is how completely myth time and real time become fused in these incantations and how, as a result, the neatness of the analytical and explicative logic of the myth becomes muddled in the incantations. The user of the incantations seems unperturbed by the myth-recognized fact that the posttransformation world cannot simultaneously be both post- and pretransformation. The sexual seduction of Yappan was an effective pretransformation strategy, and to employ the same strategy in the posttransformation world is logically impossible if one is guided by myth logic. But the curer is following a different logic from that of the myth maker. As a curer he is not concerned with metaphors that supply etiological explanations of a physical fact. He is concerned, rather, with synecdoches that activate spiritual powers. The curer's mimed copulation with the poison to deplete its vigor is sanctioned as a strategy in the myth. That sanction alone is sufficient for the curer, since his belief in the myth justifies his spiritual enterprise. The fact that the metaphorical logic of myth is concerned with a before and an after is of no importance to the synecdochic logic that disavows such categories by claiming that the one is the other.

GLOSSARIES

Glossary of Linguistic Terms

The following terms are used in the morphological and syntactical analyses and discussions in the notes and appendices. For a more elaborate treatment, see Andrews 1975.

Absolutive state. A condition of noun forms when no possessive prefix is present. Absolutive forms usually carry a distinctive number suffix and may have a distinctive stem (depending on the noun class). Compare *possessive state* (q.v.).
Action noun. A noun that names an action, e.g., *huetziliztli,* "the action of falling."
Active verb form. A verb form in which the subject confix (person prefix plus number suffix) indicates an entity (or entities) that carries (or carry) out an activity or process; e.g., *He saw her.* Compare *passive verb form* and *impersonal verb form.*
Adjunctor. The word *in,* which is used to adjoin an embedded word or clause to a matrix word or clause.
Admonitive form. A tense-mode form of a verb that admonishes one to beware of performing (positive admonitive) or of not performing (negative admonitive) an action.
Agentive noun. A derived noun form that names or signifies the one who performs an action (e.g., *fighter, actor*). Frequently such a noun is equivalent to a present participle in English (e.g., *a fighting one*). A Nahuatl agentive noun may have a present, customary present, future, or preterit verb form as the source.
Analysis of forms. Nahuatl noun forms and verb forms are analyzed into constituent parts according to formulas (hyphens separate constituents, except that parentheses replace them to isolate the stem):

Noun: person-possessor(STEM)number [an absolutive form has the possessor slot empty, i.e., filled by a zero constituent]
Intransitive verb: person(STEM)tense-number
One-object verb: person-object(STEM)tense-number
Two-object verb: person-object-object(STEM)tense-number
Three-object verb: person-object-object-object(STEM)tense-number

In two-object and three-object verbs, only one object can be manifested if two or all three are specific projective objects, the secondary object prevailing over the primary and the tertiary object prevailing over the secondary.

The above analyses are not to be confused with the mere citing of a wordstem. The notation for the latter is:

Noun: (STEM)-number
Intransitive verb: (STEM)
One-object verb: object-(STEM)
Two-object verb: object-object-(STEM)
Three-object verb: object-object-object-(STEM)

The number suffix on a cited nounstem has the appropriate absolutive singular shape (-TLI, -TL, -IN, -ø). The projective object prefix(es) on the cited verbstem has (have) the nonspecific shape (TĒ-, TLA-), while a reflexive object is given in the specific non-first person shape (MO-). Note that here a hyphen may occur with an opening or closing parenthesis, as is not the case with the analytical formulas above.

Applicative verb. A derived verb that indicates the relation of an action to a beneficiary or receiver.

Appositive. A noun or clause used as an explanatory or clarifying equivalent of a noun or pronoun, both having the same syntactic relation to the other elements in the sentence.

Basic object. Any of the verb objects (primary, secondary, or tertiary) marked in the transitive verbword by a prefix. Verb object prefixes are obligatory on transitive verbs.

Basic subject. The subject that is marked in a verbword or nounword by a subject confix (person prefix plus number suffix). The presence of such a subject is obligatory in Nahuatl in both verbwords and nounwords.

Causative verb. A derived verb that indicates causing or producing an action that is named in the original verb; e.g., *to fell* from *to fall.* The subject of such a verb names the causer of the action, and the verb object brought into the construction by the derivation names the agent of the original action: *He felled the tree = He caused the tree to fall.*

Clitic. A word having no independent accent, but pronounced as part of a contiguous word.

"Connective *-cā-*" compound. A compound verb form that contains a *preterit agentive noun* (q.v.), in its combining form (ending in *-cā*), as *embed* (q.v.).

"Connective *-ti-*" compound. A compound verb form that contains a *preterit tense theme* (q.v.) as *embed* (q.v.) linked to the *matrix* (q.v.) verbstem by means of the infix *-ti-*. The infix becomes *-t-* before a stem with an initial vowel.

Cross reference. The relationship between a *supplement* (q.v.) and its *head* (q.v.).

Customary present agentive noun. An *agentive noun* (q.v.) that has the form of a customary present verbword.

Double-nucleus form. A construction that consists of two nuclei, i.e., two separate subject-plus-predicate constructions, where the subject of each is basic (see *basic subject*). Such a construction may have a *single-nucleus form* (q.v.) as a synonymous variant.

Double-object verb. A transitive verb that must take two objects.

Embed. A constituent (morpheme, phrase, or clause) that is added to another, functionally more important, constituent (called the *matrix,* q.v.); for example, in the compound noun *fishhook, fish* is the embed. In Nahuatl compound words (as in English ones) the embed always precedes the matrix. When the constituents are clauses, the embedded clause is often equivalent to what is traditionally called a "dependent clause."

Embedded clause. A clause that functions as an *embed* (q.v.) in a larger construction.

Flaw form. A noun form derived from a defect-signifying noun by using the -ø number suffix instead of -TLI, -TL, or -IN in the absolutive singular. A flaw form refers to an entity that has the imperfection, deformity, blemish, or flaw signified by the source noun.

Frequentative verb. A verb form denoting repetition or intensity of the action or multiplicity of agents, patients, occasions, or places separately involved in the action. Such a form is created by a reduplicative prefix (i.e., a prefix that repeats the initial vowel or initial consonant and vowel of the stem) on the verbstem, without or with either a glottal stop (q.v.) or vowel length.

Future agentive noun. An agentive noun (q.v.) derived from a future tense verbword.

Future tense theme. The part of a future tense verbword consisting of the *imperfective stem* (q.v.) and the future tense suffix *-z-*.

Gentile noun. A noun that names a member of a kin-based unit or a tribal society based on it. The term derives from Latin *gens,* "patrilineal clan."

Glottal stop. The audible release of a complete closure at the glottis, often used in English (e.g., it may be heard in adjacent vowels in such words as *re-educate* and *co-operate* when pronounced carefully). In Nahuatl regularized spelling, it is represented by an *h.*

Head. A word that is syntactically dominant in a group and could have the same syntactic function as the whole group if it stood alone.

Honorific form. A grammatical form indicating inferiority or humbleness of the speaker.

In noun words the suffix *-tzin* is used; verbwords use either an *applicative* (q.v.) or a *causative* (q.v.) formation plus a reflexive verb object, or, in the instance of a reflexive source verb, a derived stem ending in *-tzin-oa.* It is signified by (H) in translated stems.

Imperfective stem. A verb stem that serves as the base for the present, customary present, imperfect, and future indicative tense forms and the present and past optative forms. Compare *perfective stem* (q.v.).

Imperfect tense theme. The part of an imperfect tense verbword consisting of the *imperfective stem* (q.v.) and the imperfect tense suffix *-ya-.*

Impersonal patientive noun. A *patientive noun* (q.v.) that has the object-prefix characteristics of an impersonal verb form (q.v.).

"Impersonal *tla-*" stem. An impersonal verbstem created from an intransitive verb by prefixing *tla-* without changing the intransitive nature of the verb.

Impersonal verb form. An inherently impersonal verb or a nonactive verb form derived from either an intransitive or a transitive source in such a way that the subject confix (person prefix plus number suffix) is only third person singular with no reference to a particular, nameable entity. The subject of an inherently impersonal form is translated as *it;* e.g., *It is raining.* The subject of a derived impersonal verb form is translated as *people (in general)* or *things (in general).* Compare *active verb form* (q.v.) and *passive verb form* (q.v.).

Inbound purposive form. A *purposive form* (q.v.) indicating movement toward the speaker. Compare *outbound purposive form* (q.v.).

Incorporated adverb. A nounstem that is included as an *embed* (q.v.) in either a nounword or a verbword in the function of an adverbial modifier.

Incorporated object. A nounstem that is included as an *embed* (q.v.) in a verbword as its direct object.

Inflectional affix. A prefix or suffix added to a nounstem or verbstem.

Matrix. A constituent (morpheme, phrase, or clause) to which another, functionally less important constituent (called an *embed,* q.v.) is added; for example, in the compound *houseboat, boat* is the matrix; in *boathouse, house* is the matrix [the former item is basically a boat, the latter a house]. When the constituents are clauses, the matrix clause is often equivalent to what is traditionally called a "main clause."

Matrix clause. A clause that functions as a *matrix* (q.v.) in a larger construction.

Modifier. An adjunct (adjective or adverb) that limits or qualifies a head word (noun or verb).

Morpheme. A minimum meaningful unit of language; e.g., *boldly* consists of two morphemes, *bold-* and *-ly.*

"Named-partner" construction. A noun-centered or verb-centered construction in which the subject confix (personal prefix plus number suffix) on a noun or a verb, the possessive prefix on a noun, or an object prefix on a verb is plural but a supplementary subject, possessor, or object names only a singular noun which must be understood to be the partner of (one of) the unnamed participant(s) in the subject, possessor, or object function. The translation of such a construction has the form *X and I, X and we, X and you,* etc., *X's and my, X's and our,* etc., or *X and me, X and us,* etc.

Name form. A special form of a noun that may be used as a personal name. It is marked by the replacement of an absolutive number suffix by zero (i.e., a silently present constituent).

Nounstem. A *stem* (q.v.) that takes affixes characteristic of nouns.

Number suffix. A suffix on a noun form or on a verb form that indicates whether one entity (singular) or more than one (plural) is involved in the subject function.

Optative form. A tense-mode form of a verb that expresses a wish. The optative is also used to express a command.

Organically possessed form. A noun form in the *possessive state* (q.v.) marked by the stem-final constituent *-yo* indicating that the possessed item is organically connected to the possessor. For example, *nonacayo,* "my flesh (part of my body)" stands in contrast to *nonac,* "my meat (that I bought)."

Outbound purposive form. A *purposive form* (q.v.) indicating movement away from the speaker. Compare *inbound purposive form* (q.v.).

Passive patientive noun. A *patientive noun* (q.v.) that has the object-prefix characteristics of a *passive verb form* (q.v.).

Passive verb form. A verb form derived from a transitive source in such a way that the subject confix (person prefix plus number suffix) indicates the entity (or entities) that is (or are) the patient or undergoer (*or* patients or undergoers) of the action expressed by the verb, e.g., *She was seen.* In Nahuatl, the subject of the source form (i.e., the agent of the action) cannot be mentioned (i.e., one cannot say literally *She was seen by me,* only *She was seen*). Compare *active verb form* (q.v.) and *impersonal verb form* (q.v.).

Patientive noun. A derived noun form that names or signifies the one who is a "patient" of an action (i.e., one who has undergone or "suffered" it). Frequently such a noun is equivalent to a past participle in English. A patientive noun may have a *verb root* (q.v.), a past verb form, or a present verb form as a source.

Perfective stem. A verbstem that serves as the base for the preterit and the pluperfect tense forms and the admonitive forms. A perfective stem has only one shape for each verb. Compare *imperfective stem* (q.v.).

Person prefix. A prefix on a noun form or a verb form that indicates whether the first, second, or third person is involved in the subject function.

Place name. A noun that names a village, town, or area.

Possessive prefix. A pronominal prefix that indicates the possessor in a possessive state noun.

Possessive state. A condition of noun forms marked by the presence of a possessive prefix. Possessive forms carry a distinctive number suffix and may have a distinctive stem (depending on the noun class). Compare *absolutive state* (q.v.).

Present agentive noun. An *agentive noun* (q.v.) that has the form of a present tense verbword.

Preterit agentive noun. An *agentive noun* (q.v.) that has the form of a preterit verbword.

Preterit agentive noun of possession. An *agentive noun* (q.v.) that has the form of a preterit of a verb of possession. Such a verb has a nounstem signifying a possessed entity as an *embed* (q.v.) and the *preterit tense theme* (q.v.) of one of three verbs as a matrix (q.v.): *TLA-(E) and *TLA-(HUA), "to own something" and *TLA-(YOA), "to own something abundantly."

Preterit-as-present agentive noun. An *agentive noun* (q.v.) that has the form of a *preterit-as-present tense* (q.v.) verbword.

Preterit-as-present tense. A special verb form that has the shape of a preterit tense form and the meaning of a present tense form. Such a tense is possible in only a limited number of verbs.

Preterit tense theme. The part of a preterit tense verbword that consists of the *perfective stem* (q.v.) and the preterit tense suffix -ø- (i.e., zero, a silently present constituent).

Primary object. The object prefix that is present on a *single-object verb* (q.v.).

Progressive form. A compound verb formation that represents continuing action. Such a form is marked by a "connective *-ti-*" infix.

Projective object. A verb object that does not refer back to the subject. Contrast *reflexive object* (q.v.).

Purposive form. A verb form that indicates movement toward or away from the speaker for the purpose of performing an action.

Reflexive object. A verb object that refers back to the subject. Contrast *projective object* (q.v.).

Relational noun. One of a small group of nouns that function as *matrix* (q.v.) of a noun word and serve to indicate relational ideas similar to those expressed by English prepositions.
Root patientive noun. A *patientive noun* (q.v.) that is formed on a *verb root* (q.v.).
Secondary object. The object prefix added to the company of a primary object by an applicative or causative derivation that creates a *double-object verb* (q.v.).
Single-nucleus form. A construction that consists of a single nucleus, i.e., a single subject-plus-predicate construction, where the subject is *basic* (q.v.). Such a construction may have a *double-nucleus form* (q.v.) as a synonymous variant.
Single-object verb. A transitive verb that can take only one object.
Stem. That which is left of a word when all inflectional affixes have been removed (see *inflectional affix*).
Supplementary object. A noun (word or clause) that stands in apposition to an object prefix (the basic object) and clarifies its reference.
Supplementary possessor. A noun (word or clause) that stands in apposition to a possessive prefix (the basic possessor) and clarifies its reference.
Supplementary subject. A noun (word or clause) that stands in apposition to a subject confix (pronoun prefix plus number suffix, the basic subject) and clarifies its reference.
Supplementation. The relationship existing between an appositive and a pronominal suffix (subject, object, or possessor). The closest construction possible in English is the so-called "expletive *it*": "*It* is reported *that they have lost the battle.*" The clause *that they have lost the battle* stands in apposition to the pronoun *it* or, in other words, supplements it.
Supportive vowel. A vowel (usually *i*) used to break up initial and final combinations of consonants, since these are not permitted in Nahuatl.
Tense theme. The part of a verb consisting of the perfective or imperfective stem and one of the correlated tense suffixes.
Tertiary verb object. The object prefix added to the company of a *secondary object* (q.v.) by an applicative or causative derivation that creates a *triple-object verb* (q.v.).
Triple-object verb. A transitive verb that must take three objects.
Verb classes. Nahuatl verbs can be classified into four classes depending on the relationship of the *perfective stem* (q.v.) to the *imperfective stem* (q.v.) that serves as the base form.

Class A: no change; e.g., (CHŌCA) > (CHŌCA)
Class B: loss of final vowel; e.g., (COCHI) > (COCH)
Class C: replacement of final vowel with glottal stop; e.g., (CHOLOA) > (CHOLOH)
Class D: addition of a final glottal stop; e.g., (YA) > (YAH)

Verb-object embed. An embedded nounstem that is incorporated into a verbword and functions as the object of a verb. See *embed.*
Verb root. The morpheme within a verbword that carries the main lexical information; e.g., (POL-), "destroyed," in (POL-IHUI), "to become destroyed."
Verbstem. A *stem* (q.v.) that takes affixes characteristic of verbs.
Vocative. A noun used in naming or calling the entity (*or* entities) being spoken to.

Glossary of Nahuatlisms and Hispanisms

Nahuatlisms are Nahuatl words that have been "borrowed" into Spanish (in Spanish they are called *aztequismos*), usually with changes in shape to accommodate them to Spanish phonological and morphological principles. Some of these have been further "borrowed" from Spanish into English. Hispanisms are Spanish words that have been "borrowed" into English. Since Nahuatlisms and Hispanisms name items that are peculiar to Aztec and Hispanic cultures, they have no easy equivalents in foreign languages such as English, and we have, therefore, kept them in our translation. In the following, Hispanisms are indicated by (S). The unmarked words are Nahuatlisms.

Achiote [*āchiyōtl*]. The seeds of a small tropical tree, *Bixa orellana*, which has alternate, simple, broad leaves and reddish flowers. The seeds, contained in a fruit that looks like a small hedgehog, are used as a food colorant and also in some foods as a condiment instead of chili pepper.

Alcalde (S). An Indian official of a town who often acted in the capacity of judge.

Alguacil (S). A political official of a barrio.

Atole [*ātōlli*]. A maize-meal gruel of varying consistency and flavor. See *Atolli* in Appendix D.

Beneficiado (S). A secular priest supported by endowed assets.

Cabecera (S). The head town of a political district.

Camote [*camohtli*], *Ipomea batatas (L.).* Sweet potato.

Camotillo, *Curcuma longa.* Turmeric, the tuberose rhizome of a herbaceous perennial plant of the ginger family.

Chicubite [*chiquihuitl*]. A basket of willow twigs, almost cylindrical in form and slightly wider at the base than at the top. Also spelled *chicobite.*

Chili [*chīlli*]. The very pungent fruit of certain red peppers, *Capsicum frutescens*, used as a seasoning.

Cimate [*cimatl*]. A plant whose roots are used as a condiment. It is added to *aguamiel* to give a good taste to pulque.

Comal [*comālli*]. An earthenware griddle for cooking tortillas and toasting beans, coffee, and so forth.

Compadre (S). A godfather (seen from the perspective of the child's godmother or parent) or an intimate friend.

Congregación (S). A concentration of scattered Indian populations brought together by the Spanish authorities.

Copal [*copalli*]. The name common to a variety of resins used principally as incense for burning in the temples and before the altars and also used for medicinal purposes. See *copalli* in Appendix D.

Cura (S). A secular priest who administers a parish.

Doctrina (S). A parish administered by a regular priest.

Doctrinero (S). The regular priest who administers a *doctrina* (q.v.).

Elote [*ēlōtl*]. The ear of ripe, tender maize.

Fiscal (S). A political official of a barrio.

Gobernador (S). The head political officer of a *cabecera* (q.v.).

Huipil [*huīpīlli*]. A closed-sewn, sleeveless woman's tunic (Anawalt 1981:52).

Jicamilla, *Jatropha macrorhiza.* A wild plant whose root is used as a purgative.

Mandón (S). A political official of a barrio. The Nahuatl equivalent is the preterit agentive noun (TĒ-YAC-ĀN-ø)-QUI, "one who has taken people by the nose," i.e., "a leader."

Mezquite [*mizquitl*]. Mesquite, i.e., any of several spiny leguminous shrubs or small trees of the genus *Prosopis*. See *Mizquitl* in Appendix D.
Nahual, *pl.*, ***nahuales.*** See *Nahualli.*
Nahualli [*nāhualli*]. An Indian sorcerer who supposedly is able to transform himself/herself into an animal. See *Nahualli* in Appendix C.
Petate [*petlatl*]. A mat woven of reeds or of fine palm, having many uses among the Mexican natives, such as a rug, a mattress, a bedspread, lining for boxes, or the seat or back for a chair.
Peyote [*peyōtl*]. The name of diverse kinds of cactaceous plants used for medicinal purposes. Martínez lists sixteen varieties of the same family, the principle ones being *Lophophora williamsii* Coult., a poisonous medicinal plant described by Sahagún; *Ariocarpus fissuratus*, Schum; *Astrophytum asteras*, Lam.; different varieties of senecios; and some mammillarias. See *Peyotl* in Appendix D.
Piciete [*piciyetl*]. The common name of the ordinary tobacco used by country people, a solanaceous plant (*Nicotina rustica*, L.). See *Piciyetl* in Appendix D.
Poquiete [*pōquiyetl*]. Tobacco for smoking. See note VI:24:7 of the *Treatise.*
Principal (S). A Spanish word used to designate certain native nobles. See note I:2:9 of the *Treatise.*
Pulque [*poliuhqui*]. An intoxicating drink of a white translucent color and thickish consistency. It comes from the fermentation of *aguamiel* extracted from the maguey. The word *pulque* was used by the Spaniards to refer to *octli*, "maguey wine." It has been hypothesized that the word is a Spanish distortion of the Nahuatl word *poliuhqui*, a preterit agentive noun meaning "a thing that has become spoiled."
Quetzal [*quetzalli*]. A long, flowing green tail feather of the resplendent quetzal *Pharomachrus mocinno.* The word *quetzalli* is a patientive noun meaning literally "a thing that can be stood upright," from the verbstem TLA-(QUETZA), "to stand something upright."
Tamale [*tamalli*]. A pone of maize dough and fried chopped meat wrapped in maize husks and steamed. There are different kinds depending on the condiments or the kind of meat used.
Tecomate [*tecomatl*]. A cylindrical gourd or pottery vessel used for drinking.
Tenamastle [*tenāmāztli*]. One of the three rocks set into a triangular configuration on which cooking utensils are set over the fire. The word *tenāmāztli* consists of the nounstem (TENĀMI)-TL, "wall," plus the instrumental ending (-ĀZ)-TLI (see Andrews 1975:371).
Tenexiete [*tenexiyetl*]. Tobacco mixed with lime, usually in proportions of ten to one. See *Tenexiyetl* in Appendix D.
Teponaztli [*teponāztli*]. A horizontal wooden drum. See note I:3:5 of the *Treatise.*
Tequixquite [*tequixquitl*]. Natural salt that appears in the form of efflorescences when water evaporates from brackish lakes. The composition varies according to the nature of the waters containing it in solution. See *Tequixquitl* in Appendix D.
Tianguez [*tiānquiztli*]. An Indian village market or fair in which merchandise is sold or bartered.
Tlameme [*tlamēmeh*]. An Indian carrier. The word is a preterit agentive noun meaning "a person who has carried things," from the verb TLA-(MĒME), "to carry something on one's back."
Tomate [*tomatl*]. A small, green tomatolike fruit. See *Tomatl* in Appendix D.
Tonal, see *Tonalli.*
Tonalli [*tōnalli*]. A day-name; loosely, a soul. The word *tōnalli* is a patientive noun meaning "a thing that has become sun-lighted *or* sun-warmed" from the verb (TŌNA), "for the sun to shine; to be sunny; for the weather to be warm."
Tzoal, see *Tzoalli.*
Tzoalli [*tzohualli*]. Dough of amaranth seeds.

Visita (S). A minor town within a *doctrina* (q.v.).
Xicara [*xīcalli*]. A hemispherical vessel or bowl made from the shell of certain gourds.
Xilote [*xīlōtl*]. The immature ear of maize.

NOTES

LETTER TO FRANCISCO MANSO DE ZÚÑIGA

[1] Francisco de Manso y Zúñiga was archbishop of Mexico from 1627 to 1637 (Bravo Ugarte 1965:62). The flyleaf of the MS says: "He was the 8th archbishop, 1629–1637." This clearly refers to Manso y Zúñiga.

[2] The *congregación* [i.e., congregation] was the program of forced resettlement of scattered Indian populations, resulting from depopulations caused by epidemics, into compact communities, primarily for Spanish administrative efficiency and ease of religious conversion. The largest were in the 1590s and early seventeenth century (Gibson 1964:282–83).

PROLOGUE

[1] I.e., secular law and ecclesiastical law.

FIRST TREATISE

Chapter 1

[1] The word *nahuales* is the plural of the Nahuatlism *nahual.* The corresponding Nahuatl word is *nānāhualtin,* the plural of *nāhualli.* See Appendix C.

[2] Ponce reports that midwives continued to perform native baptismal ceremonies. See Appendix A.

[3] I.e., *Cuāuhtli.*

[4] I.e., *Cōātl.*

[5] The Spanish is *poniendole su nombre,* which may also be translated "giving him his name."

[6] Despite this statement, Ruiz de Alarcón does not report any personally witnessed event in this section but only retells secondhand accounts. Furthermore, he later implies that the source of his first example may not be absolutely trustworthy, although he initially asserts the contrary.

[7] In I:6, Ruiz de Alarcón identifies Antonio Marques as his notary.

[8] I.e., *Cacahuatepēc.* See Appendix E.

[9] Friar Andrés Girón was auxiliary *cura* of Taxco from 1622 to 1655 (Toussaint 1931: 240).

[10] *Tēxōxqueh, tēyōllohcuānih,* and *tētlachīhuiānih.* See Appendix C.

[11] I.e., *nahuales.* See note I:1:1.

[12] Ruiz de Alarcón's discussion of *nāhualli* is mistaken. The word is not derived from any of the verbs he mentions. The first one, "to command," is TĒ-(NĀHUA-T-IA), which is an applicative verb derived from (NĀHUA-TI), "to have a loud, clear sound," derived from (NĀHUA)-TL, "a loud, clear sound; a clearly perceptible sound." The second one, "to speak with authority," is TLA-(NĀHUA-T-IA), which has the same derivation as the first. The third, MO-TLA-(NĀHUA-L-TIA), "to hide oneself behind something," is not the source of (NĀHUA-L)-LI but, on the contrary, is derived from it. For a discussion of *nāhualli,* see Appendix C.

Chapter 2

[1] Although it is unclear what source Ruiz de Alarcón is using, references to Peru were not uncommon for writers of the colonial period. For example, Torquemada (1976: 199–205, 239–42) relied on the work of Acosta (1979).

[2] This is the only mention of *cuexpalli* in the MS. Molina lists the word only with the meaning "long hair that they leave on the back of the neck of boys when they shear them." *Cuexpalli* is a compound stem which may either result from the combination of the embed (CUEX)-TLI and the matrix (PA-L)-LI or be derived as the patientive noun directly from the compound verbstem (CUEX-PA), whose matrix TLA-(PA) means "to dye something." The stem (CUEX)-TLI is also found as an embed in the word (CUEX-COCH)-TLI, "occiput, back of the head," and in the place name (CUEX-TLĀN)-ø (e.g., see Sahagún 1954: 64).

[3] *Yāōtl, Tītlācahuān;* these are two separate names, although Ruiz de Alarcón translates them as if they formed a unit. See Appendix B.

[4] The word *potōn* is a preterit agentive noun from the verb (POTŌ-NI), which is defined in Molina as "to stink, or smell bad." Although Molina does not list *potōn,* he does give its alternative form, *potōnqui* [the *-qui* is a variant singular number suffix for preterit verb forms],

which he defines as "an odiferous or stinking thing; or dry, finely ground powder, or finely sifted flour." He gives the derived causative form of the verb as TLA- or TĒ-(POTŌ-NI-A), "to put a plaster made of small feathers and turpentine on something or someone, or to feather something or someone." Therefore, the word *potōn,* in the meaning of "loosely woven cloth," is a metaphorical usage.

[5] September 29, commonly called Michaelmas Day, dedicated to the archangel Michael (Butler 1956, III:677).

[6] *Teolōchōlli,* "cairn," a compound noun consisting of (TE)-TL, "rock, stone," as embed and (OLŌCH-Ō-L)-LI, "mound," as matrix.

[7] *Mātlapōuhqui.* This should have been the plural form *Mātlapōuhqueh.* See Appendix C.

[8] *Tlaōlxīniānih.* See Appendix C.

[9] *Principales* [i.e., "principal ones"] was the term used by the Spaniards to designate the *pipiltin* (nobles), in contrast to the *tlahtohqueh* (caciques) (Gibson 1964:154–55). Molina gives *tecutli* [i.e., *tēuctli*] as the equivalent of *principal.*

[10] Ceremonial bathing was an integral part of the sacrificial ceremony in classical times (see the many occurrences of *tlaāltīltin,* "bathed ones," in Sahagún). The notion of the purification of someone being sent as a messenger to the gods is here being continued in a different dimension: dedication of someone to the service of a god. In this light, Ruiz de Alarcón's remark, "as if offering him to the river," is interesting in that, while it captures the symbolic import, it is probably made in ignorance of the classical parallel. In Sahagún (1954:64) there is a reference to bathing as a part of the ceremony for installing a *tlahtoāni* ("a ruler"): *niman īc huih in māltīzqueh in tlahtoāni īhuān tēuctlahtohqueh,* "immediately thereafter the ruler and the lords go in order to bathe," and then, again in the same paragraph, after making blood offerings to Huitzilopochtli: *īhuān māltiāyah,* "and then they bathed." But these bathings seem more for the purpose of a postritual cleansing than for a dedicatory purification.

[11] The MS has *tecomatillos,* which is a Nahuatlism with the Spanish diminutive suffix *-illo.* We have translated it as "little *tecomates.*"

[12] The MS has *ytlàpial,* which would be rewritten as *ītlahpial.* The word, however, is a patientive noun from the verb TLA-(PIYA), "to guard something." There is, then, no justification for the glottal stop, and we have rewritten the word, here and elsewhere, as *ītlapial,* although *ītlahpial* was undoubtedly a valid dialectal form; one finds, for example, the entry *tlajpia* [i.e., *tlahpia*], which would presuppose the verbstem TLA-(IH-PIYA), in Brewer and Brewer (1962:231), which they translate as *cuida* ("he takes care of"), although the compound forms show a glottal stop (which Brewer and Brewer spell *j* and we spell *h*) only if it belongs to the embed; compare *purojpia* ("he takes care of burros"), where the embed is *puroj-,* and *tomapia* ("he takes care of *tomates*"), where the embed is *toma-.* Also, they list the verb with a specific object as *quipia* (1962:197), that is, without a glottal stop, but the meaning is also different, "he has it, it contains it." The word *ītlapial* does not mean "those who have the obligation of guarding such a thing," but rather "his guarded thing." Ruiz de Alarcón translates it more accurately later in the chapter as "his inheritance." Also, *notlapial* is later correctly translated as "my inheritance." Instead of the patientive noun, the expected form here would be the agentive noun, *tlapixqui* ("one who has guarded something"), a form that, incidentally, Carochi (1904:406, 454) gives as *tlàpixqui* [i.e., *tlahpixqui*], which again presupposes the problematic verbstem TLA-(IH-PIYA).

[13] *Santohcalli* (literally, "saint-house"); a compound, having the Spanish word *santo* ("saint"), Nahuatlized to *santoh,* as embed and the Nahuatl word *calli* ("house") as matrix.

[14] See note I:2:11.

[15] *Ahmō notlapial. Ca zan īpan nehcōc.* "It is not my guarded thing. Indeed I have only come upon it." Concerning the spelling *notlapial,* see note I:2:12.

[16] *Īpampa ca ahmō notlapial.* "Because it indeed is not my guarded thing." Concerning the spelling *notlapial,* see note I:2:12.

[17] The MS has *ensierran* ("they put under lock and key"), for which we read *entierran* ("they bury"), first, because locking something up was not an effective way to hide it from Ruiz de Alarcón and, second, because of the mention of "beneath the earth" in the next part of the sentence.

[18] The *cuezcomatl* was usually a vasiform grass-and-daub granary; it was one of several

types of granaries used in pre-Columbian Mexico (Hernández Xolocotzin 1949:164–65). See note III:5:4.

[19]The MS has *Quauhchinalla,* a copyist error for *Quauhchimalla,* i.e., *Cuauhchimallan.* See Appendix E.

[20]*Ītlapial;* see note I:2:12.

Chapter 3

[1]I.e., *Huāuhtli.* See Appendix D.

[2]Several varieties of maize were cultivated in Mexico, with growing periods ranging from three to six months. Three-month maize is advantageous in dry conditions where the short growth period minimizes the danger of drought, but its yield is less than that of longer-growing varieties (Kirkby 1973:57–58).

[3]One *vara* equals 0.838 meters, or 32.99 inches (Carrera Stampa 1949:10).

[4]See note I:2:12.

[5]*Teponāztli,* a hollowed-out log drum having an H-shaped cut forming tongues that are beaten with rubber-headed drumsticks. The word consists of (TEPON)-TLI, "tree trunk" and (-ĀZ)-TLI, "instrument." See Andrews 1975:371.

[6]See note I:2:12.

[7]*Tlatōtoyāhuah,* literally, "They persistently pour something liquid out." Perhaps Ruiz de Alarcón should have written *tlatōtoyāhualiztli,* i.e., the action noun meaning "the act of persistently pouring something liquid out," although it was common to name actions by means of Nahuatl verbwords.

Chapter 4

[1]Autosacrifice was common in Mexican religion. Cutting themselves with thorns or obsidian blades, penitents frequently drew thorns or twigs through their flesh, or cut their ears, drawing blood as an offering to the gods (Sahagún 1951:184–85).

[2]*Tlamahcēuhqueh* ("penitents"), a plural preterit agentive noun from TLA-(MAH-CĒHUA), "to obtain or merit what is desired; to perform penance."

[3]The MS reads *todos llaman aseñor delmundo* [b]*cuyos,* Tlalticpaque *cautivos somos Dios. de* [b]Yaotl tiytlācahuan, *las batallas.* [c]*el coxqui* [c](Moquequeloatzin) *lloso—como si dixeran—el que no sufre coxquillas, ò el zeloso—.* The correct ordering of this (given by Paso y Troncoso 1892:138) is: *todos llaman a Señor del mundo,* Tlalticpaque; *cuyos cautivos somos,* tiytlacahuan; *Dios de las batallas,* Yaotl; *el coxquilloso,* Moquequeloatzin, *como si dixeran: el que no sufre coxquillas, o el zeloso;* our translation follows this corrected reading. The garbled sequencing in the MS suggests that the source manuscript had a different format, the lines of which the copyist has shuffled. He apparently did not understand the text, as Paso y Troncoso (1953:13) has noted.

The Spanish *zeloso* [i.e., *celoso*] is ambiguous. It may mean "zealous, jealous; fearful, distrustful." We have arbitrarily selected "jealous"; the Nahuatl word offers no guidance in choosing among the various alternatives.

[4]*Tlacāuhqueh,* "those who have abandoned something," a plural preterit agentive noun from TLA-(CĀHUA), "to abandon something." Perhaps the word intended was *tiahcāhuān,* which Molina (under the entry *tiacauan*) translates as "valiant men, spirited and brave soldiers."

[5]*Tenexiyetl.* See Appendix D.

[6]Serna (1892:390) specifies that *tenexiete* was "green tobacco mixed with lime."

[7]I.e., *Tlālticpaqueh.* See Appendix B.

[8]Serna (1892:390) has "do not go along playing" (*no vaias jugando*) before "do not detain yourself in vain."

[9]The word *nocōmihchic* is the possessive form of *cōmihchictli,* a compound noun whose embed is (CŌMI)-TL, "bowl," and whose matrix is (IHCHIC)-TLI, "a scraped-off thing," the patientive nounstem from the verbstem TLA-(IHCHIQUI), "to scrape something." It is possible that this word is the informant's misunderstanding of what should have been *nocuahchic* ("my warrior's feather ornament," a metaphor for "my warrior").

[10]The MS has *timàahuiltitiuh,* a form that contains conflicting signals: the second person singular prefix *ti-* following *mā* signals the admonitive, but the verb *-uh* after the connective *-ti-* signals the optative (when following *mā*). The context clearly calls for the admonitive, and we have changed the verb accordingly.

[11]The word *nitlacuepalohticah* is a "connective *-ti-*" compound whose embed is the preterit theme of (TLA-CUEPA-L-OA), "to produce a returned thing," i.e., "to burp," from the pa-

tientive noun (TLA-CUEPA-L)-LI, "a returned thing."

[12] I.e., *tenexiyetl.* See Appendix D.

[13] Instead of "might take [it]" (Spanish, *fueze tomando*), Serna (1892:390) says "might exert himself" (Spanish, *se fuesse esforçando*).

[14] I.e., *tenexiete,* the Nahuatlism for *tenexiyetl.* See Appendix D.

[15] The plural ("your uncles") in the preceding sentence shifts to the singular ("he") here.

[16] The *acxoyatl* [i.e., *acxōyatl*] of the MS is not just any kind of branch, as Ruiz de Alarcón believes, but a ritually significant fir bough used in penitential bleeding ceremonies. Reports of its use can be found, for example, in the *Florentine Codex* (Sahagún 1953:4): *Auh in yehhuātl, Tēucciztēcatl, in īpan tlamahcēhuaya mochi tlazohtli; īacxōyauh quetzalli,* "And all that upon which Teucciztecatl did penance was expensive; his fir bough was quetzal plumes." Hernández (1959a:13) defines *acxōyatl* as *abeto* ("fir").

[17] The MS has *mochiquacel,* which we have rewritten as *mochicuahcol* (see the entry *chiquacolli* in Molina). The glottal stop has been added under the hypothesis that the stem is (CHICU-AH-CO-L)-LI, "a shoulder to one side, an additional shoulder," i.e., "a walking staff." The embedded CHICU- is a variant of the adverb *chico,* "at/to one side," and is also found in (CHICU-ĒI)-ø, "three on the [other] side," "[one hand and] an additional three [digits]," i.e., "eight"; compare CHIC- in (CHIC-ŌME)-ø, "two on the [other] side," "[one hand and] an additional two [digits]," i.e., "seven." The variation of /kʷ/ and /k/ is frequent in Nahuatl.

[18] The MS has *Motlàtlàhuan,* that is, *motlahtlahhuān,* a distributive/varietal possessive plural form (because of the reduplication plus glottal stop) of the stem (TLAH)-TLI, "uncle." The meaning is "your separately located uncles" or "your uncles of various kinds." The reading is suspect because there is no apparent justification for the notions of distribution or variety either here or in any of the other instances of the form in the work (II:7:1; II:7:4; II:13:1; II:16:1; II:16:2; II:17:1; III:6:1). We have nevertheless kept it because there are other occasions in the MS where the expected form *motlahhuān,* "your uncles," is used (II:6:1; II:6:2; II:7:2; II:10:1; II:11:1; II:11:2; II:14:3), suggesting the possibility of a legitimate contrast in usage. However, the fact that in III:7:1 the form *notlatla* is used in the MS for the singular makes our decision to keep the reduplicated syllable even more questionable. See note III:7:3. One should, furthermore, consider that the distributive/varietal plural formation was apparently accepted, at least in certain dialects, as a simple plural; see, for example, the numerous instances in Arenas (1862).

[19] Siméon lists the intransitive verbstem (MĀY-AHUI) [listed under *mayaui*] as meaning "to drive back, to remove, to set aside," all of which sound curiously transitive and none of which fit the context here. The word seems to mean "to use one's hand(s)" and is presumably a denominative verb from the nounstem (MĀI)-TL, "hand." It is also found in II:8:10.

[20] The MS has *tlahcanahualli* here and *tlacanahualli* three sentences later. The word might be *tlahcahnāhualli,* ("daytime-*nahualli*"), except that the pilgrimage is supposedly at night. We have chosen to read *tlācanāhualli* ("person-*nahualli*" or "lord-*nahualli*") on the assumption that it is formed in analogy to *tlācatecolōtl* ("person-owl" or "lord-owl"); see note I:5:12. The evil, aggressive connotations implicit in the latter word are the same as those found in *tlācanāhualli.* Note that Molina's entry *tlacanaualli* ("a trimmed-down-thing") represents *tlacanāhualli,* a patientive noun from the verb TLA-(CANĀHUA), "to trim something down," and has nothing to do with the word in the MS.

[21] The phrase *cuauhtlah chānehcācah* means "he is in the manner of one who has owned a home in the forest," i.e., "he is a forest-dweller." The word *chanehcācah* is a "connective *-cā-*" compound; that is, it has the preterit agentive noun of possession (CHĀN-EH-ø)-ø, "one who has owned a home," in its combining form, (CHĀN-EH-ø-CĀ)-, as an adverbial embed, and the verb (CAH), "to be," as the matrix.

[22] The *tlanmahalactic* of the MS has the frequently found dialectal spelling of *-nm-* instead of a single *-m-*. The word is a compound, consisting of the adverbial embed (TLAN)-TLI ("tooth"), and the matrix *ahalactic* ("slippery"), with the reduplicative *ah-* indi-

cating distributive application (which is equivalent to saying that it indicates the plurality of "teeth"). Apparently a number of Ruiz de Alarcón's informants pronounced a stemfinal 'n' as an [m] before a following vowel even where the *n*-sound would expectedly be maintained. See Karttunen and Lockhart (1976: 10–14) on the gemination of syllable-final nasals in colonial texts.

[23]The word in the MS, *xicquahuihuītequi*, is ambiguous. It may be XI-C(CUAUH-HUIH-HUĪTEQUI)ø-ø ("strike him repeatedly with a stick" or "strike him with a variety of sticks"), where the embed is (CUAHUI)-TL, "tree, wood, piece of wood, stick, board" [which becomes XI-C(CUA-HUIH-HUĪTEQUI)ø-ø because /W/ + /w/ becomes /w/] or it may be XI-C(CUĀ-HUIH-HUĪTEQUI)ø-ø ("strike him repeatedly on the head"), where the embed is (CUĀI)-TL, "head." We have chosen the second possibility while Ruiz de Alarcón has chosen the first.

[24]The MS has *Tichualcuih*, which would ordinarily be rewritten *tichuālcuih*, "we bring it." This, however, is obviously an error since the first person plural does not fit the context. We have therefore changed the final *-h* to the future tense suffix *-z: tichuālcuiz*, "you will bring it."

[25]The MS has *intlapoztectli* for *in tlapoztectli* ("the broken-off thing"), where *tlapoztectli* is a patientive noun from the transitive verb TLA-(POZ-TEQUI), "to break something (such as a stick)."

[26]This explanation, which may be Ruiz de Alarcón's own invention or his native informant's rationalization, is doubtful. It seems to imply that a branch from any kind of tree would serve the purpose. See note I:4:16. Also notice that the explanation contradicts the claim that the old man was clairvoyant.

[27]The informant has erred in splitting *Cipactonal* into two beings, *Cipac* and *Tonal*, and apparently Ruiz de Alarcón was uncertain about the translation since there is little correlation between the Spanish and the Nahuatl. Possibly "I am the one of superior science" is translating *niCipac*, and, if so, it may be that Ruiz de Alarcón was being guided by a belief that may have been current in his day (since it was presented several years later by Jacinto de la Serna) that *Cipactli* "is derived from these three words *cen, icpac, thatli* [i.e., *tahtli*], which mean 'the Father superior to all'" (Serna 1892:315), where Serna's claimed "syncope" has, among other impossibilities, kept only the number suffix of (TAH)-TLI. It should be mentioned that *Cipactli* was a different entity from *Cipactonal*. See note V:3:5 and Appendix B.

[28]"And we would almost say" is not translating any Nahuatl words, but is a rephrasing of Ruiz de Alarcón's comment "as if he said," and is not part of the incantation. The Latin, *Ego vir videns*, "I a man seeing," has been omitted.

[29]See note I:4:28.

[30]We have omitted Ruiz de Alarcón's comment "as if he said, *Ego vir videns*," since it is not a part of the native informant's text.

[31]In V:2, where there is another mention of the pair, *Ohxomoco* and *Cipactonal*, one finds the equivalent expressions *Old-woman* and *Old-man*. Apparently either Ruiz de Alarcón or his informant omitted the word *nIlamah* ("I am Old-woman"). Accordingly, we have emended the text. Note that the old man who is speaking is assuming the sexually ambivalent role of both *Ohxomoco* and *Cipactonal*. See Nicholson (1971:398) concerning the sexual identity of *Ohxomoco* and *Cipactonal*. Also see note I:4:27.

[32]For purposes of polite address, certain kinship terms in Nahuatl may reverse the relationship so that an older, highly respected person is addressed as if he or she were a younger kinsman or kinswoman. The attributed kinship is, of course, fictional. Pérez (1713:163) has a remark that is pertinent here: "[In the hotlands] they use the noun *Icniuh* to explain all kinds of kinship, because just as in Castilian we say *mi deudo* ["my relative"] to any kinsman, in Mexico [City] they say *nohuayolqui* [i.e., *nohuān yōlqui*, "one who lives with me"], and in other places *Nocniuh*, and even when speaking Castilian many of them, being, for example, second cousins, say *Es mi hermano* ["He is my brother"], *lo veo mi hermano* ["I see my brother"], *lo llamo mi hermano* ["I call my brother"]. And in Mexican [i.e., Nahuatl], *Nicitta nocniuc* [*sic*, i.e., *Niquitta nocniuh*], *nicnotza* [i.e., *nicnōtza*]." Pérez also makes a similar remark on page 141.

[33]The word in the MS, *nihcauhtzine* (i.e., *nihcāuhtziné*), is a variant spelling of *niccāuhtziné* and shows a very common de-gemina-

tion from /kk/ to /hk/. Both spellings are found in Molina; in his Spanish-Nahuatl section he lists, under the entry *ermano menor* ("younger brother"), the word *teiccauh* (i.e., *tēiccāuh*, literally, "someone's younger brother") and in his Nahuatl-Spanish section he lists *icauhtli* (i.e., *ihcāuhtli*) with the same meaning (although now spelling *hermano* with an *h*). Actually, the /kk/ > /hk/ shift is not the whole story, since there is really a three-step process: /kʷk/ > /kk/ > /hk/; that is, (IUC-CĀUH)-TLI > (IC-CĀUH)-TLI > (IH-CĀUH)-TLI. The justification for this statement is found in Molina's entry *ermana menor.teicu* [i.e., *tēiuc*]; the same word is listed in the Nahuatl-Spanish section under the two entries for *icuh.n.* [i.e., *niuc*, where the *n-* is the first person singular possessive prefix, "my"], meaning *mi hermano, o hermana menor.*[*dize la hermana mayor*], "my younger brother or sister [said by the older sister]," and *mi hermana menor.*[*dize el hermano mayor*], "my younger sister [said by the older brother]." Notice that Molina is using a spelling convention that allows syllable-final /kʷ/ to be spelled *cu* or *cuh* (see Andrews 1975:407). The word for "younger brother" found in the MS is a compound noun whose embed is (IUC)-TLI and whose matrix is (CĀUH)-TLI. See note I: 4:32.

[34] See note I:2:4.

[35] *Cuauhāmatl* (literally, "tree-paper").

[36] I.e., "as elsewhere."

[37] This is an error for *nacaztecòcoyocpol* [i.e., *nacaztecohcoyocpōl*, the pejorative form (the suffix *-pōl* expresses contemptible largeness) of *nacaztecohcoyoc* ("a person with holes in the earlobes"), the "flaw form" of *nacaztecohcoyoctli* ("holes in the earlobes"). See "flaw form" in the Glossary of Linguistic Terms. Garibay (1947:248, note 69) says, "*nacazcocoyoc*, 'a person suffering with earache,' perhaps rather in a moral sense: one who does not understand," a statement that mistakes the underlying verb (COYŌ-NI), "to become a hole," for (COCO-YA), "to become sick."

[38] This should read *tlapoztecacxōyatl nēzcayōtl* ("a broken-off fir bough that is a sign"), where *tlapoztec-* is the embed form of (TLA-POZ-TEC)-TLI ("a snapped, broken thing"); see note I:4:25. The "sign" is probably not signifying what Ruiz de Alarcón claimed. See note I:4:26.

Chapter 5

[1] *Āyahualco tlamahcēuhqueh* ("the penitents at the water-circle-place [perhaps, eddy]").

[2] This should read *ācuetzpalchīmalli, nāuhcāmpa tzontecomeh* ("the shielded thing in the shape of a water-lizard, the owner of a four-sided head").

[3] The word "these" seems to refer to the pilgrimages "in the water," but must be understood to refer to those of the previous chapter as well, since Diego de Mendoza's speech mentions only "the sacrifices and offerings on the heights of the hills."

[4] The *l.* is the abbreviation of the Latin *lege*, literally "read," i.e., "or preferably."

[5] The form *tocizhuan*, which Ruiz de Alarcón indicates as a preferable reading for *tocìhuan* [i.e., *tocihhuān*] ("our grandmother"), is listed in Molina under *teciztli* [i.e., *tēciztli*] as "mother of someone." Siméon lists *ciztli* and then incorrectly gives the possessive form as *teciztli* [i.e., *tēciztli*]. The absolutive form *ciztli* would give the possessive form *tēciz* ("someone's mother"). The form *tēciztli* is an absolutive form of a "secondary possessive formation" (see Andrews 1975:154) and would be expected to occur in a possessive state, e.g., *notēciz*, "my mother." The word in the text is the plural possessive form of (CIZ)-TLI, with the first person plural possessive prefix *to-*.

[6] The spelling of this word in the MS is not clear. Paso y Troncoso (1892:141) reads it as *quenami* [i.e., *quēn amih*], which has the same translational value as the *quenin* [i.e., *quēn in*] that we have read.

[7] The MS has *chicahuac quiahui* [i.e., *chicāhuac quiahui*], which is problematical. Since *chicāhuac* ("a thing that has become strong") is an adjective, its headword should be the noun *quiahuitl* [i.e., "rain"], creating the phrase *chicāhuac quiahuitl*, "heavy rain." This does not fit the context, however; therefore, the form in the MS, *quiahui* (a verbword meaning "it is raining"), must be assumed to be correct, with the consequence that *chicāhuac* must be replaced by the adverb *chicāhuacā*, "in the manner of a thing that has become strong," i.e., "strongly." We have so written it in the respelled version in note I:5:14.

[8] In our rewritten version of this speech in note I:5:14, we have spelled out the ab-

breviation *tty°. D.* as *ToTēucyo, Dios* ("Our Lord, God") despite the fact that *tty°* in this usage is generally spelled *totecuiyo.* The latter spelling, which occurred as early as Molina (1571:f11v) and is vouched for by Carochi (1904) in the seventeenth century, is apparently a misunderstanding of the earlier spellings *totecujo, totecuio,* and *totecuyo.* The problem results from the inadequacy of the early spelling conventions: (1) *-cu-* was used to represent the /kʷ/ sound in both syllable-initial (before /e/ and /i/) and syllable-final position (the spelling involves other ambiguities but they are not pertinent here); (2) the spellings *jo, io,* and *yo* were ambiguous, representing both /yo/ and /iyo/ (as well as /io/, which does not enter the present discussion). Given the proclivity of Spaniards to read *-cu-* as syllable initial (since the syllable-final position is foreign to them), it is not difficult to hypothesize that, very early, Spanish priests and religious began to read *-cujo, -cuio,* and *-cuyo* as /-kʷiyo/ rather than as /-kʷyo/ and eventually wrote it *-cuiyo,* especially since their usage of the word would tend to urge a distinction between the divine *totecuiyo* ("Our Lord") or *notecuiyo* ("My Lord") and the secular *toteucyo* ("our lord") and *noteucyo* ("my lord"). Except for such a hypothesis, it is difficult to justify, either etymologically or morphologically, the existence of the syllable *-cui-* (an accented syllable, furthermore) in the word. Its root is (TĒUC)-TLI, "lord," which, when serving as the embed to a (-YŌ)-TL formation, should, and does, produce (TĒUC-YŌ)-TL, "lordship," the possessive form of which, with, for example, a first person singular possessor, is *notēucyo,* /note:kʷyo/, "my lord." The intrusion of an /i/, as if the source were (TĒCU-I)-TL, is anomalous. The form *totēcuihyo* [with a glottal stop, presupposing the stem (TĒCU-IH)-TLI], which Andrews (1975:472) found attested in a no longer remembered source, is equally unjustifiable, although the intrusive *-ih-* is an unidentified morpheme that occurs frequently at the beginning of stems and is perhaps found in the word *xōchihcualli,* "fruit," literally, "flower food," which, morphologically represented, would be either *xōchi-h-cua-l-li* or *xōch-ih-cua-l-li.*

[9]The segment *caymahuizçotzin yxquich yteoyotzin tlacatl. tty°. D. noyxquich tomàcehual* is obscure. One might be tempted to translate it as "the honor and all the divinity of the Lord, Our Lord God, are also all our reward," with the possessive prefix on *ymahuizçotzin* and *yteoyotzin* both being supplemented by *tlacatl. tty°. D.* However, the grammar does not support such a reading since *ca* marks *īmahuizzōtzin* as the matrix clause. We have translated it as "all the divinity (H) of the Lord, Our Lord, God, and also all our reward are His glory (H.)" (see note I:5:14).

[10]The MS has *titotlahcali* [i.e., *titotlahcalih*] which is problematical because of the two object prefixes, *to-* and *tla-*. Molina lists only single-object verbs using this stem: the reflexive verb M-(IHCALI), "to skirmish," and the projective verb TĒ-(IHCALI), "to attack someone." Siméon further lists TĒ-CA NI-(TLA-HCALI), "to knock someone over, to jostle someone, to dismiss someone with anger or disdain." Brewer and Brewer (1962:159), however, list the double-object form *motlajcali* [i.e., *motlahcali*] ("to lie down"). We have, therefore, not tampered with the word in our rewritten version in note I:5:14, although we have translated it rather freely as "we are indifferent" rather than strictly as "we lie down."

[11]The Spanish is *boca de lobo,* "wolf's mouth," a metaphor meaning "deep darkness." Our translation, "pitch black," does not capture the connotations of danger implicit in the expression.

[12]Ruiz de Alarcón's translation for *tlācatecolōtl* is the usual one: *demonio* ("devil"). Undoubtedly it was the meaning intended by the speaker, since the Spaniards early on preempted the word, giving it a transcendental denotation that was absent in the native usage, where it denoted merely a malignant sorcerer. The word is a compound: the embed is (TLĀCA)-TL, "person, human; lord"; the matrix is (TECOLŌ)-TL, "owl." The literal translation, therefore, is "person-owl" or "lord-owl." Garibay (1944:309, note 6) says "perhaps it is to be better translated: 'man who injures people.'" The translation is wrong on three counts: (1) it reverses the embed + matrix arrangement of the constituents of the compound ("man" is not the matrix but the embed);

(2) the *te-* of *tecolōtl* is not *tē-*, "people"; (3) the idea of "injury" is not present. To justify claiming its presence, Garibay says that *tecolōtl* comes from "*coloa,* to bend, to fold; the source of the reduplicated *cocoloa,* to be sick." But *cocoloa* [more properly, TLA-(COH-CŌL-OA)] does not mean "to be sick" but rather "to go somewhere by means of numerous detours." The verb meaning "to be sick" is (COCO-YA), and this has no relation to the verb *coloa* [more properly, TLA-(CŌL-OA)]. Furthermore, even if there were a relationship between these verbstems, it would not be pertinent, since *tecolōtl* has the syllable *-co-* (with a short vowel) whereas TLA-(CŌL-OA) has the syllable *-cō-* (with a long vowel). The remarks in Sahagún (1963:42) suggest that *tecolōtl* is onomatopoeic.

[13] "His divine majesty" has no counterpart in the Nahuatl. It is standing where the word "God" should stand, but "God" was used in the preceding clause where there was no counterpart for it in the Nahuatl.

[14] *Ca ōtiquincaquilihqueh tocōlhuān tocihhuān* (or *tocizhuān*), *in huēhuētqueh in ilamatqueh, in quēn in tlahuenchīhualōya tepēticpac in tecōllālco, in teolōchōlco. In mā nel icah yohuac, mixtecomac, tlacomōni, in quēmman chicāhuacā quiahui, yeh ahmō quicāhuayah in tlahuenchīhualiztli; huel conahxītiāyah. Auh tleh in īmmahcēhual? Ca zan tētlapolōltīliztli. Ca zan tlācatecolōtl quitlātlauhtiāyah. Auh in āxcān, ca Īmahuizzōtzin ixquich Īteōyōtzin Tlācatl, ToTēucyo Dios, nō ixquich tomahcēhual. Auh zan cāmpa tiquittah, auh zan nēpa titotlahcalih. Ca huel tētlapolōltih. Ca tētequipachoh. Ca huēi totlahtlacōl Īīxpantzinco in Dios.* ("We have heard from our grandfathers and our grandmothers (*or* our mothers), the old men and the old women, how people used to make offerings on the mountaintops at the mounds of stone, at the piles of stone. Even though at times it was dark, pitch black, thundering, when it was raining hard, they would not leave off the act of making offerings; they would carry them there successfully. And what was their reward? Indeed it was only foolishness. They were only praying to the Devil. But now, all the divinity (H) of the Lord, Our Lord, God, and also all our reward are His glory (H). And we see it just anywhere, but we are indifferent just everywhere. It is a very scandalous thing. It is a worrisome thing. Our sin is big in the presence (H) of God.")

[15] I.e., "as with an iron pen."

Chapter 6

[1] *Pahini.* See Appendix C.

[2] Ruiz de Alarcón's words "another small root" and "that other seed" are inappropriate because *ololiuhqui* is not a root as the "another" implies, nor is peyote a root or a seed as "that other" implies.

[3] It sounds here as if there were a whole treatise on "the idols and superstitious *tecomates.*" Ruiz de Alarcón should have said "Chapter." The topic was discussed in I:2.

[4] *Ōninomauhtiāya.* "I was afraid."

[5] *Ahzo nēchtlahuēlīz.* "Perhaps he will hate me."

[6] A *fanega* is a dry measure equal to 90.815 liters, or 2.58 bushels (Carrera Stampa 1949: 15).

[7] "Minister," a person responsible for carrying out the orders of the judge; frequently the *alguacil.*

[8] This should read *quae societas luci ad tenebras* ("what fellowship hath light with darkness?"), 2 Corinthians 6:14. The *conventio* in the MS is found in verse 15: *Quae autem conventio Christi ad Belial?* ("What accord hath Christ with Belial?").

[9] This should read *compelle intrare* ("compel them to come in"), Luke 14:23.

Chapter 7

[1] The MS has *indiciade* [i.e., *indiciado*] ("suspected of the crime"), which we have changed to *indicado* ("indicated") because of the words *por la sospecha* ("by the suspicion").

[2] I.e., *Tepēcuācuīlco.* See Appendix E.

[3] Based on Molina's entry for *profeta,* the expected phrase would be *huehca ontlachixqui.* See Appendix C.

[4] This refers to the divining spirit at Endor consulted by Saul, 1 Kings 28:7–21.

[5] I.e., *Tlaxcallān.* This is a compound noun consisting of (TLA-XCA-L)-LI, "a baked thing," i.e., "bread," the patientive noun of TLA-(IXCA), "to bake something," and the relational noun (TLAN)-ø, "beside." The name is usually written *Tlaxcala* and refers to the area roughly encompassed by the present-day state

of Tlaxcala. The Bishopric of Tlaxcala extended from coast to coast and included much of the area in which Ruiz de Alarcón worked.

[6]I.e., *Nahui-Tōchco.* See Appendix E.

[7]I.e., *Ocuillohcān.* See Appendix E.

[8]A Nahuatlism for *tiānquiztli,* an Indian market, originally meeting daily in large cities or on a 5-day cycle in smaller towns. Following the Conquest, the 5-day markets gave way to markets based on the Christian 7-day week.

[9]Juan Pérez de la Serna was archbishop of Mexico from 1613 to 1625 (Bravo Ugarte 1965:62).

[10]"Last year, 1617" indicates that Ruiz de Alarcón was writing this treatise as early as 1618.

[11]This last sentence appears to be a comment by Ruiz de Alarcón and not part of the report of Mariana's declaration. If there is no irony involved (and there does not seem to be any), it means that Ruiz de Alarcón has accepted Mariana's declaration as being truthful and factual.

[12]This should read *dignus est enim operarius mercede sua* ("the laborer is worthy of his hire"), Luke 10:7.

[13]*Īpampa ahmō nēchtlahuēlīz.* "So that he will not hate me."

Chapter 8

[1]Ruiz de Alarcón is aware of the danger implicit in a book such as his.

Chapter 9

[1]*Tētzāhuitl,* "a shocking or frightful thing, or an augury."

[2]This reflects the Spanish belief of that time that foul-smelling air causes disease.

[3]The form in the MS, *èpatl,* would be *ehpatl* in the standard spelling, but the accent is possibly in error. *Epatl* means "skunk." See Sahagún 1963:13.

[4]The Spanish is *paxarillo depluma.* We have been unable to identify the bird.

[5]*Huāctzin* and *huāctōn* are affective forms of (HUAC)-TLI, "Laughing Falcon" (for a description of the bird, see Davis 1972:25). Also see note VI:19:4.

[6]*Xiuhquihquimiltzin* (literally, "the little sack of blades of grass").

[7]*Tēcuāntocatl* (literally, "man-eating spider"). See Sahagún 1963:88.

[8]*Tzīntlātlāuhqui* ("a thing that is red at the bottom").

[9]*Cōātl ōnēchohhuiltequih.* "The snake has crossed over the road in front of me." The verbform is from the stem TĒ-(OH-HUIL-TEQU-IA), the applicative of (OH-HUIL-TEQUI), "to cross over the road."

[10]*Mazācōātl* ("deer-snake"). See Sahagún 1963:79–80.

[11]*Metlapilcōātl* (literally, "mano-snake"). See Sahagún 1963:82. The *mano,* represented here by *metlapil-,* is the cylindrical upper grindstone held in the hand (Spanish, *mano*) to grind grain on a *metate.*

[12]The word in the MS, *çelcoatl* [i.e., *celcōātl*], meaning "burgeon snake," is apparently an error. Later it is given as *colcoatl* [i.e., *cōlcōātl*], meaning "curve (*or* hook) snake." Serna (1892: 380) also gives *colcoatl.* But this too is apparently an error for *çolcoatl* [i.e., *zōlcōātl*], "quail snake," a very poisonous snake described in Sahagún 1963:78.

[13]Ruiz de Alarcón has not "just mentioned" a reason for this. The reason is given in the second paragraph below.

[14]*Tleh in quihtoa? Tleh in quinequi īn? Ahzo nēchyāōchīhua, ahzo nēchmiquītlani in tlācanāhualli.* "What is it that is it saying? What is it that this one wants? Perhaps the person-*nahualli* is making war against me, perhaps he wants to kill me." Concerning *tlācanāhualli,* see note I:4:20.

[15]See note I:9:12.

[16]See note I:3:3.

[17]The MS has *nahuri,* which is an error for either *nāhualli* or Spanish *zahorí* ("a diviner"), both of which fit the context.

Chapter 10

[1]Another tradition holds that there were four ages before the present one. See the discussion of this in the Introduction. Also see the *Leyenda de los Soles* (Velázquez 1975:119–28).

[2]Another version of this myth is found in Sahagún 1953:4–7. Ruiz de Alarcón's version differs, among other things, in the antagonism shown in his comments about "*mandones* and potentates" and in his presentation of the fire as a furnace, possibly reflecting his aware-

ness of the biblical story of the casting of Shadrach, Meshach, and Abednego into Nebuchadnezzar's burning fiery furnace (Daniel 3:12–30). Another, briefer version of the myth is found in the *Leyenda de los Soles* (Velázquez 1975:121–22).

[3] *Centeōtl, Icnōpiltzintli* ("Ear-of-Maize-God, Orphan-child (H)"). It should be pointed out that Ruiz de Alarcón's interpretation of *Centeōtl* as "Sole God" is linguistically viable since *cen-* is the combining form of *cē* ("one"). Ruiz de Alarcón, however, is allowing himself to be swayed by a Christian preconception. The accepted translation, and the one we think is correct, takes the *cen-* to be (CEN)-TLI, "dried ear of maize." See Appendix B.

[4] Matthew 25:3–13.

[5] We have been unable to identify the bird *huinaxcatl.* Serna (1892:365) says that it is a kind of "hungry young sparrowhawk" (*gauilansillos hambrientos*). This would seem questionable in view of the bird's nocturnal habits mentioned in the text. It is apparently a nighthawk. The word is not listed in the dictionaries, but a possible formation is (HUEN-ĀX-CA)-TL, "a person from Huenaxco," with *Huenaxco* being (HUEN-ĀX-CO)-ø, "Offering-made-place," from (HUEN-ĀX)-TLI, "an offering-made-thing," the patientive noun from the verbstem (HUEN-ĀI), "to make an offering," from the embed (HUEN)-TLI, "offering," and the matrix TLA-(ĀI), "to do or make something." Compare the name *Popotecatl* for ants (see note II:13:3) and the name *Comontecatl* for quail (see note VI:22:4).

[6] Ruiz de Alarcón's informants apparently no longer recognized a word that was in use earlier. Molina lists *tahui?* with the meaning *ola, oya? para llamar a otro* ("hello! listen! used for calling someone").

SECOND TREATISE

Chapter 1

[1] I.e., *Iguala.* See Appendix E.

[2] This was a continuation and extension of pre-Columbian practices in which the Indians owed tribute to their ruler. The amounts changed through time (Gibson 1964:194–211).

[3] The MS has *canto* ("song") for which we have read *encanto.*

[4] The Spanish has *las armas que eran* ("the weapons which were"), which suggests that the text is incomplete, since only one weapon is mentioned here. The Nahuatl mentions three things that served him as weapons: His-*tonal* is One Water (the wooden staff), One Death (rocks), and One Flint (knife?). It may be that One Flint is an alternative (preferable?) possibility rather than a third entity. Later, only His-*tonal* is One Water and One Flint are mentioned. One Death is again used in II:5:4 as a calendrical name for rocks.

[5] Ruiz de Alarcón translates the boast formula *Nohmatca nehhuātl* as a phrase, "I myself in person" or "I in person"; we translate it as a sentence, with *nehhuātl* ("I am the one," "It is I") as the matrix and *nohmatca* ("in person") as an adverbial modifier. Siméon lists *noma* and *nomatca* [i.e., *nohmah* and *nohmatca*] under a single entry, with the meaning "still, even, always, spontaneously." These adverbial translations reflect the fact that both words are nounstems, *(NO-H-MAT)-TLI and *(NO-H-MAT-CA)-TL, that have been adverbialized by the replacement of the number suffix (*-tli* and *-tl,* respectively) by zero (i.e., silence). Their nounness is witnessed by their ability to occur in the possessive state, e.g., *nonohmah* and *nonohmatca,* "my person, my character," which may function as a supplement (translated "I myself" or "me myself") or as an adverb (translated as "on my own accord, by my own will"). From *nohmah* one can form the denominative verb MO-(NO-H-MAH-HUIA), The noun *(NO-H-MAT)-TLI presumably has as its matrix the passive patientive noun (IH-MAT)-TLI, from the verb TLA-(IH-MATI), "to handle something with skill or prudence" [compare the impersonal patientive nounstem (TLA-IH-MAT)-TLI, "a thing prepared or made ready with care or prudence"]. Presumably the word *nō,* "also" (itself originally a noun), has become embedded in the passive patientive nounstem to create *(NO-H-MAT)-TLI (concerning the shift of the stem-final /t/ to /h/ when followed by a zero suffix, see Andrews 1975:61). This compound stem *(NO-H-MAT)-TLI also had the option of being embedded in the stem *(CA)-TL (see Andrews 1975:157) to form *(NO-H-MAT-CA)-TL (notice that *nohmatca* is *not* the adverbial form of the preterit agentive noun, since the possessive state form is *not,* e.g., *nonohmatcāuh).*

[6]The function here is not to taunt his enemies but to transform reality by means of words and to convince himself of that transformation. Notice that at no point in the incantation does the speaker directly address his adversaries. The entire rhetorical orientation is speaker-to-self and speaker-to-allies. See Appendix F.

[7]The words for "the ones who" and "them" are masculine (*los que* and *-los*) in the MS, although the antecedent is the feminine word *hermanas.*

[8]Ruiz de Alarcón translates *notlacaxillohuan* as "the ones who are of my very nature" and "those similar to me in nature," translations that contradict the thrust of the incantation. The point of the rest of the speech is precisely that the speaker is *not* human and cannot be hurt by mere human beings. The matrix stem, (XĪLŌ)-TL, means "immature ear of maize," and in Olmos (1972:212) we find its organically possessed form (see Andrews 1975: 243), *texiloyoa* (i.e., *tēxīlōyōhuān*), used as a metaphor meaning "one's kinsmen." Olmos's word means, literally, "one's organically possessed personified immature ears of maize" (with the personification indicated by the plural suffix on the inanimate stem [see Andrews 1975:143]); the metaphor pretends that the possessor is a maize plant and the kinsmen are the ears it produces. The word in Ruiz de Alarcón does not show organic possession (to do so, the form would read *notlācaxīlōyōhuān*) and so the metaphor, now meaning that the possessor is someone who has cultivated or purchased the ears, is intended to imply a flawed kinship, that is, "human kinsmen," meaning "my kinsmen who are human, not divine like me." Incidentally, the Nahuatl word corresponding to Ruiz de Alarcón's translation would be *notlācapohhuān.*

[9]The coordinate phrase *tlapalli eztli,* literally "color and blood," is defined by Molina as a metaphor meaning "nobility of blood and of lineage." Ruiz de Alarcón, however, takes the metaphor, here and elsewhere, to mean "fragility of flesh and blood" (or simply "flesh and blood"), a meaning that does seem appropriate to the context.

[10]The MS has *yaoyòque,* which respelled would give *yāōyohqueh,* "enemy-owners," and by extension, "war-owners." That Ruiz de Alarcón saw the word as being this is evident in his translation, "warrior gods." But this is an instance where the spelling is misleading. In early texts, word-initial *ya* was frequently used to represent /iya/ (since /y/ between /i/ and /a/ was commonly left unspelled, and an initial /i/ was frequently spelled with *y*); furthermore, the *o* of *yao-* undoubtedly originated from an earlier spelling which had *u* since *u* had the ambivalent function of representing either /o/ (e.g., *teutl* [i.e., *teōtl*] or /w/ (e.g., *quautli* [i.e., *cuāuhtli*]). Given this ambiguity and given a situation in which the correct reading, *iyāuhyohqueh,* "*iyauhtli*-owners," no longer had meaning, the choice of *yāō-* instead of *iyāuh-* is not surprising. For the phrase *ōllohqueh, iyāuhyohqueh,* see Sahagún (1969:35), where Dibble and Anderson translate *in ōllohqueh, in iyāuhyohqueh, in copallohqueh* as "the lords of rubber, the lords of incense, the lords of copal." The expression is a metaphor for "gods."

[11]The Nahuatl has a third person plural form, but it is being used as part of the vocative phrase.

[12]Ruiz de Alarcón confuses the word relationships here. He reads *tetl* as the supplementary subject of *tlapalloaz* rather than of *ihuintíz.* He establishes the following collocations: (1) *tlapalloaz tetl,* (2) *ihuintíz quahuitl,* (3) *ihuintíz tlalli,* (4) *ihuintíz tonèhuã.* But the correct phrasing has *tlapalloaz* belonging to the sequence *achtotipa ezçoaz, achtotipa tlapalloaz,* and thus the collocations are (1) *tetl ihuintíz,* (2) *quahuitl ihuintíz,* and (3) *tlalli ihuintíz.* The word *tonèhuã* then stands as a word apart from the rest; but see note II:1:15.

[13]In Molina we find the entry *iuhquimma tetlyuinti quauitlyuinti ictimochiuaz* [i.e., *iuhqui in mah tetl īhuinti cuahuitl īhuinti īc timochīhuaz*] ("you will be like the one who takes up sticks and stones to kill himself, i.e., you will do yourself great harm [metaphor]"). The expression in the incantation is a threat.

[14]The *onicual* . . . of the MS has *cu* representing the consonant cluster /k/ + /w/. The standard spelling is *onichual* . . . . Both spellings are found throughout the MS.

[15]The MS has *tonèhuã,* which, respelled, would be *tonehhuan.* Ruiz de Alarcón, however, accepted this as *tonehuān* ("the two of us together, both of us together"). However, if this follows other instances of this formula, the wording would be *in nonehuiyān* ("at my

will"), as we have rewritten it. See note VI: 3:19.

[16]The MS has *hermanos* ("brothers") where it should read *hermanas* ("sisters"), as in every other instance. This permits the next phrase *hombres como yo,* to be translated "men like me" rather than "humans like me" as in the next sentence.

[17]The Spanish *sea* ("let it be") may be a copyist's error for *será* ("it will be"), a reading that matches the Nahuatl *yez.*

[18]Ruiz de Alarcón's explanation of the metaphors is unsatisfactory; while the first one ("balls of yarn" = "rocks") is reasonable, the second one ("canes" = "clubs") must be rejected since canes are not mentioned in either the Nahuatl text or the Spanish translation.

[19]The MS has *ìhiyo,* where the glottal stop is redundantly spelled with both the grave accent and the *h.* In our rewritten version, *iihīyo,* the first *i* is the third-person singular possessive prefix *ī-;* it has lost its length because of the following glottal stop. One could also represent the word as *ihīyo* since the double *i* has no implication for pronunciation; it is a sheerly graphic device to remind one of the difference between the noun *iihīyo* [i.e., ø-ɪ(ɪʜ-ī-ʏᴏ)ø, "his breath"] and the preterit agentive noun of possession *ihīyoh* [i.e., ø-ø(ɪʜ-ī-ʏᴏʜ-ø)ø, "breathful, spiritual"]. The double-*i* spelling is also justified by the fact that the initial *i* of the stem is not a merely supportive vowel but a "real" one. Compare note II:17:6.

[20]See note II:1:11.

[21]We read this sentence as the speaker's comment on his action of summoning the priests, so that the "them" refers to the priests just addressed.

[22]The MS has *tonacametzin* for *Tōnacāmetztzin.* The doubled consonant *tztz* was almost invariably simplified to *tz* in writing.

[23]Possibly under the pressure of the two preceeding sentences, the MS has the singular *tlaxihuallauh* [i.e., *tlā xihuāllauh*], where the plural *tlā xihuālhuiān* is clearly required.

[24]The Spanish reads *estas enpie o cara arriba hechado de bruças* [*sic*] ("you are standing or face up lying face downward"). The *hechado* is a copyist's error for *échate* ("throw yourself"), which matches the imperative construction in the Nahuatl. We have translated the corrected reading. The problem in the MS must have been in the original since Serna (1892:393) also has trouble with the reading. His Spanish is *estás en pie y ponte voca arriba, que estás hecho de yerbas* ("you are standing and put yourself face up, for you are made of herbs"). The *y ponte* is in the wrong place, the *hechado* has become *hecho de,* and the *bruças* has become *yerbas.* With the correction we have made, the Museo MS is closer to the Nahuatl than is Serna.

[25]Serna's text (1892:393) has a parenthetical explanation for this phrase: "here he invokes the god Tonacateuctli, who is the god of the heat, one of those of the signs in the fourth house." He has not understood.

[26]"At the shins" is a mistranslation of *īmītzcalco.* Ruiz de Alarcón seems to have confused (īᴛᴢ-ᴄᴀ-ʟ)-ʟɪ, "side," for (ᴛʟᴀɴ-īᴛᴢ)-ᴛʟɪ, "shin," as he does again in the following line.

[27]The MS has *Ia,* which we read as *Ea.*

[28]Serna's text (1892:393) has a parenthetical explanation for this phrase: "here he invokes the god Huitzilopochtli, to whom this sign belongs, and it is lucky." Again he has not understood.

[29]Notice the shift from the plural possessor of *īmītzcalco* ("at their sides") to the singular possessor of *īītzcalco* ("at his side").

Chapter 2

[1]For a discussion of hypnotism used by the *tēmācpalihtōtihqueh* ("those who cause people to dance in the palm of their hands") and for a discussion of its use in the following incantation, see López Austin (1966).

[2]Ruiz de Alarcón's translation fails because he does not understand *chicnauhtopa.* The *-pa* is not the directional suffix *-pa* (therefore, not "from nine parts") nor the frequency suffix *-pa* (therefore, not "nine times") but the relational stem *-pan,* most often translated into English as the preposition "on." The word, in standard spelling, is *ChiucnāuhTopan,* where *Topan* is a possessive phrase ("our surface," i.e., "above us"), meaning the skyward spirit world. Ordinarily such a phrase would not be capable of serving as a matrix in a compound formation, but it has become a name, and, as such, here takes *chiucnāuh-* ("nine") as an embed. Freely translated, it

means "the nine heavens" and is paralleled in this paragraph by the "number + name" phrase *ChiucnāuhMictlān* ("Nine-Deadman-land"), which Ruiz de Alarcón translates as *los nueve profundos* ("the nine depths").

[3]The Spanish is *sueño encantador,* which Ruiz de Alarcón may have intended as "Sleep, Enchanter." Perhaps the word *Tēmicxōch* is an error for *Tēmicxōx,* which would be the name form of (TĒMIC-XŌX)-TLI, "dream-trance," the matrix of which, (XŌX)-TLI, "trance, enchantment," is not attested in Molina or Siméon but is presupposed by the verbstem TĒ-(XŌX-HUIA), "to use a trance on someone," i.e., "to entrance someone, to hypnotize someone."

[4]The comment "a fable of antiquity" seems to be out of place.

[5]At the same time that the words *quahuili* and *oc celome* stand as proof of the antiquity of this incantation, the deterioration from the correct forms *quauhtin* [i.e., *cuāuhtin*] and *ocelome* [i.e., *ocēlōmeh*] suggests that the informant had no understanding of their ancient meanings ("eagle warriors" and "jaguar warriors"). Ruiz de Alarcón's translation ("and the rest of the town, the prince and the most powerful ones") shows that he too did not understand them clearly.

[6]I.e., the eagle warriors and the jaguar warriors.

[7]The form in the MS is nonstandard. *Moyohualihtoatzin* is a name, and, therefore, in the standard formation, its reflexive prefix *mo-* does not change to *no-* to match a first singular subject. Usage with such names in the text is not consistent, at times showing the standard formation and at times the nonstandard one.

[8]We assume that the MS is corrupt and that words are missing here and possibly in other places in this incantation since the language in these sentences seems to stumble. We have been unable to remedy the situation. The antiquity of the incantation (mentioned above in note II:2:5) may possibly justify the faulty transmission. Our translation is to be looked upon as doubtful.

[9]The MS has *ayhehuel,* for which we have read *ayāc huel.*

[10]The MS has *ami mançebo,* which we have translated as "me, a youth," rather than as "my young man" since the Nahuatl has a counterpart here only for "me" and Ruiz de Alarcón's translation of II:2:1 has identified the speaker as "the youth."

[11]The MS has *en (o) de tinieblas, i. de sueño.* Serna (1892:411) reads *en tinieblas, v, de tinieblas (que es lo mismo que de sueño)* ["in darkness, or, with darkness (which is the same as with sleep)"].

[12]Serna (1892:411) adds a parenthetical remark to *Cē Tecpatl:* "He invokes the flint because it is a fire-making instrument, principally at night for illumination." López Austin (1976:8–9) says that it represents "an unidentified deity whom the sorcerer asks to take care of the sleep of the victim." But all the speaker asks is that the entity find out whether the victim is asleep. We believe that One Flint is again (as in II:1:3) a knife. Here the sorcerer presses it into the victim's flesh as a test of the depth of the trance.

[13]The applicative verb TĒ-(ĒL-ĒHU-IA), "to lift one's liver (i.e., emotions) with regard to someone," i.e., "to covet someone," is used in these texts in the sense of "to harm someone," as Ruiz de Alarcón suggests in II:3:3.

[14]The expected translation of *in īc nāuhcān,* "the fourth place," does not seem to fit the context.

[15]We have changed *ye huallahuanizque* to *yohuallāhuānazqueh* under the pressure of the *niYohuallāhuāntzin* in II:2:3 and also because Ruiz de Alarcón's translation suggests the change: "they become drunk, lost in (or with) darkness." Notice also our replacement of *a* for *i* at the end of the stem; the matrix verbstem, (TLĀHU-ĀNA), "to become slightly inebriated," is itself a compound stem in which the nounstem (TLĀHUI)-TL, "red ocre," has been embedded as an incorporated verb object in the matrix verbstem, TLA-(ĀNA), "to take something," (compare English slang, "to have a glow on"). The second person singular form of the future tense *tiyohuallāhuānaz,* "you will become inebriated in the night," is found in VI:16:1. See also Appendix B.

[16]The construction is strange since one would expect a past tense verb form to match the others in the sentence.

[17]*Ea* is a Spanish intrusion.

[18]The verb object prefix *-quin-* is plural, and the only mentioned supplementary object (*yehhuātl*) is singular. The construction belongs to the "named-partner" type of sup-

plementation (see Andrews 1975:201); notice our translation.

[19] I.e., "in the name of the lord."

[20] The MS has *ycpallitl*, an obvious error for *icpalli.*

[21] "Why?" (*por que*) has no counterpart in the Nahuatl. Serna (1892:412) has *mas* ("but").

[22] Serna (1892:412) adds, "Comc on, for already the maligned one comes, &," even though there is nothing in the Nahuatl to support this. Perhaps there was in the source he used.

[23] I.e., "in order that I may speak thus," or, more loosely, "so to speak."

[24] The MS should read *Tlaltiçapan*, that is, *Tlāltīzapan.* See Appendix E.

Chapter 3

[1] We translate Ruiz de Alarcón's colloquial expression *el perrito de las bodas* ("the little dog that shows up at all the weddings [for a free meal]") rather pedantically, preserving the idea but losing the pejorative connotation. On another occasion, Ruiz de Alarcón himself (VI:3) uses the phrase *sine qua non*, not about tobacco but about water (in the ceremony for restoring the soul). Tobacco in that instance is merely an adjunct that may be used instead of fire. In II:8, Ruiz de Alarcón uses a different metaphor to express the idea of the ritual importance of tobacco: it is "the common ferment of these brews."

[2] The MS has *Eare y ven*, an error for *Ea ya ven.* Compare II:2, beginning of second paragraph of the incantation. Serna (1892: 445) has *Ea, ven ya.*

[3] The justification for reading *Mictlānmati* and *Topanmati* as compound words is found in V:2:2, *NiMictlānmati, niTopanmati,* "I am knowledgeable about Mictlan, I am knowledgeable about Topan."

[4] "As mentioned above."

[5] The MS has *chama*, an obvious error. Ruiz de Alarcón translates it as a command, *huelgate* ("amuse yourself"). We assume his translation is correct and therefore emend the text to *Ximahāhuilti.*

[6] Apparently Ruiz de Alarcón has confused *mītzcac* ("your side") for *motlanītz* ("your shin"). Also see note II:1:26.

[7] I.e., the woodcutter is right-handed.

[8] The MS has *ma*, which is followed by a future tense form, a construction that creates the future optative, but this is not appropriate to the context since a negative is needed. We have therefore changed *ma* to *Ahmō.*

[9] The verb *tinēchēlēhuilīz* is a double-object applicative form, with the primary object silently present. Ruiz de Alarcón ignores this and translates it as if it were a single-object form. The non-metaphorical meaning of the sentence is "Tree, do not harm my ax" (see note II:2:13).

[10] Ruiz de Alarcón is creating a false problem here since the difference between "minister" and "priest" exists only in his translation. The word in the Nahuatl text is simply *tlamacazqui.*

[11] Ruiz de Alarcón's explanation is questionable since any implement, faculty, or means that has a potential for action is called *tlamacazqui* in these incantations.

[12] Ruiz de Alarcón has shifted the word *demonio* ("devil") away from the idol or entity behind the idol to the one who attends it.

Chapter 4

[1] The word *montes*, which we have translated "mountains" here, is ambiguous, also having the meaning of "forests," so the sense here may be "in the forests and on the hills."

[2] López Austin (1969:109, note 5) says "the suffix *-cihuiztli* or *-cihuiliztli*, which is used so much when referring to sicknesses, comes from the verb *cihuia* and can mean 'press' or 'excitement,' although in some cases it seems to indicate paralysis or numbness. López Austin has allowed himself to be misled by Siméon's erroneous entry, "*ciuia . . . nitla* —to pursue, to hasten, to spur something on." This is merely the causative stem TLA-(IHCIHUI-A), in which the initial *i* is a prosthetic vowel, from the intransitive verb (IHCIHUI), "to hurry." The word in the text, *cōahcihuiztli*, is a compound noun with (CŌĀ)-TL, "snake," as an adverbial embed and (IHCIHUI-Z)-TLI, "the action of hurrying," the action nounstem of (IHCIHUI), as matrix. The proof of this is seen in instances in which the embed ends in a consonant, e.g., *tlaxcalicihui* (Sahagún 1970:17) which, rewritten, is *tlaxcalihcihui* ("he has the tortilla-sickness"). There are many compound words naming illnesses that have the matrix (IHCIHUI). Ap-

parently this stem, when occurring in these compounds, also has the meaning "to suffer." *Cōahcihuiztli* thus means literally "snake-suffering," i.e., "suffering like that caused by snake bite." We have translated it rather loosely as "palsy."

[3]It is curious that no translation for *yāyāhuic cōahcihuiztli* ("dusky palsy") occurs in Serna's version (1892:446). Its reappearance here, unaccompanied by its previous companion, *xoxōhuic cōahcihuiztli* ("green palsy"), is unexpected. It is useful, however, in that, being clearly in a vocative function, it confirms the vocative function of *yāyāhuic cōahcihuiztli, in xoxōhuic cōahcihuiztli* in the preceding sentence. The importance of this is that it is the only instance in any of these incantations where *cōahcihuiztli* is presented as an ally of the speaker.

[4]The phrase *ynteo chamecan tlahual* in the MS is garbled. We have read it as *in teōchānehcān notlahhuān,* "my uncles from the place of the temple owners." For a similar sequence, see *in ītlahtlahhuān tēcuānchānehcān,* "his various uncles from the place of the stinging dwellers," in III:6:1. The placement of the constituents is, to be sure, better in the latter than in the former, but Ruiz de Alarcón's translation, "the feet and hands of those that live with the gods," supports the reading. Another possibility for *tlahual* would be to read it as *Tlā cuēl!,* "Come on!" (as in II:4:4), but this would leave the third person plural possessive prefix *īm-* on *īmmāctzinco* and *īmicxictzinco* without a supplement that would explain its meaning. Note that this reading also involves a change of *m*-plus-vowel (in *-chāmeh-*) to the expected form of *n*-plus-vowel (in *-chāneh-);* see note I:4:20. For another example of *-chameh-,* see III:6:1; for an example of *-chaneh-,* see II:7:4. The word *teōchān-* ("god home") is surprising since the usual word is *teōcalli* ("god house," i.e., "temple") or *teōpantli.* We believe that the original was quite different and that the informant ("who hardly knew how to write") has muddled the text.

[5]The word in the MS is *hallare* [i.e., *hallaré*] ("I will find"), but in the margin one finds *hollare* [i.e., *hollaré*] ("I will tread on").

[6]The MS mistakenly has *su rostro soso* ("its inane face") and *tierra soso* [*sic*] ("inane land") instead of *su rostro fofo* ("its spongy face") and *tierra fofa* ("spongy land"), as is found in Serna (1892:446). We have translated the corrected forms since we believe that this is a copyist's error. Even so, Ruiz de Alarcón has made an error (see our translation below). He apparently thought that *īxcapactli* was *īxcapaxtli; capaxtli* means "a spongy thing." He was unaware that *tlālli īīxcapactzin* is a variant of *tlālli īīxcapānīltzin* (in II:4:7), which he translated more-or-less correctly as "lady earth, face-beaten-one." *Īxcapactli* and *īxcapānīlli* are simply variant forms of the patientive noun of the verb *īxcapāni.* See note II:4:8 and note II:4:23.

[7]The translation is problematic. The MS has *el seguear en la tierra* ("the measuring with a rope on the land"). We have read *ceguear,* since Ruiz de Alarcón is translating *tlalli yxcapactzin,* and we assume that he understands the *yx-* to mean "eye" rather than its alternative meaning "face, surface."

[8]The Spanish is confusing because it is rendering the Nahuatl poorly. It reads *no me ha de dañar la desigualdad del suelo ò la tierra. A la letra dize su rostro soso que verdaderamente no es tierra soso {tambien dize el seguear en la tierra}*. This should read *no me ha de dañar la desigualdad del suelo o la tierra. A la letra dize su rostro fofo que verdaderamente no es tierra fofo {tambien dize el ceguear en la tierra}* (on the reading of *fofo* for *soso,* see note II:4:6). There is a slight possibility that the agreement error of *tierra fofo* (feminine noun, masculine adjective) has resulted from an omission. Ruiz de Alarcón's original version may have read *la tierra ([otra vez, a la letra, su rostro] fofo) {tambien dize . . .}*. This rewriting permits a more intelligible English version: "And the unevenness of the ground or earth (literally it says "its spongy face"), will not hurt me, for it really is not land ([again literally, its] spongy [face]; it also says . . .)." This at least fits the Nahuatl somewhat better. In Serna (1892:446), the section reads *No me à de dañar la desigualdad del suelo, de la tierra, y su rostro fofo, que verdaderamente no es tierra fofa* (thus not including the marginal note *tambien dize, etc.;* that is, "The unevenness of the ground, of the earth and its spongy face, which truly is not spongy earth"). Since Serna seldom includes Ruiz de Alarcón's parenthetical remarks, it would seem that he did not understand the passage.

[9]The words in the MS, *tlalli yxcapactzin,* may be read as an appositive phrase, *Tlālli, Īxcapactzin* ("Earth, Face-Slapped-One (H)"), or as a possessive phrase, *Tlālli Īīxcapactzin* ("Earth's Face-slapped-one (H)"), (where *tlālli* is a supplementary possessor in cross reference with the possessive prefix *ī-* on the possessed word). We have chosen the second reading. It was quite common to write *īīx* as *ix.* For example, in Molina, we find under the entry *cegajoso* ("bleary-eyed") the item *ixmococoa,* which stands for the two words *īīx mococoa* ("his eyes are sick"). And in Ruiz de Alarcón's work, we find in the last line of the speech in I:5 *yxpantzinco yn Dios,* that is, *īīxpantzinco Dios.* Also see *Tlālli Īīxcapānīltzin* in II:4:7. Furthermore, our reading of *tlālli* as a supplementary possessor is supported by the word *Tlālīxcapān* at II:7:1.

[10]The phrase in the MS, *cē teotlalò ê,* would be rewritten as *cē teohtlāloheh.* This is impossible. The only meaning for the final *-eh* would be as the matrix for a preterit agentive noun of possession, which would be incorrect since there is a preceding glottal stop (which we represent by *h*), and the permissible preterit agentive noun of possession ending would be *-huah.* We have, therefore, rejected *-ê* for the absolutive singular suffix *-tli.* We have also rewritten the *cē* as *cen-.*

[11]The phrase in the MS, *cé comolihui e,* would be rewritten as *cē comōlihuieh.* The *-eh* ending, however, is impossible because what would be its embed is a verbstem rather than a nounstem. We have changed the *-e* to the preterit tense singular number suffix *-c* (for another use of the word *comōlihuic,* see II: 9:1). We have also rewritten the *cé* as *cen-.*

[12]The MS has the intransitive verb *niquiçaz* [i.e., *niquīzaz*], "I will exit," which is meaningless in the context. We have changed it to the transitive verb *niquiczaz,* "I will tread upon it," thus permitting *in Tlālli Īīxcapactzin* to function as a supplementary direct object.

[13]Garibay (1971:316–17) translated this segment. His version is: "Please, Nanahuatzin, come here: / first I will go, first I will walk the road; / later you will go, later you will follow the road. / Before you finish, behold the road has already come to an end, / behold the ravine has already been passed. // I shall go to go [toward?] level land, / let it not hinder me, because not except the level land: / for I shall go and I shall walk in the sky." Our rendering attempts to be faithful to the Spanish. The virgules mark what Garibay considers to be lines of verse, since he thinks this is a poem.

[14]This is written in the MS as if it were a subtitle. The part in brackets was omitted, with the MS reading . . . *conla y dize.*

[15]The MS has *tietic.* The initial *ti-* carries a helping vowel that is lost before vowel-initial stems. The form, therefore, is not respelled *tiyetic* but *tetic.*

[16]This is written in the MS as if it were a subtitle.

[17]The wording *yahuih in tēteoh īmpiltzin centzontlamacazqueh* ("the son of the gods and the four hundred priests are going") is somewhat surprising. One would have expected the verb to be first-person plural and *īmpiltzin* to have been first-person singular: *tiyahuih in tēteoh nīmpiltzin centzontlamacazqueh* ("we who are I, the son of the gods, and the four hundred priests are going").

[18]The phrase *in ahmō nezzoh* ("I do not have blood") has been inserted to regularize this passage with other instances of the pair *ezzoh tlapalloh* (see the examples in II:2 and see in the next Nahuatl segment below).

[19]The MS has *este cerro aparente ven cantando* ("this apparent hill, come singing"), which is translating *yn nahual tepèxitl.* Serna (1892:447) has the correct reading, *este serro aparente o encantado* ("this apparent or enchanted hill"). We have translated the correct version.

[20]The MS has *que yo no* ("for I did not"). Serna (1892:447) has *quién, sino yo?* ("who, if not I?"), which is closer to the idea of the Nahuatl.

[21]We have read *nictlalloz* as *nictlalōz.* Although the dictionaries list only the reflexive stem MO-(TLALOA), "to run, to flee," the projective counterpart found here, TLA-(TLALOA), "to run with something," can be postulated from the double-object verbstem TĒ-TLA-(TLALŌCHTIA), "to grab something from someone and to run with it." Compare TLA-(CŌLOA) and TĒ-TLA-(CŌLŌCHTIA) in Andrews (1975:91). The verb in the MS cannot be the verb (TLĀL-LŌ-HUA), spelled in Molina *tlalloa* (meaning "to become filled with dirt"), since the future tense of this verb would be *nitlāllōhuaz,* and, furthermore, it is intransitive.

[22]The MS has *nacayollo* [i.e., *nacayōlloh*],

which we have read as *nacayolle* [i.e., *nacayōleh*] in view of *īyōl* in II:8:7 and *yōleh* in II:8:8. Molina lists *yollo* [i.e., *yōlloh*] as meaning "clever and sharp-witted," which is not the idea being expressed here. Incidentally, this *yōlloh* is a preterit agentive noun of possession and should not be confused with the past patientive noun stem (YŌL-LOH)-TLI mentioned in note II:8:40. Contrast the rejected *nacayōlloh* with *yōllohtzin* discussed in note VI:3:24.

[23]See note II:4:6. The nouns (ĪX-CAPĀ-NĪ-L)-LI and (ĪX-CAPA-C)-TLI are variant forms of the patientive noun derived from the intransitive verb (ĪX-CAPĀ-NI), "to emit a slapping or popping sound at the face," i.e., "to become slapped at the face." Both nouns mean the same thing.

Chapter 5

[1]Ruiz de Alarcón understands *anquitlătizque* as *anquitlatīzqueh* ("you will burn him"), while we understand it as *anquitlātīzqueh* ("you will hide him," a metaphor for "you will kill him"). The idea of "burn" is not appropriate to the context: the ax is to chop down, i.e., kill, the tree.

[2]There is no word in the Nahuatl corresponding to "ax." Ruiz de Alarcón is bringing the Red Chichimec metaphor from the segment above down to this segment and demetaphorizing it.

[3]We have changed this slightly. In the margin of the MS, these two marginal remarks are run on. Paso y Troncoso (1892:158) has placed them in a single set of parentheses after *conmigo* (i.e., "with me"). We have divided this marginal material into two segments and placed them in the appropriate positions.

[4]"Genie" (Spanish *genio*) is translating *tlamacazqui.* Serna (1892:445) has the more expected *espiritado* ("possessed one").

[5]The form *milīnticah* is the progressive [formed with the connective infix *-ti-* and the verb (CAH) ("to be")] of the verb (MILĪ-NI). Although this verb is not listed in either Molina or Siméon, we see no reason not to accept the translation proposed by Ruiz de Alarcón, "to sparkle, to scintillate." In Sahagún (1951:148), the stem (MILĪ-NI) occurs in a "connective *-ti-*" compound with the stem (O), "to lie, to be recumbent," as the matrix: . . . *Milīntoc, zan nō yeh in tletl.* Dibble and Anderson do not translate the word: "Milintoc . . . . He likewise was (god of) fire."

[6]Concerning the translation "Yellow-hair," which appears to reverse embed and matrix of the word *Tzoncōztli* where the embed is (TZON)-TLI, "hair," and the matrix (CŌZ)-TLI, "yellow thing," see Andrews 1975:264. The words say literally "at-the-hair-yellow-one," and thus the translation "yellow-haired-one" is also possible.

[7]We assume that "quickly" has been omitted through an oversight. The Nahuatl requires it and Serna (1892:446) has it (*passar de prissa).*

[8]The MS has the third person singular form *acah,* where the first person singular *nacah* is required.

[9]The MS has *xictlaỳcihuiti,* an impossible form since the stem is a single-object verb TĒ-(IHCIHUĪ-TIA), "to cause someone to hurry," while the *-ctla-* claims a double-object form. In spite of the *-ctla-*, Ruiz de Alarcón apparently looked upon this word as an intransitive purposive "go in order to hasten" or "go to hasten," which assumes that the intransitive verb is (IHCIHUI-T-ĪUH). We have replaced the *-tla-* with the directional prefix *-huāl-*, which is needed to corroborate the *huāl-* in both *xihuāllauh* and *huālihcihui.*

[10]The MS has *-qu-*, a common misspelling of the consonantal sequence /k/ + /w/. We have, therefore, rewritten *xiqual-* as *xichuāl-*. Compare note II:1:14.

Chapter 6

[1]Ruiz de Alarcón's failure to recognize these words is even more surprising since the usual forms (*olchipinque, olpeyauhque*) are used in II:17, where he has no trouble translating them correctly. Concerning the spelling of /l/ by the symbol *r,* see Karttunen and Lockhart (1976:14–15) where it is referred to as hypercorrection. Inconsistent ways in which the forms are treated by Ruiz de Alarcón may be due to his having relied on his native informants rather than translating them himself. One informant understands; the other does not (or pretends not to).

[2]See note II:5:10.

[3]Garibay (1971:318) translates *īcal* as *el gorro* ("[her] cap"). However, in view of the phrase *nocal ītilmah* ("my house's blanket") in VI:21:2, which is a metaphor for 'net', *in nonān īcal īhuīpīl,* is to be translated "my

mother's house's *huipil*"; it, too, serves as a metaphor for 'net.'

[4]Garibay (1971:318) gives his own translation of this segment, which he regards as a poem. Instead of "I will cause him to enter [her] throat, etc." (i.e., I will drive the stake into the water), Garibay has reversed it to "My mother *Chalchiuhcueye* will be inserted into his [i.e., "the priest who has One-Water for a sign"] shoulder, into his belly, into his armpits" (i.e., "I will drive the water into the stake"). Garibay disregards the purpose of the incantation and says that *notlahuan tlamacazque* "are the Tlaloques, masters of the vapors and of the rains."

Chapter 7

[1]I.e., *Xīcohtlān.* See Appendix E.

[2]I.e., *tīcitl tlamatini,* "a wise doctor." See Appendix C.

[3]Ruiz de Alarcón was apparently troubled by *tlalocxochitl* [i.e., *tlālocxōchitl*]. He translated it twice: "fruit or flower of the land" or "flower of the wine." The first of these, "flower of the land," ignores the *oc-*, i.e., *tlālxōchitl;* the second ignores the *tlāl-*, i.e., *ocxōchitl* [from (OC)-TLI, "pulque; wine"]. See note II: 7:6.

[4]See note II:5:10.

[5]Serna (1892:440) says that Seven-jaguar is the "net or sack in which everything goes. Because it is ordinarily woven of several colors, he calls it seven times jaguar, made of *ichtli* [maguey fiber] or maguey rope, which comes from the magueys, flower and fruit of the earth, and that gives wine. This is inferred, because of saying that it should carry inside of itself that which they put in it, which is the piciete, and the green *colelecti* which is some little idol wrapped up in an infernal bundle." López Austin (1967:23) considers the meaning doubtful. Caso (1959:92), justifying his remark by this instance in Ruiz de Alarcón, says: "7. Ocelotl. The magical name for the squash." It is not clear how he arrived at this conclusion. Seven-jaguar is apparently the calendrical name for maguey fiber and, therefore, by extension, stands here for a carrying net made of maguey fiber (see note II:7:6).

[6]With regard to *tlalocxochitl,* López Austin (1967:23) says: "Etymology doubtful. Possibly the flower of wild wine [*vino montaraz*]. Meaning doubtful. Serna interprets it as the net in which small objects are carried." The word *tlālocxōchitl,* "land-wine-flower," is a compound word whose embed is (TLĀL-OC)-TLI, "land-wine," and whose matrix is (XŌ-CHI)-TL, "flower." The nounstem (TLĀL-OC)-TLI occurs again as the embed of *Tlālocci-huātl* in VI:22:3, a metaphorical name for the maguey plant. Here *tlālocxōchitl* is a metaphorical name for maguey fiber and, by extension, the carrying net made of maguey fiber. The word is standing in apposition with *Chicōmocēlōtl* (see note II:7:5). It should be remarked that *tlālocxōchitl* has no relation to the god-name *Tlāloc.* In the first place, this name is a preterit agentive noun; consequently, a single-word formation having it as embed would have to use its combining form, *Tlālocā-*, thus yielding *Tlālocāxōchitl,* "Tlaloc-flower" (compare *Tlālocātēuctli* in II:12:1). In the second place, a two-word construction, *Tlāloc xōchitl,* is to be rejected since the only grammatical relation possible between the two words would be (1) apposition (i.e., "*Tlāloc,* in other words, *Xōchitl*") or (2) coordinate sequence (i.e., "*Tlāloc* and, in addition, *Xōchitl,*" or "*Tlāloc,* or else *Xōchitl*"). Neither of these solutions is possible here.

[7]Serna (1892:440) says that *in Xoxōhuic Tzitzimitl, in Xoxōhuic Cōlēlectli* ("the Green Air-spirit, the Green Demon") is "the piciete" and "some little idol wrapped up in an infernal bundle." The phrasing and the singular object prefix *-c-* on *xichuālcui* suggest that this is an appositive construction and that Serna's interpretation is wrong. At no other place in these incantations does "Green Air-spirit" represent *piciete.* In II:14:1, it represents cane.

[8]To say that the bees are "people from *Tollantzinco*" is a metaphor that calls the hive a "little" *Tollan.* The *-tzin* suffix is here doing what "new" does in names like "New England," "New Jersey," and so forth. The metaphor thus recognizes the skill of the bees as workers, since *Tollan* was famed for the skill of its craftsmen.

[9]Following the hint of "land" in Ruiz de Alarcón's translation, we have rewritten *tla xilcapan* as *tlālīxcapān.* Ruiz de Alarcón translated the word as if it were *tlālīxcapāntli* (i.e., as a patientive noun) while we see it as *tlālīx-*

capānqui (i.e., as an agentive noun). What is being spoken to here is not the slappee (the earth), but the slapper (the sandal or sandals), the same as "One Grass" in the next section.

[10]The MS has *tontiazque*, which is meaningless. One may have either *tonyazque* [i.e., *tonyāzqueh*] or *tiazque* [i.e., *tiyāzqueh*]. We have chosen the former possibility.

[11]The *me* at the end of the word in the MS, *coçauhqueme* [i.e., *cōzauhquēmeh*], is not a plural suffix as it has apparently been accepted to be. The word is a singular-number preterit agentive noun of possession in which the stem (CŌZAUH-QUĒMI)-TL ("yellow clothing") serves as a verb-object embed to the verb stem *TLA-(E) ("to possess, to own"). The word in the text should, however, be plural, so we have added the plural suffix *-queh*.

[12]"And I am to bring them" has no counterpart in the Nahuatl unless it can be considered part of an inflated translation of *niquimānaco*, which has already been rendered as "I who come for [them]."

[13]One-Grass is a metaphor for "sandals." Caso (1959:89), referring to this instance in Ruiz de Alarcón, says that it is "A name of the land," but the context does not support this interpretation.

[14]For *tecoatl*, *cuauhcoatl*, see Sahagún (1959: 13), where it is explained that they symbolize "rocky road" and "mountain road," respectively.

[15]The MS presents a problem here. What we have read as *nicel yatl niicelti ytlacahuan* [i.e., *nīcēl Yāōtl*, *nīcēl Tītlācahuān*, "I am Yaotl's solitary one, I am Titlacahuan's solitary one"], Paso y Troncoso (1892:160) has read as *nicel yaotl*, *ninelti ytlacahuan* [i.e., *nīcēl Yāōtl*, *niNelTītlācahuān*, "I am Yaotl's solitary one, I am True-Titlacahuan"]. Although the MS is not perfectly clear, it does seem certain that at least the last part of what Paso y Troncoso has read as *n* is *c*. This, coupled with the fact that Nahuatl style almost demands the pairing of *nīcēl* and *nīcēl* in such a context, has prompted our reading. Ruiz de Alarcón's translation *yo solo la misma guerra o el guerrero, yo cuyos son los esclavos* ("I alone, the very war or the warrior, I to whom the slaves belong") does not help: (1) he translates *nicel* [i.e., *nīcēl*] as if it were *nocel* [i.e., *nocēl*], which would force *Yaotl* [i.e., *Yāōtl*, "he is Yaotl"] to be *niYaotl* [i.e., *niYāōtl*, "I am Yaotl"]; and (2) he does not translate the contrast of *niicel* and *ninel*, which is where the real problem is.

[16]We have changed *ynnò chitzipihuā* (which, respelled, would be *in nohchitzīpihuān*, an obvious error) to *in notzihtzīpihuān*, where the reduplicated syllable with a glottal stop indicates distributive or varietal plurality. However, neither a reference to each individual of the bee hive nor one to different sorts of bees seems valid here, and the words probably should be rewritten as *in notzīpihuān*. Nevertheless, we have chosen to keep the distributive/varietal form since in both II: 7:1 and II:7:4 one finds the equally awkward distributive/varietal form *notlahtlahhuān*, "my separate/various uncles," referring to the bees (see note I:4:18). Molina lists *tzipitl* [i.e., *tzīpitl*] with the meaning "the child who is sick or without appetite because his mother is pregnant." More to the point here, he lists *tzipitlatoa* [i.e., *tzīpitlahtoa*, or, using a stem notation, (TZĪPI-TLA-HT-OA)] with the meaning of "to lisp," (*literally*, "to speak like a sickly child," or "to speak like a child who lisps").

[17]The MS has *cecoatl*. This could be a vocative, but it is more reasonable to accept Ruiz de Alarcón's comment that it is functioning as an appositive. For this reason, we have changed it to the first-person singular form *niCē-Cōātl*. Caso (1959:83-84), referring to this instance in Ruiz de Alarcón, says "1. Coatl . . . Name of the wizard who seems to represent Tezcatlipoca." It is not clear how he arrived at this conclusion.

[18]In Serna (1892:440), the text is different: "white spiders, painted *xochua* spider; green, yellow spiders" (*arañas blancas, araña xochua pintada; arañas verdes amarillas*). For a reference to the spider called *xōchhuah*, "flower-owner," by Ruiz de Alarcón, see VI:16:14.

[19]The MS has *ma ayac quimmianti* [i.e., *Mā ayāc quimihyānti*]. The form *quimihyānti* is the third person singular admonitive form from the verb TĒ-(IHYĀNA), "to hide someone." The *-ti* suffix on a singular admonitive form is nonstandard, since the standard formation has singular number forms that are identical to the singular preterit forms for verbs of classes B, C, and D, while class A

verbs take a final glottal stop. The verb in the second part of the sentence, *quintlapachoh,* shows the standard (class B) formation. The standard (class C) formation of TĒ-(IHYĀNA) would be *quimihyān.* It should be noted that, in addition to the substandard form, the syntax of this admonitive sentence is strange. The *ma ayac* in the MS [i.e., *mā ayāc*] would expectedly occur in a negative admonitive (meaning "let someone be sure to hide them"), while the context demands a positive one ("let no one dare hide them"); concerning the negative value of a positive admonitive and the negative-of-a-negative value (i.e., an emphatic positive value) of a negative admonitive, see Andrews 1975:56–58. We have replaced the negative *ayāc,* "no one," with *acah,* "somebody," both here and in the following clause (compare note II:7:24 and note II:7:25).

[20]In the MS, this line is incongruously written as a subtitle.

[21]Since we have taken this to be a name word, we have changed the *no-* to *mo-*, since in name words the reflexive prefix does not change to reflect the number of subject. See note II:2:7.

[22]See note I:5:4.

[23]The use of "them" (*-quin-* in the Nahuatl) is surprising. One would have expected "you [pl]" (*-amēch-*). Ruiz de Alarcón's translation disregards the Nahuatl and gives *os* ["you (pl)"].

[24]The MS has *mayaca nechinmacìti,* which would be respelled as *mā ayacah nēchīmahcihti,* which is impossible since the verb TĒ-(AHCI), "to overtake someone," is a single-object verb. The form might be intended to be *nēchīmacacihti,* apparently for the third person singular admonitive form of the verb TĒ-(ĪMACACI), "to fear someone, to have reverential fear and respect for someone." However, this verb's perfective stem is (ĪMACAZ), not (ĪMACACIH), so the singular admonitive form (using the nonstandard singular *-ti* of note II:7:16) would be *nēchīmacazti,* which is the way we have written it. Note that we have also replaced the negative *ayacah* with the positive *acah* (see note II:7:19).

[25]The MS has *nechmauhcahuati,* which is meaningless. We have emended it to *nēchmauhcāithuahti,* which would be a variant of *nēchmauhcāittahti,* just as *quithuatīhuih* in the next sentence is a variant of *quittatīhuih.* The form *nēchmauhcāithuahti* is a nonstandard third person singular admonitive form (see note II:7:19). Note that, as in the preceding sentence, we have again replaced the negative *ayacah* with the positive *acah* (see note II:7:19).

[26]It is rare in Ruiz de Alarcón's writing to allow the native explanation to appear in the original Nahuatl. Segments II:7:8–9 are, of course, not incantations.

[27]See note I:5:8.

[28]These last two verbs, translated literally, are "they lie loving themselves, they lie considering themselves great." Both are "connective *-ti-*" compounds using the verb (O), "to lie, to be recumbent," as the matrix. They are reflexive formations used for the purpose of expressing the passive idea.

Chapter 8

[1]The Latin is garbled. If one reads *pace* for *peca,* the meaning is apparently "at peace in the soul in every way."

[2]The MS has *cosa* ("thing") for *casa* ("house").

[3]I.e., *tenāmāztli,* the three rocks in a fireplace set in a triangular formation to support a cooking utensil. The word consists of (TENĀMI)-TL, "wall," and (-ĀZ)-TLI, "instrument." See Andrews 1975:371.

[4]As stated in the Editorial Procedures, we have incorporated marginal notes in the text at appropriate places, enclosing them in braces.

[5]Ruiz de Alarcón's metaphor actually speaks of "doughs" (*amacijos,* which brings in a possibly pejorative connotation since the word can also mean "hotchpotch"). See the earlier metaphor for the same idea in II:3.

[6]See note II:8:4.

[7]The MS has *xohuiqui,* which might be *xonhuiqui,* with the directional prefix *-on-* ("thither"). However, we have chosen to rewrite it as *xihuiqui,* since this is the usual form found in the MS. The form *xihuiqui,* analyzed as XI(HUI-QU-I)ø-ø, is the imperative of the in-bound purposive stem (HUI-QU-ĪUH), "to come in order to go" (see Andrews 1975:127). The stem (HUI) is a variant of the stem (YA), "to go" (see Andrews 1975:65).

[8]Ruiz de Alarcón has given the non-figurative equivalent, "earth," instead of the name "Din of the earth" (his translation of *tlalte-*

cuintli at the beginning of this segment).

[9]Ruiz de Alarcón's justification for the name reveals an ignorance of the naming system. This justification may be not Ruiz de Alarcón's but his informant's.

[10]The MS has *titatacacpol* [which should read *titlatatacpol* (literally, "you are a miserable hole-dug one")] *mitznemītia yntlamacazq̃*, which Ruiz de Alarcón translates quite freely as "to see yourself wounded in as many places as the possessed ones . . . go digging you." The translation suggests that the text is defective. *Mitznemītia* ("he makes you live"), which Ruiz de Alarcón has rendered "[they] go digging you," does not repeat the idea of "digging" as would be expected. If a strict parallel should exist between this segment and II:8:4, the words *in cān* should be inserted after *titlatatacpōl* and an adverb (possibly *iuh*, "in such a way") should be added, yielding "at the place where you are dug-out holes, [in the place where] they . . . make you live [in such a way]." In our translation below, however, we have chosen not to change the text. See note II:8:13.

[11]The word in the MS, *tlaltecuintli* [i.e., *Tlāltecuīntli*] is a patientive noun. One finds *tlaltetecuin* [i.e., *Tlāltehtecuīn*] in II:1:5, which is the same form that is found in Sahagún (1970:35), where it apparently is understood as an agentive noun since it is translated *el que salta, hiriendo la tierra* ("he who jumps striking the earth"), which Dibble and Anderson render as "the Earth-stamper." The agentive translation of Sahagún takes the embed *tlāl-* to be an incorporated adverb and the matrix *-tehtecuīn* to be derived from an intransitive verb. The agentive translation of Dibble and Anderson takes *tlāl-* to be an incorporated object and the matrix to be derived from a transitive verb. The latter does not seem acceptable, since the verbstem (TECUĪNI) is listed in Molina as intransitive (meaning "for the fire to catch, throwing off flames"). In our rewritten version we have changed the word to *Tlāltecuīn* (which we would translate as an intransitive-sourced agentive noun: "He-who-flames-up-on-the-land"). It may be that Ruiz de Alarcón's informant has confused *Tlāltecuīn* and *Tlāltēuctli*, thus amalgamating the names. This seems likely since the salutation here (which is repeated verbatim in II:8:22), *nonān, Tlāltecuīntli, notah, Cē Tōchtli, Tezcatl in zan huālpopōcatimani*, appears in II:8:10 as *nonān, Tlāltēuctli, notah, Cē Tōchtli, Tezcatl [in] zan huālpopōcatimani.* If the patientive noun form *Tlaltecuīntli*, is the valid form (meaning "One-who-has-become-flamed-up-on-the-land"), *Tlatecuīn* would be merely its "name form" (by virtue of the loss of the absolutive singular-number suffix *-tli*). Since the source verbstem is intransitive, there is little difference in the translation value of the patientive and agentive formations.

[12]Ruiz de Alarcón did not recognize *Ācaxōch* (literally, "Reed-flower") as another name for the deer (see Sahagún 1963:15). He accepted *ynacaxoch* [i.e., *in Ācaxōch*] as if it were the possessive state word *īnacaxōch* (literally, "her meat-flower"). After giving the unfounded translation here (II:8:2) of "[her] place of amusement," he later renders it as "whose meat is fat and tasty" (II:8:12), as "whose fat meat" (II:8:20), and then as "the one who is delicious (or enchanted) meat" (II:9:1).

[13]We read *titlatatacpōl*, which is a second person singular form, as the verb-object complement to the second person singular object prefix *mitz-* on the verb *mitznemītiah* (see Andrews 1975:298–300). See note II:8:10. Concerning the use of the "flaw form" of a defect-signifying noun to refer to the person with the defect, see note I:4:37.

[14]The MS reads *mizcoacihuatl* (literally, "puma-snake-woman") which Ruiz de Alarcón translates as "the goddess, snake with the face of a puma." Since we can find no reference to such an entity, we have changed this to *Mixcoacihuatl* (literally, "Cloud-snake-woman"); see Appendix B. The spelling with *x* instead of *z* occurs in II:8:20 and in the material following II:9:1.

[15]The Spanish is *espiritu* ("spirit") but should be *espiritado* ("possessed one").

[16]The words "the God of the first age" are a comment by Ruiz de Alarcón and should have been put in parentheses.

[17]The MS has *ytexòtlalpan* which would be rewritten as *ītexohtlālpan* ("in his blue-land"). But this has been corrected to *in teohtlālpan* ("in the desert") to match other instances (see, for example, II:8:12).

[18]The words *in motlahuēl* have been inserted to maintain the parallel between this segment and II:8:2.

[19]The MS has *como te des jindas?* for which

we read *como te deslindas?* ("how do you demarcate yourself?") only because Serna's version (1892:434) has it. A more likely reading would be *còmo te diviertas?* ("how are you amusing yourself?") since this would be a more expected translation by Ruiz de Alarcón of *tleh ticmati?* See II:8:1 above, *que descuidado que estas* ("how inattentive you are") and later in this segment, *que descuydado que estays* ("how inattentive you are") and at II:8:9 *en que estays divertidas?* ("in what are you amused?").

[20]The words "the rest of the stakes and enchanted wood" are translating the Nahuatl *yntlaco quau tli.* Apparently Ruiz de Alarcón was reading *quau[h]tli* as *quahuitl* [i.e., *cuahuitl*] ("wood") instead of *quauhtli* [i.e., *cuāuhtli*] ("eagle"). Pérez (1713:190) says: "In all the Coast and Hotlands 'stick' or 'wood' is *Quauhtli.* In Mexico [City] it is *Quahuitl,* and *Quauhtli* is in Mexico [City] 'Eagle.'" Pérez ignores vowel length and therefore fails to distinguish between the two words. Apparently Ruiz de Alarcón has made the same error (see the similar confusion with *Chicōme-Cuāuhtzin* in note III:3:2). The dialectal usage of *cuauhtli* for *cuahuitl* is not manifested at any point in the MS, but the principle it illustrates, the substitution of /Wλ i/ for the standard /wiλ/, is abundantly evident in such dialectal forms as *xiuhtli* for *xihuitl, chiquiuhtli* for *chiquihuitl,* and *chālchiuhtli* for *chālchihuitl.* The use of /Wλ i/ instead of /wiλ/ was possibly invited by the fact that the nonabsolutive form of subclass 2 *-tl* stems ending in /wi/ is /W/ (see Andrews 1975:151). As pointed out in the Editorial Procedures, we have chosen to respell these dialectal forms in the standard manner. See note II:8:26.

[21]The words "hidden and burned" are translating *maon motlāti* and show that either Ruiz de Alarcón was unable to choose between *mā onmotlāti* ("let it be hidden") and *mā onmotlati* ("let it be burned") or that he was not aware of the vowel-length contrast that keeps these verbs from being homonyms.

[22]Ruiz de Alarcón's translation of *tlapalli* (included in *nitlapallo*) as "humor" shows him working with the European concept in which the four humors determine health and personality (Siegel 1968:217–18). See our introductory remarks.

[23]The grave accent is superfluous since both it and the *h* indicate the glottal stop.

[24]Notice that (YŌL)-LI, "life," has been added to the pair (EZ)-TLI, "blood," and (TLA-PA-L)-LI, "color," used to indicate human frailty (see note II:10:9).

[25]The erroneous subject prefix *ni-* on the source Nahuatl has been corrected. The word is a third person singular passive form.

[26]The word *tlacōcuāuhtli,* literally "twig eagle," is translated by Dibble and Anderson (in Sahagún 1963:40) as "Marsh hawk," i.e., *circus cyaneus.* It is serving here as a metaphor, possibly for the trigger of the snare. See note II:8:20.

[27]The verbword *nēchēlēhuihti* is a third person singular admonitive form using the nonstandard formation (see note II:7:19).

[28]In Serna (1892:435) we find "Come, you, my Father, the four flaming reeds; come, you, my Father, the four reeds that throw flames." In the MS the Nahuatl is only *Tlaxihuiqui ynnotâ nahui acatl milintica* ("Come, my father, Four Reed, He-is-scintillating").

[29]The MS has *centellado,* "covered with sparkles." Serna (1892:435) has *sentelleando,* "sparkling."

[30]Ruiz de Alarcón's translation "whose body" is erroneous. The *tlac-* of *tlacça-* is not the stem (TLĀC)-TLI, "body." The word in the text is a form of the verbstem TLA-(ICZA), "to tread on something."

[31]The MS has *las sobras* ("the left-overs") while in Serna's (1892:435) version, we find *las obras* ("the works"), which is an error.

[32]The Spanish is *Ea ya queya nos bamos,* and is translating *tla huiyan* ("Let them go"). Apparently the *Ea, ya que ya* is translating the *tla,* which Ruiz de Alarcón usually translates with *Ea.* The *nos vamos* incorrectly shifts the third plural form *huiyan* to the first plural. It may well be, however, that the original read *tla tiuiyan* (with the *ti-* being later misread by the copyist as *h-*). Since this fits the context, we have chosen to follow the lead of Ruiz de Alarcón's translation and have rewritten the word as *tihuiān* in our version.

[33]The last three sentences create images of the fire and smoke. The first sentence presents the fire god lying supine with his mouth centered beneath the hearth puffing smoke and sparks upward with the fire. The second presents the changing shape of the smoke and flames as they rise. The third presents the hearth as the mouth of the god, through which he spews forth the smoke as if it were water.

34 Under the entry *matentinemi,* Siméon gives the expression *nochoquiz, nixayo nicmatentinemi* [i.e., *nochōquiz, nīxāyo nicmātēntinemi,* literally, "I go filling my weeping and my tears into my hands"] as meaning "I go shedding tears." The verb in the MS, *quimatentoqueh* has replaced (NEMI), "to go," with the verbstem (O), "to lie, to be recumbent," as the matrix of the "connective *-ti-*" construction. The embedded verbstem, TLA-(MĀTĒMA), means "to fill something into the hands." The entire last sentence creates yet another image of the fire, this time that of the firewood as it burns, with the flames and sparks being represented as its weeping and its tears. Serna (1892:435) sees this as referring to the tears of the people around the fire, crying because the smoke gets in their eyes. It is difficult to see this as valid.

35 Concerning our respelling of *xiuhtli* as *xīhuitl,* see note II:8:20. The not uncommon use of /-Wλi/ as an alternative for /-wiλ/ was possibly invited by the fact that the nonabsolutive form of subclass 2 *-tl* stems ending in /-wi/ is /-W/ (see Andrews 1975:151).

36 The MS has *tle muchitl* [i.e., *tlemochitl*] in the meaning of "sparks." This is not attested in either Molina or Siméon. We have changed it to *tlemōyōtl* which is the expected word for this meaning.

37 The MS has *yniqua,* which expectedly would be rewritten as *in īcuā* ("his head"). But *īcuā* in this form can have no function in the sentence. We have rewritten it as *īcuāc,* "at his head."

38 Ruiz de Alarcón reads the first syllable of *-quahuac cacauhtin* as if it were the combining form of (CUĀ)- of (CUĀI)-TL, "head," since he translates the word as *las sobras delos de mal aliñadas cabeças* ["the leftovers of those of badly adorned heads"]. It is not clear how he arrived at "badly adorned," but "leftovers" is translating *-cauhtin.* The word, however, is the plural of the nounstem (CUA-HUĀC-ø-CĀ-CĀUH)-TLI, which is doubly compound. The embed is the preterit agentive noun (CUA-HUĀC-ø)-QUI, "dry like a stick," and thus, "a dry stick" (see Andrews 1975:264), in its combining form, (CUA-HUĀC-ø-CĀ)-, whose embed is the stem (CUAHUI)-TL, "tree, wood" [which is in the combining form *cua-* instead of *cuauh-* because the next constituent begins with *hu-,* and there is a phonological rule that /W/ + /w/ > /w/] and whose matrix is the preterit agentive noun (HUĀC-ø)-QUI, "a thing that has become dry," from the intransitive verbstem (HUĀQUI), "to become dry." The matrix of the entire word is the passive patientive noun (CĀUH)-TLI, "an abandoned thing," from the verb TLA-(CĀHUA), "to abandon something." The stem therefore means literally, "one who has been abandoned in the manner of a dry stick" or "a stick-dry-abandoned-entity," a meaning we have rendered freely as "emaciated derelict."

39 The adjective *totōnic,* "a warm one," is not listed in the dictionaries. It is a variant of *totōnqui.* Both words are preterit agentive nouns from the source verbstem (TO-TŌ-NI), "to be(come) warm" [which is also unlisted]; *totōnic* treats it as a class A verb and *totōnqui* as a class B verb.

40 The expected form would be either *īyōllo* [from the present patientive nounstem (YŌL-LŌ)-TL] or *īyōlloh* [from the past patientive nounstem (YŌL-LOH)-TLI]. However, (YŌL)-LI is here participating in an idiomatic doublet, other instances of which are found in II:4:6 and II:8:8. See also the form *yōllohtzin* in VI:3:10.

41 For other examples of the coordinate phrase "chili pepper and salt" (meaning "food"), see I:7.

42 The word *cihuātequihuah* is translated by Ruiz de Alarcón as "the one who performs the offices of a woman" or "the one who works like a woman," which suggests that he would take the immediate constituents to be *cihuātequi-* and *-huah,* with the embed being (CIHUĀ-TEQUI)-TL, "female work"; see, for example, *amocihuātequiuh,* "your (pl) female work," in Carochi (1904:522). Our translation takes the immediate constitutents to be *cihuā-* and *-tequihuah,* with the matrix being (TEQUI-HUAH-ø)-ø, "a tribute-owner," i.e., "a valiant warrior." Compare *tēlpōchtequihuahqueh,* "young seasoned warriors," in Sahagún 1952:7.

43 The MS has *ynahua,* which is *not* to be read as *in āhuah* ("the water-owner"). It is a copyist's error for *in ahcan* [i.e., *in ahcān*], which is needed as part of a parallel construction in support of the idiomatic doublet *yōleh, tzontecomeh* (for other instances of the doublet, see II:4:6 and II:8:7).

44 The last two sentences contain first person singular admonitive forms: the first, *nitlacxihuih,* is formed in the standard manner;

the second, *nitlacohcotōnti*, in the nonstandard manner (see note II:7:19).

45 The sequence *nohueltiuh, yn antlàçotēteo* presents two problems: (1) Ruiz de Alarcón reads it as an appositive phrase ("my sisters, the lesser goddesses") thus reading *nohuēltīuh*, "my sister," as if it were *nohuēltīhuān*, "my sisters." But, in addition to the fact that *nohuēltīuh* is singular, it also is a third-person form (with a vocative function here), while *antlàçoteteo* is a second-person form. This lack of agreement in person and number precludes apposition. It also precludes (in view of the vocative function) a coordinate construction. We have, therefore, placed them in separate sentences in our rewritten version. (2) Ruiz de Alarcón has translated *antlàçoteteo* as "[you] the lesser goddesses," apparently insisting on the glottal stop (the grave accent on the *a*) but intending the *ç* to be a *c*, since the word (TLAHCO)-ø means "half" (another explanation for the glottal stop which disregards the translation of "lesser" is given below). In II:8:17, we find *tlàçotèteo* with the translation "lesser gods and goddesses." In II:15:2, we find *tlacolteteo* (with no grave accent, but with *c* and with *l*), translated as "lesser gods," suggesting that it is formed with the stem (TLAHCO-L)-ø, "half," found as the matrix of (CEN-TLAHCO-L)-ø, "one half." And finally, in VI:16:2, we find *xoxouhqui tlacolteyotl* (again with no grave accent, but with *c* and with *l*), translated as "forest Gods or lesser green [gods]" (there is, however, a problem here; see note VI:16:18). This insistence on "lesser" as a translation for both *tlàço-* and *tlacol-* is all the more puzzling since in II:8:15 we find *tlaçòteteo* (with a *ç* and with a grave accent on the *o*), with the translation "the goddesses worthy of esteem," apparently representing the standard *tlazohtēteoh*, "beloved goddesses" [where the embed is (TLA-ZOH)-TLI, "a valued or beloved thing"]. And, furthermore, in IV:3:1, we find *antlaçolteteo*, with the translation "you gods of love," apparently representing the standard *anTlahzoltēteoh*, "you Filth-goddesses," i.e., "Love goddesses" [where the embed is (TLAHZOL)-LI, "filth"]. For these various forms, López Austin (1967:9) lists three items: *tlazolteteo, tlacolteteo*, and *tlazoteteo*. He says that *tlacolteteo* means "curved divinities" and identifies them as "divinities who protect the fishhooks" (so he is referring to II:15:2). The word *tlacōltēteoh* can conceivably be a viable formation. Although its embed, (TLA-CŌL)-LI, is not listed in the dictionaries, it is a legitimate root-patientive noun [see Andrews 1975:246] meaning "a thing that has been curved," from the verb TLA-(CŌL-OA), "to curve or bend something." However, in II:15:2, *tlacolteteo* is referring not to fishhooks but to the house, and the idea of "curved" is not appropriate (see note II:15:4), nor is it appropriate for *xoxouhqui tlacolteyotl* in VI:16:2. We have, therefore, considered *tlacol-* as a misspelling. If we disregard Ruiz de Alarcón's translation of *tlàco-* as "lesser," another possibility presents itself. The number of times the MS has *tlàço-*, plus the fact that in VI:25:3 we find *tlahçotli*, leads us to believe that the presence of the glottal stop after the *tla-* is a dialectal variant similar to that of *itlàpial* discussed in note I:2:12. Given the problems in the text, in our rewritten version we have chosen to read *tlàço-* as *tlaçò-* [i.e., *tlazoh-*] and *tlacol-* as *tlàçol-* [i.e., *tlahzol-*] in every instance, depending on the absence or presence of an *-l-*.

46 The MS says *uno de los dioses mejor tejera* for which we read *uno de los dioses. Mejor te será*. Serna (1892:436) has *vno de los Dioses: mejor será* ("one of the gods: it will be better").

47 The words *q. d. allanandose* ("which means by acquiescing") are in the body of the text but are not part of the incantation. Serna (1892:436) does not have them. Ruiz de Alarcón is trying to explain his translation of "for you to humble yourself to me."

48 We have added *in* and changed *huel* to *huāl-* to make this passage consistent with that in II:8:2. There are two formulas involving *Tezcatl* ("mirror") used in this work. The first is found here and in II:8:2, II:8:22, and V:1:1: *Tezcatl in zan huālpopōcatimani* ("Mirror that just lies smoking hither"). The second is found in II:10:1 and III:2:4: *Tezcatl in īīx zan huālpopōcatimani* ("Mirror whose surface just lies smoking hither"). In II:10:1 the mirror is in the possessive state: *nonāhualtezcauh* ("my *nahualli*-mirror"). The reference to the god *Tezcatl-Ihpoca* ("Mirror that smokes") is implicit in these formulas, but the symbolic meaning is "the land."

49 The form *nonmāyauh* is a first person singular admonitive form using the standard formation (see note II:7:19). Concerning the stem

(MĀY-AHUI), "to use one's hand(s)," see note I:4:19.

[50]The MS has *apositive* for the Latin *appositive* ("functioning as an appositive").

[51]It is difficult to understand Ruiz de Alarcón's use of the words "you well saw and knew about my coming and arrival to this place" unless he is merely giving a different (alternative) version of "with your consent and pleasure, I have come here," i.e., giving a second translation of *Amīxpan, amotlamatiyān in ōnihuāllah* ("It is before your eyes, before your knowing-place that I . . . have come.").

[52]See note II:1:26 about Ruiz de Alarcón's confusion of (ĪTZ-CA-L)-LI, "side," with (TLAN-ĪTZ)-TLI, "shin." The word *amītzcac* is formed on the locative nounstem (ĪTZ-CA-C)-ø, which is equivalent to (ĪTZ-CA-L-CO)-ø, "at the side." See note II:3:6. Molina lists it only in the form *mītzcac* ("your side").

[53]The MS has *antlalloque*, which Ruiz de Alarcón translates as "owners of the earth" apparently seeing a preterit agentive noun of possession, i.e., AN-ø(TLĀL-YOH-ø)QUEH, but this would mean "you are owners of dirt in every part," or "you are covered with dirt." The expression "you are owners of the earth" would be AN-ø(TLĀL-HUAH-ø)QUEH. We have, therefore, rewritten the word as *anTlāloqueh*, i.e., "you are the (supernatural) priests of *Tlaloc.*" In the *Treatise*, as in Ponce (see Appendix A), *Tlāloqueh* is used as a metaphorical name for the mountains (because that is where the rain clouds gather).

[54]The MS has *amylhuicatl quitzquitoque*, which Ruiz de Alarcón translates as "you are supporting the skies" (*estays sustentando los cielos*). The grammatical difficulty can be resolved in two ways: (1) *ilhuicatl anquiquītzquihtoqueh* (with *ilhuicatl* being placed outside the verbword as a supplementary object in cross reference with the basic object *qui-*), or (2) *amilhuicaquītzquihtoqueh* (with *ilhuicatl* losing the absolutive singular suffix *-tl* and becoming embedded in the verbword as the incorporated object. Both solutions would mean "you [pl] lie gripping the sky."

We have chosen the second alternative. This choice is backed up by the word *ilhuicatzitzque* found in Durán (1967, 2:229). This is an error for *ilhuicatzitzquique* [i.e., *ilhuicatzītzquihqueh*], since Durán translates it as "the ones who hold the sky." According to Durán these were certain large figures that supported the block that contained the idol atop the pyramid to Huitzilopochtli in Tenochtitlan. They undoubtedly symbolized mountains. The verb TLA-(QUĪTZQUIA), which has the same meaning as TLA-(TZĪTZQUIA), "to grip something," is not listed *per se* in either Molina or Siméon, but appears as the matrix of the verbs TLA-(TLACUĀUH-QUĪTZQUIA) and TLA-(TE-TEUH-QUĪTZQUIA), which Molina lists as *tlaquauhquitzquia.nitla.* and *teteuhquitzquia.nitla.*, respectively, both of which mean "to grasp something strongly in the hand." It occurs again in the *Treatise* in III:5:1 (*xitlaquītzqui*) and in VI:1:3 (*toconquītzquīcān*).

[55]The MS has *ynimitzcac ynimopochcopa*, which would be rewritten as *in īmītzcac in īmopōchcopa*, "on their left side," except that this would mean that in midsentence the second-person plural has shifted to the third-person plural and that instead of talking to the mountains the speaker abruptly begins talking about them. We have seen this as a textual error and have rewritten it as *in amītzcac in amopōchcopa*, "on your left side." Contrast this with the construction in II:8:21, where the third-person plural possessive is appropriate.

[56]"The fertile land" is translating *teohtlālpan.* Molina lists *teotlalli* [i.e., *teohtlālli*] as meaning "valley or desert of flat, wide land."

[57]The MS has *del espū*, i.e., *del espiritu* ("of the spirit"). Serna's (1892:436) version has *de el espiritado* ("of the possessed one"), which is a more likely reading.

[58]See note II:8:53.

[59]The MS reads *yeonechcoc*, which is meaningless. Since Ruiz de Alarcón translates it as "I have arrived," we have changed it to *ye ōnehcōc.*

[60]The MS has *la* ("her/it"), which we have emended to *las* ("them"). The singular feminine pronoun is unjustified since the Nahuatl has a plural (*-quim-*). The use of the feminine is unexpected, but possibly it is reaching forward to the feminine word *ovejas* ("sheep").

[61]The MS has *el espū*, i.e., *el espiritu* ("the spirit"), but again this should read *el espiritado* ("the possessed one") since it is translating *tlamacazqui.* Serna (1892:437) does not have a word here.

[62]The mistranslation, "Lord God of the

earth," comes as a surprise after the many times Ruiz de Alarcón has given a fairly acceptable translation, "Dweller of the forest," for *teohtlālhuah* (literally, "Desert-owner").

[63]The form *yāznecti* is a third person singular admonitive form using the nonstandard formation (see note II:7:19).

[64]The MS has *ynin tla ce ya canal,* which Ruiz de Alarcón translates as *suvnico guion y governador* ("their only leader and governor"). This agentive translation does not match the Nahuatl since the stem (TLA-CEN-YAC-ĀNA-L)-LI is a patientive noun and would mean "one who has been totally led or guided." The agentive counterpart would be the stem (TLA-CEN-YAC-ĀN-ø)-QUI, "one who has led or governed things totally," giving the possessive form *īntlacenyacāncāuh,* "their total leader," which resembles Ruiz de Alarcón's translation. The question is whether the Spanish translation or the Nahuatl text is correct. If the Spanish is accepted and the patientive form is replaced by the agentive form, it makes sense to have the plural possessive prefix *īn-* ("their"), which would refer back to the metaphorical "sheep" of II:8:14, so that the particular deer sought by the hunter would be the foremost example of the herd. Also, the form *īntlacenyacāncāuh* would come at the beginning of the series, "the priest, Desert-owner" (i.e., it would be a variant name for the deer). If the Nahuatl is accepted and the patientive noun is kept, the *īn-* referring back to the "sheep" makes less compelling sense. It might, therefore, be a mistake for the singular possessive prefix *ī-* ("his"), which would refer to *in tlamacazqui* ("the priest"), so the resultant *ītlacenyacānal* would now come at the end of the series "his flower-mantle, his flower necklace" (i.e., as clothing or trappings). The parallel phrasing at II:8:19, however, omits this word, and that omission may well be due to the lack of a contextual mention of "sheep," so that the reference to them here in the *īn-* may be essential to what is being expressed. Faced with these problems, we have left the Nahuatl text as it stands, not certain of the exact significance of "their totally guided one."

[65]The MS has *selo vestira, yselo pondran mis her* [*man*] *as* ("he will dress himself in it, and my sisters will put it on him"). Serna (1892: 437) has *se lo vestirán, y pondrán mis hermanas* ("My sisters will dress him in it and put it on him"). We have translated the plural forms.

[66]Ruiz de Alarcón's explanation that "dust" stands for "desire" seems unjustified in the context.

[67]The MS has *teuh yohuâ,* which would be rewritten as *teuhyōhuah,* "it is an owner of dustiness" (that is, a preterit agentive noun of possession). We have chosen, however, to read it as the verb *teuhyōhua,* "it becomes filled with dust" (see Andrews 1975:358).

[68]The MS has *tócô,* which would be rewritten as *tocoh,* a third person (animate) plural passive, "they are followed." The context, however, requires a third person singular form, *toco,* "it is followed."

[69]Ruiz de Alarcón may have thought that by saying "my sister," the "woman" (i.e., *cihuā-*) of *cihuācōātl* did not need translating, although he has translated both constitutents of the word in other instances.

[70]Ruiz de Alarcón has literalized the text, giving "stake" for *Cē-Ātl Ītōnal* and "branches" for *xoxōuhqui tlamacazqui.*

[71]The MS has *titetlayecolticahuan,* which would be rewritten as *tītētlayecōltihcāhuān,* "we are his servants." This is unlikely, however, because *tī-* [i.e., *ti-* + *-ī-*] ("you are his," "we are his") is almost always represented in this work as *tii-* or *tiy-*. Because of the preceding word *titētlācahuān,* "we are someone's slaves," we have chosen to rewrite the word as *titētētlayecōltihcāhuān,* "we are someone's servants," the possessed form (using the nonspecific possessor TĒ-, "someone's") of the preterit agentive noun (TĒ-TLA-YEC-Ō-L-TIH-ø)-QUI, "one who has served someone, a servant," from the verbstem TĒ-(TLA-YEC-Ō-L-TIA), "to serve someone."

[72]We have added the word *īhuān* to make this phrase conform with other instances of the expression (see VI:12:1 and VI:25:1). The verb phrase TLA-(HUĀN) M-(OH-HUI-MŌL-OA), "to combine (H) perilously with something, to join (H) perilously with something," is not listed in Molina or Siméon, nor is its source stem, TLA-(HUĀN) MO-(MŌL-OA), "to cause oneself to become combined with something," i.e., "to combine (H) or join (H) with something" (the reflexive causative formation is used for the purpose of creating an honorific expression). The intransitive (nonhonorific) form is found in the phrase *īhuān timoh-*

mōliuhtiuh in VI:25:1 (see note VI:25:4). In the form given here (II:8:16) and twice in VI:12:1, the embed (OH-HUI)-TL has an adverbial function. The glottal stop, marked by the grave accent in the MS, suggests derivation from the stem (OH)-TLI, "road," through the fusion of its possessive singular number suffix -HUI and the stem (a procedure not as rare as one might think, but this is not the place to discuss the matter further). The hazards associated with travel (see II:4) would, furthermore, justify this derivation since the resultant stem means "danger, peril." It is found only as an embed and in denominative verbs [namely, (OH-HUI-TI), "to be in danger," and (OH-HUI-A), whose existence is attested only by its commonly used preterit agentive noun (OH-HUI-H-ø)-ø, "a dangerous thing"]. Since the embed has an adverbial function here, we have translated it "perilously," although "under threat of danger" might express the intended meaning more exactly.

[73]We have rewritten *ynehuan* not as *īnehuān* but as *īhuān*, to accord with the parallel construction in II:15:5.

[74]The purpose of this parenthetical explanation is not clear. It may be that the informant is explaining a word whose meaning he did not think was known. The verbs for "to embrace someone" in Molina are TĒ-(NĀHUAH-TEQUI), listed as *nauatequi.nite,* and TĒ-(QUECH-NĀHUA), listed as *quechnaua.nite.* The verb given here, TĒ-(QUECH-NĀHUAH-TEQUI), which seems to be an amalgam of those two verbs, is listed in Brewer and Brewer (1962:200): *quiquechnōhuajtequi* ("he hugs him around the neck"). Of course, the form given in the MS is reflexive. In II:1:5, we find the projective form *xicnāhuahtequi.* In II:15:5, the expression (again reflexive) reads *īhuān timonāhuahtequiz,* "you will embrace him."

[75]Ruiz de Alarcón's marginal explanation is questionable. The reason the informants spoke of the hands as "owners of five *tonals*" is, we believe, because of the lunules on the fingernails. However, we have found no justification for such an assumption in any text. It should be noticed that Ruiz de Alarcón's translation "the five solar beings" (*los cinco solares*) and his preceding marginal explanation "for the hand" are inaccurate. He translates *mācuīltōnalehqueh* as if it were merely *mācuīltōnalli,* obscuring the fact that this latter word is only the embedded element (it is the incorporated direct object of the possessive verb *TLA-(E), "to own something"). So he talks of only five fingers when he should be talking of ten, since both hands are involved (the word is plural). But in fact, the Nahuatl focuses on the hands (the owners of the fingers) and not, as Ruiz de Alarcón suggests in his translation, on the fingers themselves. He sometimes translates the word more correctly as "the ones of five solar beings." It should be understood that "owners of five *tonal*s" means each owner possesses five *tonal*s.

It should *not* be thought that the word *mācuīltōnalehqueh* can be translated "the owners of a fifth *tonal,*" i.e., "the owners of an ill-omened *tonal*" (see Sahagún 1975:29, regarding the fact that any day-name containing the number "five" was considered unlucky in classical times; this is echoed in such statements as *Quēn nel nōzo? Mācuīltōnaleh.* "What can be done? He has a *tonal* in the fifth position." (Sahagún 1957:49)). The context of usage here negates such an interpretation.

[76]"Lesser gods and goddesses" is translating *tlàçotēteo* [i.e., *tlazohtēteoh*]. See point 2 of note II:8:45.

[77]López Austin translates *mācuīltōnalehqueh* as *los de los cinco destinos* ("the ones of the five destinies"). See note II:8:75.

[78]Concerning the rewriting of *tlàçoteteo* as *tlazohtēteoh,* see point 2 of note II:8:45. Notice that a problem somewhat similar to that of II:8:9 occurs in the sequence *nohueltiuh macuiltonelleque tlàçoteteo,* where *nohueltiuh* is singular while *macuiltonelleque* (a mistake for *macuiltonalleque*) and *tlàçoteteo* are plural. Ruiz de Alarcón sees the sequence as a coordinate construction ("my sister and the five solar beings, and you, lesser gods and goddesses") with *nohueltiuh* representing "the hand" and *macuiltonelleque* "the [five] fingers." His interpretation for both words is incorrect, since two hands are involved (see note II:8:75). We have again created two sentences in our rewritten version, with the singular number *nohuēltīuh* in one and the plural number *macuīltōnalehqueh* and *tlazohtēteoh* in another. We, however, have no interpretation for *nohuēltīuh.* It may refer again to the rope as in the preceding segment, or the snare mentioned later in this segment, or it may be an error for the plural *nohuēltīhuān* (as

in II:8:15), in which case the sequence in question would be an appositive construction ("my older sisters, Five-*tonal*s-owners, Beloved-goddesses").

[79]The MS has *anmotlaihuitzanal,* which would be rewritten as *amotlaihhuitzanal.* But two changes are required. First, there is an error of *n* for *u* (i.e., *hu*), since the source of this patientive noun matrix is (TZĀHUA), "to spin," so this would give *amotlaihhuitzāhual* ("your feather-woven-stuff") (see *amotzāhual* in II:8:8). Second, Ruiz de Alarcón has translated the word as "your festival garment" and, following this lead, we have changed the embed from *ihhui-* ("feather") to *ilhui-* ("holiday"). The final corrected version is, therefore, *amotlailhuitzāhual* ("your holiday-woven-stuff" or "your holiday fabric").

[80]*Ōtlamic. Nāuhcāmpa toyōhuaz. Ticyehecōz.* That is: "It has ended. You will bellow. You will test it." The inclusion of these words is unusual in that they do not belong to the incantation, but are directions for the performance of the ritual.

[81]The MS reads *el delas Rosas,* which is translating the Nahuatl . . . *yn xochitl.* Serna (1892:437) has *El de las siete rosas,* which suggests that his Nahuatl copy read *in Chicomexochitl* [i.e., *in Chicōme-Xōchitl*], which is what we have translated. See note II:8:84.

[82]It is curious that the Nahuatl verb TĒ-(TĪTLANI), "to send someone as a messenger, to dispatch someone," is used here in an extended meaning that parallels English and Spanish ("to dispatch" and *despachar*), "to kill." For another instance of sending a messenger to a god, see the section, "The Farmers," in Ponce's *Brief Relation* (Appendix A).

[83]Ruiz de Alarcón's translation, "night has caught you," is impossible. *Yohualli* cannot be the subject of *ōtitītlanīhuac,* which is a passive with a second person singular subject. *Yohualli* may have an adverbial function (meaning "in the night") but is not marked for it. We have, therefore, chosen to see it as a separate sentence.

[84]We have rewritten the text to fit Serna's translation (1892:437). See note II:8:81.

[85]In Garibay's translation (1971:319) of this segment, he has included the word *toyōhuaz* from the following sentence, despite Ruiz de Alarcón's indication that it does not belong to the incantation. Garibay's translation reads "Priest 7-Flower, owner of the steppe-ish land: / you made the night to come upon men. / Where is 1-Flower? He was beseiged. / Ha, ha, ha!; already he was thus trapped in our net." Garibay has disregarded the syntax. Also notice that he translates *toyōhuaz* as "our net" because *to-* can at times mean "our" and *az-* [more correctly, *-āz-*] can, at times, indicate an instrument. The virgules indicate lines of verse since he regards this as a poem.

[86]*Toyōhuaz.* "You will bellow."

[87]The Spanish is . . . *las caras y cabezas.* Serna (1892:437) has the singular forms *la cara, y cabeza.*

[88]The four verbs of this segment are second person singular admonitive forms. The first two (*tihuēxcāpēhuaznecti* and *tihuēxcātlahtlacōznecti*) and the last one (*titlachiaznecti*) are formed according to the nonstandard construction, while *timomauhtih* has the standard formation (see note II:7:19).

[89]The MS has *nahuianpa* [i.e., *nāhuiyāmpa*], an unusual formation that might be an error for *nohuianpa* [i.e., *nōhuiyāmpa*] ("from everywhere," "toward everywhere"), except that Ruiz de Alarcón translates it as "in the four parts of the world." We have changed it to the more usual *nāuhcāmpa,* "in four places" or "toward four directions," to echo the usage in the preceding clause.

[90]The word in the MS, *nochiauhtepec,* poses problems. The context demands that it have positive, desirable connotations, but its embed, *chiauh-,* does not allow this, as can be seen in the discussion of the stem (CHIAHUI)-TL in note VI:15:2. A comparison of the sequence beginning with *amīxpan* and ending with *ōnihuāllahtiyah* with the similarly bounded sequence in II:8:11 suggests that *nochiauhtepec* is an error for *noxiuhtepēc.* We further hypothesize that it should be in the plural, *noxiuhtepēhuān* ("my turquoise mountains"), to match *nomāquīztepēhuān* ("my bracelet-like mountains"), just as *anxiuhtētepeh* ("you are turquoise mountains") matches *ammāquīztētepeh* ("you are bracelet-like mountains") in II:8:11.

[91]Being possessed, the form in the MS cannot have the absolutive plural formation according to grammars of the standard practice.

[92]The word in the MS, *moopochcopa* [i.e., *mopōchcopa*] ("toward your left") has been

changed to *īmopōchcopa* ("toward their left") to match the third person plural possessor of *īmītzcac.*

[93]We have rewritten *niytlaca chihual* not as *nīntlācachīhual* but as *nīntlachīhual* for consistency with other occurrences. Also see II: 15:1.

[94]Notice that here and generally in this segment Ruiz de Alarcón gives the nonmetaphorical equivalent of the word in the Nahuatl.

[95]Ruiz de Alarcón's explanation that *cemmalīnalli* represents "the grassy place" seems questionable, as does Caso's remark (1959: 89) that it is "a name of the land." Elsewhere it represents the ropes (e.g., II:8:2) and the sandals (II:7:2).

[96]See note II:8:11.

[97]The *in* has been inserted to bring this expression into conformity with that in II:8:2.

[98]The MS has *vozes* [i.e., "voices, words"], but we have read *vezes* [i.e., "times"].

Chapter 9

[1]In this incantation, Ruiz de Alarcón changes the metaphors to their literal counterparts: *Cē-Ātl Ītōnal* (a metaphor for wood and wooden things) to the bow; *y ācayo* [i.e., *īācayo*] ("its reed") to the arrowshafts; and *ītzpāpālōtl* ("obsidian butterfly") to the arrowhead. Paso y Troncoso (1892:166) has read *y ācayo* as *ynacayo* [i.e., *īnacayo*] ("its flesh"), apparently assuming that the copyist had mistakenly placed a tilde over the *a* instead of over the first *y.* The diacritic, however, is not a tilde but a macron and is correctly placed. If the word were *īnacayo,* "its flesh," the metaphorical meaning would be "its bowstring," not "its arrowshafts."

[2]The verbs "made and devised" are singular in Spanish, as is the verb *ōquichihchīuh* which they translate. The problem is that Ruiz de Alarcón's translation, "the goddess *Tōnacācihuatl* {Ceres} and the one called *Xochiquetzal* {Venus}," requires a plural verb. However, the Nahuatl is not a coordinate phrase but an appositive phrase.

[3]Concerning *principal,* see note I:2:9.

[4]This is an expression of "accompanying possession" (see Andrews 1975:197).

[5]The *cihuātl* may be a mistake. In II:16:2, where the sequence *Tonacacihuatl Xochiquetzal* occurs again, it does not appear. Perhaps this is a parenthetical reminder to the speaker that the goddesses represent his wife. Compare the parenthetical use of *eztli* discussed in note VI:17:2.

[6]*Oyōhuaz, coyōtzahtziz. Quihtōz "Tahui"* (or *"Mixcōācihuātl"*). "He will bellow, he will howl. He will say, 'Halloo' (*or* 'Cloud-snake-woman')."

[7]This should read *ut infra* ("as below").

[8]Ruiz de Alarcón calls the word barbaric because, as he stated toward the end of II:8, he thought it was brought into the language by the Devil. Also see note I:10:6.

[9]*Xihuālmīlacatzo.* "Turn towards me."

[10]Cicero *In C. Verrem* 2.1.15.40 (Greenwood 1928:164). The Latin should read, *Non enim potest ea natura quae tantum facinus commiserit hoc uno scelere esse contenta; necesse est semper aliquid eius modi moliatur:* "For a being that has wrought a thing like this cannot rest content with this single wickedness: it must for ever be seeking to compass some such purpose." Ruiz de Alarcón has interrupted the quotation with a Spanish translation of part of the Latin.

Chapter 10

[1]Ruiz de Alarcón's translation ("by the gods") suggests that *Tēteoh* has inadvertently been omitted. While this is possible, we have retained the singular possessive prefix *ī-* ("his") on *nītītlan* and *nīcahuān* as possibly referring to the owner of the field. The word *nīcahuān* is a possessive state form of the patientive nounstem (CAHUĀ-N)-TLI, "one who has become famous, a celebrity," from the verbstem (CAHUĀ-NI), "to become illustrious, to make a name for oneself," listed as *cauani* by Siméon.

[2]Garibay (1958:253) has printed *ni ititlan ni icahuan nican niquintemoz in notlahuan,* which he translates (disregarding person and number) as *busco a los enviados y a los mensajeros de mis tios,* "I seek the ones sent and the messengers of my uncles." This translation ignores the logic of the segment by taking "the messengers" to be possessed by "my uncles." Contrast Ruiz de Alarcón's and our translations.

[3]Although our translation of *tlīlpotōnqueh* as "black stinkers" (or "inky stinkers") seems appropriate, since the word applies to pec-

caries (which are a blackish-brown color and have a large gland on the back that exudes a noxious odor; see Leopold 1972:493–94) and is morphologically justifiable, since the embed *tlīl-* means "ink" or "black" and the matrix, *potōnqueh,* is a preterit agentive noun meaning "stinking ones," from the verb (POTŌNI), "to stink or smell bad," there is a problem in that *Tlīlpotōnqui* was another name for *Topiltzin Quetzalcoatl* (see Sahagún 1952: 62). Although the meanings given for *potonqui* [i.e., (POTŌN-ø)-QUI] in Molina and Siméon do not support the definition, it is generally accepted that *tlīlpotōnqui* means "feather-plastered in black" (i.e., "plastered in black feathers"). For example, Durán (1967 1:146) translates *ītlīlpotōncāuh* as *el servidor emplumado de plumas negras suyo* ("her servant feathered with black feathers"). Ruiz de Alarcón himself seems vaguely aware of this since, in III:3, he translates it as "caparisoned in black" (see note III:3:4). As pointed out in note I:2:4, the derived causative form of (POTŌNI) is TĒ- or TLA-(POTŌNI-A), "to put a plaster made of small feathers and turpentine on someone or something" or "to feather someone or something." This implies that (POTŌNI) means "to become plastered with a plaster made of small feathers and turpentine" or "to become feathered." The preterit agentive noun *potōnqui* would thus mean "one who has become plastered with feathers" or "one who has become feathered." Garibay (1958:253) translates *tlīlpotōnqueh* as *los emplumados de negro* ("the feather-adorned ones in black"). In a note (1958:254), he says: "It is the name given to Quetzalcoatl in his worshiped form presiding over the education establishments called *calmecac.* In this place the poem speaks of several [Quetzalcoatls]. Ruiz de Alarcón gives 'wild pigs' without much basis. One must think rather of the various aspects of Quetzalcoatl." Despite Garibay's belief that this incantation is a deteriorated and misapplied temple poem, a careful consideration of it and others in Ruiz de Alarcón's work shows that this is a functional, workaday formula with a clearly delimited purpose. The incantation is indeed about "wild pigs," as Ruiz de Alarcón states. And to subvert this and emphasize "the various aspects of Quetzalcoatl" is to miss the basic thrust of what was going on here. This does not mean, however, that there may not have been a relationship between peccaries and Quetzalcoatl.

[4]We have read the present tense form *niquintēmoa,* since we assume that the final *s* on *niquintemos* in the MS is an error. Ruiz de Alarcón's translation has the present tense "[I] come to seek [them]," as the context seems to require. Garibay (1958:253) has chosen the future-tense form *niquintemoz* [i.e., *niquintēmōz*] but translates this as the present tense, "I seek."

[5]The *inixcehual* in the text has been rewritten as *in īīx zan huāl-* to bring this expression into conformity with those of II:8:22 and III:2:4. Garibay (1958:254) sees no problem; in a note, he says: "In this line we find the identity of Tezcatlipoca with greater clarity. He has his magic mirror, *nahualtezcatl,* which emits smoke like a mist or shadow (*cehualli*)." Except for the reference to *Tezcatl-Ihpoca,* this is incorrect. See note II:8:48. Although Ruiz de Alarcón believes that the metaphor refers to water, we believe that here, as in every other instance in the incantations, it refers to land, or, in this instance, more specifically to magic earth that has the power to protect the field.

[6]*Tlamacazqueh, tlīlpotōnqueh* ("the priests, the black-stinkers"). See note II:10:3.

[7]*Tlamacazqueh yāyāuhqueh* ("the priests, the dusky ones" or simply "the dusky priests").

[8]*Tlamacazqueh cōcōzauhqueh* ("the priests, the yellow-ones" or simply "the yellow priests").

[9]This is the only time in the MS that an incantation is not given in the same chapter in which it is promised. This is, of course, different from the problem discussed in note VI:26:1.

Chapter 11

[1]There is no mention of "dusky" incense in the Nahuatl text, which suggests *yāyāuhqui copalli* has been erroneously omitted.

[2]Serna (1892:432) has inserted this segment (II:11:3) into the body of the incantation between "bring" and "the white and dusky and yellow incense."

Chapter 12

[1]Ruiz de Alarcón's translation of *tlalloca teuctli* as "owners of the caves" (*dueños de las*

cuebas) is as curious as it is untenable. He seems not to have made the connection between this and the three mentions of *Tlallocan* [his spelling] below. Serna's version (1892:433) has "owners of the snakes" (*dueños de las culebras*), which is also impossible.

[2]Ruiz de Alarcón's translation "this unfortunate sown field" for *ītzīcamīl* ignores the fact that the word is in the possessive state, "his ant field," although "ant field" may be a metaphor for "unfortunate field." It fits into the rhetoric of claim-of-poverty-for-discouragement-of-exploitation that is found in other incantations or into that of reproachful accusation as part of shaming tactics.

[3]*Jicamilla* is Ruiz de Alarcón's translation for *tlacimatl*, which neither Molina nor Siméon lists. See note II:12:6. See Glossary of Nahuatlisms and Hispanisms.

[4]*Camotillo* is Ruiz de Alarcón's translation for *tlanelhuatl.* He understands *tlanelhuatl* to be a specific kind of root, while we consider it to be any kind of root, since Molina lists *rayz de arbol o yerua* ("root of tree or grass") as meaning *tlanelhuatl.* Also, Ruiz de Alarcón takes *intlacimatl in tlanelhuatl* to be a coordinate phrase, while we read *in tlanelhuatl* as an appositive (or a relative clause). See Glossary of Nahuatlisms and Hispanisms.

[5]"The gods of the earth" is here translating the word *tlamacazqueh* but seems to be pulling in the word *Tlālocān* in the next line, which Ruiz de Alarcón mistranslates as "deity."

[6]We have read *tlacimatl* as *tlālcimatl*, mentioned in Hernández (1959a:89), under the entry *tlalamatl* [i.e., *tlālāmatl*], as equivalent to *cimate chico* (which is how we have translated the term).

[7]We have read *tepetlauhca cihuatl* (which Ruiz de Alarcón translates as "woman bred in in the mountain") as *Tepētlāuhcacihuātl* ("Woman from Tepetlauhco," i.e., "from Mountain-ochre-place"). There is a faint possibility that the word is *Tepētlachcacihuātl* ("Woman from Tepetlachco," literally "Mountain-ballcourt-place," a town in Puebla; Gerhard 1972:280). The word is the metaphorical name for the magic earth used to erect a magic barrier around the field; the creation of the barrier is symbolized by the laying down of a line of red earth. Serna (1892:433) says the word refers to "the soil of the mountains."

[8]The derived verbstem TĒ-TLA-(ĀYĪ-TIA), here in the third person plural form *cāyītiah* (more commonly spelled *cāītiah*), looks like a causative ("to cause someone to do something"), but the context treats it as an applicative: "to do something to someone."

[9]We read *contlamiliah* as a double-object applicative verb derived from the causative verb TLA-(TLAMI-A), "to cause something to become finished," which in turn is derived from the intransitive verb (TLAMI), "to become finished." Therefore, the *c-* on the word means "to his (i.e., Tlalocateuctli's) disadvantage," but there is no ready way to express this in English.

[10]The *huicoa* in the MS is a problem since the expected form of the passive of TLA-(HUĪCA), "to carry something," is not *huīcohua* but *huīco.* We have read the word as the third-person plural present optative of the passive, i.e., *huīcōcān,* since the context requires a plural form.

[11]The words *quicenca huaz in illamatzin in huehuentzin* presents a problem. One possibility is to rewrite them as *quicencāhuaz in Ilamatzin in Huēhuēntzin,* with the verb having a singular subject and a singular object and with *in Ilamatzin in Huēhuēntzin* consequently being read as an alternative coordinate phrase meaning "Old-woman or Old-man." This permits two possible readings: (1) *in Ilamatzin in Huēhuēntzin* functions as the supplementary subject, in which case the verb is TLA-(CEN-CĀHUA), which Molina (under the entry *cencaua.nitla.)* defines as "to get something ready," in the sense of setting it in order, decking it out, or adorning it, and Brewer and Brewer (1962:201) (under the entry *quicencōhua* as "he ends it, he finishes it, he concludes it." The translation would, therefore, be "Old-woman or Old-man will deck it out" or "Old-woman or Old-man will finish it"; (2) *in Ilamatzin in Huēhuēntzin* functions as the supplementary object, in which case the verb is TĒ-(CEN-CĀHUA), which Siméon (under the entry *cencaua*) defines as "to dress [someone] out, to get [someone] ready, to adorn [someone]." The translation would, therefore, be "it will dress out Old-woman or Old-man."

Another possibility, however, is that the verbword should be read as *quiçcencahuaz,* i.e., *quizcencāhuaz,* for *quincencāhuaz,* a reading justified by the fact that /nse/ is pronounced /sse/ and geminate sounds were frequently written with a single letter in the MS. If this possibility is accepted (that is, with the verb being TĒ-(CEN-CĀHUA) and with the verb object being plural), *in Ilamatzin in Huēhuēntzin* can be read as an additive coordinate phrase, "Old-woman and Old-man," and can be seen functioning as a supplementary object. The translation would, therefore, be "it will dress out Old-woman and Old-man." It should be noticed that Ruiz de Alarcón chose the additive coordinate reading (in the mistranslated phrase "old and young"), but saw it as a supplementary subject, an impossibility since the basic subject of the verb is so undeniably singular.

Of these three possibilities, we have chosen the last, but have translated it rather loosely. None of the alternatives is wholly satisfactory. One of the difficulties is that the significance of Old-man and Old-woman is not clear. Old-man may refer to Cipactonal or to fire, and Old-woman may refer to Ohxomoco or to smoke. It is unlikely that the reference is merely to an old man and an old woman.

[12]The *aquic* of the MS has been read as an error for *aquin*, i.e., *Āc in*. If this is not the case, it stands for *Āc īc* ("He who therewith").

[13]I.e., "he would bring it upon himself."

Chapter 13

[1]Martin de Luna was mentioned in this, the Second Treatise, in chapter 2.

[2]The words "for you are all similar one to another" seem to be Ruiz de Alarcón's translation for *puputecatle*. If they are, he has misunderstood, apparently thinking of the verb TLA-(POH-POH-TIA), "to pair, match, or join one thing to another," derived from the noun (POH)-TLI, "companion, equal." However, *Popōtēcatl* has nothing to do with this word but comes from *Popōtlān* ("Beside-the-brooms"), which in turn is derived from (POPŌ)-TL, "broom." See note II:13:3.

[3]Although there is a town named *Popotlan* (Sahagún 1952:162), the word *Popotlan* here is a metaphorical place-name, similar to "Broomsville" in English slang. The expression "People-from-Broomsville" is appropriate for ants since their well-traveled pathways look as though they have been swept. Compare note I:10:5 and note VI:22:4.

[4]By leaving the main clause of the conditional sentence unspoken, the speaker gives his threat a more ominous quality.

[5]While it is not unusual in Nahuatl for a singular gentile name to have a plural referent (a form of synecdoche), in the present context (preceded by two plurals and followed by two plurals), the form *Popōtēcatl* seems stylistically awkward. The literal translation would be "Person-from-Popotlan," but the freer translation "People-from-Popotlan" is the one needed.

[6]See note II:12:8.

[7]This word is not Spanish (i.e., not the third person singular present indicative or the second person singular imperative of *suplir*) but, correctly spelled, is the Latin command *supple* ("supply," "understand"). It indicates that the word for "ants" is not in the Nahuatl text.

[8]As Ruiz de Alarcón's translation correctly indicates, the address shifts in this last sentence from the water [sg] to the ants [pl].

[9]The MS has *toconxica* which is meaningless. We have changed it to *toconxiccāhua* ("you go and abandon it/them"; the idea of "going" is implied in the directional prefix *-on-*).

[10]Garibay (1971:320) has translated this segment, which he takes to be a poem. The first two lines are "What, then, O Chalchiuhcueye? / What is the smoking one (*humeante*) doing?" However, *popōtēcatl* has no relation to (POPŌCA), "to emit smoke." See note II:13:2.

Chapter 14

[1]*Chiquihuitl,* "basket."

[2]The MS has *ceron,* underlined and with upright lines fore and aft, perhaps suggesting that there is an error. We have read the word as *cestón,* "large basket."

[3]See note II:8:75.

[4]Rhetorical questions seeking a negative answer, a common rhetorical ploy in the incantations.

[5]The MS has *nicyollalitiz,* which rewritten would be *nicyōllālītīz,* "I will cause him to console him," a double object causative form from TĒ-(YŌL-LĀLIA), "to console someone."

However, this does not fit the context. Also, Ruiz de Alarcón has the translation "I am starting." For these reasons, we have assumed an error and have changed the word to *nicyōlītīz* ("I will give life to it").

[6]We have changed *ipiltzin teuctli* [i.e., *īpiltzin tēuctli*, "the lord's child," which Ruiz de Alarcón has translated as "the prince's son"] to *Piltzintēuctli.*

[7]The verb *tiquimēlēhuihti* is a second person singular admonitive form, using the nonstandard construction (see note II:7:19).

[8]The MS has *le huelguen y alegren,* which should read *se huelguen y alegren,* as is found in Serna (1892:443).

[9]The "you" of "I am setting down for you" and "I am suspending for you" refers to the fish trap. The idea is "I am placing [the bait] in the fish trap, I am suspending [the bait] in the fish trap."

[10]Ruiz de Alarcón translates this as "food as delicious as fruit," but the Nahuatl *xōchitlacuāliztli* does not support this translation. Fruit is *xōchihcualli.* Siméon translates *xōchitlacuāliztli* as "gluttony, greediness; daintiness, epicurism, nicety, tidbit." In II:17:1, Ruiz de Alarcón's translation of the same expression is "food and the most choice of it," which is closer to the idea of the Nahuatl.

[11]The spelling in the MS, *iquetzon,* is correct since *ch* becomes assimilated to a following *tz* and the resulting double consonant is frequently spelled *tz* rather than *tztz.* We have merely spelled out the implications of the form to exhibit its makeup. It is possible, however, that the word should read *iquatzon* (i.e., *īcuātzon,* "her head-hair," or *īcuahtzon,* "her heddle"). Presumably this is a metaphor for the cord used in making the fish trap. Serna (1892:443) says it represents "the cords, from which hang the gourds that hold the fish trap in order that it not sink and from which he hangs the bait that he puts in it."

[12]We have inserted the adjunctor *in* to make the phrasing here match that of II:17:1.

[13]Although his translation is vague, Ruiz de Alarcón apparently saw this as *tiyāz timotēcaz, tiyāz timopilōz* ("You will go in order to stretch out, you will go in order to hang"). But the idea is that the bait will always be ("go") wherever the trap is. The verb *yāz* has a third person subject referring to the bait (the food); *timotēcaz* and *timopilōz* have second person subjects and are addressed to the fish trap.

[14]The verbs *tonhuēxcāpēhuaznecti* and *tonhuēxcātlahtlacōznecti* are second person singular admonitive forms using the nonstandard construction (see note II:7:19).

[15]See note II:8:39.

[16]Ruiz de Alarcón translates *nāyōuh* ["my turtle," from (ĀYŌ)-TL] as if it were *nayoh* ["my gourd," from (AYOH)-TLI]. See note II:14:17.

[17]Ruiz de Alarcón apparently translated *ye moca* as "now leaving you" (although it means literally "soon by means of you"). Although this translation makes good sense if one accepts the validity of the marginal note explaining *noxōchiāyōuh* as "the fish trap" (since the fisherman is not going to cross the river "by means of" the fish trap), it would be possible only if *ye moca* were changed to *ye nimitzcāhuaz* ("soon I will abandon you"). The solution we have chosen is to keep the Nahuatl text unchanged and reject the marginal note, seeing *noxōchiāyōuh* not as the fish trap but as a metaphor for a flotation gourd (see the first paragraph of I:5 for a reference to a gourd as a flotation device), so the translation mentioned in note II:14:16 would not be a mistranslation but rather a demetaphorization. The idea of leaving the fish trap behind is not stated explicitly in the incantation.

There is a possibility, albeit remote, that here the speaker is speaking in the person of the fish trap, projecting himself into its point of view. If this is the case, the "turtle" would be the floats on the fish trap, and the subsequent shout of joy would be an expression of the fish trap's eagerness to trap the fish. Such a dramatization by the speaker would be unique in the incantations of the collection and probably should be rejected.

[18]Compare this shout for joy with similar (but different) exclamatory expressions in the poems in Garibay (1964, 1965, 1968) and in the prose in Sahagún (1951). The presence of such an exclamation here does not, of course, define this incantation as poetry.

[19]In II:14:6, Ruiz de Alarcón translates *tecihuātlaquēmeh* as "the one of the womanly dress," and in II:17:4, he translates it as "of

the ash-colored dress." Since Ruiz de Alarcón's marginal note says that II:14:7 is addressed to the fish trap, Serna identifies the occurrence here (II:14:6) as the fish trap (1892:443) but the one in II:17:4, indirectly, as a caiman (1892:444). We see the word as representing a caiman in both instances and do not think that II:14:7 is addressed to the fish trap. The speaker has confidence in the fish trap but does not trust the caiman.

Chapter 15

[1]The word "myself" is in error. The *nohmatca* is not a supplementary object to the basic object *nēch-* that is in the verb. This idea would be expressed by *nonohmah nēchtītlani* ("It is I myself whom he sends"). See note II:1:5.

[2]We have changed *itlaca cihuatl,* which is an obvious error, *not* to *ītlācachīhual*—which may have been what Ruiz de Alarcón wrote or intended to write, since he translated it as "[her] perfect creature," apparently taking *tlāca-* ("person") to mean or imply perfection —but to *ītlachīhual* to match the corresponding form in II:3:1. Also see II:8:21.

[3]See point 2 of note II:8:45.

[4]The *tequipachtli* of the MS has been changed to *netequipachtli* to match the word in II:7:7. Notice that in II:8:9, the *tlazohtēteoh* ("beloved goddesses") were the ones to protect the house from *in zōmalli, in tlahuēlli* ("anger and hatred"), while here the *tlahzoltēteoh* are to protect it from *in zōmalli, in netequipachtli* ("anger and worry"). It would seem that Ruiz de Alarcón (or his informants) is confusing the two god terms (see note II:8:45).

[5]Ruiz de Alarcón translates *ontlatlatillo* in two different ways: first, as if it were *ontlatlātilo* ("Let things be hidden"), and second, as if it were *ontlatlatīlo* ("Let things be burned"). In our translation, we have selected the first as the more probable choice. Compare note II:8:21 for another refusal to choose between "burn" and "hide." Also see note II:5:1. Another problem with Ruiz de Alarcón's translation is that he renders the word as if it were passive (i.e., with a specific subject, which he considers to be the word "obstacles," in Spanish *estropiezos*). However, the verb in the MS is an impersonal.

[6]By his translation "because it is smoking," Ruiz de Alarcón shows that he does not understand *in xatepopotocatoc, in ihhuipopotocatoc.* He assumes that these words contain (PO-PŌ-CA), "to emit smoke." There is no hint of the "smoke" idea, however. See note II:15:8.

[7]"Let everything be lifted up; let everything be hidden away." The verbs are in the impersonal voice.

[8]The MS has *in xate popotocatoc in yhui popotocatoc,* for which we have read *in xāltepopotocatoc, in ihhuipopotocatoc.* These are "connective *-ti-*" compounds whose matrix is the verb (O), "to lie, to be recumbent," and whose embeds are (XĀL-TE-PO-POTO-CA) and (IHHUI-PO-POTO-CA), respectively. These stems are themselves compounds whose matrix is (PO-POTO-CA), the frequentative of the intransitive verb (POTŌ-NI), which may mean either "to stink" or "to become feather-plastered" (see note II:10:3). Since the idea of "to stink" seems inappropriate, we have chosen the meaning of "to become feather-plastered," in the sense of "to become decorated with stuck-on feathers." The adverbial embeds are (XĀL-TE)-TL, "pebble," and (IHHUI)-TL, "feather," respectively. Possibly the implication of these expressions is that the road was associated with Quetzalcoatl. The meaning of this segment is particularly obscure. The explication given by Serna (1892:441) is untenable since he thinks the verb (PO-PŌ-CA), "to smoke," is involved.

[9]The verb *nocontlaxiyōcotōnilihtiquīzti* is a first person singular admonitive form using the nonstandard construction (see note II:7:19).

[10]See note II:4:21. Here, however, the meaning of TLA-(TLALOA) does not seem to be "to run away with something" but "to run along on something," "to flee on something."

[11]For *notlallo,* we have given the optative verbform *nictlalo,* following the hint found in Ruiz de Alarcón's translation: "It will be well for me to go along it." The sentence may be even more erroneous and possibly should be emended to *Mā yehhuātl īpan ninotlalo!* "Let it be the one upon which I flee!" or "Let me flee upon it!"

[12]"Everybody" refers to the fish, not to the earthworms.

[13]See *īhuān timoquechnāhuāz,* "you will hug

him," in II:8:16.

Chapter 16

[1]The MS has *latela, saya* ("the cloth, skirt"). Serna (1892:442) has *la de la saya* ("the one of the skirt"), which is the correct reading and the one we have translated.

[2]Ruiz de Alarcón reads *yāhuitl* ("brown or black maize") for *āyahuitl* ("fog, mist; film on the eye"), the word in the MS. See note VI:6:11.

[3]Ruiz de Alarcón's rationalization, "for enchanted," seems to be a European reaction to the idea of darkness. It would seem that the Nahuatl word is primarily descriptive, with little or no symbolic meaning.

[4]Ruiz de Alarcón's translation "the ones sought throughout all the world walk through here" is wrong for two reasons: the Nahuatl has the fish seeking, not being sought; the word "walk," as a translation of *xīntinemi,* deals with the matrix (NEMI), "to walk," and ignores the embed *xīn-*, from the stem (XĪ-NI), "for a wall or hillside to fall down or collapse." See note II:16:5.

[5]The translation is an attempt to make sense out of a difficult passage. The Nahuatl word, according to the dictionaries, refers only to inanimate entities (a wall or something similar; see note II:16:4). The exclamation of surprised self-correction (*Tlacah!,* "But wait!" or "But on second thought!") suggests that the speaker has found what he is seeking. The translation therefore assumes that (XĪ-NI) is being used in a metaphorical sense of downfall after defeat. There may be a mistake in the Nahuatl. In the original source *xīntinemih* may have read *nentinemih,* "they go walking along," which would justify Ruiz de Alarcón's translation "walk" (see note II:16:4), although *nehnentinemih* would render his Spanish more exactly.

[6]His wife is mentioned in the next sentence, i.e., the first sentence of II:16:2.

[7]"The resplendent woman" is a strange translation for *tonacacihuatl.* In II:9:1, Ruiz de Alarcón left the name untranslated but indicated in a marginal note that she was Ceres as he does below in II:16:2. Torquemada (1976:87) identifies *Centeotl* as Ceres.

[8]Ruiz de Alarcón's translation makes the mother the possessor of the rug, which is not the case (i.e., the MS does *not* read *innan ixiuhpetlatzin*). "Rug of grass" *(la alfombra de yerba)* is standing in apposition to "their mother." Serna (1892:442) says, "The prepared mat is the river-bank with flowers, and a rug where the fish are to be taken out."

[9]The MS says *o reçongues.* Serna (1892: 442) has *o no resongues, y eches en rissa estas cosas* ("or do not grumble and turn these things into a joke").

[10]The verb *tihuēxcāpēuhti* is a second person singular admonitive form using the nonstandard formation (see note II:7:19).

[11]The MS omits the first two syllables of *achtotipa.*

[12]I.e., "Thou shalt rule them with a rod of iron," Psalms 2:9.

Chapter 17

[1]In the MS, this sentence is a statement, but in Serna (1892:443), it is a question. There is no counterpart in the Nahuatl text.

[2]The MS is illegible here. Paso y Troncoso (1892:172) suggests *poner, aquí* as the missing words. But the readable fragments do not seem to support this completely.

[3]The MS is illegible here. Paso y Troncoso (1892:172) supplies *on-*, and we follow this reading in our rewritten version.

[4]"Troupial" is a metaphor for "beautiful" or "precious" because of the bird's highly prized plumage. Anderson and Dibble (Sahagún 1963:20, note 20) identify the *zacuan* as a member of the troupial family, the *Gymnostinops montezuma.* This is listed in Davis (1972:186) as the *Montezuma oropendola.*

[5]The MS has *inammoçaquan cihual,* which is an error. Since Ruiz de Alarcón translates it as "a beautiful gallery" *(un hermoso mirador),* we have read it as *amozacuānithual* ("your troupial-courtyard").

[6]The MS has *itic,* which we have rewritten not as *ihtic* but as *iihtic* (where the initial *i* is the third-person possessive prefix *ī-*, which has lost its length because of the following glottal stop). The spelling *ihtic* is also reasonable since the double *i* has no implication for pronunciation, but the double-*i* spelling is justified by the fact that the initial *i* of the stem is not a merely supportive vowel but a "real" one. Compare note II:1:19.

[7]The words "because my sister, the goddess Xochiquetzal" have no counterpart in the Nahuatl. It may be that the Nahuatl was omitted by the copyist.

[8]Ruiz de Alarcón's translation, "she is waiting for you to give you some of her drink," is an inadequate rendering of *amēchhuālchialtihticah.* This word is the progressive form of the double-object causative verb *amēchhuālchialtih* ("she has caused you [pl] to await it"); thus, she is not the one who is waiting, as Ruiz de Alarcón has it; the fish are.

[9]The MS is damaged here. Paso y Troncoso (1892:173) has *ave*[IS DE TOMAR] and has added this note: "Damaged in the original. The part that has been put in small capitals . . . has been supplied to complete the ideas expressed in the speech." However, Serna (1892:444) has *aveis de comer y beber* ("you are to eat and drink"), which matches the Nahuatl.

[10]Ruiz de Alarcón translates *itlapan cauqui* as if it were a single word. It is, in fact, two: *ītlapāncāuh* [a possessed form of the preterit agentive noun *tlapānqui* ("a thing that has become broken," i.e., "a broken thing")] and *qui* ("he/she drinks it"). Ruiz de Alarcón gives no translation for the latter word.

[11]One might have expected this *qui* ("she drinks it") to come after "her *atolli*-water" with the word *quicua* ("she eats it/them") in the place where the *qui* is now. Of course, it is remotely possible that the informant did not know that the *qui* was a separate word and did not feel the incongruity of drinking "broken-off things" (i.e., crumbs or scraps). See note II:17:10.

[12]Ruiz de Alarcón's translation "flower of heat" has transposed the matrix (flower) and the embed (heat); the correct order would be "heat of flower." But the proper translation is "flower-*tonal.*" Serna (1892:444) says that "flower of heat" represents the caiman "because it is born with the heat of the sun on the sandy shores, where the females lay their eggs, and from there they come out for the water." The identification is undoubtedly correct, but the justification is wrong, since the word is a calendar-related name.

[13]See note II:14:19.

[14]"The dusky harmful ones" is an interpretive translation of *yāyāuhqui conohtli* while the accompanying *xoxōuhqui conohtli* is translated literally as "the green otters."

[15]The verb *tihuālyahti* is a second person singular admonitive form using the nonstandard construction (see note II:7:19). *Tihuālyahti* is a variant spelling of *tihuāllahti.*

[16]This verb, *neyahualōlohti,* and the following one, *netlatilohti,* are impersonal (and therefore third person singular) admonitive forms, using the nonstandard formation (see note II:7:19).

[17]We suggest that Ruiz de Alarcón or his informant omitted these words. Compare II: 1:3 and II:14:7.

[18]The MS is damaged. The problematic sentence reads *Hecho este conjuro se sigue p...on el encomendar.* We suggest that it should read *se sigue por fin con el encomendar,* which is how we have translated it.

[19]The sense of this sentence is particularly opaque. Molina lists *aamoxtli* [i.e., (AH-ĀMOX)-TLI] with the meaning "long hair that they leave on the side [of the heads] of young girls when they crop them" [where the syllable AH- is apparently the embed form of the stem (Ā)-TL in the meaning of "crown of the head" rather than in that of "water"]. This seems inappropriate in the present context, and, therefore, we have translated it as "water-book," without understanding, however, what it signifies. Also, the stem (AH-Ā-TĒC-PAN)-ø is troublesome because of the reduplicative prefix, which we take to indicate variety or distributive plurality (see Andrews 1975:147), although it is not clear why this should be appropriate in the present context. Of course, it is possible that the AH- of (AH-ĀMOX)-TLI is also a reduplicative prefix in which case the translation of *nahāmoxco* would be "my books-place." There is a faint possibility that some form of the much repeated formula *in nāmox, in notezcauh* ("my book and my mirror," i. e., "my devices of divination") was originally meant. The possibility that the word is a misspelling that should read *nahāmāxco* should be rejected since the source stem (Ā-MĀXA)-TL "bifurcation of a stream," has the locative form *āmāxac,* "place where a stream bifurcates." Also the possibility that *nahātēcpan* is an error for *nahātēnpan,* "on my various shores," is not very comforting, since this reading does not shed a satisfactory light on the problem.

THIRD TREATISE

Chapter 1

[1]The MS reads *Conjuro Primero* ("First Incantation") instead of *Capítulo Primero* ("First Chapter").

[2]The MS reads *nuestar ia menu.* Our translation is a mere conjecture.

[3]The MS is damaged. Paso y Troncoso (1892:174) suggests the word *procura* ("he seeks").

[4]Unlike other instances in which Ruiz de Alarcón names a native plant, the word *maguey* is not, as he appears to suggest, the Nahuatl term, which is *metl.* The word *maguey,* of Taino origin, was imported from the West Indies by the Spaniards.

[5]The MS is damaged. Paso y Troncoso (1892:174) supplies the word *espiritado* ("possessed one"), a reasonable choice since it translates *tlamacazqui,* and *espiritado* is also found in Serna (1892:429).

[6]Ruiz de Alarcón is convinced that *chicuetecpaciuatzin* is *chicuē-* ("eight"), plus *tecpān-* ("row"), plus *cihuātzin* ("honorable woman"), and he always translates it as "you worthy woman, the one of eight in order" or "the worthy woman, the one of eight in a row." He gives rationalizations to justify his readings. Of the seven occurrences of the word in the incantations of this chapter, one is even written *chicuetecpanciuatzin.* The lack of the *-n* in the other six instances could be explained by a phonological rule: an /n/ preceding an /s/ is assimilated to it and the resultant /ss/ is frequently written as if it were only a simple /s/ sound. Nevertheless, Ruiz de Alarcón is wrong. Molina reports that *tecpān,* when carrying a number prefix, is a numeral meaning "twenty persons." Therefore *centecpāntli* means "one-times-twenty," i.e., "twenty"; *ētecpāntli* means "three-times-twenty," i.e., "sixty." So *chicuētecpāntli* would mean "eight-times-twenty," i.e., "one hundred sixty." The word in the MS, then, does not contain *-tecpān-* but *-tecpa-* [(TE-CPA)-TL, "flint"], so that *chicuētecpacihuātl* means "Eight-flint-woman," where "Eight-flint" is a calendrical name. Caso (1959:94) apparently accepted Ruiz de Alarcón's reading since he does not refer to this incantation when he lists *Chicuēi-Tecpatl,* although it would be an excellent justification for his identification of this calendrical name: "The name of the maguey. For that reason the name 8 Tecpatl is on the upper rim of the Bilimeck jar. The representation of this date." The reference Caso gives for this is Seler 1904:922.

[7]We have inserted the dash since this material is not part of the incantation but is a comment by Ruiz de Alarcón. It is not included in Serna's version (1892:429).

[8]Since the word given in the MS, *tic teco pehuazque,* is meaningless, we have followed the hint of the next word and have read it as a "connective *-ti-*" compound whose matrix is (ĒHUA), "to begin" (or "quickly"), and whose embed is the perfective stem of TLA-(TE-COPĪ-N-A) ("to extract something from among rocks").

[9]The MS is damaged. Paso y Troncoso (1892:175) suggests the emendation *v hecha.* We suggest that this *v* should be *y* ("and") and accept the *hecha* ("made").

[10]The MS has *ticmixqualtiliz* as a double-object verb, but it should be only a single-object causative verb derived from the intransitive verb stem (ĪX-QUA-L-TI), "to become good (i.e., clean) at the face." The reflexive object *-m-* should not be used (it is not on the five subsequent verbwords).

[11]After the *metl,* or maguey, is full sized, they remove its heart and hollow out a cavity into which aguamiel is exuded. Drawn off and fermented, the aguamiel becomes pulque (Motolinia 1973:197–98).

[12]Serna's version (1892:430) continues: "And when it is already time, etc." This does not sound like part of the incantation. It seems to be commentary but does not correspond to the commentary following the incantation in the Museo MS. Serna's version has no final commentary (unless these words were part of an intended but unexecuted commentary).

Chapter 2

[1]*Nāhualtōcāitl* ("*nahualli*-name"). This is the term used to denote disguised or metaphorical names.

[2]The *coa* (a word imported from Cuba by the Spaniards) is a digging stick. The Nahuatl term is *huictli.*

[3]Molina lists the verb *caua.nitla.* [i.e., TLA-(CĀHUA)] as meaning both "to leave something" and "to carry something to another

place." Ruiz de Alarcón has chosen the first meaning, and we the second.

[4]The form in the MS, *oyecoque,* is a colloquial version in which the initial *e* on the verb stem takes a "bridging" *y* after the preceding *ō-* prefix.

[5]Ruiz de Alarcón takes *tonaca-* to mean "the goddess of bread" apparently because he believes this is a shortened form of *tōnacācihuātl.*

[6]López Austin (1967:23) says that this represents "the granary, as the mother of the maize who guards it in her bosom."

[7]The form *-chiquiuhtli* in the MS has been changed to *-chiquihuitl.* See note II:8:20.

[8]See note III:2:4.

[9]This is another instance of Ruiz de Alarcón giving an explanation that is foreign to the real meaning. We do not know whether the explanation is his own or of his informant or some other native.

[10]The Spanish word *carilabrado* consists of a combining form *cari-* (from *cara,* "face") and the past participle of the verb *labrar* ("to work a material to give it form" and "to plow, to till, to cultivate"). Serna's version (1892: 430) has *cari lavado* ("face-washed") but in a note explaining the metaphor, the word *carilabrado* occurs despite the fact that the explanation ("because the water cleans it") deals with *carilavado.* The Nahuatl word, *yxahual,* was not understood by either Ruiz de Alarcón or Serna. See note III:2:12.

[11]The MS has "7," which Paso y Troncoso (1892:177) has misread as *y* ("and"). The Nahuatl word being translated is *Chicōme-Cōātl* ("Seven Snake"). Serna (1892:430) has "siete" ("seven").

[12]We have changed *yxahual* to [*in*] *īīx zan huāl-* and *poztocatimani,* which is meaningless, to *-popōcatimani* to bring the sequence into conformity with II:8:22 and II:10:1. Not recognizing that the construction belongs to a formula, Garibay (1958:255) accepts it as it stands and translates *tezcatl ixahual poztocatimani* as "the one who has a mirror as facial decoration." This apparently leaves the erroneous *poztocatimani* untranslated (unless it is his "has"). See note II:8:48.

Chapter 3

[1]*Tlamacazqui, Chicōme-Cuāuhtzin* ("the priest, Seven Eagle (H)").

[2]The word *iquaquauh* [i.e., *īcuācuauh*] means "its horn(s)" as Ruiz de Alarcón suggests. But his explanation is not valid. He has read *cuauhtzin* as if it were from *cuahuitl,* not realizing that *Chicōme-Cuāuhtzin* [i.e., Seven Eagle (H)] is a calendrical name. Ruiz de Alarcón's confusion may be due to the dialectal use of *cuauhtli* for *cuahuitl* mentioned in note II:8:20.

[3]*Tlamacazqui, Tlazohpilli, Tlīlpotōnqui,* ("the priest, Beloved-Prince, One-who-has-become-feather-plastered-with-black"). *Tlīlpotōnqui* was another name for *Topiltzin Quetzalcōātl* (see Sahagún 1952:62). Also see note II:10:3.

[4]The Spanish is *encubertado de* ("caparisoned in") and is somewhat strange since it is a term ordinarily associated with horses.

Chapter 4

[1]The Spanish is *capataz* ("foreman").

[2]The translation makes *-cihuātl* ("woman") equivalent to "seed," so that Ruiz de Alarcón has demetaphorized the name.

[3]It is interesting to see how early the erroneous translation of *tonaca-* as "*our* subsistence" (and "*our* sustenance") occurred. It is an error that translators still make. The *to-* is *not* the first person plural possessive prefix ("our") and the *naca-* is *not* from (NACA)-TL, "meat." The word is the combining form of (TŌNA-ø-CĀ-YŌ)-TL, "agricultural produce, sustenance," and usually applies to sustenance *par excellence,* "maize." It is derived from (TŌNA), "to be sunny."

[4]Serna's version (1892:431) is different. After "by falling into fault," his text has "do not make this a matter for laughter and do not sin by laughing at it."

[5]The MS has *que es* ("which is"), but Serna's version (1892:431) has *que è de* ("because I am to"). This corresponds to the Nahuatl and is what we have translated.

[6]The Spanish *ver con gusto* ("to see with pleasure") is not a good equivalent for the Nahuatl *nicmahuiçoz* [i.e., *nicmahuizōz*] ("I will honor her"). Serna's version (1892:431) has *venir con gusto* ("to come with pleasure"), which is probably truer to what was originally intended.

Chapter 5

[1]See 3 Kings 17:10–16.

[2]See note III:4:3.

[3]Ruiz de Alarcón reduces the metaphor to literal terms.

[4]Although the common *cuezcomatl* granaries were vasiform (see note I:2:18), there were also rectangular granaries, both imperial (before the Spanish conquest) and family (Hernández Xolocotzin 1949:160–70).

[5]Ruiz de Alarcón has compounded the error of "our" (discussed in note III:4:3) by changing it to the singular "my." Serna's version (1892:432) has "our."

Chapter 6

[1]*Tamalayohtli* ("tamale-squash").

[2]Ruiz de Alarcón's wording "I speak to you. . . . And I speak to you" implies two entities are being spoken to, but the Spanish word he uses for "your" is *tu,* second person singular, not *vuestro,* second person plural. This matches the singular possessive in the Nahuatl.

[3]It is not clear whether, in this instance, "One Flint" is a calendrical name or a metaphor. Ruiz de Alarcón translates it as the latter. López Austin (1967:21) says "Although this apparently refers to the calendrical name 'One Flint,' it is certain that it should be interpreted simply as 'one piece of flint.'" On the two previous occasions when "One Flint" occurred (II:1:3 and II:2:2) it seemed to represent a knife. In this instance, if that equation is still valid, the knife is standing as a metaphor for the squash seed.

[4]We have changed the *m* to *n;* see note I:4:22 and note II:4:4.

[5]The problem of the erroneous translation "our sustenance" (see note III:4:3) is here compounded by the failure to associate it correctly with the matrix *mecatl* ("rope" or "cord"). See note III:6:8.

[6]Again Serna's version (1892:431) is different. After "by falling into fault," his text has "do not begin to laugh and take little notice and thereby to fail." He comments on this by saying, "They usually translate this last part differently because the word is *Acmotihuexcatlatlacoz* [*sic*], and they say do not grumble and growl like those who work unwillingly (*no resongues y gruñas como los que obran de mala gana.*" This is closer to the MS, *no empieçes a reçongar y reçongando dexes de cumplir con tu obligaçion,* but still differs.

[7]The word in the MS, *moximecaniznazque,* is meaningless. It should represent the "connective *-ti-*" compound *mocximecanihtāzqueh,* which we have rewritten in the full form *mocximecanihtiyāzqueh.* The embed is the verb MO-(ICXI-MECA-NI-A), "to get one's feet entangled." The use of *-ta-* as a variant for *-tia-* [i.e., *-tiya-*] is attested in Molina; see the entry *quataz.nic.* [i.e., *niccuahtāz*], which is a variant of the entry *quatiaz.nic.* [i.e., *niccuahtiyāz*]; both forms have the meaning "I shall go along eating something."

[8]The MS has *tonaca me catlal* which possibly could be *tonacamecatlāl,* "our meat-rope-land," but this does not make sense in the context. Paso y Troncoso (1892:178) reads *tonacamecatl* [i.e., *tōnacāmecatl*] "sustenance rope," which is the reading we have chosen.

[9]The word in the MS, *moxitepotlaminazque,* is meaningless. It should represent the "connective *-ti-*" compound *mocxitepōtlamihtāzqueh,* which we have rewritten in the full form *mocxitepōtlamihtiyāzqueh.* See note III:6:7. The embed is the verb MO-(ICXI-TEPŌ-TLAMIA), "to stumble."

[10]The word *nāhualtzontecommēmeh* is a preterit agentive noun whose embed is (NĀHUA-L-TZON-TECOMA)-TL, "*nahualli*-head" (which is functioning in the compound as an incorporated object), and whose matrix is the preterit of the verbstem TLA-(MĒME), "to carry something." The word means literally "one who has carried a *nahualli*-head." A variant spelling would be *nāhualtzontecommāmah.*

[11]*Huēxcātlahtlacōz,* "He will spoil things by grumbling."

Chapter 7

[1]Serna (1892:432) says "He calls the land embracing flower and mouth biter because, before the conversions and transformations of things, one into another, they claim that it was called flower; the embracing and biting which he mentions is a metaphor, because, into itself as into a mouth, it receives the seed, whose sprouting forth is called 'exhaling'." This mention of transformations

refers to those reported in the myth in I:10, but Serna adds details not found there. However, it would seem that the added details are based, at least in part, on a misreading of the verb *reçollar* [i.e., *resollar*], "to breathe, to exhale," in its use in the next sentence. The one doing the breathing (or exhaling) is the farmer (compare English, "to breathe easily"), not the earth.

[2]We have loosely translated the Spanish, *Porque se aiuda una con otra.*

[3]Here and three sentences later the MS has *notlatla,* a reduplicative stem for a singular-number word. This may indicate a dialectal variant *(TLĀ-TLAH)-TLI, "uncle," instead of (TLAH)-TLI, corresponding to the dialectal (TĀ-TAH)-TLI, "daddy," for (TAH)-TLI, "father" (see *motötajtzi,* "your father," under the entry *itajtzi* in Brewer and Brewer (1962:134)). Or it may be a mistake. We have, of course, rewritten it in the expected form, *notlah.* See note I:4:18 concerning the distributive/varietal plural *motlahtlahhuān.* It seems unlikely that the singular form intended here would have a glottal stop rather than length on the reduplicated syllable.

[4]The *noconigria* of the MS is an obvious error that we have rewritten as *noconilpia,* "I am tying it there" or "I am going in order to tie it."

[5]The MS has *temaco chihuia* [i.e., *tēmācochihuia*], which is not listed in either Molina or Siméon. Both, however, list the reciprocal verb MO-(MĀ-COCH-OA), "for two people to embrace, with one putting his head next to the neck of the other" (a word on this stem is found in VI:22:3). From this, one can, consequently, hypothesize the corresponding intransitive verb (MĀ-COCH-IHUI), "to become embraced," and from this we can derive the causative verb TĒ-(MĀ-COCH-IHUI-A), "to cause someone to become embraced," i.e., "to embrace someone." This verb occurs again in VI:32:10, but in the optative form.

[6]The MS has *nihiouiz* which would be respelled as *nihīyōhuīz.* The form is improper, however, since the stem is transitive, TLA-(IH-Ī-YŌ-HUIA), "to suffer difficulties," and the word in the MS shows no object prefix. We have changed the stem to (IH-Ī-YŌ-CUI), "to catch one's breath, by resting."

FOURTH TREATISE

Chapter 1

[1]The only indication that a new treatise has begun is the heading for Chapter I.

[2]I.e., do not have free will, are not human.

[3]The MS says *en vltimo lugar* ("in last place"). This is inappropriate since there are two more treatises after this one. Perhaps Ruiz de Alarcón envisioned a different organization of his work when he was writing this part.

[4]I.e., "bad things are not to be done in order that good might come," a common saying derived from Romans 3:8.

[5]This appears to be another instance of Ruiz de Alarcón voicing an awareness of the danger of publishing these incantations.

[6]"The heart inflamed (with anger)" is translating *coçauhqui yollotli* [i.e., *cōzauhqui yōllohtli*] ("yellow heart"). Ruiz de Alarcón is giving a demetaphorized translation.

Chapter 2

[1]The MS reads *laparen,* for which we read *se aparecen,* as one finds in Serna's version (1892:407).

[2]It is unlikely that Ruiz de Alarcón's interpretation "one snake" (in the sense of "a snake") is correct, since this is evidently a calendrical name. But it is also questionable that the calendrical name stands for *Xochiquetzal,* as Caso (1959:83–84) suggests as a possibility, since it would seem that here *Xochiquetzal* is a metaphor for the beloved and therefore the subject of the sentence. It is also possible that "already I accompany . . . *Xochiquetzal*" is word magic of a different sort, that of obtaining *Xochiquetzal* as an ally. If this is the case, there is a break in the continuity since the "She" of the next sentence refers not to *Xochiquetzal* but to the speaker's beloved. We believe that "One Snake" is a metaphorical name for feminine apparel.

[3]The three verbs appearing in the MS as *apantiuitz, cuitlalpitiuitz,* and *tzonilpitihuitz* are impossible forms. Being transitive verbs, they must have an object prefix—in the present instance, a reflexive one, which is the way they appear in our rewritten version.

[4]Other instances of this formula are found

in II:8:8 and II:8:12. In these examples, the formula begins *in yalhua ye huiptla.*

[5]Although *porel florido y trasparente sexo feminil* [i.e., "for the sake of the elegant and transparent feminine sex"] has no counterpart in the Nahuatl, it may be translating the omitted portion referred to by "etc."

[6]This is an instance of hysteron proteron, a rhetorical figure found occasionally in the *Florentine Codex* (Sahagún 1951–75). The logical sequence would be "I have dawned and I have sunshined."

[7]Presumably the East.

[8]We have inserted the word *niquittaz* to complete the identical wording of the first seven sentences of IV:2:2 and the first seven sentences of IV:2:3.

[9]The question mark in the MS is an error.

[10]Molina lists *ciuayotl* [i.e., *cihuāyōtl*] with the meaning "matrix where the woman conceives." The word *Cihuāyoh,* however, means "a person who makes use of women." As the context makes clear, the MS is using the former word with the meaning of the latter, possibly under the pressure of the sound *-ōtl* at the end of *Yāōtl.* The MS could be corrected to *Cihuāyoh,* but we have decided to let it stand as written. There is a slight possibility that the word in the MS is an error for *cihuayaotl* [i.e., *CihuāYāōtl*], but we have rejected this since (CIHUĀ)-TL, "woman," as an embed of compound nouns has such a strong gender-defining function that, even in this context, the reader would have to struggle against "Female-*Yaotl*" rather than going easily to "*Yaotl*-of-women," i.e., "Enemy-of-women." Moreover, the internal development argues against the notion of antagonism to women and argues for that of devotion to women. See Appendix F.

Chapter 3

[1]The MS has *occurrentes,* for which we read *concurrentes.*

[2]Serna (1892:408) adds *de pies, y manos* ("with feet and hands").

[3]The Spanish is *para heuitar* ("in order to avoid").

[4]This should read *tlàçolmiquiztli* [i.e., *tlahzolmiquiztli*] "filth-death," that is, "death due to filth (i.e., illicit sexual conduct)."

[5]This should read *tlaçolmimiquiliztli* [i.e., *tlahzolmihmiquiliztli*], "variety-of-filth-death" or "filth-annihilation" [i.e., annihilation due to illicit sexual conduct]. The reduplicative prefix *-mih-* may indicate variety or distributive plurality of the adverbial embed or may indicate intensity of the action of the matrix.

[6]*Netēpalhuīliztli* ("the act of doing something by someone's grace," i.e., "the act of being dependent on someone").

[7]The MS has *parese* for *parte* ("part").

[8]The MS has *assi* ("thus") for *a su* ("at their").

[9]The MS has *del* § *&c. presedente.*

[10]This should read *tlaçolmiquiztli* (i.e., *tlahzolmiquiztli).* See note IV:3:4.

[11]See note IV:3:6.

[12]*Tētlahzolāltilōni* ["the instrument (or means) of washing someone with regard to filth" (i.e., sexual misconduct)].

[13]The MS has *sepreuiene elfuego* for *se previene de fuego.*

[14]This is a copyist error.

[15]These four goddesses (*Cuātōn, Caxxōch, Tlāhui,* and *Xāpel*) are not mentioned in any source not derived from Ruiz de Alarcón. However, they appear to be locally variant names of the four goddesses mentioned in Sahagún (1970:23) in the discussion of the *Tlahzolteoh.* See Appendix B.

[16]More correctly, Ruiz de Alarcón should have written *diosas* ("goddesses").

[17]Ruiz de Alarcón mistranslates the god *Tlaloc* as *terrestridad.*

[18]"Filth" is a metaphor for illicit sexual conduct.

[19]López Austin (1970:16, note 17) proposes emending *techuat* to *teehua.* Our reading, *tēhuahti,* is based on *īca tēhua* in IV:3:3, but the form *tehēhuahti* can be justified by *īca tehēhua* in VI:3:3. The word is a second person singular admonitive form, using the nonstandard formation (see note II:7:19).

[20]The verb *timīlacatzohti* is a second person singular admonitive form, using the nonstandard formation (see note II:7:19).

[21]The Spanish view of medicine of the time attributed much illness to unhealthy air. Also see note I:9:2.

[22]See note II:8:75.

[23]We have translated *nicān* here and in the second sentence following, as a temporal ad-

verb, "now," "at this time," because of the directional prefix *-o* (a variant of *on-*) ("thither") on the verb. Ruiz de Alarcón has ignored the prefix and translated *nicān* as a locative adverb, "here." This does not seem appropriate. Another translation that could be valid is "from here."

[24] López Austin (1970:16, note 18) says "It should say *toconitquican*." The word in the MS is, however, a correct form. See Andrews 1975:49, note.

FIFTH TREATISE

[Preamble]

[1] In the MS, the word for "fifth" is missing.

[2] The specific citations for the preceding references are Leviticus 16:8–10; Numbers 26:55, 33:54, 34:13, 36:2; Deuteronomy 1:38; 1 Kings 10:19–22; Jonas 1:7–9.

[3] This is an error. It should be Acts 1:26.

[4] This is not true. For example, see 1 Kings 28.

[5] This should be *De Divin.* for *De Divinatione* ("On Divination").

[6] The translation of the Latin is ". . . about the casting of lots? It is much like playing at mora, dice, or knuckle-bones, in which recklessness and luck prevail rather than reflection and judgement. The whole scheme of divination by lots was fraudulently contrived from mercenary motives, or as a means of encouraging superstition and error" (Falconer 1922:466–67).

[7] This reference is to *Summa Theologica* 95.8.

[8] This is a garbled version of Jerome's commentary (Migne 1844–64: P.L. 25, 1126): *Nec statim debemus sub hoc exemplo sortibus credere, vel illud de Actibus Apostolorum huic testimonio copulare, ubi sorte in Apostolatum Mathias eligitur,* which, translated, says "We should not, following this example [of Jonah], believe in lots, or add to the testimony of this case from the Acts of the Apostles, where Matthias was chosen with a lot."

[9] I.e., "Not by the example of Matthias, or by the fact that Jonah the prophet was apprehended by lot, should there be an indiscriminate belief in lots, for the concessions made to individuals cannot be made a common law for all." (Migne 1844–64: P.L. 92, 945).

[10] I.e., "Sorcerers are those who, in the name of a feigned religion, carry out the science of divination through the use of lots, which they call the practice of saints or apostles" (Lindsay 1911:P.L. 8.9.28). Note that this passage is from book 8, not book 4.

[11] I.e., "Sorcery is a certain kind of cultivation of idols, predicting future events from consultation with demons" (reference uncertain).

[12] I.e., "They pretend to be filled with divinity, and with a certain fraudulent craftiness they forecast future things for men [or other people]" (Lindsay 1911:P.L. 8.9.14). Note that this passage is from Isidore, not Augustine.

[13] I.e., "All arts of this sort, therefore, are either nullities, or are part of the guilty superstition, springing out of a baleful fellowship between men and devils, and are to be utterly repudiated and avoided by the Christian as the covenants of a false and treacherous friendship." *On Christian Doctrine* (Shaw 1956, 2: 547).

[14] I.e., "Also against worshippers of idols, and soothsayers, and diviners, we very earnestly exhort your Fraternity to be on the watch with pastoral vigilance," Epistle 65, to Januarius, Bishop of Caralis (Barmby 1956, 13:17-18).

Chapter 1

[1] I.e., "Therefore all inquiry, and all healing, which is pursued through godless magic arts from demons in the cultivation of idols, are more to be called death than life." Although attributed to Augustine, this passage is actually from Rabanus Maurus, *De magicis artibus* (Migne 1844–64: P.L. 110, 1097).

[2] I.e., *tīcitl.* See Appendix C.

[3] The MS reads *si sienta en limpio.*

[4] López Austin (1970:3) translates this as "the one made to give off a cracking sound (Spanish, *restallado*) against the rocks in nine places." He takes the embed *chiucnāuh-* ("nine") in this word and the other names for tobacco, such as *Chiucnāuhtlatetzohtzonalli* and *Chiucnāuhtlamātelōlli,* to be an adverb of place. We, on the other hand, see it as an adverb of temporal repetition, as does Ruiz

de Alarcón. We base our interpretation on the belief that it is a truncated form of *chiucnāuhpa* ("nine times"), since the fuller form occurs in *Chiucnāuhpatlatetzohtzonalli* (VI:3:7), *Chiucnāuhpatlatetzohtzon* (VI:4:3), and *Chiucnāuhpatlamātelōlli* (VI:3:7).

[5]The MS has *titzotzotlacatoc*, which presents a problem. The occurrence of the second person singular prefix *ti-* on only this one word in the vocative sequence is anomalous. All the names here function as vocatives and all would be expected to be either in the third person or in the second person. A solution to the problem could be obtained by stopping the vocative sequence with *Ahquetztimani* and reading *Titzotzotlacatoc, Tezcatl in zan huālpopōcatimani* as a separate sentence, with *Titzotzotlacatoc* now functioning as a verb rather than as a preterit agentive noun: "You lie glittering, Mirror that is just smoking hither." The problem with this is that it breaks up the unity that should exist between the summons *(Tlā xihuālhuiān)* and the subsequent future-tense commands (the last two sentences of the segment). We, therefore, have chosen to solve the problem differently, that is, by removing the second-person prefix.

[6]The verb *huēxcāpēhuaz* is intransitive (see II:16:3). The *tla-* of the MS is in error.

[7]In this instance, since only one hand is spoken of, Ruiz de Alarcón's translation "the five solar beings" is correct. See note II:8:75. Also see note V:1:8.

[8]López Austin (1970:16, note 22) says: "It should say *macuiltonaleque*" [i.e., making the word plural]. However, the singular number of *mācuīltōnaleh* cannot be thought to be a slip of the pen because it is corroborated by the singular object prefix *-c-* on the verb. This agreement between the supplementary direct object and the basic direct object with which it stands in cross reference strongly suggests that the singular number is intended. The speaker seems to be pointing fastidiously to the fact that when one clasps one's hands and kisses the crossed thumbs, only one hand is actually kissed.

[9]The Nahuatl simply says "them" *(-quin-)*. Our translation, "him and the other one," attempts to make clear that in this sentence both hands are now being spoken of, in contrast to the single hand mentioned in the preceding sentence.

[10]As pointed out in note II:8:75, the hands, not the fingers, are being addressed.

[11]The meaning is that each owner has one face.

[12]"Jade, jewel, and quetzal-feather" is a metaphor for one's child and is here applied, as Ruiz de Alarcón suggests (except that his explanation seems to refer only to "jade"), to the sick person, since the curer pretends to be in a parent-child relation with the patient.

[13]López Austin (1970:16, note 24) says, "It should say *tzoneptzitzinhuan.*" However, the *-huān* suffix signals plurality on a possessive state form and the form intended here is in the absolutive state, which properly carries the plural suffix *-meh.* Note also that in Ruiz de Alarcón's text this word has an *-i-* after the *-p-*, as if the stem were (EPI)-TL instead of (EP)-TLI, "pearl."

[14]The MS has *-totocon ecahuican*, which is a mistake. It should read *tocon ecahuican* (i.e., *toconehcahuīcān*). There is a further problem. Ruiz de Alarcón translates this as "let us go up [it]." The same verb is used with the same translation in V:2:3. But the verb TLA-(EHCA-HUIA) means "to cause something to arrive," derived from the intransitive verb (EHCO), "to arrive." If the idea of climbing is valid, as it seems to be, the verb should be TLA-(TLEHCA-HUIA), derived from the intransitive verb (TLEHCO), "to ascend." Molina lists this verb with only a causative meaning ("to lift something"), as do Brewer and Brewer (1962:211): *quitlejcabia* ("he lifts it up, he raises it up"). However, it is used in an applicative meaning in Sahagún (1963:269): *njctlecavia in teucalli* (i.e., *nictlehcahuia in teōcalli*), "I climb up the temple" (*literally,* "I climb in relation to the temple"). We have changed the MS accordingly in our rewritten version. The problem with *toconehcahuīcān* may be related to the fact that the word for ladder is (EHCA-HUĀZ)-TLI, literally, "breeze-instrument"—ladder-like racks were used for drying things in the wind—(see the following word *tochālchiuhehcahuāz*), so that the verb intended here may have been TLA-(EHCA-HUĀZ-HUIA), "to use a ladder on something."

[15]The MS has *nimimatca tiçitl* [i.e., *nimihmatcātīcitl*], but the word is not a "name form," and therefore the reflexive prefix standardly changes for person of subject: *ninihmatcātīcitl.*

[16]The "upwards" of the earlier remark (V:

1:4), "he measures the forearm upwards," is now clarified as meaning from the bend of the arm to the fingers. See also the statement in the next-to-the-last paragraph to the Preamble to the Fifth Treatise that it was "by measuring the left forearm from the elbow to the tips of the fingers." Compare this with Ponce (Appendix A): "Others measure with a straw from the inside of the arm to the middle finger."

[17] *Oc huetztoc* (literally, "Still he lies having fallen," i.e., "He will be abed for a while").

[18] *Nohmatca nehhuātl. NiMictlānTēuctli. Nitlamacazqui.* "It is I in person. I am Lord-in-Mictlan. I am the priest."

[19] We have broken up the run-on paragraph in the MS for purposes of clarity.

[20] *Nināhualtēuctli.* "I am the *nahualli*-lord."

[21] *Nohmatca nehhuātl. NiXōlōtl.* "It is I in person. I am Xolotl." Concerning Xolotl, see Appendix B.

[22] *Tochālchiuhehcahuāz* ("Our jade-ladder").

[23] *ToMictlānehcahuāz* ("Our ladder-to-Mictlan").

[24] The MS reads *que sepa* ("that he know [it]"). Serna (1892:401) reads *que se sepa* ("that it be known").

[25] Commenting on V:1:8, Ruiz de Alarcón says that *ca* is an "adversative particle." He has translated it here as *o no, antes* ("or not, rather"). This usage is not attested by Molina or Siméon. Molina lists it with the meaning "because. A conjunction to give a reason for something." While there may be occasions where one may translate the word in this way, it is not a conjunction and "because" is not its intrinsic meaning. Siméon defines it as "adv[erb] or conj[unction]. Already, where, indeed, because, why, since." The "where" is a mistake: it applies to *cān*, not *ca* (a confusion made possible by the fact that a final /n/ was frequently voiceless and thus not spelled and vowel length was normally not indicated). Of all the other meanings given by Siméon, only "indeed" is strictly valid. *Ca* is an emphatic particle that marks a sentence matrix. This usage is confirmed repeatedly in the incantations. There are, however, four instances (V:1:6, V:1:8, V:3:2, V:3:3) where this standard usage seems not to apply. These instances may be explained by Pérez's (1713:189) remark that "In Mexico [City] in order to say *no*, they say *Ahmó* [i.e., *ahmō*], and outside of Mexico [City] they say *Câh* [i.e., *cah*], putting a glottal stop after the *A*." Apparently Ruiz de Alarcón has jumped from the negative idea to an adversative one. We have followed his lead but have rewritten the word as *cah.*

[26] The sentence is incomplete. Our suggested reading is based on a similar remark in the next-to-the-last paragraph of the Preamble to the Fifth Treatise.

[27] *Dios ōnēchmomaquilih.* "God gave (H) it to me."

[28] The Spanish is *Pero como tienen tan assentado sucredito, y el enfermo, o muere, o, sana* ("but since they have their reputation so established and the sick person either dies or gets well").

[29] I.e., *ololiuhqui.* See Appendix D.

[30] We have followed Paso y Troncoso (1892:189) in placing the following series of short paired statements in a paragraph format rather than in parallel columns as they are in the MS.

[31] The words *Tla tiquitilican* have been included here through error. They do not precede the rest of the quoted material (they occur in a later incantation; see V:1:7, which is the next sentence quoted in the text; see note V:1:32) and are not included in the translation. On the other hand, the words that translate "Immediately, right away" (i.e., *Zan niman axcan* in V:1:4) have been omitted. The corrected reading is *Zan niman āxcān toconittazqueh āc yeh quimictia,* "It will be immediately now that we will see who is the one who is killing him."

[32] *Tlā tiquittilīcān tēteoh īmpiltzin, ahzo quināmiquiz, ahzo quihuelmatiz in pahtzintli, iztāc ātl īnān, cihuātzintli,* etc. "Let us see for the child of the gods whether the medicine (H), white 'its-mother is water,' the lady (H), will match [i.e., be appropriate to] the son (H) of the gods, or whether he will get on well with it."

[33] "Daughter of the water-herb" *(Hija del aguayerba)* is a mistranslation. See note V:1:32.

[34] The MS has *tlacopati,* which should read *tlacopatli* [i.e., *tlacōpahtli*] ("stick-medicine") and is here symbolized by *cōzauhqui tlamacazqui* ("yellow priest").

[35] *Ahzo quihuelmatiz in cōzauhqui tlamacazqui ahnōzo xoxōuhqui tlamacazqui.* "Perhaps he will get on well with the yellow priest

[i.e., *tlacōpahtli*] or the green priest [i.e., the *piciete*]."

[36]The MS has *yoformo* for *ya formó.*

[37]Ruiz de Alarcón's translation does not recognize that *tiquittilīcān* is a double-object verb.

[38]The MS reads "sepamos donde esta v donde sefue? *La muger ola hija,*" with the words *La muger ola hija* standing to the right of the question mark, underlined, and over in the right-hand column (the Nahuatl column) and separated from *tlatiquiti* (which is the only part of the word permitted by the available space) by a short upright mark. We have followed Paso y Troncoso (1892:189) in dealing with the problem (we have, however, replaced the question mark with a period).

[39]The MS has °*ca.* Paso y Troncoso (1892: 189) emended this to *onca.* But this emendation is erroneous as can be seen by the identical wording of the phrase *ca ye oc onca* in V:3:2. Moreover, as can be seen by Ruiz de Alarcón's translation, *sino que* (i.e., "but rather"), he was reading the word *ca* [i.e., *cah*]. See note V:1:25.

[40]See note V:1:25.

[41]See note III:2:1.

[42]I.e., *Yauhtepec.* See Appendix E.

[43]The Spanish is *alamujer consultante.* The consulting is understood to be with the Devil.

[44]The MS has *sortilegios* ("sorceries") for *sortílegos* ("sorcerers") as in other instances in this treatise.

[45]I.e., *ololiuhqui.* See Appendix D.

[46]The Spanish is troubled: *porque mediante elpacto que en latal beuida el* ololiuqui *interuiene . . . les Responde el demonio alas Dudas.* We have read *porque mediante el pacto que con la tal bebida del* ololiuhqui *interviene. . . .*

[47]The words "in the mirror of my spell" are translating *inamoxco* [i.e., *in nāmoxco*] ("in my book"). Serna (1892:401) has "in the mirror and paper of my spell." It is possible that the original text had *in notezcac in nāmoxco,* "in my mirror and in my book.

[48]These references appear to be to Mary, the mother of Jesus, the Wise Man Caspar, and John the Baptist. Conventionally understood to be (in Latin) Gaspar, Balthaser, and Melchior (Jacobus de Voragine 1941, 1:85), Caspar (Gaspar) is not named in the Bible, nor is he officially recognized as a saint by the Roman Catholic church. However, in the folk tradition, he was considered a saint and was associated with the curing of epilepsy (Réau 1955–59, 2:2:239). Of the many Saint Johns, John the Baptist seems most closely related to the other figures chronologically, and he is also associated with epilepsy, as well as with headaches (Réau 1955–59, 2:1:437).

[49]This is put differently in Serna (1892: 402): "or perhaps you are another Saint (and they mention here the Saint of the village they are from) or Saint John, &."

[50]Notice the shift from the second person in the first question to the third person in the others. One would have expected *tiTo-TlazohNāntzin, tiSanGaspartzin,* and *tiSan-Juantzin,* as suggested by Ruiz de Alarcón's translation.

[51]The MS has *sortilegio* ("sorcery") for *sortílego* ("sorcerer").

[52]The words "the owners of the earth" are a mistranslation of *āhuahqueh* ("the owners of water," i.e., the clouds).

[53]The MS has *no nonan,* which would be rewritten as *nō nonān,* "also my mother," but since what would be *nō* occurs at the end of a line, and also since in no other instance in the MS does the formula *notah, nonān,* "my father, my mother," contains *nō,* we have considered it a copyist's error and have omitted it, as does Paso y Troncoso (1892:190).

Chapter 2

[1]The discrepancy of plural number (in "four reeds") and the singular number (in "throws") is present in the Spanish: *las cuarto cañas que hecha* [for *echa*] *llamas.*

[2]It should read "ten solar beings." See note II:8:75.

[3]The two words in the MS, *no nahuatl teteo huan, noztac teteohuan,* present problems. In both, the embed has a singular number suffix: the -TL of the absolutive nounword and the -C of the preterit verbword. But *-nahuatl-* is simply a scribal error for *-nahual-*. The problem of *-ztac-* is different. According to a general rule, before serving as the nominal embed of a compound formation, a preterit verbform must nominalize its preterit tense theme by embedding it in the matrix (-CĀ)-TL, a procedure that allows the embedded verbform to

be disencumbered of the notions of person and number. For example, the third person singular preterit form ø(MIC)ø-QUI has the preterit theme -(MIC)ø-, which becomes (MIC-ø-CĀ)- to form *nomiccāmā* [i.e., ø-NO(MIC-ø-CĀ-MĀ)ø], "my dead-man hands" (II:1:4). All four verb classes follow this rule. On occasion, however, Class A verbs (whose singular number suffix is -C is a post-vocalic variant of -QUI) may forgo the nominalization by means of (-CĀ)-TL and merely keep the singular number suffix. For example, Molina lists *Iztac teocuitlauia.nitla* [i.e., TLA-(IZTĀ-ø-C-TEŌ-CUITLA-HUIA)], "to silver something"; in Sahagún (quoted in Sullivan in 1972:190) we find *yztaccac* [i.e., ø-Ī(ZTĀ-C-CAC)ø], "his white sandals," and *ychayauaccuzqui* [i.e., ø-Ī(CHAYĀ-HUA-ø-C-CŌZ-QUI)ø], "his scatter necklace"; and in Durán (1971: 233) *Iztactlamacazcauh* [i.e., ø-Ī(ZTĀ-ø-C-TLA-MACA-Z-CĀ)UH], "her white priest." We have therefore left *-ztāc-* as it is in the MS without changing it to *-ztācā-*, despite the fact that this means that a singular embed is cooperating with a plural matrix. This brings us to the next problem with the two words in the MS: both have a matrix stem pluralized by reduplication, which, since these are possessed forms, should represent distributive or varietal plurality: *-teh-teō-*. This seems inappropriate to the context and we have therefore rewritten the words as *nonāhualteōhuān, noztācteōhuān.*

[4]The word in the MS, *inchayanacauh*, is an impossible form since it presupposes the absolutive form **chayanac*, a nonexistent word. We have changed the text to read *īnchayāhuacāuh*, which presupposes the absolutive form *chayāhuac* "a thing that has become scattered." Molina lists *quauhchayahuac* [i.e., *cuauhchayāhuac*] ("a wooden balustrade"), a word which occurs along with its illustration in the *Códice Sierra* (León 1933:26).

[5]The MS has *Luego aora heilz lo hedever.* We have not tried to decipher *heilz* since it has no counterpart in the Nahuatl (nor do any of the other words quoted here except *Luego aora*). Serna (1892:403) has *Luego ahora lo è de ver* ("Immediately now I am to see it").

[6]The MS has *todo lo ando* ("I walk it all"). Serna (1892:403) has the same reading. There is nothing in the Nahuatl that would justify this. Ruiz de Alarcón probably intended to write *todo lo mando* ("I command it all") which would be more reasonable in the context.

[7]Ruiz de Alarcón does not know the meaning of *nihocomoniz nicepactonal*, as can be seen by the translation "in whom the splendor and whiteness of the snow is." He may have been translating only *nicepactonal* since he may have thought that *-cepac-* was somehow related to (CEPAYAHUI)-TL ("snow"), and that *-tonal* had to do with "splendor." If this is the case, "I who walk it all" is presumably translating *nihocomoniz.* See note V:2:19.

[8]Serna (1892:403) has "a wise experienced old man (if it is a man who is performing this office; and if it is a woman, she says); a wise experienced old woman, for *I* know [Spanish: *yo conozco*] even what there is in Hell and in the heights."

[9]Ruiz de Alarcón is correct; there is no such word. The problem is that the word should not be *nihocomoniz*, but *noxomoco* [i.e., *nOhxōmoco*]. He seems unaware that the combination of *Ohxomoco* and *Cipactonal* has occurred in I:4:3. López Austin (1970:16, note 35) says "It should say *nioxomoco.*" However, the *i* is only a supportive (or prosthetic) vowel and should be omitted before another vowel. Concerning the spelling *nihocomoniz*, see note V:2:19.

[10]Paso y Troncoso (1892:191) gives *huehueel* as *"huehue el" (sic).* Referring to the *el*, López Austin (1970:16, note 37) says "this word has no meaning." We have read *huehueel* as *huehue uel* [i.e., *huēhueh* vel], with the *vel* being the Latin word for "or," in view of the alternative implicit in Ruiz de Alarcón's later marginal remark "if it is a woman."

[11]Speaking of Ruiz de Alarcón's "explanation that these two last words are said if the conjurer is of the feminine sex," López Austin (1970:16, note 38) says, "It is to be doubted." If we are correct in reading *el* as *vel* ("or"), the objection becomes less viable. Furthermore, there are other instances of alternative formulations in the MS. It should be noted, however, that if, as we believe, there is an alternative formulation, it must be carried forward to include a choice between *nOhxomoco* and *niCipactonal.* The result would be similar to that found in V:3:1, where the MS has only *niCipactonal, niHuehueh,* without the alternative *nOhxomoco, nIlamah* being mentioned.

[12]Ruiz de Alarcón's translation, "a wise experienced old man or a wise experienced old

woman" takes *Huēhueh* and *Ilamah* to be the subjects of the two occurrences of *nicmati*, a reading that would be possible only if the nouns were *niHuēhueh* and *nIlamah*. As the MS stands, *Huēhueh* and *Ilamah* have to function as the supplementary objects of the basic object *-c-* in the verbwords. This means that the speaker, immediately after claiming to "be" *Ohxomoco* or *Cipactonal*, now claims merely to be "acquainted with" one or the other. Also notice that the wording (if parallel ordering applies) identifies *Ohxomoco* as Old-man and *Cipactonal* as Old-woman. See note I:4:31.

[13]The MS has *pintado* which we have read as *pintadas* referring to the skirts (*nahuas*, i.e., *naguas*).

[14]"Ten solar beings." See note II:8:75.

[15]The *nochpar-*, for *nōchpal-*, is another instance of the *l* to *r* shift. See note II:6:1.

[16]I.e., "Carmine-colored-skirt-owners." *Nōchpal-*, meaning "carmine-colored," is found in the *Florentine Codex* (e.g., Sahagún 1954:23, *nōchpaltilmahtli*, "carmine-colored cape"; 1953:72 *nōchpalmāxtlatl*, "carmine-colored breech clouts"). The stem (NŌCH-PA-L)-LI means, literally, "prickly-pear-fruit colored-thing."

[17]On the change of *toconecauican* to *tocontlehcahuīcān*, see note V:1:14.

[18]It is surprising to hear such a remark from a Catholic churchman living at that time since one of the differences between newly established Protestantism and Roman Catholicism was the former's use of the vernacular so that the congregation could understand both the service and the Bible. Also, one of the rhetorical devices found in the priests' sermons to the Indians was the use of Latin quotations from the Bible and the church fathers as a means of impressing their audiences. See also Ruiz de Alarcón's remarks in the paragraph preceding VI:16:1.

[19]The word *Socomoniz* and the subsequent mention of its initial *s* suggest that the earlier spelling *nihocomoniz* (in V:2:2) was a copyist error for *nisocomoniz* (see note V:2:9 and note V:2:21).

[20]*Nōchpalcuēyehqueh* ("Carmine-colored-skirt-owners"). See note V:2:15. The name *Nōchpalli Īcuē*, which is a variant of *Nōchpalcuēyeh*, is found in *La Leyenda de los Soles* (Velázquez 1975:119–28).

[21]The use of the symbol *s* to represent the sound /š/ was very common as an alternative to the symbol *x* among the writers of Nahuatl. See its extensive use in the *Florentine Codex* (Sahagún 1951–75), where frequently on the same page, the spelling of a word will shift between *s* and *x*. (See Anderson, Berdan, and Lockhart 1976:35.) Concerning the use of *r* instead of *l*, see note II:6:1.

[22]The MS has *eser* for *es en*.

[23]See note I:1:7.

[24]I.e., *Tasmalaca*. See Appendix E.

Chapter 3

[1]The MS has *duraçiones* for *curaçiones*.

[2]The MS has *inicacion* for *invocación*.

[3]Ten solar beings. See note II:8:75. Ruiz de Alarcón's commentary, both before and after V:3:1, mentions only one hand, but the word in the Nahuatl text is plural, so both hands are involved.

[4]I.e., to his death.

[5]Ruiz de Alarcón's informant speaks as if *Cipactonal* were two entities, *Cipac* and *Tōnal*. Serna (1892:265) does the same. Before "I command it thus," Serna introduces a parenthetical remark that says, "He invokes Cipactli; he also remembers the fire." He has confused *Cipactli* with *Cipactonal*. See note I:4:25.

[6]See note II:17:6.

[7]I.e., *Ohuapan*. See Appendix E.

[8]The words "On the contrary, no? On the contrary" are translating the word *ca* [i.e., *cah*], again instancing Ruiz de Alarcón's statement that *cah* is an adversative particle. See note V:1:25.

[9]See note II:17:6.

[10]See note V:1:25.

[11]See note V:1:25.

[12]I.e., in order to find out who has bewitched them and caused their illness.

[13]I.e., *ololiuhqui*. See Appendix D.

[14]I.e., according to his will.

Chapter 4

[1]The MS has *tetonaltia* [i.e., *tētōnaltiah*], which is the present agentive noun. The preterit agentive noun *tētōnaltihqueh* would have

been more expected (see note VI:2:2). See Appendix C.

[2] *Tōnalli,* a patientive noun derived from (TŌNA), "to be(come) warm, for the sun to shine." It means, literally, "that which has become warm." However, it has several extended meanings, among which are "day-name" (as in the possessive form in the name *Cē-Ātl Ītōnal,* "His-*tonal* Is One Water") and "soul," which is the usage here.

SIXTH TREATISE

Chapter 1

[1] The title is missing in the MS. Paso y Troncoso (1892:195) used "About the Superstitious Doctors and Their Frauds," as this Treatise was referred to in IV:3.

[2] I.e., *tīcitl.* See Appendix C.

[3] *Ohhuihcān chānehqueh.* See Appendix B.

[4] *Tēpalēhuiāni;* see Appendix C.

[5] *Tēmīxihuītiāni;* see Appendix C.

[6] The translation is mistaken since ten fingers (or better, two hands) are being spoken to. See note II:8:75.

[7] The word *ticyōcoyaz,* "you will create it," seems to cast the earth in an antagonist role, though the implication may be that it, as the one responsible for the pain, is the patron of the birthing process.

[8] I.e., *piciete.* See Appendix D.

[9] Ruiz de Alarcón translates *mācuīltōnalehqueh* properly as the hands ("the ones of") but then puts this in jeopardy by his explanation "the fingers." See note II:8:75.

[10] The words "who all look toward one direction, all of you" are a mistranslation of *cemithualehqueh* ("owners of one courtyard").

[11] Serna (1892:394) has the following note: "Goddesses of the midwives. They call them with these primitive proper names that the Devil gave them in order to make their invocations more mysterious, or because they [pre]suppose some of the old fables which are no longer known. Or because *Quato* signifies 'disheveled head' and signifies the disordered pains close to childbirth. And *Caxoch* means 'vase of roses', and as a metaphor it is the fount that the midwives invoke" [Spanish: *es la fuente que llaman las parteras*]. See note IV:3:15.

[12] Since Ruiz de Alarcón translates this word in the singular, and since the referent is in fact singular (the vagina), we take the reduplication (which would indicate distributive plurality) to be an error in the MS.

[13] The first person plural object, *-tēch-,* and the phrase *tēteoh īmpiltzin,* "the child of the gods," are cooperating in a named-partner construction (see Andrews 1975:201).

[14] Ruiz de Alarcón's explanation is dubious.

[15] I.e., *tlacuātzin,* "opossum." See Appendix D.

[16] As Serna (1892:395) puts it: "that her own saliva enter *intra vas.*"

[17] The MS has *disonçia* for which we have read *disonancia* ("faultiness").

Chapter 2

[1] "Star" is included here in the sense of astral influence over personal destiny. The word reveals Ruiz de Alarcón's European bias.

[2] *Tētōnaltihqueh,* a preterit agentive noun meaning "ones who have provided someone with a *tonal* (i.e., a soul)," that is, "*tonal* providers" (or "soul providers"). See Appendix C.

[3] *Ātlān tlachixqueh;* see Appendix C.

[4] The *o-* of *ochalchiuhtli* is an intrusive Spanish word, *o* [i.e., "or"], inserted, we assume, by Ruiz de Alarcón to indicate an alternative wording found in another version. The problem is that one cannot know for certain how much material is covered by the "or." But, since the appositive sequence *Chālchiuhcuēyeh, Iztāc-Cihuātl,* meaning "water," is found, for example, in VI:3:1, we suggest that it covers the four-item sequence *Chālchihuitl Īcuē, Chālchihuitl Īhuīpīl, Xoxōuhqui Īcuē, Xoxōuhqui Īhuīpīl* (notice that this is really a compound two-item sequence in which each item consists in turn of two items). For another instance of *Chālchihuitl Īcuē, Chālchihuitl Īhuīpīl,* see VI:5:1.

[5] It is unclear whether the word *Icnōpiltzintli* is used here as a name referring to the god (and thus functions as a metaphor for the child) or whether it is a common noun to be translated as "the pitiful little child" or "the little orphan."

[6] The MS has *chalchiuhe,* which Ruiz de Alarcón translates as "precious stone." But the form is a preterit agentive noun of possession, *chālchihueh* ("Jade-owner"). We have

chosen to read it as *Chālchiuhcuēyeh* since at no other point in the work is the goddess called *Chālchihueh*, and, furthermore, the MS immediately presents the alternative, double-nucleus version, *Chalchiuhtli icue* [i.e., *Chālchihuitl Īcuē*].

[7] On the change of *Chalchiuhtli* to *Chalchihuitl*, see note II:8:20.

[8] The MS has *perodando caso que interuenga elpacto* ("assuming that the pact intervenes"), which we have read as *pero dando caso que no intervenga el pacto* ("assuming that the pact does not intervene").

[9] *Ōquicāuh ītōnal*, "His *tonal* has left him."

[10] The Spanish word is *genio*, which here is merely standing for the Latin word *genius*, "the guardian spirit of a man or place."

Chapter 3

[1] The words "hindrance or anger" seem to be an inflated translation for a single instance of *tlaelpan* [i.e., *tlahēlpan*] but should be understood to be plurals since Ruiz de Alarcón says "causes" in the marginal remark. Note that for him to translate *tlaelpan* as anger suggests that he thought the word contained *tlahuel-* [i.e., (TLAHUĒL)-LI "anger, hatred"]. He has not recognized the adverbial nature of *tlaelpan* ("in the filth") and sees it as an agent. López Austin (1970:6) translates *tlaelpan* as "excrement" and then says (1970:16, note 51), "A very doubtful version. *Tlaelli* is 'excrement'; *tlaelpan* is literally 'on the excrement' (Spanish '*sobre el excremento*')."

[2] The letters of this word are not clear in the MS. Paso y Troncoso (1892:198) has read *oniquizaco*, where we read *oniquesaco*, although the copyist probably intended to write *oniquetzaco*. But since the verb TLA-(QUETZA), "to stand something up," is transitive, we have spelled the word *ōnicquetzaco* in our rewritten version (see the Editorial Procedures concerning the spelling *cqu* or *qu* for /kk/).

[3] The MS has *acitlal cueye*, which would be rewritten as *Ācītlalcuēyeh*, "Dewdrop-skirt-owner," a compound preterit agentive noun of possession whose embed is (Ā-CĪTLAL-CUĒI)-TL, "dewdrop skirt," from (Ā-CĪTLAL)-IN, "star in the form of water," i.e., "dewdrop," and (CUĒI)-TL, "skirt," and whose matrix is *TLA-(E), "to possess something." Although this form is morphologically viable, we have chosen to read the word in the MS as an error for *Cītlalcuēyeh*, "Star-skirt-owner," since the latter is the goddess's name in every other instance in the MS. Ruiz de Alarcón's translation also accepts it as simply *Cītlalcuēyeh*.

[4] See note III:2:3.

[5] The words "is destroying" are a mistranslation of *-quipolocayotia* [i.e., *quipolōcayōtia*]. Ruiz de Alarcón is confusing this verb with *quipoloa*, "he destroys it" (or possibly *quipolohtiyah*, "he went along destroying it"). The verbstem is TLA-(POLŌ-CA-YŌ-TIA), "to fill something with chaff." It is formed from (POLŌ-CA-YŌ)-TL, from (POLŌ-CA)-TL, "chaff," from *(POLŌ)-TL, from (POLŌ-NI), "to stammer."

[6] *Tlāuhtzin*, "Red-ochre (H)," the honorific "name form" of (TLĀHUI)-TL, "red-ochre." Serna (1892:398) identifies this as "the fate in one of the four houses dedicated to the four Gods, the third of whom is Tonatiuh, which is a lucky one," and then, on its second occurrence, as "the fire." López Austin (1967:7) says it is "the water."

[7] *Tlāuhcalco*, "Red-ochre-house-place," from (TLĀHUI)-TL, "red-ochre," plus (CAL)-LI, "house," plus the relational noun (CO)-ø, "place." López Austin (1967:7) says this is "the place of the knowledge that is obtained by supernatural means."

[8] See note VI:3:6.

[9] We have read *in tlamacazqui, Tlāuhtzin* as the supplementary direct object in cross reference with the basic object *-c-* in both *ticpahpācaz* and *ticyēctilīz*. Ruiz de Alarcón has read it as a vocative.

[10] Since the words *centepētl* and *cemixtlāhuatl* are not marked for an adverbial function, some means to indicate that function would be expected. We have chosen to insert *īpan*, "upon it/them." Compare the phrase *ixtlāhuatl īpan*, "upon the plains," in VI:5:1.

[11] The verb *timopīnāuhti* is a second person singular admonitive form, using the nonstandard formation (see note II:7:19).

[12] Ruiz de Alarcón again does not recognize *Tlaloc* as a god.

[13] This list of *tonal*s has no grammatical relation to either the preceding or following sentences, both of which contain verbs with second person singular subjects addressed to Chalchiuhcueyeh. The only solution is to

read the list as a statement, "He is X," where the named *tonal*s are suggested alternatives (i.e., with "or" being understood between each), as if the speaker were identifying the missing *tonal* [whose owner is the "vassal" mentioned in "go wash my vassal"] to Chalchiuhcueyeh. It may be that the text is defective and that a verb such as *Tlā xictēmōti* ("Go in order to seek him") is missing.

[14]The verb TĒ-(CĀHUA) has the meaning "to carry someone to another place" (see note III:2:3).

[15]Concerning the jump from *Cē-Ātl* to *Ōme-Ācatl,* López Austin (1970:16, note 55) says, "Possibly it [i.e., *atl*] is *acatl.*" This is indeed possible, but we have chosen to take this as a *lapsus calami* of the informant and not of Ruiz de Alarcón since in the latter's translation we find "one water" also jumping to "two reeds" with the further confirmation that the former is followed by the parenthetical "or the sea" (even though his explanation is wrong). Another problem here is why the copyist underlined only *ceatl* and none of the other *tonal*s.

[16]The *-llin* ending in the MS is structurally impossible since a geminate *l* can arise only by means of assimilation through the juxtaposition of either *l* and *tl* or *l* and *y.* Despite this fundamental rule, there is a widespread persistence in the use of the word-final *-llin* spelling (e.g., *ollin* is a common error for *olīn,* a preterit agentive noun). López Austin (1970: 16, note 57) correctly says, "It should say either *cuetzpalli* or *cuetzpalin.*" Note that the MS also has an erroneous *qu-* instead of *cu-.*

[17]The MS has *chicaz,* which is an obvious error. López Austin (1970:16, note 58) says, "It should say *chihuaz.*" His translation therefore reads "What will you do?" But to justify his translation, the word would have to read *ticchīhuaz* (i.e., with the subject prefix *ti-* and the object prefix *-c-*). Ruiz de Alarcón has translated this sentence as "in what are you entertained and idle?" which is similar to the translations he has given to *tleh ticmati?* We have, therefore, chosen to read *chicaz* as a total error (with nothing salvageable) as *ticmati.*

[18]A rhetorical question that expects the answer "Nothing." This is equivalent to the expression *ahtleh īpan nitlamati,* "I consider things as nothing," i.e., "I fear nothing," or "I respect nothing," in II:1:1.

[19]The MS has *in nicā nēnemi no tehuan no nehua,* which permits any number of readings. Ruiz de Alarcón's translation "Tie [pl] me here for I am as much as another" has no valid relation to the Nahuatl. As can be seen in II:14:7 and II:17:4, the expression *tetl īhuinti, cuahuitl īhuinti* would be expected to be followed by *in nonehuiyān* ("at my will"). Notice that in II:1:3 it was followed by *tonèhuā,* which we have rewritten as *in nonehuiyān* (see note II:1:15). However, in light of the present problem, some other expression may have been intended there. Here the *no nehua* may well be another instance of *nonehuiyān* (spelled *nonehuian* or even *nonehuia* in the seventeenth century), but that would leave the problem of the meaning of *in nicā nēnemi no tehuan* unresolvable. Our rewriting has been encouraged by Molina's entry *Teuan neua* [i.e., *tēhuān nēhua*], "to join someone's faction."

[20]The words "whichever it may be" are reflecting *xoxoqui* [i.e., *xoxōuhqui*] and *iztac* [i.e., *iztāc*] as types of possible *tōnalli* choices.

[21]Ruiz de Alarcón again misreads *ChiucnāuhTopan,* this time by trying to read it as if it were structured like *achtopa.* See note II:2:2.

[22]A child in a mother-and-child relationship is generally spoken of as (CONĒ)-TL and in a father-and-child relationship as (PILTZIN)-TLI.

[23]The shift from the third person in the preceding sentence to the second person in this one indicates that the speaker has found the *tonal.*

[24]See note II:4:22 and note II:8:40. *Yōllohtzin* here is the honorific form of (YŌL-LOH)-TLI, "heart."

[25]I.e., *tōnalli.* See note V:4:2.

[26]The MS has *lazos delsueño,* which is probably a copyist's error. Serna (1892:397) has *bostesos del sueño,* i.e., "yawns of sleep."

[27]López Austin (1970:16, note 62) says, "It should say *cochcamachalolíztli.*" The MS is correct, however, as it stands. The word *cochcamachāl* is the name form of *cochcamachālli,* "sleep-jaw," i.e., "jaw affected by sleep," which serves as the source for the intransitive verb (COCH-CAMA-CHĀL-OA), "to yawn," from which López Austin's suggested

emendation is derived as an action noun. The speaker is not addressing the action but the sleep-filled jaw itself [(CAMA-CHĀL)-LI].

[28] See note V:1:12.

[29] See note VI:2:10.

Chapter 4

[1] The chapter title should read simply "About Superstitious Cures . . . ."

[2] Here "those of the five fates" would be the two hands. Ruiz de Alarcón's marginal remark ("the fingers") would have to apply only to the words "the five fates" and is therefore misleading. See note II:8:75.

[3] See note VI:1:10.

[4] The MS has *ello* ("it") but it should probably read *ella* ("her"). Serna (1892:413) also has *ello*.

[5] Because of the shift from third-person to second-person forms, we have created a new sentence beginning with *In tiCuātōn*. Compare note V:1:5.

[6] See note I:5:8.

[7] I.e., *Tecuācuīlco*. See *Tecuaquilco* in Appendix E.

[8] I.e., *iyāuhtli*. See Appendix D.

[9] I.e., *chālalahtli*. See Appendix D.

[10] We have changed *nehua* to *Nohmatca nehhuātl* in keeping with the repeatedly used formula.

[11] With his translation of *tiChiucnāuhehehcatl* as "you, winds," Ruiz de Alarcón has ignored the fact that this is a calendrical name, "Nine-wind." Caso (1959:81) says that it is the "Name of the obsidian lancet or razor (Ruiz de Alarcón 206 [i.e., VI:13:1]) and invoked against the headache (Id. 200 [i.e., VI: 4:4, to which the present note refers])." The basis for his conclusion about the lancet is not clear. See Appendix B.

[12] The spelling *-qu-* represents /k/ + /w/, which in the standard representation is *-chu-*. See note II:5:10.

Chapter 5

[1] The MS has *ó*, the Spanish word for "or." Ruiz de Alarcón has *y* [i.e., "and"] in his translation. We have omitted the word, reading the construction as an appositive rather than as an alternative.

[2] Concerning the applicative translation of *ticāītia*, see note II:12:8.

[3] On the respelling of *chalchiuhtli* as *chālchihuitl*, see note II:8:20.

Chapter 6

[1] The words "or dusky or yellow" have no counterpart in the Nahuatl text. This suggests that the copyist omitted the Nahuatl. If this is the case, the MS would read *xoxouhqui coacihuiztli, yayauhqui coacihuiztli, coçauhqui coacihuiztli* (i.e., *xoxōuhqui cōahcihuiztli, yāyāuhqui cōahcihuiztli, cōzauhqui cōahcihuiztli*).

[2] López Austin (1970:7) changed the correct spelling *-uc-* to the erroneous *-cuh-*. The MS has *ni nahualteuctli;* this should not be changed to read *ninahualtecuhtli*. See Andrews 1975:407. Because of the continuing belief that the word is *tecuhtli* (i.e., /te:koh ƛi/) rather than *tēuctli* (i.e., /te:kʷ ƛi/), it might be well to point out evidence to the contrary. The /kʷ/ sound in syllable-final position has /k/ as a variant. One finds, therefore, forms such as *tēcpilli, tēcciztli, tēcpan,* and *totēc,* all of which contain the stem (TĒUC)-TLI in its variant shape (TĒC)-TLI. The syllable /koh/ never permits reduction to /k/.

[3] See note V:1:13.

[4] López Austin (1970:16, note 68) says, "It should say *tzoneptzine*." There is, however, no need for the vocative "suffix" *-é* for the word to function as a vocative.

[5] The reduplication of *ac teotl* exists in the MS, but since the first *ac teotl* ends a page, it is probable that the second one is a copyist error. Or it may be that the first one should have been written as a catchword for the following page.

[6] *Texihxihuitl*. See Appendix D.

[7] *Xoxōuhqui Pahtēcatl* ("Green Medicine-lander"). The phrase is derived from the place name *Xoxōuhqui Pahtlān* ("Green Medicine-side") which is derived in turn from *xōxōuhqui pahtli* ("green medicine"). The place name is figurative for a place where green medicine is found in abundance. Concerning *Pahtēcatl,* see Appendix B.

[8] "Green medicine" is a nonfigurative translation. See note VI:6:7.

[9] *Iztāc-Cihuātl* ("White Woman"). See Appendix B.

[10] I.e., *tlachihchinoa.* See Appendix D.

[11] Ruiz de Alarcón has confused *āyahuitl* ("fog, mist; cloud on the eye") with *yāhuitl* ("brown or black maize"). The appropriateness of the name has to do with the "cloud on the eye" meaning of the word. See note II: 16:2.

[12] Concerning the embed (POLŌ-CA)-TL, "chaff" (here with a reduplicative prefix for plurality), see note VI:3:5.

[13] The possessive state word *amoneoncāhuīl* is assumed to be a passive patientive noun, (NE-ON-CĀHU-Ī-L)-LI, "one who is accompanied to his dwelling," from the applicative verb ON-MO-TĒ-(CĀHU-IA), "to accompany someone (H) to his dwelling," from the stem ON-TĒ-(CĀHUA), "to accompany someone to his dwelling," which is listed in Molina as *caua.nonte.*

Chapter 7

[1] The verb *ticchīuhti* is a second person singular admonitive form, using the nonstandard formation (see note II:7:19).

[2] See note II:17:6.

[3] The MS has *nochicnauh oztoc* [i.e., *noChiucnāuhōztōc*], "my Nine-caves-place," an apparent error for *no chicomoztoc* [i.e., *noChicōmōztōc*], "my Seven-caves-place." We have given the corrected form in our rewritten version.

[4] The MS has *quitoticalaquiz,* an obvious error for *quitocaticalaquiz;* see *xictocaticalaqui* in the second sentence of this segment.

Chapter 8

[1] The MS has *tenexcu* for *tenexiete.*

[2] The MS has *en* for *es.*

[3] The words "four small reeds" (Spanish, *quatro cañuelas*) seems to be an appositive for "the one entrusted to me." Serna (1892:415) reads differently, letting this segment of the incantation end with "the one entrusted to me" and omitting the parenthetical remark "here she is talking to the gum." The commentary following the segment reads, "Here with four small reeds she wounds the gum, making it bleed and goes on with the incantation, saying." The problem can be made clearer by juxtaposing the two Spanish versions. Museo MS: *quatro cañuelas {aqui conlas [sic] encia hablādo}, hiere saca sangre iprosigue con los dedos* ("four small reeds {here talking to the gum}, she stabs, draws blood, and continues with the fingers"). Serna: *Aqui con quatro cañuelas yere la ensia sacandole sangre, y prosigue su conjuro diciendo* ("Here with four small reeds she stabs the gum, drawing blood from it, and continues her incantation saying").

[4] Instead of *con las [sic] encia* ("with the gum"), the Museo MS should have *de la encia* ("about the gum").

[5] López Austin (1970:16, note 72) says, "Possibly a word is missing here which Ruiz de Alarcón translates as 'four small reeds.'"

[6] The MS has *-xitocaticalaqui,* which is not possible since the embed of this "connective *-ti-*" compound is a transitive verb and no object prefix is showing. We have rewritten it with the verb object prefix *-c-*. See *xictocaticalaqui* in VI:7:1.

[7] The verb *timopīnāuhtihti* is a second person singular admonitive form, using the nonstandard formation (see note II:7:19).

[8] The verb *ticchīuh* is a second person singular admonitive form using the standard formation.

[9] More correctly "to the hands."

[10] Ruiz de Alarcón translates the *tlen ye* [i.e., *tleh in ye*] as *porque razon* [i.e., "for what reason"], as if the text had *tlen ic* [i.e., *tleh in īc*], "what is the reason that," suggesting a copyist error. The error would not, however, have been in reading *ye* for *yc* but rather of omitting *yc* before the *ye* since the Spanish reads *porque razon . . . ya* (where *ya* is translating *ye*). In our rewritten version, we have chosen to ignore this possibility, choosing to follow the MS as it stands.

[11] The MS has *y ne tlayecolayan,* which is meaningless. López Austin (1970:16, note 73) says "It should say *inetlayecoloyan.*" However, assuming that the form is built on the impersonal stem TLA-(YEC-Ō-LO), from the active stem TLA-(YEC-OA), there is no way to justify the object prefix *ne-;* MO-TLA-(YEC-OA) does not exist. Besides, a locative created on an impersonal stem should appear in the absolutive state only, but the word in the MS is in the possessive state. See note VI:8:14.

[12] *Vel* (Latin, "or"). The word was, of course, added by Ruiz de Alarcón. As his

translation (*porque razon echa yaaperder . . . oPorque haze blandear . . .* , i.e., "Why is it now ruining . . . or Why is it making . . . become soft") suggests, he apparently intended the words *nonahual yao tepan mitl quihuehueloa* as an alternative for *ye quiixpoloa in nonahual metl yne tlayecolayan,* possibly indicating that one version of this incantation had one wording and another the other. Although there are other possible explanations, we have opted to insert another *tleh in* in brackets in our rewritten version to spell out this reading of the alternative construction.

[13]López Austin (1970:8) translates *nonāhualmetl* as "my magic maguey." However, the matrix is not (ME)-TL, "maguey," but (METLA)-TL, "quern," since the word shows the nonabsolutive form of the stem. If the matrix had been (ME)-TL, the word would have been *nonāhualmeuh.*

[14]Paso y Troncoso (1892:203) has read the marginal material as part of the text, creating the sequence *nonatlayecoltzayan, hual yaotepanmitl,* thus splitting *nona* from *hual,* which is left as a meaningless word. Furthermore, what we read as *tlayecoltiayan* he has read as *tlayecoltzayan.* This, if standing alone, might be a possible formation, consisting of the embedded nounstem (TLA-YĒC-Ō-L)-LI, "a completed thing," and the matrix verbstem TLA-(TZAYĀ-N-A), "to rip or tear something up"; the resulting compound verbstem, (TLA-YĒC-Ō-L-TZAYĀ-N-A), would mean something like "to tear up a completed thing." But while this stem is theoretically possible, its derivative, *tlayēcōltzayān,* an absolutive preterit agentive noun, meaning "one that tears up completed things," can serve neither as an alternative nor as a replacement for the *tlayecolayan* of the possessed noun *inetlayecolayan* in the text. We, however, having read the marginal material as *tlayecoltiayan* [i.e., *tlayecōltiāyān*], see it as a corrective replacement for the erroneous *tlayecolayan,* creating *īnetlayecōltiāyān,* a locative noun based on the imperfect active tense theme of the verbstem MO-TLA-(YEC-Ō-L-TIA), "to seek and earn what is necessary for life."

[15]The sequence in the MS, *nonahual yao tepan mitl,* presents a problem. It cannot be rewritten as *nonāhualyāōtepāmitl* [i.e., with (TEPĀMI)-TL, "wall," serving as matrix] since the absolutive singular suffix *-tl* cannot co-occur with the possessive prefix *no-* ("my"). We have, therefore, rewritten it as *nonāhualyāōtepāmmetl,* "my *nahualli*-war-wall-quern" [i.e., with (METLA)-TL, "quern," being the matrix, as in *nonāhualmetl;* see note VI:8:13]. There is, however, the slight possibility that the word intended was *nonāhualyāōtepān,* "my *nahualli*-war-wall."

Chapter 9

[1]Ruiz de Alarcón again translates *tlamacazqui* as "spirit" *(espiritu)* when his normal translation is *espiritado* ("possessed one").

[2]It would seem that the MS is corrupt; see our rewritten version.

[3]The grave accent is an error since the word has no glottal stop. López Austin (1970: 16, note 74) says, "Literally, 'I came to burn him'; but 'I came to kill him,' metaphorically." As can be seen, Ruiz de Alarcón also translates "I have come . . . to burn him." But the word used here is not TLA-(TLATIA), "to burn something," but TLA-(TLĀTIA), "to hide something." The metaphor for "to kill" is "to hide," not "to burn." Brewer and Brewer (1962:212) list *quitlötia* ("he kills it") and (1962:210) *quitlatia* ("he burns it"). See note II:5:1 and note II:8:21.

[4]The word in the MS, *coconectin,* is a problem. Ruiz de Alarcón apparently thought that it was the plural of (CONĒ)-TL ("child") since he translated it as "his pages." This translation is wrong for several reasons, one of which is that the word is not in the possessive state. López Austin (1970:8) translates it as "the children." But the word is standing in apposition to the singular noun *tlamacazqui* ("priest") and is modified by the singular form *yāyāuhqui* ("dusky"). We have, therefore, read it as *Tzoneptzin,* since the speaker holds the tobacco on the tooth with his finger, "Nacre-as-hair."

[5]This instance of *xoxōuhtli* is unique in the *Treatise.* The word is a past patientive noun meaning "a thing that has become green," from the verbstem (XO-XŌ-HUI), "to become green." Although not listed in the dictionaries, its legitimacy is supported by the fact that it occurs as the embed of the place name *Xoxōuhtlan* (see Appendix E). In every other instance in the *Treatise,* we find

either *xoxōuhqui* or *xoxōhuic*, the variant agentive nouns from (XO-XŌ-HUI), the first treating the verb as belonging to class B and the second as belonging to class A. Since the verb is intransitive, there is no translatable difference between the patientive and agentive nounstems. It is also possible that the word should be rewritten as the present patientive noun (XO-XŌ-HUI)-TL, which Siméon lists as *xoxouitl*, "sky-blue color made with some flowers and used for dying cloth" (in other words, it would be an instance of /wi/ versus /W/; see Editorial Procedures and note II: 8:20), but the question is academic since the words should mean the same thing, a color that ranges from sky-blue to green. Molina lists *xuxuhqui* [i.e., *xoxōuhqui*] as meaning "green or raw" and then, in the Spanish-Nahuatl section, defines *azul color de cielo* ["sky-blue color"] as *xoxouhqui*.

6 The sequence in the MS is obviously defective since the speaker has not brought *xoxōuhtli cōahcihuiztli* but is seeking to get rid of it. Also the formula at the end of the sequence is incomplete. In our rewritten version, we have enclosed a possible reconstruction in brackets.

7 "The hands" is an overstatement for "a finger."

Chapter 10

1 *Tzopilōtl.* See Appendix D.

2 More correctly, "the hands." See note II:8:75.

3 See note V:1:12.

Chapter 11

1 See Glossary of Nahuatlisms and Hispanisms.

2 The words "in all the rest" are not part of the incantation; they are a comment by Ruiz de Alarcón to the effect that the material he has omitted from this incantation is the same as that found in the foregoing one.

3 The MS has *nonahual coco.* Molina lists the matrix under the possessive form *tococouh* [i.e., *tococōuh*] ("the gullet," *lit.*, "our gullet"). We have, therefore, changed the text to *nonāhualcocōuh.*

Chapter 12

1 *Mayānallān.* See Appendix E.

2 *Tepēcuācuīlco.* See Appendix E.

3 Cupping is a curing procedure associated with phlebotomies, in which a glass cup, heated to create a vacuum, is applied to the skin in order to draw blood to the surface. In dry cupping, no blood is actually removed from the body: the vacuum causes the skin to tumefy. In wet cupping, dry cupping is followed by making incisions in the skin and reapplying the cupping glasses to collect the blood (Davis and Appel 1979:17). The latter method was followed here.

4 López Austin (1970:9) translates this as "Deign to unite yourself here with my father," and then (1970:16, note 76) says, "A doubtful version." It is not clear why he considers this unsatisfactory. The meaning is that the cotton should join the fire, that is, ignite and burn to create the vacuum in the cupping glass.

5 See note II:8:72 and note VI:25:4.

6 The form in the MS, *tzonco çahuiztica* [i.e., *tzoncōzahuizticah*], a "connective *-ti-*" compound, is correct, but we have replaced it with a more common representation (*x* instead of *z* for the perfective stem ending). López Austin (1970:16, note 105) says, "It should say *tzoncozahuitica.*" However, the imperfective stem of the embedded verb is (CŌZ-AHUI-YA), "to become yellow," which is intransitive and belongs to Class B, not Class C. On verb classes, see Andrews (1975:19–21, 384–87).

7 The MS has *ico papallotzin.* We agree with López Austin (1970:16, note 79) that it should read *Itzpapalotzin* (i.e., *Ītzpāpālōtzin*), which means Obsidian Butterfly. Ruiz de Alarcón's translation, "point similar to the wing of a butterfly," should possibly be considered a demetaphorized translation (although he mistakes the matrix of the Nahuatl word for the embed).

8 The MS has *chico moztococ,* which we have read as *chicōmōztōc,* deleting the final *oc* as a copyist error. There is, however, a slight possibility that the *oc* should be placed in the next sentence, giving *Oc ticquīxtīzqueh,* "We will yet cause it to leave."

9 I.e., to replay verbally the event or procedure.

10 *Tlā cuēl. Tlā xihuāllauh, Iztāc-Cihuātzin.*

"Let it be soon. Come, White Woman (H)."

[11]The MS has *indice,* which is an error. We have read *indica* ("it indicates"), but possibly *induce* ("it induces") was intended.

Chapter 13

[1]*Cōānenepilli.* See Appendix D.

[2]See note II:8:75.

[3]At this point, Serna (1892:416) inserts the parenthetical comment "Here he pretends that he is seeking."

[4]The words "the green pain" occur where the Nahuatl text has "&." Serna's version (1892:416) continues with "the dusky pain." This suggests that the Nahuatl text originally had *xoxouhqui coacihuiztli, yayauhqui coacihuiztli* (i.e., *xoxōuhqui cōahcihuiztli, yāyāuhqui cōahcihuiztli*).

[5]The MS has *coa* (with a superscript *a* joined to the *o*). It is an obvious copyist error. Paso y Troncoso (1892:205) omits it, as do we.

[6]*Chiucnāuhehcatl* ("Nine-breeze") is a legitimate, if rarely used, variant of *Chiucnāuhehehcatl* ("Nine-wind"). In our rewritten version below we have, however, chosen to use the more common form.

[7]The MS has *pàtecal.* The final *l* is a mistake for *tl.* Also since the word is standing in apposition to *titlamacazqui,* it should have the second person singular subject prefix *ti-*. We have therefore rewritten the word as *tiPahtēcatl.*

[8]The MS has *xihualtotocati* [i.e., *xihuālto-tōcati*] ("Go in order to run hither"). But, as suggested in note VI:13:4, the original MS probably included more material, and the missing additional words would have functioned as direct objects. Furthermore, Ruiz de Alarcón translated this verb as a transitive like the verb in the preceding sentence. We have therefore inserted the direct object prefix *-c-: xichuāltohtocati.* ("Go in order to pursue it hither"); thus, instead of the verb (TO-TŌ-CA), "to run," we read the verb TLA-(TOH-TOCA), "to pursue something."

Chapter 14

[1]The words "and in the spine" have no Nahuatl counterpart. It is highly likely, given the problem in the Nahuatl text, that the copyist omitted material. See note VI:14:7.

[2]The form in the MS *(nonahualtzontecomatl)* is impossible since it contains both a possessive prefix *no-* ("my") and the absolutive form *tzontecomatl* (the possessive form of which is *-tzontecon*). As explained in note VI: 14:7, we assume a *lapsus calami.*

[3]This is an instance of the "named-partner" construction (see Andrews 1975:201).

[4]We have inserted this material in order to bring the phrasing into conformity with other instances of the formula.

[5]The MS has *tlàcotli* which Ruiz de Alarcón has translated as "you who are worthy of esteem," so the copyist should have written *tlàçotli.* Compare this with *tlahçotli* (which Ruiz de Alarcón translates as "the precious one") in VI:25:3. We have rewritten the word as *tlazohtli* (see point 2 of note II:8:45).

[6]See note II:17:6.

[7]López Austin (1970:16, note 86) says, "Perhaps it should say *nonahualelchiquiuh,*" which he translates as *mi caja torácica encantada* ("my enchanted thoracic box"). Then in a further comment (1970:16, note 87) he says, "The text, possibly mistaken, speaks of the head." It is, however, unlikely that the original MS would have used the emendation López Austin suggests since Ruiz de Alarcón translates the word as "my enchanted coffer [Spanish, *arca*] of ribs {the chest}." The word in the MS was, then, a metaphor that needed explanation by a marginal note, and López Austin's suggested replacement needs none (since *ēlchiquihuitl* is the usual word for thorax). Also, since the MS is speaking in metaphors and because of the problem with *nonahualtzontecomatl* mentioned in note VI: 14:2, perhaps the idea of "head" should be kept. Ruiz de Alarcón's Spanish is *estara dentro de mi encantada arca de costillas {el pecho}, y en el espinaço entrate tras la encantada cabeça.* Assuming a *lapus calami* whereby *nonahualtzontecomatl* includes *nonahual . . . nahualtzontecomatl* (that is, a skip from one instance of *-nahual-* to a later one), we have reconstructed the text to match Ruiz de Alarcón's Spanish by reading *nonāhual[omicicuilpetlacal ōmotēcato. Ītepotzco nāhual]tzontecomatl tictocaticalaquiz.* This assumes that Ruiz de Alarcón was not sure about the translation of *en el espinazo* and also that the text is using a double-nucleus form (see Andrews 1975:134) of the verb TĒ-(TEPOTZ-TOCA) ("to follow someone at his

back," i.e., "to follow or go after someone"). This leaves the problem of why "*nahualli*-head" was mentioned. Serna (1892:416) says it means "the pain."

Chapter 15

[1] *Pachōliztli* means "a thing that is capable of being pressed down on (or compressed)." It is likely that *tlapachōliztli* ["the act of pressing down on (or compressing) something"] was intended.

[2] Although Ruiz de Alarcón is not certain of the translation of this word (giving us the choice between "large sloughs" and "pretty green fields") and although Molina is of no help, since he defines *chiauitl* [i.e., *chiahuitl*] as "another viper, or plant louse that nibbles at vines," the word is found in Sahagún (1952:9) in its embedding form in the word *chiauhtlālli* ("marshy land"), corroborating Ruiz de Alarcón's first translation, "slough." López Austin, in commenting on his translation (1970:9), "the place of the legitimate plant-louse," says (1970:16, note 90): "This seems meaningless. Surely the word Chiahuitl is mistaken. It is the name of a plant louse and of a serpent. Ruiz de Alarcón translates 'in the large sloughs,' and, not satisfied, gives a second version 'in the pretty green fields.'" We do not know the reason for Ruiz de Alarcón's uncertainty (possibly it was owing to his recognition of the rhetorical inappropriateness of enticing someone to leave by inviting him to an unpleasant place), but it seems certain that his first translation is correct.

[3] "The laying on of hands."

[4] *Huitzōcco.* See Appendix E.

Chapter 16

[1] The MS does not include the symbols, except for the symbol "X" toward the end of VI:16.

[2] See note V:2:18.

[3] "Your disheveled hair" (Spanish, *v[ues]tras melenas*) is translating *ammoquentzon,* which Ruiz de Alarcón did not understand. It is supposed to be *amocuahtzon.* This word and the next one, *amoxiyōuh,* constitute an idiomatic doublet (i.e., *Cuahtzontli xiyōtl,* "warp and heddle"), meaning "example."

[4] The MS has *v[ues]tros liços, primideras y tempiales* [i.e., *vuestros lizos, premideras, y tempiales* (sic)]. Serna (1892:307) has *vuestras lisas ramas* ("your smooth branches"). The words *primideras y tempiales* have no counterpart in the Nahuatl.

[5] López Austin (1970:16, note 92) says, "Metaphor that means food." He translates *ayohhuachtli* as "squash seeds" *(la pepita de la calabaza),* which is more accurate than Ruiz de Alarcón's "seeds" *(pepitas).*

[6] The letters in the MS are in the margin. We have inserted them in the text to match their placement in Ruiz de Alarcón's subsequent commentary.

[7] We have inserted the word *Nohmatca* in keeping with the general formula.

[8] We have changed the third person form to the needed first person form.

[9] The use of *ye* here is unique in the text and may be the result of a copyist error. The text may originally have read *Ye āxcān yez,* "It will be the time [for action]," or some similar formulaic phrase.

[10] We have changed the possessive *to-* ("our") of the MS to *no-* ("my") in conformity with *annohuēltīhuān* and the rest of VI: 16:1.

[11] On our change of *r* to *l,* see note II:6:1 and note V:2:15.

[12] Since *Nōchpalcuēyehqueh* and *Cōācuēyehqueh* are standing in apposition to *annohuēltīhuān,* we have introduced the second person plural prefix *an-* before each.

[13] The MS has "Dioses silvestres, O, *omenores verdes.*" Either the captial *O* or the initial *o* of *omenores* is an error. "Forest Gods or lesser green [gods]" is an "undecided" translation for *xoxouhqui tlacolteyotl* (but see note VI:16:18).

[14] The omission of letters between {H} and {Q} suggests that material is missing from the MS.

[15] López Austin (1970:10) translates this as "I will carry you" (as if the word were *nimitzhuīcaz*), possibly because he allowed himself to be persuaded by Ruiz de Alarcón's erroneous translation. It is a third person form, not a first person form.

[16] In both this sentence and the following one, we have read the plural verb plus singular vocative as a "named-partner" construction (see Andrews 1975:201).

[17] The verb in the MS *tictetemoliz* [i.e., *tic-*

tehtēmolīz] is a frequentative form (because of the reduplicative prefix *te-* [i.e., *teh-*], here indicating repetitive action) of a double-object applicative verbstem TĒ-TLA-(TĒM-O-LIA), "to seek something for someone." Ruiz de Alarcón translates it as a single-object verb: "you . . . seek . . . that which harms . . . this unfortunate one," as if the verbstem were merely TLA-(TĒM-OA), "to seek something." We have read *mācēhualli* as the indirect object ("for the vassal," i.e., "for the vassal's benefit") and the clause *ye quīxpoloa* as the direct object ("the one who is already destroying him").

18 The MS has *tlacolteyotl*, which would be rewritten *tlahzolteōtl* ("filth-goddess"), although *tlahzolteōyōtl* ("filth-divinity") might also be theoretically possible. There are, however, a number of reasons for believing there has been a mistake on the part of the informant or a misunderstanding on the part of Ruiz de Alarcón: (1) there is the problem of the misspelling; (2) the form *-teōtl* is singular (although Ruiz de Alarcón translates it as a plural, "forest gods or lesser green [gods]"; see point 2 of note II:8:45), while in all the other instances in the incantations the word is in the plural, *tlahzoltēteoh;* (3) there is no apparent justification for *Tlahzolteōtl*'s being an obstacle to the speaker's enterprise since in every other instance in the incantations the *Tlahzoltēteoh* are presented as beneficent figures; (4) the other entities addressed in the parallel sentences following this one are spiders, typical hindrances to curing efforts. For these reasons, we have chosen to read the word as *tlaçoltocatl* [i.e., *tlahzoltocatl*], "filth-spider" (a large spider, according to Molina).

19 The verb *namēchīxpolohti* is a first person singular admonitive form, using the nonstandard formation (see note II:7:19).

20 The MS has *que habla*, an indicative construction, meaning "that he speaks," when a subjunctive construction, *que hable*, "for him to speak," would be expected. But the problem is further complicated by the fact that the translation referred to speaks of drinking, not talking. The text probably was intended to read *que beba*, "for him to drink," which is how it reads in Serna (1892:308).

21 The Spanish has *a*, "to"; but *tocante a*, or *con respecto a*, or some other expression meaning "about" would be expected.

Chapter 17

1 "And it now swoons" is another mistranslation for *ye tlapolōcayōtia.* See note VI:3:5.

2 The word *eztli* ("it is blood"), being parenthetical, seems to be a prompting to the native speaker, reminding him of the meaning of the metaphor.

3 The Spanish word *Spiritu*, combined with its identification as a bird, seems to be a projection of Christian symbolism (the dove as a symbol of the Holy Spirit) into the native symbolism. See *Códice Sierra* (León 1933:25, 31, 38, 54, 59) for usage of this symbol to represent Easter. Notice that here it is antagonistic to the patient.

4 The MS has the verb in the preterit (which in the rewritten form would be *Tleh ticmah?* "What did you learn?"), but this idiom always occurs in the present tense (except here and later in this incantation). We have changed it accordingly (in both places). López Austin (1970:16, notes 97 and 98) makes the same change.

5 The MS has *titlamachtzitzquiz* but the word is transitive (with *-tlamach-* functioning as an adverbial embed meaning "carefully," "gently") and must have an object prefix. We have inserted the prefix *-c-: Tictlamachtzītzquīz.*

Chapter 18

1 *Ātl īnān* ("Its mother is water"). See Appendix D.

2 I.e., *tzopilōtl.* See Appendix D.

3 In the MS, this is run on into the text of the incantation.

4 Serna (1892:419) has "Come on, come you, white woman, here I apply you, etc." It is not clear whether he is simply spelling out the implications of the text or whether he is copying exactly what he finds in his source.

Chapter 19

1 The MS has *le echaron aire* and later in the same sentence *le tornaron a echar ayre*, which we have translated as "they fanned him" and "they again fanned him," because of the statement in the second paragraph below, *la Veronica le echo ayre con un lienço*, "Veronica fanned him with a cloth." The

first two instances with *echar aire* are referred to three sentences later, however, as an act of blowing: *auiendole soplado como antes,* "having blown on him as before."

[2]This should read *xitlamahuiço* [i.e., *Xitlamahuizo*], "Be amazed." As the &c. after the word indicates and the translation in the text confirms, Ruiz de Alarcón chose to give only the first word of their speech in Nahuatl.

[3]The MS has *-cuetlacoxcolli,* an obvious error for *-cuetlaxcolli,* which is the reading given by Paso y Troncoso (1892:210).

[4]Concerning the Laughing Falcon, or *huāctzin,* see note I:9:5. The metaphor of the falcon is apt since the bird preys on snakes.

[5]Ruiz de Alarcón mistranslates *Cōzahuic Tlamacazqui* as "dusky conjured one," instead of his usual translation "yellow possessed one." Serna (1892:296) says that this represents the *piciete.* Compare VI:3:2.

[6]Serna (1892:296) says that "green possessed one" [i.e., "Green Priest"] represents *atl inan.*

[7]Serna (1892:296) says that "dusky possessed one" [i.e., "Dusky Priest"] represents "anise" [i.e., *iyāuhtli*].

[8]The word in the MS, *çomolli,* has been corrected to *xomolli.* The use of the symbol *ç* to spell the sound /š/ was sporadic in colonial times.

[9]The form in the MS, *contocataz* (i.e., *contocatāz*), here and again in the next sentence, is correct, but we have emended it to a more explicit representation of the matrix, (YA), "to go." López Austin (1970:16, notes 102 and 103) says, "It should say *contocatinemiz,*" but the text is adequate as it stands. See also note III:6:7 and note III:6:9.

[10]See note VI:19:9.

Chapter 20

[1] *Tlāltīzapan.* See Appendix E.

[2] *Cōlōpahtli.* See Appendix D.

Chapter 21

[1] *Tēpahpachōliztli,* "the act of pressing down on (or compressing) someone thoroughly" or possibly "with medicine." Compare VI:15.

[2]The *-cc-* should be *-cç-* (that is, *-cz-*): *tētleiczaliztli,* "the act of treading on someone with fire (i.e., heat)."

[3]"My spongy heel or callus" is a demetaphorized translation of *nopoçoloac* [i.e., *nopozolcac*] ("my foam sandal," i.e., a sandal made of unspun cotton). This was part of ceremonial attire before the Conquest, and it is unlikely that Ruiz de Alarcón would understand this meaning. See Sahagún 1954:62–63; 1970:7; passim.

[4]The Spanish is *no te emplees en el.* Serna (1892:418) explains that this means "do not just heat it" (Spanish *no solo lo calientes á el*). The meaning should be, however, "do not hurt it," since it is translating *àmo tinechelehuiz,* which Ruiz de Alarcón translated correctly in the preceding sentence as "watch out that you do not covet me." The problem in the Spanish may be related to the curious use of parentheses around the Nahuatl source.

[5]López Austin (1970:11) translates this correctly as "I will kill you" and then, commenting on this (1970:16, note 107) says, "Metaphorically, because it says literally 'I will burn you'." However, the word is *nimitztlahtlātīz* ("I will hide you"), not *nimitztlahtlatīz* ("I will burn you") despite the fact that here, with the use of heat, the idea of burning might seem appropriate. See note VI:9:3. For another instance of the reduplicative prefix (creating a frequentative form signifying intensity of action) on the verbstem TĒ-(TLĀTIA), "to hide someone; to kill someone," see VI:30:1: *quitlahtlātīznequi,* "he wants to hide him thoroughly."

[6]See note VI:12:6.

[7]The MS has *ó* [Spanish, "or"], which Paso y Troncoso (1892:212) reads as a question mark. We have omitted it in our rewritten version.

[8]The MS has *noçalitilma,* which Ruiz de Alarcón translates "my drag-net." López Austin (1970:11) translates it "my sticking blanket" (Spanish: *mi manta adherida,* lit., "my blanket that has become stuck"). He is obviously relating *-zali-* to the verb (ZĀL-IHUI), "to become stuck," "to become glued." However, the source stem of this verb is (ZĀL)-LI, not *(ZĀLI)-TL or *(ZĀLIH)-TLI. The solution to the problem is that there are two words here, not one; furthermore, the *-ç-* is a mistake for *-c-*. The phrase should read *nocal*

ītilmah ("my house's blanket"), which is a metaphor for a hunting net. See *īcal īhuīpīl,* in II:6:2, which Ruiz de Alarcón also translated as "net."

[9] See note II:17:6.

Chapter 22

[1] *Poztecpahtli.* See Appendix D.

[2] The MS has *deestallia.* Serna (1892:426) has *de estrallido* [*sic*]. Serna also lacks the words "*oruido,* o, *alboroto*" ("or noise or uproar"), which, except for the *o* between commas, are in italics in the MS.

[3] López Austin (1970:11) respells *tecuçoline* as *tecuhzoline,* again creating the syllable *cuh* from the single consonant sound /k^w/, here spelled *cu,* although Ruiz de Alarcón for the most part uses the preferred spelling *uc* when /k^w/ occurs at the end of a syllable. See note VI:6:2.

[4] "Person-from-Comontlan" is a metaphor, as if in English slang we were to say, "He is from Cracklingsville." *Comōntlān* means, literally, "Beside the crackling fire," from the patientive noun (COMŌ-N)-TLI, "crackling fire" [from the verb (COMŌ-NI), "for a fire to burn, throwing out flames"], plus *-tlan,* "near, beside." The metaphor is apt because of the loud whirring noise made by a covey of quail when flushed. Compare note I:10:5 and note II:13:3.

[5] López Austin (1970:11) translates *tonacaomitl* of the MS as "the bones of our body." He reads the initial *to-* as the first person plural possessive prefix, "our," and the *-naca-* for the noun stem (NACA)-TL. However, the matrix of the word, i.e., (OMI)-TL, "bone," is in the absolutive state, and a basic rule of Nahuatl word formation establishes that any possessive prefix on a noun word refers to the matrix, which must then, of course, be in the possessive state. The *tonaca-* in the word is *tōnacā-,* which is derived from the verb (TŌNA). See note III:4:3.

[6] The verb *ticāītia* has the form of a causative, but the context demands that it have an applicative meaning. See note II:12:8.

[7] The MS has *nictilitzaco,* which is an error for *nictitilitzaco,* an in-bound purposive form of the stem TLA-(TI-TILI-TZA), "to tighten something," which is the frequentative of TLA-(TILĪ-NI-A), "to pull on something, to stretch something, to tighten a knot or fastening, to draw the string of a bow."

[8] Ruiz de Alarcón's explanation is not valid. Although in the next incantation mention is made of Quetzalcoatl's visit to Mictlan, Ruiz de Alarcón seems not to have grasped the reference to the myth. A version of the myth contained in the *Leyenda de los Soles* (Velázquez 1975:120–21) reports that Quetzalcoatl, moved by the sadness of the gods because there were no men in the world to worship them, went to Mictlan to get the jade bones from MictlanTeuctli (the Lord of Mictlan), who allowed him to take them. After Quetzalcoatl left with them, MictlanTeuctli ordered his servants to mar them. Quail frightened Quetzalcoatl, causing him to faint and drop the bones, whereupon the quail pecked and broke them. At that instant, Quetzalcoatl regained consciousness, saw the damage, and wept. He gathered up the bones and continued his return trip. After arriving at Tamoanchan, he used the damaged bones to create man. Another version of the myth is reported in Clavijero (1979, 1:245–246) in which Xolotl rescues the bones from MictlanTeuctli, but breaks them in his flight. Quail are not mentioned. The myth is an explanation of human fragility and perishability. Human mortality is owing to imperfections in the very framework, the hardest part of the body. MictlanTeuctli's perfidious action is motivated by his realization that if man were made from perfect material, he would never die. By putting his mark on the bones, he brands them as his property so that they must return to him. Quetzalcoatl's weeping comes at the recognition that, in creating life, he will be creating death. By naming Mictlan as the source of the bones, the myth presents mortality as implicit in human life. The narration of the marring simply spells out that inherent mortality by metaphorically dramatizing it.

[9] Ruiz de Alarcón's translation of *tlalo çiuatl* as "the woman like a macaw" is erroneous. The embed here is not (ALO)-ø, "macaw," but *tlalo-* (see note VI:22:15).

[10] The MS has *se bajan,* which we have read as *sé bajar,* as it is in Serna (1892:426).

[11] The MS has *subi* which we have changed

to *subir* to match the *sé bajar* with which it is in parallel construction. Serna (1892:426) also has *subir*.

[12]The MS has *la superior* ("the upper one"). Serna (1892:426) has *lo superior* ("the upper part").

[13]The MS reads *los muchos pajaros quebrantado han quebrado*. Serna's version (1892:426) is *los muchos pajaros quebrantado àn, y quebradolo* ("the many birds have cracked and broken it").

[14]See note III:1:6.

[15]López Austin (1970:12) translates *tlalo ciuatl* [relying on Paso y Troncoso's (1892: 213) spelling, *tlalocihuatl*] as "woman who runs" and he says (1970:16, note 111) "'woman who runs,' 'woman who flees,' a very doubtful version. It might be a bad spelling of *tlaloccihuatl*, 'female aquatic divinity.'" His first translation is not viable since its equivalent in Nahuatl would be the two-word construction *motlaloa cihuātl*. And his alternative translation, relating the word to the god *Tlāloc*, is not valid since that name is a preterit agentive noun, and consequently the construction would be possible only as (1) *Tlāloc cihuātl* (two words, meaning "*Tlāloc*, the woman" or possibly "*Tlāloc* or the woman") or (2) *Tlālocācihuātl* (one word, using the combining form (TLĀL-O-ϕ-CĀ)- and meaning "*Tlāloc*-woman"). Since the word in the MS stands in apposition to *Chicuetecpacihuatl*, who is associated with maguey (see note III:1:6) and thus with pulque, we have chosen to read it as *Tlāloccihuātl*, "Land-wine-woman," a compound noun whose embed is (TLĀL-OC)-TLI, "land-wine," and whose embed is (CIHUĀ)-TL, "woman." Compare *Tlālocxōchitl* in note II: 7:6.

[16]The MS has *oma naloque oma co choque* and Ruiz de Alarcón translates this as "They have caught and detained [him]." López Austin (1970:12) echoes this with "They have made [him] a prisoner, they have caught [him]." Neither is correct. The first word must be the passive of the verb TLA-(MANA) ["to set something (flat or flat-bottomed) down"] and must be translated "They have been set down." It cannot come from the verb TLA-(ĀNA) ("to seize something") or from M-(ĀNA) ["to grow (in body size)," or, referring to an inanimate object such as a rope, "to give"]. The second word is malformed and, as is, means nothing. The verbstem is transitive and, according to both Molina and Siméon, takes a reciprocal object, MO-(MĀCOCH-OA), "for two entities to hug one another." Therefore, the word must read *ōmomācochohqueh*, which means "they have hugged one another." In view of this, and since *ōmanaloqueh* ("they have been set down") makes no compelling sense in this context, we have chosen to see these words as a synonymous pair, taking the first one to be an error for *ōmonāpalohqueh* ("they have held each other in their arms") (see the use of *xicnāpalo* and *ticnāpalōz* in VI:22:1). The plural subject affixes in both these verbs under discussion are participating in a "named-partner" construction (see Andrews 1975:201).

[17]Ruiz de Alarcón translated the embed of this word, *teuh-*, as "many" and it is true that the verb (TEUH-TI), "to become like dust," has the metaphorical meaning of "to be many." But in the present context, such a translation does not seem valid. In other incantations "dust" has served as a symbol of evil (although it usually refers to sexual misconduct), which may be involved in the present context. It may be that, since the reference is to quail, the word is simply descriptive of the birds' dusty-brown coloration. There is even the possibility that the text should read *tēuctōtōmeh* ("lord-birds") since in VI:22:2 we find *tēuczōliné*, the vocative form of *tēuczōlin* ("lord-quail"). The replacement of /k^w/ with /W/ was a dialectal variation; for example, in Arenas (1862) *teuc-* is consistently rendered *teuh-* (see, for example, pages 23 and 24).

[18]The form *xontlapixto* is the optative form of the "connective *-ti-*" compound TLA-(PIX-ϕ-T-O), "to lie guarding something," where the matrix verb is (ON-O), "to lie there."

[19]The verb *tontlahtlacoh* is a second person singular admonitive form, using the standard formation (see note II:7:19).

[20]Basing his remarks on this statement of Ruiz de Alarcón, Caso (1959:94) says, "8. Tecpatl. Name of the macaw who was the perpetratress of the breaking of the bone Quetzalcoatl brought from hell. She was the wife of Tlaloc or [in other words, she was] Tlaloccihuatl." However, see note VI:22:9 and note VI:22:15.

[21]See note III:1:6.

[22]Ruiz de Alarcón's explanation is false.

It is based on a mistranslation.

[23]The MS has "Cogido an (dice) *y deteniendo al hijo delos dioses*" [that the *cogido an* is not in italics is presumably a copyist error]. The *dice* indicates that this is a quote from VI:22:3, but there the MS reads *cogido han y detenido al hijo delos dioses.* The *deteniendo* is, then, a copyist's error, and we have translated the sentence using *detenido.*

[24]Ruiz de Alarcón's explanation is again mistaken, guided as he was by his religious presuppositions. "Bone from Mictlan" is a mythological and metaphorical way to say "broken bone." See note VI:22:8.

Chapter 23

[1]The MS has *casad* for which we have read *cesad.* Serna (1892:425) has *mirad* ("look"). There is no counterpart in the Nahuatl.

[2]The MS has *iztac quauh tzotzopitzal,* which would be rewritten as *iztāc cuāuhtzotzopitzal.* But the phrase presents a problem. Ruiz de Alarcón translates it as "the white strong pricker" and López Austin (1970:12) as "the white and hard puncheon." Both translations present *cuāuhtzotzopitzal* as an agentive noun. But the word is the "name form" of *cuāuhtzotzopitzalli,* a patientive noun, which would refer to the thing that is pricked rather than to the thing doing the pricking. The context asks for an agentive noun. Therefore, since the matrix is built on the verbstem TLA-(TZO-TZOPI-TZA), "to puncture something repeatedly or strongly," a frequentative form derived from TLA-(TZOPĪ-NI-A), "to puncture something," what is needed is the preterit agentive nounstem (TLA-TZO-TZOPI-TZ-∅)-QUI, "one who has repeatedly or strongly punctured something," i.e., "a repeatedly or strongly puncturing one." The nounstem (CUĀUH)-TLI, "eagle," embedded into this as an incorporated adverb produces (CUĀUH-TLA-TZO-TZOPI-TZ-∅)-QUI, "a repeatedly or strongly puncturing one like an eagle" or "an eagle-like repeatedly or strongly puncturing one," which yields the word we have given in our rewritten version. The resulting phrase, *Iztāc Cuāuhtlatzotzopitzqui,* is ambiguous since the adjective *Iztāc,* "White," may modify either the compound as a whole or only the embed. We have chosen the latter possibility, since *iztāc cuāuhtli,* "white eagle," is the name of a particular kind of eagle (see Sahagún 1963:40) and this fits the metaphorical context.

[3]See note II:17:6.

Chapter 24

[1]The MS has the first person singular verb form *dexare* [i.e., *dejaré*], "I will leave," which also causes the subjunctive form *ande* to be first person singular. The Nahuatl has a third person singular, so the verb here should be *dexara* [i.e., *dejará*], "it will leave," thus permitting *ande* to be "it will walk," i.e., "it will visit."

[2]The MS has *intonacayo cuetlax coliztac,* which Ruiz de Alarcón translates as "the one who has white tripe similar to ours." It is difficult to justify such a translation, since, if the nounstem is, in fact, (NACA-YŌ-CUITLA-XCOL)-LI, "meaty-guts," with the embed being (NACA-YŌ)-TL, "a thing pertaining to meat, meatiness," the translation of *tonacayōcuitlaxcol* would be only "our meaty-guts," with the *to-* being the possessive prefix meaning "our." This does not fit the context. We suggest that, again, the word involved is not (NACA-YŌ)-TL but (TŌNA-∅-CĀ-YŌ)-TL, "a thing having to do with abundance," i.e., "sustenance." If this is the case, it means that the expression in the MS is one word, *Tōnacāyōcuitlaxcōliztāc,* where the embed is (TŌNA-∅-CĀ-YŌ-CUITLA-XCOL)-LI, "sustenance-guts," which functions adverbially to modify the matrix, (IZTĀ-∅)-C, "a white thing." The word in the MS, therefore, is another name for the needle (because of its thread): "White-sustenance-guts" (for the apparent reversal of embed and matrix in the translation, see Andrews 1975: 264–65; it is the same construction as *tlālcōzahuitl* and *tocatlātlāuhqui* in VI:25:5).

[3]The MS has *donde ai agribo buenas.* Serna (1892:421) has *donde ay abrigo de buena cassa* ("where there is the shelter of a good house"). In our translation of the Spanish, we have assumed this to be the correct reading.

[4]The MS has *como casa abundante.* Serna (1892:421) has *en cassa abundante* ("in an abundant house"). The latter is closer to the Nahuatl.

[5]The MS has *humos olores.* Serna (1892: 421) has *humos olorosos.* We have accepted the latter.

[6] López Austin (1970:12) translates *totetzon* as "our hair of people." However, the *-te-* is not *-tē-* "people," but *te-*, from (TE)-TL, "rock." The stem (TE-TZON)-TLI, which has the variant (TE-ZON)-TLI, literally means "petrified hair." It is listed in Siméon with the meaning "a porous rock valued for constructions." This compound stem serves as the source of the verb TLA-(TE-TZON-TI-A), which Molina lists as the entry *tetzontia.nic* with the definition "to hoard up or lay by wealth for the future, or to put a support under a large earthen jar or an earthen jug so that it does not tip over, or to put a foundation of rock and mortar to a wall on which something is to be built." His first definition is metaphorical. We have taken advantage of that metaphor to translate *totetzon* as "our hoard," i.e., "that which serves as our economic foundation."

[7] López Austin (1970:16, note 114) says, "All the metaphors indicate a prosperous place, a capital, a place of established government." Santamaría (1974:882) says that the Nahuatlism *poquiete* [from *pōquiyetl,* which in the rewritten version is represented by the possessive form *topōquiyeuh*] means "Reed in which the ancient aboriginal Mexicans smoked tobacco in rolled leaves; perhaps the same as *acayete* or *acayote.*" Molina lists *acayetl* [i.e., *ācaiyetl*] as "cane for incensing," a translation that erroneously reverses embed and matrix. The expected form for such a meaning would be *iyeācatl,* "tobacco reed," which apparently does not occur. *Ācaiyetl* would expectedly mean "tobacco for (*or* in) a reed (*or* cane)" or possibly "tobacco in the shape of a reed." *Pōquiyetl* consists of the embed (PŌC)-TLI, "smoke," and the matrix (IYE)-TL, "tobacco," thus giving "smoke-tobacco," i.e., "tobacco for [creating] smoke." We take this to be rolled tobacco leaves, not a pipe. See Robicsek 1978:17.

[8] Paso y Troncoso (1892:215) read the word as *tipactiezque.* The form in the MS reads *to pactiezque* [i.e., *tompāctiezqueh*], which is a "connective *-ti-*" compound whose embedded verb is (PĀQUI) "to be happy." The initial *to* of the MS is the first person plural prefix *t-* plus the directional prefix *on-* [i.e., "thither" or "there"].

[9] The MS has *tlaizcaltiticac* [i.e., *tlaizcaltihtihcac*], "its stands nurturing something." This makes no sense in the context. As Ruiz de Alarcón's translation suggests, the word should be *tlaītzcaltitihcac,* "everything stands being cold," i.e., "everything is steadily cold." It is a "connective *-ti-*" compound, whose matrix is the preterit-as-present verb (IHCA), "to stand," and whose embed is an "impersonal *tla-*" stem (TLA-ĪTZ-CAL-TI), "for everything to be cold," from the intransitive stem (ĪTZ-CAL-TI), "to be cold."

[10] The MS says *estregando lo mucho las partes punçadas* which we read as *estregándolo mucho en las partes punzadas* or *estregándole mucho las partes punzadas.*

[11] López Austin (1970:12) translates *Chiucnāuhpahpatlāntzin* as *el venerable cambiado en nueve lugares* ("the venerable one changed in nine places"). However, without the honorific suffix, the word is *chiucnāuhpahpatlān,* which consists of the adverbial embed *chiucnāuh-* ("nine [times]") and the matrix *pahpatlān,* "one who has fluttered," i.e., "a flutterer," the preterit agentive noun of (PAH-PATLĀ-NI), "to flutter," which is the frequentative form of (PATLĀ-NI), "to fly" (compare *Xiuhpahpatlāntzin* in II:13:3). This has no relationship with TLA-(PATLA), "to change or exchange something." Since the word is a name here, it has the special privilege of taking the honorific suffix *-tzin* directly without the intervention of *-cā-*, normally required by preterit agentive stems for the creation of affective forms.

[12] The MS has *ojo* [i.e., "note well!"] in the margin.

Chapter 25

[1] In the MS, *campa oquitlalli ini tleuh nota xiuhtli milintica nahui acatl tzoncoztli* was left untranslated. In Serna's version (1892:422), it is translated as a subordinate clause: "There where my father, the comet that scintillates, the four reeds with blond hair set his fire," which modifies "you are to put it out."

[2] The MS has *ojo* [i.e., "note well!"] in the margin.

[3] See note II:5:6.

[4] The phrase *īhuān timohmōliuhtiuh,* "you go thoroughly joining or combining with her," uses an intensified (because of the reduplicative prefix) form of TLA-(HUĀN) (MŌL-IHUI), "to become joined or combined with something." The transitive stem (used honorifi-

cally and manifesting an embedded adverb) is found in the phrases *īhuān timohhuimōlōz* (II:8:16) and *tlā īhuān ximohhuimōlo* (VI:12:1). See note II:8:72. López Austin (1970:13) has *con ella vas como surgiendo* ("you go with her as if surging"), apparently relating the embedded verb (MOH-MŌL-IHUI) with (MO-MOLŌ-NI), "for the water to bubble up." We see the verb as related to (MŌL)-LI, "stew," *literally,* "a combined thing."

[5]See note II:1:19.

[6]The MS has *quimocamahahuiltizquia,* which is meaningless. We have changed it to *quimocamanālhuīltīzquia* from the double-object honorific verb MO-TĒ-(CAMA-NĀL-HUĪ-L-TIA), from the single-object verb TĒ-(CAMA-NĀL-HUIA), "to joke with someone," "to jest with someone."

[7]The Spanish is *quando alaba esta parte del conjuro,* which means "when she praises this part of the incantation." We have read *llega a* for *alaba.*

[8]The MS reads *el colorado overmejo bolador.* Ruiz de Alarcón's translation *bolador* ("flying one") is a misunderstanding of *tlapahpalācatl,* which he seems to relate to (PATLĀ-NI), "to fly," which is impossible. Serna's version (1892:422) omits the word *bolador,* reading only *el colorado bermejo* (i.e., "the ruddy bright-red one").

[9]The MS reads *ha uendo* [i.e., *ha venido* ("he has come")] for *he venido* ("I have come"). Serna (1892:422) has *E venido* [i.e., *he venido*], which is how we have translated it.

[10]The repetition of "yellow heat" is not in the Nahuatl. It is also not in Serna's version (1892:422).

[11]This marginal note is apparently a copyist error. It is repeated directly below in an appropriate position. In our rewritten version, we have omitted it.

[12]"My ninth reed" is a mistaken translation of *nochicnauh acatl* (which should read *nō chiucnāuhācatl,* "also Nine-reed"; the *no-* is not a possessive prefix) but the adverb *nō* ("also"). López Austin (1970:13) also gives the translation: "my Nine Reed." If this were valid, the word would be *nochiucnāuhācauh.* For a similar use of *nō,* see VI:25:4.

[13]Ruiz de Alarcón translates "yellow heat, . . . white heat" as the thing being drunk by the medicine (the *axin*), a translation that has a certain logic if "heat" represents the rash, but he has upset this logic with a marginal note identifying "yellow heat," etc. as "medicinal herbs," an identification that is difficult to understand. Serna (1892:422) cleverly resolves the difficulty by inserting a parenthetical remark: "She speaks with irony, because she considers the drinks that she gives him cool." The translation of the rest of the segment becomes obscure. We have made two changes. First, we have chosen to see "yellow heat," etc., as the inflammation of the rash, since from the beginning of the incantation fire has been a metaphor for rash. Second, we have read "yellow heat," etc., as a vocative, so that it becomes the one who will drink the medicine, a reading of *-mitz-* (i.e., "you," as verb object) that is supported by the fact that the same prefix in the following sentence necessarily refers to "yellow heat," etc.

[14]This is another instance of the rare inclusion of an indication of ritual that accompanies the verbal action of an incantation.

[15]In the MS, this comment by Ruiz de Alarcón is run on into the incantation but is underlined.

[16]Concerning the respelling *tlazohtli,* see point 2 of note II:8:45. Also see note VI:14:5.

[17]The verbs in the last two sentences, *ticchīuh* and *timopīnāuhtih,* are second person singular admonitive forms using the standard formation.

[18]In the MS, this comment by Ruiz de Alarcón is run on into the incantation.

[19]This is the Latin command *supple* ("supply," "understand"). See note II:13:7.

[20]Concerning this translation that appears to reverse embed and matrix, see Andrews 1975:264–65.

[21]Concerning this translation that appears to reverse embed and matrix, see Andrews 1975:264–65. Serna (1892:423) says, "He calls the sickness metaphorically with the name of the spider because half of its body is bright red [*encendido*], and, when it bites, its poison is such that it inflames [*enciende*] all the body."

[22]Like Ruiz de Alarcón (see the *suple* in his translation), we feel that this sentence is incomplete. We have, therefore, rewritten *xinelhuayo cotonati* [i.e., *xinelhuayōcotōnati*], "go in order to cut the root" (where the embed *nelhuayō-,* "root," is functioning as an

incorporated direct object) as *xicnelhuayōcotōnati,* "go in order to cut it at the root" (where the verb object is the prefix *-c-*, "it," and *nelhuayō-* is functioning as an incorporated adverb of place).

23 The verb *ticāītia* has the form of a causative, but the context demands that it have an applicative meaning (see note II:12:8).

24 Instead of "&c.," Serna (1892:423) continues: "Look, for here is the white woman, in whom you may be enraptured and occupied. In another house or in another place you will be more at pleasure, and you will have more enjoyment, bright-red Chichimec." The Nahuatl that these sentences are translating has been omitted in the MS and its absence is not marked with "&c."

Chapter 26

1 Hinz (1970:21) suggests that an incantation found in Serna (1892:421) but without a counterpart in the Paso y Troncoso edition (nor in the Museo MS) was originally located here. The incantation referred to reads: "Come here you, white woman: appease or calm down this thing that desires to turn the bones of the flesh into dust: go destroy this cruel inflammation. Come on now, my mother, the one of the skirt of precious stones, you who had a skirt and a *huipil* of stones. Come and drown this one and cool off God's creature, and destroy this evil and make it disappear." And, although Hinz does not point this out, the Serna text continues with additional necessary commentary material that also does not appear in the Museo MS: "With this, they put the poultice over the swelling or inflammation, which they name with a quite obscure metaphor, because they call it *Xiutli tlachinoltotonqui* [i.e., *xīhuitl tlachinōltotōnqui* ("comet, fiery hot fever")], the comet that burns—for the heat that the comet conserves within itself, and for the one who is sick." If Hinz's suggestion is correct (and it does have considerable merit), it means that the source used by Serna was quite different in this chapter from the source used by the Museo MS, not just in the omission of this material, but also because, if Chapter 26 really did have this incantation (as well as the associated commentary, although perhaps with a somewhat different wording), the original phrasing of almost the entire chapter would have been different. The wording of the last sentence has a chapter-final tone and style (compare the tone of the end of VI:21 or VI:31). And furthermore there are other instances where Ruiz de Alarcón does not give an incantation because of its similarity to one used earlier, "changing only one word or another" (see, for example, III:1 and IV:3). And there are others in which he gives only those parts of an incantation that are distinctive (see, for example, V:1 or V:2), but he is careful to point this out. As Chapter 26 stands in the Museo version, an incantation is, therefore, not only not expected but would be somewhat surprising if included. While it is indeed possible that Hinz may be right, another possibility is that this is an instance of material from one of those loose sheets that Serna (1892:264, 448) said he used, so that this incantation was never part of Ruiz de Alarcón's *Treatise* but was one of the many incantations he collected but chose not to include.

Chapter 27

1 The MS has *quatecuhpol* which must be read *quateuhpol* (i.e., *cuāteuhpōl*). The *-tecuh-* must not be confused with the frequent erroneous spelling of (TĒUC)-TLI, a spelling that is never used in Ruiz de Alarcón's text. See note VI:6:2. Both *cuāteuhpōl* and its companion *cuāpachpōl* are "flaw forms." See Glossary of Linguistic Terms.

2 As a rule, Serna does not give Ruiz de Alarcón's commentary and it is not particularly significant that he (Serna 1892:420) does not include the idea of this sentence in his text. Instead we find the following, which has no counterpart in the Museo MS: "Others add an invocation to the fire, in the ordinary form, saying, 'Come on, come, my Father, the four canes that throw off flames, etc.'" Serna's text then continues: "Others give *piciete* with the herb *yauhtli* to be drunk, and they say: 'Come on, come, my Mother, the one of the skirt of precious stones, companion, green woman, for I already send you to the seven caves, in order that you take out from there the green pain, etc.'" These incantatory fragments have no counterpart in the Museo MS.

[3]*Īca motlātlauhtia in ātl* ("with it the water is prayed to").

[4]The phrase "the ire of Heaven, justice" is an inflated translation of *ilhuicac Justicia* ("the justice in Heaven"). The interesting thing is that Christian heavenly justice is taken to be a vengeful power. The encroachment of Christian ideas is seen in this incantation, not only by *Justicia* but also by *Dios*, the name among the natives for the foreign god. See Ponce, Appendix A.

[5]Serna (1892:420) includes at this point an incantatory segment not found in the Museo MS: "Come on already, white woman, accompany the green woman, and together with her go down to the stomach of God's creature in order to placate and temper the ire and justice of heaven."

[6]See note II:17:6.

Chapter 28

[1]This "yellow root" is later identified as *tlacōpahtli* at the end of VI:28.

[2]The MS has *mi presea joya y rica esmeralda* ("my gem, jewel, and rich emerald"), translating *noquetzal &.*, which suggests that the &. is standing for *nocōzqui noquetzal.* See note V:1:12. It is probable that the &. covers even more material. Serna's version (1892: 424) continues, "Well, I will fix it and return it to its former being and beauty; not tomorrow or the day after but immediately right away, for I am the one who commands it, the Prince of the spells."

[3]I.e., *tlacōpahtli.* See Appendix D.

[4]*Tlacuātzin.* See Appendix D.

Chapter 29

[1]The MS should read *tlanechicolpàtli*, [i.e., *tlanechicōlpahtli*] which Molina lists as meaning "an unguent composed of many medicinal things." See Appendix D.

[2]*Huēi nacaztli; xōchimecatl; cōānenepilli; xiuhcohcōlin.* See the entries in Appendix D for each item.

[3]The MS has *abuso* ("abuse") for *abusion* ("superstition").

[4]I.e., the Holy of Holies.

[5]This Mazatec woman's name was Isabel Luisa earlier in the chapter.

[6]Neither *ololiuhqui* nor peyote is a "root" *(raiz).*

[7]This is, of course, not the answer to the preceding question but a presenting of credentials as a justification of the authority to ask it.

Chapter 30

[1]*Chīlāpan.* See Appendix E.

[2]For another instance of the reduplicative prefix on the verbstem TĒ-(TLĀTIA), "to hide someone; to kill someone," see VI:21:1: *nimitztlahtlātīz*, "I will hide you thoroughly."

[3]The verb TĒ-(CĀHUA) is again used in the sense of "to carry someone to another place"; see note III:2:3.

[4]The MS has *-xo con matlalloti* [i.e, *xoconmātlāllōti*], which means "go in order to separate it/them with your hands." While this may have been the word intended (even if somewhat strange), Ruiz de Alarcón's translation, "go rub [them] with your hands," suggests that the more expected word would be *xoconmātelōti*, "go in order to rub it/them with your hands." We have changed the text accordingly.

[5]The MS has *teotl* at the bottom of the page as a catchword but fails to repeat the word in the text at the top of the next page.

[6]Paso y Troncoso (1892:219) reads *inchialo* as *inchialoca* [i.e., *īnchialōca*, "it is their act of being awaited"], apparently the result of having written the *ca* following *inchialo* twice.

Chapter 31

[1]*Cuahcuauhtiliztli* ("cramp, stiffness").

[2]The words *y tetleiça* should read *y tetleicça* (i.e., *in tētleicza*), "he treads on someone with fire (i.e., heat)." Compare note VI:21:2.

[3]The MS has *quauhtiliztli*, but it would appear from Ruiz de Alarcón's translation that this is a repetition (as would be expected) of the preceding noun. We have therefore assumed that it should be *quaquauhtiliztli* (i.e., *cuahcuauhtiliztli*). We have, however, left *cuauhtiliztli* in the next incantation.

[4]The MS has *dar . . . por* for *dan . . . por* ("they consider").

[5]*Huitzōcco.* See Appendix E.

[6]*Tzopilōtl.* See Appendix D.

[7]The words *quihtōznequi cuauhtiliztli* are

not part of the incantation but a reminder to the speaker of the meaning of the metaphor. Siméon shows a different meaning for *cuahcuauhtiliztli* (which was mentioned in the previous segment) and *cuauhtiliztli.* The former is defined as "stiffness of the members" and the latter as "pain in the side." Ruiz de Alarcón's translation, "fatigue," seems inadequate.

[8] *Necēhualiztli* ("act of cooling oneself off," i.e., "act of becoming refreshed").

[9] I.e., "with a rod of iron," from Psalms 2:9.

Chapter 32

[1] We take *Yappan* to be *Yāuhpān* (since /w/ followed by /p/ can assimilate to create /pp/). The *Yāuh-* is the embedding form of (YĀ-HUI)-TL, "brown or black maize." We assume the matrix to be the "name form" of *pāmitl* ("flag"). *Yāppān* would accordingly be equivalent to "Black-maize-flag," in the sense of "Flag having the color of black-maize," and would refer to the fact that burrowing scorpions hold their tails up like flags. Concerning the "first age," see the "first world" in I:10.

[2] *Tehuēhuētl* ("stone-drum"). Unlike the *teponāztli* mentioned in the second paragraph of I:3, the *huēhuētl* is an upright drum whose upper end is covered with a taut hide which is beaten with the hands.

[3] *Yāōtl* ("Enemy"). This, of course, is not the god.

[4] *Cītlalcuēyeh.* See Appendix B.

[5] *Chālchiuhcuēyeh.* See Appendix B.

[6] After "Brother," Ruiz de Alarcón has omitted the name *Yappan.*

[7] In the Spanish part of the MS, Ruiz de Alarcón has supplied the speech assignments that are lacking in the Nahuatl text. We have set them out in paragraph format, which is in keeping with the format of the Nahuatl.

[8] We have added the *oc,* "yet, still," since Molina lists *oc xicchia* (and not *xicchia* alone) as meaning *espera vnpoco* [i.e., "wait a moment"], as if it were a set expression.

[9] See note II:2:2. Even though the *-n* is present, Ruiz de Alarcón apparently continues to believe that the word ends in the directional suffix *-pa.*

[10] The MS has *colotl.* But the word is complementing the second person singular object-prefix *-mitz-* and should have the second person singular subject prefix *ti-.* We have therefore changed the text to *tiCōlōtl.*

[11] This segment differs from all the others in the retelling of the myth in that it is not dialogic, but narrative. Ruiz de Alarcón has recast all the other narrative content into Spanish.

[12] *Tzontecommāmah* is a preterit agentive noun whose embed is (TZON-TECOMA)-TL, "head," and whose matrix is the verb TLA-(MĀMA), "to carry something." It means, literally, "one who has carried a head." Compare note III:6:10.

[13] *Tlāhuitzin,* "Red-ochre (H)." Serna (1892:382) adds an explanation omitted by Ruiz de Alarcón: "for that reason there are red scorpions." The myth thus offers an etiological explanation for both brown scorpions (from *Yāppān*) and red scorpions (from *Tlāhuitzin*). *Yappan's* wife is not a goddess, but it is curious that one of the *Tlahzolteteoh* was called *Tlahui* (See Appendix B). See the somewhat different recounting of this myth in Clavijero (1979 I:260) where *Yappan* is transformed into a white (!) scorpion.

[14] It is likely that this focus on sin and retribution is manifesting Ruiz de Alarcón's Christian biases and preoccupations; see the comments following the paraphrases of the incantations of this chapter in Appendix F.

[15] *Āhuacachapolin* ("avocado locust"). Concerning the *-llin* at the end of the word in the MS, see note VI:3:16.

[16] The MS has *tzonteconmamama,* which would be respelled *tzontecommahmāmah.* The reduplicated syllable after *tzontecom-* is presumably an error since the word would mean "heads-carrier." In VI:32:6, the form used was *tzontecommāmah.* See note VI:32:12.

[17] The MS has *punta,* the basic meaning of which is "point." Ruiz de Alarcón later uses *aguijon,* "sting of a bee, wasp, etc; prick, spur, goad; thorn (plants)."

[18] López Austin (1970:16, note 135) says, "It should say *huitzcoltic.*" However, the word in the MS, *huizcol* [i.e., *huitzcōl*], is a "name form" of *huitzcōlli.*

[19] The Spanish sentence is incomplete.

[20] *Chīlāpan.* See Appendix E.

[21] *Piltzintēuctli.* See Appendix B.

[22] *Cōlōtl* ("scorpion").

[23] *Chicōme-Xōchitl* ("Seven Flower"). See Appendix B.

[24] At times, (NE-ZAHUA-L)-LI meant only abstinence from food and, at times, abstinence from food and sex.

[25] Ruiz de Alarcón thinks that the *-huehue-* in *Tehuehueticpac* is *huēhueh* ("old man") from which he gets "ancient rock" (notice that he reverses embed and matrix). The matrix is, however, (HUĒHUĒ)-TL, "drum." See note VI: 32:2.

[26] The MS has *chicomexochitl*. But the word is in apposition with *nitlamacazqui* and should have the first person singular prefix *ni-*. We have therefore changed the text to *niChicōme-Xōchitl*.

[27] The MS reads *ahmo tle tlein*. While in another context the wording could be valid, here, because it is supposed to be in parallel construction with the following *Ahmō tleh in*, we have seen it as a mistake which we have changed to *Ahmō tleh in*.

[28] López Austin (1970:16, note 141) says, "Undoubtedly the word *pelxayaque* is poorly written. Ruiz de Alarcón interprets it as 'curve-faced' and as 'shaved-face.' One can suppose, very remotely, that it may be *picilxayaque* ("owner of the small face")." However, the word *pelxāyaqueh* is a legitimate formation and the translation "shaved-face-one" (given by Ruiz de Alarcón in VI:32:10) is an adequate one. A more accurate translation, however, would be "Bare-mask-owner," since (XĀ-YACA)-TL means "mask" and (PE-L)-LI, which is unattested as an isolated lexical item, means "bare" or "smooth." With regard to the stem (PE-L)-LI, see, for example, the entry *quapepelli* [i.e., (CUĀ-PEH-PE-L)-LI], "a cleric's tonsure," in Molina, where it has a reduplicative prefix. Brewer and Brewer (1962:123) list *cuōpejpetztic* [i.e., (CUĀ-PEH-PE-TZ-TI-ø)-C] with the meaning "hairless, bald." The morpheme *-pe-* is found in a number of words having to do with bareness, smoothness, and shininess, e.g., (PE-TLĀ-NI), "to become polished," (PE-TLĀ-HUA), "to become naked," (PE-TZ)-TLI, *"pyrite,"* (PE-PE-TZ-CA), "for silk or rich feather to have a sheen," (XĪ-PE-TZ)-TLI, "a smooth thing." It is also found in the god-name Xipe (see Appendix B). Compare also *Xāpel*, note IV:3:15 and Appendix B. The word *pelxāyaqueh* is a denigrating name since, while, like the names *Yāppān* and *Huitzcōl*, it names the scorpion in reference to the tail, it points to its penile appearance and thus memorializes the cause of *Yāppān's* downfall. See VI:32 in Appendix F.

[29] The MS has *cuix huiptla*, which we have changed to *cuix quin huīptla* to match other instances of the formula.

[30] The MS has *viene* ("he comes") instead of *vine* ("I came").

[31] See note VI:32:25.

[32] See note III:7:5.

[33] *Icxitl* means "foot," so the present use must be metaphorical.

[34] The MS has *tzonipilhuaztli* for *tzonilpihuāztli* ("instrument with which one ties up one's hair; hair binding"). Concerning the instrumental-noun ending (-HUĀZ)-TLI, see Andrews 1975:371.

[35] The MS has *pintando* ("painting") for *pintado* ("painted").

[36] As Paso y Troncoso notes (1892:223), the symbol evidently was in the author's original text, but is not in the Museo MS.

[37] In Serna (1892:424), the text reads: "And tightening the cord or head ribbons, he/she goes along making a circular character, encircling the ligatures, the ones next to the others, as if he/she is tying off and girdling it, saying."

[38] Serna (1892:424) adds, in parentheses, "*idest*, as I have tied you."

Appendix A

[1] *Tzompanhuahcān* ("Skull-rack-Owner-Place") modern name: Zumpahuacan, Michoacan, Mexico (Gerhard 1972:170–71).

[2] *Ōme-Tōchtli* is a mistake for *Ōme Tēuctli*. See Appendix B.

[3] *Taras*, probably the Tarascan word *Thares*, "idol" (Gilberti 1975:107). It may refer to *Tares* [sic] *Upeme*, the god of Cumanchen (Comachuen, Michoacan, Mexico [Gerhard 1972:352]), god of wine (Tudela and Núñez 1977:112).

[4] *Michhuahcān* (Place-of-fish-owners), now spelled Michoacan.

[5] *Xippilli* for *Xiuhpilli*. See Appendix B.

[6] *Xoxeptzin*, *Ximeontzin* for Joseph (H) and Simon (H), i.e., St. Joseph and St. Simon.

[7] *Tocentah* ("Our-one-father," "Our-total-father," or "Our-common-father").

[8] *Tlahzolcōātl* is a mistake for *Tlahzoltēotl.*

[9] *Āhuahqueh* ("Water-Owners"), i.e., the clouds.

[10] *Tlāloqueh* is a mistake for *Tlāloc.* See Appendix B.

[11] *Tlāloqueh tlamacazqueh* ("*Tlalocs,* the priests").

[12] *Tzoal* is a Nahuatlism, for *tzoalli* or *tzohualli* ("amaranth seed dough").

[13] The description of the eating of Huitzilopochtli in Sahagún (1952:5–9) offers no help in deciphering the erroneous *vxcucoeyotiah.*

[14] It sounds as if a description of how they beheaded sacrificial chickens was intended. Possibly the text is incomplete.

[15] *Tlaquechcotōnaliztli* ("the act of cutting off something at the neck," i.e., "the act of beheading").

[16] *Poquietes* is a Nahuatlism for *pōquiyetl* ("smoke-tobacco"). See note VI:24:7 of the Ruiz de Alarcón text.

[17] *Xicara* is a Nahuatlism for *xicalli* ("a gourd or wooden drinking cup").

[18] *Teōpan tlācah* ("the people in the church," i.e., "the church people").

[19] *Ītleuh quīzaz in piltzintli* ("the child's fire will exit").

[20] *Ehcatl* ("Breeze"), *Cōātl* ("Snake"), *Xīcoh* ("Bee"), *Xoco* ("Fruit").

[21] *Cualāni in Sāntoh.* "The Saint is angry."

[22] *Cualāni in Huēhuēntzin.* "The Old-Man (H) [i.e., the fire] is angry."

[23] *Tenamastles* is a Nahuatlism for *tenāmāztli* ("the three hearth stones used to support a cooking vessel"). See note II:8:3 of the Ruiz de Alarcón text.

[24] *Motēnciāhuaz in Huēhuēntzin.* "The Old-Man (H) [i.e., the fire] will wet his lips."

[25] The word in the text, *matlalcueyeque* (i.e., *Matlalcuēyehqueh*), is a mistake because of the plural suffix *-queh.* It should be *Matlalcuēyeh,* "the Blue-Skirt-Owner." See Appendix B.

[26] *Cualāni in tōnacāyōtl.* "The sustenance (i.e., the maize) is angry."

[27] *Tētōnalmacanih* ("ones who customarily give a *tonal* to someone," i.e., "*tonal*-givers"). The singular form is *tētōnalmacani.* This is a customary-present agentive noun from the verb TĒ-(TŌNA-L-MACA), "to give a soul to someone," a compound verbstem whose embed is (TŌNA-L)-LI, "day-sign," and by extension, "soul," which has been incorporated in the verbstem as a direct object. The matrix is TĒ-TLA-(MACA), "to give something to someone." A curer who attempts to effect a cure by retrieving a patient's truant soul. Compare *tētōnaltih* in Appendix C.

[28] *Tlacōpahtli* ("stick-medicine"). See Appendix D.

[29] *Cualānih in ehehcameh; cualānih in Āhuahqueh.* "The winds are angry; the Water-owners (i.e., the clouds) are angry."

[30] *Cuātlapānqueh* ("those who have become broken open at the head"). This is a plural preterit agentive noun from the intransitive verb (CUĀ-TLAPĀ-NI), "to become broken open at the head."

[31] *Xilote* is a Nahuatlism for *xīlōtl* ("immature ear of maize").

[32] *Miyāhuatl* ("corn tassel").

[33] *Elote* is a Nahuatlism from *ēlōtl* ("a ripe green ear of corn").

[34] *Tlaxquiztli* ("the action of roasting something"). This is the action noun from the verb TLA-(IXCA), "to roast something."

[35] The text seems to be incomplete although Paso y Troncoso makes no comment about the problem.

[36] *Ule* is a Nahuatlism from *ōlli* ("rubber").

[37] *Texāmatl* ("maize-dough paper").

[38] *Xicōlli* ("clothing, jacket of painted material that the ministers of the idols wore in their office").

[39] *Tehtelli* ("rock mounds").

[40] "*Xōlōtl* was the god of double or monstrous things, and even in order to invoke him, they used to go, as it says here, to road junctions, which without doubt were also dedicated to him." (Paso y Troncoso's note). See Appendix B.

[41] The text has *temporal* ("tempest; weather, long rainy spell of weather") for which we have read *temporada* ("season").

[42] *Tequixquitamale* is a Nahuatlism for *tequixquitamalli* ("saltpeter tamale").

[43] *In tiXōlōtl, ximohuīcatiuh. Mā xicmonāhuatilīti in Iztāc-Cihuātl, ca in mochīhua, motequipanoa in quimonequīltia.* "O Xolotl, go along (H). Please go tell White Woman that what she wants (H) is being done, is being wrought." Notice that *ximohuīcatiuh* is a progressive form while *xicmonāhuatilīti* is an outbound purposive form.

[44] *Chicōme-Cōātlé, ca ōnihuāllah; in titēquetzal, in titēcencōzqui, ca ōnichuālitquic in noteōcuitlachiquiuh, in noteōcuitlamācpal.* "O Seven

Snake, I have indeed come; O someone's plume, O someone's total necklace [i.e., beloved child], I have indeed brought my gold-basket, my gold-palm [of the hand]" [i.e., the harvest basket].

45 *Tlā xihuāllauh, Tlāltēuctli. Nicān mopan nocontēma in Chicōme-Cōātl. Ahmō cē toconēlēhuīz.* "Come, Tlalteuctli [i.e., the earth]. Here I fill Seven Snake [i.e., the maize] upon you. You will not covet [i.e., harm] a single one of them." Possibly *nocontēca* ("I will stretch it out") was intended instead of *nocontēma.*

46 *Nicān catqui, in antlamacazqueh, achitzin neuctzintli. Īc ammohuellamachtīzqueh.* "Here is, O priests, a little honey (H). With it you will be happy."

47 *Huitztli* ("thorn").

48 *Huitzmanaliztli* ("the act of setting down thorns" or "the act of offering thorns").

49 *Nicalchālia.* "I inaugurate a house."

50 The text has *sus morillos del jacal o cubierta.* The word *morillos* ("andiron, firedog") seems strange unless he means with this word the *tenamastles* mentioned earlier, although apparently the ceiling of the house is intended.

51 As Paso y Troncoso's *"sic"* indicates, material seems to have been omitted from the text.

52 *Calchālia* ("he inaugurates a house") or *calchāliah* ("they inaugurate a house").

53 The Spanish is *unas rayas como aspas* ("some marks like crosses").

54 *Cuauhtlahtohqueh* ("they are the speakers [i.e., the rulers] of wood").

55 *Acxōtlahtōlli* ("the words of *acxōtl* (?)"). (AC-XŌ)-TL occurs as the embed of (AC-XŌ-YA)TL, "fir bough," (see note I:4:16 of the *Treatise*) but its meaning is uncertain.

56 The Spanish is *cimarrón,* which is not a native word although the text leads the reader to expect one.

57 *Teciuhpeuhqueh* is an error for *teciuhpēhuihqueh* ("those who shoo away hail").

58 *Cōātequitl* ("public work, work that is done in common").

59 *Tētōnalmacanih,* see note 27.

60 *Ātlan tlachixqueh* ("those who have looked into water"). See Appendix C.

61 The text says *miden una paja con tres paños y medio,* instead of *tres puños.*

62 *Ololiuhqui.* See Appendix D.

63 *Tlihtlīltzin* ("the very black one (H)"). This is the word for both the individual morning-glory seeds and a hallucinogenic decoction made from them.

REFERENCES

Ackerknecht, Erwin H.
1971 *Medicine and Ethnology: Selected Essays.* H. H. Welser and H. M. Koelbing, eds. Baltimore, Md.: Johns Hopkins Press.

Acosta, Joseph de
1979 *Historia natural y moral de las Indias.* Mexico City: Fondo de Cultura Económica.

Acosta Saignes, Miguel
1946 "Los teopixque." *Revista mexicana de estudios antropológicos* 8:147–205.

Aguirre Beltrán, Gonzalo
1947 "La medicina indígena." *América indígena* 7(2):107–27.
1963 *Medicina y magia.* Mexico City: Instituto nacional indigenista.

Anawalt, Patricia Rieff
1981 *Indian Clothing Before Cortés: Mesoamerican Costumes from the Codices.* Norman: University of Oklahoma Press.

Anderson, Arthur J. O., Frances F. Berdan, and James Lockhart
1976 *Beyond the Codices.* Berkeley and Los Angeles: University of California Press.

Anderson, Edward F.
1980 *Peyote: The Divine Cactus.* Tucson: University of Arizona Press.

Andrews, J. Richard
1975 *Introduction to Classical Nahuatl.* Austin: University of Texas Press.

———, and Ross Hassig
N.d. "Medical Astrology in Pre-Columbian Mexico," *Homenaje a Thelma Sullivan,* forthcoming.

Arenas, Pedro de
1862 *Guide de la conversation en trois langues: français, espagnol, et mexicain.* M. Charles Romey, trans. Paris: Maisonneuve et Cie.

Banton, Michael, ed.
1966 *Anthropological Approaches to the Study of Religion.* London: Tavistock.

Barmby, James
1956 *Nicene and Post-Nicene Fathers.* 2d ser. Grand Rapids, Mich.: Eerdmans.

Benson, Elizabeth P., ed.
1975 *Death and the Afterworld in Pre-Columbian America.* Washington, D.C.: Dumbarton Oaks.

Bidney, David
1963 "So-called Primitive Medicine and Religion." In Galdston 1963.

Braden, Charles S.
1930 *Religious Aspects of the Conquest of Mexico.* Durham, N.C.: Duke University Press.

Bravo Ugarte, José
1965 *Diócesis y obispos de la iglesia mexicana (1519–1965).* Mexico City: Editorial Jus.

Brewer, Forrest, and Jean G. Brewer
1962 *Vocabulario mexicano de Tetelcingo, Morelos.* Mexico City: Summer Institute of Linguistics.

Brinton, Daniel G.
1894 "Nagualism: A Study in Native American Folk-lore and History." *Proceedings of the American Philosophical Society* 33:11–73.

Burland, C. A.
1967 *The Gods of Mexico.* New York: Putnam.

Butler, Alban
1956 *Butler's Lives of the Saints.* H. Thurston and D. Attwater, eds. 4 vols. New York: Kenedy.

Cárdenas, Juan de
1945 *Problemas y secretos maravillosos de las indias.* Madrid: Ediciones Cultura Hispánica.
Carochi, Horacio
1904 "Arte de la lengua mexicana con la declaracion de los adverbios della." *Colección de gramáticas de la lengua mexicana.* Mexico City.
Carrera Stampa, Manuel
1949 "The Evolution of Weights and Measures in New Spain." *Hispanic American Historical Review* 29:2–24.
Case, Bradley Wheelden
1977 "Gods and Demons: Folk Religion in Seventeenth-Century New Spain, 1614–1632." Ph.D. diss., Cornell University.
Caso, Alfonso
1958 *The Aztecs: People of the Sun.* Norman: University of Oklahoma Press.
1959 "Nombres calendáricos del los dioses," *El México antiguo* 9:77–100.
Castro Leal, Antonio
1943 *Juan Ruiz de Alarcón: su vida y su obra.* Mexico City: Ediciones Cuadernos Americanos.
Chadwick, Robert
1971 "Native Pre-Aztec History of Central Mexico." In *Handbook of Middle American Indians,* 11:474–504.
Chiapelli, F.
1976 *First Images of America.* 2 vols. Berkeley and Los Angeles: University of California Press.
Ciruelo, Pedro
1977 *A Treatise Reproving All Superstitions and Forms of Witchcraft.* E. A. Maio and D. W. Pearson, trans. Cranbury, N.J.: Associated University Presses.
Clavijero, Francisco Javier
1979 *The History of Mexico.* Charles Cullen, trans. 2 vols. New York: Garland.
Coe, Michael D.
1968 *America's First Civilization: Discovering the Olmec.* New York: American Heritage.
Cook, Sherbourne F.
1946 "The Incidence and Significance of Disease Among the Aztecs and Related Tribes." *Hispanic American Historical Review* 26:320–35.
Córdoba, Pedro
1970 *Christian Doctrine: For the Instruction and Information of the Indians.* S. A. Stoudemire, trans. Coral Gables, Fla.: University of Miami Press.
Covarrubias, Miguel
1957 *Indian Art of Mexico and Central America.* New York: Knopf.
Cuevas, P. Mariano
1946 *Historia de la iglesia en México.* 5 vols. Mexico City: Editorial Patria.
Davies, Nigel
1977 *The Toltecs: Until the Fall of Tula.* Norman: University of Oklahoma Press.
Davis, Audrey, and Tobey Appel
1979 *Bloodletting Instruments in the National Museum of History and Technology.* Washington, D.C.: Smithsonian Institution Press.
Davis, L. Irby
1972 *A Field Guide to the Birds of Mexico and Central America.* Austin: University of Texas Press.
Díaz, José Luis
1976 *Índice y sinonimia de las plantas medicinales de México.* Mexico City: Instituto mexicano para el estudio de las plantas medicinales.
1977 *Usos de las plantas medicinales de México.* Mexico City: Instituto mexicano para

el estudio de las plantas medicinales.
Dietschy, Hans
1944 "La medicina de los aztecas." In Rodríguez 1944.
Dundes, Alan
1964 *The Morphology of North American Indian Folktales.* Helsinki.
1980 "Texture, Text, and Context." In *Interpreting Folklore.* Bloomington: Indiana University Press.
Durán, Diego
1971 *Book of the Gods and Rites and The Ancient Calendar.* F. Horcasitas and D. Heyden, trans. and eds. Norman: University of Oklahoma Press.
1967 *Historia de las Indias de Nueva España e islas de la tierra firme.* 2 vols. Mexico City: Editorial Porrúa.
Eliade, Mircea
1974 *Shamanism: Archaic Techniques of Ecstasy.* Princeton: Princeton University Press.
Emmart, Emily Walcott
1937 "Herb Medicine of the Aztecs." *Journal of the American Pharmaceutical Association* 26:42-45.
1940 *The Badianus Manuscript: An Aztec Herbal of 1552.* Baltimore, Md.: Johns Hopkins Press.
Ennis, Arthur
1977 "The Conflict Between the Regular and Secular Clergy." In Greenleaf 1977.
Fabrega, Horacio, Jr.
1971 "The Study of Medical Problems in Preliterate Settings." *Journal of Biology and Medicine* 10:385-407.
1978 "Ethnomedicine and Medical Science." *Medical Anthropology* 2:11-24.
Falconer, William Armistead, trans.
1922 *Cicero: De senectute, de amicitia, de divinatione.* London: Heinemann.
Fellowes, William H.
1977 "The Treatises of Hernando Ruiz de Alarcón." *Tlalocan* 7:309-55.
Furst, Peter T.
1976 *Hallucinogens and Culture.* San Francisco: Chandler & Sharp.
Galdston, Iago
1963 *Man's Image in Medicine and Anthropology.* New York: International Universities Press.
Garibay K., Ángel María
1944 "Paralipómenos de Sahagún." *Tlalocan* 1:307-13.
1946 "Paralipómenos de Sahagún." *Tlalocan* 2:167-74.
1947 "Paralipómenos de Sahagún." *Tlalocan* 2:235-54.
1958 *Veinte himnos sacros de los nahuas.* Mexico City: Universidad Autónoma Nacional de México.
1964 *Poesía náhuatl.* Vol. 1. Mexico City: Universidad Autónoma Nacional de México.
1965 *Poesía náhuatl.* Vol. 2. Mexico City: Universidad Autónoma Nacional de México.
1968 *Poesía náhuatl.* Vol. 3. Mexico City: Universidad Autónoma Nacional de México.
1971 *Historia de la literatura náhuatl.* Vol. 2. Mexico City: Editorial Porrúa.
Gerhard, Peter
1972 *A Guide to the Historical Geography of New Spain.* Cambridge: Cambridge University Press.
Gibson, Charles
1964 *The Aztecs Under Spanish Rule.* Stanford: Stanford University Press.
1966 *Spain in America.* New York: Harper & Row.
Gilberti, Maturino
1975 *Diccionario de la lengua tarasca o de Michoacan.* Morelia, Michoacán, Mexico: Balsal Editores.

Glick, Leonard B.
1967 "Medicine as an Ethnographic Category: The Gimi of the New Guinea Highlands." *Ethnology* 6:31-56.

Graulich, Michel
1981 "The Metaphor of the Day in Ancient Mexican Myth and Ritual." *Current Anthropology* 22:45-60.

Greenleaf, Richard E.
1965 "The Inquisition and the Indians of New Spain: A Study in Jurisdictional Confusion," *Americas* 22:138-66.
1969 *The Mexican Inquisition of the Sixteenth Century.* Albuquerque: University of New Mexico Press.
1977 *The Roman Catholic Church in Colonial Latin America.* Tempe: Arizona State University Center for Latin American Studies.

Greenwood, L. H. G., trans.
1928 *Cicero: The Verrine Orations.* Vol. 1. New York: Putnam.

Guerra, Francisco
1953 *Historiografía de la medicina colonial hispanoamericana.* Mexico City: Abastecedora de Impresos.
1963 "Medical Colonization of the New World." *Medical History* 7:147-54.
1966 "Aztec Medicine." *Medical History* 10:315-38.
1967 "Mexican Phantastica—A Study of the Early Ethnobotanical Sources on Hallucinogenic Drugs." *British Journal of Addiction* 62:171-87.
1969 "The Role of Religion in Spanish American Medicine." In Poynter 1969.

Haring, C. H.
1963 *The Spanish Empire in America.* New York: Harcourt, Brace and World.

Hernández, Francisco
1959a *Historia natural de Nueva España.* Vol. I. Mexico City: Universidad Nacional Autónoma de México.
1959b *Historia natural de Nueva España.* Vol. II. Mexico City: Universidad Nacional Autónoma de México.

Hernández Xolocotzin, Efraim
1949 *Maize Granaries in Mexico.* Harvard University Botanical Museum Leaflets 13, 7:153-211.

Hinz, Eike
1970 *Anthropologische Analyse altaztekischer Texte, Teil 1: Die magischen Texte im Tratado Ruiz de Alarcons (1969).* Hamburg: Kommissionsverl. Klaus Renner.
1978 *Analyse aztekischer Gedankensysteme: Wahrsageglaube und Erziehungsnormen als Alltagstheorie sozialen Handelns auf Grund des 4. und 6. Buches der "Historia General" Fray Bernardino de Sahaguns.* Wiesbaden: Franz Steiner Verlag.

Jacobus de Voragine
1941 *The Golden Legend of Jacobus de Voragine.* Granger Ryan and Helmut Ripperger, trans. 2 vols. New York: Longmans, Green.

Jarcho, Saul
1957 "Medicine in Sixteenth Century New Spain as Illustrated by the Writings of Bravo, Farfan, and Vargas Machuca." *Bulletin of the History of Medicine* 31:425-41.

Joralemon, Peter David
1971 "A Study of Olmec Iconography." *Studies in Pre-Columbian Art and Archaeology,* no. 7. Washington, D.C.: Dumbarton Oaks.

Karttunen, Frances
1983 *An Analytical Dictionary of Nahuatl.* Austin: University of Texas Press.

———, and James Lockhart
1976 *Nahuatl in the Middle Years.* Los Angeles and Berkeley: University of California Press.

Kirkby, Anne V. T.
1973 *The Use of Land and Water Resources in the Past and Present Valley of Oaxaca, Mexico.* Memoirs of the Museum of Anthropology, University of Michigan, no. 5.

Klein, Cecelia F.
1975 "Post-Classic Mexican Death Imagery as a Sign of Cyclic Completion." In Benson 1975.

Kluckhohn, Clyde, and Dorothea Leighton
1962 *The Navaho.* Garden City, N.Y.: Doubleday.

Kubler, George
1967 "The Iconography of the Art of Teotihuacan." *Studies in Pre-Columbian Art and Archaeology,* no. 4, Washington, D.C.: Dumbarton Oaks.

Lanczkowski, Guenter
1970 "Different Types of Redemption in Ancient Mexican Religion," In *Types of Redemption,* R. J. Zwi Werblowsky and C. Jouco Bleeker, eds. Leiden: E. J. Brill.

Laughlin, William S.
1963 "Primitive Theory of Medicine: Empirical Knowledge." In Galdston 1963.

Lea, Henry Charles
1922 *The Inquisition in the Spanish Dependencies.* New York: Macmillan.

León, Nicolás
1933 *Códice Sierra.* Mexico City: Museo Nacional de Arqueología, Historia, y Etnografía.

León-Portilla, Miguel
1971 *Aztec Thought and Culture.* Norman: University of Oklahoma Press.

Leopold, A. Starker
1972 *Wildlife of Mexico: The Game Birds and Mammals.* Los Angeles and Berkeley: University of California Press.

Lindsay, W. M.
1911 *Isidori Hispalensis episcopi* Etymologiarum *sive Originum libri xx.* Oxford: Oxford University Press.

Logan, Michael H.
1977 "Anthropological Research on the Hot-Cold Theory of Disease: Some Methodological Suggestions." *Medical Anthropology* 1:87–112.

López Austin, Alfredo
1966 "Los temacpalitotique: brujos, profanadores, ladrones y violadores." *Estudios de cultura nahuatl* 6:97–117.
1967 "Términos del nahuallatolli." *Historia mexicana* 17:1–36.
1969 *Augurios y abusiones.* Mexico City: Universidad Nacional Autónoma de México.
1970 "Conjuros médicos de los nahuas." *Revista de la Universidad de México* 24:11:1-16.
1975 *Textos de medicina náhuatl.* Mexico City: Universidad Nacional Autónoma de México.

Madsen, William
1960 "Christo-Paganism: A Study of Mexican Religious Syncretism." *Middle American Research Institute Bulletin* 19:105–79.

Martínez, Maximino
1979 *Catálogo de nombres vulgares y científicos de plantas mexicanos.* Mexico City: Fondo de Cultura Económica.

Mendieta, Gerónimo de
1971 *Historia eclesiástica indiana.* Mexico City: Editorial Porrúa.

Mengin, Ernest
1952 "Commentoire du Codex Mexicanus, nos. 23–24," *Journal de la Société des Américanistes* 41:387–498.

Migne, J. B.
1844-64 *Patrologiae cursus completus. Series Latina.* Paris.
Miller, Arthur G.
1973 *The Mural Painting of Teotihuacán.* Washington, D.C.: Dumbarton Oaks.
Moerman, Daniel E.
1979 "Empirical Methods in the Evaluation of Indigenous Medical Systems: Comments on a Symposium." *Medical Anthropology* 3:525-30.
Molina, Alonso de
1945 *Arte de la lengua mexicana y castellana.* Madrid: Ediciones Cultura Hispánica.
1970 *Vocabulario en lengua castellana y mexicana y mexicana y castellana.* Mexico City: Editorial Porrúa.
Moreno Toscano, Alejandra
1965 "Tres problemas en la geografía de maíz, 1600-1624," *Historia mexicana* 14: 631-55.
Mota y Escobar, Alonso de la
1945 "Memoriales del obispo de Tlaxcala." *Anales del Instituto Nacional de Antropología e Historia* 1:191-306.
Motolinia [Toribio de Benavente]
1973 *Historia de los indios de la Nueva España.* Mexico City: Editorial Porrúa.
Newman, Marshall T.
1976 "Aboriginal New World Epidemiology and Medical Care, and the Impact of Old World Disease Imports." *American Journal of Applied Physiology* 45: 667-72.
Nicholson, H. B.
1971 "Religion in Pre-Hispanic Central Mexico." *Handbook of Middle American Indians* 10:395-446.
1976 "Preclassic Mesoamerican Iconography from the Perspective of the Postclassic." In *Origins of Religious Art and Iconography in Preclassic Mesoamerica.* H. B. Nicholson, ed. Los Angeles: UCLA Latin American Center Publications.
Nuttall, Zelia
1891 "The Atlatl or Spear-Thrower of the Ancient Mexicans." *Archaeological and Ethnological Papers of the Peabody Museum,* vol. 1, no. 3.
Olmos, Andrés de
1972 *Arte para aprender la lengua mexicana.* Rémi Siméon, ed. Guadalajara, Mexico: Edmundo Aviña Levy.
Paso y Troncoso, Francisco del, ed.
1892 Ruiz de Alarcón: "Tratado de las supersticiones y costumbres gentilicas que oy viuen entre los indios naturales desta Nueva España." *Anales del Museo Nacional de México* 6:125-223.
1905a *Papeles de Nueva España.* Vol. 4. Madrid.
1905b *Papeles de Nueva España.* Vol. 5. Madrid.
1905c *Papeles de Nueva España.* Vol. 6. Madrid.
1906 *Papeles de Nueva España.* Vol. 7. Madrid.
1953 Ruiz de Alarcón: "Tratado de las supersticiones y costumbres gentilicas que oy viuen entre los indios naturales desta Nueva España." In *Tratado de las idolatrías, supersticiones, dioses, ritos, hechicerías y otras costumbres gentílicas de las razas aborígenes de México.* Mexico City: Navarro.
Pasztory, Ester
1974 "The Iconography of the Teotihuacan Tlaloc." *Studies in Pre-Columbian Art and Archaeology,* no. 15. Washington, D.C.: Dumbarton Oaks.
Pérez, Manuel
1713 *Farol indiano, y gvia de curas de indios.* Mexico City.

Pérez Trejo, Gustavo A.
1959 "La medicina." In *Esplendor del México antiguo,* 1:211–20.
Poesse, Walter
1972 *Juan Ruiz de Alarcón.* New York: Twayne.
Ponce, Pedro
1892 "Breve relación de los dioses y ritos de la gentilidad." *Anales del Museo Nacional de México* 6:4–11.
Poynter, F. N. L.
1969 *Medicine and Culture.* London: Wellcome Institute of the History of Medicine.
Pozo, Efren C. del
1967 "Empiricism and Magic in Aztec Pharmacology." In *Ethnopharmacologic Search for Psychoactive Drugs.* Public Health Service Publication no. 1645, pp. 59–76.
Propp, V.
1973 *Morphology of the Folktale.* Austin: University of Texas Press.
Quezada, Noemí
1975 *Amor y magia amorosa entre los aztecas.* Mexico City: Universidad Nacional Autónoma de México.
Ramírez de Alejandro, Cleofas, and Karen Dakin
1979 *Vocabulario náhuatl de Xalitla, Guerrero.* Mexico City: CISINAH.
Réau, Louis
1955–59 *Iconographie de L'Art Chrétien.* 6 vols. Paris: Presses Universitaires de France.
Remy, Nicolas
1970 *Demonolatry.* New York: Barnes & Noble.
Riley, G. Michael
1973 *Fernando Cortés and the Marquesado in Morelos, 1522–1547.* Albuquerque: University of New Mexico Press.
Robertson, Donald
1959 *Mexican Manuscript Painting of the Early Colonial Period: The Metropolitan Schools.* New Haven, Conn.: Yale University Press.
Robicsek, Francis
1978 *The Smoking Gods: Tobacco in Maya Art, History, and Religion.* Norman: University of Oklahoma Press.
Rodríguez, Luis Angel
1944 *La Ciencia médica de los aztecas.* Mexico City: Editorial Hispano Mexicana.
Ruiz de Alarcón, Hernando
1892 "Tratado de las supersticiones y costumbres gentilicas que oy viuen entre los indios naturales desta Nueva España." *Anales del Museo Nacional de México* 6: 125–223.
1953 "Tratado de las supersticiones y costumbres gentilicas que oy viuen entre los indios naturales desta Nueva España." In *Tratado de las idolatrías, supersticiones, dioses, ritos, hechicerías y otras costumbres gentílicas de las razas aborígenes de México.* Mexico City: Navarro.
Sahagún, Bernadino de
General History of the Things of New Spain. Arthur J. O. Anderson and Charles Dibble, trans. Salt Lake City: University of Utah Press:
1951 *The Ceremonies.* Book 2.
1952 *The Origin of the Gods.* Book 3.
1953 *The Sun, Moon, and Stars, and the Binding of the Years.* Book 7.
1954 *Kings and Lords.* Book 8.
1957 *The Soothsayers and the Omens.* Books 4 and 5.
1959 *The Merchants.* Book 9.
1961 *The People.* Book 10.

1963 *Earthly Things.* Book 11.
1969 *Rhetoric and Moral Philosophy.* Book 6.
1970 *The Gods.* Book 1.
1975 *The Conquest of Mexico.* Book 12.

Santamaría, Francisco J.
1974 *Diccionario de mejicanismos.* Mexico City: Editorial Porrúa.

Sauer, Jonathan D.
1976 "Changing Perception and Exploitation of New World Plants in Europe, 1492-1800." In Chiapelli 1976, 2:813-32.

Schendel, Gordon
1968 *Medicine in Mexico: From Aztec Herbs to Betatrons.* Austin: University of Texas Press.

Scholes, France V.
1977 "An Overview of the Colonial Church." In Greenleaf 1977.

Schultes, Richard Evans, and Albert Hofmann
1979 *Plants of the Gods.* New York: McGraw-Hill.

Schwaller, John Frederick
1978 "The Secular Clergy in Sixteenth-Century Mexico." Ph.D. diss., Indiana University.

Seler, Eduard
1904 *Gesammelte Abhandlungen zur Amerikanischen Sprach- und Alterthumskunde.* Vol. 2. Berlin: A. Asher.

Serna, Jacinto de la
1892 "Manual de ministros de indios para el conocimiento de sus idolatrias, y extirpacion de ellas." *Anales del Museo Nacional de México* 6:264-480.

Shaw, J. F., trans.
1956 *The Nicene and Post-Nicene Fathers.* 1st Ser. Vol. 2, Grand Rapids, Mich.: Eerdmans.

Shiels, W. Eugene
1977 "Seventeenth-Century Legal Crisis in the Missions." In Greenleaf 1977.

Siegel, Rudolph E.
1968 *Galen's System of Physiology and Medicine.* New York: S. Karger.

Siméon, Rémi
1963 *Dictionnaire de la langue nahuatl ou mexicaine.* Graz, Austria: Akademische Druck- u. Verlagsanstalt.

Soustelle, Jacques
1970 *Daily Life of the Aztecs.* Stanford, Calif.: Stanford University Press.

Spence, Lewis
1923 *The Gods of Mexico.* London: Unwin.

Standley, Paul C.
1920-26 *Trees and Shrubs of Mexico.* Washington, D.C.: Smithsonian Institution.

Stirling, Matthew W.
1965 "Monumental Sculpture of Southern Veracruz and Tabasco." In *Handbook of Middle American Indians,* 3:716-38.

Sullivan, Thelma D.
1972 "The Arms and Insignia of the Mexica." *Estudios de cultura nahuatl* 10:155-93.

Torquemada, Juan de
1976 *Monarquía indiana.* Vol. 3. Mexico City: Universidad Nacional Autónoma de México.
1977 *Monarquía indiana.* Vol. 4. Mexico City: Universidad Nacional Autónoma de México.

Toussaint, Manuel
1931 *Tasco: su historia, sus monumentos, características actuales y posibilidades turísticas.* Mexico City: Editorial Cultura.
Tudela, José, and José Corona Núñez
1977 *Relación de Michoacán.* Morelia, Michoacán, Mexico: Balsal Editores.
Underhill, Ruth Murray
1976 *Singing for Power.* Berkeley and Los Angeles: University of California Press.
Vargas Castelazo, Manuel
1956 "La Patología y la medicina entre los mexica," *Revista mexicana de estudios antropológicos* 14:119–43.
Velázquez, Primo Feliciano, trans.
1975 *Códice Chimalpopoca: anales de Cuauhtitlán y leyenda de los soles.* Mexico City: Universidad Nacional Autónoma de México.
Warren, J. Benedict
1973 "An Introductory Survey of Secular Writings in the European Tradition on Colonial Middle America, 1503–1818." In *Handbook of Middle American Indians,* 13:42–137.
Wasson, Gordon R.
1966 "Ololiuhqui and Other Hallucinogens of Mexico." In *Summa antropológica en homenaje a Roberto J. Weitlaner.* Mexico City: INAH.
Wax, Murray, and Rosalie Wax
1962 "The Magical World View." *Journal for the Scientific Study of Religion* 1:179–88.
1963 "The Notion of Magic." *Current Anthropology* 4:495–518.

INDEX

Southern Methodist Univ.
3 2177 00183 9271